Museums and Memorials

Commemorating the Victims

of Communist Dictatorships

Museums and Memorials

Commemorating the Victims of Communist Dictatorships

Edited by Anna Kaminsky,
compiled by Anna Kaminsky, Ruth Gleinig and Lena Ens
commissioned by the Federal Foundation for the Study of the Communist Dictatorship in Eastern Germany

Sandstein Verlag, Dresden

Table of Contents

Countries with No History of Communist Dictatorship

Foreword

This book describes memorials, monuments and museums that commemorate the crimes of communist regimes and their victims worldwide. The Bolshevik coup in October 1917 marked the first attempt by a communist party to seize power in the Russian Empire. Under Lenin's leadership, the Bolsheviks shattered existing political, economic and social structures and established Soviet power after a bloody civil war that claimed millions of lives and devastated the country. Trotsky, one of Lenin's former comrades-in-arms, later declared that what had been established was not a "dictatorship of the proletariat", but rather a "dictatorship over the proletariat".

Lenin and his comrades saw the overthrow and transformation of the state and society as nothing less than the prelude to global revolution and the model for the establishment of communist rule worldwide. They hoped that the revolutionary spark from Russia would ignite fires first in Western Europe and then on the remaining continents. This expectation failed to materialise at first. Only after the Second World War, in which the Soviet Union shouldered the main burden in the defeat of Nazi Germany, thereby suffering the greatest human losses, did further communist dictatorships emerge in Eastern Europe. Most of these countries were occupied by the Soviet Union; in others, such as Albania, communist parties based on the Soviet model took power. However, communist rule was not limited to Europe: other communist regimes were also established in China, Cambodia, North Korea, Vietnam and Cuba. At the height of communist power in the 1970s and 1980s, about a third of the world's population lived under communist rule.

These dictatorships were as varied as their attempts to fulfil their totalitarian claim to power. Communist ideology was based on the promise of a utopia in which the abolition of private property in the means of production would, as a matter of historical inevitability, solve all of humanity's problems. For the people, this utopian vision heralded salvation from oppression, poverty and exploitation and — given the required "insight into the objective necessity" — promised the free development of every individual. And these "necessities" were defined and redefined by the leaders of the communist parties according to their convictions.

For most people, however, the reality of living under communist rule was an experience of terror, repression, surveillance, humiliation and intimidation. However, the communist dictatorships of Joseph Stalin in the Soviet Union, the "Great Helmsman" Mao Zedong in the People's Republic of China, Kim Il-Sung and his descendants in North Korea, "Brother Number One" Pol Pot in Cambodia, Mengistu Haile Mariam in Ethiopia, Enver Hoxha in Albania, Nicolae Ceauşescu in Romania, Fidel Castro in Cuba, the rulers of the Soviet Occupation Zone and the GDR, the Baltic states and Poland were very different in their individual manifestations. The "Great Terror" in the Soviet Union in 1937/38 alone took hold of all strata of society without exception within just a few months. Not only were all the "elements" deemed dangerous within the state and party apparatus removed during the "Great Purge", but the Stalinist excesses of mass terror claimed the lives of at least 700,000 people who were arrested, tortured and killed while innocent or on trumped-up charges.

More than two million people were arrested during this period and sent to Gulag camps. An estimated 20 million people endured the horrors of the forced labour system between 1918 and the final dissolution of the Gulag in 1991. These camps spanned the entire territory of the Soviet Union, from the Solovetsky Islands in the White Sea to Magadan and Vladivostok in the far east, from Murmansk and Vorkuta on the Arctic Circle to Alma-Ata and Ulaanbaatar in Central Asia. Unlike the "Gulag Archipelago", the Laogai, a vast network of "reform and re-education camps" in the People's Republic of China, still exists today in a modified form. Since the camps were established in the early 1950s under Chairman Mao Zedong, an estimated 50 million people have been imprisoned in them. In the dictatorial state of North Korea, deportations and imprisonment in camps characterised by forced labour, terror, torture and death are to this day still common practice in the so-called judiciary to this day.

The long list of communist atrocities also includes disasters such as the Holodomor, the Great Famine of 1932/33. As a direct result of the forced collectivisation, "dekulakisation" and forced industrialisation practised under Stalin, around seven million people fell victim to a catastrophic famine on the territory of Ukraine, along the Don and in Stavropol, along the Lower and Middle Volga, in the Southern Urals, in Western Siberia and on the vast steppes of Kazakhstan. All mention of these crimes was taboo; they were covered up for decades and their victims slandered. The Great Chinese Famine from 1959 to 1961 cost the lives of at least 20 million people in the wake of Mao's "Great Leap Forward". The many crimes committed by communist regimes also include the genocide of the Cambodian population by the Khmer Rouge. Dictator Pol Pot's reign of terror, which lasted only three years, claimed the lives under horrific circumstances of approximately 1.4 to 2.2 million people between 1975 and 1978. At least until the death of Stalin, mass terror was also common practice in the governance of most Eastern European states.

The excesses of repression and terror differed markedly in the individual countries. They also gradually underwent a change in intensity. As the governments stabilised, everyday oppression took on a different form—censorship of the media and the systematic isolation of dissidents and nonconformists—but the memory of terror lingered among the population in all communist states. The history of repression and persecution also includes those men and women who resisted and often paid for their courage with their lives or long prison sentences.

Only after the collapse of the communist regimes in Europe did it become possible to publicly commemorate the crimes and their victims. It became apparent that, in Western Europe in particular, there was little knowledge of, or interest in, what had taken place behind the former Iron Curtain. The ensuing engagement with, and memorialisation of, communist crimes in all former Eastern Bloc countries was often met with apprehension and incomprehension in Western Europe. All too often, those in Eastern Europe who campaigned to commemorate the crimes of the second great totalitarian system after National Socialism were accused of relativising Nazi crimes and the Holocaust.

In 2005, Buchenwald survivor Jorge Semprún expressed the hope "that at the next commemoration in ten years, in 2015, the experience of the Gulag will have become integrated into our collective European memory [...]. One of the most effective ways to pave the way for the future of a united Europe, or rather a reunited Europe, is to share our past, our memory, our memories, which have previously been divided. The recent accession [to the European Union] of ten new countries from Central and Eastern Europe—the other Europe trapped in Soviet totalitarianism—can only truly take hold, culturally and existentially, when we have shared and united our memories."[1]

It is in this spirit that this book presents 119 memorial sites in 35 countries that commemorate the injustice suffered by millions of people under communist rule. May this book contribute to keeping the memory of their fates alive.

As always, we had a great deal of support in preparing this book. On the one hand, we received important information about memorial sites from numerous people and institutions from all countries. On the other, we were able to draw on the expertise of many of the people who were involved, especially when composing the introductory texts for the individual countries. We would therefore especially like to thank Oktav Bjoza, György Dalos, Vera Dubina, Juri Durkot, Adam Hudek, Alexandar Jakir, Matthias Kiesler, Fanna Kolarova, Hartmut Koschyk, Norbert Mappes-Niediek, Meelis Maripuu, Maria Matschuk, Georg Meusel, Valters Nollendorfs, Markus Pieper, Corneliu Pintilescu, Viera Polakovičová, Stojan Raichevsky, Krzysztof Ruchniewicz, Bernhard Seliger, Darius Semaska, Ashot Smbatyan, Thomas Sindilariu, Claudia Vollmer and Felix Wemheuer. Without their assistance, this book would not exist in its present form.

Of course, such a book also requires professional editing, translation and design. We are very grateful to have found such competent partners in Sandstein Verlag and its employees and partners. Our special thanks go to Lutz Stellmacher for his prudent project management, Sina Volk for proofreading and Katrin Hoyer for the production.

Last but not least, we would like to thank you, the readers of this book, and invite you to send us further information, which we will gladly include in a second edition.

Anna Kaminsky · Ruth Gleinig · Lena Ens
Berlin, February 2018

1 Speech available online at: www.zeit.de/2005/16/BefreiungBuchenw_/seite-2 (German, last accessed: 01/03/2018).

Museums and Memorials

Commemorating the Victims of Communist Dictatorships

Countries with a History of Communist Dictatorship

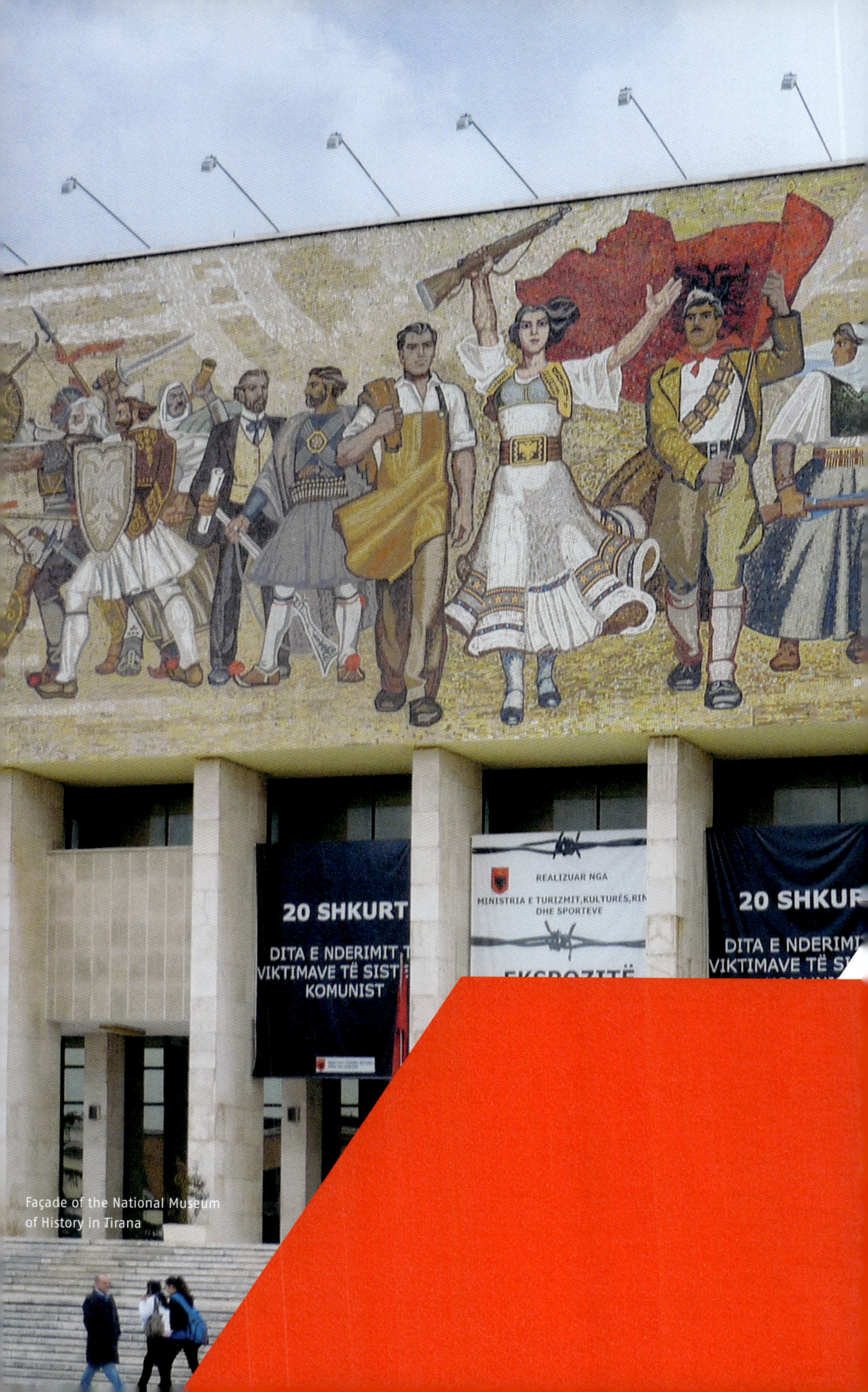

Façade of the National Museum of History in Tirana

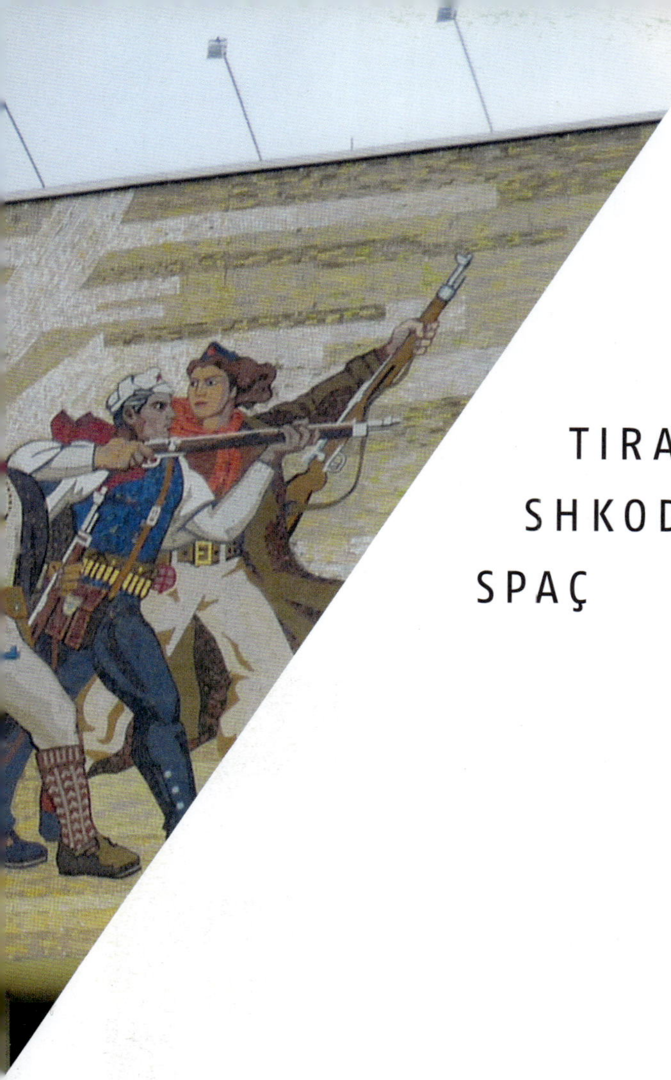

TIRANA
SHKODRA
SPAÇ

Albania

Albania gained its independence from the Ottoman Empire in 1912. In the First World War, during which the country was formally neutral, Albania experienced various occupations. Even after the war had ended, the country did not settle down; conditions akin to civil war continued to shape its post-war history until Ahmet Zogu took power in 1925 and proclaimed himself king in 1928. In April 1939, Albania was occupied by Italy, which was allied with Nazi Germany. During the Second World War, in 1941, the territories of Kosovo and Western Macedonia and parts of Northern Greece were also annexed to Albania. The resulting "Greater Albania" came under German occupation following the surrender of Italy in September 1943.

Various partisan movements formed from the very beginning to resist the occupations. After the German Wehrmacht withdrew from Albania at the end of 1944, Communist-dominated partisan units under the leadership of Enver Hoxha took power in the country and established a dictatorship based on the Stalinist model. Purges began as early as 1944, the first phase of which claimed the lives mostly of fighters and sympathisers of the Republican partisan movement Balli Kombëtar.

This was all grist to the propaganda mill of the Communist Party of Albania, founded in 1941, which was able to disseminate the myth that the communists were the only faction to oppose the fascist and national socialist occupation of the country. Representatives of pre-war bourgeois parties, former members of parliament, members of previous governments, factory and land owners, clergymen and intellectuals fell victim to continued reprisals.

On 11 January 1946, Enver Hoxha proclaimed the People's Republic of Albania within the borders of 1912. The constitution adopted on 14 March 1946 banned all non-Communist organisations and imposed severe sanctions on any dissenting expression or activity. In the course of the land reform carried out in the summer of 1945, all landholdings were expropriated without compensation. In 1948, Enver Hoxha proclaimed the "aggravation of the class struggle against the kulaks". Thousands of people were arrested and executed in the early post-war years on false accusations of war crimes or trumped-up political charges.

Under the rule of Enver Hoxha, over 170,000 bunkers were built in communist Albania.

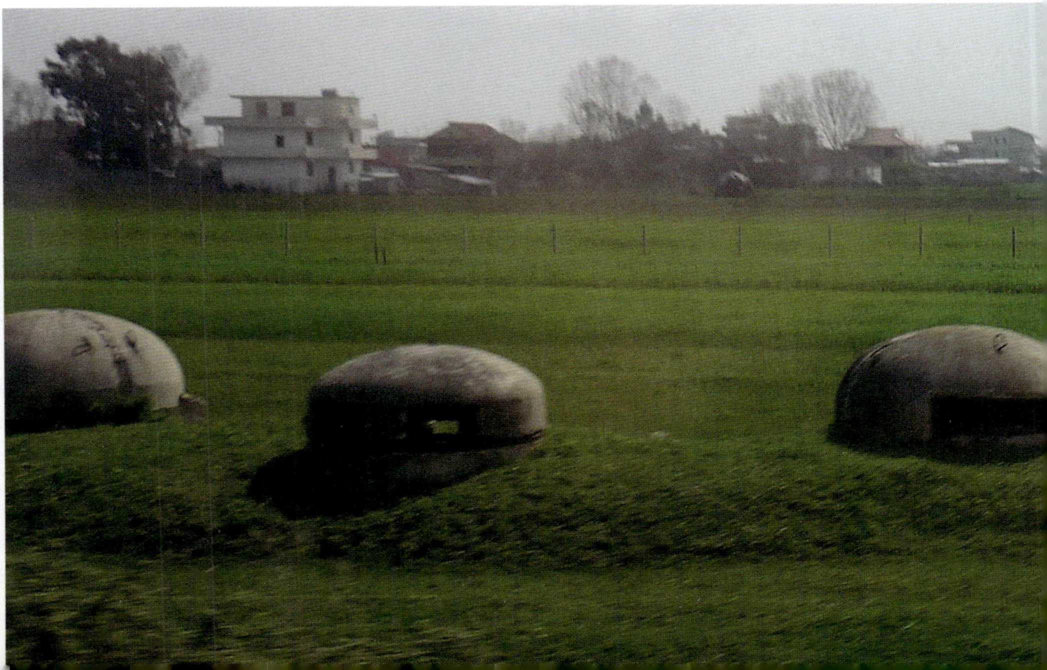

No-one in Albania was safe from persecution, exile or death. The application of the principle of collective punishment meant that both the accused and their families were expropriated and often sent away for decades to the forced labour camps that were spread throughout the country. In addition to actual and alleged opponents, followers of Hoxha and members of the party leadership and the government were also arrested and executed.

Whenever the course of foreign policy changed, those who had supported the previous policy were persecuted and systematically eliminated. For instance, after Yugoslavia's break with Stalin's Soviet Union in 1948, the Soviet regime not only terminated the treaty with the Titoist state concluded one year before but also initiated a massive wave of repression against pro-Yugoslav factions and alleged agents. 1961 saw a rift between Albania and the Soviet Union, which had begun to de-Stalinise after the 20th Congress of the CPSU in 1956. Albania now began to align itself more closely with China. As a result, all those who had studied in the Soviet Union or were deemed pro-Soviet were persecuted. When Albania also severed relations with China after the Chinese leadership distanced itself from Mao, allegedly pro-China factions and their families suffered the same fate.

The ubiquitous oppression was exacerbated by the total isolation and surveillance of the population by thousands of informants and agents of the Albanian secret police, the Sigurimi. While the Orthodox patriarch and the Muslim Grand Mufti were still able to reach an agreement with the state authorities in the late 1940s, the Catholic Church was subject to extensive repression. In 1949 alone, almost half of all Catholic clergymen were executed. In 1967, Albania declared itself the first atheist country on earth. All churches, monasteries, synagogues and mosques were closed or repurposed as sports facilities, stables or warehouses. Anyone who practised religious rites or owned religious literature or objects was officially persecuted as an "enemy of the people and the party".

Albania was hermetically sealed off from its neighbours by a deadly border regime. Between 1945 and 1990, more than 14,500 people were arrested during attempted escapes, and more than 1,000 people died. Out of a population of less than three million, an estimated 100,000 were held as political prisoners, 10,000 of whom did not survive imprisonment. 50,000 families—or several hundred thousand people—were expropriated because a relative had been declared an

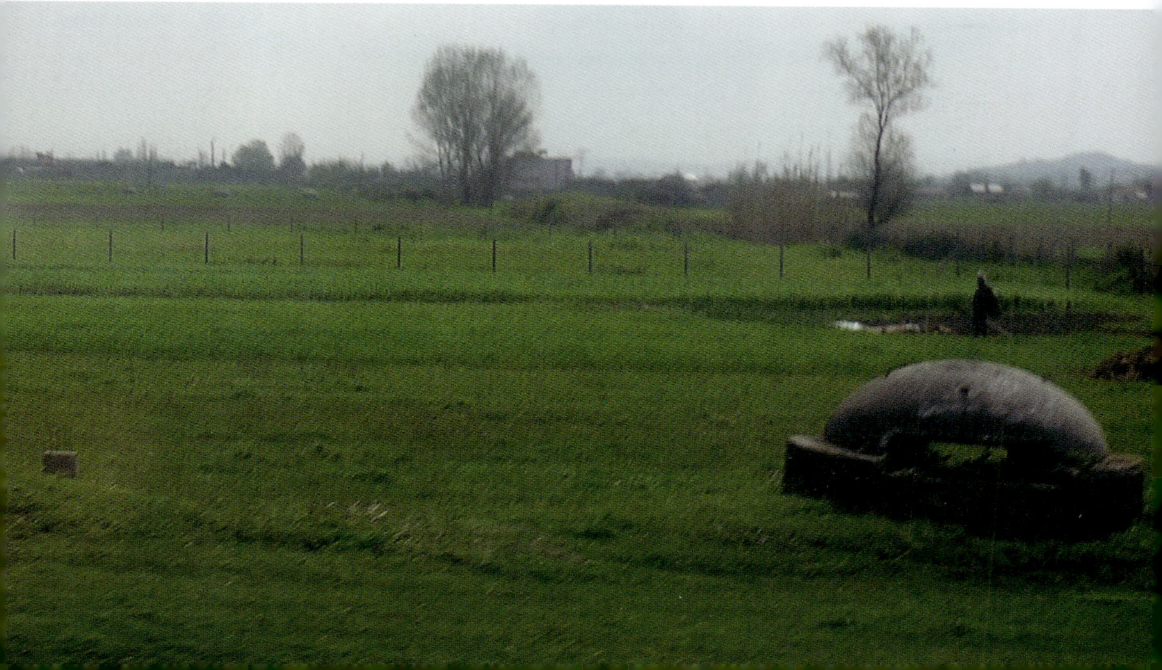

enemy of the state and were consequently deported to forced labour camps, where even children had to perform hard labour. More than 5,000 men and 450 women were executed for political reasons. The death penalty was imposed in Albania not only for murder or embezzlement, but above all for political offences such as treason, espionage or anti-Communist activity and "enemy propaganda", which also included the practice of religion.

As in other Communist-ruled countries, the late 1960s/early 1970s brought about a timid liberalisation. Television programmes with modern music were produced and censorship was relaxed. Efforts were also made to reduce external isolation. This phase came to an abrupt and brutal close at the end of 1972: artists were arrested and detained for years in forced labour camps on the grounds of allegations that they were painting in too modern a style and not representing socialist realism sufficiently faithfully. Singers and directors were persecuted because their art was deemed too un-Albanian or too Western. No accusation was too absurd to be used as a pretext for purges. Cultural luminaries such as the head of state television, along with musicians and writers, were arrested along with their families.

After Enver Hoxha's death in 1985, many people hoped in vain for an easing of the repression. Although Hoxha's successor Ramiz Alia, the last communist leader, introduced some initial economic reforms and ushered in the diplomatic opening of the country, for the most part he maintained the overall policy of the Communist Party. In January 1990, inspired by the uprisings taking place throughout the Eastern Bloc, resistance against the rulers spread across the country, starting from Shkodra in the north. In the spring, the government removed the practice of religion from the list of offences subject to the death penalty and allowed religious acts. In the summer, security forces violently broke up student protests in Tirana, and thousands of Albanians sought refuge in foreign embassies. However, the anti-communist movement could no longer be stopped. In mid-December 1990, the Communist Party relinquished its right to the monopoly on power. The first newly registered party was the Democratic Party of Albania (PDSh), which was founded on 12 December.

The Socialist Party of Albania (PSSh), a direct successor to the Stalinist Communist Party, won the first free elections in 1991. On 20 February 1991, angry protesters tore down the six-metre-high statue of Enver Hoxha on Skanderbeg Square (Sheshi "Skënderbej") in the centre of the capital Tirana. Countless students died when the police opened fire on the crowd. Ongoing unrest led to new elections barely a year later, which the PDSh won with a two-thirds majority under the leadership of Sali Berisha. The subsequent government of national unity introduced reforms and signed the CSCE Final Act. The term "Socialist" was removed from the name of the state, a pluralist party system and freedoms of speech and assembly were approved, and the release of political prisoners was initiated. Following the 1992 elections, the PDSh took control of the government. Unrest, economic stagnation and corruption dominated the country in the years that followed, with the PSSh and PDSh taking turns at the reins of power.

First attempts to come to terms with the past ran aground as no one was being held to account for the crimes committed under communist rule. Instead, the old elites re-established their foothold in positions of power. Although an exhibition on communist crimes in Albania opened at the National Museum of History as early as 1991, little progress was made in the compensation and rehabilitation of victims of political persecution or the criminal investigation of the regime's transgressions. It was particularly painful for many former victims of persecution that high-ranking members of the Communist Party, prosecutors and judges involved in reprisals and the imposition of death sentences under the communist regime regained political power.

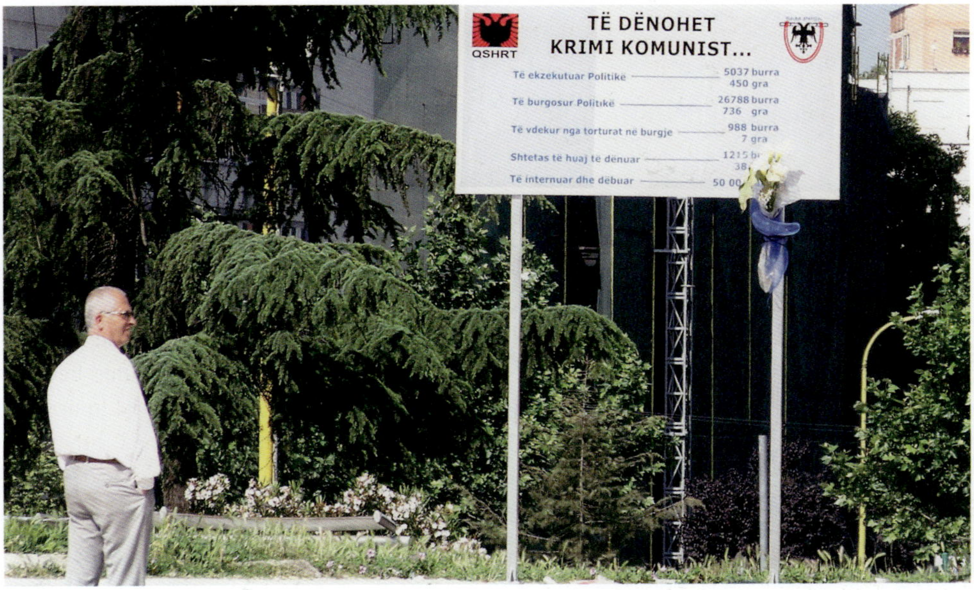

Sign on Skanderbeg Square with information about victims of persecution

The survivors united in victims' associations, but for a long time their aspiration to compensation and rehabilitation was ignored. Even today, some of them have yet to receive their meagre compensation. Some of the property of expropriated families was returned, but this process, too, was arduous, as it was often difficult to provide evidence of the expropriations.

The Institute for the Studies of Communist Crimes in Albania was founded in 2010. Run by former victims of persecution, it collects the testimonies of contemporary witnesses. The institute's mission is to provide information about the dictatorship with educational and contemporary witness programmes in schools.

It took more than 20 years after the end of communist rule for memorials and commemorative plaques to be installed at sites of terror. In 2013, a first monument commemorating the crimes and the overthrow of the dictatorship was inaugurated in the capital at the entrance to Blocku, the secluded residential quarter of the communist elite, and in 2014 the only memorial to be installed to date in a former Sigurimi prison was opened in Shkodra, a hotbed of anti-communist resistance.

The opening of the Sigurimi files was a long and controversial chapter in Albanian history. These were only compiled and made accessible on a separate official site in 2017. In the former Sigurimi headquarters in Tirana, the "House of Leaves", a memorial was opened commemorating the surveillance of society and its victims. In Lushnja, a monument to the victims of the internment camps there was inaugurated in the spring of 2017. Other initiatives of former prisoners and exiles, but also of young people, are attempting to erect memorials and monuments in former camps (e.g. in Tepelenë) and prisons such as Spaç or Burrel. In Tirana, two large exhibitions in the notorious bunkers that Hoxha forced hundreds of thousands of people to erect throughout the country from the 1970s now provide information about the practice of repression under the communist dictatorship.

National Museum of History

Tirana. The National Museum of History was constructed according to the designs of Albanian architect Enver Faja and ceremonially inaugurated on 28 October 1981. With an exhibition area of 27,000 square metres, it remains the largest museum in the country. The collection, which comprises over 5,000 objects, sheds light in eight thematic areas on Albanian history from prehistoric culture and the Middle Ages to the collapse of the communist regime. A sub-exhibition, which was completed in 1991 and focused exclusively on the 40 years of Communist dictatorship under Enver Hoxha and Ramiz Alia, was the first exhibition to address communist crimes in the national museum of a post-communist state.

This exhibition was closed in 2011 as part of the renovation of the museum. Since its reopening, a pavilion located on the second floor has been dedicated to the topic of communist persecution. Using original documents, photographs and authentic objects, the history of the communist regime of terror in Albania from 1944 to 1991 is told in chronological order. In addition to the communist takeover of the state, which was accompanied by systematic "cleansing campaigns" and the elimination of the legitimate opposition, it also portrays attempts to resist the established dictatorship. The uprising in Postribë on 8 September 1946 was the largest-ever armed revolt against communism in Albania. The strongest remaining partisan and resistance groups in the country, such as the Republican Balli Kombëtar and the monarchist Legaliteti, had joined forces under the slogan "For faith and fatherland. Down with the communists!" Troops loyal to the government quashed the uprising.

A further focus is on the system of labour and detention camps. Since traditional prisons were overcrowded due to the rapid rise in the numbers of political detainees, and the conditions of detention in them were considered too good, a network of labour camps was established. By 1947, there were already four such complexes. They were mostly built near major construction sites—railway lines, airports or canals—or, like the notorious camp in Spaç, which was built at a copper and pyrite extraction site, mines. In the Maliq camp, some 1,000 inmates were enslaved to drain the marshlands. Relatives of political prisoners were also persecuted and sentenced according to the principle of collective punishment. In concrete terms, this meant exile to completely isolated areas, so-called "closed villages", which were strictly guarded. While a political "thaw" began in the other communist states in March 1956 following the revelations at the 20th Congress of the CPSU, Albania remained faithful to Stalinist ideology and practice until the late 1980s.

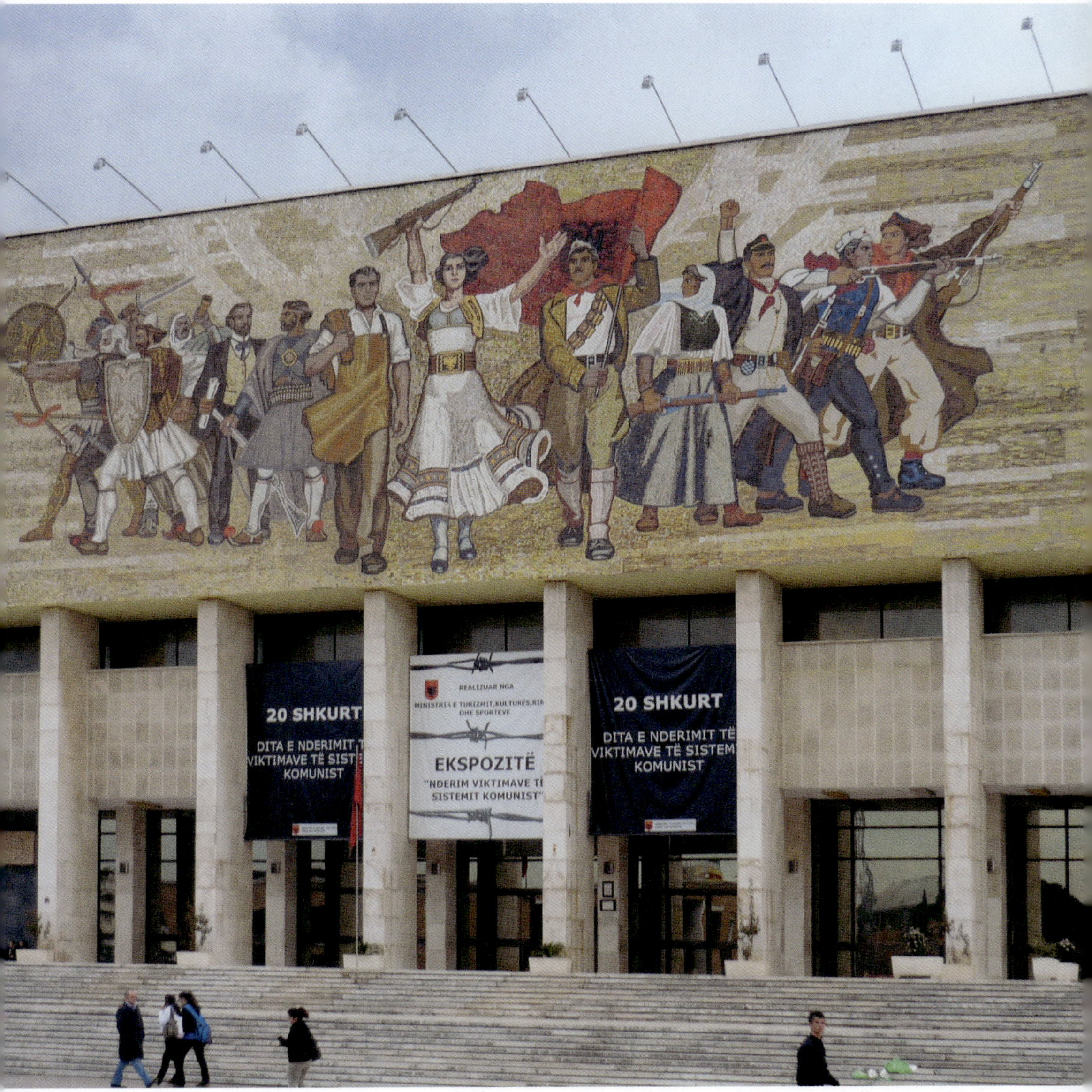

Location: Tirana, at the intersection of Sheshi "Skënderbej" and Bulevardi Zogu I
Internet: www.mhk.gov.al

Façade of the National Museum of History

"House of Leaves"

Tirana. On 23 May 2017, 26 years after the fall of the communist regime in Albania, the first memorial to the victims of the communist dictatorship was opened in the former Sigurimi headquarters. The initiative to erect a memorial in this building was taken by survivors of the communist dictatorship and has been supported by the Ministry of Culture since 2013.

The building was constructed in 1931 by well-known Albanian doctor Jani Basho, who used it as a clinic. During the German occupation, the building was used by the Gestapo as its headquarters and prison. Following the incursion by Communist partisan groups under the leadership of Enver Hoxha, the Albanian communist secret police, the Sigurimi, took control of the building. In 1945 and 1946, hundreds of people were imprisoned, tortured and murdered here.

From 1950 onwards, the building served as the headquarters of Section V of the Albanian secret police. It was responsible for monitoring foreigners and diplomats living in Albania. Within walking distance of all-important party offices, the only hotel approved for foreigners, and the embassies, the surveillance of foreign missions and locals who had contact with foreigners was organised from this building. An underground passage connected the "House

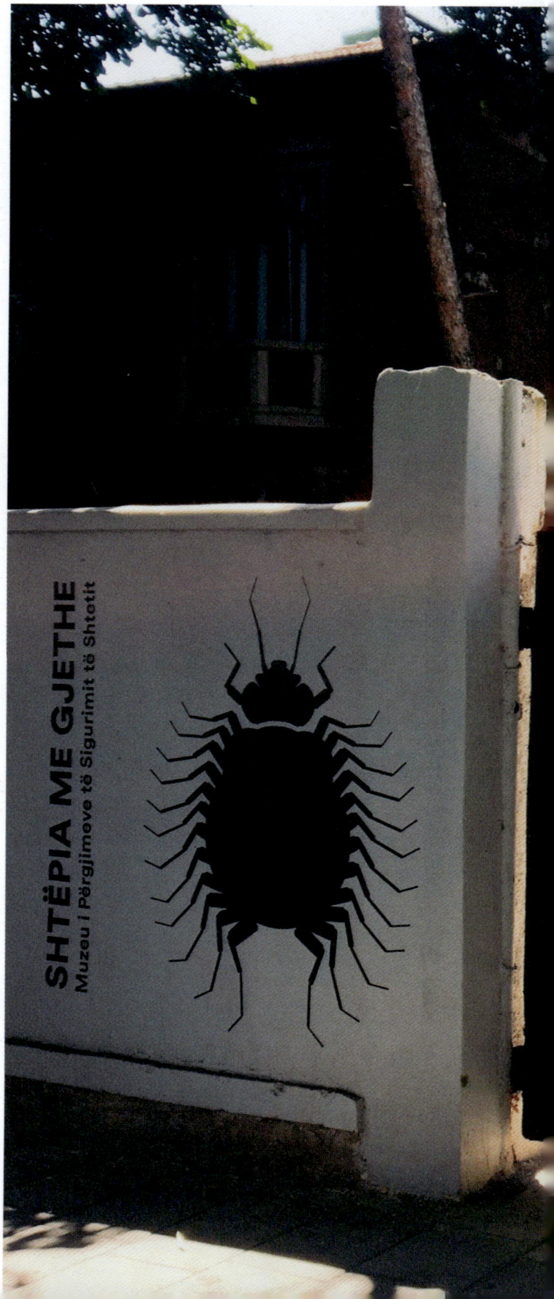

►
Entrance to the "House of Leaves"

View of the museum's exhibition

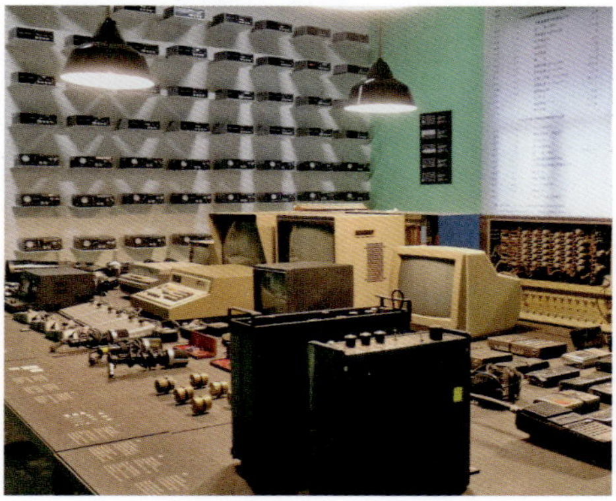

of Leaves", which got its name from the dense growth of climbing plants on the façade, to the nearby Ministry of the Interior, to which the Sigurimi was subordinated.

Location: Tirana, Muzeu Kombetar "Shtepia me Gjethe"; Rruga Dëshmorët e 4 Shkurtit
Internet: www.muzeugjethi.gov.al

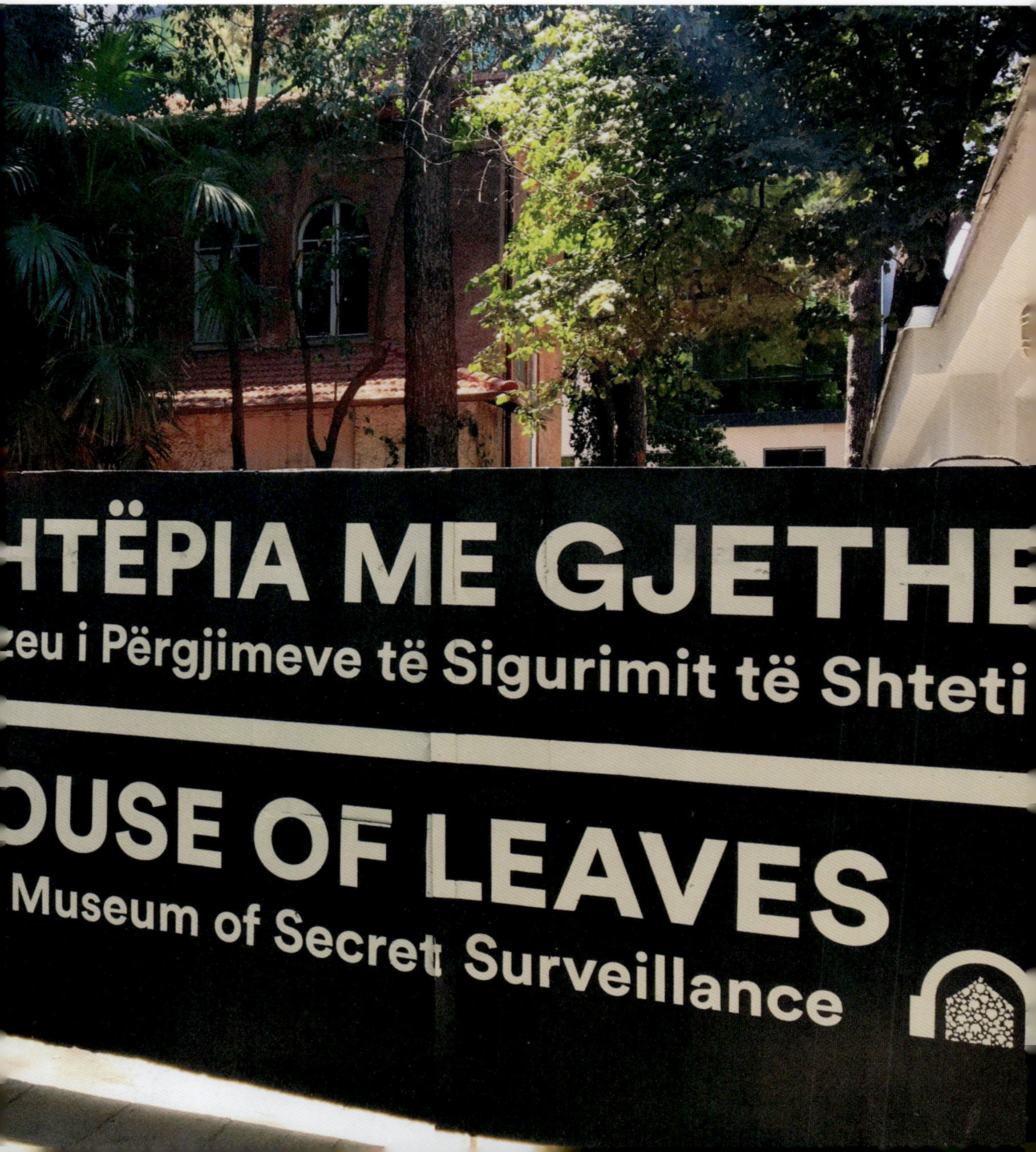

"Post-Bloc" Memorial Ensemble

Tirana. A memorial was inaugurated on 26 March 2013 in the Albanian capital Tirana to commemorate the overthrow of the communist dictatorship and to recall its victims.

The art installation, which was erected on the former exclusion zone in today's night-life district in the centre of Tirana, consists of an original segment of the Berlin Wall, a concrete support from the mining tunnels of the Spaç labour camp and a bunker, which is symbolic of the more than 170,000 bunkers still scattered throughout Albania today. The memorial was designed by Fatos Lubonja, a political prisoner of the regime who spent 19 years in labour camps and solitary confinement, and Ardian Isufi.

Location: Tirana, Bulevardi Dëshmorët e Kombit

Full view of the "Post-Bloc" memorial complex

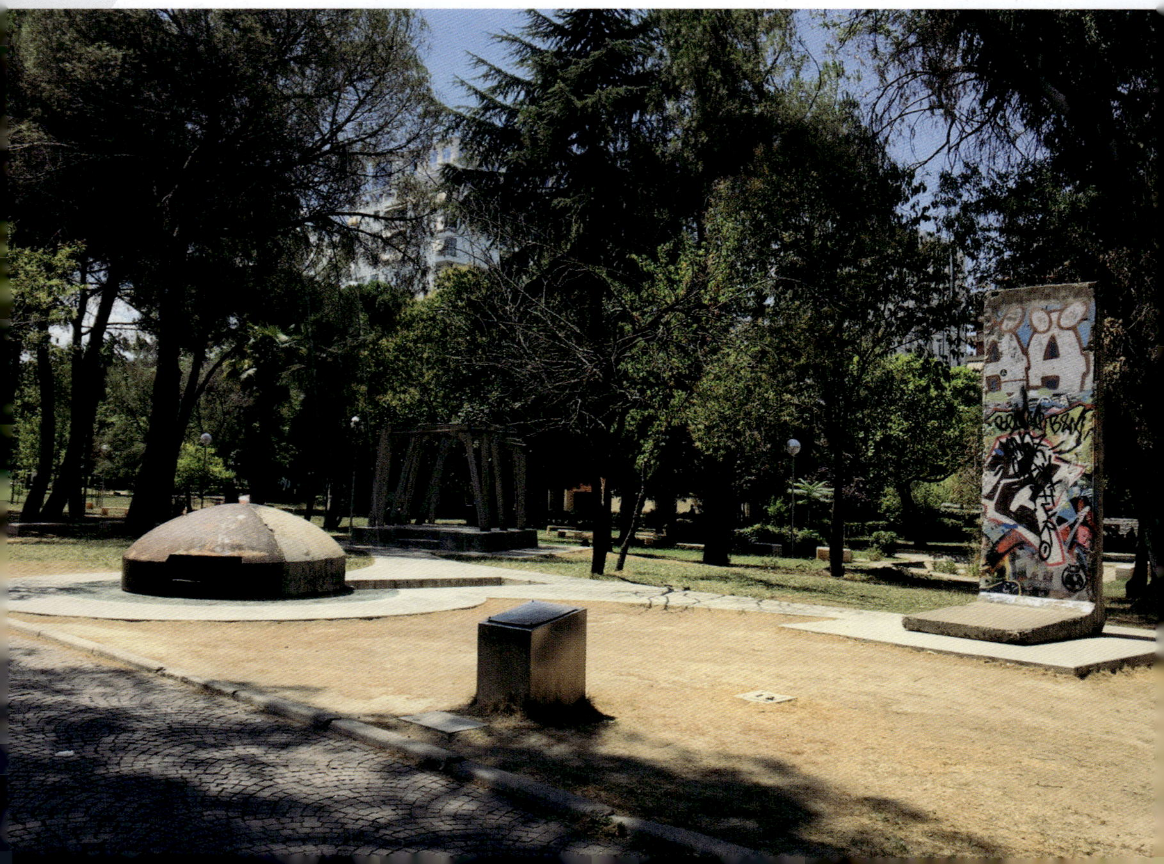

"Bunk'Art I" and "Bunk'Art II"

Tirana. The multimedia exhibition "Bunk'Art I" was opened to the public on 22 November 2014. It is located in a bunker several storeys underground on the outskirts of Tirana, which was built in the 1970s as a shelter for the highest state leadership in the event of a nuclear attack on Albania. "Bunk'Art I" comprises over 100 rooms, some of which have been converted into historical and museum exhibition halls, while others are used for art installations. Concerts, seminars and conferences take place in an assembly hall integrated into the bunker. Visitors can learn in 13 historical exhibition rooms about the Albanian communist armed forces and the everyday life of the population.

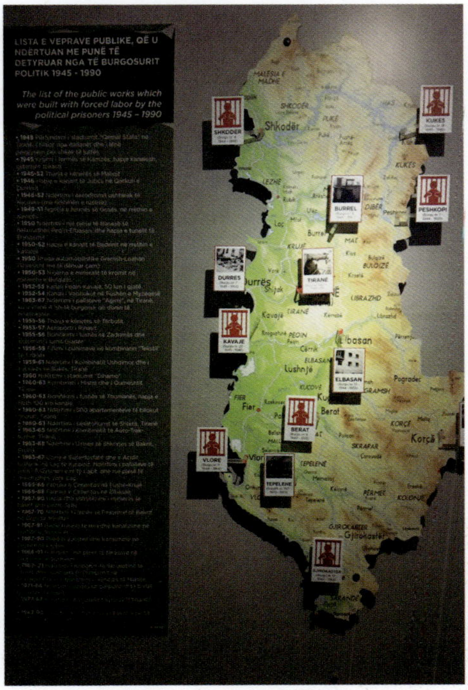

Map with camp and prison locations in the permanent exhibition "Bunk'Art I"

The 18 rooms, some of which have been preserved in their original state, show various facets of everyday life in socialist Albania. The broad-based measures for the literacy of the population after the end of the Second World War and the subsequent shaping of the educational system by the ideology of Marxism-Leninism are presented here. Other thematic modules deal with the importance of sports culture, its state support, regulation and instrumentalisation. The original offices of Enver Hoxha and Prime Minister Mehmet Shehu are also on display. Finally, the bunker construction programme, which was stepped up between 1975 and 1983, is also addressed. Of 221,143 planned bunkers, to be built mainly along the country's borders and on the coast, a total of 173,371 were built.

On 19 November 2016, a branch of the "Bunk'Art" Museum was opened in the centre of Tirana. "Bunk'Art II" is located in the shelter tunnels built between 1981 and 1986 by the

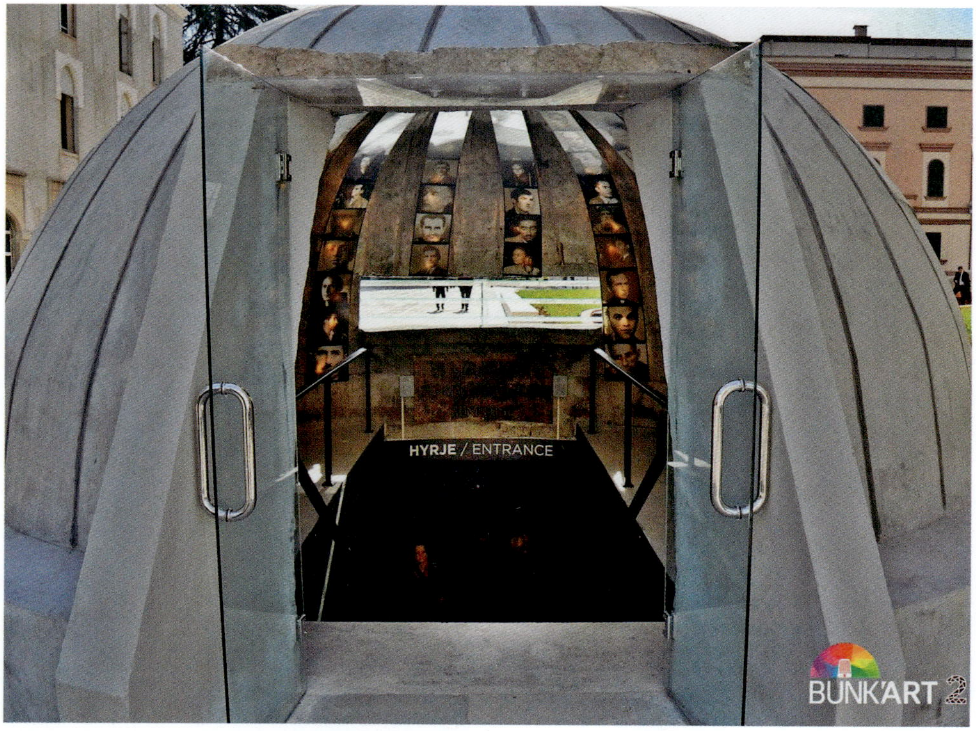

Entrance to the exhibition in "Bunk'Art II"

Albanian Ministry of the Interior. "Bunk'Art II" recounts the history of the Albanian Ministry of the Interior in the years between 1912 and 1991 and that of the notorious secret police, the Sigurimi, which was subordinated to it from 1944. The initiator and current curator of both "Bunk'Art" exhibitions is Italian journalist Carlo Bollino.

In addition to the history of the state apparatus of repression and deterrence, the new complex also illustrates the surveillance and espionage methods used by the Sigurimi secret police. Originally code-named "Objekti Shtylla", the facility comprises 24 rooms, the living and working quarters of the Ministry of the Interior and a command centre installed for internal communication. Like many other bunkers of this size, the premises were built to withstand an attack with nuclear, biological and chemical weapons. Like the "Bunk'Art I" exhibition, the curators have divided the exhibition into a historical and a museum section. The history of the Albanian police forces under the fascist Italian and Nazi German regimes of occupation is retraced and made accessible to the public. The Albanian communist secret police, the Sigurimi, is the centrepiece of the exhibition. A map shows the prisons distributed throughout the country separating political and "regular" inmates, the labour and detention camps, and the inhumane conditions the prisoners had to endure.

The institution provides an online database on its website with the names of victims of political repression in Albania. The exhibits in both complexes are labelled in Albanian and English.

Location: Tirana, Rruga Fatil Deliu and Rruga Sermedin Said Toptani
Internet: www.bunkart.al

"Site of Witness and Memory" Memorial

Shkodra. The "Site of Witness and Memory" was opened in Shkodra in September 2014 to commemorate the victims of the Communist regime of terror. It is located in a historic building that was used between 1946 and 1992 as the headquarters of the local department of the Albanian Ministry of the Interior and as a prison.

The building, which was constructed in 1850, was originally used by the Austrian order of the Christian Brothers as a dormitory for children attending the nearby Franciscan school. Between 1918 and 1930, the town council converted the building into a hospital, and, from October 1930 onwards, Franciscan monks used it as an educational institution. After the establishment of communist rule, the Franciscan Order, like many other religious institutions throughout the country, was expropriated and driven out. The building then served as the headquarters of the local department of the Ministry of the Interior.

After reconstruction, holding cells and interrogation rooms were set up in the former store rooms in the basement. A total of 29 dark cells, each no larger than three square metres, were lined up in two corridors about four metres long. The cell block had an adjoining inner courtyard from which the detainees were led through a connecting door to the interrogation room. During their pre-trial detention, the prisoners remained imprisoned in the cells on the ground floor. One of the "special features" of communist "jurisdiction" in Albania was that pre-trial detention could be extended indefinitely—often for years. At the same time, any behaviour could be branded "treasonous". After sentencing, the prisoners were transferred either to other prisons or to internment camps. Those sentenced to death were held in a separate room until the sentence was carried out.

In the 1980s, cells were set up on the second floor for regular detention. An additional storey was added to accommodate the offices. The Ministry of the Interior maintained the building until the change of government in 1992, after which it became the property of the local police force. In 1997, the state returned the building to the Albanian Franciscan Order.

Today's entrance to the cell block leads through a gallery with documents and art objects designed to give expression to the suffering of those imprisoned in this place. At the end of the gallery is the exhibition room with objects made by the prisoners during their detention. The first anti-communist protests in Albania, the radical persecution of the clergy, the internment of political prisoners and the numerous punitive measures are presented here. The documents, letters, manuscripts, utensils and valuables on display were donated by survivors and relatives of the victims.

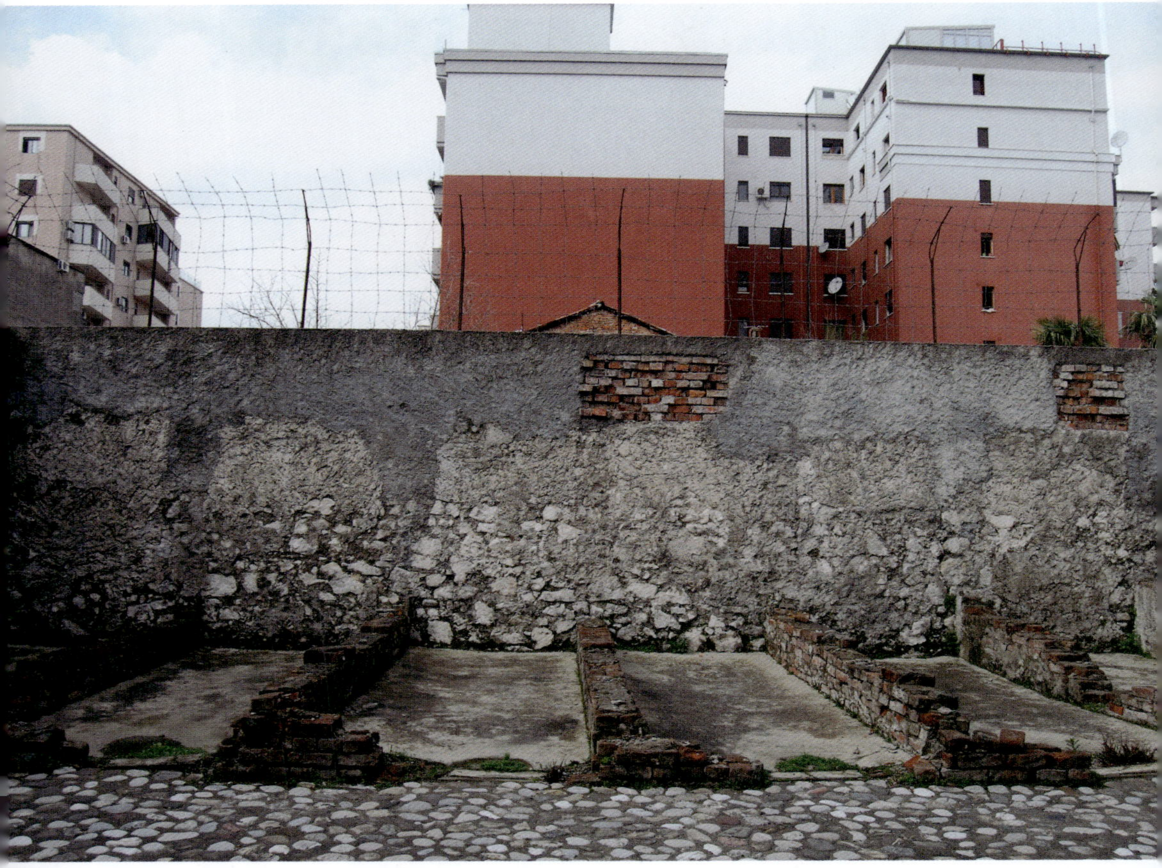

Exercise yard in the former prison in Shkodra

A room with audio-visual media and a small library provide the opportunity to investigate the topic in greater depth.

Location: Shkodra, Bulevardi Skënderbeu 26
Internet: www.vdkshkoder.com

Spaç Memorial Project

Spaç. The grounds of the notorious labour and internment camp at Spaç, known during communist rule as "Unit for Re-education 303", are located in a mountainous area near the northern Albanian municipality of Mirditë. Most of the buildings that fell victim to harsh weather conditions and vandalism after the camp was finally closed are still in ruins. Spaç Prison, established in 1968, whose inmates were enslaved and forced to work in the nearby copper and pyrite mines, was one of the cruellest prisons in communist Albania, alongside the prison in Burrel and the camp complex in Ballsh. Many of the men detained here were political prisoners: artists, writers, intellectuals and clergymen. Among them were prominent personalities such as the author and dissident Fatos Lubonja and architect and painter Maks Velo. After the collapse of the communist regime and the lifting of the ban on religion, Catholic priest Simon Jubani, who, like the Roman Catholic Cardinal Ernest Simoni, was among the prisoners, officiated over the first Christian service in the country. The National Restoration Council of Albania announced in 2009 that it would convert Spaç into a museum complex. However, no funding has been made available to date. In 2015, the historic site was included in the list of the 50 most endangered sites of the World Monument Fund, an international non-profit organisation dedicated to the preservation of monuments and historical sites.

Spaç Prison is located on a steep slope in the northern Albanian mountains. The buildings of the camp guards and the administration are among the better-preserved structures of the complex. The area assigned to the camp prisoners, including housing units and barracks, a parade ground and an inner courtyard, was surrounded by barbed wire and extends all the way to the watchtowers located down in the valley. It is bordered by a deep gorge. At maximum occupancy, there were about 1,400 prisoners in Spaç.

Throughout the country, prisoners were deployed as slave labour in construction projects: draining swamps, building blocks of flats and refineries, constructing canals and roads, mining precious metals and minerals, and quarrying. In addition to the pursuit of purely economic goals, forced labour was designed not only to purge the prisoners of "wrong thoughts" but also to re-educate them to become "new socialist men"—with unattainable labour standards and inhumane working conditions. No consideration was given to the health of the prisoners. In the pyrite and copper mines of Spaç, the prisoners worked in three shifts in sweltering heat and icy cold with the most primitive of tools, without any safety precautions. It was common practice to send the men

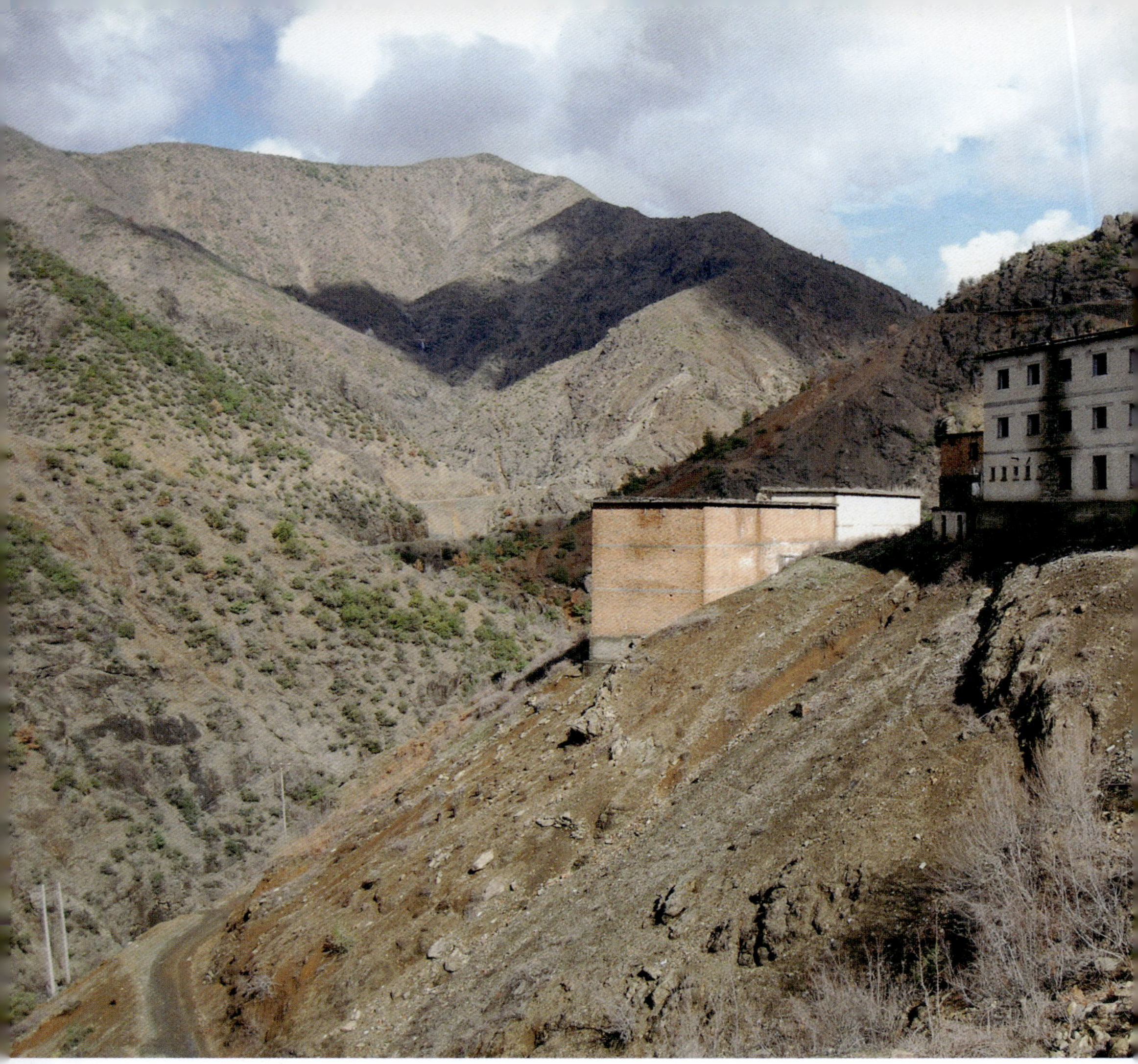

Ruins of the former labour and internment camp in Spaç

back into the tunnels immediately after the detonations—when the mines were still suffused with poisonous dynamite vapours.

Due to the inhumane detention and working conditions, the prisoners organised a revolt in May 1973. For two days, from 21 to 23 May 1973, they managed to take control of the camp. As a sign of protest, they raised the Albanian flag without the socialist star above the two eagle heads. After the uprising was finally suppressed, the leaders of the revolt were executed. Another 130 people were sentenced to longer prison terms under even stricter conditions. Twelve years later in 1985, another protest erupted in Spaç against the abuse and humiliation of the prisoners by the guards. Special forces of the Ministry of the Interior were flown in from Tirana to Spaç to quell the uprising. Three men were sentenced to death, one man died as a result of ill-treatment and torture during the interrogation, and another 36 prisoners received extended prison sentences of between six and twenty years. Dead prisoners were buried in unmarked graves. To this day, many of the victims' families still do not know the whereabouts of the bodies of the deceased. In Spaç, the remains of the former prisoners are said to be buried on the

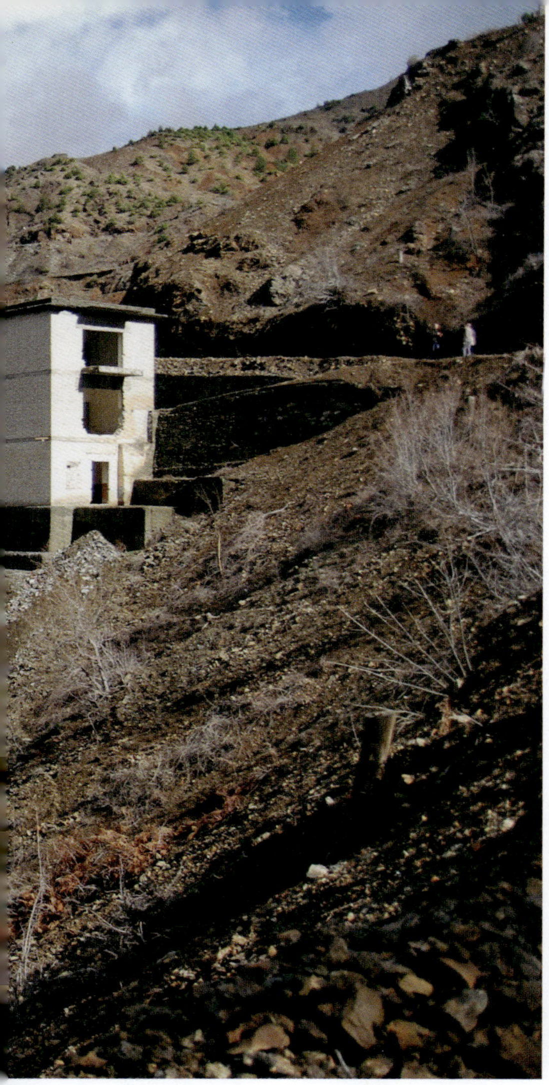

site where the bare mountain slope was planted with young tree seedlings.

In late 1991, after the Communist regime in Albania officially ceased to exist, the work and internment camps for political prisoners throughout the country—including in Spaç—were closed.

Location: Spaç, 60 kilometres north of Tirana on the SH40 main road

Further reading:
Idrizi, Idrit: Zwischen politischer Instrumentalisierung und Verdrängung: Die Auseinandersetzung mit dem Kommunismus in Öffentlichkeit, Geschichtspublizistik und Historiografie im postkommunistischen Albanien. In: Mählert, Ulrich et al. (ed.): Jahrbuch für Historische Kommunismusforschung. Berlin 2014. / Justice and Peace Commission Albania: Spaçi Prison. Why a Museum? Shkodra 2015. / Mirdita, Pierin (ed.): "Site of Witness and Memory"; from a place of suffering and tortures to a museum in commemoration of the victims of the communist regime 2016. Available online at: www.academia.edu/31408339/Site_of_Winess_and_Memory_-_Vendi_i_D%C3%ABshmis%C3%AB_dhe_Kujtes%C3%ABs.pdf (last accessed: 14/11/2017). / Niegelhell, Anita/Ponisch, Gabriele: Wir sind immer im Feuer. Berichte ehemaliger politischer Gefangener im kommunistischen Albanien. Vienna, Cologne, Weimar 2001.

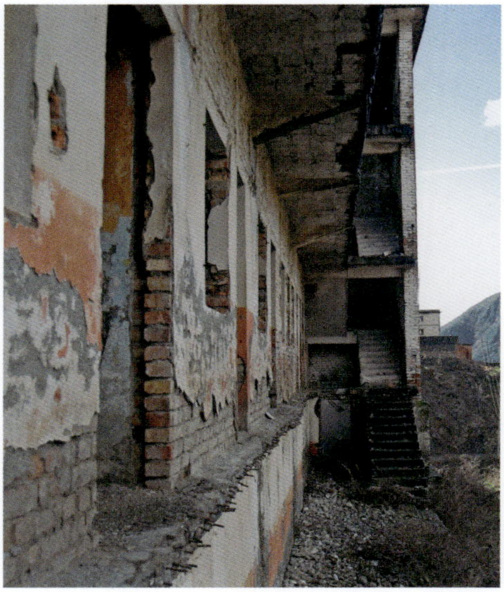

Weathered ruins of the camp in the Northern Mountain Range in Albania

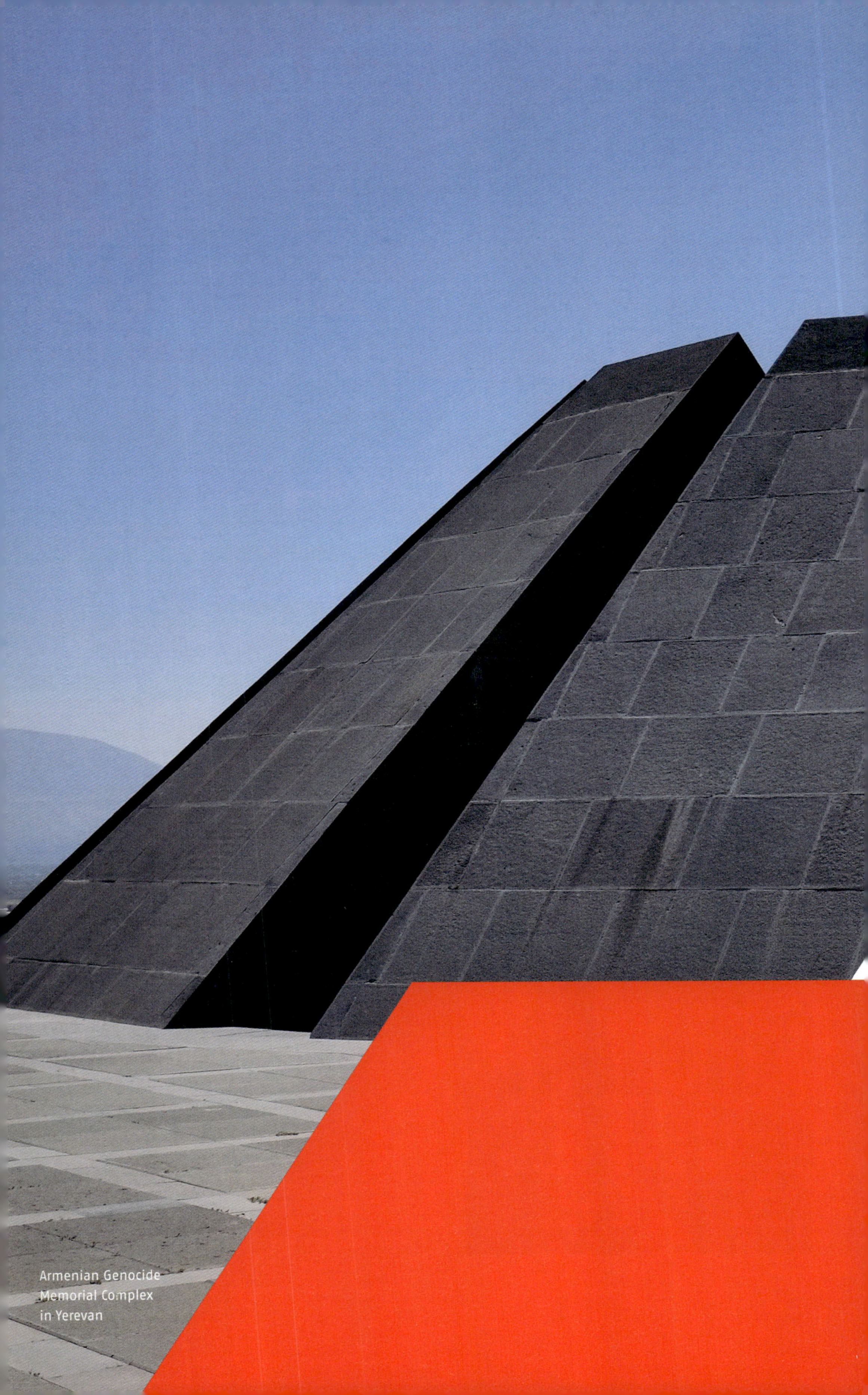

Armenian Genocide
Memorial Complex
in Yerevan

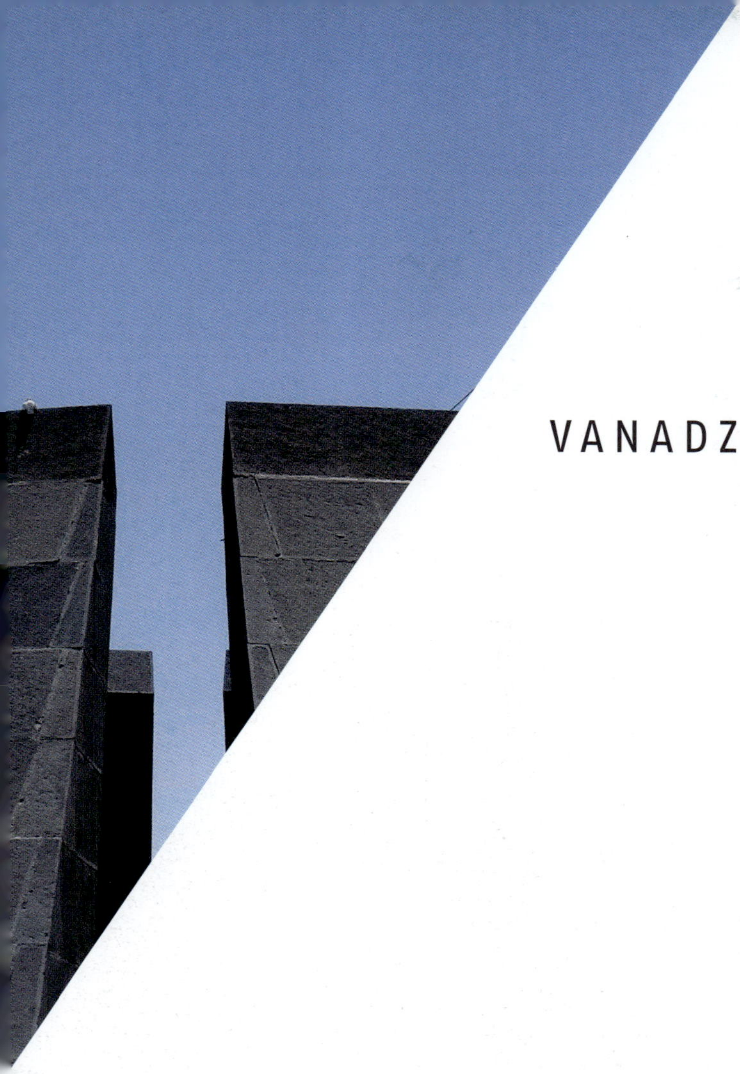

VANADZOR

Armenia

After the First World War, on 28 May 1918, the first Armenian democratic republic was founded but lasted for only two years. In late November 1920, Armenian communists took power in the country in a coup. They received military support from Red Army troops occupying Armenia. The Armenian Soviet Socialist Republic, founded in December 1920, formally retained its autonomy until, under pressure from Soviet Russia, it merged with Georgia and Azerbaijan in March 1922 to form the Transcaucasian Socialist Federative Soviet Republic. Part of the Armenian territory was ceded to Turkey in 1923 under the terms of the Treaty of Lausanne. Likewise, in the early 1920s, the Soviet government decided to give areas inhabited by Armenians, such as Nagorno-Karabakh, to Azerbaijan.

The implementation of Soviet rule was accompanied by extensive reprisals. The Bolsheviks declared war on everything they perceived as "backwards", including many regional and national traditions in all occupied territories. Whoever resisted the new power was subjected to persecution. With the establishment of Soviet power, all other political associations were banned: genuine and alleged supporters of the previous ruling party, Dashnaktsutyun, were persecuted and executed. These included representatives of the church as well as worshippers, owners of industries and land, and members of political parties and nationalist groups.

When collectivisation began in 1929, thousands of Armenian "kulaks" were also expropriated and persecuted. Some 25,000 farmers who opposed forced collectivisation were deported to Siberia. As part of the "Socialist Construction Service" introduced in Armenia in the early 1930s, all citizens were subject to compulsory relocation and forced labour in national construction projects. The aim was to promote the industrialisation of the country and the development of socialism.

In the 1930s, reprisals intensified once again. Around 300,000 people, a quarter of the population, were murdered or deported to the Gulag camps in the Great Terror of 1937/38. Virtually the entire Armenian intelligentsia was wiped out. The cultivation of national memories, the commemoration of the Armenian Genocide of 1915 under the sway of the Ottoman Empire or the discussion of arbitrary cessions of territory were suppressed and denounced as nationalist propaganda.

The campaign against the church began immediately after the Communists took power in December 1920. The Armenian Apostolic Church was expropriated, religious education in schools was banned, and clergy were stripped of their right to vote. Countless priests were arrested and murdered. Of the approximately 800 churches and monasteries to be found on the territory of what was to become Soviet Armenia at the beginning of the 20th century, a mere four were still open in the spring of 1938. The others had been desecrated, repurposed as cattle stables, storage rooms, cinemas or cultural centres, or destroyed. The repression of the churches during the Great Terror culminated in the assassination of Catholicos Khoren I, the spiritual head of the Apostolic Armenian Church, on the night of 5 – 6 April 1938.

At the beginning of the Great Patriotic War in 1941, Soviet policy towards Armenia changed. In order to bolster the morale and fighting spirit of the population during the war years, the Soviet state and party leadership relaxed its policy towards the churches that had previously been persecuted. As Moscow relied on the financial support of the Armenian diaspora, general repression was also eased.

Migration policy was similarly ambivalent. Especially after the end of the Second World War, Soviet Armenia initiated a campaign to repatriate the diaspora to compensate demographically and economically for the high casualties of the war. Between 1946 and 1948, some 90,000 people—around ten percent of Armenians living abroad—accepted the Soviet government's invitation to return. Most of them were survivors of the 1915 genocide. However, their integration proved difficult. It soon became clear that the life promised by Soviet propaganda had nothing to do with what really awaited them. To compound matters further, the re-immigrants were considered dangerous. Not only did they raise questions about the appropriate commemoration of the 1915 genocide—a heavily sanctioned taboo whose disregard was punishable by arrest and deportation—but they also undermined the myth of "catastrophic conditions and tyranny in the capitalist West". As a result of a decision of the Soviet government on 29 May 1949, thousands of returnees were swiftly re-exiled. During the deportations on the night of 13 to 14 June 1949 alone, 12,000 people were exiled to Altai and the Western Siberian city of Tomsk.

After the death of Stalin in 1953, political terror in Armenia and the other Soviet republics died down. Following the amnesty of 27 March 1953, some 5,600 people returned to Armenia from exile. It was not until 1962, almost ten years after Stalin's death, that the largest monument to Stalin in the Soviet Union was taken down in Yerevan. With the easing of repression following Stalin's death, previously taboo topics such as the 1915 genocide could be cautiously broached without immediately risking arrest and deportation. However, both the genocide and Stalinist repression and the question of border demarcations remained officially taboo. For opposition activists and dissidents, the focus was less on the enforcement of artistic freedoms—Armenian cultural policy was generally considered more liberal than that of the Soviet Union as a whole—or the observance of human rights. They concentrated instead on the recognition of the crimes of 1915 as genocide, reunification with separated territories such as Nagorno-Karabakh, and the preservation of national consciousness and traditional cultural monuments.

The process of strengthening Armenian national consciousness that began under the conditions of Khrushchev's "thaw" reached its climax on 24 April 1965. Disregarding state regulations not to hold any official commemoration ceremonies for the 50th anniversary of the genocide, 200,000 people gathered in Yerevan for an unofficial memorial rally. A year earlier, the Armenian Church had already advocated the introduction of 24 April as the official day of commemoration for the victims of the genocide. On posters and banners, protesters demanded recognition of the crimes as genocide and the erection of a memorial in the Armenian capital. It was inaugurated only two years later in 1967. They also demanded the return of Armenian territory, such as Nagorno-Karabakh, which had been ceded to Azerbaijan. The rallies were permitted as an outlet for political dissatisfaction and promoted a new national self-confidence, which was fuelled by the grief for, and memory of, the Armenians killed in the genocide.

On 24 April 1968, the underground National United Party of Armenia (NOP) was able to broadcast a message on the radio during the official commemoration ceremony for the victims of the genocide. In it, the activists called on the population to fight for the country's independence. Following this campaign, many members of the NOP and other underground organisations were arrested and sentenced to years in the infamous DubravLag in the Mordovian Soviet Republic. Many of them later described their experience in the work and reform camps as "a school of civil disobedience". Between 1961 and 1972, DubravLag was the only camp complex in the USSR where individuals alleged to be "particularly dangerous state criminals", i.e. persons convicted of "anti-Soviet agitation and propaganda", "treason", or "involvement with an anti-Soviet organisation", were detained. It was here that the Armenian opposition established contacts with dissidents from Russia, Ukraine and other Soviet republics. In the early 1970s, the first reports on opposition work in Armenia were published in the underground information bulletin of the "Chronicle of Current Events" human rights movement in Moscow.

As in other Eastern Bloc states, the CSCE Conference led to the establishment of a local Helsinki Group in Armenia in early 1977, which, citing the Helsinki Final Act, called for the granting of human and civil rights. In the first half of 1979, all members of the Armenian Helsinki Group were arrested. In the years to follow, the reprisals intensified again.

It was not until the perestroika era that many formerly taboo topics were opened up for public discussion. In 1987, Gorbachev issued an amnesty after which thousands of political prisoners returned to Armenia. This mainly affected Nagorno-Karabakh where the Armenian majority population attempted to break away from Azerbaijan and military conflict between Armenia and Azerbaijan broke out in February 1988. In the same year, thousands of Armenians were killed in anti-Armenian pogroms such as those in Sumgait on 28 February; as a result, 400,000 people fled to Armenia. At the same time, pogroms ensued against the Azeris living in Armenia, who in turn fled to Azerbaijan. In 1988, an earthquake devastated Armenia, killing 25,000 people and destroying about 40 percent of the country. This disaster was officially covered up, as the catastrophic accident at a nuclear power station in Chernobyl had been three years earlier. In 1991, the democratic movement finally achieved its most important political goal: in a referendum on the country's withdrawal from the Soviet Union, the majority of the population voted for national sovereignty. On 21 September 1991, the Republic of Armenia proclaimed its independence.

Armenian Genocide Memorial Complex
in Yerevan

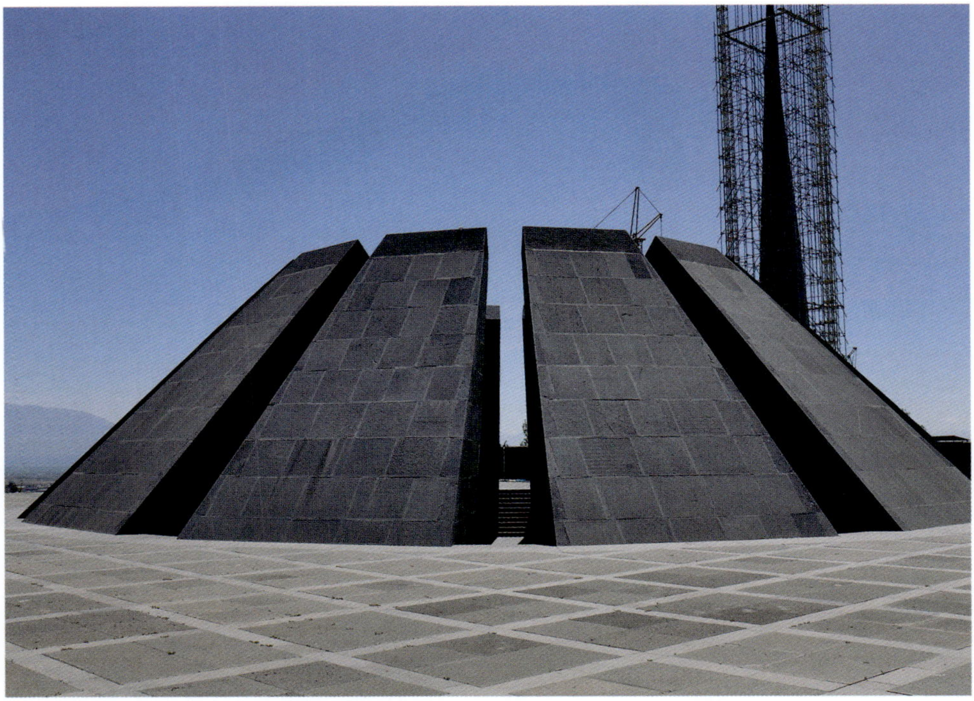

The collapse of the Soviet Union reignited conflicts that had been suppressed for decades but never resolved. This applied in particular to the dispute over the affiliation of Nagorno-Karabakh, which had been ceded to Azerbaijan under Stalin against the wishes of the majority Armenian population. Moscow had redrawn the borders in all the Caucasian republics. Part of the Armenian population thus found itself outside the borders of Soviet Armenia. Nakhchivan, the exclave settled by Azeris and claimed by Armenia, was also ceded to Azerbaijan. With the collapse of the Soviet Union, this political arrangement was upended, leading to bloody conflicts. After September 1989, all roads and railways from Azerbaijan to Armenia were closed, the supply of oil and gas was stopped, and the Nagorno-Karabakh War erupted in 1992. Since 1994, this conflict has been considered "frozen" under a ceasefire agreement, with no real solution in sight. This meant considerable hardship for the Armenian population until the end of the 1990s. As the flow of resources had stopped, people had to survive the winters in temperatures as low as 25 degrees below zero for years on end without electricity or fuel.

National memory is focused on the genocide of the Armenians by the Ottoman Empire in 1915/16, to which more than 1.5 million people fell victim. 24 April is the official Genocide Remembrance Day, while 14 June is the official day of commemoration of the victims of political repression in Armenia. Memorials to the repression of the Soviet era and its victims are still few and far between.

The Ethnological Institute at Yerevan University runs a research department on Stalinist repression. Among other things, it has issued a publication with the names of 23,000 people murdered. Books on the deportations and political repressions between 1922 and 1953 have also been published.

Memorial to the Victims of Political Repression 1920 – 1991

Vanadzor. In memory of the victims of political repression in Armenia, a memorial was erected on 9 October 2001 on the initiative of the Armenian Memorial Society, "Gushamatyan". The grey marble sculpture designed by Gerasim Tumanyan sits on a pedestal and depicts the figure of a man stretching his arms towards the sky in a defensive posture.

Inscription on the base of the monument
Armenian: աղաքական / ճնշման / զոհերին

Russian: Жертвам / политических / репрессий

English: *To the victims / of the political / repression / 1920 – 1991*

Location: Vanadzor, in the city park near the railway station

Further reading:
Hofmann, Tessa: Annäherung an Armenien. Geschichte und Gegenwart. 2. Aufl. München 2006. / Lehmann, Maike: Eine sowjetische Nation: Nationale Sozialismusinterpretationen in Armenien seit 1945. Frankfurt, New York 2012. / Sarkissian, Ani: Religion in Postsoviet Armenia: Pluralism and Identity formation in Transition. In: Religion, State, Society, 2008, Vol. 36, No. 2, pp. 163 – 180.

►
Memorial to the Victims of Political Repression

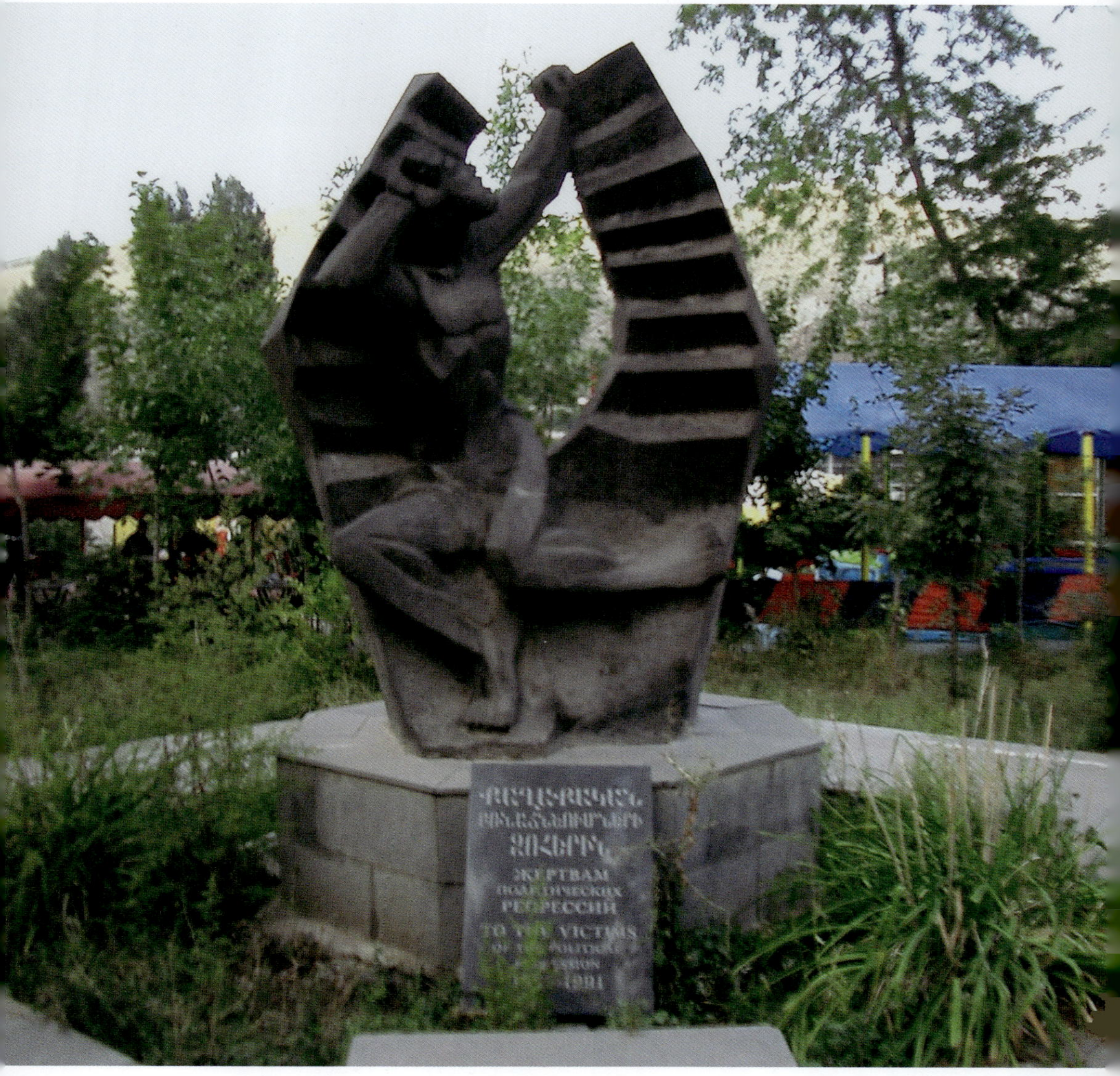
ЖЕРТВАМ
РЕПРЕССИЙ
VICTIMS
1991

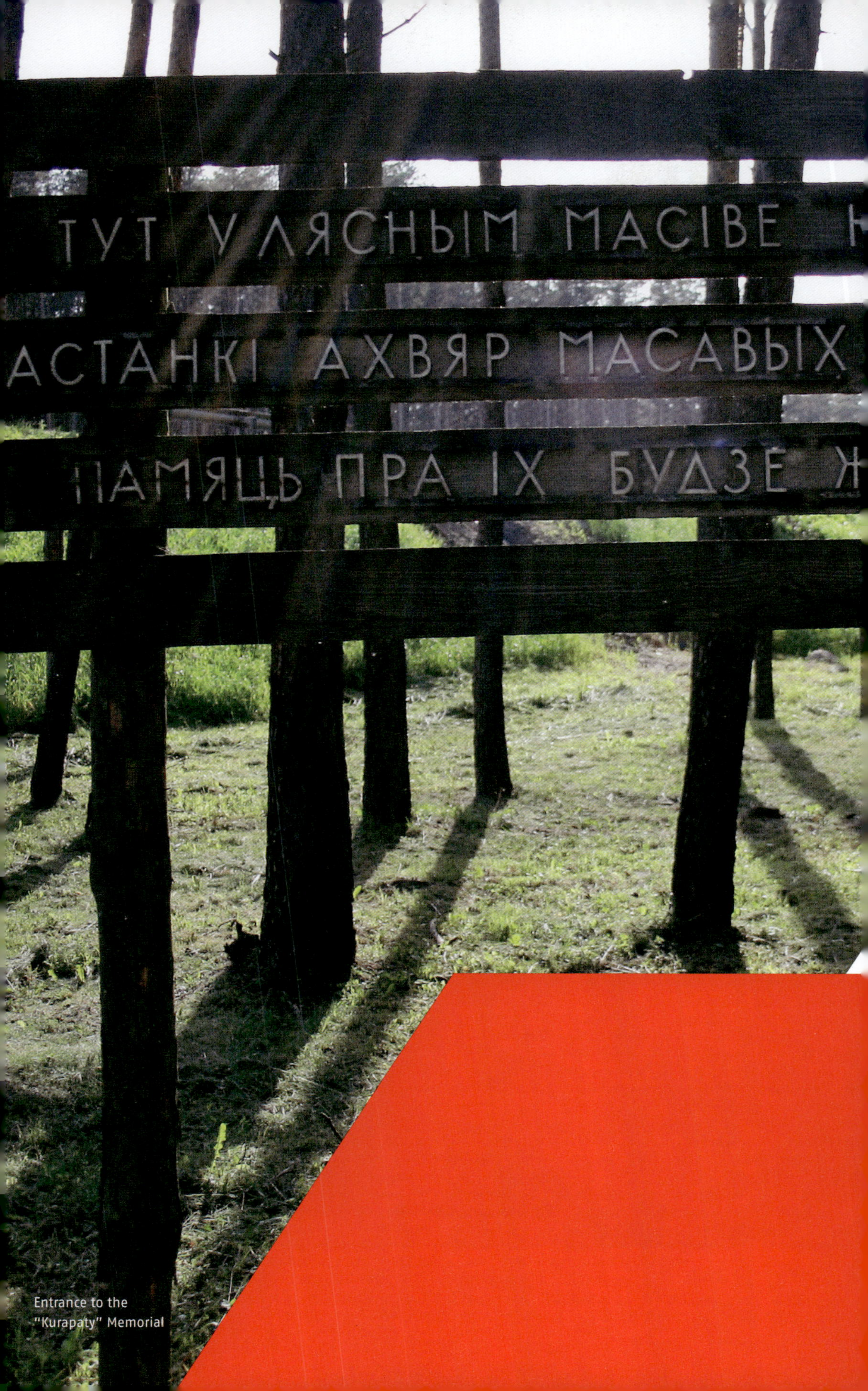

Entrance to the "Kurapaty" Memorial

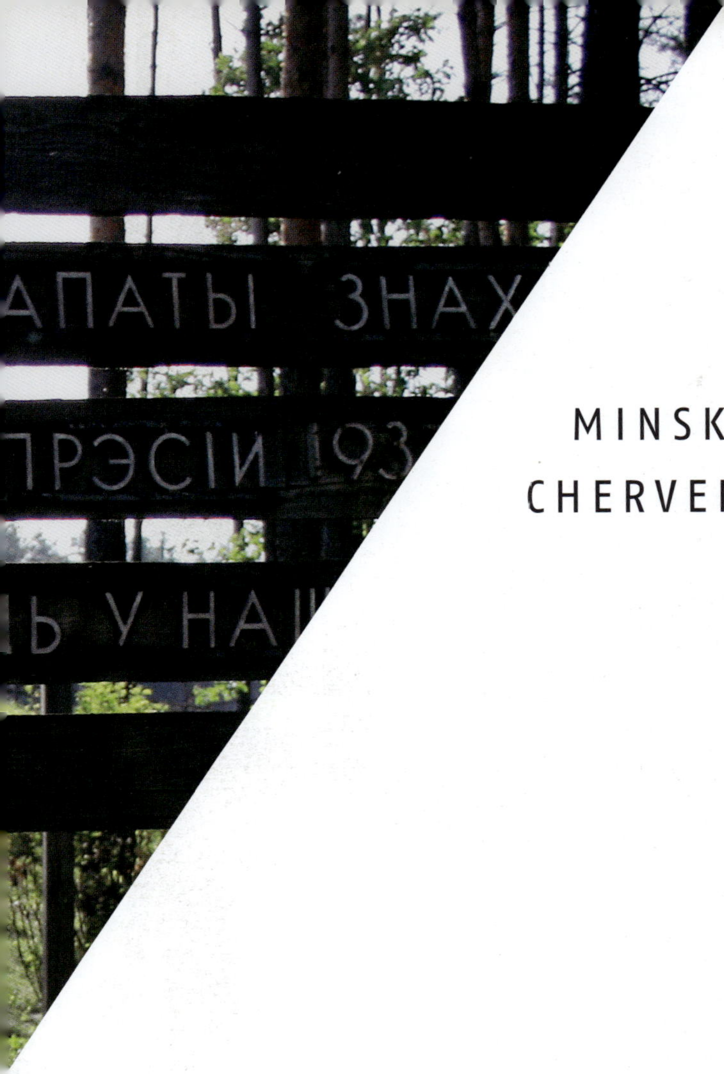

MINSK
CHERVEN

Belarus

Until the end of the 18th century, present-day Belarus was part of the Commonwealth of Poland-Lithuania. Under Catherine the Great, the country was annexed to the Russian Empire, where it remained until the end of the First World War. After a short period of independence following the Polish-Russian War, which raged from 1918 to 1920, the western parts of the country were integrated into newly independent Poland, while the eastern parts, including the capital Minsk, came under Soviet administration and became part of the Soviet Union as the Byelorussian Soviet Socialist Republic (BSSR) at the end of 1922.

In accordance with the border demarcations agreed between the Soviet Union and Nazi Germany in the secret additional protocol to the Molotov-Ribbentrop Pact of 23 August 1939, the Red Army occupied the parts of Belarus previously belonging to Poland at the end of September 1939 and annexed them to the BSSR. When Soviet troops invaded the west of the country, the Soviet regime was installed here as well. The eastern part of the country had experienced all the repressions of Soviet rule, including the persecution of the kulaks—farmers with land and livestock—who were to be dispossessed and destroyed as a class in the course of collectivisation, as well as forced industrialisation and the persecution of intellectuals, people of faith and artists. Tens of thousands of people were murdered during the "Great Terror" of 1937 and 1938. One of the few large execution sites to have been located so far is in Kurapaty near the Belarusian capital Minsk. Countless victims of the killings were buried in mass graves here.

With the introduction of Soviet rule in the western parts of the country that had been occupied in 1939, repression and terror became an everyday political tool here too. Prior to the invasion of the Soviet Union in 1941 by German troops, the economy was nationalised, and farms were converted into kolkhozes. Anyone who opposed Sovietisation or was suspected of such opposition was persecuted. Tens of thousands of people were arrested, deported to Siberia or murdered in the torture cellars of the Soviet secret police. When the German troops invaded, Lavrentiy Beria, the head of the Soviet secret police, the NKVD, ordered the evacuation of the prisons and torture cellars. The prisoners were driven east in so-called death marches. Thousands of inmates who could not be evacuated in time before the German invasion were shot either in the prisons or during the marches. By the end of 1941, the territory of the BSSR was completely under German occupation, and the occupiers set about ravaging the country in a campaign of murder and terror. Many thousands of people were deported to Germany as forced labourers. Almost the entire Jewish population fell victim to murder by German Einsatzgruppen troops and the SS. By the time the Red Army drove the Wehrmacht out of Belarus in 1944, the entire country had been devastated. About 2.25 million people, a whole quarter of the Belarusian population, had lost their lives.

With the return of Soviet power to Belarus, Stalinist repression resumed. In new waves of purges, tens of thousands of people were arrested, deported to Siberia or murdered. After Stalin's death in 1953, the forms of repression changed: open terror gave way to more subtle methods. Notwithstanding the dissolution of the Gulag, people were arrested for being "nationalists" and deported to penal camps because of their opposition to continued Sovietisation.

The opposition in Belarus remained relatively weak compared to other communist states. While opposition activities in the first decades were limited to protests by individuals or expressed in subcultural movements, especially among young people, the signing of the Helsinki Final Act in 1976 gave a boost to civil rights groups as it did in other countries. A Belarusian Helsinki Group was founded; the documentation of human rights violations and environmental destruction began. Until the mid-1980s, the few opposition activities did not meet with a broad response in society. After the Chernobyl reactor disaster in 1986, the protests finally spread to large sections of society. Under the influence of Gorbachev's policies of glasnost and perestroika, a civil rights movement dedicated to reckoning with Stalinist repression also formed in Belarus. Like the "Memorial" group in Moscow, the Martyrology Society of Belarus ("Martyraloh Belarusi") investigated the silent crimes of the Stalin era, located mass graves and campaigned for the rehabilitation of the victims.

In 1990, the first laws on reparation and compensation were passed: 53,000 people who had been persecuted for political reasons were pardoned in 1988 and 1989 alone. When textbooks were revised for the 1993/94 school year, they already referred to the Soviet Union as a totalitarian regime.

After getting off to a promising start in the early 1990s, the process of working through the Soviet past ground to a halt under the impact of the economic crisis and the problems associated with it. Aleksandr Lukashenko's election as president in 1994 marked the beginning of the rehabilitation of Soviet history. Commemorating the victims of repression became increasingly marginalised as a political issue. Many of the Soviet rituals were reintroduced and used as points of identification for a population suffering from the political and economic upheavals following the dissolution of the Soviet Union. After years of what had been experienced as chaos in the aftermath of communism, Lukashenko's authoritarian rule promised stability. Human rights groups and those who campaigned for the historical reappraisal of the past were excluded from public debate and persecuted as political opponents of the Lukashenko regime.

Even despite this marginalisation, however, it proved impossible to completely deny the memory of the victims of repression. Thanks to the persistent commitment of civil rights groups, there are now over 100 smaller memorials and monuments, which were described for the first time in the volume "Erinnerungsorte an die Opfer des Kommunismus in Belarus" (Memorials to the Victims of Communism in Belarus) compiled by the Foundation for the Study of the Communist Dictatorship in Eastern Germany.

Due to public attention, the Belarusian authorities had no choice but to officially recognise some large burial grounds, such as the execution sites of the Stalin era in Kurapaty near Minsk, Gomel and Vitebsk, as memorial sites. Their existence is, however, under constant threat. Today, the narratives of the "Great Patriotic War" and the victory over German fascism, which were already decisive in the Soviet era, dominate the country's politics of remembrance. The crimes of the Stalin era and repression have not yet found their due place within this narrative.

"Kurapaty" Memorial to the Victims of Repression

Minsk. The memorial is located on the northern outskirts of Minsk on the site of a burial ground where tens of thousands of people were executed by the Soviet secret police between 1937 and 1941. Since the discovery of the burial ground in the summer of 1988, a number of associations and parties in Belarus have been trying to transform the area into a national memorial. So far, this project has failed because of the resistance of the state, which has to this day not officially recognised the memory of the victims of Stalinist terror. Nevertheless, the name Kurapaty has become synonymous in large parts of Belarusian society with the crimes of Stalinism.

Following the outbreak of mass terror in 1937, the secret police of the BSSR began to search for a suitable site where the execution of several thousand people could be carried out unobserved. Previously used execution sites scattered throughout Minsk, such as modern-day Chelyuskintsev Park and Loshitskiy Park, were deemed unsuitable for this purpose. In June/July 1937, Kurapaty forest outside the city was selected and enclosed by a three-metre-high wooden fence. The area of about 30 hectares was located at some distance from the village of Brod, whose inhabitants were able to witness the nightly executions from August 1937. The NKVD's prisoners were initially brought to Kurapaty only at night, later also during the day. They were shot upon arrival and buried in pre-dug mass graves.

According to eyewitnesses, the number of executions increased in the winter of 1937 and spring of 1938. It has not yet been possible to determine exactly how many people died in Kurapaty during these months. According to estimates, several tens of thousands of people were killed here. After the annexation of the former Polish territories in Western Belarus by the Soviet Union in the autumn of 1939, the mass executions resumed. The main victims were members of the Polish social, military and political elite who were taken to the BSSR's central prison in Minsk and subsequently shot in their thousands in Kurapaty. More than 4,500 Polish soldiers and civilians from the prisoner-of-war camps of Kosielsk and Oshtakov were murdered in Minsk in connection with the atrocities committed in Katyń in the spring of 1940.

The executions in Kurapaty only ended after the German invasion of the Soviet Union in the summer of 1941 and the subsequent withdrawal of Soviet troops. The inhabitants of the surrounding villages tore down the wooden fence for fuel and discovered the mass graves. The German occupying forces were not interested in Kurapaty. After the withdrawal of German troops and the liberation of Minsk by the Soviet army in the summer of 1944, members of the Soviet secret police began to cover up the graves. The sunken mass graves were partially filled in, and the entire area was reforested. In the 1960s, a road and a gas pipeline were built through the burial site. The human remains found in the course of this work were disposed of. In the 1970s, a new housing estate was built which extended as far as Kurapaty. The forest area became a popular destination for local residents.

At about the same time, archaeologist Zianon Pazniak from Minsk began to study the history of the burial site in Kurapaty. He collected reports from contemporary witnesses in the surrounding villages confirming the executions. But it was not until the late 1980s that he was able to make his findings available to a broader public. In May 1988, a small team of archaeologists, including Yauhen Shmyhaleu, Mikola Kryvaltsevich, Aleh Ioŭ and Pazniak, conducted their first exploratory excavations with the permission of the military prosecutor's office. The report, published in excerpts at the beginning of June 1988, came as a shock to large sections of the population. The crimes committed during Stalinism, which had until then been taboo, were brought back into public consciousness.

After the formation of a fact-finding commission, further investigations were carried out. In the new excavation report, the commission stated that at least 30,000 people had been executed by the Soviet secret police in Kurapaty. Pazniak, on the other hand, stressed that, in his opinion, the death toll was actually more than 200,000. Distrustful of government authorities, artists, writers and scientists had a few months earlier founded the Martyrology Society of Belarus ("Martyraloh Belarusi"), which advocated an independent reinvestigation of the Stalinist past. The conflicts with the authorities escalated on Memorial Day 1988, when a commemoration ceremony with several thousand participants was forcibly broken up by the police. The increasing decline of power in the spring of 1989 forced the state and party leadership to officially acknowledge the crimes and grant the burial site the status of a national memorial. A memorial stone inaugurated by the Council of Ministers of the BSSR was erected in January 1989 as an expression of this concession. The first commemorative symbols, such as a six-metre-high wooden cross, were accompanied by about 50,000 people in a procession to Kurapaty and consecrated there. The redevelopment of the site began in spring 1990. Opposite the Cross of Martyrs, a four-by-six-metre sign was set up, and crosses were placed on the individual graves.

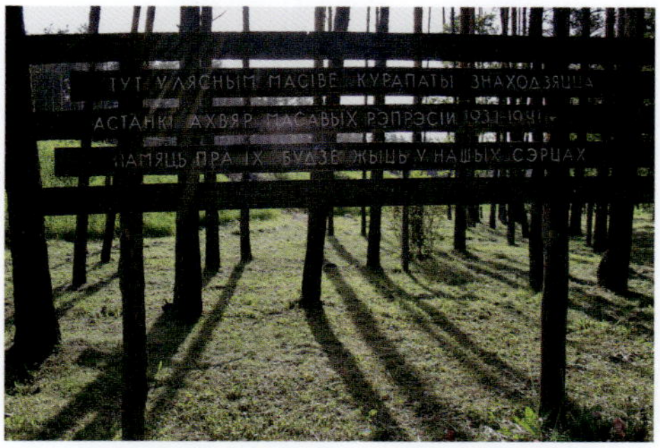

Entrance to the memorial with the inscription: "Here in the Kurapaty forest lie the mortal remains of the victims of the mass repressions of 1937–1941. Their memory lives on in our hearts".

The importance of the site and the question of who was to blame remained controversial. Although an investigation had been ordered, archives including those of the Ministry of the Interior and the secret service remained closed, with the effect that hardly any documents were made available to the investigation. It was accordingly impossible to ascertain the names of the victims. Moreover, in the summer of 1991, the state's fact-finding commission declared that, contrary to previous findings, the executions in Kurapaty had taken place during the German occupation from 1941 to 1944; the

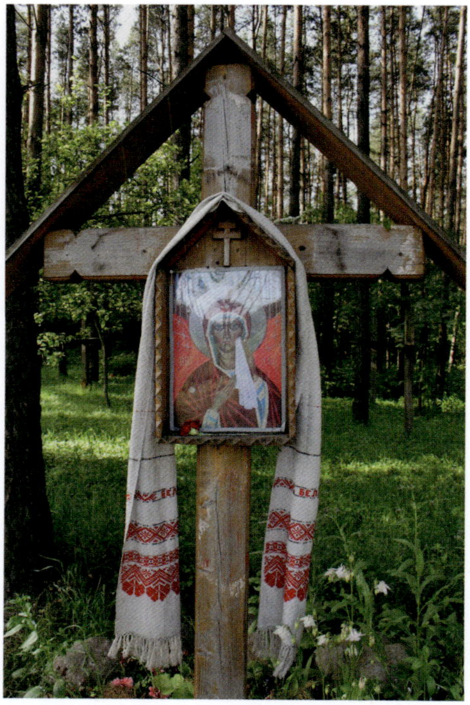

"Mother of God of Kurapaty" icon

victims were said to have been deported Jews from Hamburg who had been murdered by German Einsatzgruppen. Until final clarification, the burial ground was not to be turned into a memorial.

Despite many years of archival research, during which experts from Israel and Germany were consulted, this hypothesis concerning the dead in Kurapaty could not be confirmed. The fact-finding commission ordered new exploratory excavations in October 1997. During the exhumations, which continued in May 1998, several dozen mass graves were reopened and the human remains examined by forensic scientists. Based on the discoveries in mass graves, it was possible to prove once again without a doubt that only the Soviet secret police could have carried out the executions. For the first time, two victims were identified by name. Moreover, there were indications that Kurapaty had still been in use as an execution site even after the end of the Second World War.

However, the debates about Kurapaty were no longer causing the public furore with which they had been greeted in the late 1980s. In a process accelerated by domestic political developments, Stalinist crimes increasingly took a back seat. This changed in the autumn of 2001, when a presidential decree ordained the extension of the road leading through the burial site. In late September, various organisations and opposition parties joined forces to launch a joint initiative for "the Preservation of the Kurapaty Memorial", which sought to harness a nationwide press campaign to prevent the construction work. Opposition youth organisations, for their part, set up the "Youth for Kurapaty" association, which initiated a permanent vigil from September 2001. Despite these protests, construction work began. There were some violent clashes between security forces and protesters. Notwithstanding all their efforts, the protesters were unable to prevent the extension of the road, and the construction work was completed one year later. The only concession took the form of an underpass through which the burial site can be reached today. Various organisations, religious communities and relatives of the victims encouraged the erection of countless new crosses.

Location: Minsk, in the northeast of the Zyalyony Luh district

Memorial for the Victims of the "Minsk Death March"

Cherven. Since 1989, four memorials have been erected in the vicinity of the city of Cherven, to the south-east of Minsk, commemorating the victims of the "Minsk Death March" of June 1941, who were murdered during the evacuation of the NKVD prisons in the summer of that year. Among them were Polish, Lithuanian and Belarusian prisoners. They were rounded up from the prisons in the front-line areas—including the prison in Kaunas, Lithuania—and initially taken to a forest near Minsk from where they were to march towards Cherven. About half a kilometre to the right of the road to Dubrova is a mass grave, which has become a memorial to the victims of the death march.

After the discovery of this mass grave, the first memorial cross in memory of Jonas Petruitis was erected in June 1991. The colonel of the Lithuanian officer corps imprisoned by the NKVD managed to escape in June 1941 shortly before arriving in Cherven. Two years later, after the inauguration of the memorial cross in 1991, a chapel-like shrine, built according to plans by Stanislau Bandalevitch, was ceremonially inaugurated. This memorial sign was erected on the initiative of the Belarusian Martyrology Society. Set on a wooden pole about four metres high, it displays an image of the historical Belarusian equestrian coat of arms, "Pahonia". It is covered by a small roof and crowned by a four-armed cross. In memory of the Lithuanian victims, the Association of Lithuanian Students in London and the Algiras Society erected a simple wooden cross commemorating the victims with epitaphs in Belarusian and English. The wooden cross has since been replaced by a two-barred metal cross that only bears a Belarusian inscription. On the same day, relatives of Polish victims consecrated a metal cross of their own, funded by donations collected in Poland. The last cross was erected for Tadeusz Giedroyć on 26 June 1995.

After the German invasion of the Soviet Union on 22 June 1941, Beria ordered the evacuation of all prisons in the front-line areas, which began immediately. If an evacuation was not possible due to the rapid advance of German troops, all political prisoners were to be executed. On the night of 22–23 June 1941, the central prison in Minsk, with over 1,000 inmates, was evacuated after several prisoners had already been murdered. The other prisoners were rounded up in a forest outside the city where the NKVD also gathered prisoners from other prisons in the Minsk region and the prison in Kaunas (Lithuania). Up to 10,000 people were marched eastwards to Cherven in smaller groups. On the way, the marches repeatedly came under German fire, which claimed the lives of many of the prisoners. Others used the general chaos that ensued to escape. By this time, the NKVD's security forces had been

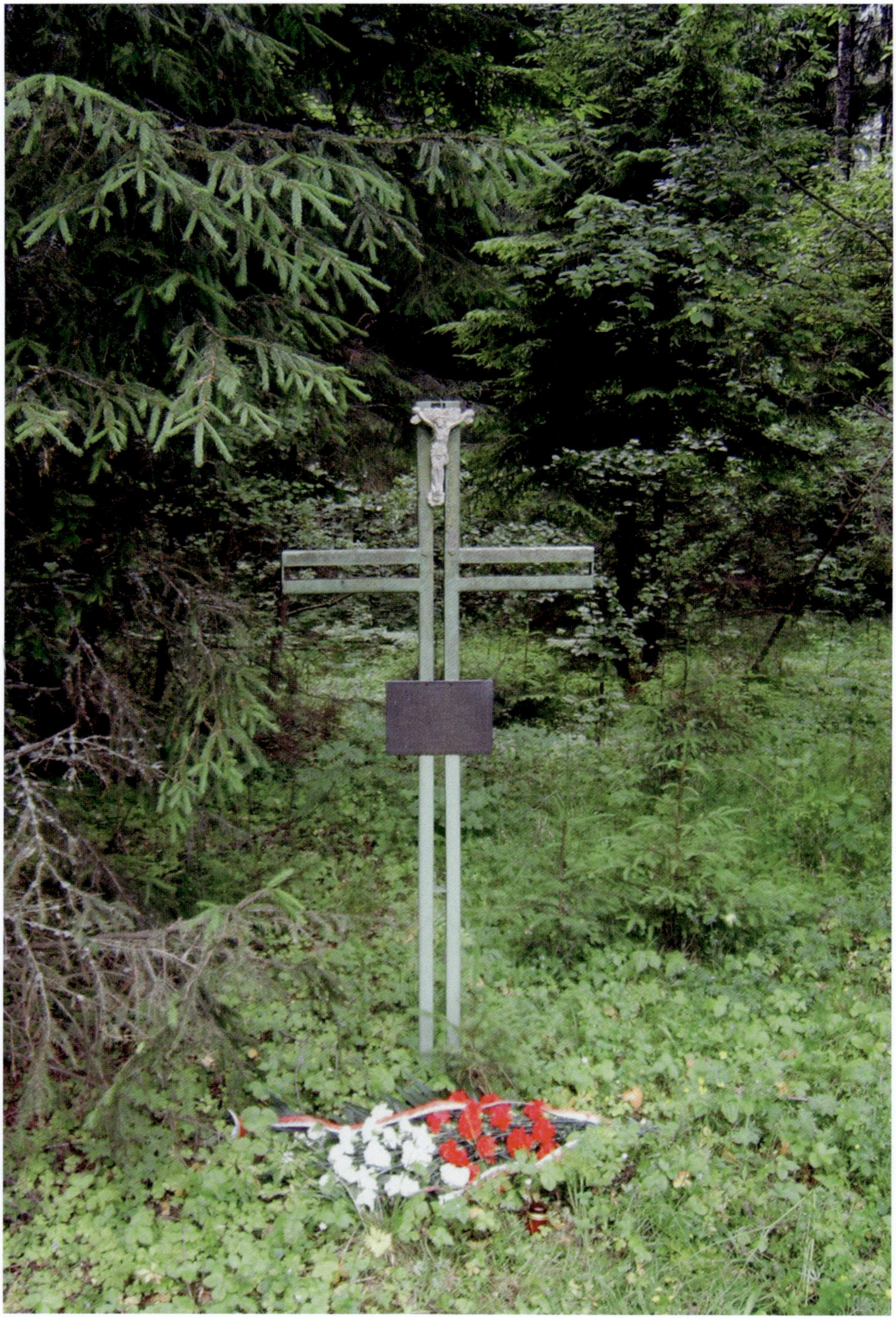

Memorial cross for the Polish victims

ordered to begin the execution of political prisoners. As a result, several thousand people were murdered on the way to Cherven. According to the Soviet secret police, only 2,200 prisoners arrived at the transit prison in Cherven on 26 June 1941. Of these, several hundred people, mainly political prisoners, were once again singled out and murdered in various sites outside the city. The remaining prisoners, especially women, children and the elderly, were released by the NKVD. Others were sent to Red Army penal battalions to fight the German troops. Few people survived this massacre known as the "Minsk Death March". The total number of victims is estimated at 5,000 to 7,000.

Until the 1980s, the crimes of the NKVD in Cherven were barely discussed. It was only in the Polish, Lithuanian and Belarusian diasporas that the memory of the victims was kept alive. Not until the late 1980s did freedom and civil rights movements spur in earnest the public discussion in Poland and Lithuania of Soviet crimes during the Second World War. In Belarus, local historian Uladzimir Darahush from Cherven studied the events of June 1941. After the discovery of the Kurapaty burial site in Minsk and the beginning of a public movement to come to terms with the Stalinist crimes, Darahush's first ground-breaking article appeared in the local press in the summer of 1989.

In the following years, relatives of victims from Belarus and especially from Poland and Lithuania came to Cherven to commemorate their murdered relatives. Associations of former victims of persecution from all three states tried to transform the mass graves located by eyewitnesses into memorial sites. Initially supported by local authorities, public commemoration of the victims is now considered undesirable. Nevertheless, since 1989, a commemorative procession ("Ihumenski shliakh") has been held regularly on the anniversary of the massacre, organised by Belarusian, Lithuanian and Polish victims' associations and some parties. Efforts to convert the remaining building of the NKVD prison in Cherven into a memorial to commemorate the victims of the repression have so far failed due to resistance from the authorities. In Poland and Lithuania, the NKVD massacre was also addressed in connection with the criminal prosecution of Soviet crimes in the mid-1990s. However, the proceedings were discontinued, as it was no longer possible to apprehend the people who were responsible at that time.

Inscriptions

Belarusian / on the cross of the Algirdas Society: Вы не памёрлі, бо будзеце жыць / у нашых сэрцах / Algirdas Society

English: *You are not dead as long as you live on in our hearts / Algirdas Society*

Polish / on the Polish cross:
Ofiarom / mińskiej / szosy śmierci / zamordowanym / w 1941 roku / —Rodacy

English: *For the victims of the Minsk Death March, murdered in 1941.*
From their compatriots

Location: 0.5 km outside of Cherven, to the right of the road to Dubrova

Further reading:

Kaminsky, Anna (ed.): Erinnerungsorte an die Opfer des Kommunismus in Belarus. Berlin 2010. / Kashtalian, Irina: The Repressive Factors of the USSR's Internal Policy and Everyday Life of the Belarusian Society (1944–1953). Wiesbaden 2016.

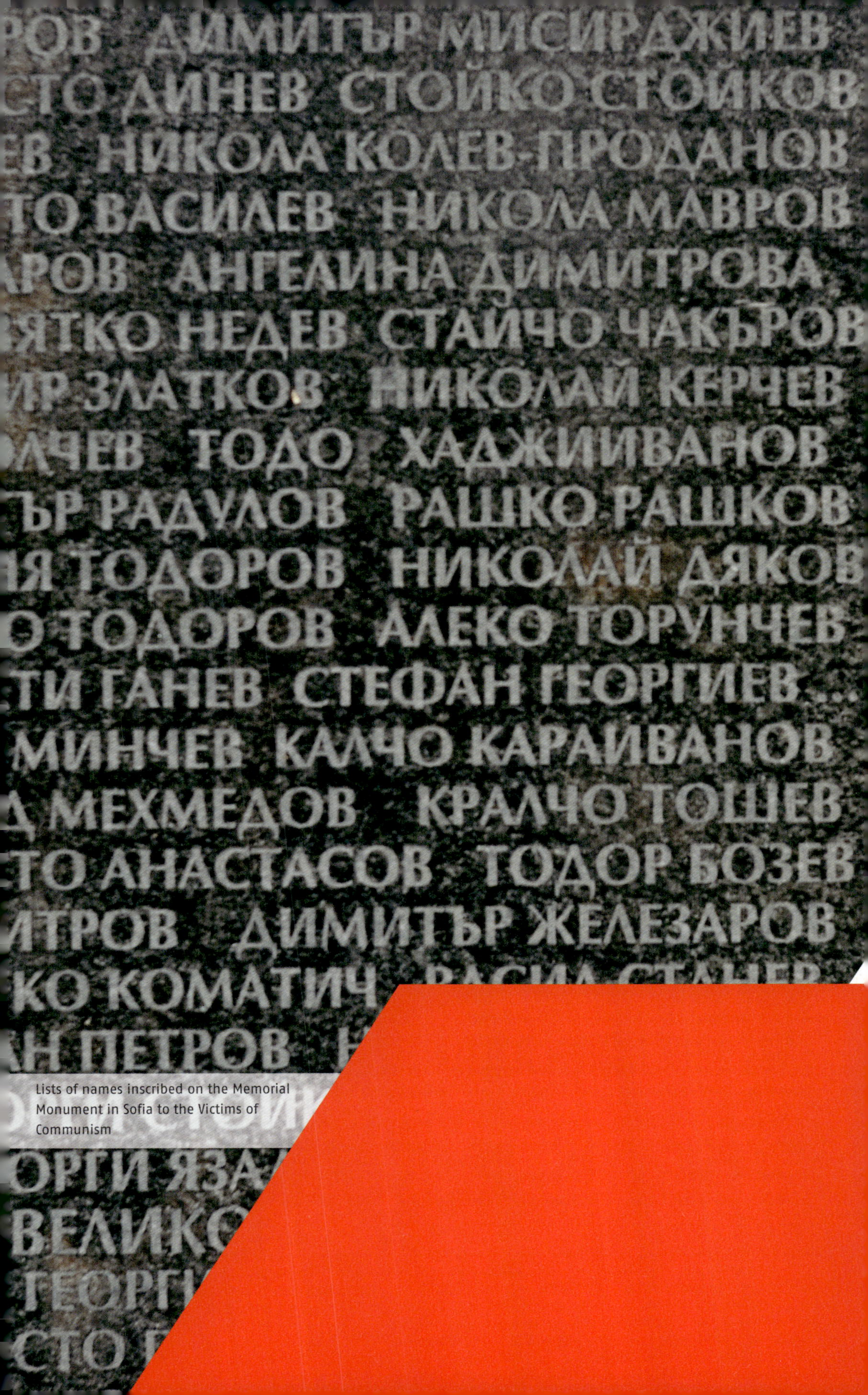

Lists of names inscribed on the Memorial Monument in Sofia to the Victims of Communism

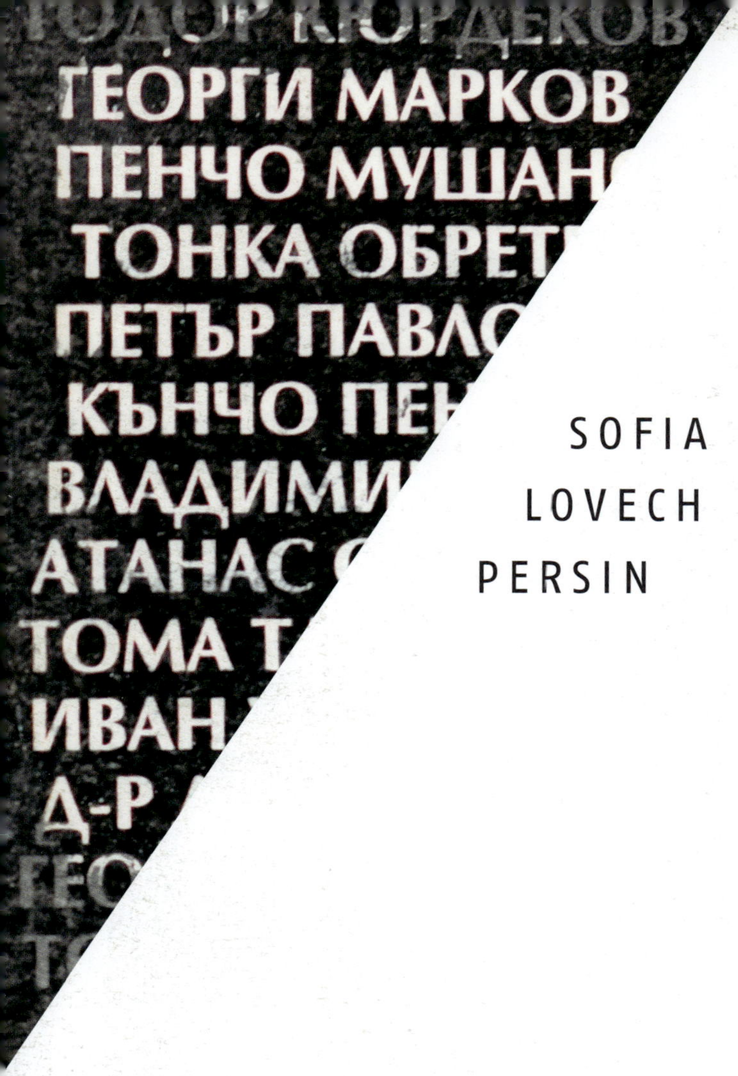

SOFIA
LOVECH
PERSIN

Bulgaria

After the end of the First World War, during which Bulgaria fought on the side of the German Reich and its allies, the country was ruled by a succession of authoritarian regimes and governments. In 1934, a military organisation seized power before being forced in turn in 1936 to relinquish it to Tsar Boris III, who reinstated the constitution which had been repealed in 1923. The years of the "royal dictatorship" brought stable political conditions for the Bulgarian population. Between the outbreak of the Second World War and February 1941, Bulgaria remained neutral before entering the war alongside the Axis powers. German troops immediately advanced into Bulgarian territory. Bulgarian troops in turn participated in combat operations against Greece and Yugoslavia and occupied Thrace and Macedonia. While Bulgaria had already passed an anti-Jewish law in 1940 ordering the expropriation of Jews and their deportation from the cities to camps, the Jewish populations of the occupied territories in Thrace and Macedonia were extradited and deported to German extermination camps.

On 27 August 1944, Bulgaria withdrew from the Tripartite Pact, whereupon the Soviet Union declared war on the country on 5 September. On the night of 8 – 9 September—the day after the Red Army had crossed the Bulgarian border and begun its occupation of the country—the government under Prime Minister Konstantin Muraviev was overthrown in a coup. The Kremlin-backed coup propelled the National Council of the communist-dominated Fatherland Front into power. Subsequently, with Moscow's support, the Bulgarian Communist Party (BCP) asserted its claim to leadership. This was accompanied by a rigorous "cleansing" of the state apparatus under the pretext of an "unreserved liquidation of all fascist nests of resistance".

Violence, terror and repression came to shape the social, economic and political life of the country within a very short time. The country's administrative apparatus was completely replaced. The principle of a non-partisan legal system was abolished, and the offices of judges and public prosecutors were filled with people who were approved by the Communist Party. The newly founded People's Army recruited its personnel from the ranks of the BCP and members of so-called "combat groups". Anyone branded as a "fascist" or an "enemy of the people" was executed or disappeared without a trace. From September to October 1944 alone, the number of people who were executed or disappeared without a trial or court ruling was around 25,000. All those branded as enemies by the BCP—teachers, priests, wealthy farmers, industrialists, traders, lawyers and doctors—were systematically eliminated.

On the pretext of punishing those responsible for Bulgaria's entry into the Second World War alongside the Axis powers, a general reckoning was staged against politicians, members of the army, intellectuals, scientists, journalists, writers and other public figures. All those who might be able to resist the Communist Party's course of Sovietisation were to be discredited, isolated or destroyed. Between December 1944 and April 1945, a specially established "People's Court" sentenced over 11,000 defendants, 2,700 of whom were executed. More than 1,200 people received life sentences, and at least 4,300 were sentenced to up to 20 years in prison. Retribution was also practised by the repressive organs of the state in line with the principle of collective punishment and directed at relatives, spouses and children of those sentenced. Thus it was that more than 28,000 people were forcibly resettled between September 1944 and May 1945 by order of the Committee for State Security. A further 184,300 people were deported to forced labour camps during the same period.

By 1962, more than 23,500 people, including over 2,300 women, had disappeared into these camps, where they were to be "re-educated" by hard labour. Among the prisoners were not only "politically dangerous persons", "hostile elements", and "counterrevolutionaries", but also young people branded "hooligans" and "antisocial elements" whose "offences" consisted of dressing according to Western fashion, listening to "Western music" or having "fashionable" haircuts. A total of 83 camps existed on the territory of the People's Republic of Bulgaria. In addition, 22 prisons were used for the internment of political prisoners until 1989. Under inhumane conditions, subjected to physical and psychological torture and without medical care, the camp inmates were used for forced labour in quarries and mines as well as in the construction of railway tracks and roads. To this day, many of the mass graves of the victims of political repression remain unaccounted for.

However, the regime's campaign was directed not only against so-called "hostile elements" but also against the peasants. In a society in which 80 percent of the approximately seven million inhabitants lived from subsistence farming, manual labour and small businesses, forced collectivisation inevitably meant long-term demographic, economic and social damage. Peasants were defamed as "kulaks" and expropriated, their land and livestock transferred to kolkhozes and sovkhozes. Anyone who resisted expropriation or compulsory levies had to reckon with fines, corporal punishment, imprisonment, torture, forced resettlement or banishment to labour camps.

However, agriculture was not the only sector affected by nationalisation. In the spring of 1946, in a sweeping campaign to enforce the "dictatorship of the proletariat", the BCP set about the rigorous abolition of private property in industry, banking and trade. The churches were also seized or completely destroyed. Hundreds of priests, monks and bishops had already been executed in the immediate aftermath of the Communist coup in September 1944. In show trials, clergymen were sentenced to years of imprisonment in labour camps and workhouses. The Denominations Act enacted on 16 February 1949 legalised the confiscation of church property and placed severe restrictions on religious life. Until the collapse of the Communist regime in November 1989, the Bulgarian Orthodox, Catholic and Protestant churches of the country were also subject to special surveillance by the "Clergy and Sects" group of the First Department of State Security. The penal and forced labour camps, above all the quarry in Lovech and the remote Danube island of Persin opposite the town of Belene, are emblematic of the violence and dehumanisation practised in the People's Republic of Bulgaria.

In the summer of 1945, armed resistance groups were formed against the establishment of communist rule—the "Goryani" (English: ones of the forest). The underground fighters were recruited from all strata of society. Almost half were farmers seeking to actively oppose compulsory expropriation and collectivisation. The armed resistance was supported by networks in the country's urban centres and associations of political exiles such as the Bulgarian liberation movement, which organised, among other things, the smuggling of partisans into the territory of the People's Republic. By the early 1960s, almost all "Goryani" groups had been infiltrated and wiped out by the secret police, the army and forces of the ministry of the interior.

After Stalin's death in March 1953, a process of political easing and de-Stalinisation began in Bulgaria, but this was reversed immediately after the suppression of the Hungarian revolution by Soviet troops in November 1956. Since the uprising against communist rule and Soviet occupation in Hungary had also met with great sympathy in Bulgaria, the rulers feared an upsurge of anti-Communist opposition. The omnipresence of the state apparatus of repression and, especially, the Bulgarian secret police would go on to make any form of resistance against the regime impossible.

Despite comprehensive surveillance of the entire population, Bulgarian officers and party cadres tried to overthrow the chairman of the BCP, Todor Zhivkov, in 1965. The attempted coup was suppressed, and the repression was further intensified. Even after Bulgaria joined the CSCE in 1976, the human rights situation did not improve. Only a small group of dissidents dared resist the regime, paying for their courage with persecution and imprisonment. Among them were the human rights activist Lyubomir Sobadzhiev and Nikola Popov, a comrade-in-arms of the Bulgarian Charter 77. Volodya Nakov wrote a series of protest letters to Amnesty International, the UN, and Bulgarian authorities in the early 1980s. They all were sentenced to prison for this act. Grigor Bozhilov, Iliya Minev and Eduard Genov also chose this form of protest and appealed to the Vienna meeting of the CSCE in 1986.

The victims of the communist dictatorship in Bulgaria also include students and pupils who were denied higher education because of their background or oppositional stance, refugees who tried to escape to Turkey or Yugoslavia, people who were barred from their profession for political reasons in the 1980s, and ethnic Turks who were to be forcibly Bulgarianised. It is estimated that the victims of Bulgarian communism totalled several hundred thousand.

On 10 November 1989, head of state Todor Zhivkov was overthrown. As the longest-serving head of state in the entire Eastern bloc, he had led the BCP since 1954. The philosopher and former opposition leader Zhelyu Zhelev took over as head of state in 1990. Democratic reforms were carried out in the period that followed. However, wrenching power from the ruling elite proved an impossible task. Instead, a form of "laissez-faire" capitalism was established in which the former communist elites secured economic predominance for themselves and held onto political power.

Corruption, mafia-esque structures and mismanagement led to hyperinflation and a banking crisis in the mid-1990s, which wrought misery and impoverishment on the vast majority of the Bulgarian population. High unemployment, a lack of prospects, corruption and mafia-esque structures in politics and business gave rise to nostalgic yearnings for the communist era, which came in retrospect to be perceived as stable. In the following years, the government of Bulgaria changed hands a number of times in rapid succession.

Bulgaria's accession to the EU in 2007 gave rise to widespread hopes of an improvement in the political and economic situation and the fight against corruption and "wild west capitalism". Disillusionment with the lack of democratic development led to mass protests against the government in 2013.

Given these circumstances, the process of coming to terms with the history of communism in Bulgaria was a disappointing one. The former Bulgarian Communist Party had renamed itself the Bulgarian Socialist Party as early as 1990. At the same time, a variety of new communist parties and associations emerged. Attempts to condemn communism and its crimes repeatedly failed.

As early as 1989, political prisoners were granted amnesty and the acts of which they were accused annulled. In 1991, a law on political and civil rehabilitation was passed, which was amended again and again in the following years. This law allows persons who were oppressed due to their ethnic background or their political or religious beliefs to be rehabilitated and for their confiscated property to be returned or compensation to be paid. Several individuals in positions of power and other perpetrators were put on trial but in no cases were convictions were handed down.

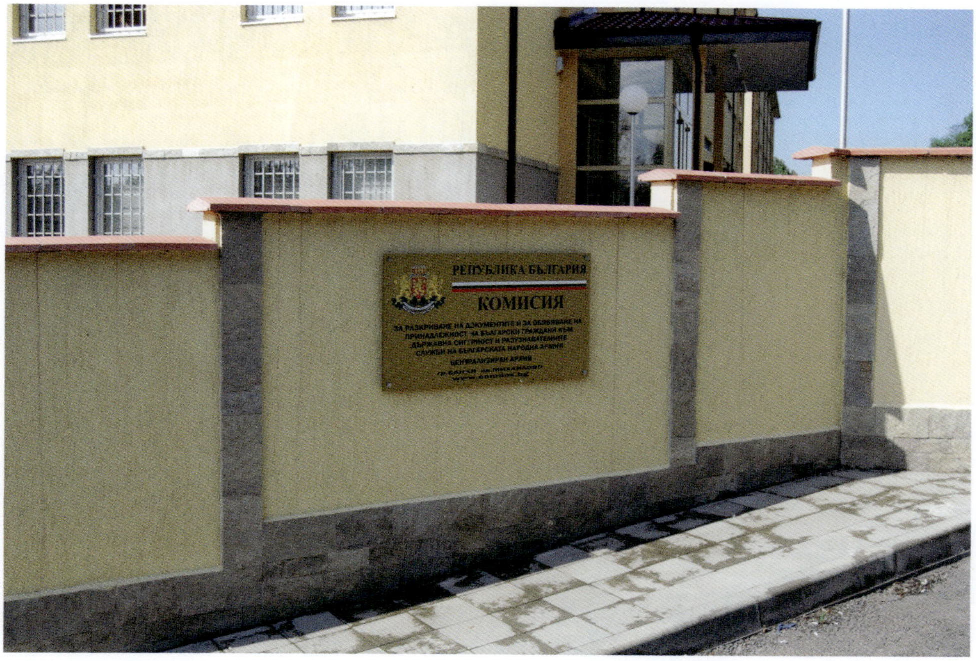

Entrance to the "Committee for the disclosure of the documents and the affiliation of Bulgarian citizens to the State Security and intelligence services of the Bulgarian National Army" (COMDOS)

The first lustration law was passed in 1997, but it was not until December 2006 that a decision was taken to open the documents of the Bulgarian Committee for State Security and to establish an independent authority to oversee its implementation. To this day there has been no political or social acknowledgement; nor has there been any recognition of the victims in the form of official commemoration ceremonies or by state-sponsored institutions officially appointed to publicly perform this task. Although 1 February was established as an official day of commemoration for the victims of political persecution, the main events on this day are commemoration ceremonies staged by the various victims' associations, which have little public influence. Many former victims still suffer even today from the effects of persecution and their lack of compensation and recognition.

Memorial Monument to the Victims of Communism

Sofia. A memorial to commemorate the victims of the communist regime was inaugurated in the central park of the Bulgarian capital on 11 September 1999. A 58-metre-long wall of black marble bears the names of 7,526 people who were executed or perished in prison in Bulgaria between 1944 and 1990. The memorial was designed by Bulgarian architects Atanas Todorov and Dimitar Krastev. The complex is complemented by an orthodox chapel dedicated to "all Bulgarian martyrs". Every year on 23 August, the European Day of Remembrance for Victims of Stalinism and Nazism, 1 February, the Day of Remembrance and Respect to Victims of the Communist Regime in Bulgaria, and 9 September, the date the communist regime took power in Bulgaria, memorial services are held there.

Inscription

Bulgarian: ПОКЛОНИ СЕ, БЪЛГАРИНО! / В ТАЗИ СТЕНА Е ВГРАДЕНО СТРАДАНИЕТО НА НАШИЯ НАРОД. / МЕМОРИАЛЪТ Е ИЗДИГНАТ В ПАМЕТ НА НАШИТЕ СЪОТЕЧЕСТВЕНИЦИ, / ЖЕРТВИ НА КОМУНИСТИЧЕСКИЯ ТЕРОР: ЛИШЕНИТЕ ОТ ЖИВОТ, / БЕЗСЛЕДНО ИЗЧЕЗНАЛИТЕ, / ИЗПРАТЕНИТЕ НА РАЗСТРЕЛ ОТ ТАКА НАРЕЧЕНИЯ «НАРОДЕН СЪД». / ТОЙ НАПОМНЯ ЗА ЛАГЕРИСТИТЕ, ПОЛИТИЧЕСКИТЕ ЗАТВОРНИЦИ, / ИЗСЕЛЕНИТЕ, ПОДЛОЖЕНИТЕ НА ПОЛИТИЧЕСКИ РЕПРЕСИИ И / ТЕХНИТЕ ЗЛОЧЕСТИ СЕМЕЙСТВА И БЛИЗКИ. / НЕКА СПОМЕНЪТ ЗА НЕВИННО ПРОЛЯТАТА КРЪВ / ГОРИ СЪРЦАТА НИ КАТО ВЕЧЕН ОГЪН. / НЕКА МИНАЛОТО ДА НЕ СЕ ПОВТАРЯ! // УСПОКОЙ, ГОСПОДИ, ДУШИТЕ НА ТВОИТЕ МЪЧЕНИЦИ. / ВЪЗДАЙ ИМ ТВОЯТА ПРАВДА. / ПРИЕМИ ГИ ЗА НАШИ ЗАСТЪПНИЦИ, СВЕТИ И БЕЗСМЪРТНИ— / СЕГА И ВО ВЕКИ ВЕКОВ. АМИН.

► Memorial chapel next to the monument

English: *Kneel before this wall, Bulgarians! It symbolises the suffering of our people. This memorial was erected for our fellow citizens, victims of communist terror: those who lost their lives, those who disappeared without a trace, those who were shot by the so-called "People's Court". It commemorates the prisoners of the concentration camps, the political prisoners, those who were interned, those who were subjected to political repression and their unfortunate families and relatives. May the memory of the innocently shed blood burn in our hearts like an eternal flame. May the past never repeat itself! Lord, give peace to the souls of your martyrs, grant them your righteousness, accept them as our guardians, holy and immortal—now and forever. Amen.*

Location: Sofia, in the city's central park

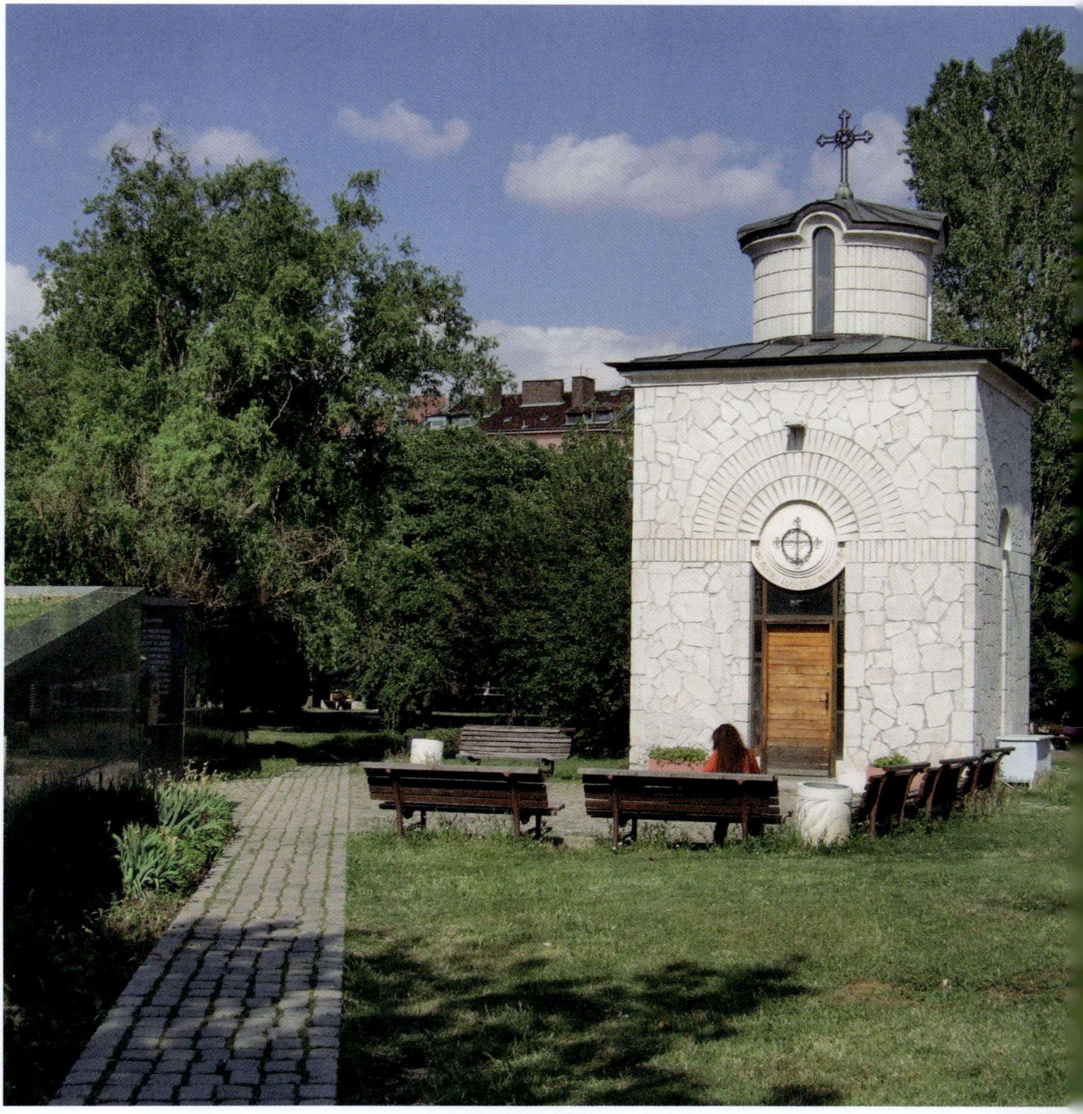

Monument Commemorating the Victims of the Prison Camp in Lovech

Lovech. After the collapse of the communist regime in Bulgaria in November 1989, the local group of the Union of Democratic Forces (SDS)—an alliance of various opposition parties and groups against the Communist regime—organised the first pilgrimage to the quarry at the site of the former Lovech labour camp in March 1990. On 19 April 1990, the diocese of the town of Lovech inaugurated two commemorative plaques on the rocky slope of the quarry and erected a cross at the highest point of the rock to commemorate the victims of the labour camp. Since then, a memorial service has been held at the foot of the rock every year in March.

With the provisional closure of the Belene penal camp on the Danube island of Persin on 27 August 1959, the majority of the approximately 1,400 detainees were released. However, on 7 September 1959, a group of 166 prisoners who were regarded as "incorrigible recidivists, a danger to the social order" were transferred to the newly established prison camp of Lovech in northern Bulgaria. Within a few months, about 1,000 prisoners had joined their ranks. Both political prisoners and "ordinary" criminals were interned here. Almost all of them were brought to the camp as a result of extrajudicial punitive measures with no trial or sentence. They constituted the "work brigade" for forced labour in the quarry near the town of Lovech. The prisoners here were to be "re-educated" as socialist citizens through brutal hard labour in the spirit of communist ideology. Notorious in local parlance as a "death camp" and cynically referred to by the guards as the "Sunny Beach" after a coastal resort on the Black Sea, Lovech was the location with the cruellest conditions in the system of Bulgarian penal and labour camps. Driven by unattainable compulsory quotas, the inmates—among them numerous intellectuals, writers and artists—were enslaved in the quarry under inhumane conditions. There was no medical care, and the prisoners were maltreated and tortured by the guards. Many did not survive their imprisonment.

The names are known of 151 people who were brutally killed in the camp between 1959 and 1961. They died as a result of torture and gruelling hard labour. As was common practice, false causes of death were given in the death certificates and their remains buried in secret places without identification under the supervision of the People's Police. On 5 April 1962, a special commission appointed by the Politburo decided to dissolve the Lovech camp

► A memorial service is held every year at the foot of the rock.

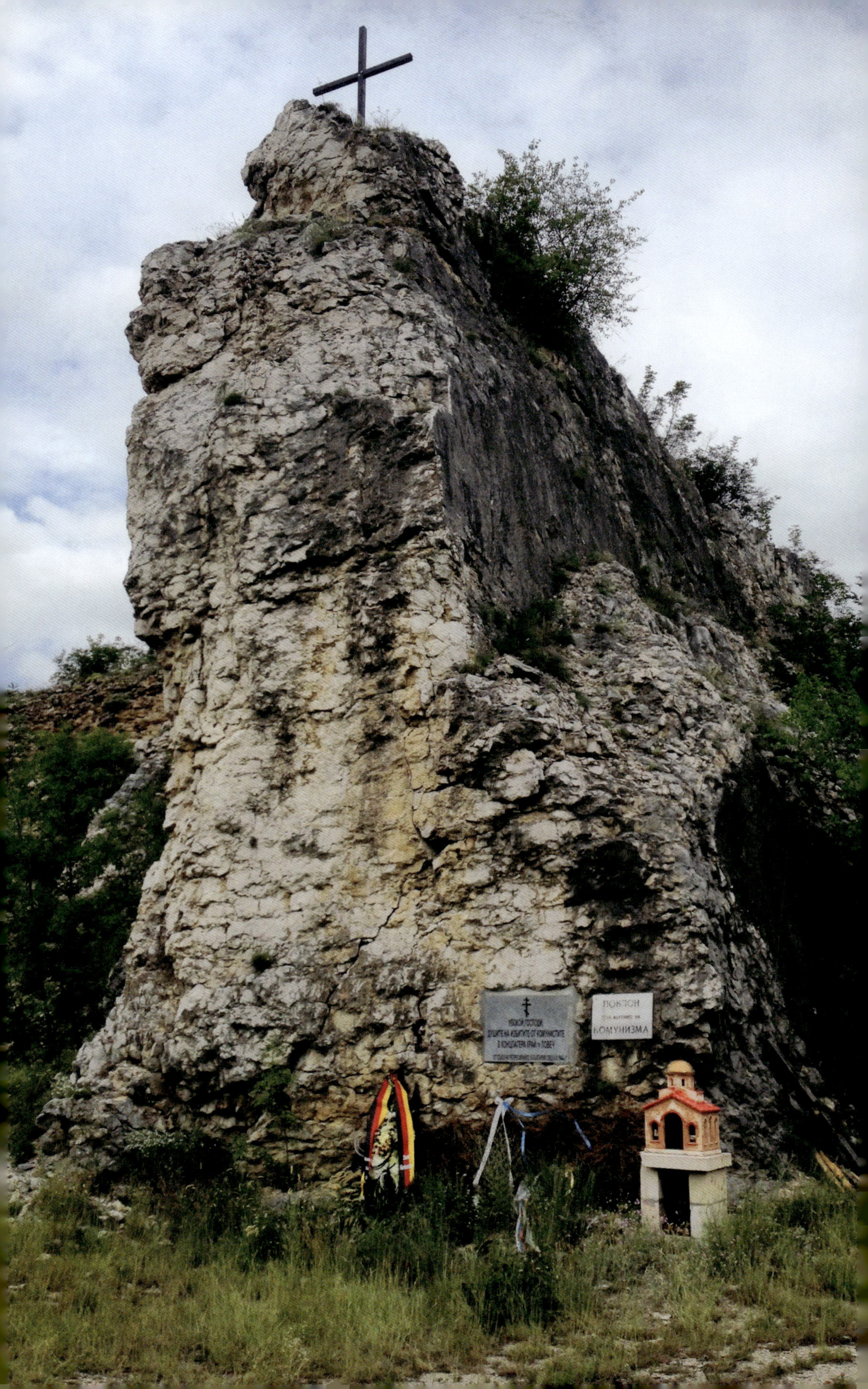
ПОКЛОН
КОМУНИЗМА

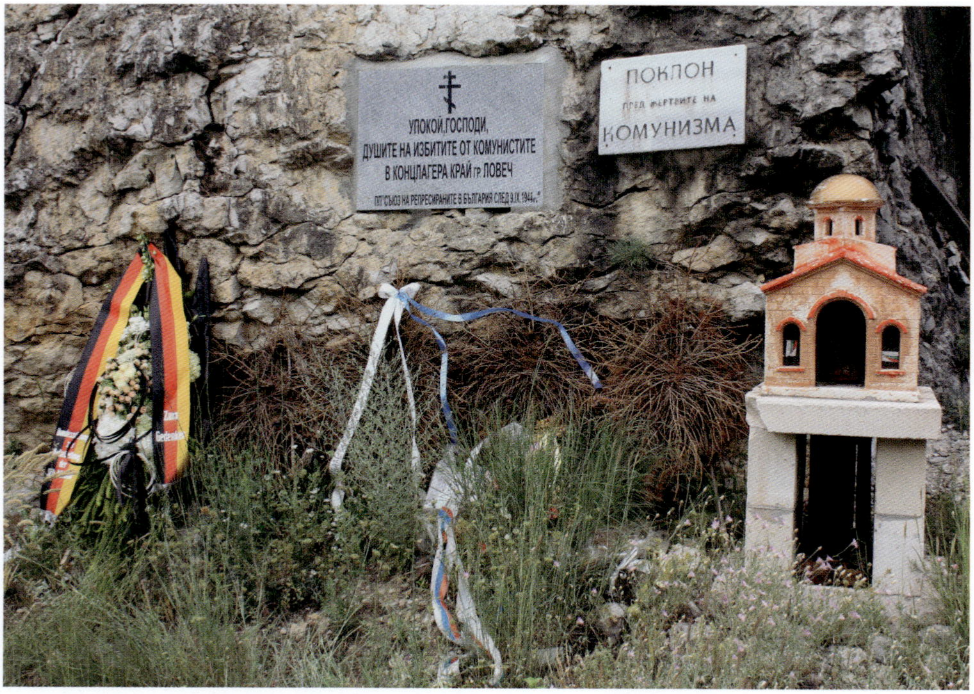

Memorial by the former quarry
of the Lovech penal camp

and release some of the prisoners. The remaining prisoners were only released two years later by an amnesty law issued on 9 September 1964.

Inscription

Bulgarian: УПОКОЙ, ГОСПОДИ, / ДУШИТЕ НА ИЗБИТИТЕ ОТ КОМУНИСТИТЕ / В КОНЦЛАГЕРА КРАЙ ГР. ЛОВЕЧ // ПП »СЪЮЗ НА РЕПРЕСИРАНИТЕ В БЪЛГАРИЯ СЛЕД 9. IX 1944 Г.«

ПОКЛОН / ПРЕД ЖЕРТВИТЕ НА / КОМУНИЗМА

English: *Lord, calm the souls of those killed by the Communists in the concentration camp near Lovech. Political Party "Union of Repressed by Communism in Bulgaria after 9 September 1944"*

A bow to the victims of Communism

Location: Lovech

Memorial to the Victims of the Belene Labour Camp

Persin. Since 2005, a memorial to the victims has been located on the site of the former Belene forced labour camp. On the initiative of the Bulgarian Agrarian National Union, two adjacent concrete steles and a memorial wall were erected. After the collapse of the communist regime in Bulgaria in November 1989, the largely disused camp complex started to decline. Since 2014, the Belene Island Foundation, founded by Catholic priest Paolo Cortese, has been working to establish a memorial to the victims of totalitarian regimes on the former camp grounds and to initiate a project to document and study the Bulgarian penal camp system. The island where the prison building was erected in 1952 is still in use under the regular Bulgarian penal system and can be entered only with the consent of the Ministry of the Interior and the Prison administration.

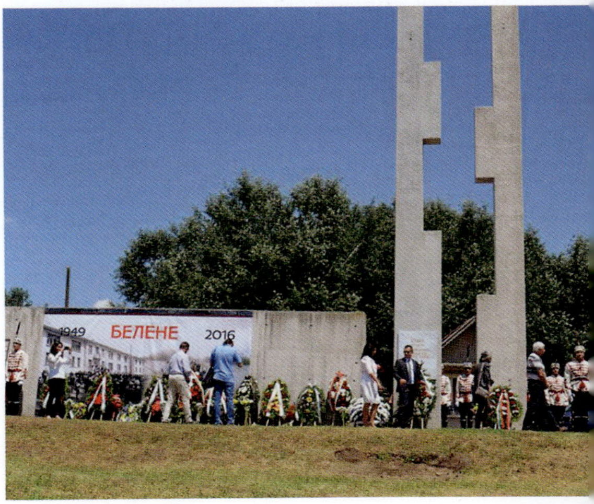

Memorial to the victims of the Belene forced labour camp

The Belene Concentration Camp was founded as a camp for political opponents by a decree of April 1949. It ordered all the Danube islands opposite the village of Belene—Persin, Golyama Barzina, Shturcheto, Magaritsa, Belitsa, Sovata and Predel—to be placed under the authority of the Ministry of the Interior for the construction of a camp complex. Within a few weeks, detention operations began on Persin, the largest Bulgarian island on the Danube. Belene, popularly known as the "Bulgarian Gulag", quickly developed into the largest camp for political prisoners in Bulgaria. The first prisoner transport, with 300 detainees, reached the island in July 1949. Designed for a capacity of up to 3,000 prisoners, more than 9,900 men and women were interned here with sentences ranging from six months to seven years. In addition to the camp on the archipelago, which stretched for ten kilometres inland, there was also a prison complex on the western coastline from the end of 1952.

After Stalin's death in March 1953, Belene was temporarily shut down. Immediately after the suppression of the Hungarian Revolution in November 1956, operations were resumed.

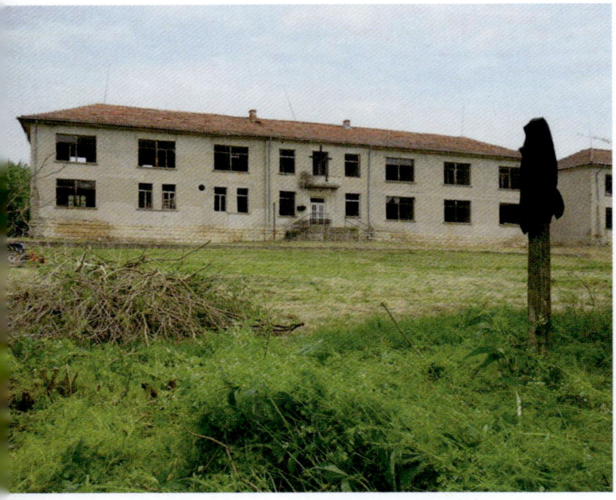

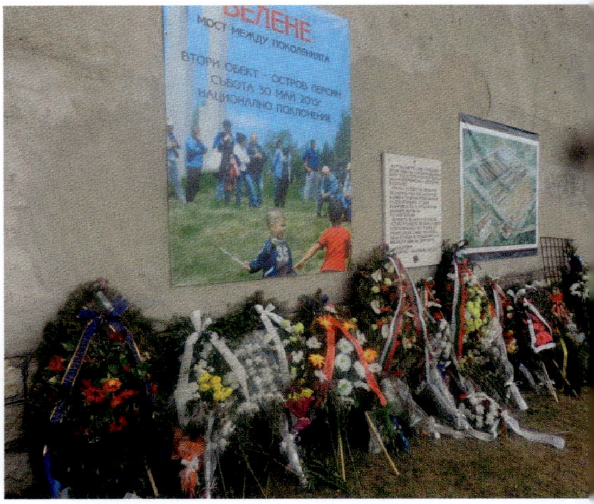

On 5 November, the security forces arrested over 370 people who had expressed sympathy with the Hungarian Revolution. Most of them were sent directly to Belene. In June 1958, there were more than 2,700 prisoners designated as "criminals" and "counterrevolutionaries" on the island. The forced labour camp was officially closed on 27 August 1959. More than 1,250 of the over 1,400 people detained on the island were released. A group of about 160 prisoners —"incorrigible recidivists, a danger to the social order"—were transferred to the newly established prison camp in Lovech.

In 1984, on the initiative of the Central Committee of the Bulgarian Communist Party, a campaign was initiated to force all Bulgarian Muslims to take on new names. The almost one million Muslims in the country had to "Bulgarianise" their names and abandon their traditional dress code; ethnic Turks had to restrict their use of the Turkish language to the immediate family circle; and the sanctions for practicing religious rites were also tightened. This led to protests in January 1985, which were met with retaliatory measures on the part of the security authorities and the military, during which some 400 people were arrested and deported to the Belene camp. In April 1986, the prisoners went on a 30-day hunger strike, which led to the release or forced resettlement of most prisoners in various parts of the country in early May 1986.

After the collapse of the communist regime in Bulgaria in November 1989, Belene became a symbolic memorial to all victims of the Bulgarian penal and forced labour camps. Every year on 9 September, the anniversary of the communist takeover in Bulgaria, commemorative events in honour of the victims of the communist dictatorship are held on the former camp grounds.

Location: Persin Island, across from the town of Belene
Internet: www.beleneisland.org

◄

left: Deserted barracks at the former camp site

right: Wreath-laying ceremony at the memorial

►

Sketch of the camp by the former inmate Krum Horozov

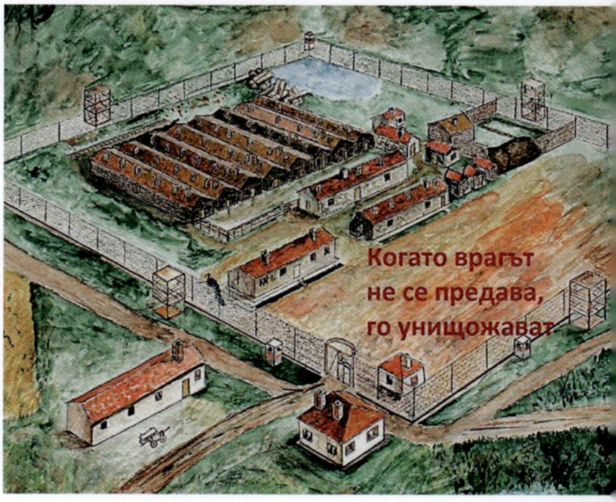

Further reading:

Kadrinov, Vasil: Case Study on Bulgaria. In: Honoring Civil Courage. Developing Suggestions to Improve the Situation of Victims of Communist State Crimes. Project Coordinator: Gedenkstätte Berlin-Hohenschönhausen 2015, Ref.-Nr.: JUST/2011/JPEN/AG/2998. Available online at: www.stiftung-hsh.de/assets/Dokumente-pdf-Dateien/EU-Projekt-Laenderstudien.pdf (last accessed on: 15/11/2017). / Nedeltschew, Michail: Geschichte der bulgarischen Opposition. In: Biografisches Lexikon Widerstand und Opposition im Kommunismus 1945–91. Bundesstiftung zur Aufarbeitung der SED-Diktatur 2017. Available online at: www.dissidenten.eu/laender/Bulgarien/oppositionsgeschichte/1/ (last accessed on: 15/11/2017). / Raichevsky, Stoyan: Bulgarien unter dem kommunistischen Regime 1944–1989. Berlin 2016. / Schwarz, Karl-Peter: Organisiertes Wegschauen. In vielen postkommunistischen Ländern herrschen noch die alten Eliten. In: Frankfurter Allgemeine Zeitung, article dated 24/6/2014. Available online at: www.memoryandconscience.eu/wp-content/uploads/2014/06/Organisiertes-Wegschauen-Zeitungsausschnitt.pdf (last accessed on: 06/12/2017). / Topouzova, Lilia: Reclaiming Memory: The History and Legacy of Concentration Camps in Communist Bulgaria. Dissertation. University of Toronto 2015.

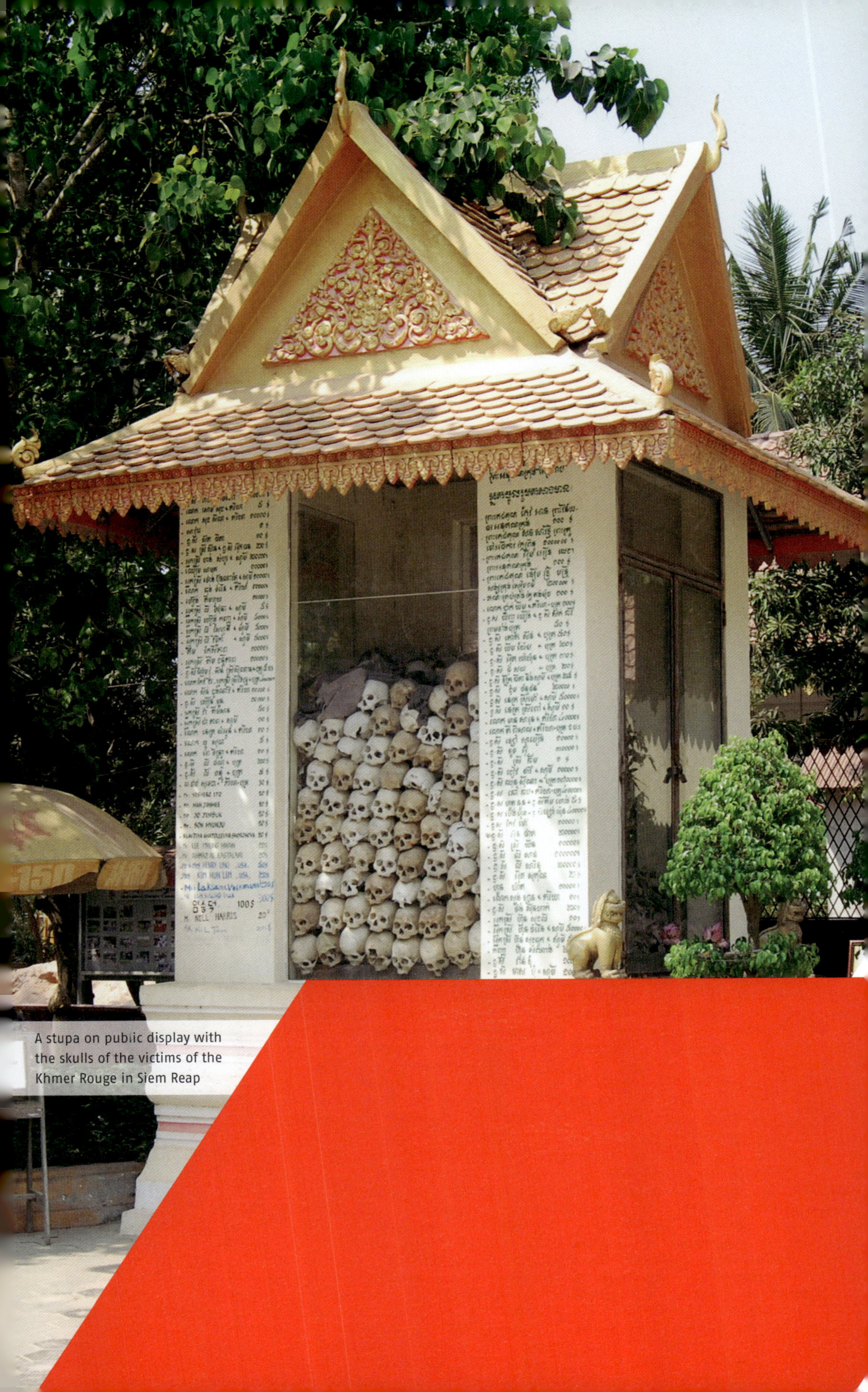

A stupa on public display with the skulls of the victims of the Khmer Rouge in Siem Reap

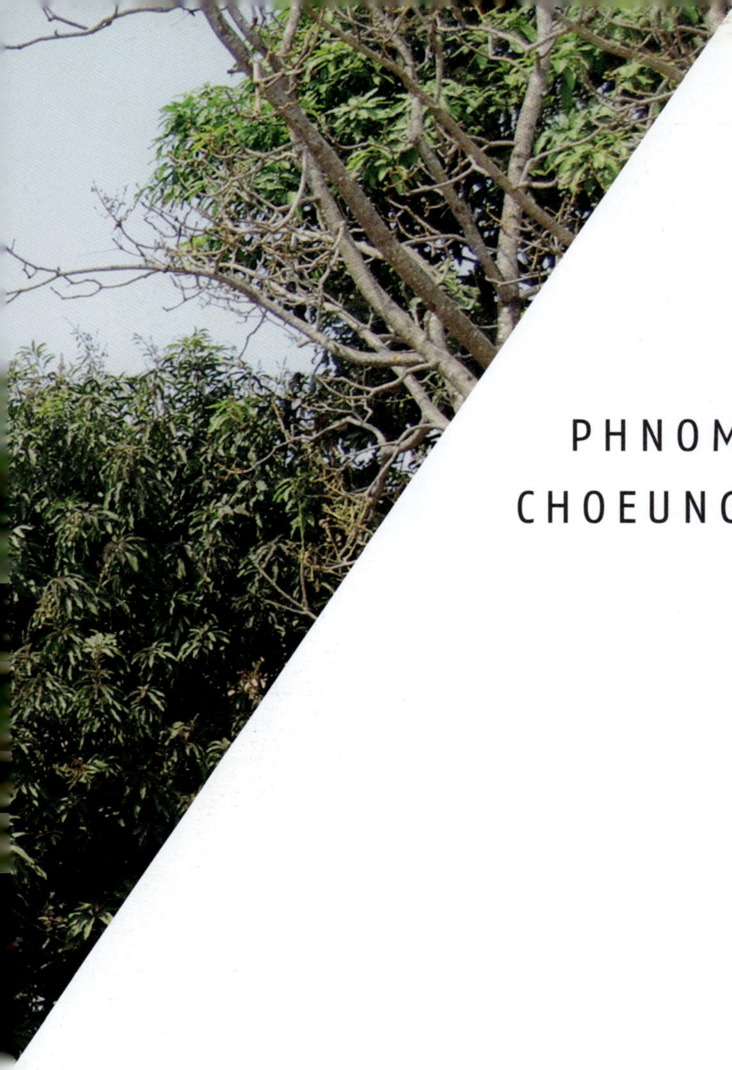

PHNOM PENH
CHOEUNG EK

Cambodia

From the mid-19th century until 1954, Cambodia belonged to the French colonial area and sphere of influence in Southeast Asia, which was known as "Indochina" or "Union indochinoise". Following independence in 1953, civil war broke out throughout the country. The Cambodian government attempted to maintain neutrality in its foreign policy. Although the country tried to stay out of the wars raging in the neighbouring countries, Cambodia eventually became one of the battlegrounds of the Vietnam War.

Vietnamese communist units moved their transport and supply routes (Ho Chi Minh trail) to Cambodian territory to escape the US bombing of Vietnam. This resulted in heavy bombing by the US Air Force. In 1970, officers supported by the USA under General Lon Nol took power and proclaimed the Khmer Republic. Together with South Vietnamese and American troops, Lon Nol fought against North Vietnamese troops and Khmer Rouge units. The US bombardments spread from the border regions with Vietnam to the whole country. In 1975, units of the Khmer Rouge occupied the capital Phnom Penh. Within a few days, the entire population, which at the time counted 2.5 million people, was evacuated from the city to the countryside on the pretext of imminent American air raids. Anyone who tried to escape deportation was shot.

In order to build the so-called "new society" according to the Maoist model, all existing social structures were destroyed, and thousands of people, predominantly intellectuals, who were deemed resistant to "re-education" were systematically murdered. Often, even being it was enough to be able to read and write or speak a foreign language or even just to wear glasses.

The entire population of the cities was deported and settled in huge labour colonies and camps in the countryside. All private property was banned; children were separated from their parents for induction into the Khmer Rouge's educational programmes, to prevent family influences and to wipe out traditions and identities. The rural population was glorified as the "old people", and the inhabitants of the cities were defamed as decadent "new people" who had to be re-educated and returned to their roots. Forced labour was compulsory for all. In order to destroy all links to the decadent past, archives, cadastres and property deeds were destroyed. Even private documents and photos fell victim to the Khmer Rouge's destructive frenzy.

The devastation of the existing economic structures caused the economy to collapse entirely. Millions of people starved to death, died of abuse or were murdered. All those who were considered "enemies" or members of the "bourgeoisie" were sent to extermination camps and executed in the "Killing Fields". It is estimated that more than 2.2 million people lost their lives in this way, amounting to about half of the population.

Following border disputes with Vietnam, the Vietnamese army invaded Cambodia in 1979, occupying the country and liberating it from Khmer Rouge rule. Even after the takeover of the capital Phnom Penh and the establishment of a new Cambodian government, the country remained under Vietnamese control. The Khmer Rouge and their supporters—including China and the USA—fled to border regions with Thailand in the north-east of the country and plunged the country into a new civil war that ended in 1998 with a ceasefire and numerous concessions to the Khmer Rouge leaders.

The Vietnamese occupiers sentenced Pol Pot and Ieng Sary to death in absentia in 1979 as the main perpetrators of the genocide in Cambodia. However, a true historical reckoning did not take place, and the perpetrators were never convicted. Pol Pot was considered "Brother No. 1" until 1997 and, in the wake of internal disputes, was sentenced to life imprisonment by a Khmer Rouge tribunal in 1997, which did not, however, address the crimes committed during the Khmer Rouge regime between 1975 and 1979. He died in 1998.

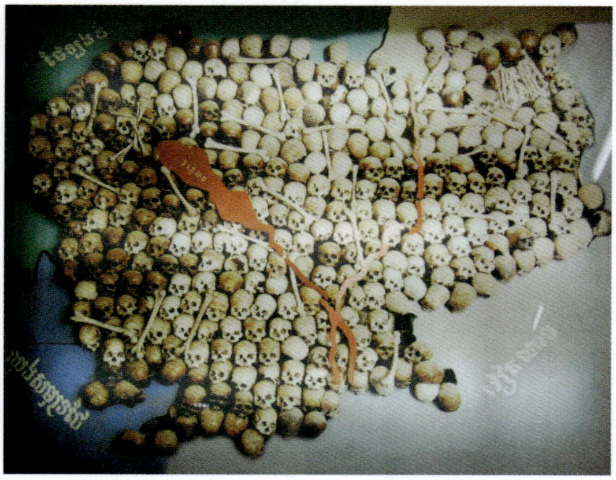

◄ A map of Cambodia made from the bones of the victims of the Khmer Rouge in the Tuol-Sleng Genocide Museum in Phnom Penh

To this day, it has proved extremely difficult to come to terms with the crimes. Many of those responsible and involved in the Khmer Rouge regime at the time are at large and have no fear of prosecution. Some of them are now members of the government and parliament. In a few cases, the perpetrators and victims live next door to one another in the same towns. Although an international criminal court consisting of Cambodian and international judges which operates in accordance with the Cambodian Criminal Procedure Code was set up in 2004, only two cases have thus far gone to trial.

In the first trial, "Comrade Duch", the director of the torture prison Tuol Sleng where over 20,000 people died, was sentenced to life imprisonment. In the second trial, a total of four Khmer Rouge leaders—Nuon Chea, Ieng Sary and his wife Ieng Thirith, and Khieu Samphan—were indicted. Only two of the accused—Khieu and Nuon—received life sentences for crimes against humanity. Ieng Sary died in prison; his wife Ieng Thirith was ruled mentally unfit to stand trial due to dementia and was released from prison. The two who were convicted did not accept the verdict and described the proceedings as a "show trial".

The last commander of the Khmer Rouge, Ta Mok, who succeeded Pol Pot as "Brother No. 1" in 1997, was detained and charged with crimes against humanity. However, he died in 2006 before the case went to trial. The Cambodian government under Hun Sen, also a former Khmer Rouge official who fled to Vietnam in 1977, rejects further trials.

After the invasion of Cambodia by Vietnamese troops in 1979 and the discovery of the "Killing Fields" and the torture prisons, the Vietnamese had bones and skulls exhibited publicly in so-called "stupas" to publicly document the crimes committed. Many of the mass graves have not yet been located. With the support of international organisations, in particular Yale University, a documentation centre was set up in Phnom Penh in 1995 to collect the names and biographies of the victims and to implement reconciliation and healing projects. A memorial was set up in the Tuol Sleng torture prison and in Choeung Ek, one of the "Killing Fields". In view of the increasingly repressive climate in Cambodia, civil society initiatives and actors find it difficult to initiate processes of reckoning with the crimes of communist rule and their consequences.

Tuol Sleng Genocide Museum

Phnom Penh. The former Tuol Svay Prey High School on 103rd Street in the Cambodian capital has housed the Tuol Sleng Genocide Museum since the defeat of the Khmer Rouge terror regime in 1979. It is located at the site where the Khmer Rouge established the notorious "Security Prison 21" ("S21") after the expulsion of the city population to the countryside in 1975. The complex, consisting of several buildings, formed the Khmer Rouge's central "security prison". Around 20,000 people from all over Cambodia, including former members of the Khmer Rouge, were tortured and murdered here.

Symbolic graves on the grounds
of the modern-day Genocide Museum
of the last victims to die in Tuol Sleng

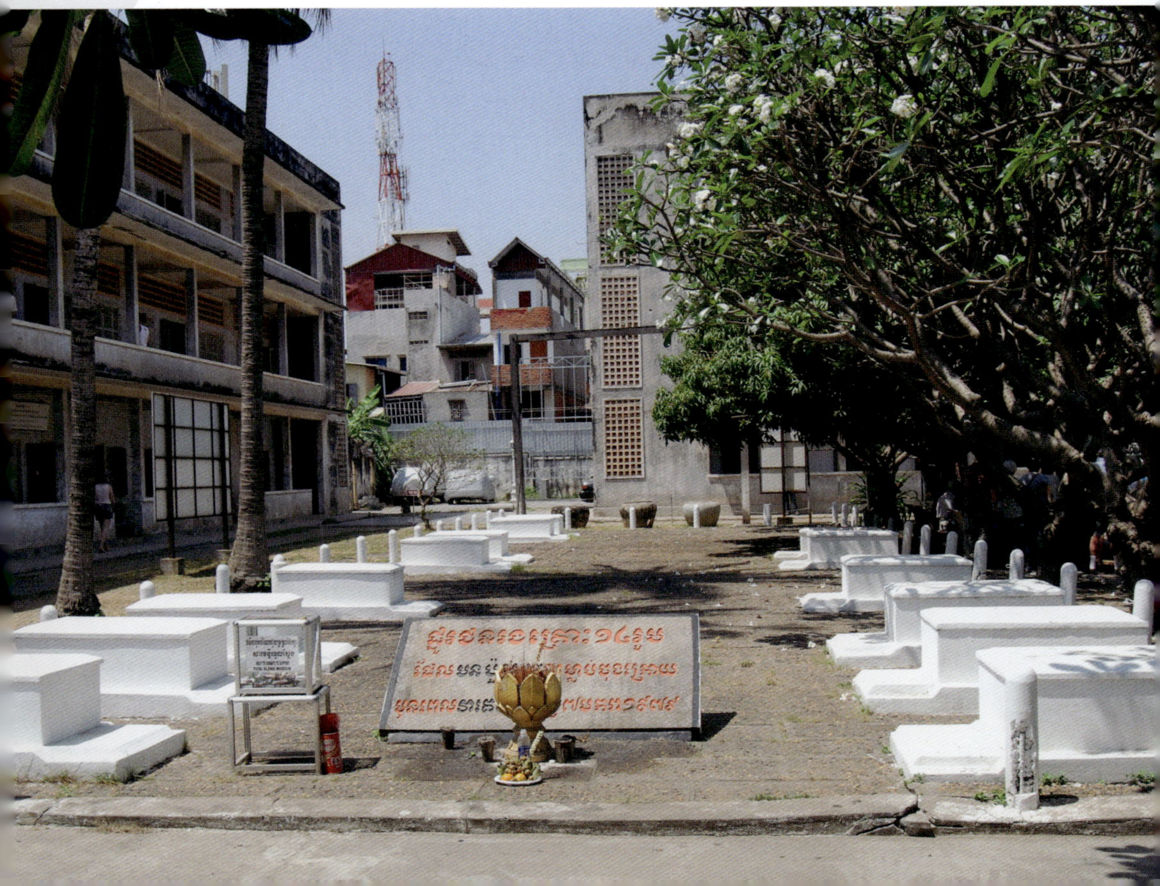

The "S21" was subordinated to the Ministry of Defence under the leadership of Son Sen. The prison complex itself also supplied several detention and execution facilities, including the Prey Sar Prison ("S24") and Choeung Ek, an execution site about 12 kilometres south of Phnom Penh. The prison staff numbered around 1,700. After the Khmer Rouge took over the school grounds, the entire campus was enclosed by an electric barbed wire fence. The corridors between the building wings and the windows of the classrooms, which were converted into prison and torture cells, were also fenced in with barbed wire. Prisoners were detained in different parts of the building, depending on their assigned category. Formerly high-ranking members of the Khmer Rouge, who were branded "traitors" by the regime, were imprisoned in two rooms on the ground floor of Building A. In the classrooms of the B, C, and D sections of the building, tiny isolation cells with a floor area of 1.6 square metres were constructed. The upper floors contained mass detention cells for 40 to 50 detainees.

Prisoners were strictly prohibited from talking to one another. They were chained to the ground, and their every movement—including getting up, sitting down or turning around—required the consent of the guards. Non-compliance with the rules was punished with torture. Buildings adjacent to the main wing were used by the prison administration for the interrogation and torture of the detainees. Those who survived the cruel torture and inhumane conditions of detention were brutally executed outside the city after forced confessions on the "Killing Fields". In many cases, the prisoners had to dig their own graves. After the collapse of the Khmer Rouge's "Stone Age Communism" and the liberation of Phnom Penh by Vietnamese troops in early 1979, only twelve prisoners, including four children, escaped execution in Tuol Sleng. The 14 white stone tombs in the inner courtyard symbolise the last 14 of the prison's torture victims found on the Tuol Sleng site.

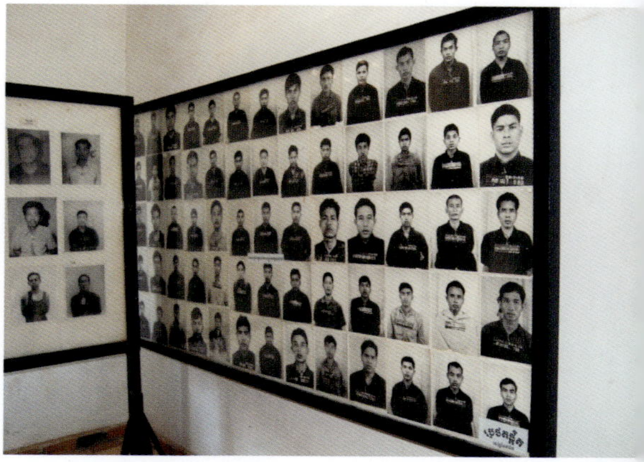

Exhibition of thousands of photos of the detainees in "S21"

The permanent exhibition at the historic site shows the classrooms of the former Tuol Svay Prey High School converted into prison cells by the Khmer Rouge. It examines in detail the history of the Khmer Rouge's reign of terror between 1975 and 1979 and in particular the crimes committed in Tuol Sleng Prison. Considerable space is devoted to displaying thousands of photos of the people detained in "S21". The museum also shows paintings by Tuol Sleng survivor Vann Nath, whose works depict the inhumane conditions of detention and torture.

Location: Phnom Penh, 113th St., Boeung Keng Kang III, Chamkarmorn
Internet: www.tuolsleng.gov.kh

"Killing Fields" Memorial

Choeung Ek. The "Killing Fields" are now considered synonymous with the mass murder by the Khmer Rouge of their own people. In the years of their reign of terror between 1975 and 1979, more than 150 such execution sites were located on the territory of the entire country. In Choeung Ek alone—the most famous of the "Killing Fields" about twelve kilometres south of the Cambodian capital Phnom Penh—some 14,000 people were brutally executed, according to estimates of the genocide documentation centre. "In order to save ammunition", the victims were beaten to death with iron bars, pickaxes and shovels, and infants were thrown against a so-called "Killing Tree for Children". Most of the people who were executed had previously been subjected to torture in the infamous Tuol Sleng Prison.

Only 86 of the 129 mass graves in Choeung Ek were excavated by scientists, archaeologists and forensic experts after the collapse of the Khmer Rouge terrorist regime in 1979 and the mortal remains of the victims of execution exhumed. The remaining untouched execution sites were cordoned off by barrier tape and marked with information plaques. Integrated into the memorial architecture of the site is an elaborately designed memorial stupa, a tower-shaped construction from the Buddhist culture of commemoration and burial. Covered by a gilded roof, the remains of the victims are laid out in the interior of the construction—according to a specific taxonomy. Stacked on top of each other, protected only by acrylic glass walls, are the remains of over 8,900 people.

Location: Choeung Ek, about 12 kilometres south of Phnom Penh

Further reading:
Documentation Center of Cambodia. Yale University Cambodia Genocide Program. Available online at: www.d.dccam.org (last accessed on: 29/11/2017). / Follath, Erich: Die Kinder der Killing Fields. Kambodschas Weg vom Terrorland zum Touristenparadies. München 2009. / Fröberg Idling, Peter: Pol Pots Lächeln. Eine schwedische Reise durch das Kambodscha der Roten Khmer. Frankfurt 2013.

►
Marked execution site on the "Killing Fields"

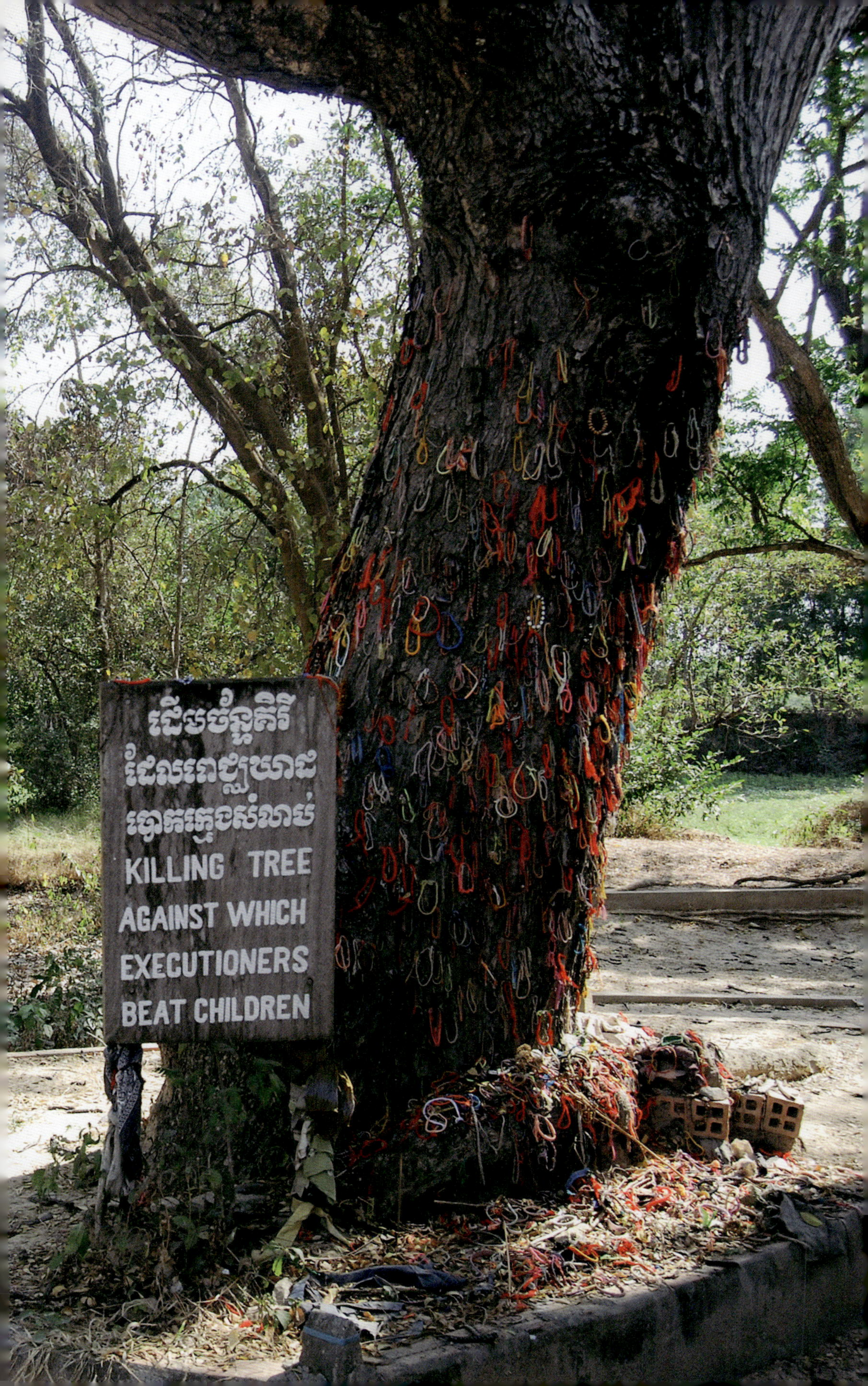
KILLING TREE
AGAINST WHICH
EXECUTIONERS
BEAT CHILDREN

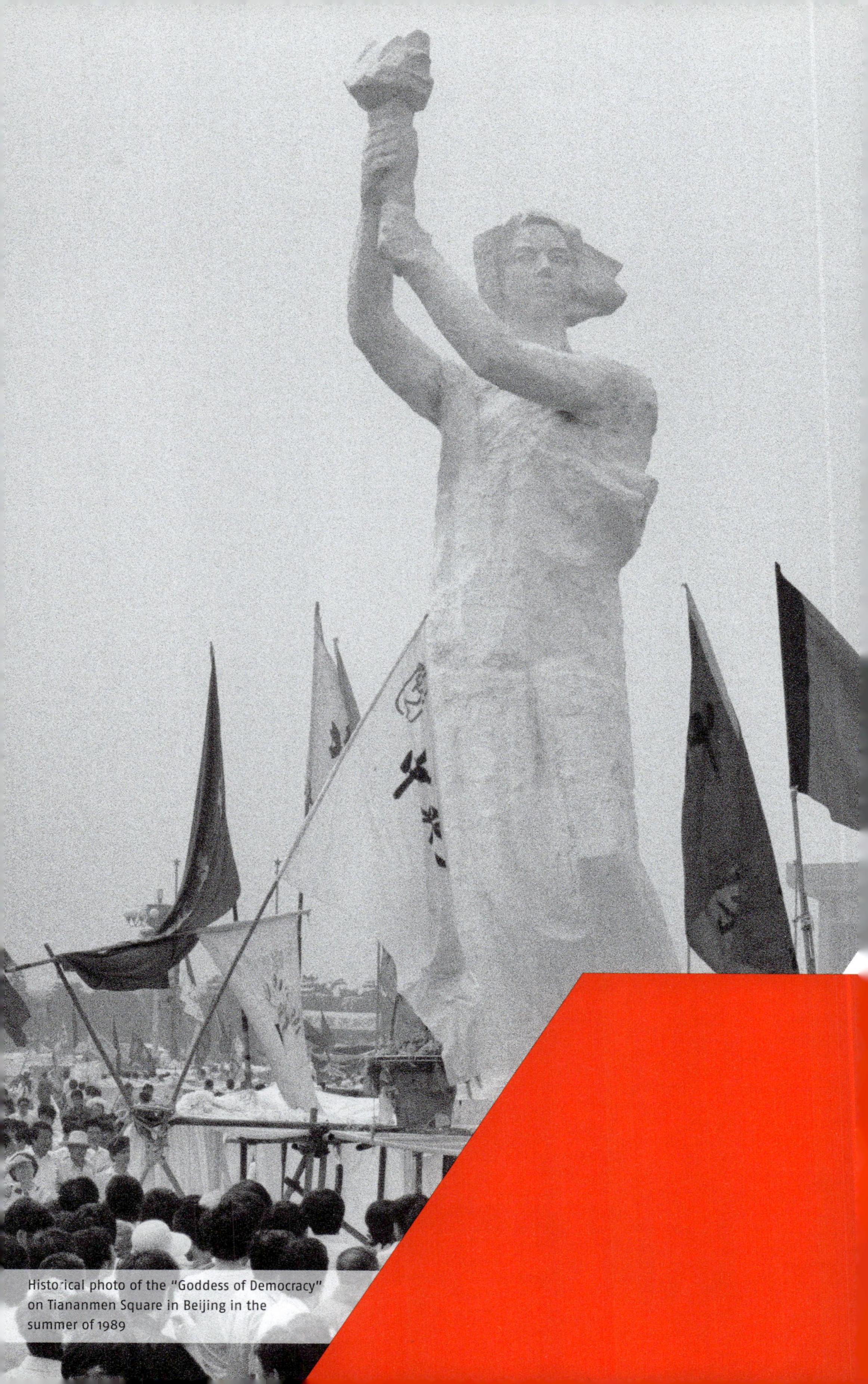

Historical photo of the "Goddess of Democracy" on Tiananmen Square in Beijing in the summer of 1989

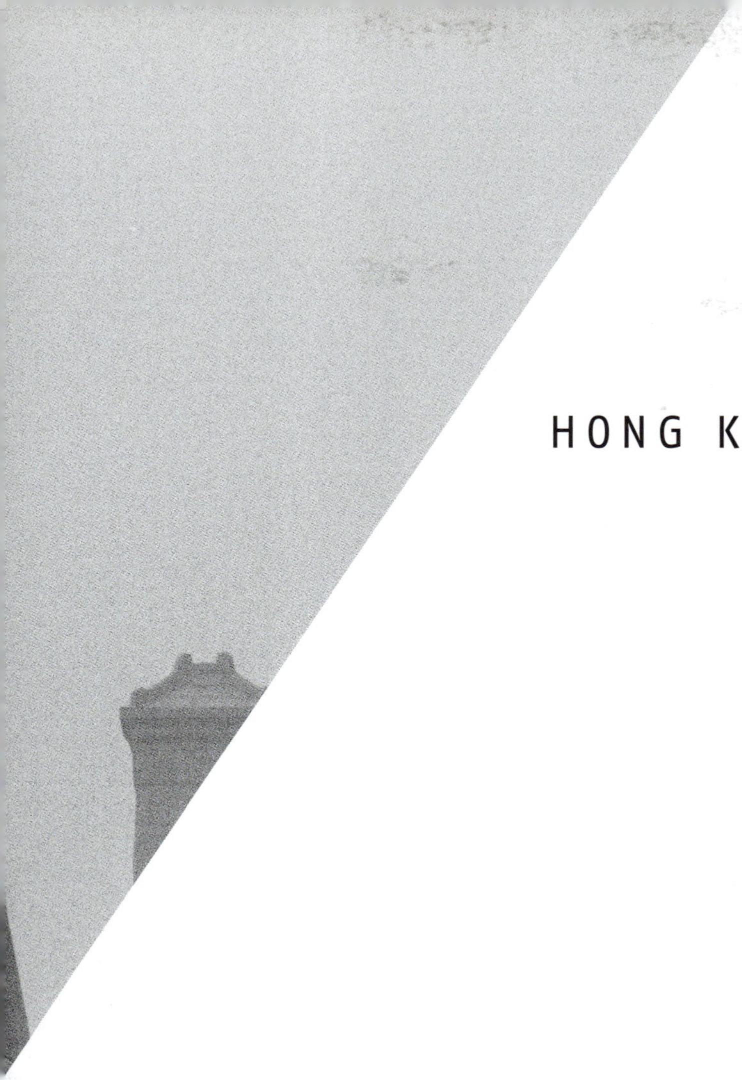

HONG KONG

China

The end of the Opium Wars of 1840 marked the beginning for China of the "century of humiliation" at the hands of the Western colonial powers and Japanese and Russian imperialism. The government lost sovereignty over parts of the country. China was plagued by wars, occupation and internal conflicts. In 1911, the Qing Dynasty finally collapsed, and China became the first republic in East Asia. After the last Chinese Emperor resigned in 1912, there was a brief hope that the country would become a democracy. However, the newly formed republic was unstable. Conflict between the Republican forces under the leadership of Sun Yat-sen and conservative forces led by Yuan Shikai weakened the republic. Yuan finally prevailed and attempted to restore the monarchy. After his death in 1916, central authority collapsed, and the Warlord Era began. The warlords effectively controlled large parts of the country with their armies. The internal conflicts were compounded by the invasion of imperialist powers from without. For example, the 1919 Versailles Peace Conference awarded the Chinese province of Shandong to Japan.

In 1921, with the support of the Comintern, the Communist Party of China (CPC) was formed. The most influential party, however, was the nationalist party Kuomintang (KMT) under the leadership of Sun Yat-sen and, after his death, Chiang Kai-shek. At first, the two parties were united in their fight against foreign powers and warlords. Between 1922 and 1927, both parties formed a united front with the support of the Soviet Union, but the massacre of communists and trade unionists in Shanghai by Chiang Kai-shek's troops tore it apart. In the early 1930s, the CPC took advantage of the limits on the power of the new KMT central government in Nanjing to found a Chinese Soviet republic in the hinterland. In 1934, however, the KMT was able to launch an effective "extermination campaign". To avoid total defeat, the communist troops fought their way north in 1936 during what became famous as the Long March. Although only about 10,000 of the original 100,000 fighters survived this march, it cemented Mao Zedong's (1893 – 1976) claim to leadership.

After the Japanese occupation of Manchuria in 1931, the KMT and the CPC once again temporarily set aside their differences to form a united front, particularly during the Sino-Japanese War of 1937 – 1945. However, this alliance fell apart within a year of the victory of the Allies over Japan in 1945. This rift ultimately provoked a factional civil war (1946 – 1949) between the Communist Party, which garnered support from the Soviet Union, and the US-backed KMT. In 1949, the CPC emerged victorious from the conflict and the Chinese Revolution prevailed. The KMT fled to Taiwan, and Mao proclaimed the People's Republic of China in Beijing on 1 October 1949.

The CPC created a centrally organised state based on the Soviet model. A central measure of the new government was the implementation of a land reform which redistributed almost half of the agricultural land from large landowners to peasant farmers. As part of a campaign to "suppress counterrevolution" (1951 – 1953), 700,000 people were executed to break resistance to the new regime. By 1956, a planned economy based on the Soviet model was introduced, industry was nationalised and agriculture collectivised.

In 1957, Mao launched the anti-rightist campaign targeting dissenting intellectuals. Around 550,000 people were branded as "rightists", and many of them were sent to the rural provinces for 20 years. In order to increase industrial and agricultural production, the CPC initiated a new economic programme in 1958 with the "Great Leap Forward". In the so-called steel campaign, industrial products were to be manufactured even in the smallest backyards and steel produced in small furnaces. Farmers were reorganised into people's communes; private farming was outlawed. Poor planning, radical restructuring and crop failure led to severe famines in 1959 and 1961, claiming an estimated 20 to 40 million lives.

After the population and the economy began to recover from this catastrophe, Mao proclaimed the so-called Cultural Revolution in 1966 to prevent "revisionism" from taking hold in the party in China, as was purported to have occurred in the Soviet Union under Khrushchev, and to prevent the country from straying from the socialist path. In the summer and autumn of 1966, young Red Guards destroyed many cultural sites and temples and terrorised teachers and intellectuals. Mao finally called on the common people to revolt against the "the power-holders on the capitalist path within the party". In 1967, after China descended into chaos, he had the army restore order. According to recent research, about one million people fell victim to the Cultural Revolution. Most of them died in "cleansing campaigns" carried out by the army after order had been restored. The Cultural Revolution ended with Mao's death in 1976.

In 1978, the so-called "reform and opening-up" began under the leadership of Deng Xiaoping. China rejoined the world market. Planned and market economies were combined and private enterprises approved. This form of Chinese economic policy was described by the CPC as a "socialist market economy". It brought the country one of the highest economic growth rates worldwide, which has continued for decades, but also resulted in immense environmental destruction and social division. In 1981, the CC passed a "Resolution on Certain Questions in the History of Our Party Since the Founding of the People's Republic of China", which critically re-assessed excesses such as the "Great Leap Forward" and the Cultural Revolution. Although many victims of the Anti-Rightist Campaign and the Cultural Revolution had been rehabilitated, political dissidents still faced persecution and prison sentences. Moreover, the absolute hegemony of the Communist Party remained untouched.

In May 1989, tens of thousands, later hundreds of thousands of students and ordinary citizens gathered at Tiananmen Square in Beijing to campaign for the democratisation of China and freedom of the press and to protest against corruption. The demonstrations were prompted by the death of party secretary Hu Yaobang who was considered a reformer and had been ousted two years previously. After the students went on a hunger strike in support of their demands, the military brutally dispersed the student protests on 4 June and cleared the square. The number of casualties is still unknown to this day. The highest estimates put the number at several thousand.

Between 1980 and 2015, the CPC implemented the "one-child policy", which imposed heavy fines on families with more than one child. Until the 2000s, women were forced to have abortions in the event of unapproved pregnancies. In 2016, China instituted a "two-child policy".

From the very beginning, the development of Communist China was accompanied by territorial conflicts with neighbouring states and autonomous areas within China. This includes the Tibet conflict, which sparked uprisings in 1959, 1989 and 2008. Hong Kong was reabsorbed into the Chinese state in 1997 as a special administrative zone, and Macao followed suit in 1999. This marked the end of the colonial era in China. Furthermore, the question of relations between the People's Republic of China and the Republic of China in Taiwan remains unresolved. Beijing considers Taiwan a renegade province and strives for "reunification". According to CPC plans, China is set to become a highly developed industrialised nation and global superpower by 2049, the centenary of the founding of the People's Republic.

"Goddess of Democracy" Monument

Hong Kong. In June 2010, a replica of the statue of the "Goddess of Democracy" was set up on the campus of the Chinese University of Hong Kong (CUHK). The original, which was erected by students of the Beijing Academy of Arts on Tiananmen Square between the Tiananmen (or "Gate of Heavenly Peace") and the Monument to the People's Heroes, was destroyed by soldiers of the People's Liberation Army in the suppression of the democracy movement on 4 June 1989. The approximately three-metre-high bronze-imitation replica, created by Chinese artist Chen Weiming, was presented by the Hong Kong Alliance in Support of the Patriotic Democratic Movement in China on Times Square in Hong Kong in the run-up to the 21st anniversary of the Tiananmen massacre in the spring of 2010.

On 29 May, the Hong Kong police confiscated the sculpture along with another replica made of white plastic, claiming that the organisers were not licensed to hold a public event. Under the pressure of massive public criticism, the decision was reversed, and the bronze

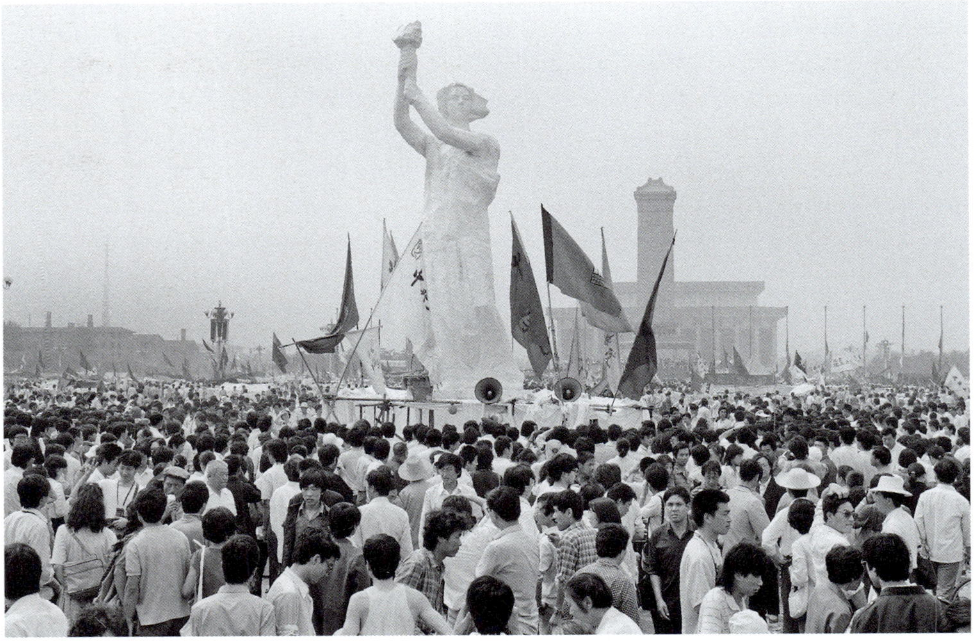

sculpture was publicly exhibited at the commemoration ceremony on 4 June in Victoria Park. The statue of the Goddess of Democracy was subsequently installed on campus on the initiative of the CUHK student union.

Whereas the democratic reform movements in the Soviet Union and Eastern and Central Europe eventually succeeded in 1989, all the efforts of the democracy movement in the People's Republic of China failed to bring about lasting change. In the early hours of 4 June 1989, more than 200,000 soldiers of the People's Liberation Army, mobilised by the Chinese government at Tiananmen Square in Beijing, brutally crushed the protest movement of tens of thousands of people. Images of the massacre went around the world. To this day, no precise figures are known regarding total death toll. Official reports give a casualty count of 241, including "hooligans", innocent bystanders, ten soldiers, and 13 police officers. However, international human rights organisations and unofficial Chinese agencies estimate that up to 3,000 people were killed that day. Tens of thousands of people who were branded "political criminals" were detained in prisons for years as a result of the crackdown. Thousands of political refugees fled the country.

Various replicas of the Goddess of Democracy around the world commemorate the victims of the Tiananmen Square massacre, for example in Washington D.C., and Arlington VA in the US, in Toronto and British Columbia in Canada, and in Sydney in Australia.

Location: Hong Kong, Campus of The Chinese University of Hong Kong

◄

Historical photo of the "Goddess of Democracy" on Tiananmen Square in Beijing in the summer of 1989

Further reading:

Shiu-Hing Lo, Sonny: Interest groups, intellectuals and new democracy movement in Hong Kong. In: Shiu-Hing Lo, Sonny (ed.): Interest Groups and the New Democracy Movement in Hong Kong. London, New York 2017. / Yiwu, Liao: Die Kugel und das Opium. Leben und Tod am Platz des Himmlischen Friedens. Frankfurt am Main 2012.

"Goddess of Democracy" monument in Hong Kong

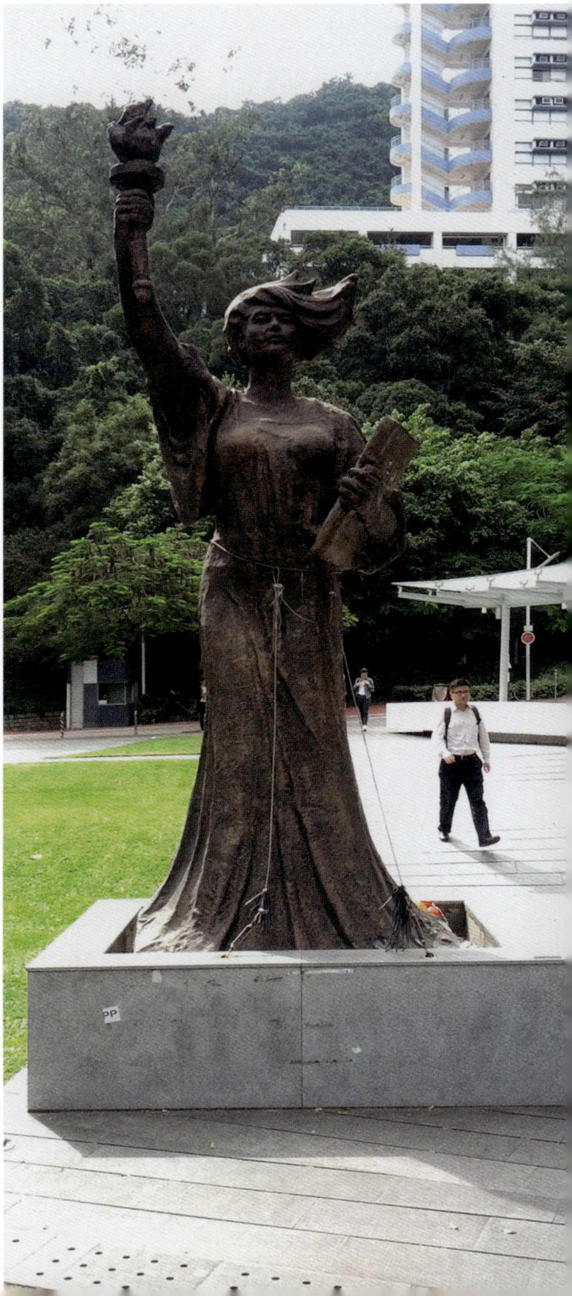

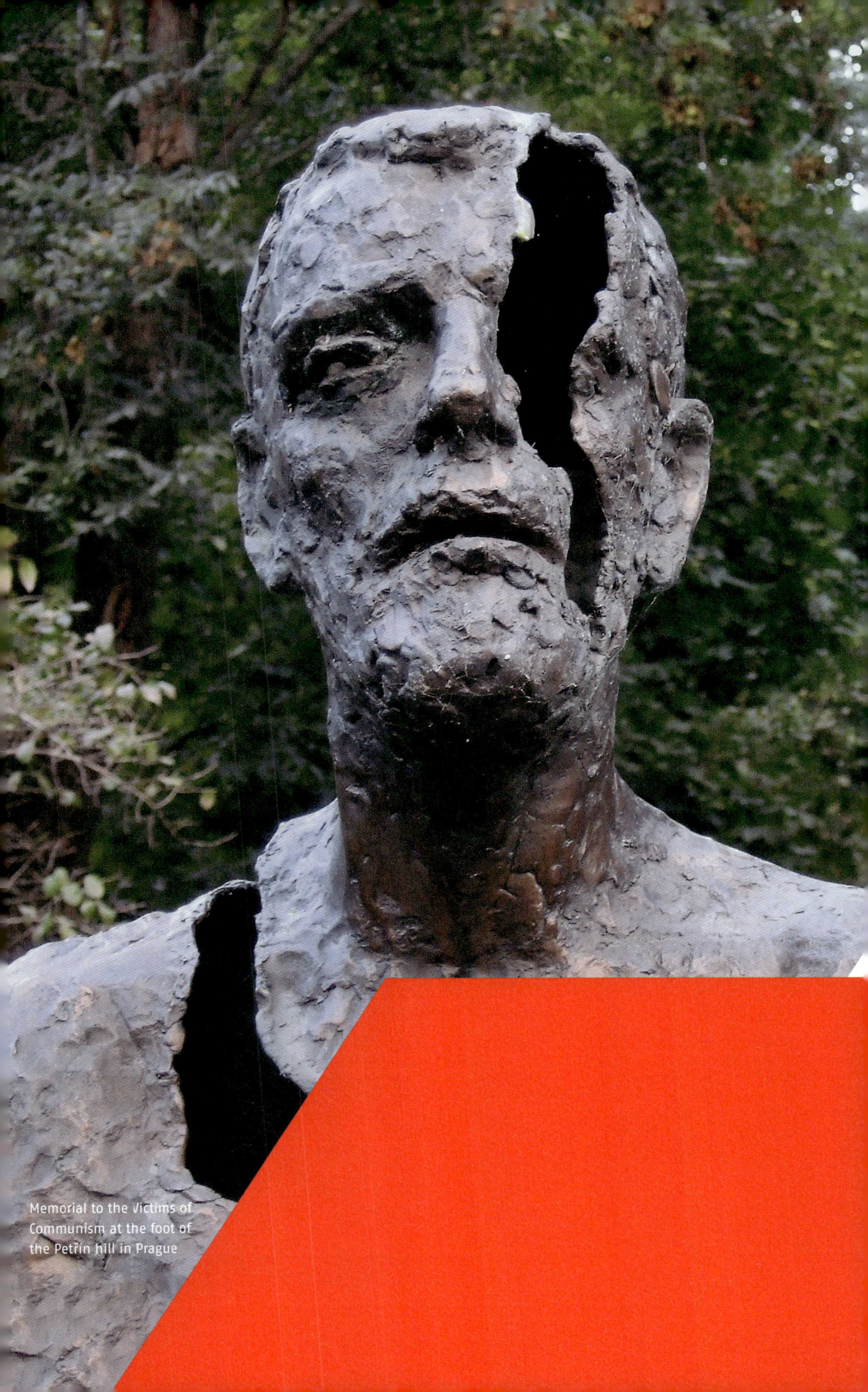

Memorial to the Victims of Communism at the foot of the Petřín hill in Prague

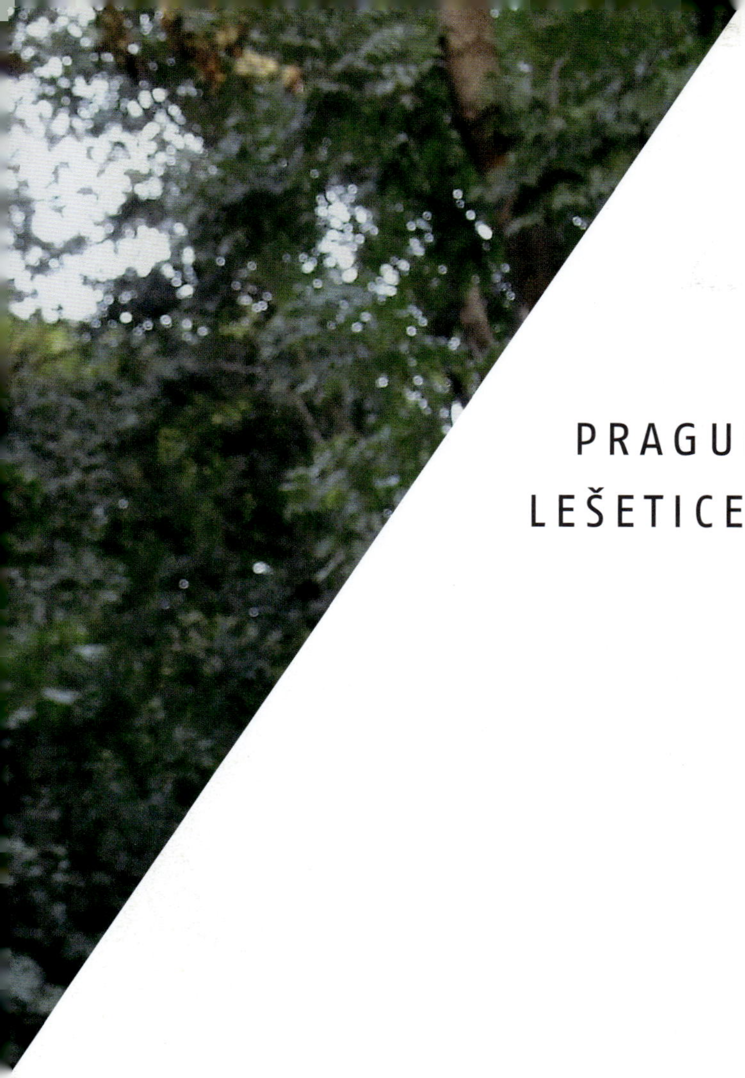

PRAGUE

LEŠETICE

Czech Republic

The first Czechoslovak Republic was founded in the aftermath of the First World War and continued to exist until 1938. As a result of the Sudeten crisis of 1938, the Sudeten region of Czechoslovakia, most of which was German-speaking, was annexed by Nazi Germany. This territorial incorporation by Germany was settled on in the Munich Agreement, to which the Czechoslovak government was not invited to be a party, which resulted from the mediation of Benito Mussolini between Great Britain and France on one side, and Germany on the other. At the same time, Hungary and Poland took advantage of the opportunity to take control of mainly Hungarian or Polish-speaking areas of Czechoslovakia. In March 1939, Slovakia finally broke away from the remaining confederation of states and declared its independence. Only the rump of the former Czechoslovak Republic remained. Members of the government, including Edvard Beneś, fled into exile. After the occupation of the remaining Czech territory, which became known as the "Protectorate", the German occupying power brutally suppressed all forms of resistance. Infamous massacres of civilians, for example in Lidice, were carried out under the pretext of retaliation against acts of resistance. Most of the Jews living in Bohemia and Moravia were deported and murdered in German extermination camps. The resistance against the German occupying forces continued until the end of the war and led to an armed uprising at the beginning of May 1945. Prague was liberated by the Red Army on 9 May 1945.

After the end of the war, Czechoslovakian territory was restored within the borders of 1937. Carpathian Ruthenia remained within the Soviet Union and was annexed to Ukraine. After the return of former president Beneš from exile, a government of national unity was formed, in which the communists were also represented. Because of their opposition to the Munich Agreement, they enjoyed great respect and support among the population. In addition, they dominated the companies and trade unions; important key departments were headed by communists. Immediately after the end of the war, massive retaliations began against the German inhabitants who were expelled from their homes, abused and robbed of their property.

After its victory in the 1946 elections, the Communist Party of Czechoslovakia (KPČ) systematically prepared for the takeover of political power. Important government positions were filled by representatives of the Communist Party, and its chairman Klement Gottwald was appointed Prime Minister. After the 1948 coup d'état that became known as the "Victorious February", which was accompanied by the resignation of several non-communist ministers, a new, communist-dominated government was formed with Klement Gottwald as president. Expropriations began almost immediately after the 1946 elections and were stepped up in the aftermath. Democratic-minded citizens were declared "class enemies", prosecuted by the State Security (Státní—StB) and sentenced to long prison terms. Between 1946 and 1964, the country's jails held about 30,000 political prisoners per year. At least 240 people were killed for political reasons. In addition to prisons, countless forced labour camps were set up.

Dr Milada Horáková became the symbol of resistance against the totalitarian repression regime of the 1950s: she was imprisoned in the Theresienstadt concentration camp from 1942 to 1944 for her work against the Nazi occupation. After her return to Czechoslovakia, she was arrested again in 1949 because of her resolute opposition to the Stalinist regime. In a staged show trial, she was sentenced to death for "anti-Soviet conspiracy", "espionage", "high treason" and "subversive behaviour" in Pankrác on 27 June 1950. Since 2009, a monument installed at the entrance to the memorial in Pankrác with a bust of Horáková designed by the Czech sculptor Milan Knobloch has borne witness to the courageous resistance fighter. A main street in Prague also bears her name.

In the first years of communist rule, armed resistance continued. The various groups, whose members had in many cases been active in the struggle against the Nazi occupation, carried out acts of sabotage in industry and agriculture, collected intelligence information, acquired weapons for a fight against the communist rulers and fought local party functionaries. Infiltrated by secret police units, these groups were wiped out; their members were arrested and either sentenced to long prison terms or executed.

The regime's continued campaign of repression made organised acts of resistance more difficult. Nevertheless, hundreds of small initiatives and individuals remained active. They prepared for escapes abroad, secured hiding places for politically persecuted persons, supported the families of detainees, produced and distributed leaflets critical of the regime, and removed propaganda slogans from public spaces. There was greater social resistance in rural areas where forced collectivisation and expropriation of the private property of the peasantry was enforced with violence.

The effects of the planned economy diktat led to spontaneous workers' demonstrations in Brno as early as December 1951. In the wake of the devaluation of the currency in 1953, the vast majority of the population lost all their savings, while the communist government, under the pretext of the class struggle against "bourgeois and reactionary elements", propped up the ailing economy, eradicated foreign debt and sought to fill the empty state coffers. Tens of thousands of people took to the streets in Prague and other cities, while 129 companies across the country went on strike to protest against the currency reform. On 1 June 1953 in Plzeň, the workers at the Škoda Works called a strike, angry protesters occupied the town hall and the city radio, and communist symbols in the streets and on buildings were torn down. It was only through the violent intervention of the army, border troops and the people's militia that the uprising was quelled. In 14 politically motivated court cases, 331 people were sentenced to long prison terms and about 200 families forced out of their homes.

After the harsh repression of the 1950s, the political situation relaxed at the beginning of the 1960s. Initial—mostly economic—reform efforts were put in place to stop the economic crisis. When these failed, dissatisfaction grew in the country: ever greater numbers of people took to criticising their poor living conditions; young people demanded reforms, and writers and artists spoke out with critical works. In 1968, the reform-minded Alexander Dubćek was elected General Secretary of the KSČ. His programme envisaged the establishment of "socialism with a human face". His reforms did not only target the economy but also, in particular, granted civil rights such as freedom of speech and assembly and permitted other parties and organisations. Politically persecuted persons were rehabilitated. The relaxation of censorship allowed for a public discussion in the media of the reprisals of the past and the course of reform. "The Two Thousand Words", a manifesto published in June 1968, condemned repression and called for more far-reaching new regulations.

While the reform debates continued in Czechoslovakia, other socialist dictatorships feared that these reform efforts would spread. The Czechoslovak Communist Party leadership was called upon to complete the reforms and to combat the "counter-revolution". On the night of 20–21 August 1968, Warsaw Pact troops finally invaded Czechoslovakia and cracked down on the reforms. Soviet troops occupied the capital Prague. Millions of people rose up against the invasion in the ČSSR. After the suppression of the Prague Spring, thousands of people fled abroad. In the ČSSR itself, supporters of the reform movement were arrested and imprisoned. Others were banned from working. Freedom of assembly and speech were restricted once again and hard-won reliefs reversed. The attempt to create "socialism with a human face" had been bloodily suppressed. On 16 January 1969, the student Jan Palach set himself on fire on Wenceslas Square in Prague to protest against the invasion.

Barely ten years later, with the civil rights movement Charter 77, critical intellectuals and artists once again publicly advocated fighting for democratic rights and freedoms and denounced human rights violations. Encouraged by the signing of the Helsinki Final Act in 1976, they supported the democratisation of society and respect for human rights. These initiatives were also answered with persecution and repression, and their authors were imprisoned for years, banned from working and harassed. Among them was the future President Václav Havel. Despite the reprisals, there were repeated protests. In 1978, the Committee for the Defence of the Unjustly Persecuted was founded, whose most prominent founders and supporters, such as Václav Benda, Václav Havel, Petr Uhl and Jiří Dienstbier, were arrested and sentenced to long prison terms.

The policy of glasnost and perestroika in the Soviet Union that started in the mid-1980s under Mikhail Gorbachev also had an impact on the opposition and dissident movement in the ČSSR. For example, in August 1988, the 20th anniversary of the suppression of the Prague Spring, thousands of students demonstrated in Prague for the democratisation of their society. In the wake of the political changes in the neighbouring countries of Hungary, Poland and the GDR, where the Wall had fallen on 9 November 1989 and hundreds of thousands of people had successfully taken their protest against the communist regime to the streets, the people in the Czechoslovak capital also began to rise up. A demonstration of more than 15,000 students on 17 November in Prague marked the beginning of the Velvet Revolution in Czechoslovakia. This was violently suppressed by the police but led to a huge outpouring of solidarity throughout the country and further revolts against the communist regime. Protest rallies took place in many cities; a general strike was joined by millions of people across the country.

On 24 November 1989, from Wenceslas Square in Prague, Alexander Dubćek and Václav Havel, two iconic figures in the resistance, demanded the resignation of the KSČ Politburo. As in the other communist countries, the fall of the communist rulers took place extremely quickly. Negotiations began on 28 November 1989 between the Civic Forum, which had been set up just a few days earlier, and the government, which eventually led to the formation of a new government dominated by representatives of the opposition. The upheaval in Czechoslovakia became known as the "Velvet Revolution" because the changes were brought about not by bloodshed but at the negotiating table. The keychains used by the people to loudly voice their protest became a symbol of the mass demonstrations against the regime. The election of Alexander Dubćek as Chairman of the Parliament and Václav Havel as President in December 1989 marked the final triumph over communism.

Communist rule in Czechoslovakia had overseen 248 politically motivated executions. 200,000 people were convicted on political grounds, and 4,500 died due to the inhumane conditions in prison. At least 327 people lost their lives trying to escape. About 250,000 people were imprisoned in internment and forced labour camps, and some three times as many were discriminated against on professional or social grounds, plus another 500,000 to 750,000 on religious grounds.

After the reorganisation of Czechoslovakia, unjustly convicted former political prisoners were rehabilitated. In addition, a lustration law was passed in 1991 that removed former high officials, state security and People's Militia members from higher administrative posts and public offices.

As early as 1993, the Czech parliament declared the communist regime illegitimate and criminal. In 2008, the trivialisation of communist crimes in the Czech Republic became punishable by law. As in all former communist countries, the prosecution of former perpetrators and those responsible for the crimes proved difficult. Of the approximately 200 charges brought, only 23 ended in prison sentences, most of which were suspended. As early as 1991, the first institute for State Security documents was established within the Ministry of the Interior. The Office for the Documentation and the Investigation of the Crimes of Communism (ÚDV) was set up in 1995. Lastly, in 2007, the Institute for the Study of Totalitarian Regimes (ÚSTR), which also owns archival holdings from the former security agencies, was established.

17 November, the day the Velvet Revolution broke out in 1989, is now a national holiday in the Czech Republic—the Day of Struggle for Freedom and Democracy. 27 June became the Commemoration Day for the Victims of the Communist Regime in the Czech Republic in 2004. It also commemorates the execution of Maria Horáková in Prague's Pankrác prison on 27 June 1950.

Memorial to the Victims of Communism

Prague. The Memorial to the Victims of Communism was inaugurated on 22 May 2002 at the foot of the Petřín hill in the Lesser Town area of Prague. The Confederation of Political Prisoners of the Czech Republic had been working to build a monument since the mid-1990s. The association was supported by the mayor of Prague and the district administration of the Prague 1 district.

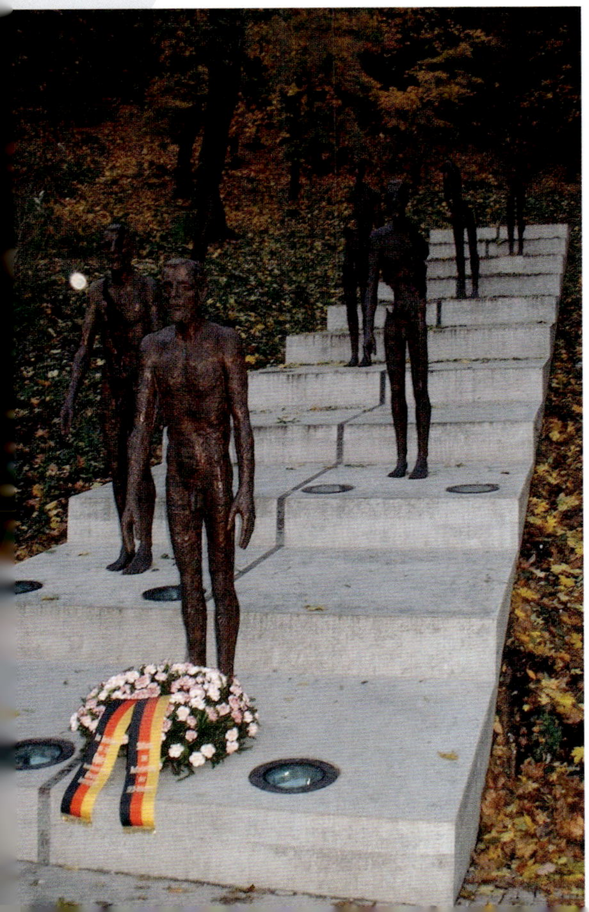

Sculptor and former political prisoner Olbram Zoulbek designed the 60-metre-long and seven-metre-wide complex. Seven stylised bronze sculptures of men stand on a 26-step white staircase that narrows as it rises. Viewed from the foot of the hill, the higher the stairs rise the more the figures dissolve, until they can finally only be seen as fragments. The male figures symbolise a person earmarked for liquidation (in Czech: "Muž určený k likvidaci", abbreviated as "Mukl"). Along the stairs runs a bronze strip with engraved information about the victims of communism in the former ČSSR. A granite base with inscriptions is located at the foot of the site. The memorial was realised by architects Zdenék Hölzel and Jan Kerel from Prague.

Inscription at the foot of the memorial
Czech: *OBĚTI KOMUNISMU 1948 – 1989 / 205486 ODSOUZENO / 248 POPRAVENO / 4 500 ZEMŘELO VE VĚZNICÍCH / 327 ZAHYNULO NA HRANICÍCH / 170 938 OBČANŮ EMIGROVALO*

English: *Victims of communism 1948 – 1989 / 205,486 were sentenced, 248 were executed, 4,500 died in prisons, 327 died on the border, 170,938 emigrated.*

◄
Memorial to the Victims of Communism at the foot of the Petřín hill in Prague

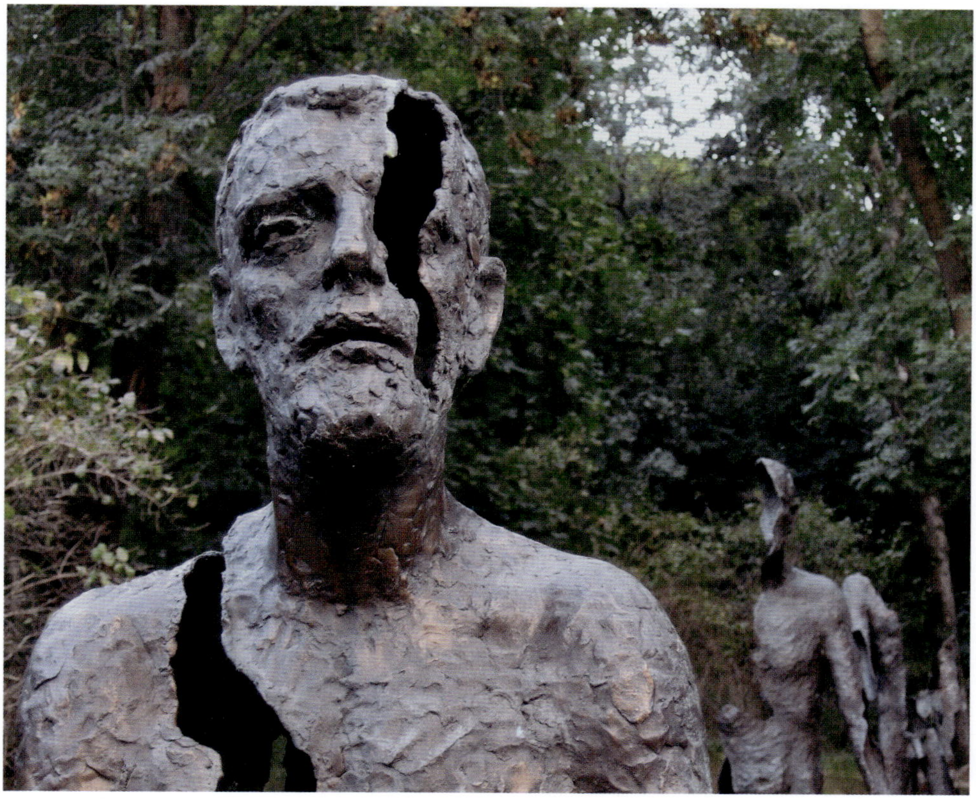

Inscriptions on the granite base
Czech: *POMNÍK OBĚTEM KOMUNISMU JE / VĚNOVÁN VŠEM OBĚTEM, NEJEN / POPRAVENÝM A VĚZNĚNÝM, ALE / I VŠEM, JEJICHŽ ŽIVOTY BYLY / TOTALITNÍ ZVŮLI ZNIČENY / ZBUDOVÁNO ROKU 2002 PÉČÍ HLAVNÍHO MĚSTA PRAHY, / MĚTSKÉ ČASTI PRAHA 1, KONFEDERACE POLITICKÝCH VĚZŇŮ / AUTOŘI: ING. ARCH. ZDENĚK HÖLZEL, AK. ARCH. JAN KEREL, AK. SOCHAŘ. OLBRAM ZOUBEK*

English: *THE MEMORIAL TO THE VICTIMS / OF COMMUNISM IS DEDICATED TO / ALL VICTIMS NOT ONLY THOSE / WHO WHERE JAILED OR EXECUTED / BUT ALSO THOSE WHOSE LIVES / WERE RUINED BY TOTALITARIAN / DESPOTISM. / THE CITY OF PRAGUE, THE MUNICIPAL DISTRICT OF PRAGUE 1 / AND THE CONFEDERATION OF POLITICAL PRISONERS BUILT / THE MEMORIAL IN 2002. / AUTHORS: ARCHITECTS ZDENĚK HÖLZEL, JAN KEREL, AND SCULPTOR OLBRAM ZOUBEK.*

Bronze sculptures as symbols of individuals destined for liquidation

Location: Prague, at the foot of Petřín hill

Monument to Jan Palach and Jan Zajíc

Prague. The monument to Jan Palach and Jan Zajíc was inaugurated on 16 January 2000 to mark the 31st anniversary of Jan Palach's self-immolation at the northern end of Wenceslas Square next to the fountain below the National Museum. After long debates about the design of this symbolic place, the design by Čestmír Houška and Jiří Veselý was finally realised. Two mound-like elevations in the cobbles symbolise the bodies of Palach and Zajíc, which are connected by a bronze cross embedded in the ground. The end of the cross points in the direction in which the burning Palach attempted to walk onto Wenceslas Square. The names and dates of birth and death of the two young men are engraved on the left arm of the cross. The inauguration ceremony was attended by the Mayor of Prague, representatives of the Society of Jan Palach and the Thimm company, which contributed to the construction costs.

Jan Palach was born on 11 August 1948 in Mělnik, the son of a merchant who was forced in the same year to give up the family business due to the communist coup. The family moved to Všetaty where Palach spent his youth. From 1963 to 1967, he attended a grammar school in Mělnik. Although he had passed the entrance exam required to study philosophy, he could not enrol at Charles University in Prague. He studied at the business school for the next two years. In the spring of 1968, he was subsequently admitted to the Faculty of Philosophy, where he came into direct contact with the political and social reforms of the Prague Spring.

After the invasion of the Warsaw Pact intervention forces on 21 August 1968, Palach took part in the student strikes in the autumn but was disappointed by the growing lethargy and indifference of his compatriots. As a sign of protest against the encroaching "normalisation", Palach decided to set himself on fire.

At the turn of 1968/69, he visited his mother and returned to Prague in January 1969. On 15 January, he returned home to attend his uncle's funeral. The following day he took the train back to Prague and went to the city centre at around 4 pm. Standing at the foot of the National Museum, he doused himself in petrol, lit a match and walked towards the busy Wenceslas Square, burning. After a few metres, he lost consciousness and collapsed. A tram driver put out the fire with his coat and Palach was taken to a hospital with severe burns shortly afterwards.

Before his self-immolation he had written several letters in which he criticised indifference and demanded the abolition of censorship. The news of the immolation and its demands, which quickly became known throughout the country, led to an outpouring of solidarity and protest. Some students, among them Jan Zajíc, held a hunger strike at the Wenceslas Memorial. Jan Palach died of his injuries on 19 January 1969. His body was laid out in Charles

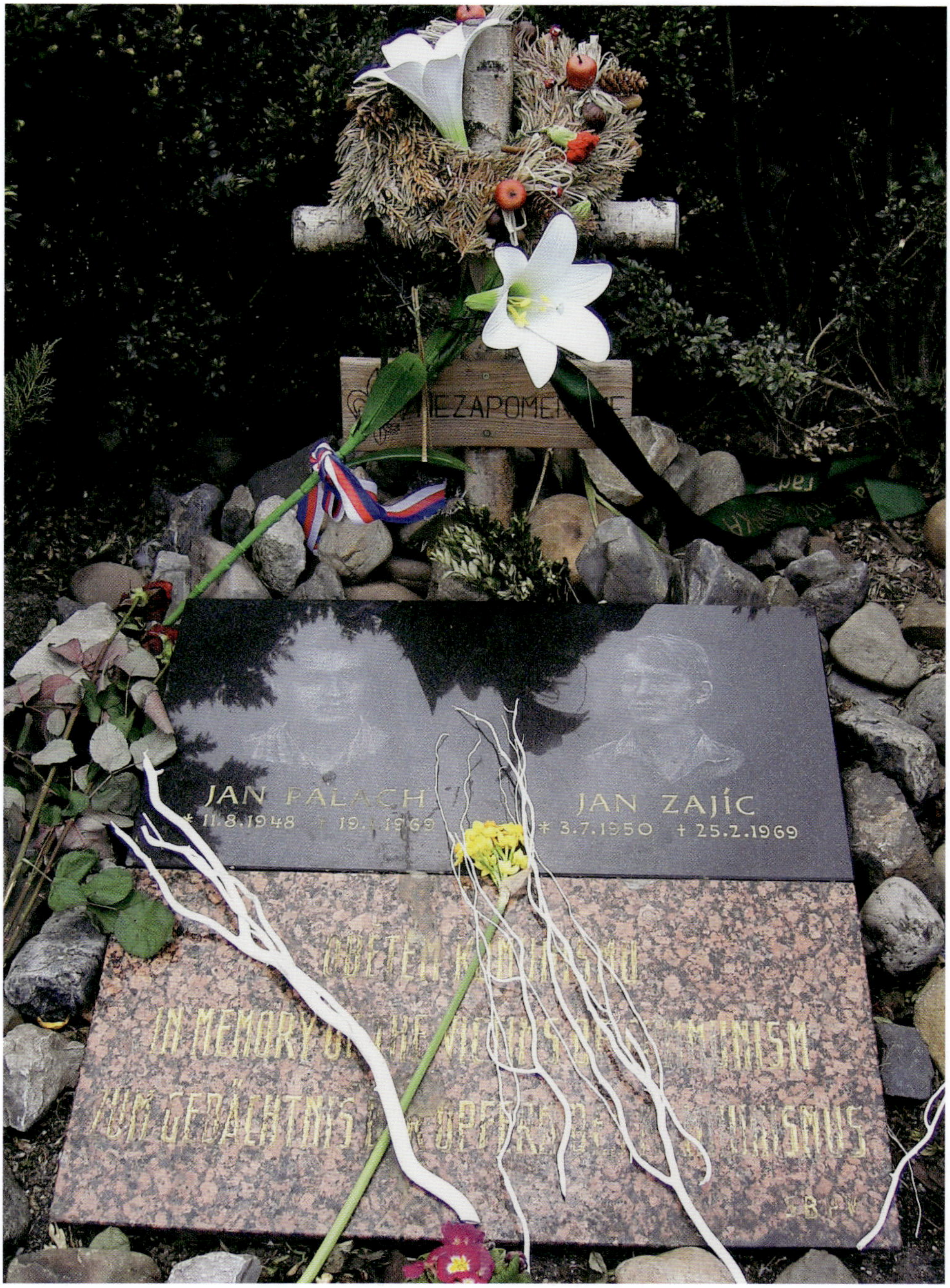

The monument in a rotunda planted with flowers and bushes was erected in 1989 during the Velvet Revolution.

University on 24 January 1969 and then buried in the Olšany Cemetrey with a crowd of thousands of people in attendance.

Jan Zajíc was born in Vítkov on 3 July 1950 as the son of a teacher and a chemist. After attending school, he began training at a school of railways in Šumperk. Zajíc registered the social and political upheavals during the Prague Spring with enthusiasm. He participated in various rallies and initiatives and was greatly shocked by the suppression of the reform movement by the troops of the Warsaw Pact. Like Palach, in the following months he lamented the indifference that had spread in Czechoslovakian society following the mood of optimism of the last few years.

When Zajíc heard of Palach's self-immolation, he joined a hunger strike in Prague to reaffirm Palach's demands. In late January, he returned to Šumperk where he resumed his studies. On the morning of 25 February 1969, the anniversary of the communist coup d'état of 1948, he went to Prague with three friends. In his luggage were several letters and resolutions. At around 1:30 pm Zajíc went to the city centre alone and ingested petrol in the cellar of building No. 39 on Wenceslas Square, dousing

Monument to Jan Palach and Jan Zajíc
next to the fountain below the National Museum

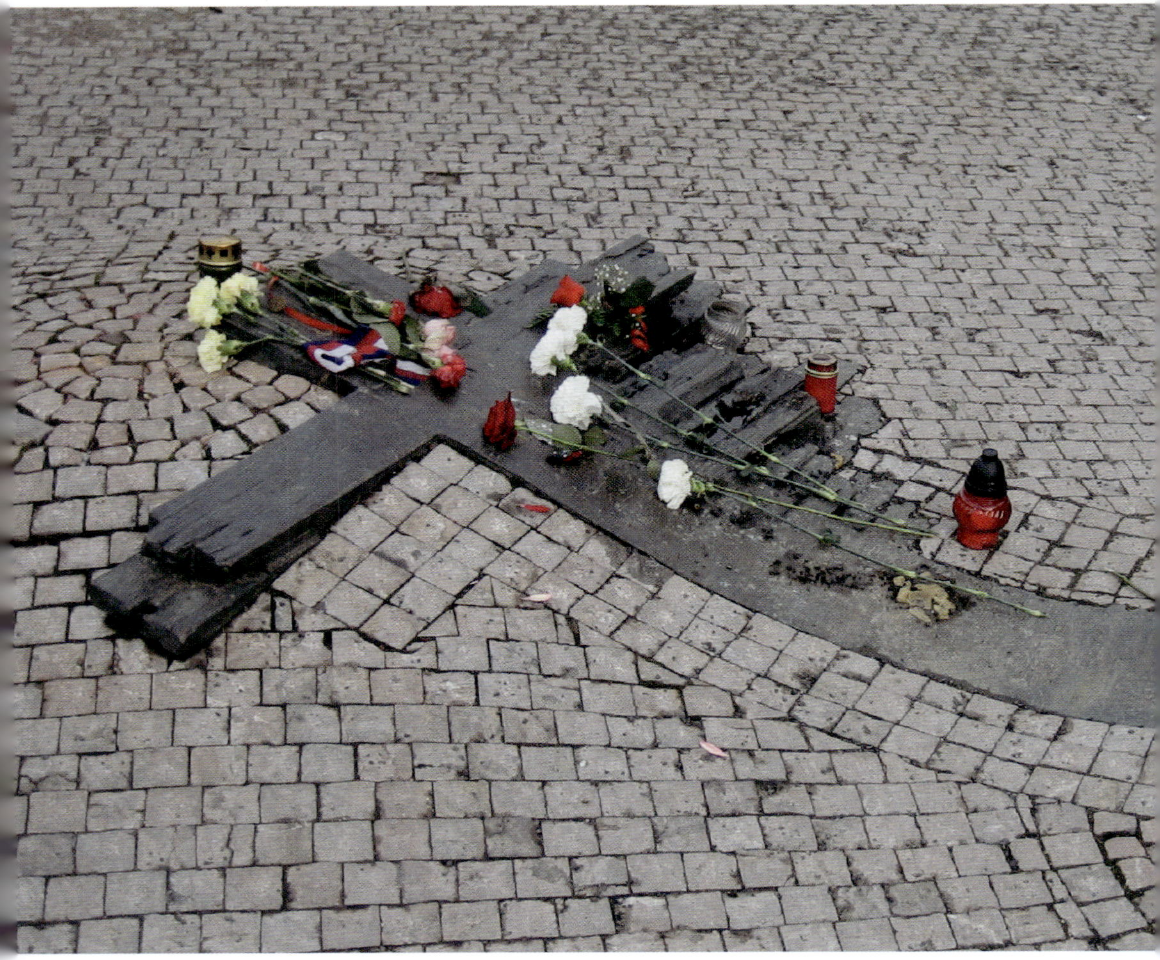

himself with the rest before setting himself on fire. Zajíc had planned to walk out of the entrance to Wenceslas Square but only made it as far as the cellar steps before collapsing and dying. Although he did not cause the same public sensation as Palach, the news of a new self-immolation spread quickly. Thousands of people attended Zajíc's solemn funeral in his hometown on 2 March 1969.

On Wenceslas Square, not far from the monument inaugurated in 2000, there is another memorial to Jan Palach and Jan Zajíc. This was built during the Velvet Revolution in 1989 and consists of a rotunda planted with flowers and bushes, in which a memorial stone with the names of Palach and Zajíc is set. Both the immediate aftermath of the tragic events themselves and the following decades saw repeated spontaneous demonstrations commemorating the suppression of the Prague Spring and the desperate acts of Palach and Zajíc.

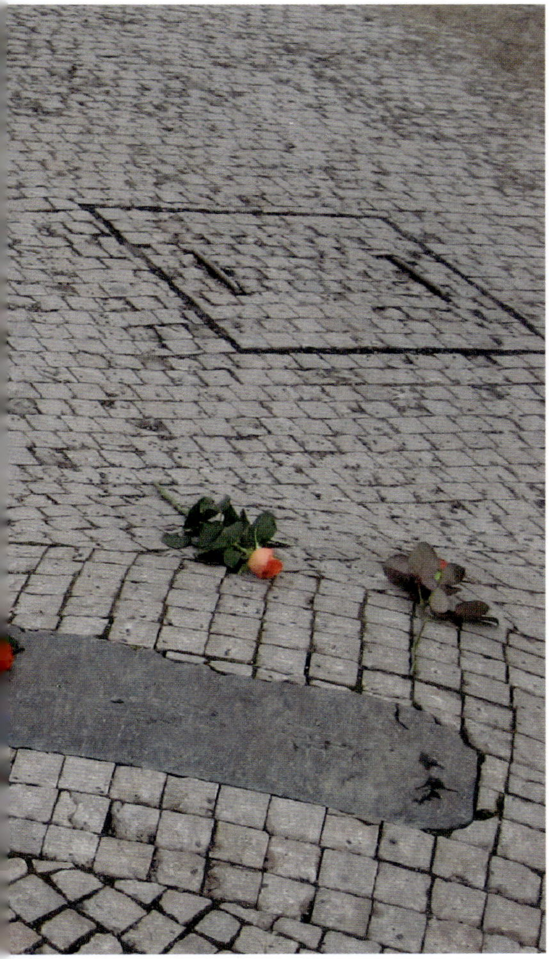

The Czechoslovak security authorities tried in vain to stop the commemoration of both events. When, on the occasion of the 30th anniversary of the self-immolation in the spring of 1989, the Czechoslovak opposition movement proclaimed the Palach commemoration weeks, large rallies were held on Wenceslas Square for the first time since 1968/69. Once again, flowers were laid down in front of the statue of St Wenceslas. Between 16 and 19 January, the police acted against more than 1000 protesters, forcing them back with water cannon and arresting them. In November 1989, tens of thousands of people gathered again in the centre of Prague. These rallies marked the beginning of the Velvet Revolution in the ČSSR.

Inscription on the base of the monument:
*Jan Palach / *11. 8. 1948 †19. 1. 1969 /*
*Jan Zajíc / *3. 7. 1950 †25. 2. 1969. //*
Obětem kommunismu / In memory of the victims of communism / Zum Gedächtnis der Opfer des Kommunismus / SBPV

Location: Prague, Prague 1 district, Václavské náměstí

Pankrác Memorial

Prague. The Pankrác Memorial is located in the building of the prison of the same name and was installed in 1995 with funds from the Prison Service of the Czech Republic. The Division for the Documentation and History of the Prison Service of the Czech Republic, the Association of Former Political Prisoners and numerous scientific and cultural institutions in the Czech Republic played a major role in implementing the memorial concept. The institution is used primarily to train employees and students of the judiciary and the police; regular visitors must register with the prison administration for a guided tour of the memorial. The permanent exhibition provides information about the history of the judiciary in Bohemia from the Middle Ages to modern times. Comprehensive documentation under the heading "From race justice to class justice" sheds light on political imprisonment and persecution under Nazi German occupation and the communist regime after 1945.

The building that houses the modern-day prison and the Pankrác Memorial was erected in 1889 on undeveloped land east of Prague city centre and was intended to replace the former St Wenceslas State Prison. After the foundation of the First Czechoslovak Republic in 1918, it housed the prison of the Prague district's criminal court. On 15 March 1939, Nazi German troops occupied the Czechoslovak territories. The occupation of the country led to the destruction of the Czechoslovak Republic with the departure of Slovakia and Carpathian Ruthenia and to the formation of the so-called Protectorate of Bohemia and Moravia.

Pankrác was used by the Nazi occupation administration between 1939 and 1945, as were other institutions. On the ground floor of the left wing of the prison, the notorious Section II/A was built to accommodate prisoners who had been sentenced to death. 20 cells—numbers 32 to 52—were reserved for this purpose, four of them for mass detention, and the others for solitary confinement. Cells 29, 30 and 31 made up the so-called "axe room"—consisting of a meeting room, an execution room and a coffin room. These authentically preserved rooms still provide visitors with the most memorable moments in the exhibition. Between 5 April 1943 and 26 April 1945, the National Socialist occupiers in Pankrác carried out a total of 1,075 death sentences by hanging and guillotine. The mortal remains of the victims were subsequently destroyed in the crematorium in Prague-Strašnice. Display panels provide information about the objects found at this place during the takeover of the prison by the Czech administration in May 1945. After the communists took power in 1948, tens of thousands of opponents of the regime were imprisoned here, many of whom were tortured, and over 1,000 people executed.

A list of the names of all the people executed for political reasons at this site between 1939 and 1960 can be found in the commemorative hall of Pankrác. An urn with earth from the Auschwitz concentration camp — where many inhabitants from Bohemia, Moravia, Silesia and Slovakia lost their lives — recalls the Nazi repressions and the terror visited on the vanquished territories by the occupying Nazi forces. Also on display are a larger-than-life photograph of the trial of Dr Milada Horáková and the original stand at which she had to defend herself at her show trial. Visitors can also see the remains of the execution board of one of the two gallows used in Pankrác, by both the National Socialist occupying power and, later, the communist regime. The purpose of the memorial room is not only to keep alive the memory of the victims of totalitarian tyranny but also to issue a warning for the future. The inscription in the room lays out this mission: "The violation of human rights is not a thing of the past. Violence and cruelty are still so close, we are all responsible for democracy and freedom, each one of us, each day, the blood of the victims of totalitarian power obligates us […]".

Location: Prague, Prague 4 district, Soudní 988/1

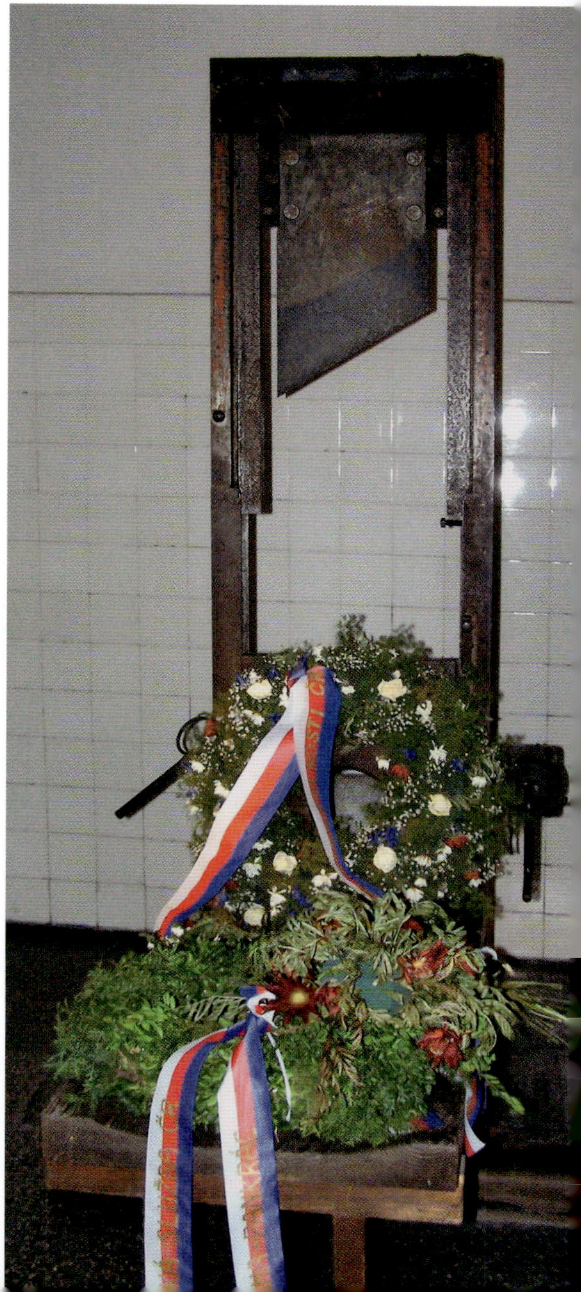

Guillotine in the so-called "axe room" of the memorial

Vojna Memorial

Lešetice. At the request of the Association of Former Political Prisoners, the government of the Czech Republic decided in July 1998 to create a memorial on the site of the former Vojna forced labour camp, whose inmates were made to mine uranium—the only authentically preserved site of this kind from the communist era. After the clearance of the site, which was used by the Czech Army until 2000, extensive reconstruction and safety work took place. In 2001, the entire area was declared a cultural monument. In May 2005, the Vojna Memorial was finally ceremonially opened to the public. As a branch of the Příbram mining museum, its intended purpose is to keep alive the memory of the injustices committed here. In cooperation with the Museum of the Third Resistance in Příbram and the Association of Political Prisoners in the Czech Republic, a permanent exhibition was created on the site of the memorial. This illustrates the political persecution which ensued in Czechoslovakia after the communists seized power on 25 February 1948, sheds light on aspects of anti-communist resistance and illustrates the history of uranium mining. Between 1945 and 1962, about 5,000 German prisoners of war, 7,000 non-resettled Sudeten Germans, 100,000 Czechoslovak

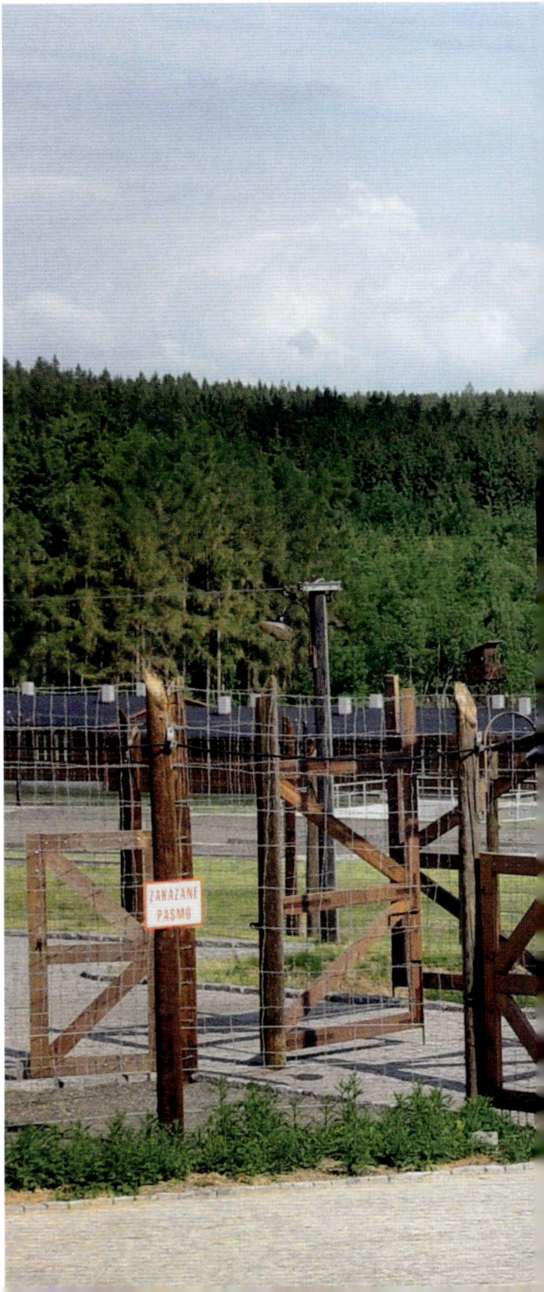

►
Entrance to the Vojna Memorial

political prisoners and some 260,000 Czech civilian workers were forcibly exploited for the Soviet nuclear weapons industry in the uranium mining areas in Jáchymov, Horní Slavkov, and Příbram.

The forced labour camp for uranium mining (Tábory Nucené Práce—TNP) Příbram-Vojna was officially established on 22 November 1949. By 3 March 1950, 530 men were interned here, and by the spring of 1951 that number had risen to 761. By 1 July 1950, the branches TNP Příbram-Brod, which was shut down again on 20 January 1951, and TNP Třebsko, which became an independent camp in the autumn of 1950, had also been established. In the same year, uranium shafts No. 4 (Lešetice), No. 5 and No. 6 in Brod, and No. 7 (Třebsko) were added.

As at the other sites—and by the end of 1949 there were 26 forced labour camps with 5,618 inmates in the ČSSR—the reckless desire for ever larger quantities of uranium resulted

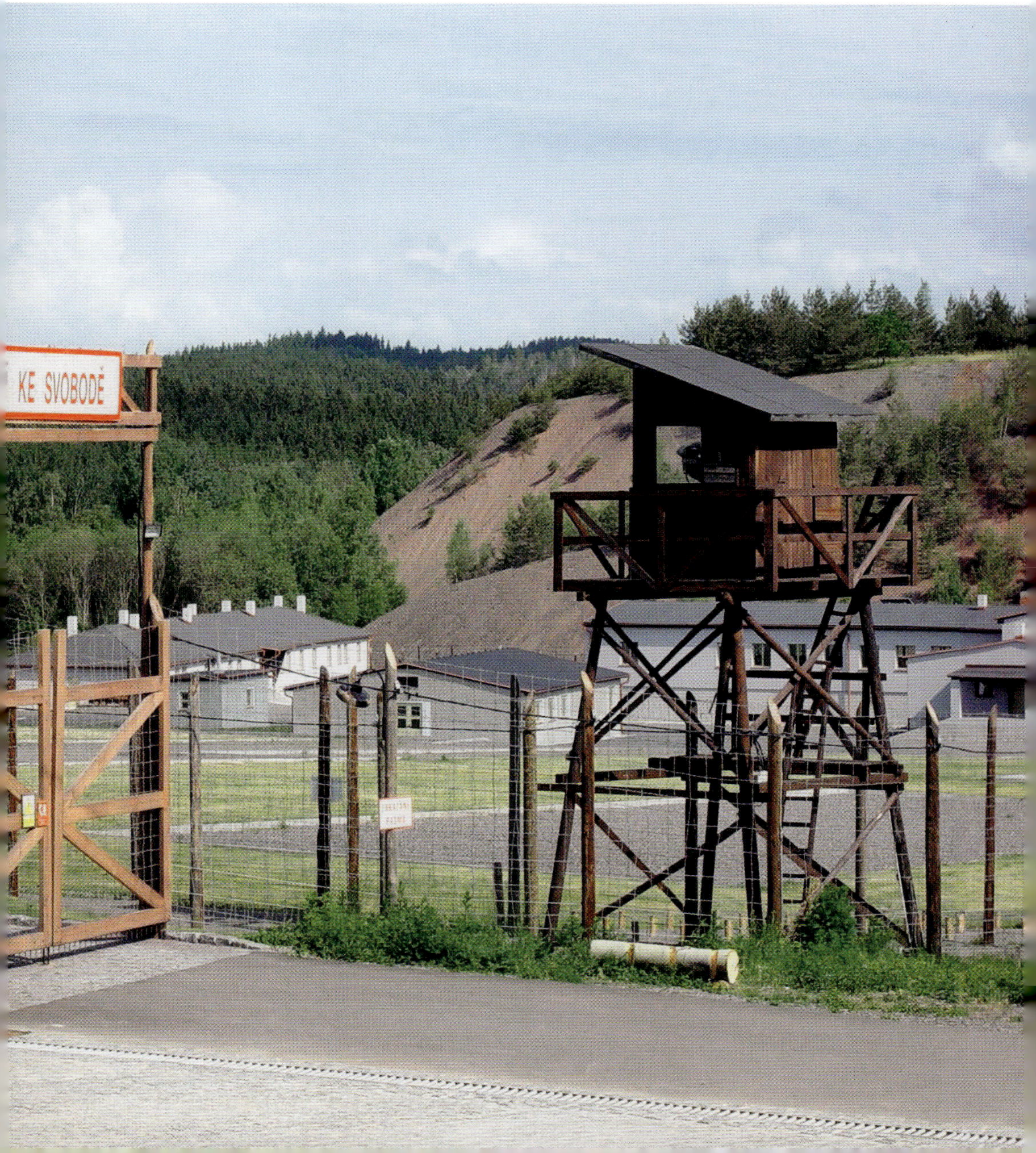

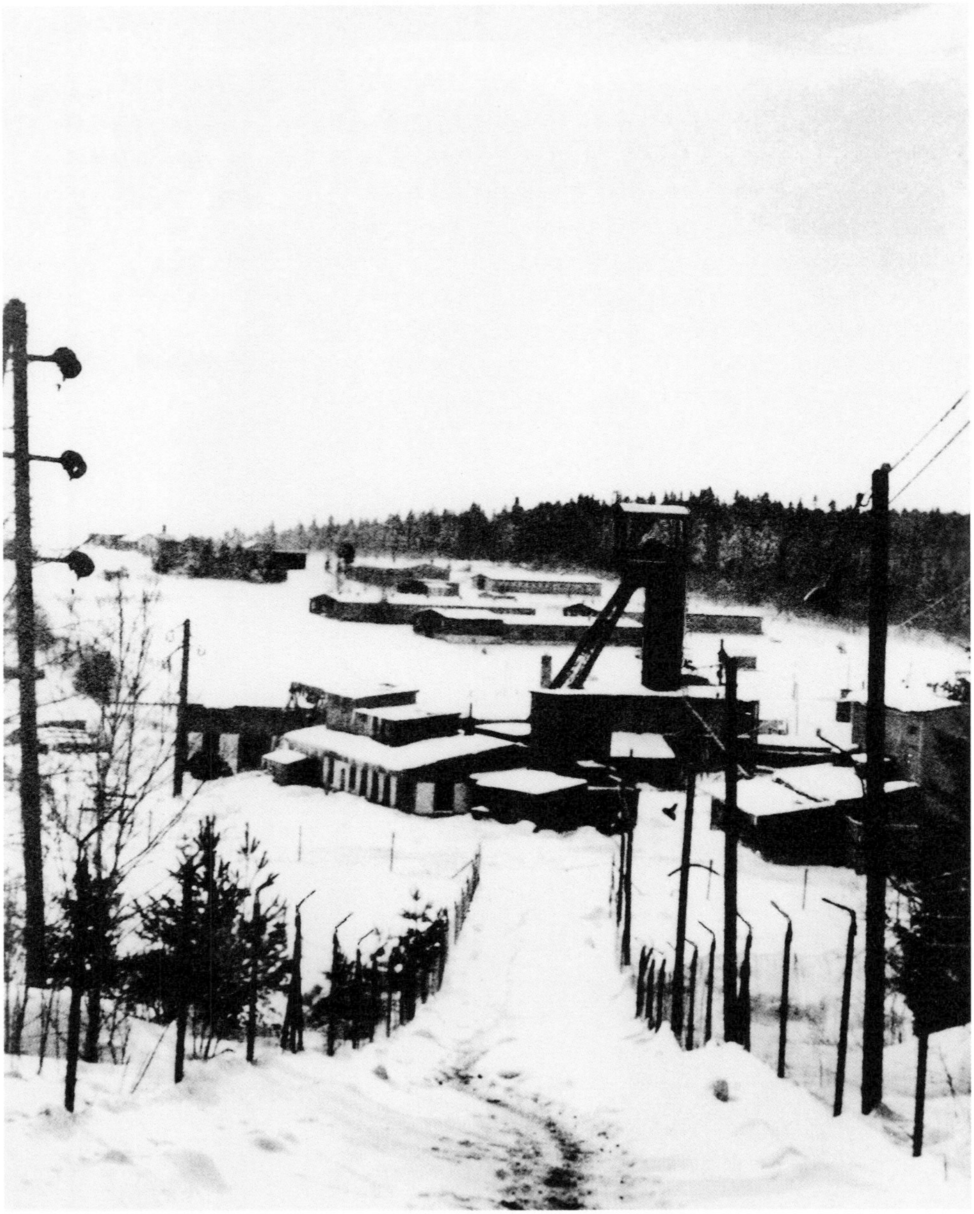

Historical photo of the camps taken in the 1950s

in inhumane working conditions. Excessive delivery rates and non-compliance with the most basic safety precautions repeatedly led to accidents resulting in serious injuries and fatalities. The work with radioactive material, the inadequate ventilation system in the shafts, the consumption of radioactively contaminated water and the inhalation of radioactive dust took a heavy toll on the health of the prisoners, with severe long-term consequences. Since the prisoner barracks were erected directly between the Vojna 1 and 2 uranium shafts for the "optimal use of the labour force potential", the detainees were constantly exposed to uncontrolled levels of direct radiation, even outside the mines.

At the beginning of 1951, the storage system was reorganised. Some sites, such as Jáchymov, were shut due to a slow-down in production. The detainees were transferred to other penitentiary institutions, called "corrective labour work camps" (Nápravně Pracovní Tábory—NPT). Thus it was that the former forced labour camp at Vojna, too, was converted into "corrective labour camp" NPT-U. The majority of inmates who were sentenced to long prison sentences were now exiled to the uranium camps.

From the perspective of the camp management, the political prisoners, whom the judiciary was turning out in particularly large numbers at that time, were much more useful for uranium mining than the detainees of the forced labour camps whose imprisonment was deemed too short. In accordance with Law No. 231/1948 "On the Protection of the People's Democratic Republic", prisoners with sentences of ten years or more were used in uranium mining. The "most dangerous criminals", especially those relevant to state security were then transferred to the NPT-U Vojna. Most of them were democratically-minded citizens of all social classes, from workers and peasants to the highest officers of the Czechoslovak Army or former factory directors who had been convicted of high treason, espionage or conspiracy against the people's democratic order. The prisoner contingent also included ordinary criminals, black marketeers and economic criminals. From May 1950, the camp was guarded by an independent company of a special unit of the National Security Corps (SNB) called "Crane 3" (Jeřáb).

After the partial amnesty in 1960, the Vojna labour camp was closed on 1 June 1961. The remaining prisoners were transferred to the nearby Bytíz prison camp—built on the largest of all uranium deposits on the territory of the ČSSR with a capacity of up to 2000 prisoners. Between 1961 and 2000, the NPT-U Vojna site was used first by the Czechoslovak (1992) and then by the Czech Army. Not least for this reason, essential parts of the complex have been preserved to this day, including the kitchen, one of the prisoner barracks, the doctor's surgery, the special police barracks, the underground "bunkr", and the machine building for the hoisting shaft. Together with the reconstructed elements, these historic buildings provide visitors to the museum with an impression not only of the conditions in the Vojna camp but also of those in the other camps in the secret area around Jáchymov.

Location: Lešetice, in the forest 5 km southeast of Příbram, on the outskirts of Lazsko, Lešetice and Příbram-Zavržice.
Internet: www.muzeum-pribram.cz

Further reading:

A comprehensive overview of memorials sites and museums commemorating communist rule in the Czech Republic is available here: www.pametnimista.usd.cas.cz / Kladnik, Ana: Case Study on the Czech Republic. In: Honoring Civil Courage. Developing Suggestions to Improve the Situation of Victims of Communist State Crimes. Project Coordinator: Gedenkstätte Berlin-Hohenschönhausen 2015, Ref.-Nr.: JUST/2011/JPEN/AG/2998Available online at: www.stiftung-hsh.de/assets/Dokumente-pdf-Dateien/EU-Projekt-Laenderstudien.pdf (last accessed on: 15/11/2017). / Kýr, Aleš: Gedenkstätte Pankrác. Ausstellung des Justizvollzugsdienstes der Tschechischen Republik. Lanškroun 1999. / Pauer, Jan: Die Aufarbeitung der Diktaturen in Tschechien und der Slowakei. In: Aus Politik und Zeitgeschichte, 2006, Vol. 42, No. 16, pp. 25 – 32. / Pustejovsky, Otfrid: Stalins Bombe und die „Hölle von Joachimsthal". Uranbergbau und Zwangsarbeit in der Tschechoslowakei nach 1945. Münster 2009.

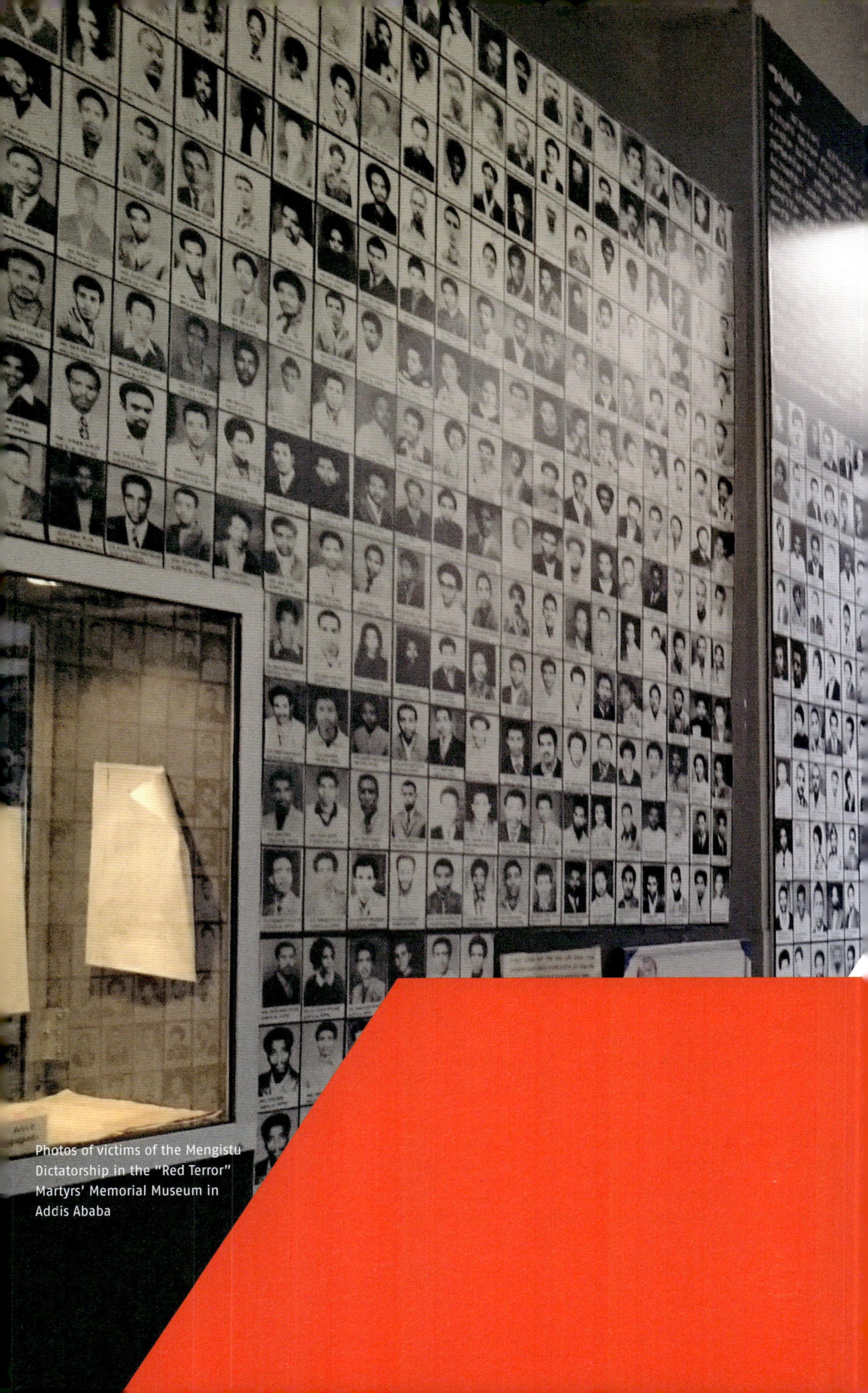

Photos of victims of the Mengistu Dictatorship in the "Red Terror" Martyrs' Memorial Museum in Addis Ababa

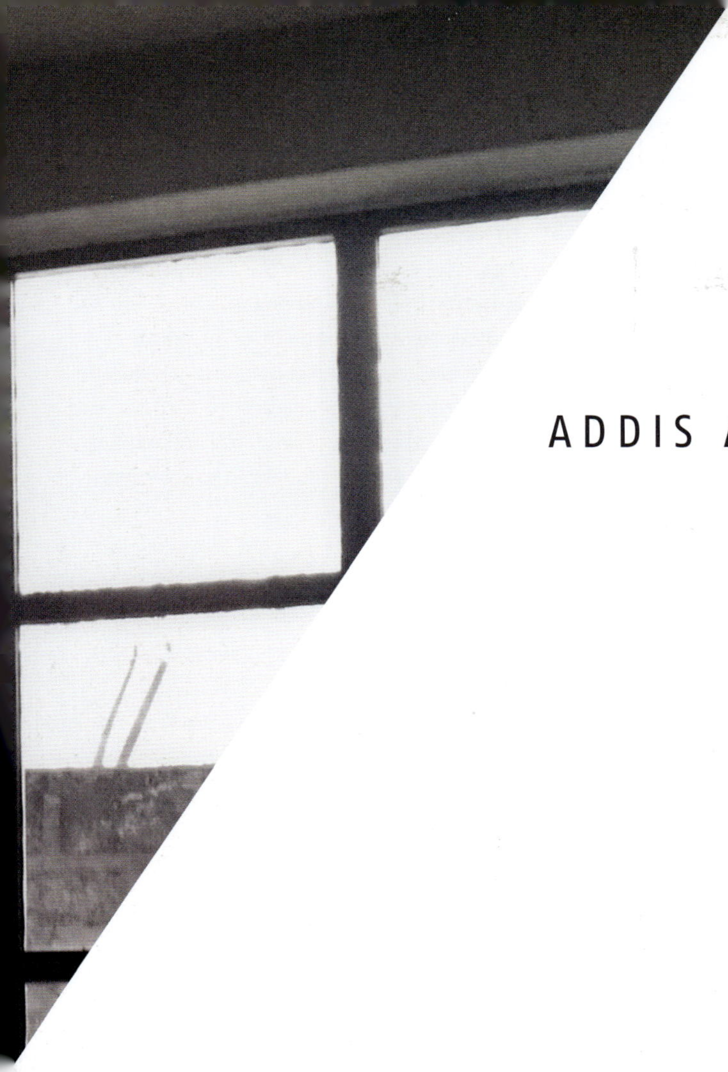

ADDIS ABEBA

Ethiopia

Ethiopia had been ravaged by civil war since 1961. This conflict had been triggered by the downgrading of the federal region of Eritrea to a mere administrative province and marked the attempt by Eritrea to reassert its independence. Emperor Haile Selassie I, who had been in power since 1930, ruled by means of brutal terror and persecution.

Protests and unrest continued in the 1960s and 1970s, culminating in a coup d'état in 1974, as a result of which the military junta, termed the Provisional Military Government (Derg), led by General Mengistu Haile Mariam, took power and declared the establishment of socialism as a political goal. The Ethiopian path to socialism outlined by the Derg found concrete expression in the nationalisation of private property, the expropriation of real estate, radical restrictions on freedom of assembly, opinion and the press, and the bitter persecution and liquidation of political dissenters. At a public performance in April 1977, Mengistu called on the population to destroy the "enemies of the revolution".

Various political and ethnic groups engaged in armed resistance against the military junta. All parties committed crimes, which mainly claimed the lives of civilians caught between the fronts. Hundreds of thousands fled their home regions and sought protection in refugee camps. Persecution and torture were the order of the day. About half a million people fell victim to the regime.

The Derg also exploited the global rivalries of the Cold War to expand its claim to power. Although the USA had sold arms to Ethiopia in 1975/76 and made additional war materiel available, under Mengistu's rule the country established itself as the most important ally of the Soviet Union in Africa. The Derg used the "humanitarian aid" provided by Moscow to combat ethnic and regional freedom movements that wanted to break away from the centuries-old structures of the Ethiopian elite. With the support of Soviet naval and air forces, the Derg succeeded in staving off the offensives of the Marxist-Leninist Eritrean People's Liberation Front after Eritrea had been forcibly incorporated into the Ethiopian Empire in 1961.

Soviet arms supplies and logistical support also allowed the Ethiopian armed forces to successfully wage war against neighbouring Somalia from July 1977 to January 1978. As with the victims of the "Red Terror", complete information is not yet available on the victims of the "total war" against the "Eritrean secessionists" that was declared by Mengistu in 1977.

When Ethiopia was hit by a severe famine in 1984/85, the Mengistu government used the catastrophe to promote a policy of "villagisation". Officially proposed as a measure for the resettlement of the population from underserved regions to the fertile lowland plains, the campaign was aimed at isolating opposition and rebel groups. At the same time, the policy of "villagisation" was designed to promote the expansion of the Soviet agricultural system. These socio-political upheavals claimed the lives of many people in Ethiopia. It was not until 1991 that the Derg was brought down by the Ethiopian People's Revolutionary Democratic Front (EPRDF), a broad coalition of rebel groups organised along regional and ethnic lines. Mengistu managed to flee to the Zimbabwean capital Harare. Leading officials of the former Communist Party, which had renamed itself the Ethiopian Democratic Unity Party in 1990, were arrested. 72 Derg officials were indicted and convicted of genocide in 2006.

The years between 1977 and 1987 went down in Ethiopian history as years of "Red Terror". The "Red Terror" Martyrs' Memorial Museum in Addis Ababa commemorates this period.

"Red Terror" Martyrs' Memorial Museum

Addis Ababa. The "Red Terror" Martyrs' Memorial Museum, which was funded by donations, opened in 2010 in the presence of Ethiopian government officials and family members of the victims of the Derg regime. A series of stamps honouring the victims of the "Red Terror" was published to mark its inauguration.

The exhibition at the "Red Terror" Martyrs' Memorial Museum sheds light on the history of Ethiopia from the coup by the Derg until its fall 17 years later. The torture and execution methods of the state terror apparatus are reconstructed using life-size models. Glass display cases show the remains of victims of the Mengistu dictatorship. Some displays contain not only bones and skulls but also photos and personal remains of the people who were murdered. Numerous photographs of the victims of execution line the walls of the rooms. On request, contemporary witnesses are available for guided tours of the museum. The exhibition is bilingual in Amharic and English. In front of the museum building, there is a bronze sculpture showing three grieving women.

Inscription on the base of the sculpture
Amharic: መቼም ቸየትም አንዳይደገም

English: Never, ever again.

Inscription on the commemorative plaque at the entrance to the building
Amharic: ይህ ለኢትዮጵያ ህዝብ ሰብዓዊና ዲምክራሲያዊ መባዩች / መከበር ሊታገሉ በፖሰቲካቂ አመሰካከትና አምኒታቸዎ / ብቻ በደርግ መንግሰት ለተጨሪጨፉ ሰማዕታት ዚጎቻችገ / ሁሉ መታሰቢያ አንዳሆን የተቋቋመጡ ፖተይ ቫብር / ለማዕታት መታሰቢያ ሙዚየምም የሰማዕታቱን ለተሶበ / በመጠከል በእንጽ ለሊት ኦሪት ልጿቻቸጡ በተገደለፐትጡ / አናት በወሮ ከበቡሽ አድማሉ የካቲዮ ዓም / ተከፈተ። // በአንደ ሰሲት የወሰደኳቸው ዶመለበ በአንድ ሰሲት ረጃቸው

English: *This is a monument erected for the citizens martyred for their beliefs / in the struggle for the Ethiopian peoples' human and democratic rights. The ›RED TERROR MARTYRS MEMORIAL MUSEUM‹ / monument was unveiled on March 7, 2010 by Kebebushe / Admasu — a mother whose four children were killed in one day. // As if I bore them all in one night, / they slew them in a single night.*

In addition to the "Red Terror" Martyrs' Memorial Museum in Addis Ababa, the martyr monuments in Bahir Dar and Mek'ele in northern Ethiopia also commemorate the victims.

Location: Addis Abeba, Meskel Square
Internet: www.rtmmm.org

Further reading:

Human Rights Watch. Backgrounders. Ethiopian Dictator Mengistu Haile Miriam. Available online at: www.pantheon.hrw.org/legacy/english/docs/1999/11/29/ethiop5495.htm (last accessed on: 20/06/2017). / Santamaria, Yves: Formen des Afrokommunismus: Äthiopien, Angola, Moçambique. In: Courtois, Stéphane et al. (ed.): Das Schwarzbuch des Kommunismus. Unterdrückung, Verbrechen und Terror. Sonderausgabe. München, Zürich 2004, pp. 748 – 771. / Toggia, Pietro: The revolutionary endgame of political power: the genealogy of "red terror" in Ethiopia. In: African Identities, 2012, Vol. 10, No. 3, pp. 265 – 280.

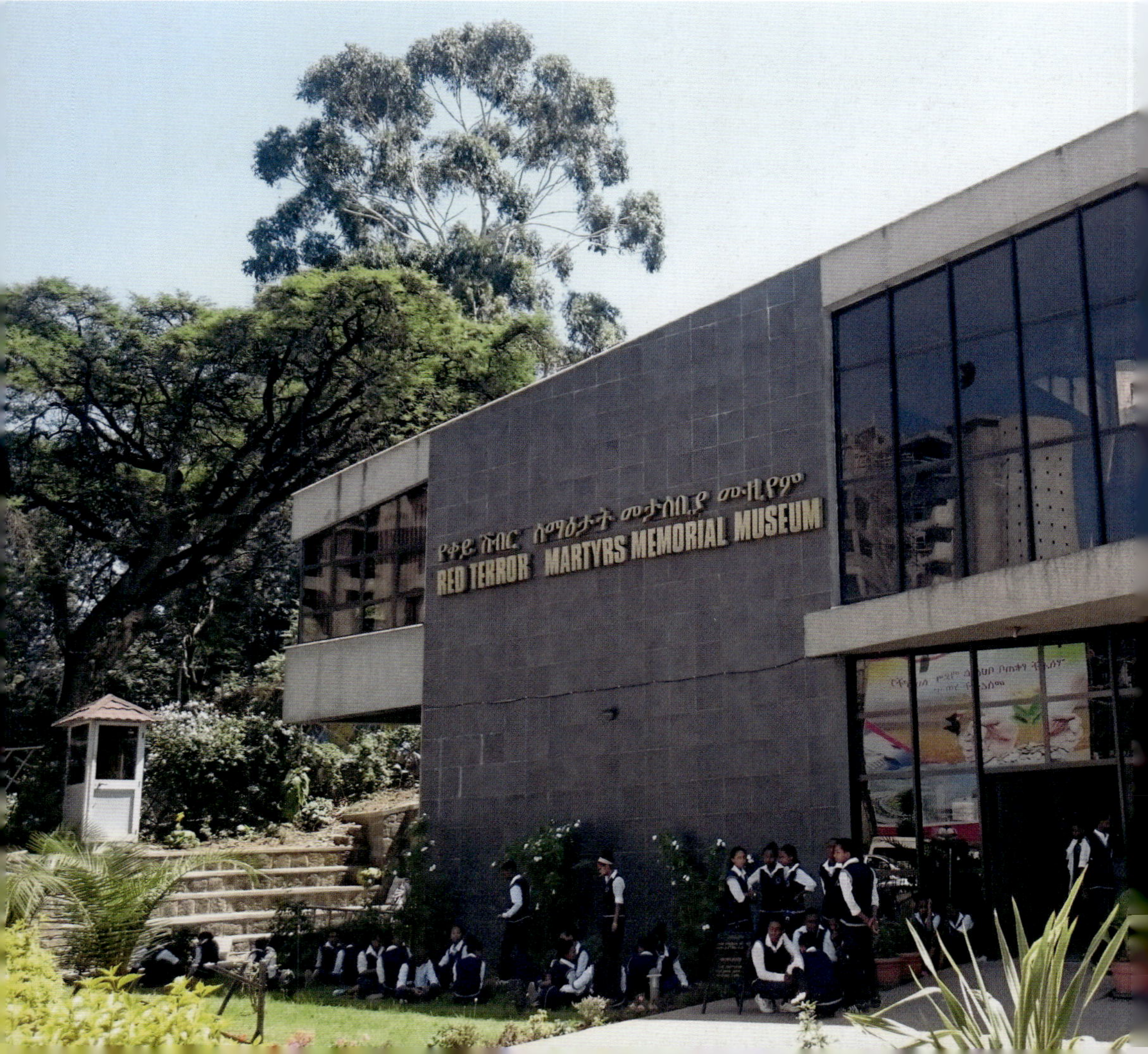

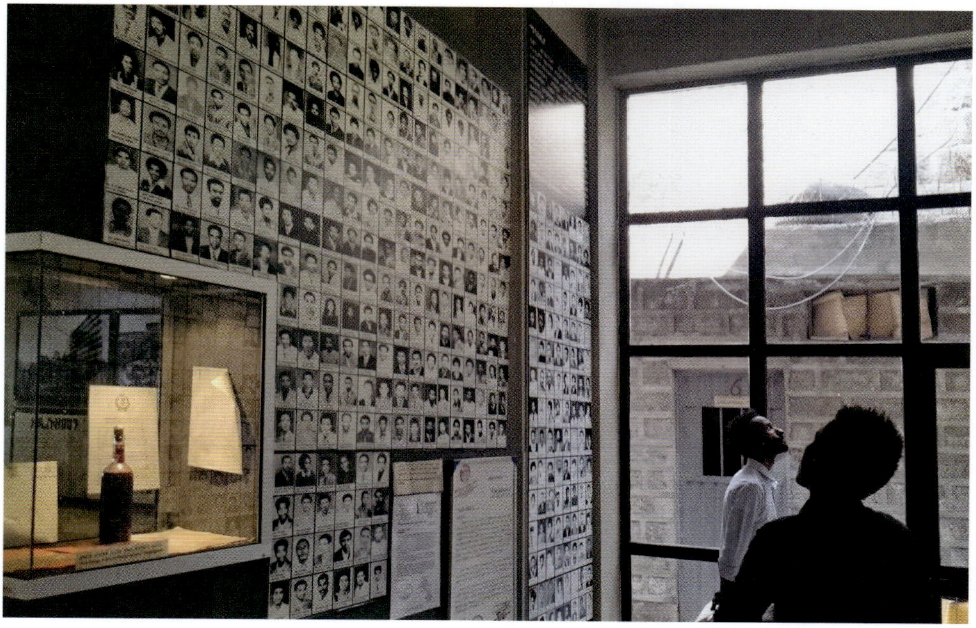

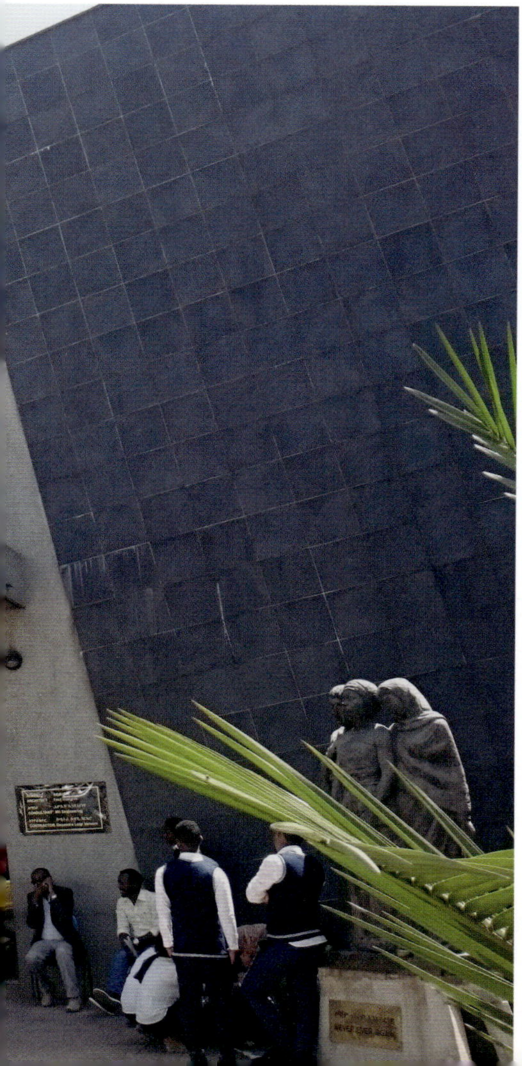

Photos of execution victims
in the exhibition area

◄

Main entrance to the "Red Terror"
Martyrs' Memorial Museum

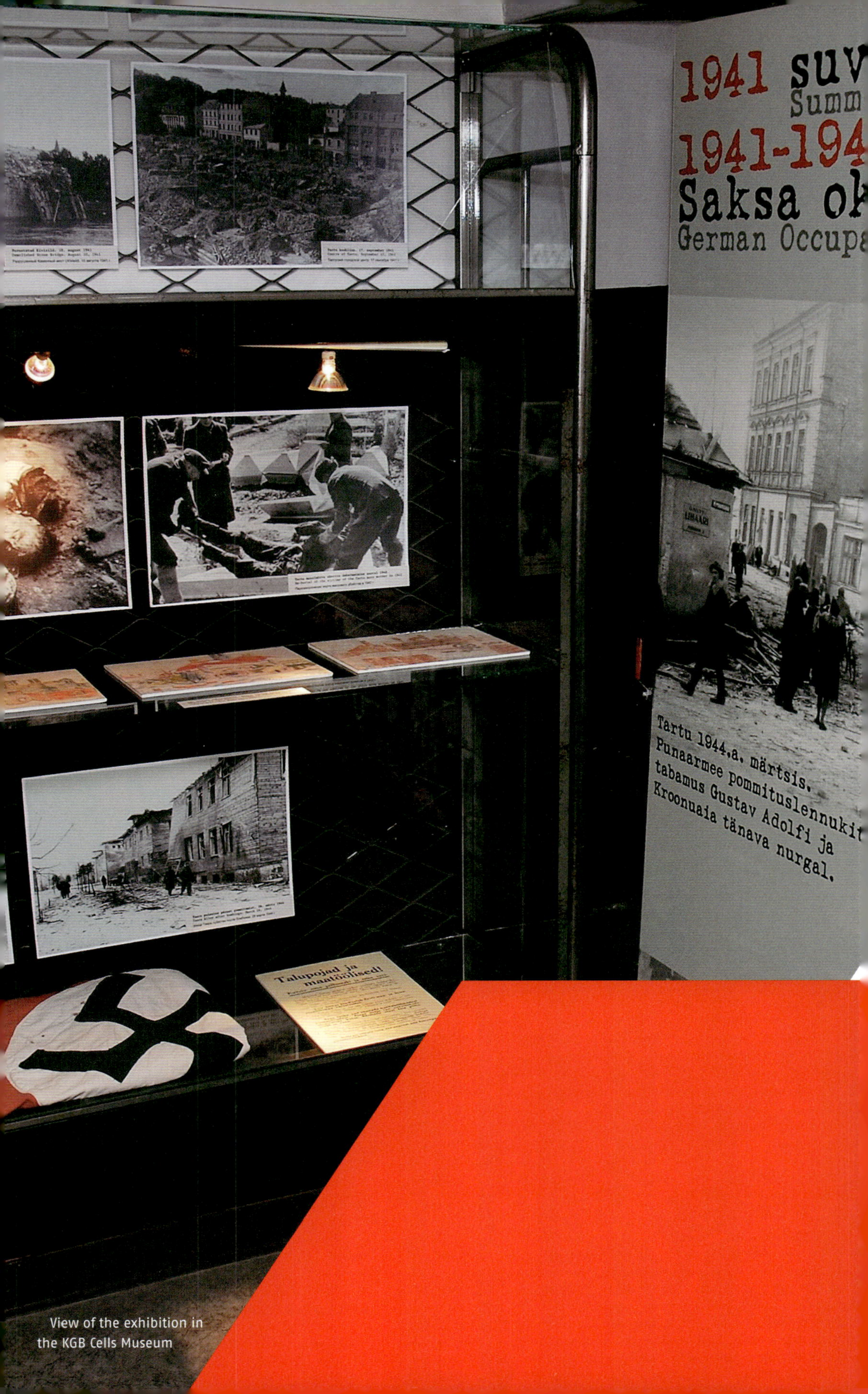

View of the exhibition in
the KGB Cells Museum

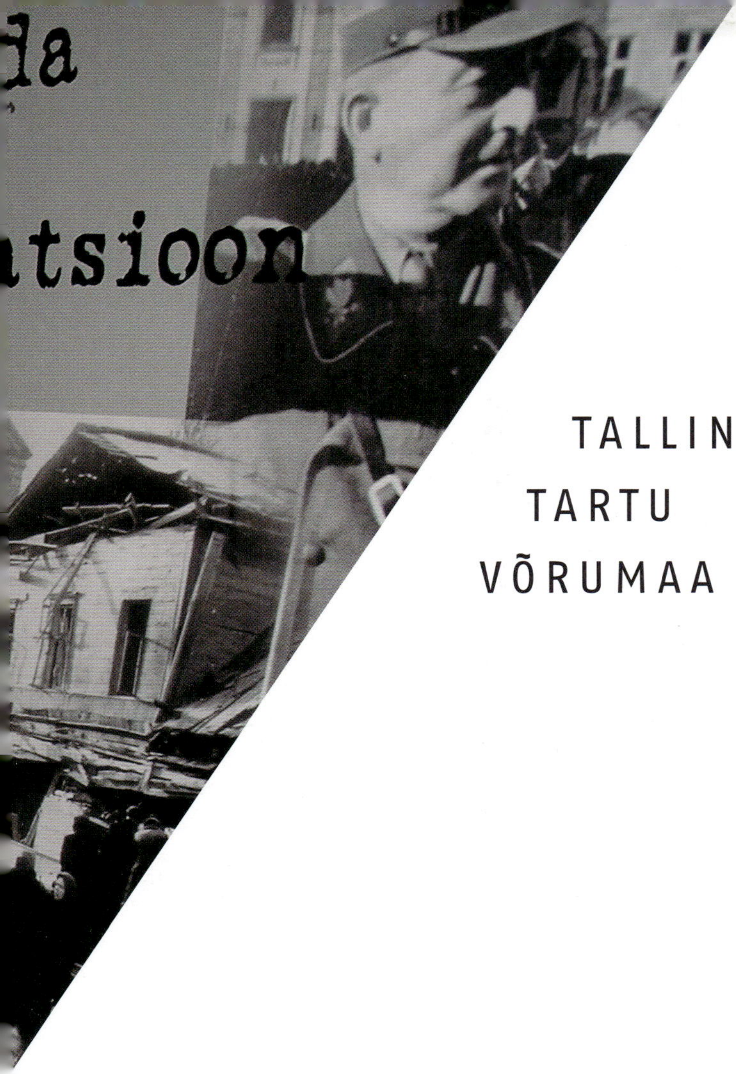

TALLINN

TARTU

VÕRUMAA

Estonia

With the signing of the German-Soviet Nonaggression Pact on 23 August 1939, which divided the states of Central and Eastern Europe between the spheres of influence agreed by Hitler and Stalin, the fate of Estonia, which had been independent since 1918, was also sealed. Red Army units occupied the country in June 1940. In Tallinn, under the leadership of political commissioner and Leningrad party leader Andrei Zhdanov, a puppet government loyal to Moscow was appointed under Estonian Prime Minister Johannes Vares. All non-Communist organisations were banned; banks, industry and land were nationalised. Members of the country's economic, cultural and political elite were arrested at will, deported to penal camps or executed. Konstantin Päts, long-time prime minister and first president of Estonia, was placed under house arrest and deported to the Russian city of Ufa in the Western Urals.

However, Stalinist purges did not only affect state officials and their families. In the course of the deportations, which took place in parallel in all the Baltic republics, over 10,000 Estonian citizens were arrested between 14 and 17 June 1941. Around 3,000 men were arrested and separated from their families. Of those arrested, about 2,500 were shot immediately by the Soviet secret police. Those prisoners who escaped an immediate death sentence were placed in custody and subsequently sent to penal camps or prisons on Soviet territory. Women and children were deported to the Kirov and Novosibirsk regions of Russia for forced labour without trial. By the spring of 1942, only a few hundred of the men arrested were still alive.

After Germany began its invasion of the Soviet Union on 22 June 1941, the German Wehrmacht marched into Estonia in August 1941. Still bearing the scars of previous Soviet repression, many Estonians welcomed the Germans as liberators and joined German associations. More than 70,000 Estonians served with the police, Waffen SS and Wehrmacht units, about 20,000 of them as volunteers. In 1942/43, Estonian SS legions were formed (from January 1944 as the 20th Waffen Grenadier Division of the SS), some of whose members were forcibly recruited. Several thousand men who had fled to Finland formed an Estonian infantry regiment and fought against the Red Army in 1944. The invasion of the Germans triggered a wave of refugees, especially among the Jewish population.

By the end of 1941, members of SS Einsatzgruppe A, with the participation of Estonian collaborators, had wiped out almost the entire remaining Jewish population of the country, about 1,000 people. In addition, about 1,800 Jews deported from the Theresienstadt ghetto in Frankfurt and Berlin were shot dead in a large-scale extermination operation in the Estonian dunes of Kalevi-Liiva in the autumn of 1942. Hundreds of Roma and Sinti, persecuted as "gypsies", also fell victim to genocide. Almost 15,000 Soviet soldiers died in the prisoner-of-war camps on Estonian territory.

After the reconquest of the country by the Red Army in October 1944, Estonia was reabsorbed into the Soviet Union. More than 70,000 people fled across the Baltic Sea. Once again, the population was confronted with deportation, tyranny and state terror. Actual and alleged collaborators with the German occupying forces were targeted, as well as people who were described as "bourgeois nationalists". Foremost among the latter group were the "Forest Brothers", armed resistance fighters in the Estonian forests who, like their Latvian and Lithuanian comrades-in-arms, fought for national sovereignty. These associations included some 15,000 armed combatants who could count on the support of the population. The hope of allied support in the fight against the Soviet occupation failed to materialise. Armed Estonian resistance was crushed in the mid-1950s.

During the height of the Stalinist terror in the immediate aftermath of the war, the arrests were followed by either the death penalty or deportation to Siberian penal camps. At the same time, the families of the "Forest Brothers" were persecuted as relatives of "class enemies". Despite the danger of draconian punishments, anti-Soviet youth movements organised underground in the larger towns of Tartu, Võru and Viljandi. Officially persecuted as "enemies of the people" and "criminals", they disseminated printed material critical of the political leadership and supported the "Forest Brothers".

By 1953, 35,000 people out of a total population of 1.1 million had been arrested for political reasons and sent to prison camps in Siberia. Several thousand were murdered. Only after the death of Stalin in 1953 did open repression cease. In the late 1950s, the survivors of deportation to Siberia were allowed to return to Estonia as part of the de-Stalinisation process. However, most of them remained in the focus of the security authorities as "second-class citizens". The returnees bore the stigma of being "previously convicted" and were subjected to various forms of discrimination. These ranged from the choice of place of residence to access to education and choice of career. In addition, Soviet population policy relied on the large-scale settlement of ethnic Russians and other peoples of the Soviet Union to make the Estonian population a minority in its own country.

Although the form of the reprisals changed, they lasted until the end of the Soviet Union and were directed against all those who questioned Soviet rule and insisted on Estonian independence. During the "thaw" period under Khrushchev, works by previously banned national poets were printed again and the regulation of cultural life was relaxed. An important part of the Estonian resistance and dissident movement was the cultivation of cultural and linguistic heritage. Writings critical of the regime were printed and distributed in underground printing houses. Song festivals took on a special role as a manifestation of the Estonian desire for independence in the 1970s and 1980s.

Illegal human rights organisations were also founded at around that time, demanding free elections and an independent Estonia. Oppressed ethnic and religious minorities, such as members of the German and Jewish minorities, increasingly spoke out and demanded the right to emigrate. Following the signing of the Helsinki Final Act, Estonian human rights groups drew increased attention to human rights violations and tried to network with likeminded groups from Lithuania and Latvia. This culminated in the publication of the Baltic Appeal in 1979. In 1983, the European Parliament adopted a resolution condemning the occupation of the three Baltic states by the Soviet Union and calling for their independence.

All these efforts strengthened the Estonian people's desire for independence. Students at the universities organised protests. These were crushed and their leaders subsequently tried in Moscow and sentenced to imprisonment in camps. In the early 1980s, repression intensified again, and the opposition, which in the 1970s had adopted an increasingly public profile, was driven back underground. However, environmental groups formed to protest against phosphorus mining in eastern Estonia and the associated environmental damage. Similarly, groups of preservationists organised to draw attention to the destruction of cultural heritage—activities that, as in other communist countries, were not formally banned but were perceived as a threat because of their condemnation of the destruction of the environment and cultural treasures.

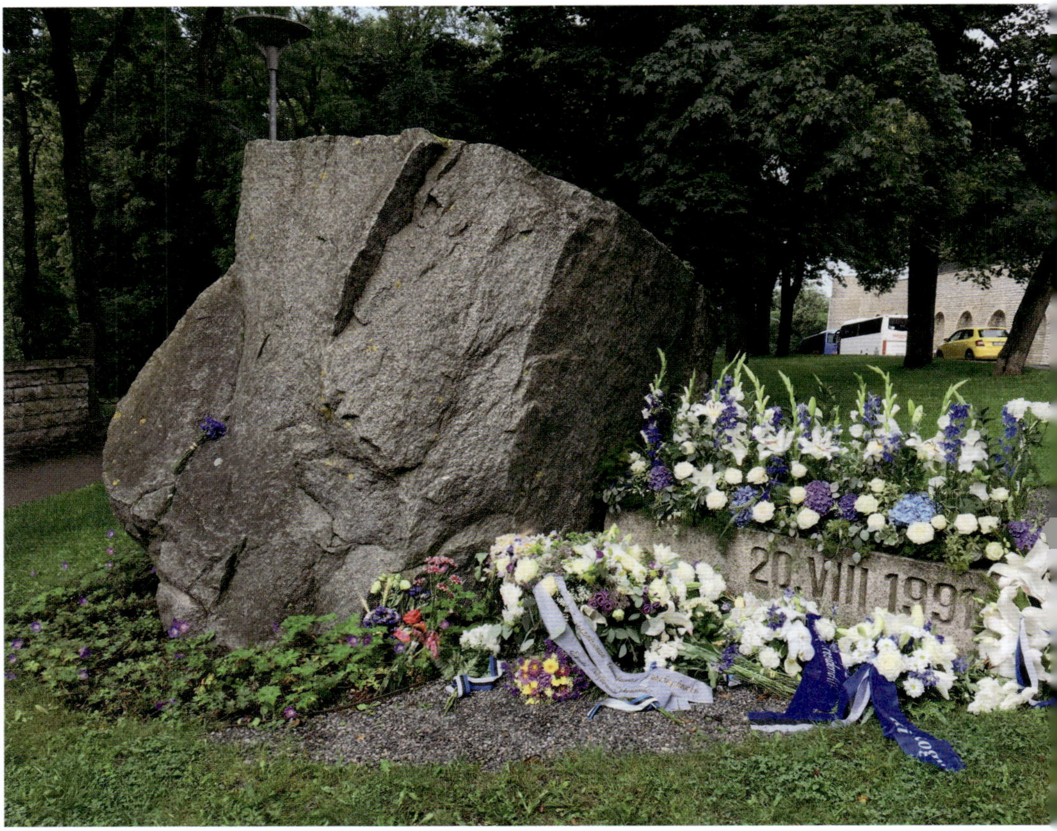

Memorial to Estonian Independence
in front of the parliament building in Tallinn

Only with Gorbachev's policy of glasnost and perestroika from 1987 did the protests against the Soviet occupation intensify. They expressed themselves in a resurgence of Estonian folk songs and the singing of the banned Estonian national anthem. The latter was sung publicly again for the first time since 1940 in August 1988 during a demonstration attended by around 300,000 people in the capital Tallinn. Faced with mass protests, the Soviet leadership changed its nationality policy in the three Baltic Soviet republics in the hope that concessions would calm the situation. For example, Estonian was incorporated into the Constitution as a national language at the end of 1988.

On 23 August 1989, the fiftieth anniversary of the Molotov-Ribbentrop Pact, several million people formed a 600-kilometre-long human chain through all three Baltic republics—Estonia, Latvia and Lithuania—to demonstrate their desire for national independence. The "Singing Revolution" was born.

In March 1990, Estonia declared itself a republic once again. Complete separation from the Soviet Union took place in August 1991 after the failed coup against Gorbachev. As a result, both the KGB and the CPSU were declared illegal in Estonia. The KGB was dissolved in Estonia on 1 December 1991 but managed to spirit away most of the personnel files, operational reports and agent logs of the former secret police into Russia. Some 28,500 KGB files containing information on political prisoners remained in the possession of the Estonian state. Unlike the two neighbouring countries, Latvia and Lithuania, the independence movement in Estonia was not opposed by Soviet tanks and troops and ran its course without bloodshed.

The Estonian government officially rehabilitated the victims of deportation and exile following the state's independence and the collapse of the Soviet Union in 1991. At the same time, it adopted a law decreeing the return of confiscated property to its former owners. Until 1995, lustration took place on the basis of the KGB documents remaining in Estonia, as a result of which Gestapo and KGB employees were removed from public offices. In 2002, the Estonian parliament declared the communist regime of the Soviet Union a criminal regime and the crimes it had committed, alongside those of the Nazi occupation, crimes against humanity. However, the legal proceedings were unsatisfactory: only twelve cases were brought to trial and eleven defendants sentenced to prison.

At the same time, the Estonian government tried to reverse the Russification of the country. Estonian became the official and national language, Soviet monuments were dismantled and streets renamed. On 15 February 2007, the Estonian parliament passed a law banning monuments glorifying Soviet rule. Disputes between parts of the Russian population and the Estonian security forces occurred when the monument to the Soviet soldiers, erected in 1947 as a symbol of the liberation of Estonia from Nazi rule, was moved to a military cemetery on the outskirts of Tallinn in April 2007.

In parallel with the renaming of streets and the removal of monuments, new monuments were erected to commemorate the oppression of the Estonian population and the loss of independence under both the Soviet and German occupations. The Museum of Occupations in the centre of Tallinn, which is supported by a private foundation, the Estonian National Museum and city and local history museums deal with the occupations and their consequences.

Fact-finding commissions were set up to document the material and human cost of the occupation. The Estonian International Commission for Investigation of Crimes Against Humanity and its successor—the Estonian Institute of Historical Memory, founded in 2008—have published numerous papers and scientific studies on the history and consequences of foreign rule in Estonia in the 20th century.

On 25 March and 14 June of each year, and on 23 August, memorial ceremonies are held to commemorate the victims of totalitarian rule in Estonia.

War of Independence Victory Column

Tallinn. The War of Independence Victory Column in the centre of Freedom Square (Vabaduse väljak) was officially opened to the public on 23 June 2009. It commemorates the struggle for independence in the years from 1918 to 1920. The 23.5-metre-high monument was conceived and designed by architects Reiner Sternfeld, Andri Laidre and Anto Savi. The monument consists of 143 glass plates and incorporates the Estonian Cross of Liberty. Thousands of small LED lights illuminate the monument at night. The Cross of Liberty, introduced by Prime Minister Konstantin Päts after the proclamation of Estonia's independence, was a special award for services to national independence between 1919 and 1925. Only after the erection of the monument did a broad social debate take place about the aesthetics of the huge victory cross, which some people consider too militaristic. Every year, on 24 February and 23 August, the official festivities for Estonian Independence Day, which is celebrated as a national holiday, take place on Freedom Square and at the monument itself.

The **inscription** on the left side of the monument complex represents the first verse of a poem by Estonian poet Gustav Suits and reads:

Eesti Vabadussõda // 1918 – 1920 // Tõsta lipp! See aja käänul / tunnistagu tuulte väänul / üle maa ja vee ja tee / tund on tulnud vannet vandu, / et ei iial enam andu / ikke alla rahvas see.

English: *Estonian Liberation War // 1918 – 1920 // Raise the flag! The vows sound out, / blown early from the winds / across the land and waves high: / The time has come to swear the oath, / that this people will rise up, / but never bow before the yoke!*

Location: Tallinn, Vabaduse väljak 9

►

War of Independence Victory Column for the Estonian Liberation War in the centre of Freedom Square

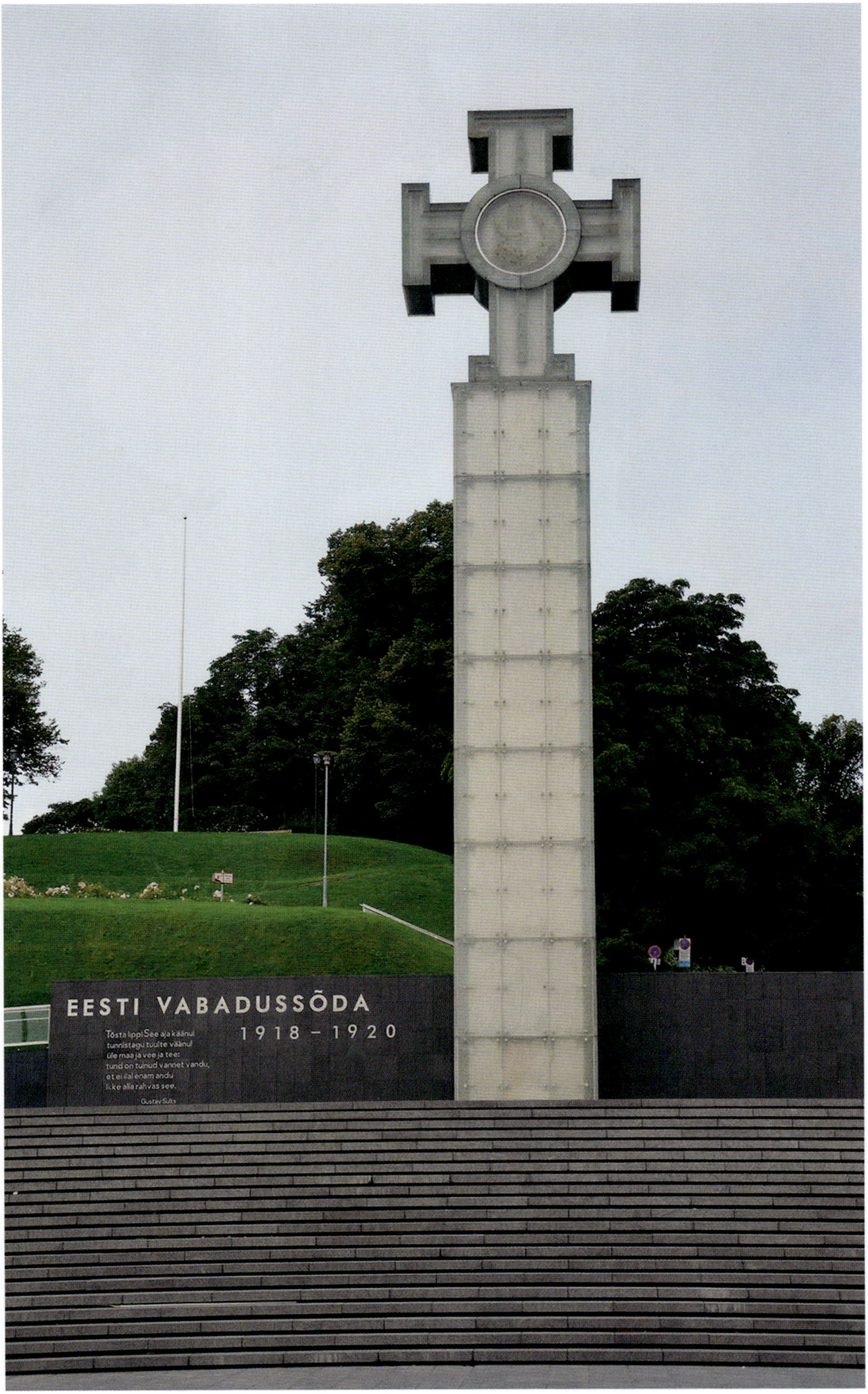

EESTI VABADUSSÕDA
1918 – 1920
Tõsta lippi! See aja käänul
tunnistagu tuulte väänul
üle maa ja vee ja tee:
tund on tulnud vannet vandu,
et ei iial enam andu
ikke alla rahvas see.
Gustav Suits

Memorial to the Victims of the "Red Terror"

Tallinn. A memorial was erected in 1989 at the Liiva forest cemetery in Tallinn on top of the mass graves of victims of the Soviet secret police, the NKVD, who were murdered in the summer of 1941. Estonian sculptor Ekke Väli designed the monument, which was built with private donations. In 1991, the site was redesigned and expanded. The memorial consists of three vertically mounted granite blocks on which the names of the victims are engraved. The structure is topped off by a horizontal stone block. The adjoining area also features several unmarked crosses, symbolically marking the graves of those who were shot.

On 14 May 1941, the Central Committee of the Communist Party of the Soviet Union and the Council of People's Commissars of the USSR gave the order to purge the territories of Moldova, Western Ukraine, the Baltic countries and the western part of Belarus, annexed by the Soviet Union under the Molotov-Ribbentrop Pact, of "anti-Soviet, criminal, and socially dangerous elements". In these areas, 200,000 to 300,000 people fell victim to mass

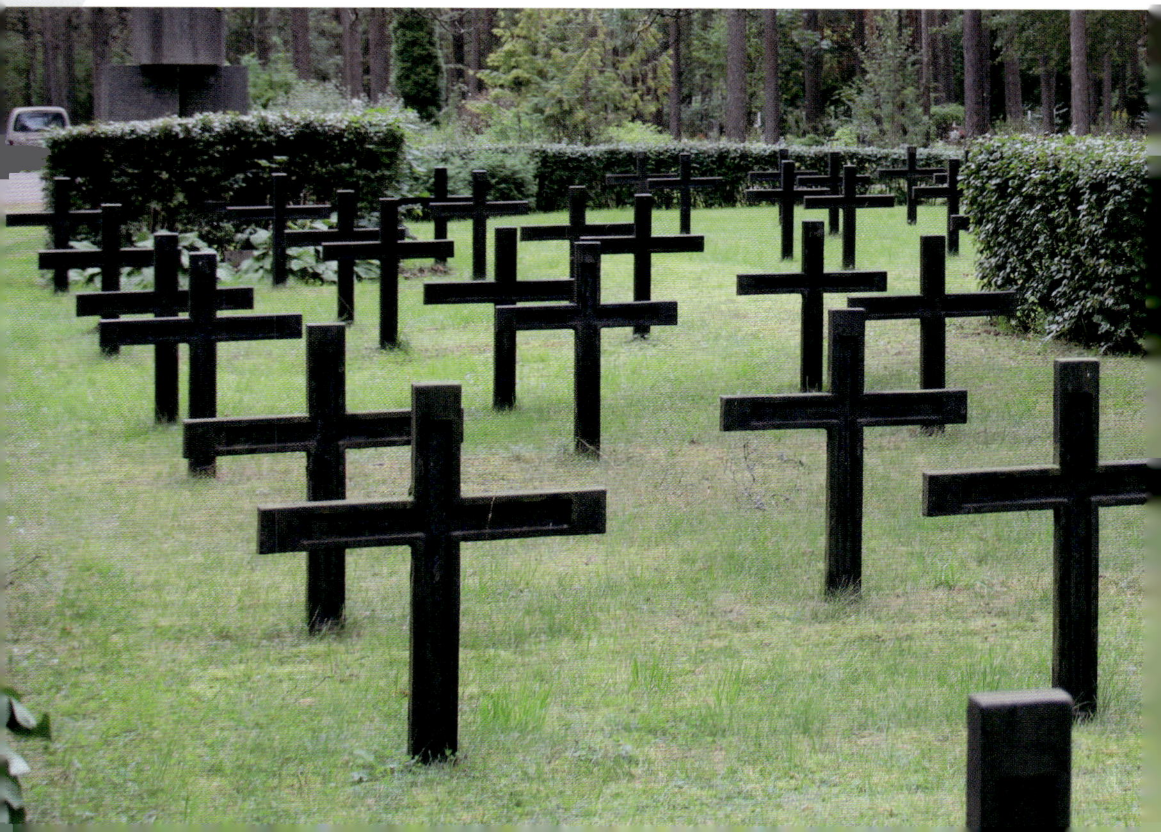

deportations and expulsions before the invasion of German troops. In addition to former government members and high-ranking representatives of the judiciary, the military and the police, party politicians, prominent members of civil society initiatives, entrepreneurs and financiers with contacts abroad, clerics, members of student associations and, basically, all citizens who came into contact with capitalist foreign countries were under suspicion.

The number of arrests reached enormous proportions within a few days during the June deportations. Between 14 and 17 June 1941, local NKVD forces in Estonia imprisoned over 10,000 people, including 400 Jews. As a rule, the victims were taken from their homes during night raids, confronted with a predetermined sentence and escorted into the unknown by armed guards. In the "deportations on official orders", members of the secret police removed the persons concerned without any pretence of formality. The victims were not informed of the destination or duration of the deportation. Families were taken in trucks to collection points at stations in Tallinn, Narva, Tartu, Keila and other major cities. Crammed into cattle cars, which were not visibly marked as prisoner transports, the prisoners and deportees were sent to remote areas along the Volga and in the far east of Siberia.

Location: Tallinn, Liiva cemetary, Kalmistu tee 34

◄ Unmarked crosses mark the symbolic graves of the victims of execution.

Memorial commemorating the victims shot by the NKVD in the summer of 1941

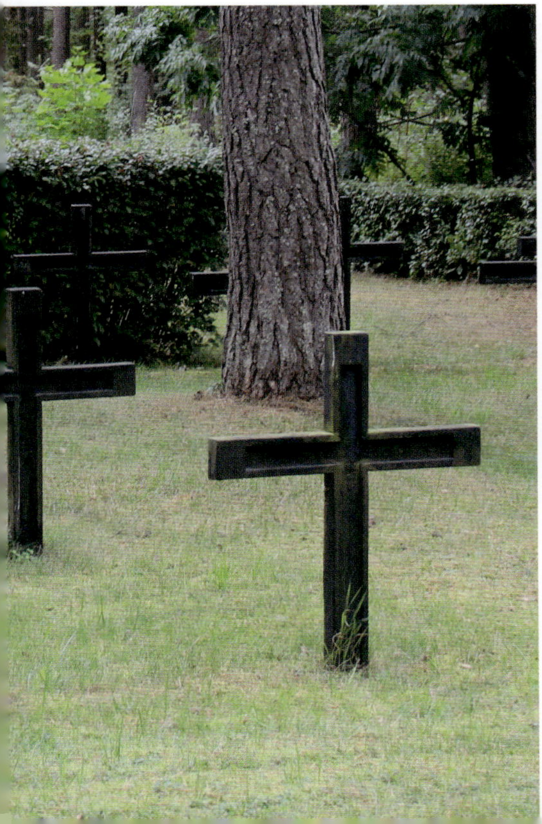

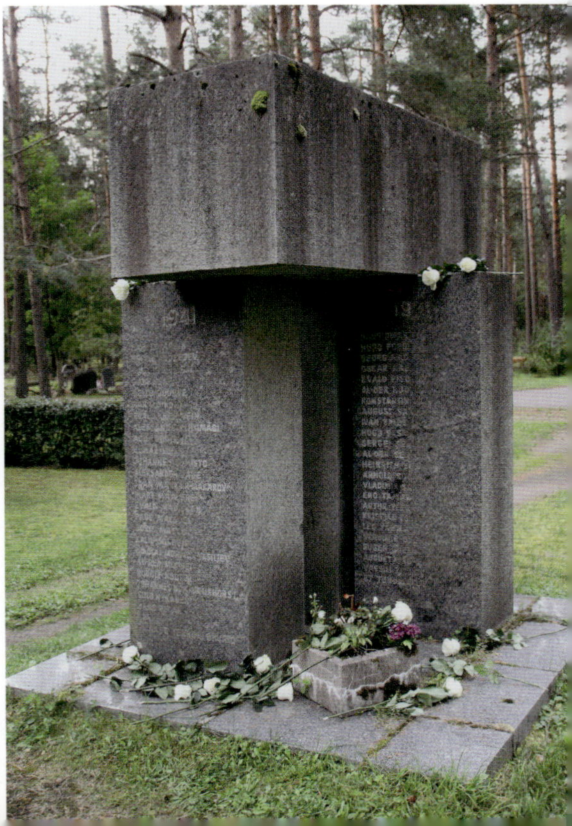

Former central prison Patarei

Grounds of the former Central Prison in Patarei

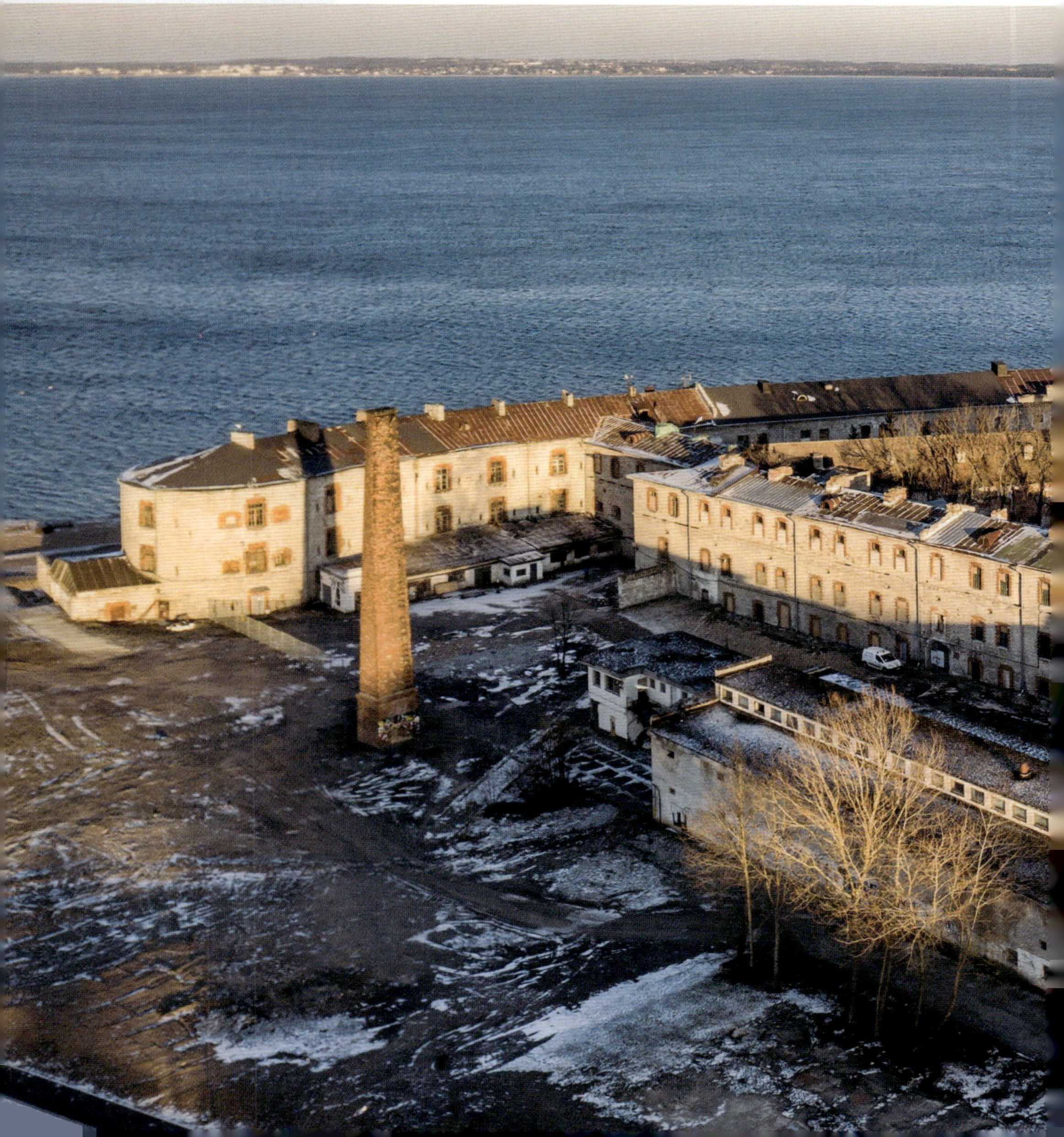

Tallinn. Commissioned in 1828 by Russian Tsar Nicholas I to secure the sea route between Tallinn and St. Petersburg, the capital of the Russian Empire, the sea fortress at Patarei was completed in 1840. The four-hectare complex on the Estonian Baltic coast has fulfilled various functions since its construction. Originally used as a fortification and cannon battery, the building complex served as a military base between 1867 and 1919. Equipped with officers' quarters, soldiers' barracks, hospital facilities, utility rooms and artillery installations, the facility could accommodate up to 2,000 people. From 1920 until its final closure in 2002, Patarei served as a prison and detention centre under both the Estonian governments and the Soviet and Nazi occupying powers that ruled the country between 1940 and 1991.

In the course of the first Soviet occupation of Estonia from June 1940, the building complex of the central prison was transferred from the local administration to that of the Soviet secret police, the NKVD. Within a few months of the occupation of the country, some 10,000 Estonian citizens had been arrested "by order of the authorities", i. e. without trial or court

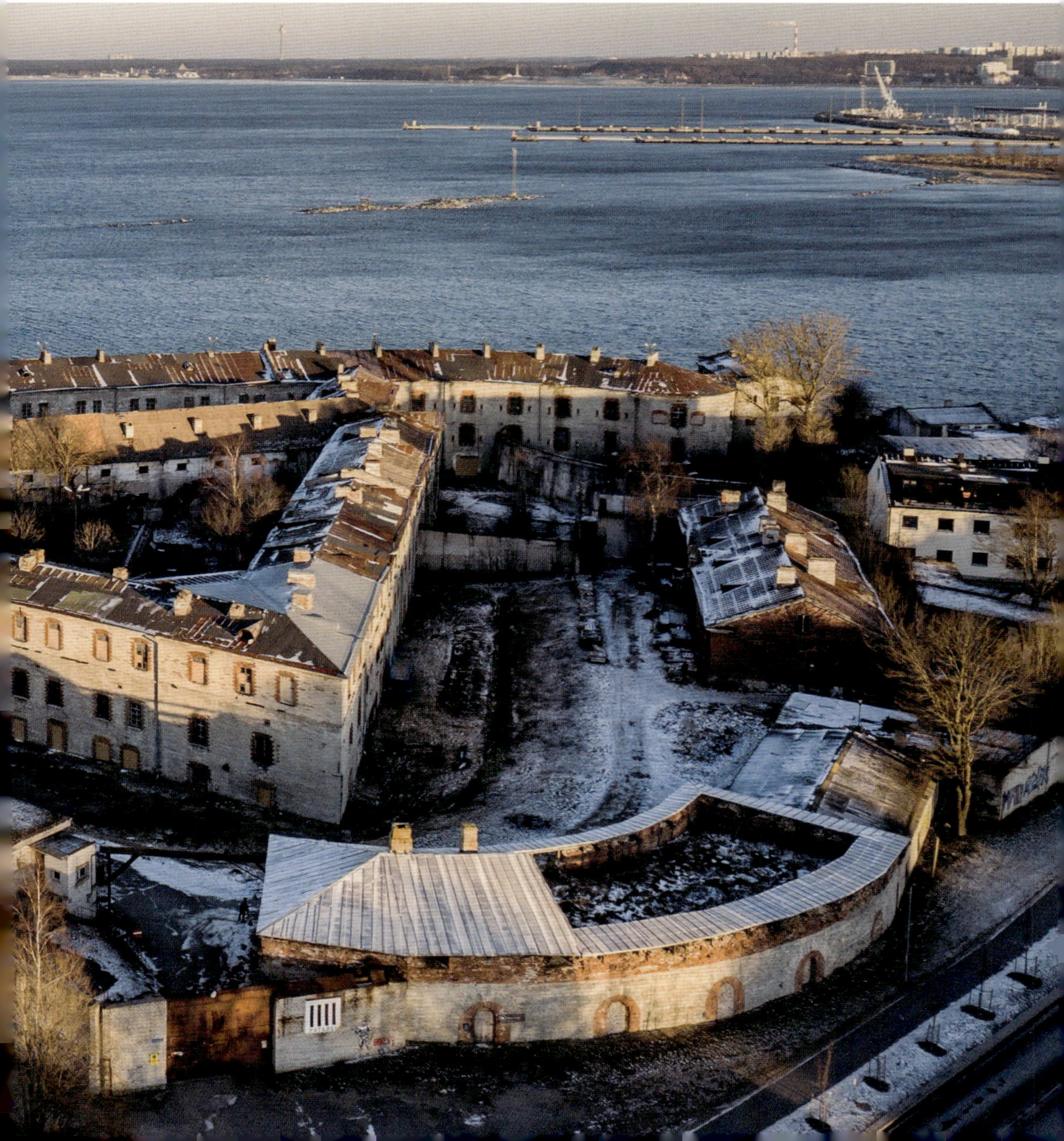

order, detained and transported in overcrowded cattle cars for forced labour to remote Soviet camps in Siberia and along the Volga. Prior to this, political prisoners, accused by the NKVD of "counterrevolutionary activity" as "enemies of the people" and "traitors to the Motherland", were subjected to an agonising ordeal of interrogation and torture at the headquarters of the secret police in Pagari Street. All those who were not killed in the execution cells of the NKVD headquarters were transferred to the prison and labour camps of the Gulag in Patarei until they were transported away. During the first Soviet occupation and in the initial phase of the second, from 1944 onwards, the central prison served as a transit point for prisoners who were to be deported to the interior of the Soviet Union.

After the German invasion of the Soviet Union on 22 June 1941, the National Socialist occupying power took just a few weeks to assign all Baltic territories to the Reichskommissariat Ostland. Thousands of detainees—Estonians, Jews and Russians—were held at the prison during this time. By the end of 1941, 1,000 people had fallen victim to the National Socialist genocide of the Jewish population in Estonia. This wiped out the entire remaining Jewish population of the country that had been unable to flee in time to the interior of the Soviet Union. At the Wannsee Conference on 20 January 1942, the meeting of high-ranking representatives of the Nazi government and SS authorities for the further organisation and planning of the Holocaust, Estonia was declared "Jew-free". Between the end of May and the beginning of June 1944, "Convoy 73", with 300 Jewish prisoners from the French Drancy concentration and transit camp, reached Patarei, which served as a temporary transit point.

On 22 September 1944, Red Army units recaptured Tallinn. The administration of the Patarei central prison passed back into the hands of the Soviet secret police, which, after a number of restructuring measures, had changed its name to NKGB. The conditions of detention remained inhumane: cells designed for 16 persons were occupied by up to 30 inmates. After the death of Stalin on 5 March 1953, the new head of state and party leader of the Soviet Union, Nikita Khrushchev, who himself had been involved in crimes during Stalinism, denounced the cult of personality surrounding Stalin and the crimes committed in a secret speech to the 20th Party Conference of the CPSU in 1956.

In the course of the step-by-step restructuring and dissolution of the Gulag system and gradual de-Stalinisation under Khrushchev, survivors of deportation and abduction were gradually permitted to return to their homes. The prison regime and internment practice in Patarei also changed. The entire facility was given a central heating system and better sanitary facilities. And yet, the conditions the detainees were forced to endure were worsened by the reconstruction, with the attendant reduction in space, of the inner courtyard, the only place where detainees could spend time outside. In the summer of 1980, the sailing competitions of the Olympic Games took place in the Bay of Tallinn. Before the start of the competitions, all cell windows on the sea-facing side were doubly secured with bars and nailed shut with boards. Any visual contact between detainees and athletes was to be prevented. Large-scale arrests, as were common in the Stalin era, were replaced by targeted punitive measures. During the interrogations in Patarei, the prisoners were subjected to torture in the form of physical and psychological pressure. The last death sentence carried out in the basement of the building was in September 1991—after Estonia had regained its independence on 20 August.

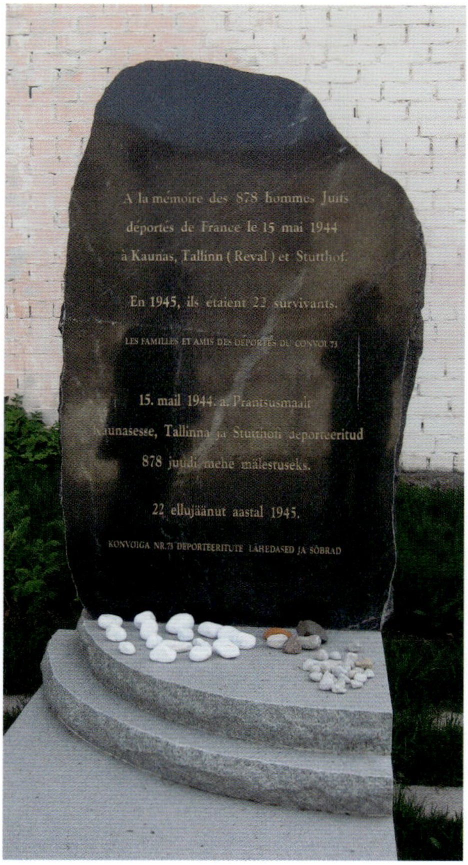

Memorial stone commemorating the Jews deported to Estonia from France

After the official dissolution of the KGB in Estonia and the transfer of all facilities under its control to Estonian state ownership in December 1991, the prison remained in operation. The closure of the complex in 2002 prompted a broad public debate regarding the further use of the site. In addition to proposals for the complete redesign and "positive" reconceptualisation of the four-hectare site, ideas for the transformation of the prison into a documentation centre were also put forward. Until 2016, the site served as the "Patarei Cultural Park", an art space for exhibitions and various cultural events. The building complex was also used as a historical excursion site. Guided tours offered visitors the opportunity to visit former cell and kitchen sections, the medical facilities of the facility, the inner courtyard and the former execution cell. In 2016, the dilapidated condition of the entire complex forced it to close. In 2017, it was decided to turn the former prison complex into a memorial.

On 14 January 2005, on the initiative of the Museum of Occupations, the Estonian Minister of Justice added a plaque in memory of the victims of Soviet occupation detained in the prison. Earlier, a memorial stone made of black granite had been placed in front of the building to commemorate the Jews deported from France to Estonia.

Inscription on the memorial stone
French: *A la mémoire des 878 hommes Juifs / déportés de France le 15 mai 1944 / à Kaunas, Tallinn (Reval) et Stutthof. // En 1945, ils étaient 22 survivants. // Les familles et amis de déportés du convoi 73*

Estonian: *15. mai 1944. a. Prantsusmaalt / Kaunasesse, Tallinna ja Stutthofi deporteeritud / 878 juudi mehe mälestuseks. // 22 ellujäänut aastal 1945. // Konvoiga Nr. 73 deporteeritute lähedased ja sõbrad*

English: *In memory of the 878 people of Jewish origin who were deported from France to Kaunas, Tallinn (Reval) and Stutthof on 15 May 1944. In 1945, there were 22 survivors. The families and friends of the deportees of Convoy 73*

Location: Tallinn, Kalaranna 28
Internet: www.patarei.org

Museum of Occupations

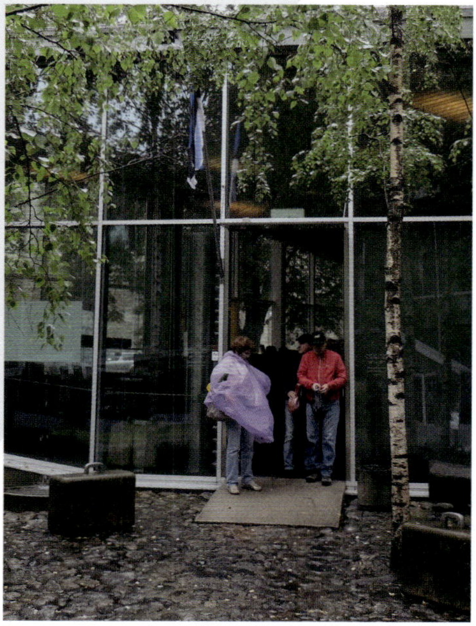

Entrance to the museum

Tallinn. The Estonian Museum of Occupations was inaugurated on 27 June 2003 on the anniversary of the first Soviet occupation in 1940. The project to establish the museum had been initiated by the American Kistler-Ritso Estonian Foundation in 1998.

The exhibition presents a chronological overview of the three occupations of Estonia in the 20th century, from the Soviet occupation of 1940/41 to the rule of the National Socialists between 1941 and 1944 and the renewed Soviet occupation from 1944 to 1991. Various aspects of oppression, adaptation and resistance are illustrated using official testimonies and the personal possessions of former prisoners and persecuted persons, as well as a variety of audio-visual media. The museum's collection comprises over 36,000 objects—including books, photographs, magazines, newspapers, clothing, sculptures, diaries, postcards, toys and artefacts—which can be viewed in digital form on the institution's website. In November 2014, an original segment of the Berlin Wall was erected on the museum's grounds.

In cooperation with the Estonian Institute of Historical Memory and the Estonian Heritage Conservation Society, the Museum of Occupations developed the exhibition in the former KGB prison cells in 1 Pagari Street, Tallinn, which opened in the summer of 2017. The basement rooms of the building constructed in 1912 were used by the NKVD above all as interrogation rooms and torture chambers. Using audio-visual elements, historical objects, documents and photographs, the elaborately designed exhibition sheds light on the history of the building and gives an impression of the conditions of detention at this site.

Location: Tallinn, Toompea 8
Internet: www.okupatsioon.ee

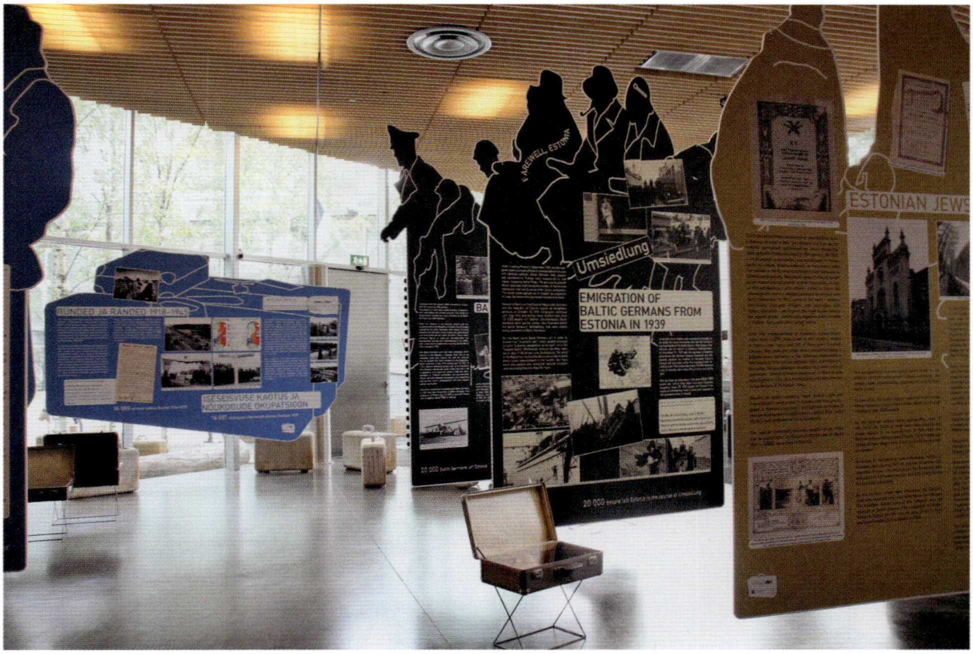

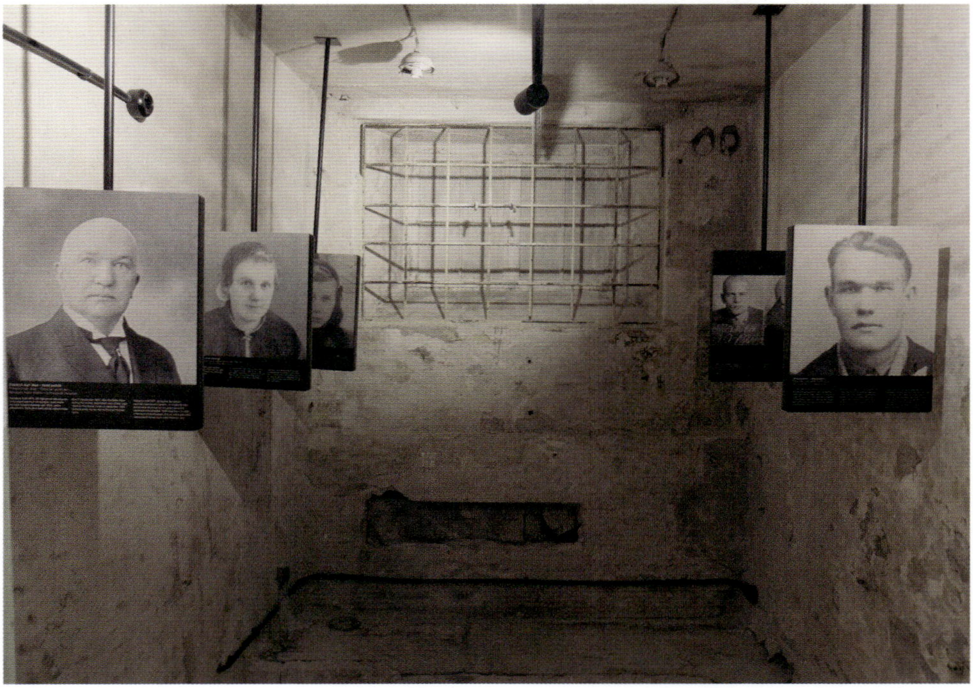

at the top: View of the exhibition
in the Museum of Occupations

down: Exhibition in the former KGB prison
cells in Pagari Street 1 in Tallinn

KGB Cells Museum

Tartu. The KGB Cells Museum is part of the Tartu City Museum and was established in the basement of the former Soviet secret police headquarters in 2001. The family of the building's former owner, Oskar Sõmermaa, donated the rooms to the City Museum. Sõmermaa was deported in 1941 and died two years later in a prison camp in Siberia. Constructed in 1938, the building served as the headquarters of the NKVD during the first Soviet occupation from June 1940 to July 1941. During the German occupation of the country between 1941 and 1944, the building was used by the SS. After the invasion of the Red Army in August 1944 and until the 1950s, the building once again served as a prison for actual and alleged opponents of the Communist regime.

After the Nazi assault on the Soviet Union on 22 June 1941, the Wehrmacht quickly advanced into the Baltic territories. Before the German troops arrived in Estonia, the NKVD ordered the shooting of many political prisoners. The largest mass execution took place in Tartu prison on the night of 8 – 9 July 1941. A few days earlier, all the prisoners had been transported to Siberia. In just one week, however, the prison filled up again. The new detainees had been neither officially charged nor brought before a judge. P. Afanasiev, the head of the local NKVD section, ordered the murder of the prisoners and personally monitored the executions. Witnesses identified another eleven NKVD agents and prison guards by name as collaborators. 192 (172 men and 20 women) of the 223 prisoners were shot. Their remains were then buried in two mass graves that had been dug in the prison yard or thrown into a well that was located on the grounds. The prison continued to operate even during the German occupation. However, reliable information on this period is still lacking to this day.

In March 1949, as part of the large-scale operation entitled "Priboi" (surf), Soviet security forces quickly deported almost 90,000 "counter-revolutionary elements", many of them women and children, from the Baltic countries to forced labour camps in Siberia. The property of those who were exiled was confiscated by the state for an indefinite period. In Estonia, some 20,500 people were affected. In 1953, several members of the black-blue-white (Estonian tricolour flag) youth resistance movement active in Tartu were detained in the "Grey House" and charged with "counterrevolutionary activity" under the dreaded Article 58 of the Russian Penal Code. Convicted as "traitors of the people", the young people were sent to prison camps in Siberia.

The exhibition housed in the restored cells sheds light on various aspects of Soviet occupation and repression policies: from the mass deportations of 1940/41 to the resistance movement and the life of exiled Estonians in the camps of the Soviet Gulag. The exhibition con-

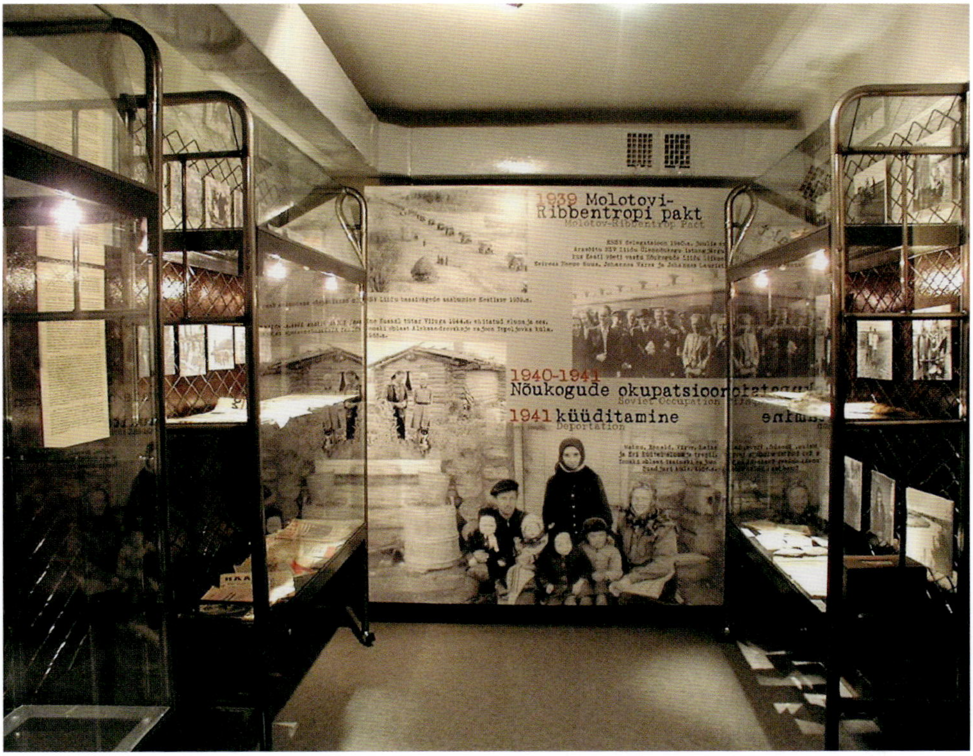

Different aspects of Soviet occupation and repression policies in the exhibition

tains official Soviet documents on the history of repression and numerous testimonies of former underground fighters and political prisoners.

Location: Tartu, Riia 15b
Internet: www.linnamuuseum.tartu.ee

"Forest Brothers" Bunker

Võrumaa. The "Forest Brothers' Farm" (metsavenna talu), 1.5 kilometres from the Latvian border, with a preserved underground hideout of the Estonian "Forest Brothers", was opened to the public in 1999. This private estate was set up by Meelis Mõttus, whose father Harry Mõttus (1921–1991) was active as a "Forest Brother" between 1940 and 1954 in the Estonian resistance against both the Nazi and the Soviet occupation of Estonia.

As in the other Baltic republics, the "Forest Brothers" resisted both the first Soviet occupation from 1940 to 1941 and the second from the autumn of 1944. During the occupation of Estonia by units of the German Wehrmacht between 1941 and 1944, there were only isolated resistance activists in the forests of the Baltic Republic. With the return of the Red Army in autumn 1944, the regime continued the previous practices of repression. The largest wave of political arrests had swept up over 17,000 people by the end of 1945. Measures resumed for forced collectivisation, systematic persecution, and the suppression of the clergy and the elimination of the intelligentsia. At the height of Stalinist repression, 20,500 Estonian citizens fell victim to the "Red Terror" within just a few days during the March deportations of 1949.

The partisan groups in the Baltic forests were associations with different political orientations, united above all by the struggle against the Soviet occupation. Between 1944 and 1953 in Estonia, some 30,000 underground fighters participated in the armed resistance against the Soviet occupation. Among the subversive activities of the "Forest Brothers" were the sabotage of Soviet state assets, the removal of communist propaganda and the circulation of a nationalist underground press. In addition, they fought locally against the development of Soviet administrative structures. 773 armed assaults by the "Forest Brothers" are documented for the period between November 1944 and November 1947 alone, killing around 1,000 Red Army soldiers and their local collaborators.

The Soviet leadership repeatedly ordered targeted reconnaissance and extermination operations. In the mid-1950s, the armed Estonian resistance was almost completely wiped out due to the lack of support from the Allies, the intensification of collectivisation measures and massive Soviet counter-offensives. To persuade the partisans to surrender, they were promised reduced sentences and amnesty. At the same time, the families of the "Forest Brothers" were subjected to repressive treatment as relatives of "class enemies", which usually went hand in hand with arrest, torture, economic ruin and deportation. The last Estonian "Forest Brother"—August Sabbe—was not found by the Soviet secret police until 1978. He was killed trying to escape arrest.

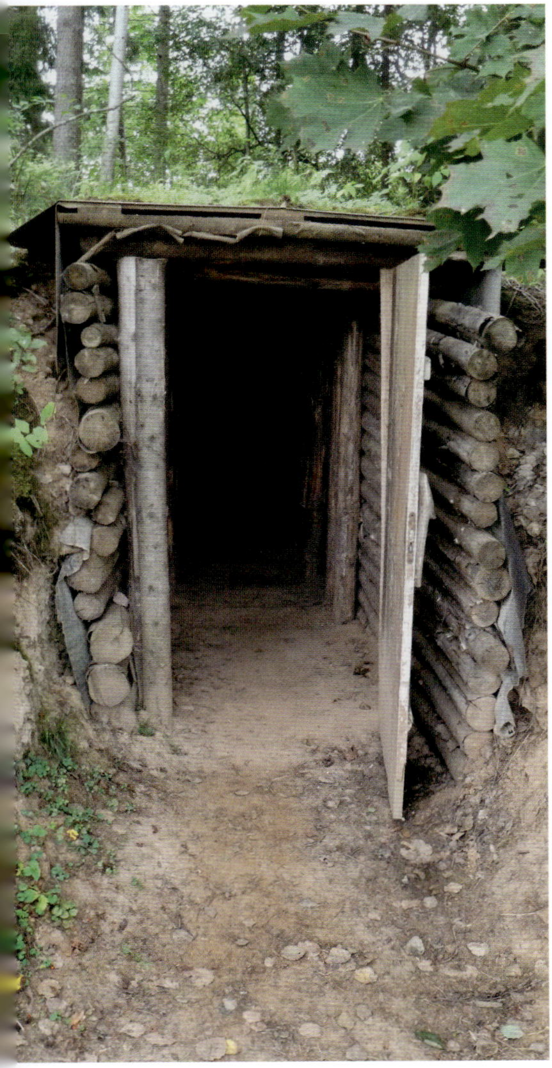

Location: Võrumaa, 1.5 kilometres from the Estonian-Latvian border near the village of Vastse-Roosa
Internet: www.metsavennatalu.ee

Further reading:
Kuusi, Hanna: Prison Experience and Socialist Sculptures—Tourism and the Soviet Past in the Baltic States. In: Kostiainen, Auvo / Syrjämaa, Taina (ed.): Touring the Past. Uses of History in Tourism. Savonlinna 2008, pp. 105 – 122. / Mertelsmann, Olaf/ Rahi-Tamm, Aigi: Soviet mass violence in Estonia revisited. In: Journal of Genocide Research, 2009, Vol. 11, Nr. 2 – 3, pp. 307 – 322. / Saueauk, Meelis: "Honoring Civil Courage". Case study on Estonia. In: Honoring Civil Courage. Developing Suggestions to Improve the Situation of Victims of Communist State Crimes. Project Coordinator: Gedenkstätte Berlin-Hohenschönhausen 2015, Ref-Nr.: JUST/2011/JPEN/AG/2998. Available online at: www.stiftung-hsh.de/assets/Dokumente-pdf-Dateien/EU-Projekt-Laenderstudien.pdf (last accessed on: 15/11/2017).

◄
Entrance to the former "Forest Brothers" bunker

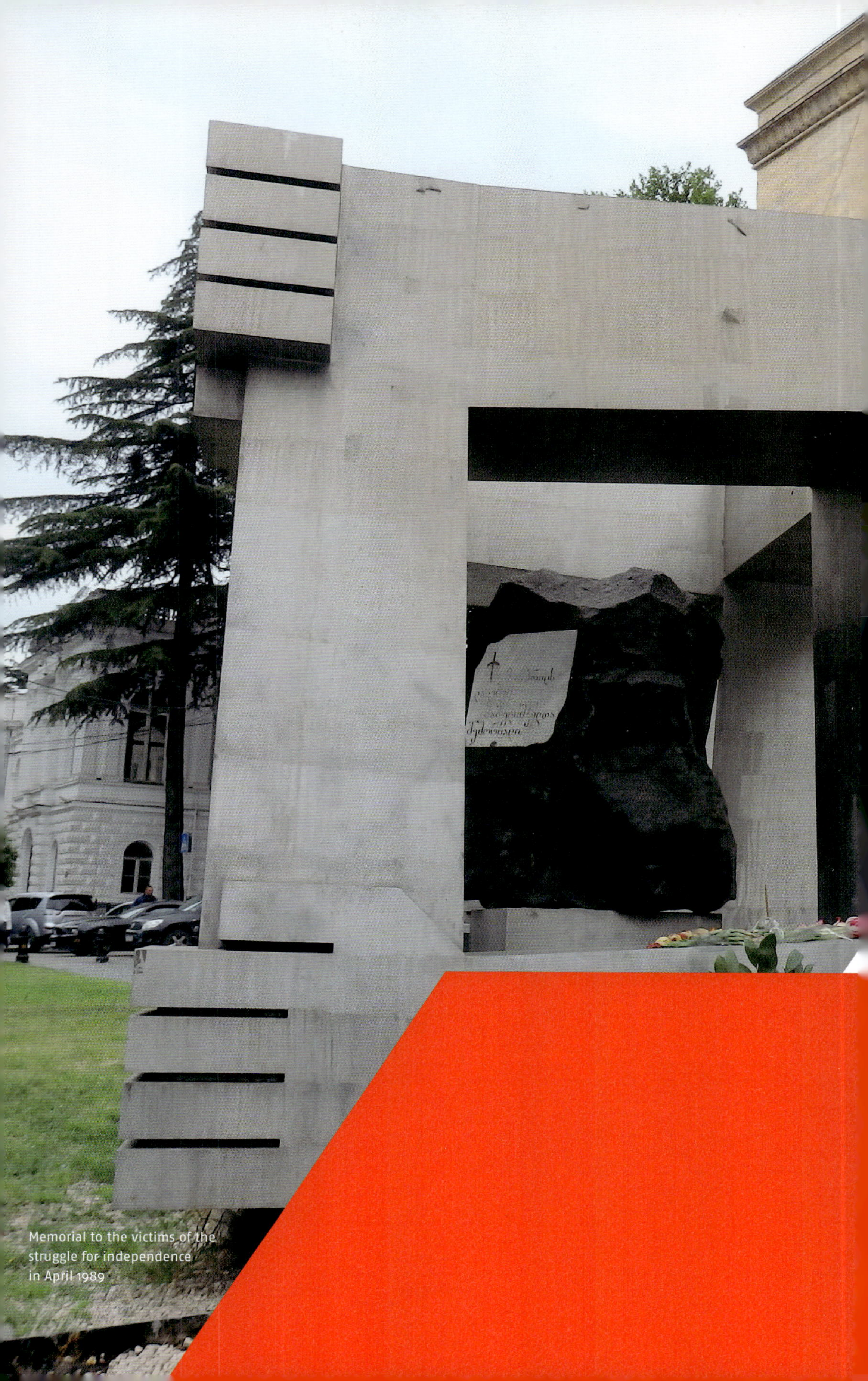

Memorial to the victims of the struggle for independence in April 1989

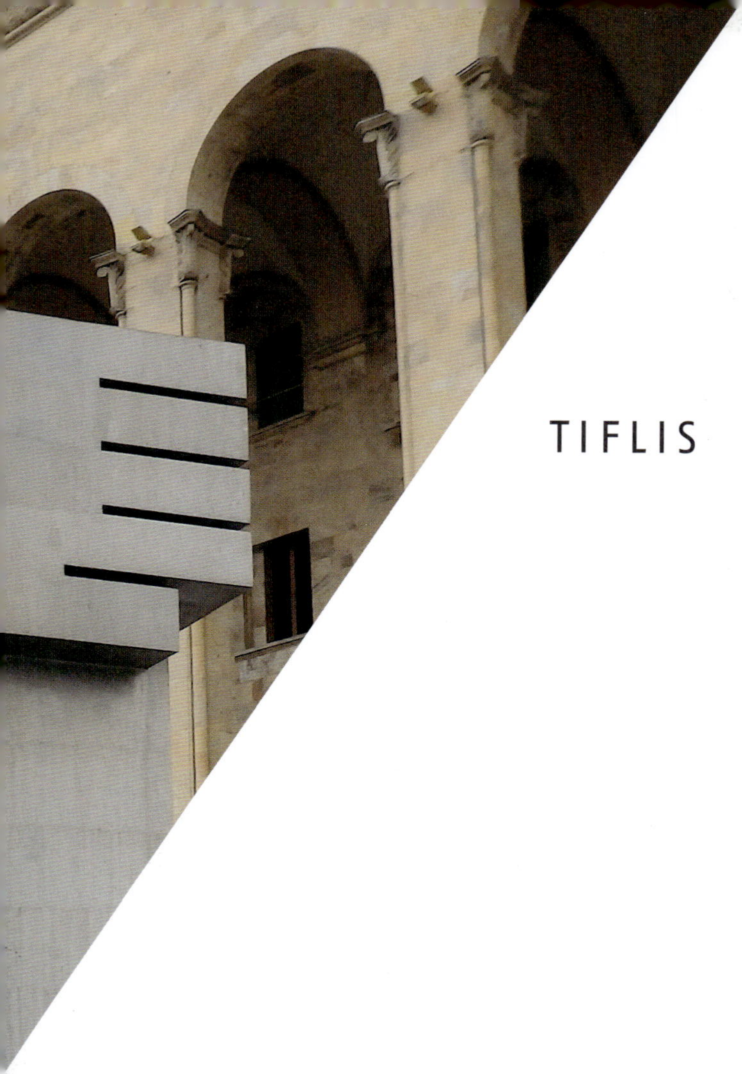

TIFLIS

Georgia

Following the February Revolution in 1917, which overthrew Tsarist rule in Russia, and the end of the First World War, Georgia, too, gained its independence. On 26 May 1918, the Democratic Republic of Georgia was founded and recognised under international law. Soviet Russia also agreed to Georgian independence in 1920. The country formed a Transcaucasian Federation with Armenia and Azerbaijan. In February 1921, Red Army troops occupied Georgia, and the government fled abroad. From that point onwards, Georgia was systematically Sovietised. Land was expropriated, and reprisals against representatives of an independent Georgia accompanied the country's transformation into a Soviet republic, which was officially founded in 1922.

The Georgian government-in-exile, which had fled the country, supported resistance against the Soviet regime. August 1924 saw the first uprising in Georgia against Soviet occupation, but it failed to reach the capital. Stalin, installed as Soviet governor in his home country of Georgia, had the uprising crushed and thousands of people arrested, deported and executed. An estimated 30,000 people were murdered between 1921 and 1924. In the later waves of terror in 1937/38, 1942 to 1945 and the late 1940s, another 50,000 people were deported to Siberian penal camps and killed. These included members of the "old" elites, land and factory owners, artists, and intellectuals, but also priests and worshippers. In Georgia, which, alongside Armenia, was one of the first countries on earth to adopt Christianity, priests and worshippers were systematically persecuted, and churches and monasteries were expropriated and deconsecrated for use as stables, barns, cinemas, gymnasiums or even prisons.

After the Second World War, the country was industrialised. A metallurgical centre, whose buildings were erected by Soviet and German prisoners of war, was established in Rustavi. As there were not enough workers in Georgia to operate such a plant, nomadic Caucasians were deported to Rustavi. In 1956, three years after the death of Stalin, there was another uprising, which was at first directed against de-Stalinisation and accompanied by chants of "Long live Stalin!" After Soviet troops intervened, the protest turned into a revolt against Soviet rule, whose violent suppression killed 150 people.

In the context of the decentralisation that began under Khrushchev at the end of the 1950s, Georgia developed into one of the most economically prosperous Soviet republics. Nationalist tendencies and the quest for state sovereignty increased. In the 1970s, the protests emanating from the country's universities were directed against the Russification of the country and promoted the preservation of the Georgian language and culture. They reached fever pitch at a time when Russian was poised to be enshrined in the constitution as the sole official language. Eduard Shevardnadze, who later became Foreign Minister of the USSR, was the interior minister and later chairman of the Communist Party in Georgia from 1964 and was largely responsible for the brutal repression of the opposition. However, despite the remand of critical intellectuals to psychiatric institutions, camps and prisons, it proved impossible to completely suppress the protests.

After Mikhail Gorbachev came to power in 1985 and glasnost and perestroika began, protests against Soviet rule and the call for national sovereignty intensified. In the autumn of 1990, free elections were held for the first time, from which the "Round Table—Free Georgia" electoral alliance emerged victorious. The referendum on national independence, held only a few months later, was adopted with over 98 percent of the votes, after which Georgia was re-established as an independent state on 26 May 1991, exactly 73 years to the day after the proclamation of the first republic.

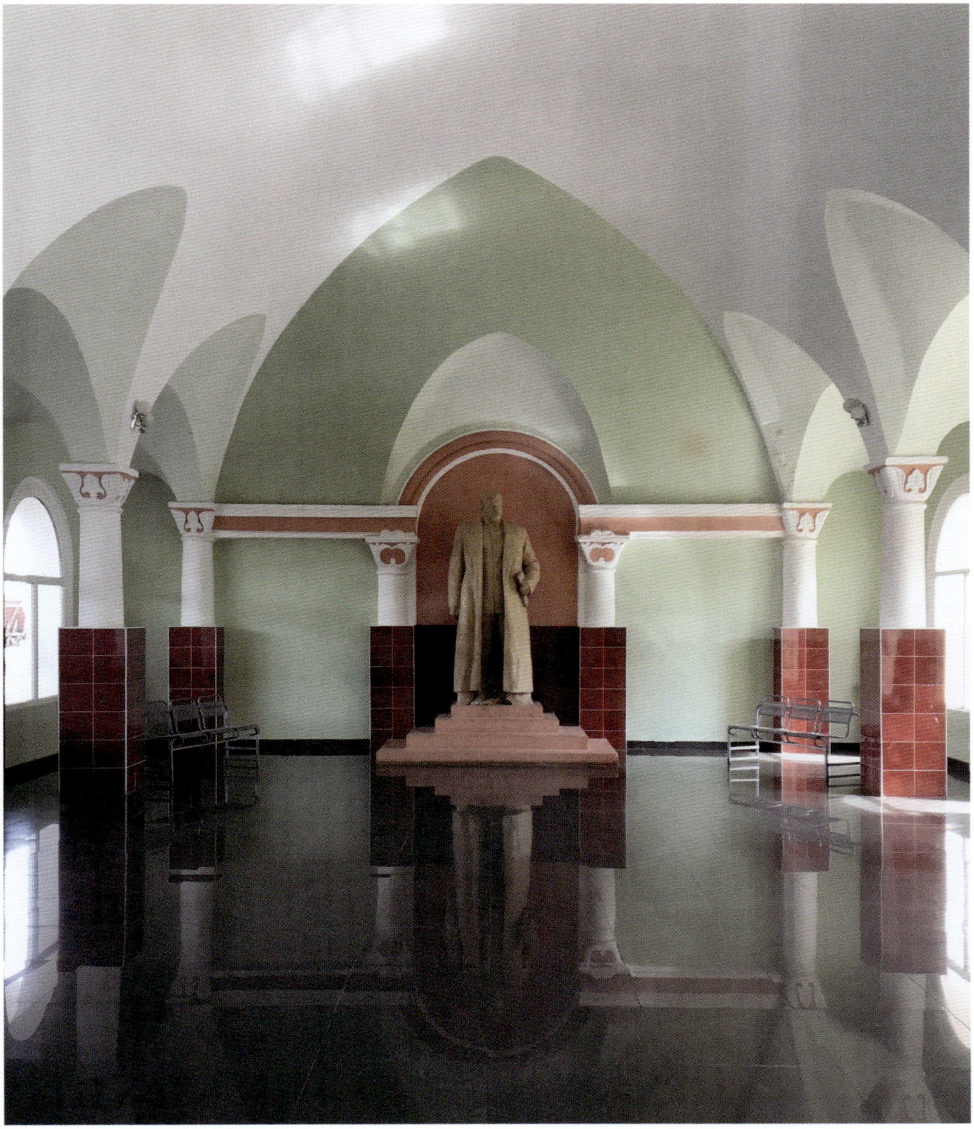

Statue of Stalin at Gori train station

The country was politically unstable and suffered from massive corruption. The confrontation with Russia led to the loss of important markets, resulting in economic and political crises. In addition, the ethnic conflicts in Abkhazia and South Ossetia, which had also been brewing during the Soviet era, flared up again with Russian support. In 2003, following popular protests against electoral fraud that favoured Eduard Shevardnadze, new elections were held in Georgia in which opposition leader Mikhail Saakashvili emerged victorious. He set about combating corruption and carried out political and economic reforms. In the 2007 elections, however, he was himself accused of electoral fraud.

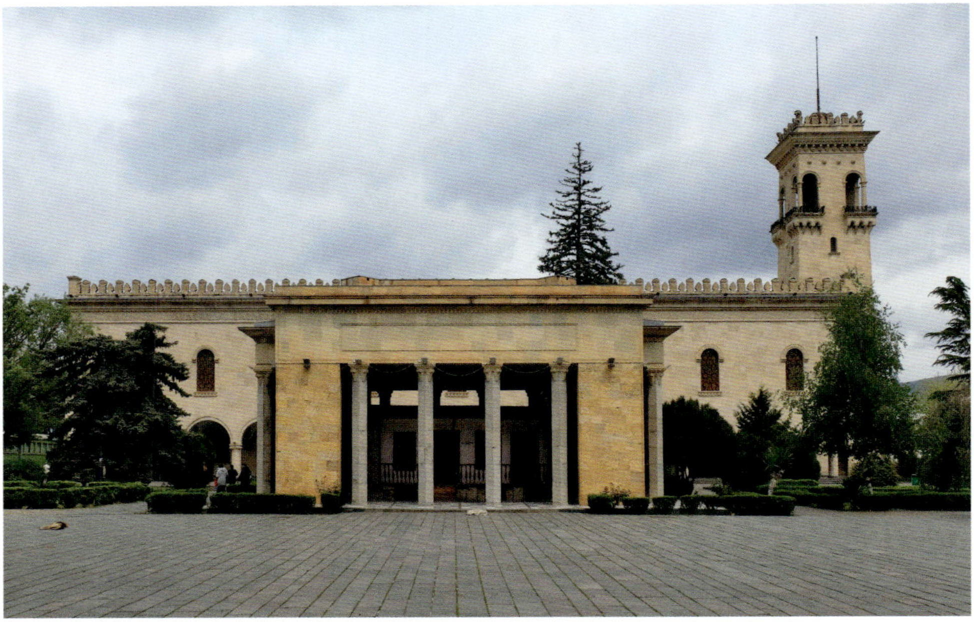

The Stalin Museum in Gori

The critical reappraisal of the past is a marginal issue in Georgia. Although the Museum of Soviet Occupation opened in 2006 as part of the National Museum, the struggle to come to terms with the communist past got off to a slow start. Communist rule was perceived as an occupation regime, and an appreciation of the extent of collaboration and Georgian participation in communist rule in Georgia was accordingly largely neglected. In Gori, Stalin's birthplace, the Stalin Museum, which dates back to the Soviet era, is still in operation, with the house where he was born as the central element of the exhibition. Stalin is portrayed as a wise and great leader. The mass crimes committed under his rule are not discussed. However, there are plans to redesign the museum in the future. Stalin-worship in Gori even goes so far as to reserve a waiting room of its own for a statue of Stalin at the local railway station.

On the other hand, there are no monuments commemorating the victims of repression or marking secret service centres, camps or prison sites. Historical reappraisal today is primarily a matter for NGOs such as SovLab, whose projects are committed to a critical examination of the past.

Museum of Soviet Occupation

Tbilisi. On 26 May 2006, an exhibition on the history of the Soviet occupation between 1921 and 1991 opened in the Georgian National Museum. The exhibition was funded by the Georgian Presidential Reserve Fund. More than 3,000 exhibits—archival documents, photographs, video material and everyday objects—and installations are presented over an exhibition area of around 700 square metres. A number of the objects on display come from public organisations, the families of victims and former dissidents.

The entrance area to the exhibition is made up of two deliberately juxtaposed displays. One is a bullet-ridden freight car in which the participants of the 1924 national uprising were shot, accompanied by pictures of Lenin to symbolise Soviet aggression against Georgia. Directly opposite is an installation that uses a portrait of Putin to evoke Russian support for the breakaway regions of Abkhazia and South Ossetia and the Caucasus War of 2008. The actual exhibition is arranged chronologically and leads visitors along a timeline illustrated with numerous photographs depicting the fall of the government under Noe Zhordania in 1921, the annexation of Georgia by the Soviet Union in 1922, the "Great Terror" of 1937/38 and the events of the Second World War, Stalin's death in March 1953 and the bloody suppression of the peaceful independence demonstration in Tbilisi by the Soviet army in April 1989. The repression of the Soviet regime is conveyed through various visual images, such as cell doors, which represent imprisonment and incarceration. An enlarged historical photograph just behind the entrance shows soldiers armed with rifles next to the bodies of executed victims. The names of the victims are written in red letters on a concrete wall. The traditional Georgian dress of the national hero Kakutsa Cholokashvili, who led the uprising in 1924 and escaped from the country after its suppression, is on display in a glass showcase.

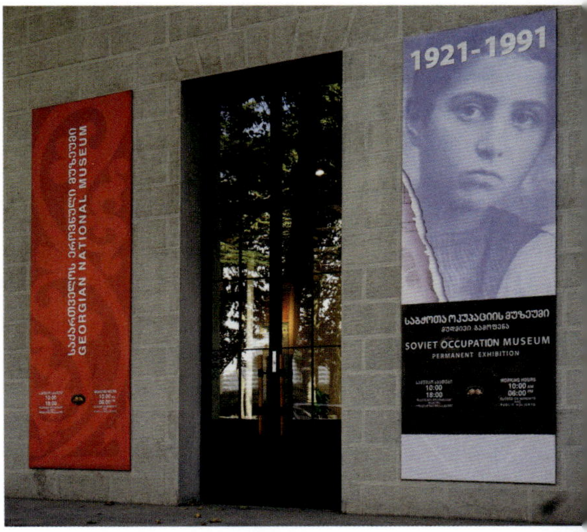

►
Entrance to the Museum of Soviet Occupation

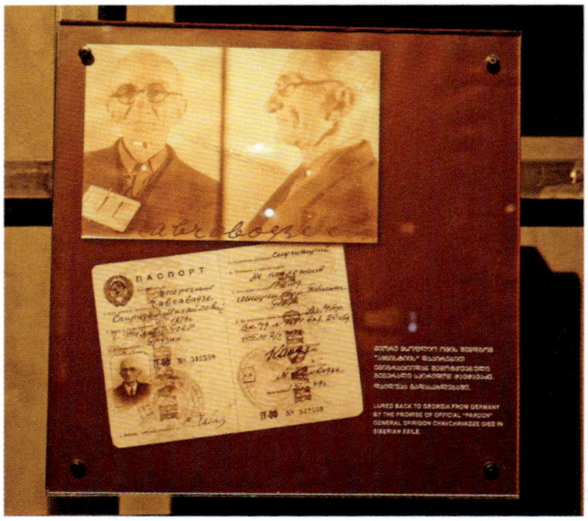

Photos of the victims of Soviet repression in Georgia

down:
View of the exhibition

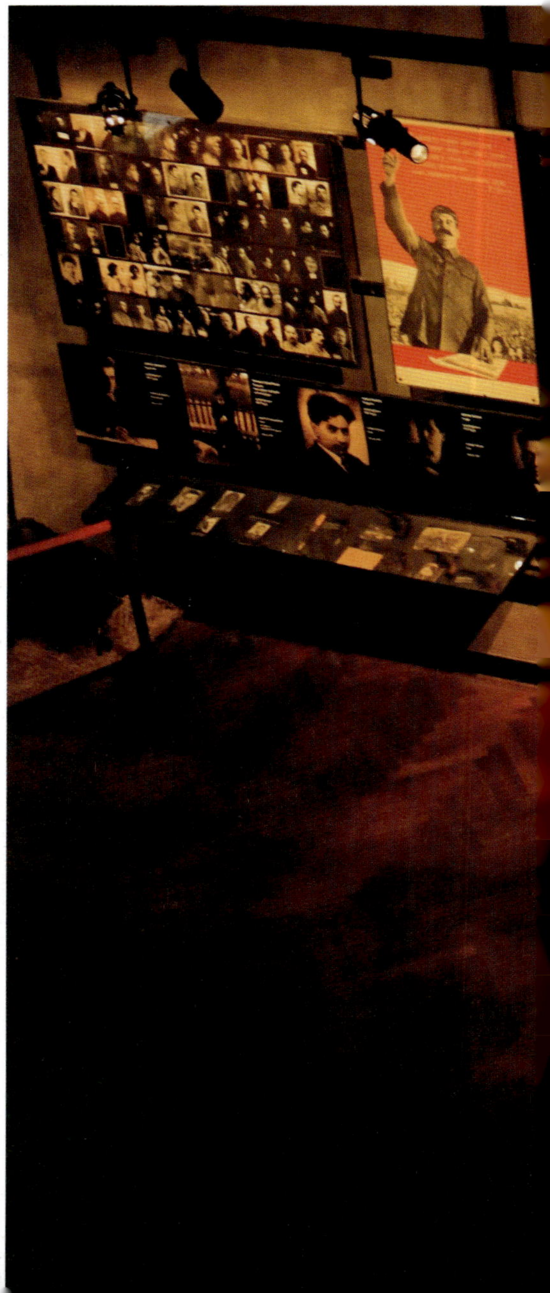

Location: Tbilisi, Rustaveli Avenue, on the fourth floor of the Georgian National Museum
Internet: www.museum.ge

Further reading:
Batiashvilli, Nutsa: Das Museum der sowjetischen Okkupation in Georgien. In: Religion und Gesellschaft in Ost und West (RGOW), 2016, No. 5, pp. 20f. / Rukhadze, Vasili: Reinterpretations of Soviet History in Georgia and the Post-Soviet Space: Never-Ending Battle. In: Eurasia Daily Monitor, 2012, Vol. 9, Nr. 212. Available online at: www.jamestown.org/program/reinterpretations-of-soviet-history-in-georgia-and-the-post-soviet-space-never-ending-battle/#.VrHVSebo_Wo (last accessed on: 01/12/2017).

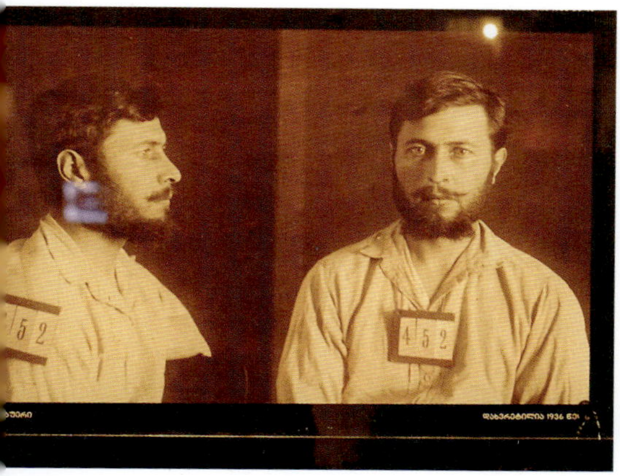
დახვრეტილია 1936

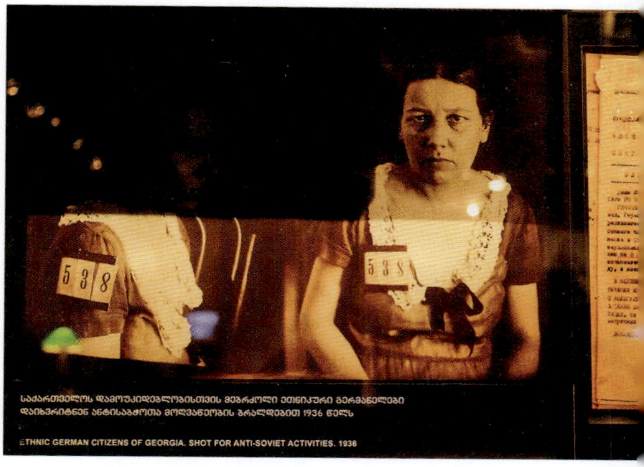
საქართველოს დამოუკიდებლობისთვის მებრძოლი ეთნიკური გერმანელები
დაიხვრიტნენ ანტისაბჭოთა მოღვაწეობის ბრალდებით 1936 წელს
ETHNIC GERMAN CITIZENS OF GEORGIA. SHOT FOR ANTI-SOVIET ACTIVITIES. 1936

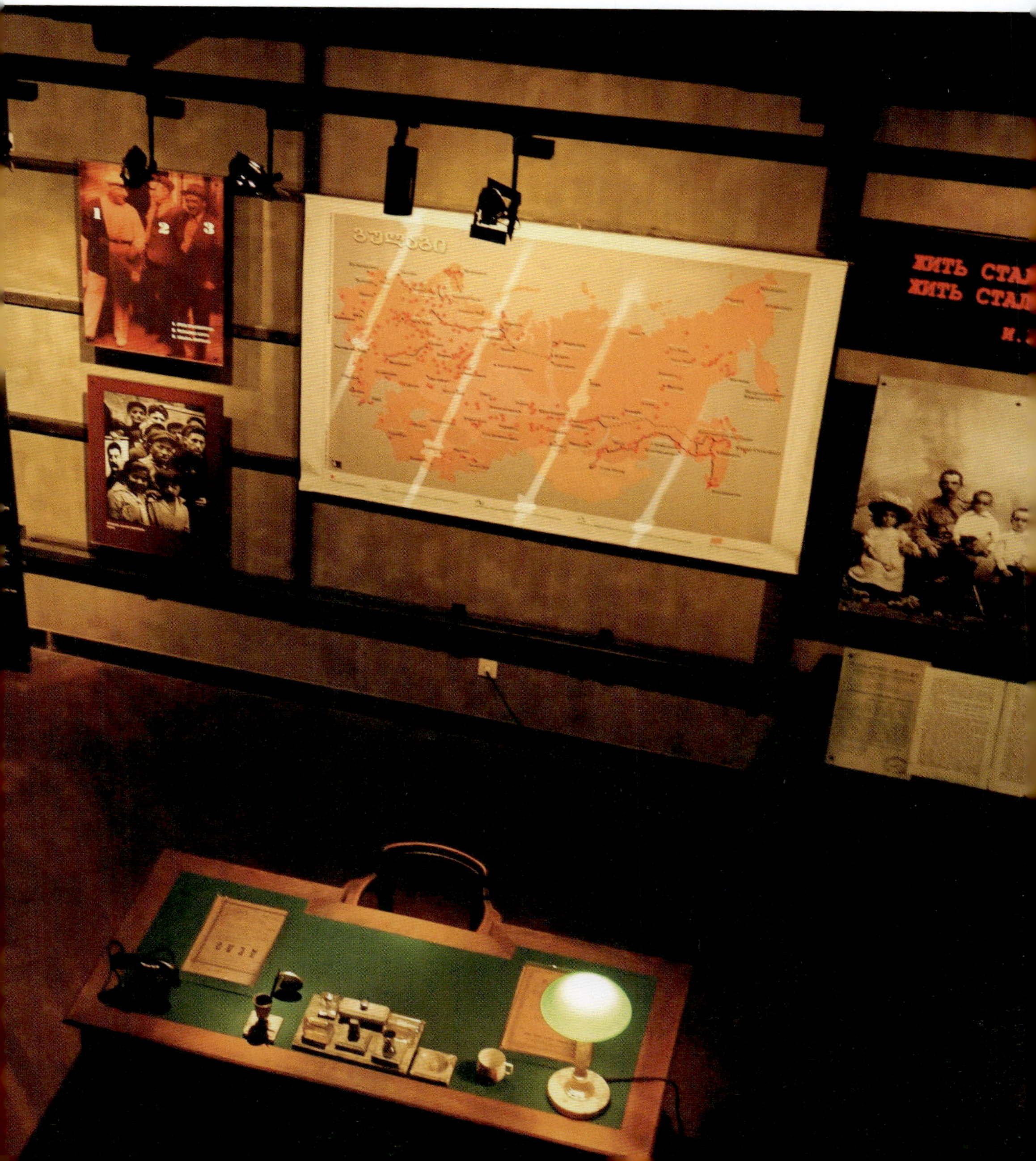
გულაგი

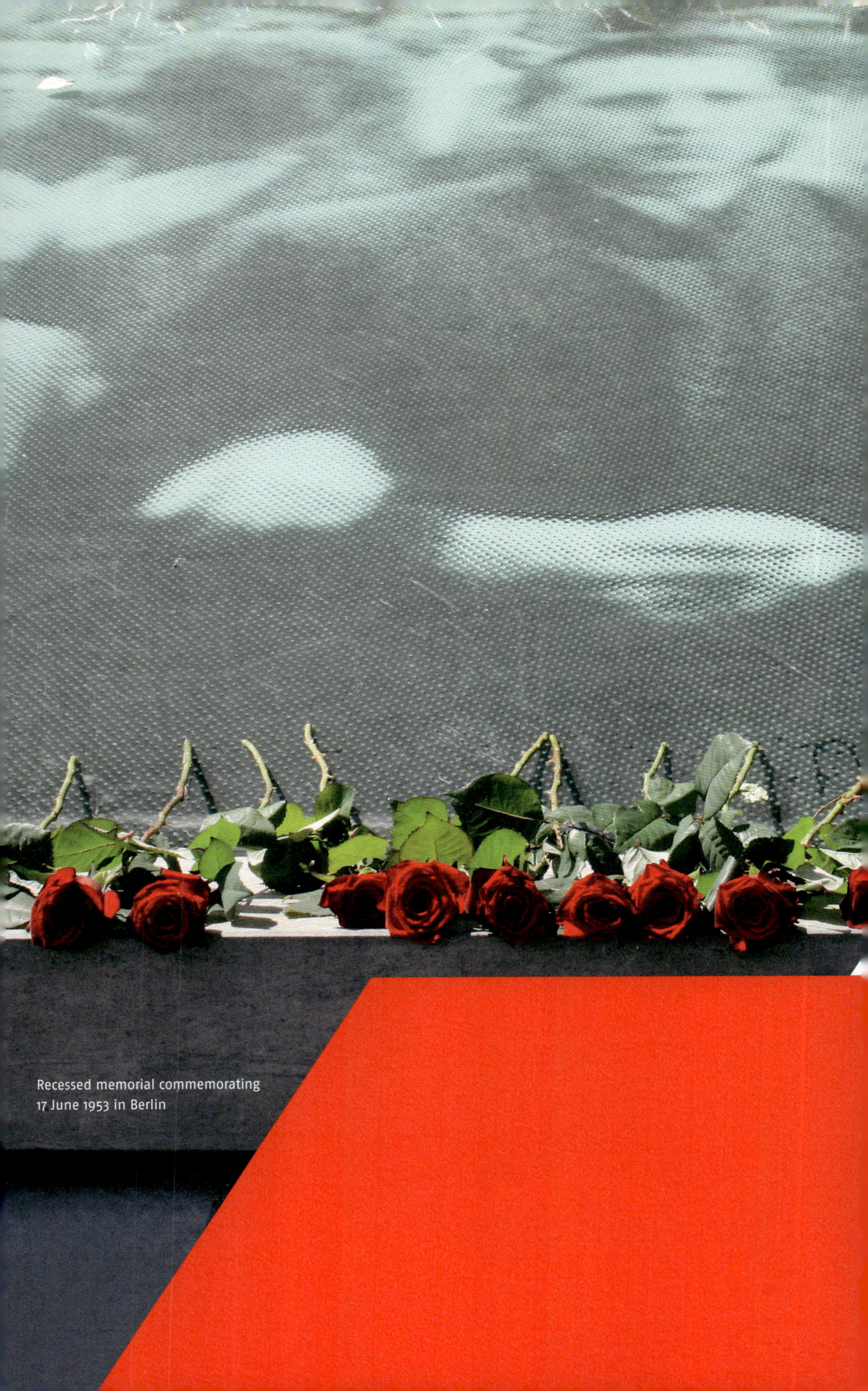

Recessed memorial commemorating
17 June 1953 in Berlin

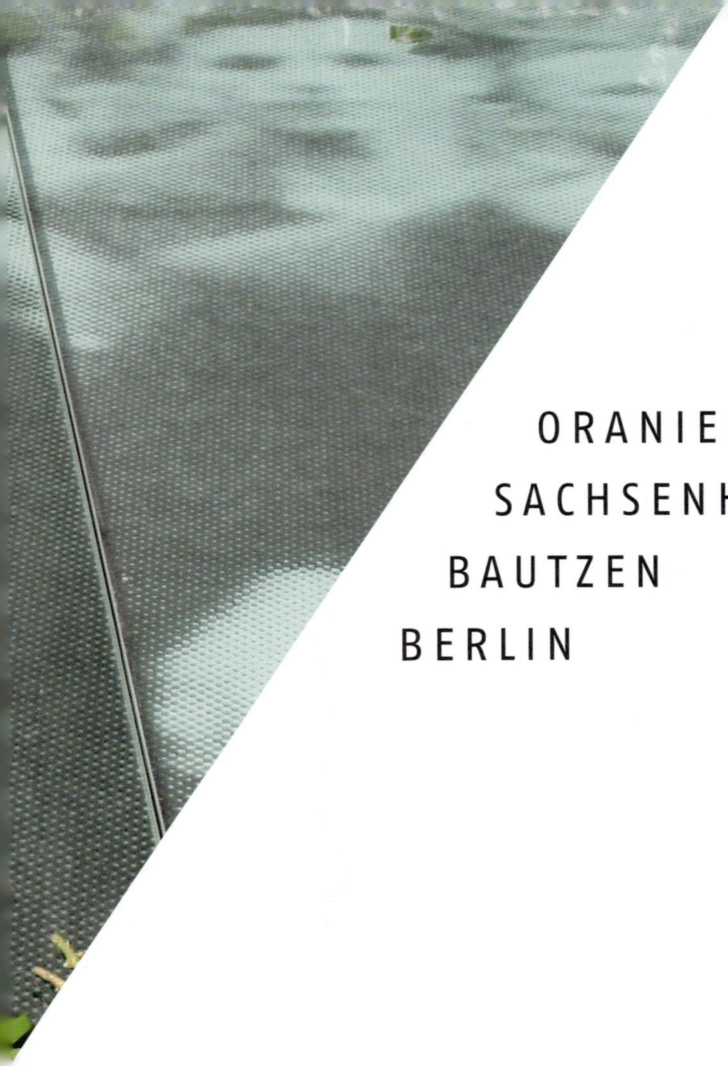

ORANIENBURG / SACHSENHAUSEN
BAUTZEN
BERLIN

Germany

Memorials and commemorative sites dedicated to the memory of resistance and persecution and to the victims of the dictatorship in the SOZ/GDR were inaugurated in Germany long before the fall of the SED regime. In West Germany and West Berlin, there were already more than 60 commemorative markers by 1989, which mainly served as reminders of the division of Germany, the victims of the border regime and the People's Uprising of 17 June 1953. The first memorial stone for the victims of Stalinism, the result of an initiative of former prisoners of the Soviet special camps who were able to flee to West Germany after their release, was set up in Berlin-Charlottenburg on 4 November 1951.

In the GDR itself, there were no official memorials to post-war resistance and political persecution until 1989. Official places and acts of remembrance, admonition and commemoration were dedicated exclusively to the victims of Nazi persecution. Politically instrumentalised and subordinated to the interests of the SED, these focused on communist resistance to the Nazi regime.

The largest space in the memorial landscape, which is dedicated to the second dictatorship and expanded rapidly after 1989/90, is taken up by the commemoration of the division of Germany. More than 300 memorials and museums along what used to be the internal German border and the course of the Berlin Wall commemorate the division and its victims. They document the forced resettlements and the many, often fatal attempts to escape through the Iron Curtain. Finally, numerous markers in the public space raise awareness of the Peaceful Revolution and the opening of the border in the autumn of 1989.

Another important place in the topography of memory is occupied by the more than 80 sites dedicated to repression and resistance and the victims of Stalinist terror in the 1940s and 1950s. These include the "memorials with a 'double past'", the redesign of which was the subject of fierce controversy in the 1990s: former Nazi concentration camps such as Buchenwald and Sachsenhausen, which remained in use as special camps under the Soviet military administration after 1945, prisons such as the "Roter Ochse" (Red Ox) in Halle, Münchner Platz in Dresden, Moritzplatz in Magdeburg, Demmlerplatz in Schwerin, and the prisons in Bautzen, where victims of political persecution were imprisoned both before and after 1945.

The fact that the Soviet occupying power imprisoned Nazi functionaries, political opponents and victims of denunciations and arbitrary arrests—one in three of whom did not survive imprisonment—alike under inhumane conditions in its special camps and prisons particularly serves to highlight the problem of "double memory". The more than 35,000 dead and those who survived imprisonment, many of whom consequently suffered from severe health effects, are seen as victims of an inhumane prison regime that cries out for appropriate commemoration. More than 40 memorial sites near former camps and prisons or mass graves alone contribute to meeting this need.

Another focus is on memorial sites and markers commemorating the injustices committed in the GDR by the Ministry of State Security (MfS), the Ministry of the Interior and the Volkspolizei (People's Police). These include in particular the exhibitions and documentation centres set up in former prisons and other State Security service buildings. One example is the museum in the "Runde Ecke" (Round Corner) in Leipzig, which was set up after the city's MfS district administration was occupied by the local citizens' committee. There are also permanent exhibitions in the former prisons and the MfS headquarters in Berlin-Hohenschönhausen, Magdeburg and Halle, and in the former MfS headquarters in Berlin's Normannenstrasse, with its "Mielke Suite", which attract many interested visitors.

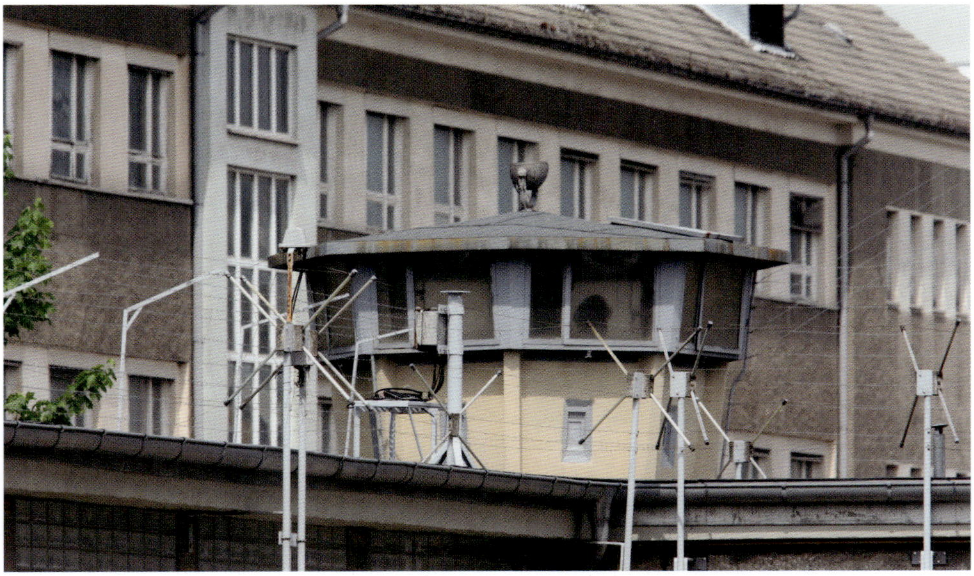

Watchtower at the former Stasi prison
in Berlin-Hohenschönhausen

In addition, 50 commemorative markers at the local and regional level commemorate persecution and repression by the state apparatus. These also include sites that were used as prisons until very recently or still are to this day, such as Waldheim, Brandenburg and Torgau. Some of these had been used to detain political prisoners since the 19th century and continued to serve this purpose, especially during the Nazi era. Even in GDR times, the buildings served as prisons for victims of political persecution; some of them are still in use as prisons to this day. In most cases, plaques or memorial stones highlight the historical background to the political persecution that occurred in these places.

Last but not least, a large group is comprised of more than 70 commemorative markers relating to the events of 17 June 1953 and its victims. More than 50 further memorials commemorate the events of the autumn of 1989, which presaged the fall of the Berlin Wall on 9 November and German Reunification.

New ways of marking historical sites have also emerged that recall political persecution, German division, opposition and resistance. These include the "Green Belt" along the 1,381-kilometre length of the former inner-German border and the "Berlin Wall History Mile", which, with its demarcation line set into streets and pavements, retraces the Wall that has been almost completely expunged from the Berlin cityscape.

Altogether there are more than 900 commemorative markers, memorial sites and museums in Germany that bear witness to the dictatorship in the Soviet Occupation Zone and the GDR. Three of them are presented below. The third edition of "Orte des Erinnerns: Gedenkzeichen, Gedenkstätten und Museen zur Diktatur in SBZ und DDR" (Places of Remembering: Memorials and Museums to the Dictatorship in the Soviet Occupied Zone and the GDR), which was published by Ch. Links Verlag in March 2016, provides an overview of all the memorial sites.

Memorial and Museum "Soviet Special Camp No. 7 / No. 1" Sachsenhausen

Oranienburg / Sachsenhausen. Only a few kilometres north of Berlin lies the extensive complex of the Sachsenhausen Memorial and Museum. Used as a concentration camp from 1936 to 1945, the Soviet secret police, the NKVD, maintained the largest of the ten special camps in the Soviet Occupation Zone here from 1945 to 1950. In 1961, the Sachsenhausen National Memorial was opened here, but, for as long as the GDR was in existence, it commemorated only the horrors of the Nazi concentration camp. After 1990, chapters of the camp's story that had hitherto been kept secret and previously taboo groups of victims were included in the public exhibition. Since 1993, the memorial has belonged to the Brandenburg Memorials Foundation and has been extensively redesigned.

Today, it is a memorial site for both the Nazi concentration camp and the Soviet special camp. The history of Sachsenhausen and its various phases is presented and documented in a decentralised museum concept. A visitor centre opened in the entrance area in 2004 introduces the complex history of the site.

In the immediate vicinity of the memorial are three mass graves of the Soviet special camp, designated as cemeteries, where 12,000 people were anonymously buried. Since the autumn of 2006, Szczypiorski House, an International Youth Venue and Youth Hostel which is located in the former official residence of the "Concentration Camps Inspectorate", has been attached to the memorial.

Sachsenhausen concentration camp was built in the summer of 1936 by prisoners from the Emsland camps. It was the first concentration camp to be founded after the appointment of Reichsführer-SS Heinrich Himmler as the chief of the German police in 1936. As a model and training camp for the SS and concentration camps in the immediate vicinity of the German capital, Sachsenhausen occupied a special place in the system of National Socialist concentration camps: in 1938, the administrative headquarters for all concentration camps under German control was moved from Berlin to Oranienburg.

The concentration camp complex in Oranienburg, covering almost 400 hectares, included extensive housing for the higher SS ranks and their families, the "Klinkerwerk" satellite camp built by the Lehnitz Lock in 1938 and extensive logistical and military areas for the SS.

Between 1936 and 1945, the National Socialists held more than 200,000 people from around 40 nations in the Sachsenhausen concentration camp. At first, the SS imprisoned political opponents of the Nazi regime here: communists, social democrats, liberal and conservative politicians, followed increasingly by socially and racially persecuted people, such as Jews, Christians, Jehovah's Witnesses, Sinti

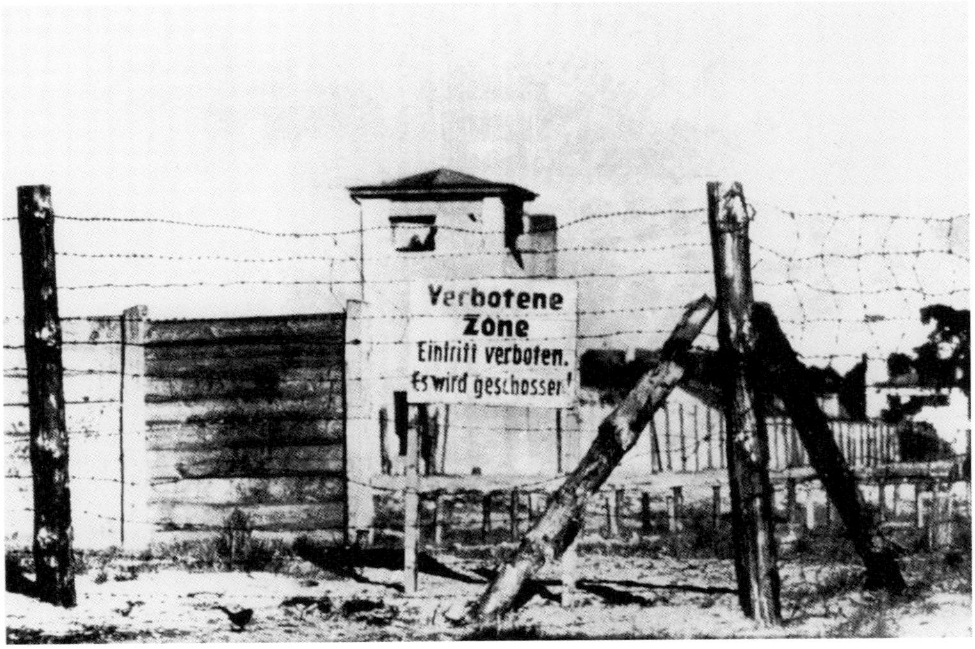

Historical photo of Sachsenhausen concentration camp

and Roma, and homosexuals. In March and June 1938, as part of the Reichskriminalpolizeiamt's "Arbeitsscheu Reich" ("workshy Reich") campaign, the SS brought 6,000 people classified as "anti-socials" into the camp. After the pogrom night of 9/10 November 1938, more than 6,000 Jews from Berlin and other parts of the German Reich were deported to Sachsenhausen.

Following the beginning of the Second World War on 1 September 1939, an increasing number of prisoners from the German-occupied countries of Europe arrived in Sachsenhausen. Due to the constantly growing number of detainees, the conditions of detention deteriorated rapidly. Thousands died of malnutrition, illness, exhaustion or maltreatment or were murdered by the SS in special "operations". In the late summer and autumn of 1941, more than 10,000 Soviet prisoners of war were killed by the SS within a few weeks in a specially built "Genickschussanlage", a facility for shooting prisoners in the back of the neck. Another 3,000 died in transit or shortly after arrival at the camp. A crematorium with incinerator had previously been installed in 1940; in 1942, the SS erected a new building in the industrial yard containing four incinerators, another facility for execution by bullet to the back of the neck and (from 1943) a gas chamber.

Countless prisoners fell victim to "extermination through labour". The prisoners had to perform forced labour for the SS or the weapons industry in SS-owned factories and in around 100 subcamps. The large arms companies such as Allgemeine Elektrizitäts-Gesellschaft (AEG), Siemens & Halske, DEMAG-Panzerwerk, Heinkel Flugzeugwerke, Daimler-Benz-Werken, and IG Farben all benefited from the greater involvement of the concentration camps in war production from 1942 onwards. Several tens of thousands of people died in the Sachsenhausen concentration camp. Shortly before the end of the war, the camp was evacuated, leaving behind about 3,000 prisoners who were not

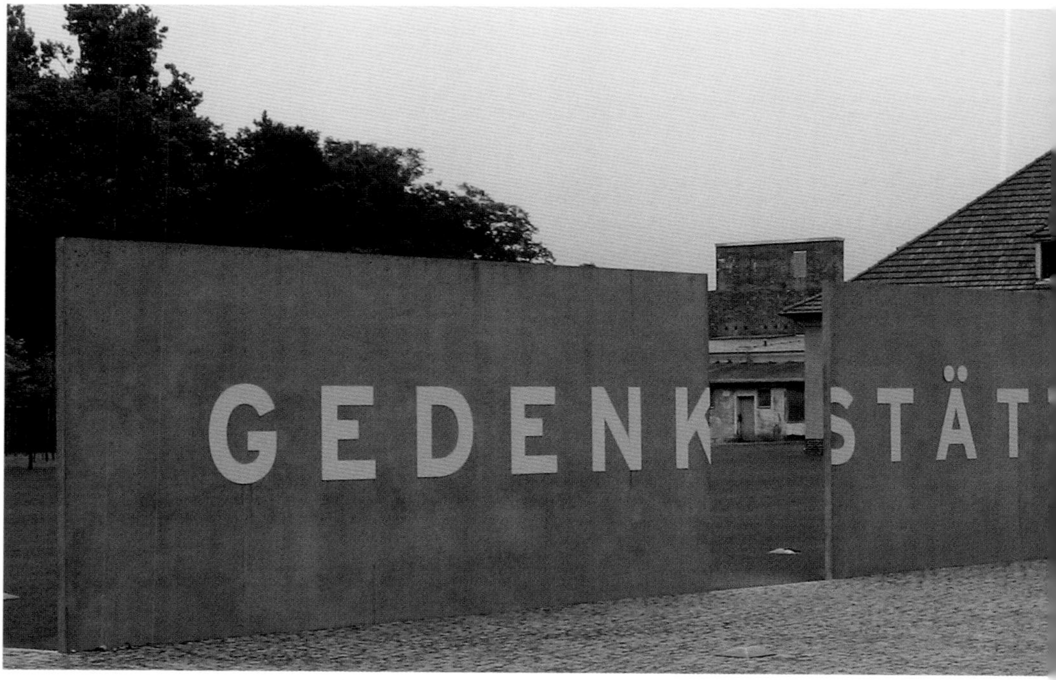

Entrance to the Memorial
and Museum Sachsenhausen

"fit to march". They were liberated on 22/23 April 1945 by Soviet and Polish units. More than 35,000 prisoners had been forced to leave the barracks two days earlier but were liberated by units of American and Soviet troops on their "death march" to Schwerin. Many, however, did not survive the march.

From August 1945, the former concentration camp was used as "Special Camp No. 7" by the Soviet secret police, the NKVD. The first transport, with 150 prisoners of the so-called "Vorkommando" (advance party), arrived in Sachsenhausen on 10 August to prepare the accommodation barracks to receive further prisoners, in particular to repair the damage to the security systems. On the morning of 16 August, 5,000 prisoners started their march 40 kilometres away in Weesow. They arrived in Sachsenhausen in the evening and were placed in the triangular barracks area in what was referred to as Zone I. By the end of 1945, more than 11,000 people had been imprisoned in Sachsenhausen.

A total of 30,000 people were brought to Sachsenhausen as detainees pursuant to order No. 00315. These prisoners had been pre-emptively arrested in accordance with the provisions of the Potsdam Agreement and remained imprisoned under inhumane conditions for years without a formal court ruling. Among them were mainly lower and middle NSDAP functionaries such as "Blockleiter" and "Zellenleiter". The internment lists also include members of the SS, Gestapo and concentration camp guards, employees of Nazi ministries and authorities, young people, ordinary members of Nazi youth organisations, political opponents and arbitrarily arrested persons.

At the beginning of 1946, a new group of prisoners arrived in the camp. These were housed in zone II, a separate area of the camp away from the other internees, and were 6,000

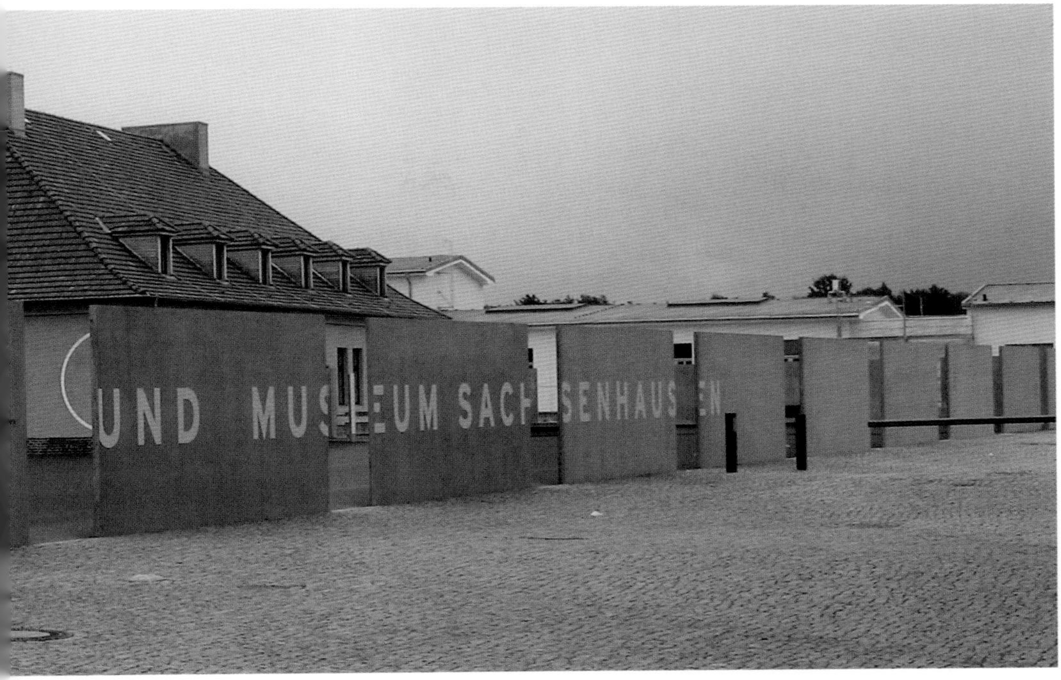

former officers of the German Wehrmacht who had been released from Western Allied captivity and re-imprisoned by the NKVD upon entering the Soviet Occupation Zone and were finally deported via Sachsenhausen to the Soviet Union for forced labour.

On 16 and 17 September 1946, the NKVD transferred the first prisoners convicted by a Soviet Military Tribunal (SMT) to the Sachsenhausen special camp. These came from the Mecklenburg prisons of Alt-Strelitz and Güstrow. In total, more than 16,500 SMT convicts were imprisoned in Sachsenhausen. Most convictions were based on the infamous section 58 of the 1927 Criminal Code of the Russian Soviet Federative Socialist Republic. The range of grounds for detention found in Soviet records is broad: espionage, possession of weapons, anti-Soviet propaganda, "werewolf" activity (resistance behind enemy lines), illegal group formation, Nazi crimes, theft, economic crimes, traffic accidents with property damage and personal injury, complicity, and many more. The legitimacy of these accusations remains unclear in many cases, but it can be assumed that the arrests were often arbitrary and the confessions extorted under torture.

Most of the prisoners were German men. The 7,500 foreigners—mainly Russians, Ukrainians and Poles—included numerous Russian emigrants persecuted by the Soviet secret services, Soviet prisoners of war, former forced labourers and soldiers of the Red Army, but also members of Vlasov's army. The camp administration kept them in separate barracks isolated from the other prisoners. Most Russian emigrants and citizens of the Soviet Union were only held in Sachsenhausen for a few months until they were transported to the penal camps of the Soviet Gulag or executed in the Soviet Union. Between 1945 and 1950, the Soviet occupying power held a total of 60,000 prisoners in Sachsenhausen. At least 12,000 prisoners died there from malnutrition, cold and disease.

Unlike their equivalents in the Soviet Union, the special camps were not labour camps, which meant that the prisoners were forced to remain inactive. The prisoners were strictly forbidden from any contact with the outside world ("silent camps"). Catastrophic hygienic and sanitary conditions prevailed, compounded by inadequate nutrition. Inevitably, diseases and epidemics spread.

Approximately 5,000 prisoners were released from "Special Camp No. 7" after the official completion of denazification in the Soviet Occupation Zone in 1948. Until the dissolution of the Soviet special camps in the GDR in the spring of 1950, the camp in Sachsenhausen remained in operation as "Special Camp No. 1". In January and February 1950, a total of about 8,000 prisoners were released, and around 260 were deported to camps in the Soviet Union. The Soviet secret police handed several thousand prisoners over to the GDR authorities. Of these prisoners, 550 were convicted in the "Waldheim Trials".

Until the opening of the memorial in 1961, the camp was used as a training ground for the National People's Army. After decades of silence about the special camp in the GDR National Memorial, the discovery of the mass graves in 1990 marked the beginning of the process of addressing the "second" history of Sachsenhausen. A first memorial stone in honour of the victims of Stalinist abuse was inaugurated in the area connecting Zone I and Zone II as early as 1990. Outside the Sachsenhausen memorial site, on Carl-Gustav-Hempel-Strasse, the victims of the special camp are commemorated with a memorial stone at the "An der Düne" mass grave. There is also another mass grave in Schmachtenhagen Forest. The largest of the three mass graves to the immediate north-east of the camp was converted into a cemetery with a memorial stone by the Arbeitsgemeinschaft Lager Sachsenhausen 1945 – 1950 e.V. (Sachsenhausen Camp Association).

In December 2001, the museum named "Soviet Special Camp No. 7 / No. 1 in Sachsenhausen 1945 – 1950" opened to the public. The permanent exhibition covers an area of over 350 square metres and documents the construction, organisation and everyday prison life in the camp as well as its public perception in the East and the West. One focus of the exhibition is on the presentation of 27 biographies of prisoners held in the special camp. The museum includes two of the original stone barracks from Zone II in the immediate vicinity. These two buildings document daily life in the camp. The memorial site also includes a library and an archive. Guided tours or themed special tours with an introductory film are available by appointment.

In 2010, a book with the names of almost 12,000 dead from the special camps in Weesow and Sachsenhausen was published with the support of the Foundation for the Study of the Communist Dictatorship in Eastern Germany.

Location: Oranienburg,
Strasse der Nationen 22
Internet: www.stiftung-bg.de

Bautzen Memorial

Bautzen. The name of this East Saxon city is closely associated in the public consciousness with political persecution and imprisonment in the 20th century. "Ab nach Bautzen" (Off to Bautzen) was a common expression during the SED regime which made it clear that this place was primarily associated with political imprisonment. In both West and East Germany, "Yellow Misery" and "Stasi Prison" have become bywords for political injustices committed during the Soviet occupation and the SED dictatorship between 1945 and 1989.

Bautzen includes Bautzen I Prison, which became known as "Yellow Misery", and Bautzen II Prison, which gained notoriety as the "Stasi Prison". Bautzen I was built from yellow clinker bricks on the outskirts of the city at the beginning of the 20th century. At around the same time, Bautzen II Prison was built in the immediate vicinity of the Bautzen District Court. The 134 cells were used as remand facilities and for prisoners serving short prison sentences. The inauguration of both prisons was intended to implement the reformist ideas of a modern, humane prison system.

After the beginning of Nazi rule, many of the reforms of previous years were reversed. Prisons in the German Reich were crucial to the implementation of the Nazi dictatorship. The Bautzen prisons, too, were placed in the service of the policy of judicial terror practised by the National Socialists. From May 1933, both prisons were officially administered by prison director Dr Rudolph Plischke as detention centres for criminals and juvenile delinquents. In addition to criminal detainees, both prisons held victims of racial and religious persecution, as well as communists and social democrats, Jews and Jehovah's Witnesses. During the Second World War, political opponents within Nazi Germany ("radio criminals", "war economy criminals", "war effort subverters", etc.) were joined by prisoners from the countries occupied by Germany: Czechs, Poles, Belgians, Dutch, Norwegians and French. These men and women prisoners were forced to work for the armaments industry during the war.

After the end of the Second World War and with the occupation of Saxony by the Red Army, the NKVD set up a so-called special camp on the site of the "Yellow Misery" in 1945. This was initially meant to serve as an internment camp on the basis of Allied resolutions to isolate functionaries and those implicated in the National Socialist regime. Soon, however, the Bautzen special camp became dedicated mainly to the imprisonment of victims of tyranny and denunciation and of political opponents of the Stalinist system, which remained its primary function until 1956. The camp's inhumane detention conditions cost the lives of over 3,000 people. From 1950 to 1989, Bautzen I

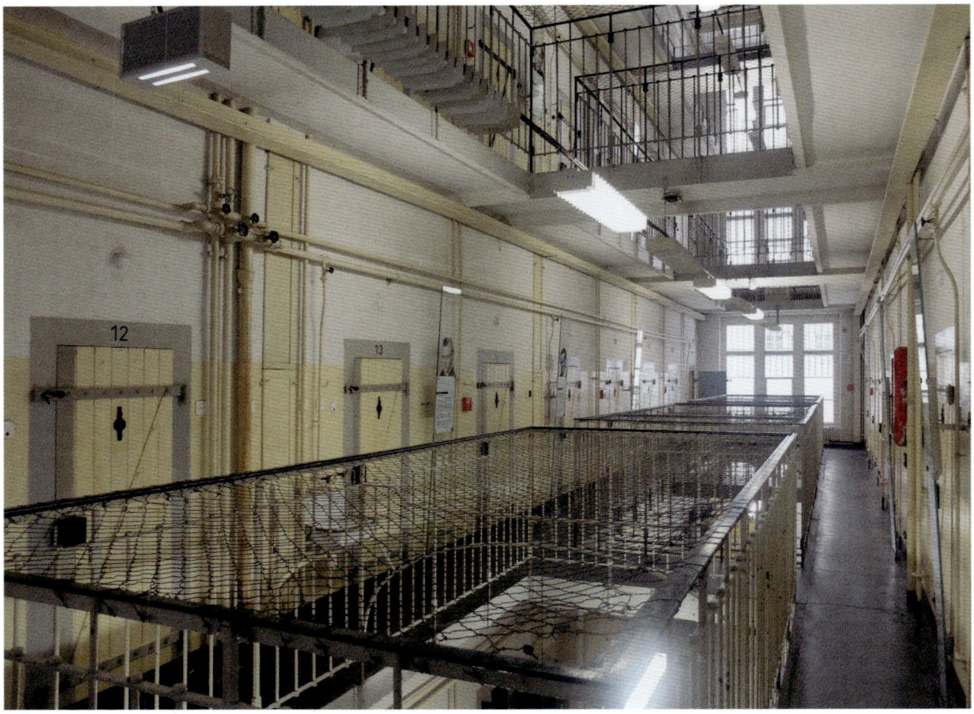

Former cell wing in Bautzen II Prison

was one of the largest prisons in the GDR, mainly holding political prisoners and criminals until the Peaceful Revolution in the autumn of 1989.

Bautzen I Prison of the Free State of Saxony has been in use since 1990 and remains a prison to this day. Bautzen II was a remand prison until 1945 and fulfilled the same function for the NKVD in the immediate post-war period. Many of the detainees were convicted by a Soviet Military Tribunal (SMT) based in the former District Court. Most of these judgements, however, were politically motivated. The charges were often fabricated, and the confessions extorted by torture. A new chapter began in 1956, when the Ministry of State Security (MfS) created its only prison with a "special facility for enemies of the state" (Bautzen II was never directly subordinated to the MfS, which had only special access rights).

Between August 1956 and the end of 1989, the GDR secret police sent around 2,000 men and 400 women to serve their sentences here. In addition to dissidents, GDR citizens and foreigners—in most cases West German citizens—who had been convicted of alleged or actual espionage, assisting refugees or "Republikflucht" (the offence of deserting the GDR) were imprisoned here. But members of the army and MfS, along with SED and economic functionaries convicted of criminal offences, were also among those detained. All inmates of the special prison were in the crosshairs of the MfS: for political reasons, they were not permitted to serve their sentences in one of the GDR's regular prisons.

Although it was located in the city, hardly any information filtered out of this "House of Silence". Many residents thought that Bautzen II was still being used as a remand prison for the neighbouring court. It was not until the collapse of the SED regime that the political prisoners were able to leave Bautzen II.

In early 1992, the former "Stasi Prison" Bautzen II was finally closed as a prison, and the dedication of the Bautzen Committee, an association of former political prisoners, finally led the following year to its declaration as a memorial site by the Free State of Saxony. Since 1994, the Bautzen Memorial has been under the patronage of the Saxon Memorial Foundation, which is dedicated to the memory of the victims of political dictatorship. The German Federal Government and the Free State of Saxony have been supporting the foundation since 1998.

The Bautzen Memorial is located on the site of the former Stasi Special Prison Bautzen II. Despite several fire safety construction measures, the building itself has largely been left as it was in the 1980s and is perceived by visitors as authentic. The prison gives first-hand impressions of the detention conditions in the late GDR. In addition to permanent exhibitions on the individual periods of persecution, the main exhibits are the former prison itself, with all its detention areas, detention cells ("tiger cages"), isolation wing, vehicle garages and prison transports, basement workshops, open exercise yards and the old cinema room, etc. Almost all areas can be freely accessed by visitors or as part of guided tours.

The historic areas of the prison are marked with information plaques. The memorial offers visitors three permanent exhibition areas: the introductory area contains a chronological overview of the history of both prisons. An exhibition area (consisting of a central exhibition room and a mocked-up cell) documents the history of the Bautzen special camp between 1945 and 1956, while another room traces that of the "Stasi prison" Bautzen II from 1956 to 1989. Another permanent exhibition on the history of Bautzen prisons and their prisoners during National Socialism is currently in preparation. Biographical stelae in the various prison wings draw on prisoner biographies to illustrate the composition of prison society and show how many varied the paths to imprisonment were. The presentation of biographies is of particular importance at the Bautzen Memorial, as the idea is for the victims to feel that their fate has been adequately acknowledged.

As an "open place of learning", the memorial offers guided tours and projects for groups of students and visitors which are tailored to the interests, available time and previous knowledge of the groups. Contemporary witness tours and discussions take place regularly. In addition to these learning opportunities, the history of both prisons and the fate of the prisoners are communicated in a variety of ways, with concerts, readings and lectures, dance and theatre performances, film screenings, special exhibitions, panel discussions and commemorative events.

Location: Bautzen, Weigangstrasse 8
Internet: www.gedenkstaette-bautzen.de

Berlin Wall Memorial

Berlin. The Berlin Wall Memorial is the central memorial to the division of the city of Berlin and of Germany. It belongs to the Berlin Wall Foundation and, over a length of 1.4 kilometres, illustrates the consequences of the construction of the Wall on the former border strip which ran along Bernauer Strasse for the state and the city of Berlin and the surrounding area, and in particular for the lives of the people living along the road. The new permanent exhibition "1961 | 1989. The Berlin Wall" at the Documentation Centre also explains the politico-historical context of the Berlin Wall and uses biographies to illustrate the human consequences of the division.

The construction of the Berlin Wall turned Bernauer Strasse into one of the central symbols of the division of the city. The border ran along the façades of the houses on the eastern side of the border, but the pavement in front of them was already part of the western sector. Many residents spontaneously decided to flee. In the first two months after the Wall was built, 113 people left the GDR via Bernauer Strasse alone, and by 1989 there had been about 500 escape attempts. People climbed out of windows, abseiled down from higher floors or jumped into the safety nets provided by the West Berlin fire brigade. Some were seriously injured: in fact, the first casualties of the border regime were recorded in Bernauer Strasse. In order to prevent escapes from the houses, the doors and windows to Bernauer Strasse were walled up and the residents forcibly relocated. After 1963, the houses were demolished down to the facades of the ground floors so that the border troops had a clear field of vision and line of fire. Finally, the border houses were evacuated, the border strip was further extended and, in 1985, the Reconciliation Church was blown up.

After the fall of the Wall, initiatives were taken to preserve a section of the Wall as a memorial site. On 2 October 1990, the East Berlin City Council declared the 212-metre-long section of the Wall along the Sophiengemeinde cemetery a monument, and, on 13 August 1991, the Berlin Senate gave the green light to the construction of the memorial. After several years of animated discussions about the form the commemoration should take, the German Federal Government launched a competition in April 1994 for the design of a national monument to the victims of the construction of the Wall and the division of Germany. The design selected integrated the remaining border installations and used artistic means to reinforce their effect.

►

View of the permanent exhibition at the memorial site

The memorial was officially inaugurated on 13 August 1998. It consists of two seven-metre-high steel walls enclosing a 70-metre-long section of the border fortifications. This is the last section of the Berlin Wall preserved in its original configuration, with the inner wall (Hinterlandmauer), signal fence, watchtower, death strip and wall, all of which now form part of the memorial. The inscription on the monument reads: "In memory of the division of the city from August 13, 1961 to November 9, 1989, and in commemoration of the victims of Communist tyranny".

The Documentation Centre opened on 9 November 1999, and one year later the Chapel of Reconciliation was consecrated on the site of the destroyed Reconciliation Church. In 2007, an international competition was held to redesign the memorial site, which was completed in 2015. Today it covers 4.4 hectares. Its features include the "Window of Remembrance", a twelve-metre-long wall made of Corten steel. Niches were embedded in the wall featuring black and white photographs commemorating the casualties of the Berlin Wall, who number at least 140. In addition, the foundations of demolished houses were exposed, and the courses of former escape tunnels marked.

An exhibition at the adjacent Nordbahnhof S-Bahn station on the "Border and Ghost Stations in Divided Berlin" shows how the building of the Wall severed the two halves of the city's public transport system from another. The Marienfelde Refugee Centre is the second site of the Berlin Wall Foundation. This refugee transit camp in Berlin-Marienfelde, established in 1953, was a point of transit for around 1.35 million people who fled the GDR for the Federal Republic between 1949 and 1990. Today, an exhibition at the historic site recalls the causes, course and consequences of flight and emigration between the two German states.

Location: Berlin / Mitte, Visitor Centre, Bernauer Straße 119; Documentation Centre, Bernauer Strasse 111
Internet: www.berliner-mauer-gedenkstaette.de

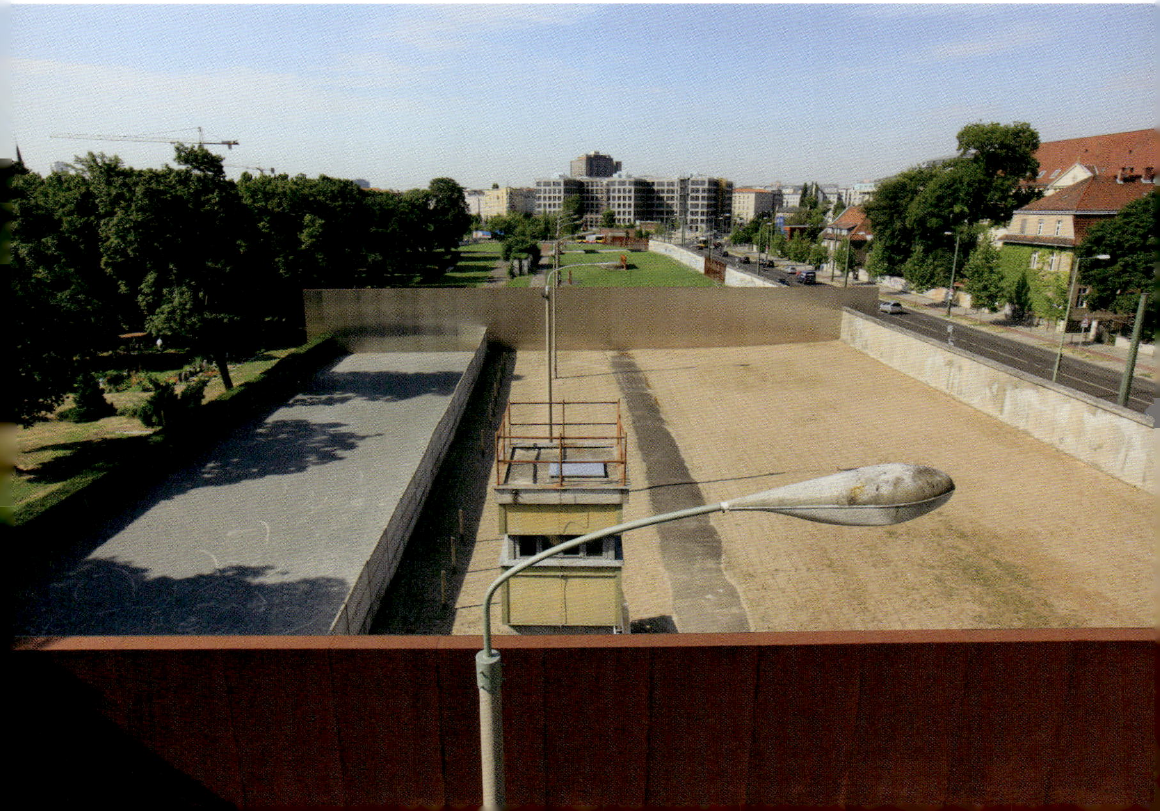

Memorial sites commemorating the People's Uprising of 17 June 1953

The People's Uprising of 17 June 1953, barely four years after the founding of the GDR, marked the first major uprising against a communist regime after the Second World War. The uprising was crushed by Soviet tanks.

According to various estimates, between 50 and 125 people, protesters and bystanders were shot and killed on 17 June in East Berlin and the GDR by Soviet soldiers and the GDR Volkspolizei (People's Police). Most of the casualties were in East Berlin, Halle, Leipzig and Magdeburg. There were also five deaths among the police and state security personnel. The victims of 17 June also included Germans who were sentenced to death and shot as "provocateurs" and "ringleaders" by Soviet courts. After the "restoration of public order", GDR courts passed four death sentences, two of which were carried out, and imposed prison sentences on about 1,800 insurgents. Soviet courts sentenced 750 protesters to forced labour. In the aftermath, the uprising and the insurgents were vilified and criminalised in the GDR. According to the official declaration by the SED leadership, the protests were a fascist coup organised and staged by Western saboteurs and provocateurs.

The desire for freedom and courage of the insurgents was celebrated in the Federal Republic. Barely two weeks after the uprising, on 3 July 1953, the German Bundestag declared 17 June the "Day of German Unity" and a public holiday. Every year on 17 June, the highest German parliament staged celebrations to commemorate the events in the GDR and the courage of the people involved. The events of June 1953 increasingly receded from public memory as time passed, superseded as they were by new uprisings in the communist sphere of influence, for example in 1956 in Hungary, 1968 in Prague and 1970 in Poland, but also due to the construction of the Wall and the policy of rapprochement and "peaceful coexistence" between East and West. Symptomatic of this is the fact that the last monument commemorating the uprising was erected in Berlin in 1963. After the construction of the Wall, beginning on 13 August 1961, the focus shifted to the division of Germany and the victims of the Wall. In 1990, 17 June was abolished as a public holiday in favour of 3 October as the "Day of German Unity"; a decision that met with consternation and was widely criticised as "historical amnesia". It is still hard to understand why the violently suppressed uprising against the communist regime in the GDR was erased from the official calendar as a day of remembrance and commemoration.

The first memorials and monuments commemorating the uprising and its victims were erected in former West Berlin. Just five days after the uprising, on 22 June 1953, the Berlin Senate decided to rename Berliner Strasse — the street running through the Tiergarten and

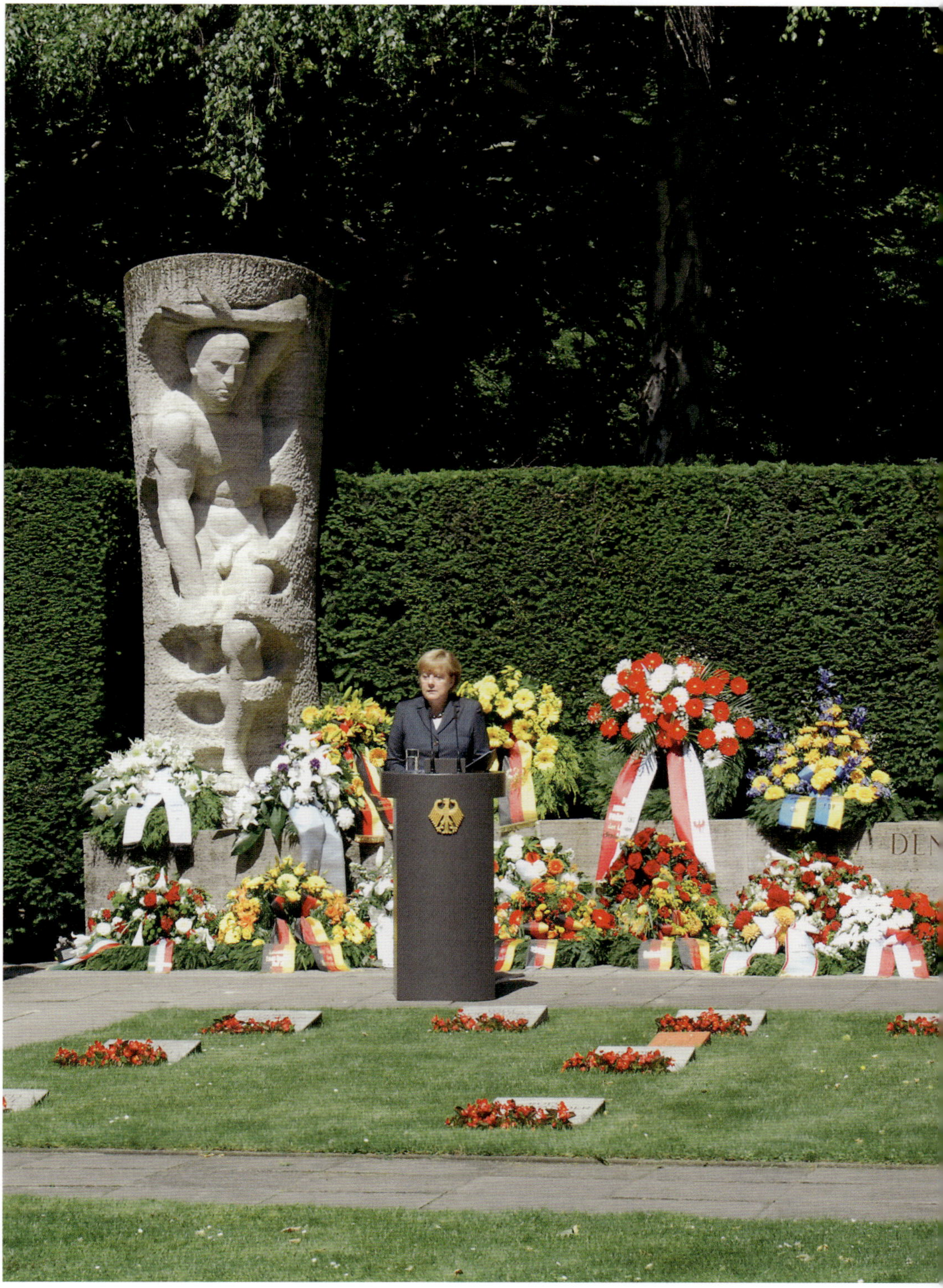

Commemoration ceremony at the central memorial
to the victims of 17 June at Seestrasse Cemetery in Berlin

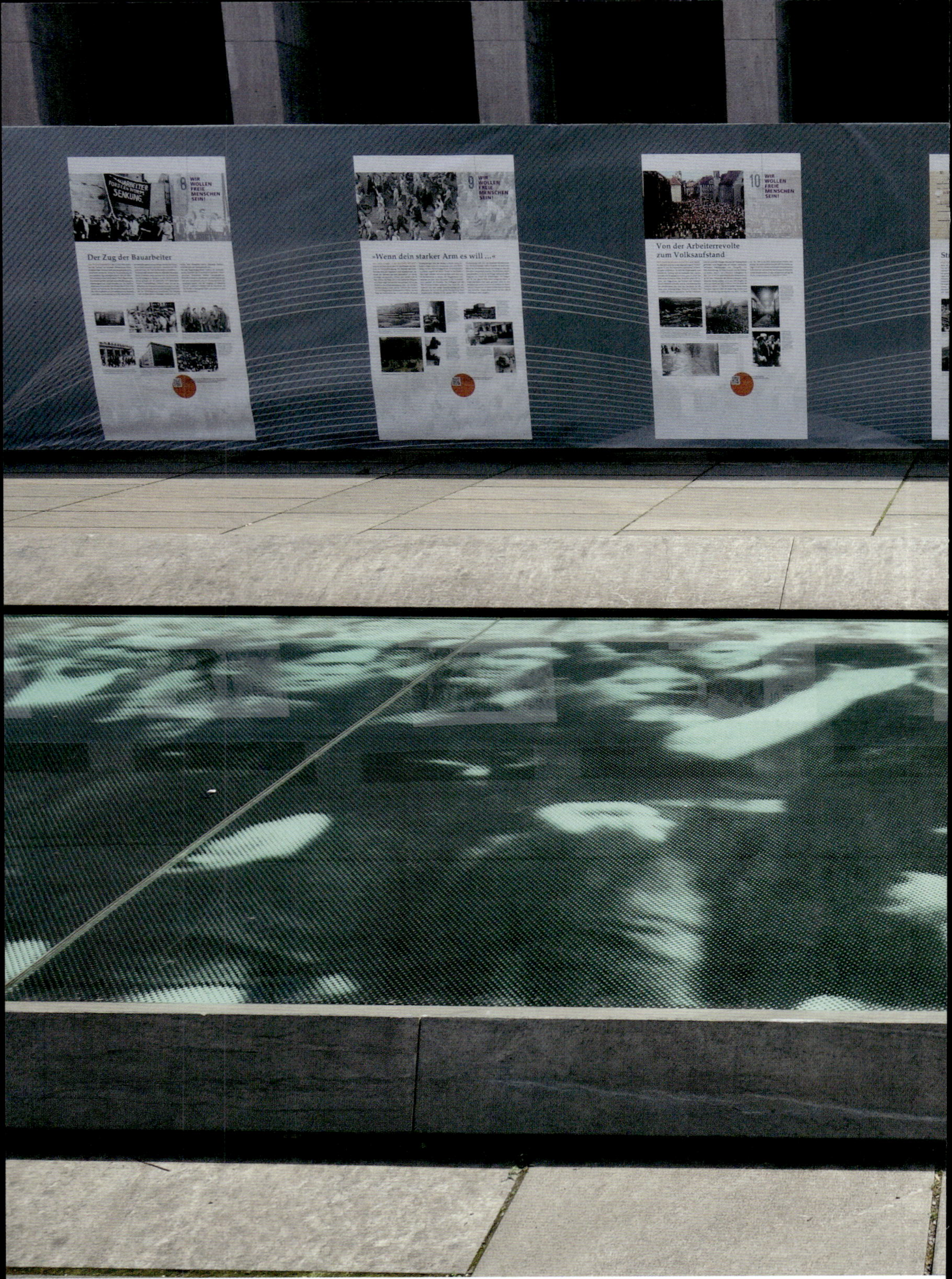

Recessed memorial and placard exhibition
"We want to be free people" by the Federal Foundation
for the Study of the Communist Dictatorship
in Eastern Germany at the Ministry of Finance

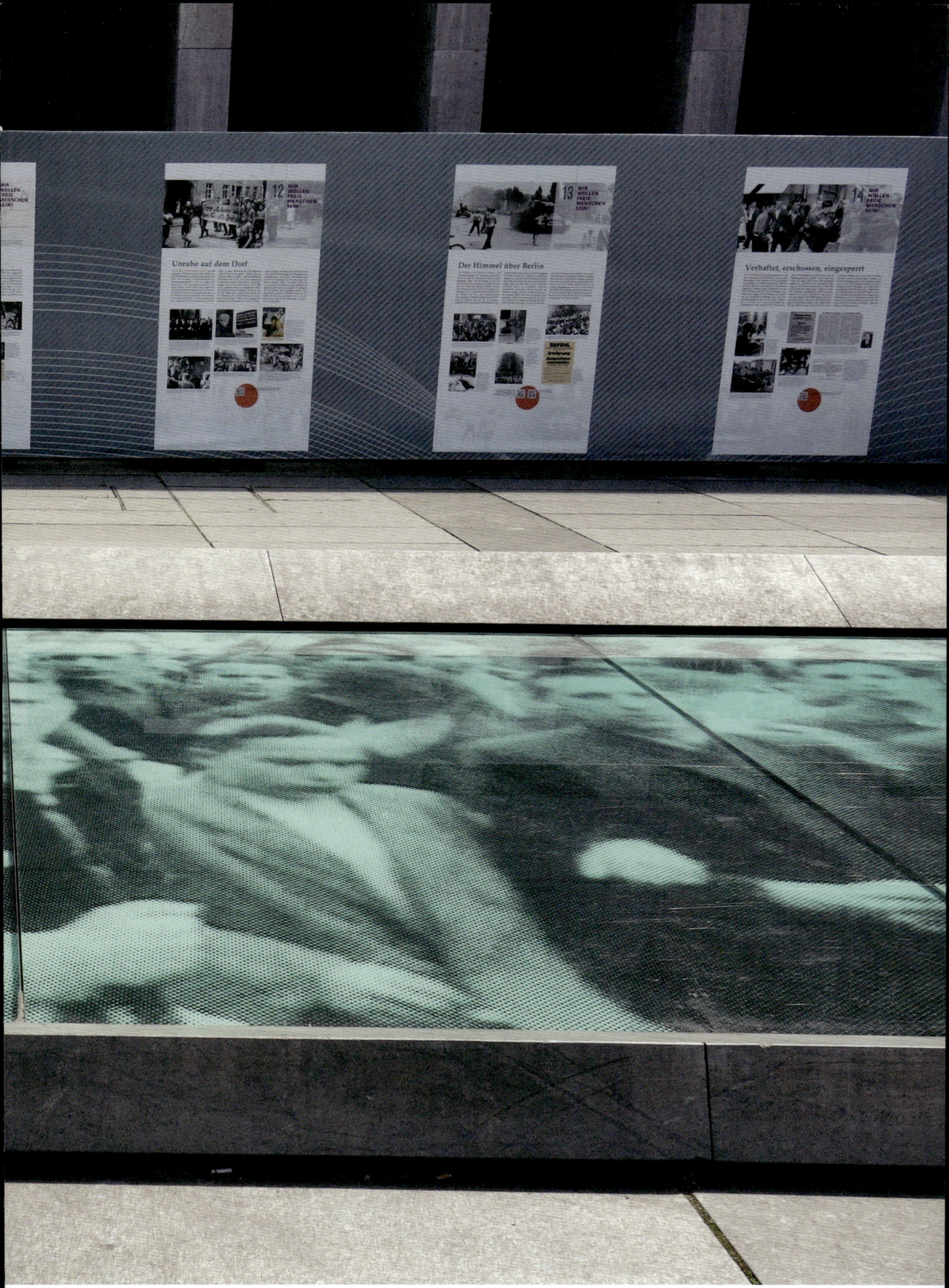
12
WIR WOLLEN FREIE MENSCHEN SEIN!
Unruhe auf dem Dorf
13
WIR WOLLEN FREIE MENSCHEN SEIN!
Der Himmel über Berlin
BEFEHL
14
WIR WOLLEN FREIE MENSCHEN SEIN!
Verhaftet, erschossen, eingesperrt

the grounds of the Technical University up to Ernst-Reuter-Platz—as "Strasse des 17. Juni". The first memorial cross was set up in Berlin-Steglitz / Zehlendorf on the road to Potsdam. Protesters erected a temporary wooden cross there barely a week after the uprising. On 20 July 1953, it was replaced by a new wooden cross with a commemorative plaque.

The municipal urn cemetery on Seestrasse in the district of Wedding became the central place of remembrance of the victims in the west of the city of Berlin. On 23 June 1953, eight victims of the uprising who had died in West Berlin hospitals were buried there. On 17 June 1955, a memorial was inaugurated on behalf of all the victims, and the official commemoration and wreath-laying ceremonies of the Federal Government and the Berlin Senate still take place there every year to this day.

There was no official commemoration of 17 June and its victims in the GDR. It was only after 1990 that the victims could be commemorated at the original sites of the uprising. Almost all the memorials and monuments created since reunification are in the eastern German states. Most of them were inaugurated around the 50th anniversary of the uprising. The renaming of streets and squares in places such as Bitterfeld, Stralsund, Görlitz and Berlin was possible only in this context. The uprising had begun spontaneously, and no leaders or symbolic personalities emerged from it. It was not possible to commemorate individuals until after 1989, as many of the names of the people involved were unknown during the SED regime. With the 50th anniversary in 2003, the focus shifted to individual fates. Several of the memorials erected at the time no longer commemorate the uprising and its victims but are dedicated to people who took part in the protests on 17 June and were killed or sentenced to long prison terms.

The commemorative markers created since 1990 often closely resemble the monuments erected in the 1950s and 1960s and draw on proven forms such as crosses, stones or simple commemorative plaques. An exception is the central monument in Berlin, which has stood on the square in front of the former House of Ministries—now the Federal Ministry of Finance—since 2000. The House of Ministries played a central role during the uprising. On 16 June 1953, thousands of construction workers marched here to deliver their demands to the government. This show of defiance has been acknowledged since 1993 by a commemorative plaque next to Max Lingner's mural in praise of the merits of socialist society. On the initiative of 17 June and 13 August associations, large photographs were mounted on the façade of the listed building in 1994, making a visible historical reference to the uprising and its suppression. In the following years, a competition was organised in which the design of artist Wolfgang Rüppel prevailed. The large-format glass image embedded in the floor shows a greatly enlarged photo of the protest march of the strikers on their way to the House of Ministries.

There are also information stelae on the corner of Leipziger Strasse / Wilhelmstrasse. On the occasion of the 60th anniversary of the uprising and at the request of the Federal Ministry of Finance, this previously nameless square was given the name "Platz des Volksaufstandes von 1953" (Square of the 1953 People's Uprising) during its official inauguration on 16 June 2013. The original proposal "Platz des 17. Juni" (Square of 17 June) was rejected by the Berlin-Mitte District Office to avoid confusion with the "Strasse des 17. Juni".

Further reading:

Kaminsky, Anna (ed.): Orte des Erinnerns, Gedenkzeichen, Gedenkstätten und Museen zur Diktatur in DDR und SBZ. Berlin 2016. / Klausmeier, Axel (ed.): Die Berliner Mauer. Ausstellungskatalog der Gedenkstätte Berliner Mauer. Berlin 2015. / Gedenkstätte und Museum Sachsenhausen/ Stiftung Brandenburgische Gedenkstätten (ed.): Totenbuch sowjetisches Speziallager Nr. 7 / Nr. 1 in Weesow und Sachsenhausen 1945 – 1950. Berlin 2010. / Stiftung Sächsische Gedenkstätten (ed.): Stasi-Gefängnis Bautzen II, 1956 – 1989. Katalog zur Ausstellung der Gedenkstätte Bautzen. Dresden 2008.

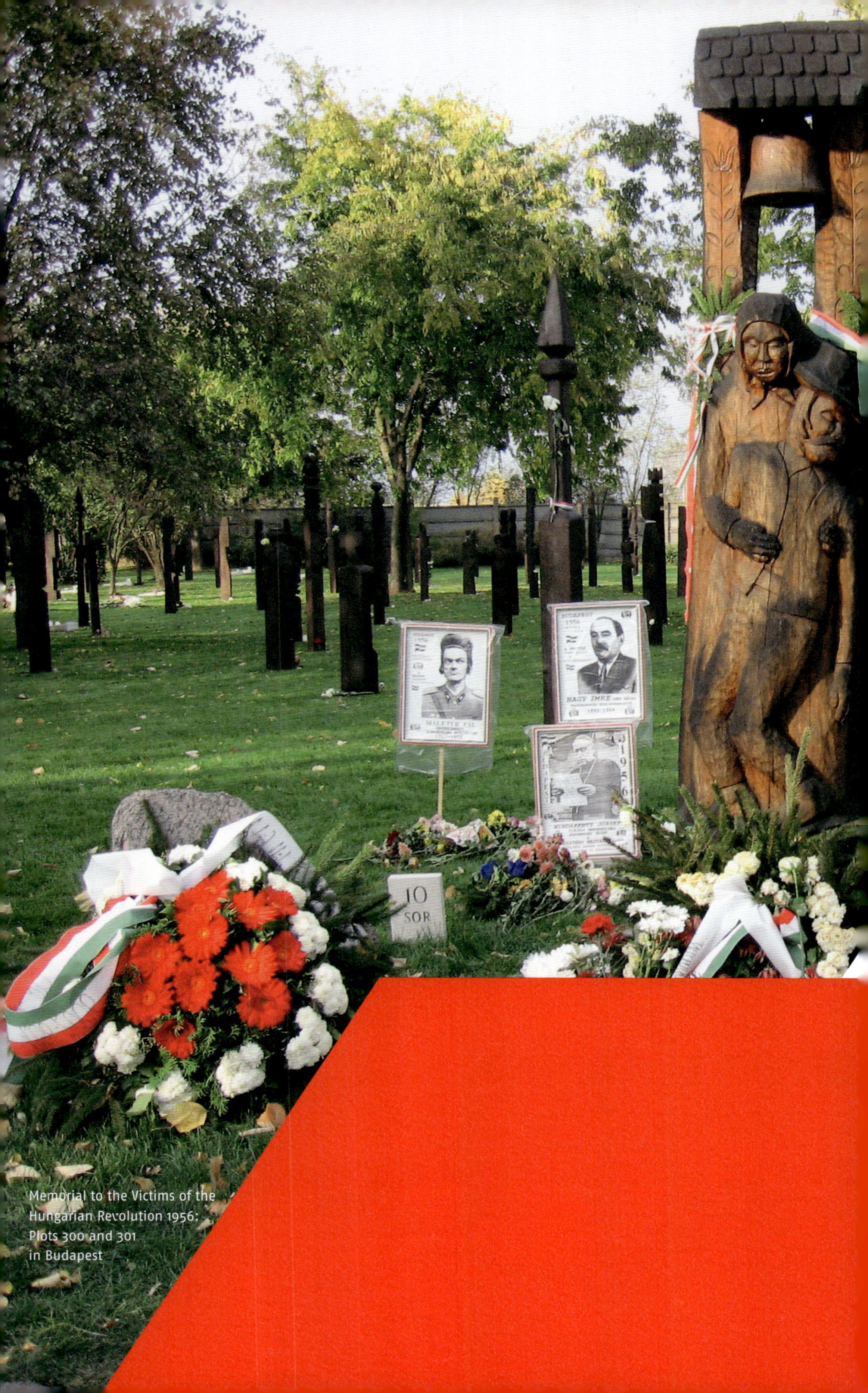

Memorial to the Victims of the Hungarian Revolution 1956: Plots 300 and 301 in Budapest

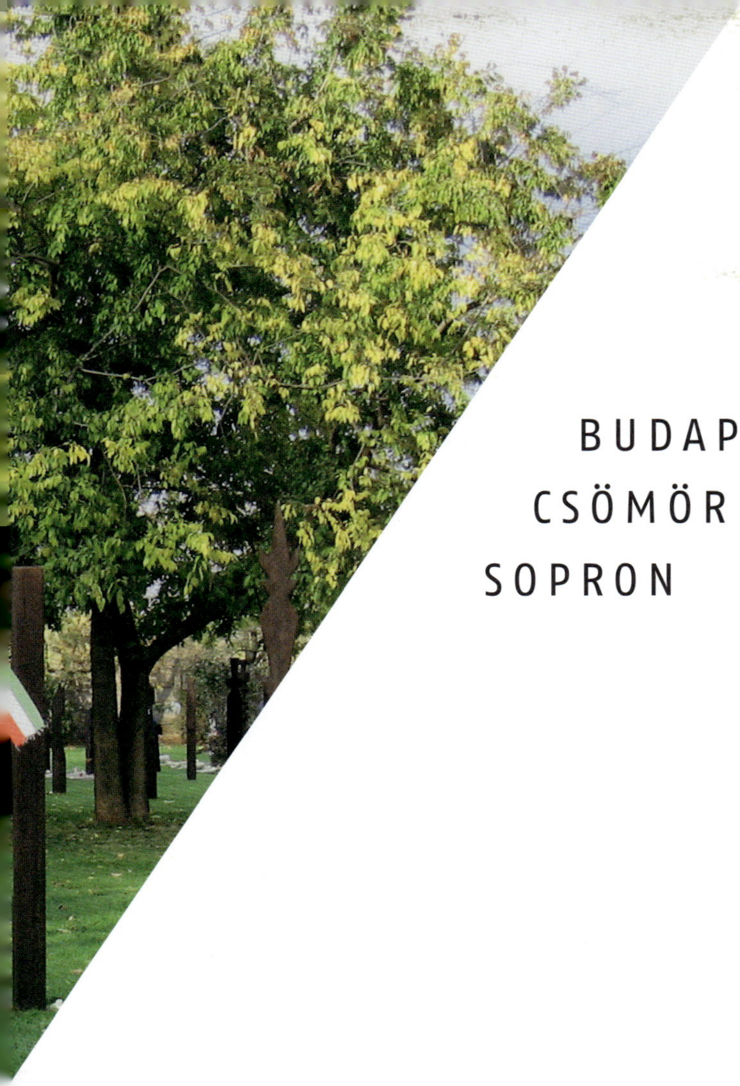

BUDAPEST
CSÖMÖR
SOPRON

Hungary

After the First World War in which Austria-Hungary had been on the losing side, while Hungary was granted independent statehood it lost about two-thirds of its territory to the newly founded neighbouring states. After the short-lived bourgeois republic of Count Mihály Károlyi and "Soviet Republic" under Béla Kun, Hungary came under the authoritarian rule of self-styled Regent Miklós Horthy. In 1934, the country concluded an economic agreement with Nazi Germany and, following the German dismantling of Czechoslovakia in March 1939, occupied areas in the Carpathians that had formerly belonged to it.

On 20 November 1940, Hungary joined the Tripartite Pact with Germany, Japan and Italy and entered the war against the Soviet Union. After the defeat of the Hungarian Second Army in 1943 in the Battle of Voronezh, the Hungarian government changed its policy and attempted to align itself with the Allies of the anti-Hitler coalition, after which German troops occupied the country in March 1944. This was accompanied by the deportation of 400,000 Hungarian Jews with the help of the Hungarian gendarmerie and state officials. Most of the deportees were murdered in German extermination camps.

In the autumn of 1944, the Red Army reached Hungary from the East. Regent Miklós Horthy concluded a truce with the Soviet armed forces in the autumn of 1944, after which he was taken prisoner by SS units and detained in Bavaria. The fascist Arrow Cross under Ferenc Szálasi took over the affairs of state. Hungary came under Soviet occupation at the end of the war. In the elections held for the first time in autumn 1945, the Communist Party did not achieve a majority. Competing parties—such as the traditionally strong party of small farmers—were then crushed or obstructed. In June 1948, the Social Democratic and Communist Parties were forcibly merged to form the "Party of Hungarian Labourers" (MDP), the only party to be admitted to the parliamentary elections of 1949.

This course of events elevated the Secretary General of the Communist Party of Hungary and long-time Prime Minister Mátyás Rákosi to power. Under the dictatorial leadership of "Stalin's best pupil", as Rákosi fashioned himself, the ruling Communists based their rule on the efficiently functioning terror apparatus that had already been established in 1945. With the help of the ÀVH (Àllamvédelmi Hatóság) secret police, democratic parties were effectively eliminated. "Internal enemies"—members of the party and state leadership, such as the Interior Minister and later Foreign Minister László Rajk—were also prosecuted in Stalinist show trials. Between 1950 and 1953 alone, over 400,000 people were sentenced to prison and many years in labour or concentration camps. Among the convicts were Cardinal József Mindszenty and Paul Esterházy.

Political terror was linked to an economic plan which was imposed on the country: overhasty collectivisation campaigns and forced industrialisation, which resulted in the arrest or banishment of tens of thousands of people, led to a drastic drop in the already low standard of living. In the light of the popular uprising in the GDR on 17 June 1953, which could only be crushed with the help of Soviet troops, the Soviet leadership was keen to prevent the destabilisation of another strategically important satellite state.

On 4 July 1953, at the instigation of Moscow, Mátyás Rákosi was forced to resign from his post as head of government in favour of Imre Nagy. The agricultural expert Nagy distanced himself from the Stalinist leadership style of his predecessor and introduced a policy of the "New Course", which made him the bearer of hope for many. He tried to bring about a socialism without state terror, with greater social freedoms and a more moderate economic policy. However, large parts of the party apparatus were still under the influence of Mátyás Rákosi and blocked his policy. This finally led to the dismissal of Nagy on 14 April 1955 on the grounds of "anti-party, anti-Marxist, opportunist and right-wing tendencies" and his expulsion from the party a few months later.

With the accession to power of András Hegedüs, a close confidante of Rákosis, many of the reform projects initiated by Nagy were reversed during a phase of restoration. From the spring of 1956, following Khrushchev's revelations about Stalin at the 20th Party Conference of the CPSU, discontent was expressed both within the Hungarian Communist Party (CP) and among large sections of the population in view of the country's obviously retrogressive political and economic development and the government's refusal to take responsibility for the consequences. The government's retrogressive course was rejected by both reformist factions of the Communist Party and the anti-Stalinist intelligentsia.

In the summer of 1956, the Petőfi Circle, which was born of the events of the time, developed into the opposition's foremost discussion forum and became the pioneer of revolution. With the founding of the independent association of Hungarian university students (MEFESZ) on 19 October 1956, political demands were for the first time expressed in addition to the desire for educational reforms.

The revolutionary events began with a demonstration in Budapest on 23 October 1956. The day before, students of the Technical University had formulated a 16-point manifesto. Under the slogan "Poland is the model, let us take the Hungarian path", the students demanded the immediate withdrawal of Soviet troops from Hungary, the formation of a new government under Imre Nagy, the removal of old functional cadres from the Rákosi era and the comprehensive democratisation of public life.

In the evening hours of 23 October, more than 250,000 people throughout the city took to the streets in support of students' demands. When these were summarily rejected, the situation escalated. Some of the protesters stormed the radio station, and there were clashes with the state security service, resulting in numerous deaths and injuries. Meanwhile, numerous insurgent groups, revolutionary committees and workers councils formed to fight the Soviet troops transferred to Budapest. Imre Nagy was reappointed Prime Minister. On 28 October, in a famous radio address, he described the uprising as "a great [...] national democratic movement" and assured the population that all warranted demands would be met. The next day, the Soviet troops left Budapest at the request of the Hungarian government.

The dissolution of the state Communist Party, the restoration of the multi-party system, the release of the political prisoners of the Rákosi era, and, above all, the withdrawal of Hungary from the Warsaw Pact announced by Imre Nagy in tandem with the declaration of state neutrality, led to the military suppression of the Hungarian Revolution by the Soviet Union: the second Soviet offensive against Hungary began in the early hours of 4 November 1956. During this bloody suppression of the uprising, 15 divisions of the armed forces throughout the country took action against the insurgents. In Budapest alone, the Red Army invaded with about 2,000 tanks and systematically destroyed the remaining active units of the Hungarian military. On 6 November 1956, the capital was placed under Soviet military administration. By 11 November, the occupation of the country was essentially over, despite fierce resistance from the population, and the revolution had finally been stifled.

The fighting had cost the lives of some 2,500 Hungarians, and almost 20,000 were injured. János Kádár, the new Prime Minister, initially promised amnesty and impunity for the supporters of the revolution. Only later were the workers' councils, which were initially tolerated, dissolved and the first arrests made. Important figures of the reform movement, including Imre Nagy, were sentenced to death and executed in show trials which culminated in 1958. A total of 800 death sentences were handed down, 400 of which were carried out. About 15,000 people were sent to internment camps and another 20,000 had to serve long prison sentences. Around 200,000 Hungarians fled abroad across the temporarily open western border.

After the suppression of the revolution, János Kádár resorted to a carrot-and-stick approach of harsh repression of opposition figures on the one hand and the pacification of the population with promises of greater prosperity on the other, for which the term "Goulash Communism" was coined. Economic reforms permitted private initiatives within certain limits in the retail and craft trades. In 1963, almost all of those involved in the revolution were granted amnesty. Censorship was relaxed, although it was not lifted until the very end.

It was not until the mid-1970s that a new system-critical public emerged from the circle of students of the philosopher Georg Lukács. Without questioning the legitimacy of the regime, they chose instead to advocate a gradual expansion of freedom. But even this criticism of the ruling system did not remain without consequences. Authors of critical writings were arrested, barred from practising their profession or sent to prison. In response to censorship, a tradition of samizdat literature developed. After the arrest of members of the Czechoslovak civil rights movement Charter 77 in 1977, three Hungarian intellectuals demanded the release of the detainees in a protest letter. By the time the latter had been sentenced to long prison terms in 1979, several hundred people had already signed a petition to the Hungarian leadership. Many of them subsequently lost their jobs or were put under pressure and intimidated.

Demonstration on József Boulevard in Budapest during the 1956 Hungarian Revolution

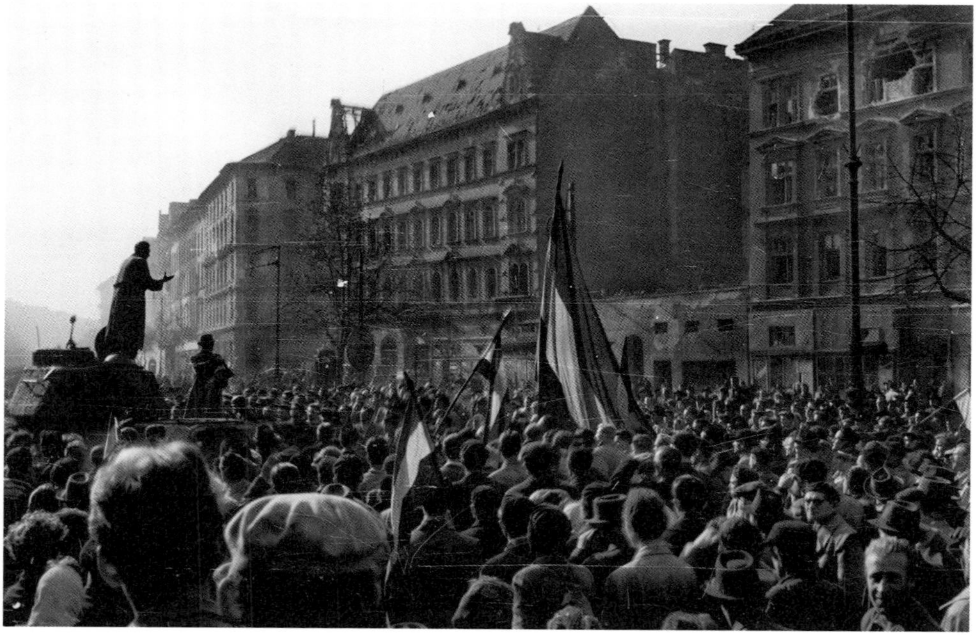

In the 1980s, the opposition activities of Hungarian society intensified. Further samizdat publications appeared and civil society and intellectual initiatives were founded. At the same time, the growing economic difficulties—especially the high level of western debt—led to the further liberalisation of Hungarian politics: an electoral reform made it possible to nominate two candidates per constituency. As early as 1985, some non-CP representatives were elected to parliament. Under the influence of Gorbachev's policies of perestroika and glasnost, fears of military intervention in Hungary by the Soviet Union progressively receded. In June 1987, the samizdat magazine "Beszélő" issued a declaration entitled "The consensus is over" and demanded the abdication of János Kádár. Another group of intellectuals founded the Hungarian Democratic Forum in the autumn of the same year.

After Kádár's replacement in May 1988, more and more protests took place, for example on 16 June 1988, in memory of the 1956 popular uprising, despite police violence and public arrests. Under pressure from the opposition, which continued to grow and organise, the party leadership increasingly conceded to the creation of constitutional structures, including parties. A symbolic turning point was the ceremonial rehabilitation and reburial of Imre Nagy and his comrades-in-arms in June 1989. Hundreds of thousands of people took part in the commemoration and turned it into a powerful demonstration. In the summer of 1989, the Iron Curtain at the Hungarian-Austrian border was abolished. Refugees from the GDR could now reach West Germany via Austria—an event that accelerated the fall of both the Honecker regime and the Berlin Wall.

In a referendum in November 1989, the vast majority of the Hungarian population voted for democratic reforms. The Hungarian Democratic Forum won the elections in April 1990. The transformation in Hungary took place via reforms, not as a revolutionary process. The smooth transition to democracy also meant, however, that issues involving coming to terms with the past were tackled only with hesitation. It is however true that the first regulations to repeal unjust judgements ("2nd Annulment Act") and to compensate those affected were adopted as early as 1990.

And yet, no prosecution took place of individuals responsible for persecution and crimes during the Communist dictatorship. By 2005, background checks had been conducted on several thousand employees in the upper echelons of government to determine whether they had held party offices during the Communist dictatorship or worked for the secret police. The outcome was disappointing: only one per cent were asked to resign their mandate or position. In most cases—with the exception of the churches—expropriated and confiscated property was not returned, although compensation was in many cases paid.

In Hungary, starting in 1989, documents belonging to the secret police were destroyed on a massive scale, and the records received by the Historical Office, founded in 1997 to take possession of the files of the secret police, were correspondingly incomplete. In 2003, the Historical Office was converted into the Historical Archives of the State Security Services. The records are available for individual access as well as scientific research.

Numerous monuments were created to pay tribute to the freedom fighters of the 1956 revolution and keep them in public memory. In 1989, 23 October was proclaimed a national holiday.

"House of Terror" Museum

Budapest. The "House of Terror" Museum opened on 24 February 2002, the day before the national Memorial Day for the Victims of the Communist Dictatorships.

Built in 1880 as a residential building according to the plans of architect Adolf Feszty, it was taken over in 1937 by the Hungarian fascist movement (Arrow Cross) and served as its headquarters from 1940. When the Arrow Cross Party, which was allied with the Nazis, came to power in the autumn of 1944, the cellars served as a prison and place of torture. After the invasion of Soviet troops and the return of leading Hungarian Communists from exile in Moscow in the spring of 1945, the Hungarian State Protection Authority took charge of the building. It also used the basement rooms as a prison and place of torture. In 1956, the State Protection Authority abandoned the building; in the following decades it served as an office complex.

The initiative to establish the "House of Terror" with the aim of creating a museum dedicated to the history and consequences of the totalitarian regimes of the Arrow Cross and the Communists in Hungary goes back to József Szájer. The Public Foundation for the Research of Central and East European History and Society, initiated by the government under Viktor Orbán, acquired the building in 2000 and began construction of the museum. Two years later, the exhibition opened. It presents a chronological overview of the totalitarian regimes in Hungary until 1989. In addition to the rule of the Arrow Cross in 1944/45 and the Holocaust, the focus is on crimes under Soviet occupation and the reprisals in the early phase of the people's democratic Hungary.

The 1956 Revolution plays a special role in the exhibition. In addition to objects that bear witness to repression and personal effects of the victims, audio-visual elements—i. e. films, photos, narratives by contemporary witnesses, music sequences and interactive installations—recall the horrors and suffering of the victims. Seminars and conferences are also held at the "House of Terror" Museum.

In 2010, an original segment of the Berlin Wall was installed in front of the "House of Terror".

Location: Budapest, Andrassy útca 60
Internet: www.terrorhaza.hu

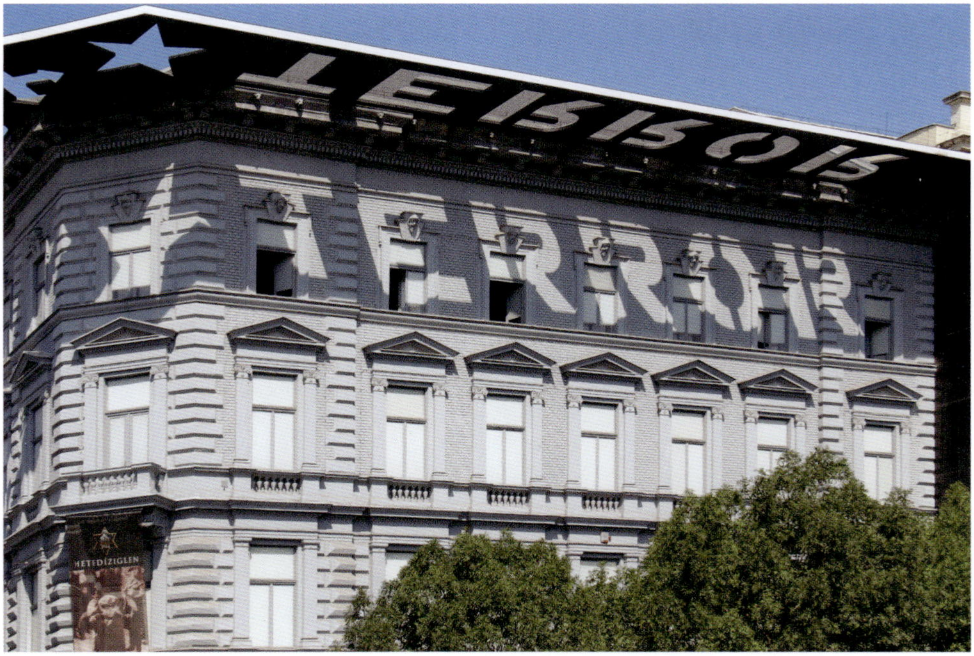

Exterior view of the "House of Terror" Museum

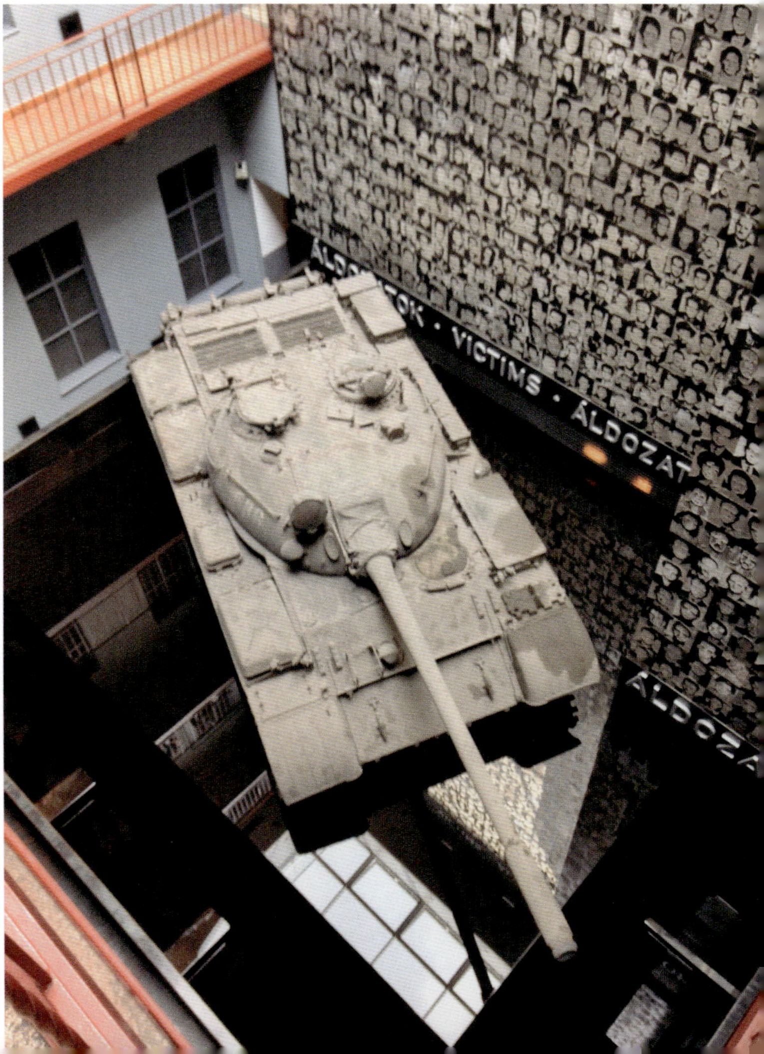

► View of the museum's exhibition

Memorial to the Victims of the Hungarian Revolution 1956: Plots 300 and 301

Budapest. The Memorial to the Victims of the Hungarian Revolution of 1956 is located on plot 301 of the New Municipal Cemetery in Budapest. It was inaugurated on the occasion of the 33rd anniversary of the uprising on 23 October 1989. Even before the official opening, the remains of Imre Nagy and other revolution leaders had already been reburied here in June of that year. During the first official celebrations in October 1989, the graves were given provisional markings. In the same year, the Hungarian government announced a national competition to transform the site into a memorial. The artist György Jovánovics, who presented a three-part concept, was awarded the contract. After two years of construction, the plot was officially inaugurated on 23 October 1992.

The central memorial is located on the edge of the plot. It consists of several coarsely hewn white limestone blocks that form a sarcophagus and is completed by a column structure. In accordance with the will of the executed insurgent István Angyal, it symbolises the "great white rock" to which Angyal compared the 1956 Revolution. An open symbolic grave in the middle of the square commemorates all the victims of the revolution. A 1,956-millimetre-high column of black marble, which rises up to ground level, was embedded in the middle. The names of the approximately 400 dead resting in the plot are engraved on a large plaque at the edge. Only individual, outstanding personalities of the revolution were given individual graves. These uniformly consist of simple white limestone blocks displaying the name and dates of birth and death. Besides Imre Nagy, the final resting places of Miklós Gimes, Géza Losonczy, Pál Maléter and József Szilágyi, who were sentenced to death alongside him, are marked. Sándor Kopácsi, the sixth victim of the trial of the revolutionary leaders, who was sentenced to life imprisonment, was also buried in plot 301 after his death in 2001. In memory of other victims, crosses and headboards were erected on private initiatives. Symbolic graves can be found for István Bibo, István Angyal, József Dudás, János Szabó, László Iván Kovács and Povl Bang Jensen.

After the suppression of the revolution in 1956, the victims of the uprising were buried in a remote part of the New Municipal Cemetery, some of them anonymously. This area, which is called plot 301, thus became one of the largest cemeteries for the victims of the revolution. After 1945, the State Protection Authority, the ÁVH, used the surrounding plots 298 and 300 to bury prisoners of the secret police who had died or were executed. For this reason, the entire area was declared a forbidden zone. In addition to those who were killed in the fighting, those condemned to death in the trials of the leaders of the revolution also found their final resting place here. Imre Nagy

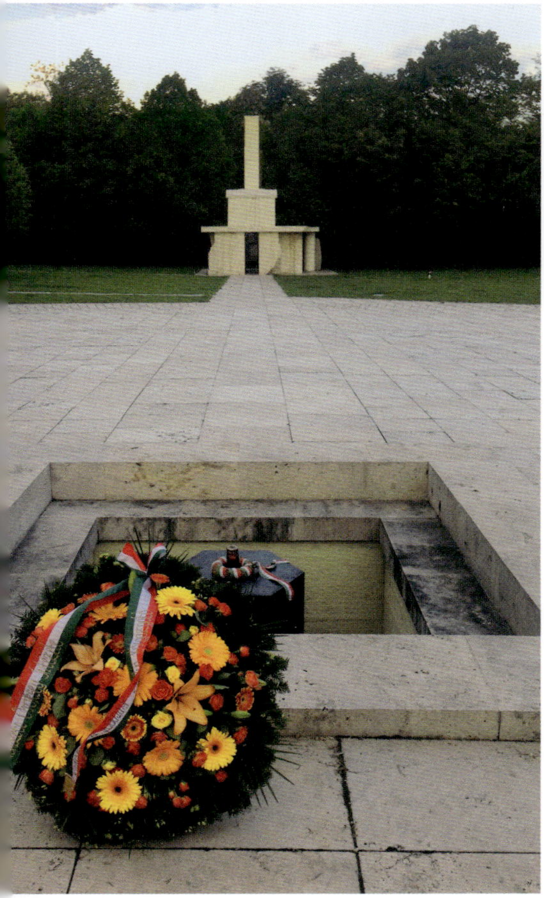

Memorial to the Victims of the 1956 Hungarian Revolution in the New Municipal Cemetery

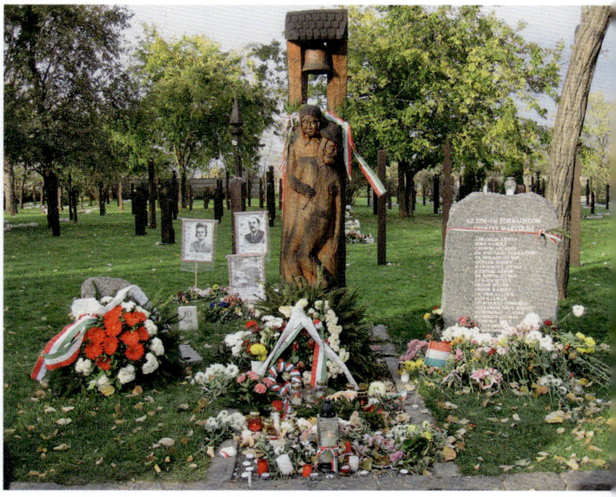

Grave markers and crosses were erected on private initiative in memory of other victims of the revolution.

and those executed with him in 1958, for example, were secretly moved to plot 301 in 1961. The population was not officially informed of the whereabouts of the mortal remains of the fallen insurgents. There were rumours, however, that they had been buried in the New Municipal Cemetery.

Time and again, small groups or individuals tried to enter the closed part of the cemetery to hold secret commemorations here. A first major rally to mark the anniversary of the death of Imre Nagy on 16 June 1988 was forcibly disbanded by the police. At the end of that year, under public pressure, a fact-finding committee was set up to investigate the whereabouts of the casualties of the revolution, above all of Nagy. In March of the following year, plot 301 was officially proclaimed a burial site. Immediately afterwards, the exhumation of the mortal remains began. The identification of the insurgents, most of whom were recorded under false names in the documents of the cemetery administration, was one of the major problems. While this work was taking place, Imre Nagy was solemnly reburied on 16 June 1989, and the conversion of the plot into a memorial site began.

Location: Budapest, Municipality X, Kozma-utca 8 – 10

Memorial to the 1956 Hungarian Revolution

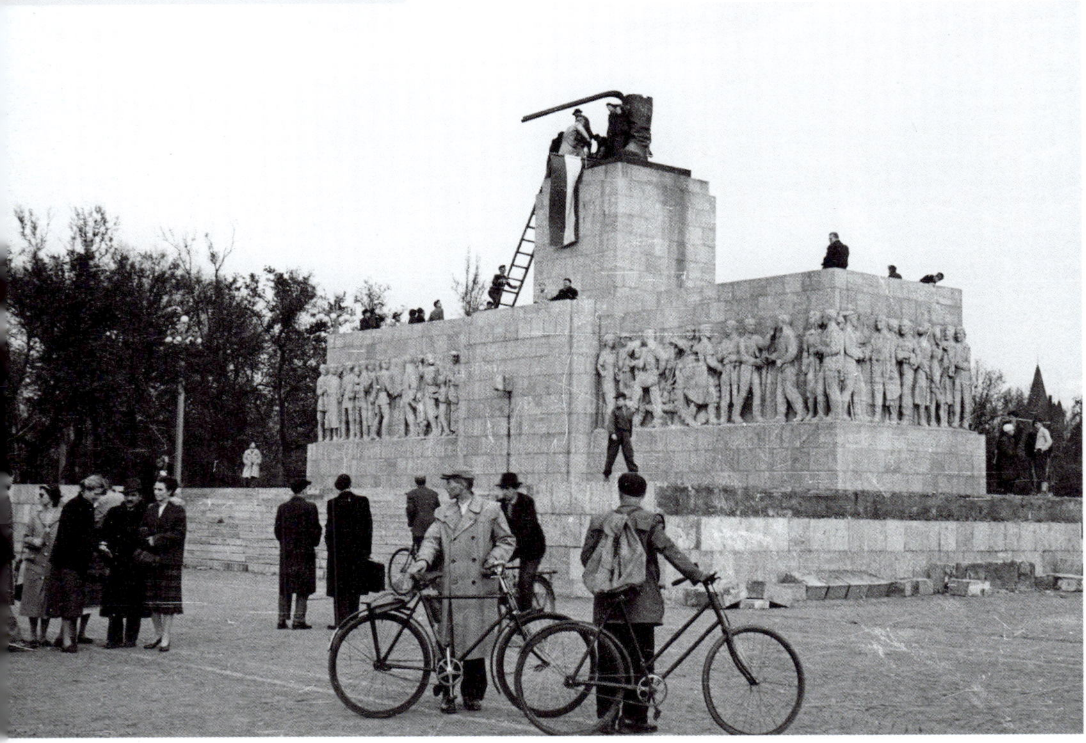

Budapest. The Memorial to the 1956 Hungarian Revolution was unveiled to the public on 23 October 2006, the 50th anniversary of the 1956 popular uprising. The wedge-shaped construction, consisting of over 2000 shaped iron and steel columns, is located where a monumental sculpture of Stalin used to stand. The latter was brought down by protesters during the revolutionary events of 23 October 1956. The new memorial symbolises the Hungarians who united to prevail over communist rule.

Evoking the year of the revolution, the memorial is shaped like a wedge at a 56-degree angle. The larger-than-life iron columns represent protesters walking hand in hand. Towards the apex of the monument, the pillars become

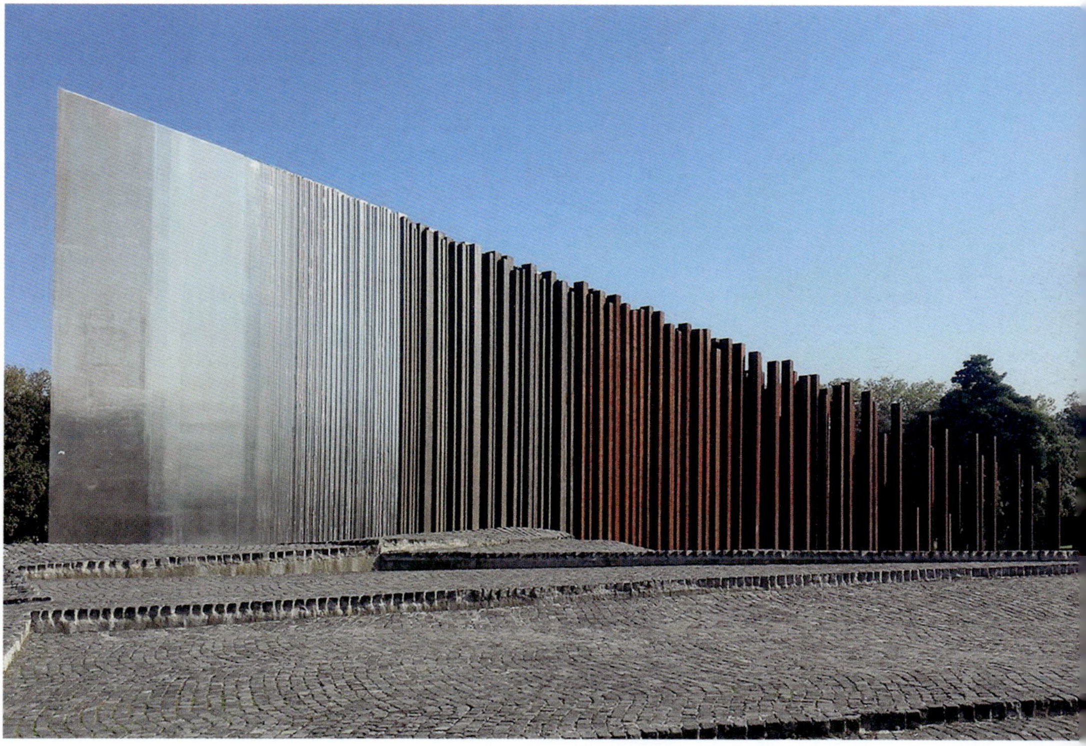

lighter in colour, and the distance between them diminishes as they approach a pointed stainless-steel construction that marks the culmination of the memorial.

Location: Budapest, Ötvenhatosok tere opposite Városliglet Park

Memorial to the 1956 Hungarian Revolution in the centre of Budapest

◄

Remains of the Stalin monument after it was taken down at the beginning of the Hungarian Revolution in 1956

Memento Park

Budapest. Opened in 1993, the open-air museum presents some of the sculptures and monuments from the Soviet era that shaped Budapest's cityscape for decades. The 42 exhibits include pioneers and famous figures of communism such as Karl Marx and Friedrich Engels, Vladimir Ilyich Lenin, the Bulgarian head of state and party Georgi Dimitrov and Hungarian revolutionary Béla Kun. On the other hand, some of the sculptures are allegorical monuments depicting certain events, ideas and individuals, such as the founding of the Soviet Republic in 1919, Soviet soldiers and communist martyrs.

After the collapse of the communist regime in Hungary in 1989, as in many other countries of Central and Eastern Europe, the question arose of what to do with the ideological-political heritage of communism—the monuments and sculptures that embodied the dictatorial claim to omnipresence and omnipo-

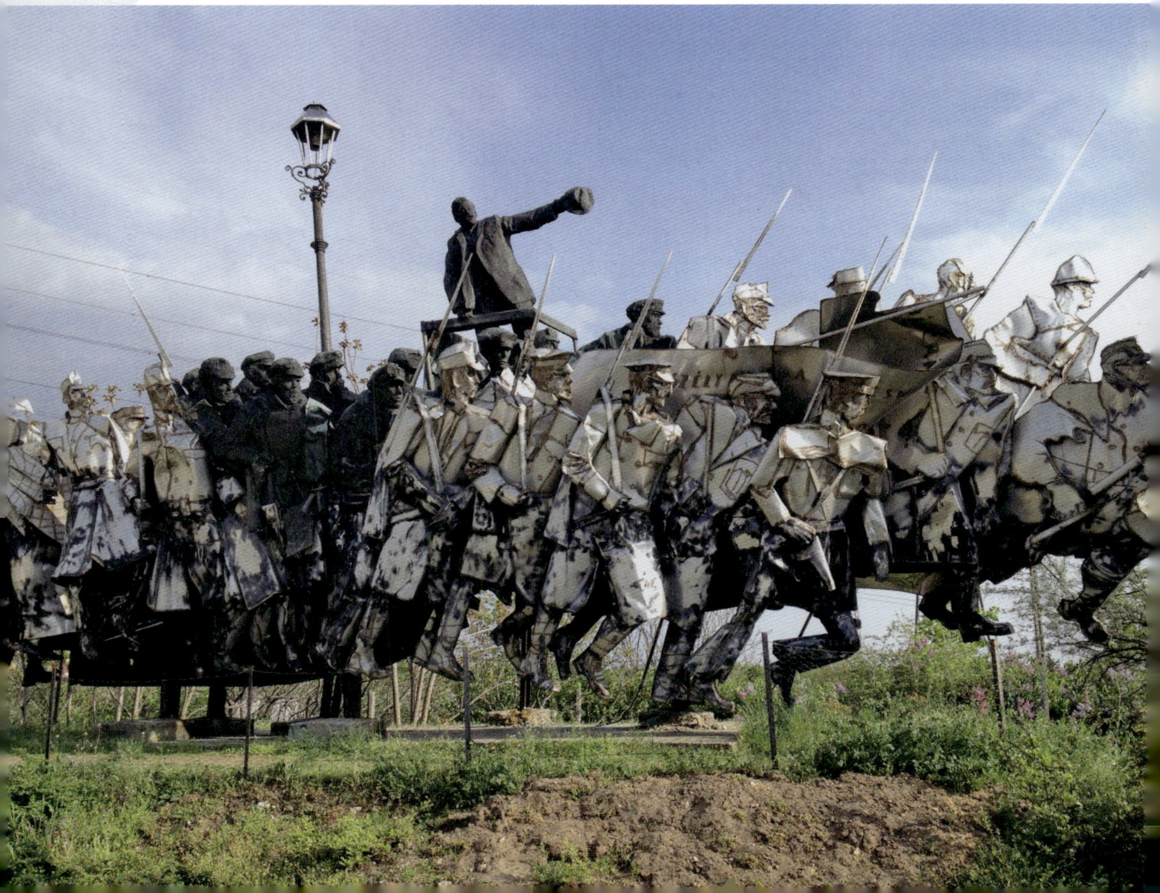

tence—found in public spaces. Several options were floated, ranging from the removal and destruction of these relics of the past to their preservation in recontextualised or even original form. In the end, it was the alternative of exhibiting these communist monuments in a sculpture park on the outskirts of Budapest which prevailed.

The idea of a monument park goes back to the literary historian László Szörényi. In the cultural magazine "Hitel" in July 1989, he proposed the construction of a "Lenin Garden" where all of Budapest's Lenin monuments could be gathered and presented in a new context. Taking up this idea, the General Assembly of Budapest decided in December 1991 that each district could decide independently on the final whereabouts of the statues. At the same time, a competition for the design of a sculpture park was announced. The contract was finally awarded to architect Ákos Eleőd whose concept was to create an attitude of ironic distance to the monuments themselves and the entire era of communist rule without any "arbitrariness or arrogance".

An "ideologically neutral" area outside the city centre on the south-western edge of Budapest was chosen as the exhibition site. In line with the design concept, the site is framed by a red brick wall with integrated stylistic allusions to popular forms of socialist realism. The entrance is marked by a gabled façade with niches in the walls containing sculptures of Marx, Engels and Lenin. Inside the park, the monuments are arranged along three circular promenades, each crossing the main axis of the exhibition path. In the centre of the complex is a circular flower bed, planted to form a red star. Among the most prominent exhibits in the Memorial Park are the boots of the huge Stalin statue, completed in 1951, which was toppled at the very beginning of the Hungarian Revolution on the night of 23–24 October 1956.

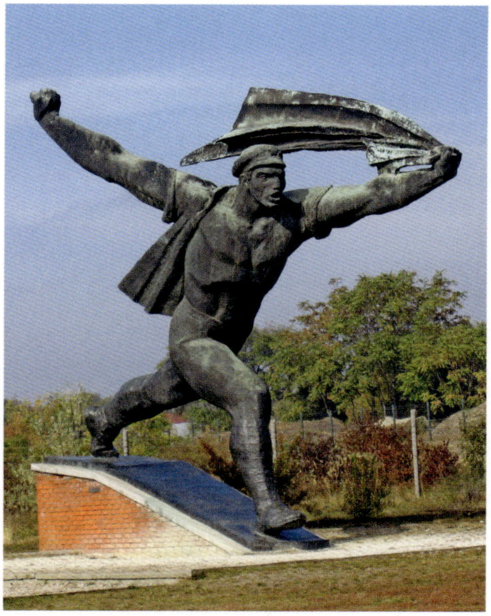

Sculpture of a Hungarian worker

Location: Budapest, XXII. Municipality, Balatoni útca—Szabadkai utca sarok
Internet: www.mementopark.hu

◄
Sculptures and statues from the Soviet era in Memento Park

Gloria Victis Memorial

Csömör. The Gloria Victis Memorial in honour of the 100 million victims of communism was ceremonially unveiled in the municipality of Csömör on the north-eastern outskirts of Budapest on 21 October 2006, on the occasion of the 50th anniversary of the Hungarian Revolution. The memorial was set up on the initiative of the Hungarian foundation of the same name and was funded by public donations and gifts from the Mayor's Office of the Municipality of Csömör.

At the centre of the memorial is a twin monument made of granite by the Hungarian sculptor János Víg. The first element is an arched wall, on which the contours of a world map, intended to express the dimensions of the devastation and annihilation wrought by the communist regimes, are engraved. Above the crown of this "world wall" are a barbed wire fence and several steel crosses. They symbolise the inhumane conditions of the camps and the victims of the communist dictatorships. The composition is completed by a steel belfry attached to the masonry. The Latin cross in the structure's vault symbolises the Christian faith that prevails over all human suffering. The knell in the belfry is regularly rung in memory of those executed by the communist regimes and all those who suffered under the totalitarian dictatorships. On the back of the wall, Resolution No. 1481 on the "The Necessity of International Condemnation of the Crimes Committed by Totalitarian Communist Regimes", adopted by the Parliamentary Assembly of the Council of Europe on 26 January 2006, is engraved in English, Hungarian and German.

Opposite the "world wall" is the arched monument of the 1956 Hungarian Revolution in the form of a "flagship". The Christian cross protruding diagonally from the wall is intended to express the burden under which the Hungarian population took up the fight against the communist dictatorship in the autumn of 1956. Right next to it, a revolutionary flag made of stainless steel rises into the sky. Instead of the socialist emblem, however, the flag has a hole symbolising triumph over the oppressive regime. At the front of the monument are hymns of praise from the Hungarian national poet István Sinka to the heroic Hungarian youth. The reverse of the arch wall bears the contours of a Hungarian map.

Other special elements of the memorial are the commemorative plaques for the victims of the Holodomor in Ukraine and the murdered Polish officers from Katyń and a plaque in memory of the 1939 German-Soviet Nonaggression Pact, which divided East-Central Europe into the spheres of influence of Hitler and Stalin. Commemorations are held every year on 23 August, the anniversary of the signing of the Pact, which the European Parliament declared the European Day of Remembrance for Victims of Stalinism and Nazism in 2008.

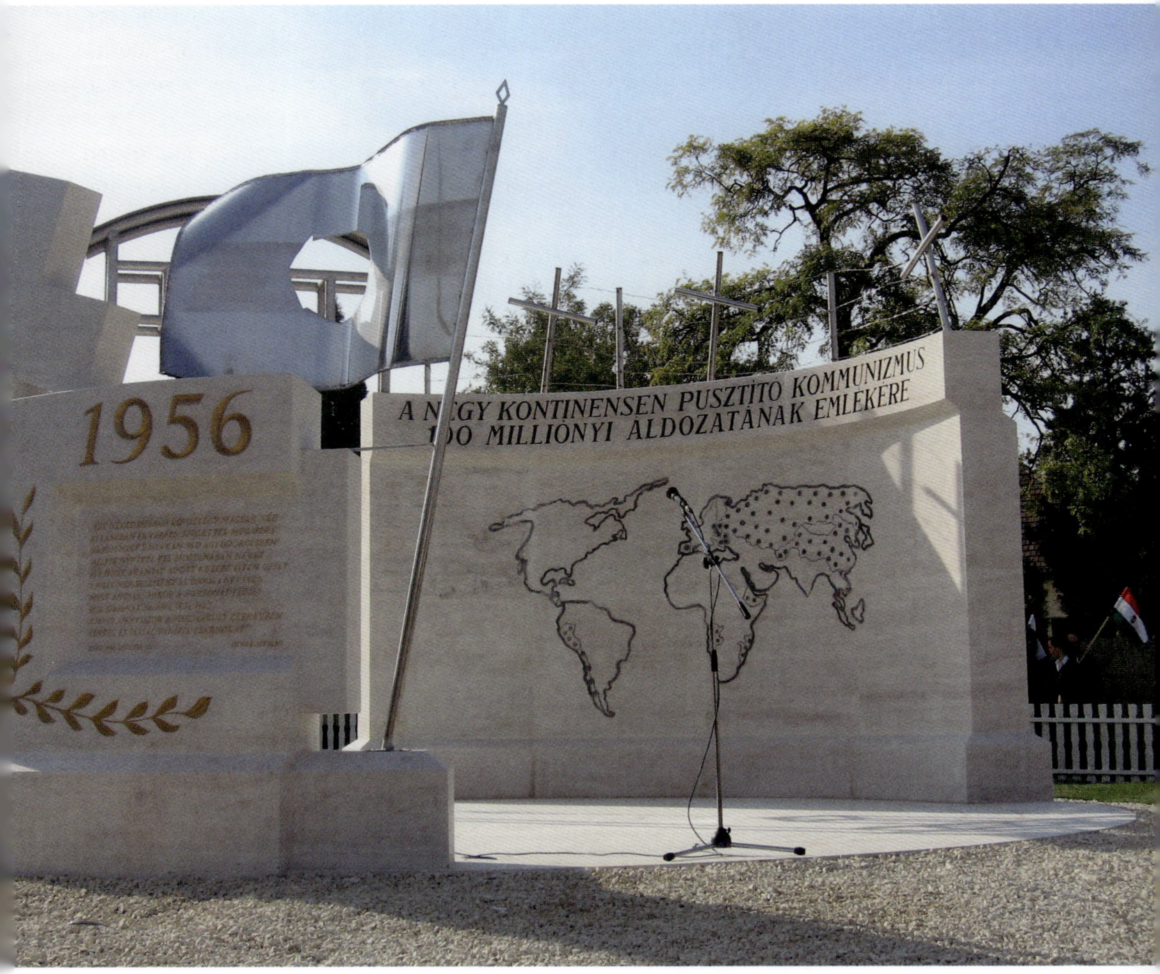

Location: Csömör, Emlékmű köz, near the municipal cemetery
Internet: www.gloriavictis.hu

Gloria Victis Memorial in honour of the 100 million victims of communism

"Breakthrough" Monument

Sopron. The "Breakthrough" monument designed by Italian-Hungarian sculptor Miklós Melocco was ceremonially unveiled in 2009. This was the first memorial site to be built in Hungary to keep the events of the peaceful revolution in the GDR in the public eye. Alongside other sculpture compositions, the monument is featured in the "Pan-European Picnic" Memorial Park located near the place where, on 19 August 1989, more than 600 GDR citizens managed to flee to the West across the Hungarian-Austrian border.

The monument unveiled in Sopron in 2009 on the 20th anniversary of the border breakthrough shows a group of people rising from the ruins of a collapsing classical temple. The memorial thus symbolises the liberation of the peoples of Eastern European from communist rule.

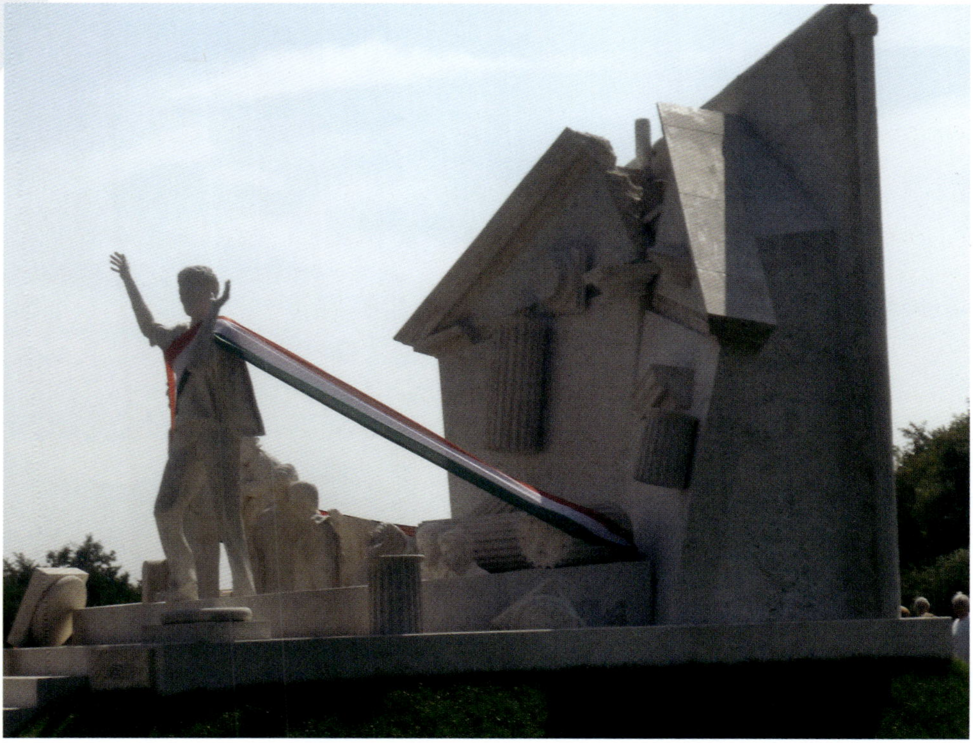

Inscriptions

On the front, Hungarian / German:
Àttörés // Durchbruch

English: *Breakthrough*

On the back, Hungarian / German:
*1989. Augusztus 19. Egy Rab Nép / Kinyitotta Börtönének a Kapuját, / Hogy Egy Másik Rab Nép Kiléphessen a / Szabadságba. //
Am 19. August 1989 öffnete ein / unterjochtes Volk das Tor seines / Gefängnisses / um einem anderen unterjochten Volk / zur Freiheit zu verhelfen.*

English: *On 19 August 1989, one subjugated people opened the gate of its prison to help another subjugated people to freedom.*

Errichtet anlässlich des 20. Jahrestages / des Paneuropäischen Picknicks / mit Unterstützung der Bundesrepublik Deutschland / der Selbstverwaltung der Stadt Sopron / mit Komitatsrechten und / des Freundeskreises Europa Berlin e. V. / zur Erinnerung an die Öffnung der Grenzen 1989, / die das Ende der Teilung Europas einleitete.

English: *Built on the occasion of the 20th anniversary / of the Pan-European Picnic / with the support of the Federal Republic of Germany / the self-government of the city of Sopron / with county rights and / the Freundeskreis Europa Berlin e. V. / in memory of the opening of the borders in 1989 / which initiated the end of the division of Europe.*

◄
"Breakthrough" Monument
in the "Pan-European Picnic" Memorial Park
near the Austro-Hungarian border

Location: Sopron, Páneurópai Piknik Emlékhely — Fertőrákos, at the intersection of St. Margarethener Landestrasse and Schuschenwald
Internet: www.paneuropaipiknik.hu

Further reading:

Hegedüs, András / Wilke, Manfred (ed.): Satelliten nach Stalins Tod: der "neue Kurs"; 17. Juni 1953 in der DDR, ungarische Revolution 1956. Studien des Forschungsverbundes SED-Staat an der Freien Universität Berlin. Berlin 2000. / An insight into the commemorative landscape of the 1956 revolution in Budapest is available at www.bundesstiftung-aufarbeitung.de/gedenkorte-zur-erinnerung-an-die-ungarische-revolution-1956-in-budapest-3300.html (last accessed on: 03/01/2018). / Nagy, László: Das paneuropäische Picknick und die Grenzöffnung am 11. September 1989. In: Potsdamer Bulletin für Zeithistorische Studien No. 23 / 2001, pp. 24 – 40. / Kerékgyártó, Béla: Identitätskämpfe im öffentlichen Raum: Budapest und seine Denkmalwellen. In: International Review of Sociology, 2006, Vol. 16, No. 2, pp. 273 – 308. / Schmidt, Mária: Das Budapester Museum "Haus des Terrors" — Museum der modernen Zeitgeschichte und lebendige Gedenkstätte. In: Knigge, Volkhard / Mählert, Ulrich (ed.): Der Kommunismus im Museum. Formen der Auseinandersetzung in Deutschland und Ostmitteleuropa. Cologne 2005, pp. 161 – 170. / Tallai, Gabor: Länderstudie Ungarn. In: Honoring Civil Courage. Developing Suggestions to Improve the Situation of Victims of Communist State Crimes. Project Coordinator: Gedenkstätte Berlin-Hohenschönhausen 2015, Ref.-Nr.: JUST/2011/JPEN/AG/2998. Available online at: www.stiftung-hsh.de/assets/Dokumente-pdf-Dateien/EU-Projekt-Laenderstudien.pdf (last accessed on: 15/11/2017).

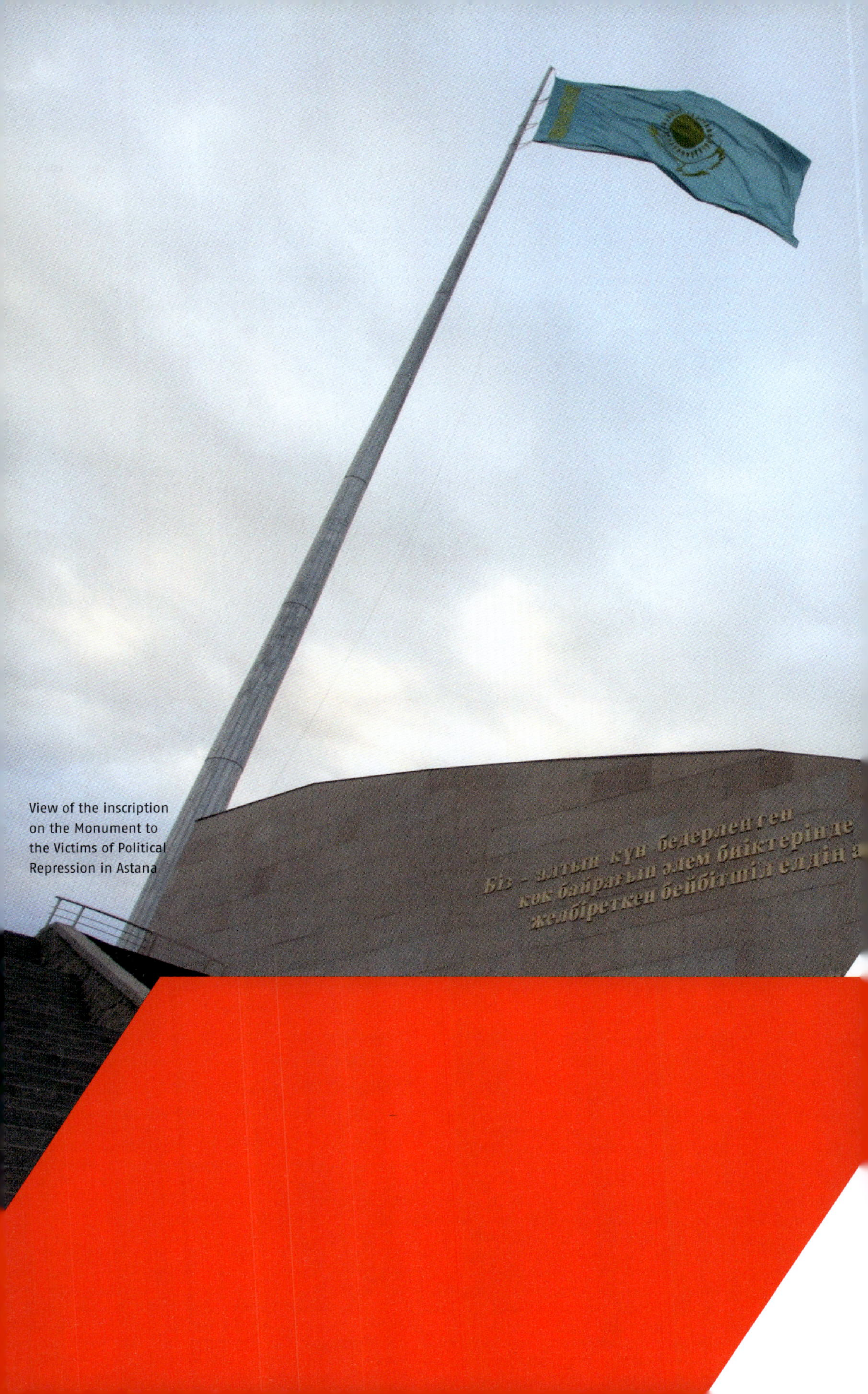

View of the inscription on the Monument to the Victims of Political Repression in Astana

ASTANA
AKMOL
DOLINKA
PAWLODAR

Kazakhstan

Kazakhstan, which had been in the sphere of influence of the Russian Empire since the 9th century, came under communist rule in 1918, although the Kazakh Socialist Soviet Republic (KSSR) was not founded until 1936. The country of about 2.8 million square kilometres was mainly inhabited by nomadic Kazakhs, most of whom were of the Muslim faith. The establishment of Bolshevik rule in the vast steppes of the country was hampered by the way of life and traditions of the many nomadic communities. A society in which most people had no permanent abode, eluded state registration and taxation, and had their most important economic resource—cattle—with them at all times was difficult to subordinate to the "dictatorship of the proletariat".

Time and time again, representatives of the Soviet government found that their authority only extended as far as local clan structures and personal networks allowed. In the eyes of the Soviet leadership, the nomadic pastoralists' way of life, based on tradition, faith and feudal clan structures, was "backward" and incompatible with Soviet governance, as were the practices of the village-based peasantry that were based on orthodox rites and customs going back many generations. This "backwardness" and "unculturedness" was to be overcome by the "Sovietisation of the Kazakh aul".

In the autumn of 1928, the first secretary of the Central Committee of the Communist Party of Kazakhstan, Filipp Goloshchyokin, initiated the brutal repression policy of the so-called "Small October". This was the beginning of the Kazakh version of dekulakisation—"debaisation"—in the Central Asian republic. The assignment of people to the category of "bais" (the Central Asian counterpart of the "kulaks") was arbitrary and used as a pretext for the indiscriminate labelling of tribal clan elders, actual and supposedly wealthy cattle breeders and members of the Kazakh upper class.

All people classified as "representatives of the land-owning class" were expropriated, with their supposed "riches" redistributed to "the poor population", and deported with their families from their home regions. Ownership of three horses, two cows, twelve goats and a yurt or residence in a somewhat more solid house were sufficient grounds for the individuals concerned to be classified as a "bais", to warrant the withdrawal of state rights and confiscation of property, and for the individuals concerned to be interned, deported or killed. Anyone who tried to rescue even the bare minimum of their grain and livestock from requisitioning brigades was forced to undergo draconian punishments.

As with other major socialist projects, the measures for "debaisation" and the forced collectivisation and sedentarisation of the nomads were brutally implemented within a very short period. All protests were suppressed, their leaders murdered or kidnapped. The transfer of private-sector production conditions to centrally administered collective farms, coupled with the amateurishly implemented settlement of the nomads, quickly escalated into an unprecedented tragedy, which ultimately claimed the lives of hundreds of thousands of people.

Between 1930 and 1933, more than 400,000 households—some two million people—would be sedentarised in the style of what would later become known in China as the "Cultural Revolution". In most cases, however, settlement of the nomads was limited to their deportation without seeds or construction materials to inhospitable steppe or desert regions where they had to live in tiny mud huts. With revolutionary zeal, the government, in collaboration with the local authorities, continued to ramp up the pace of collectivisation and the final sedentarisation of the nomadic population. In June 1932, the Kazakh leadership reported to the central government in Moscow that 73.1 percent of all private enterprises and 97.8 percent of all crop-growing areas in the country had been collectivised. Kazakhstan thus took first place in this regard among all the Soviet republics.

Only one year later, however, in the summer of 1933, Filipp Goloshchyokin's government was confronted with an economic and humanitarian catastrophe. Around 90 percent of the cattle rounded up in kolkhozes throughout the country perished due to incorrect care, water scarcity and lack of food. Within a matter of years, not only had one of the most important economic resources been destroyed, but the centuries-old tradition of nomadism had to all intents and purposes been wiped out.

From the very beginning, the measures of "Small October", collectivisation and "debaisation" met with massive resistance from the population. Between 1929 and 1931, some 80,000 people throughout Kazakhstan participated in over 400 uprisings. The protests, which were mainly directed against representatives of the Communist Party and state institutions, could be suppressed only with massive police violence. Many people chose the path of passive resistance and tried to flee the country to get away from the requisition commands, the repressions and the famine that had started in 1930. Between 1930 and 1932, more than one million Kazakhs fled to Mongolia, China, Afghanistan, Persia and Turkey.

The supply crises, which were initially limited only to certain regions, quickly spread to the entire country—not least because the central leadership in Moscow insisted on rigorously meeting the excessive tax quotas, even once the extent of the famine catastrophe had become apparent. In 1932/33, millions of people starved to death in all parts of the Soviet Union: in Ukraine, the Northern Caucasus, the Volga, the Urals and the steppe regions of Kazakhstan. In terms of the proportion of its total population affected, the Central Asian country was the Soviet republic most affected by starvation. An estimated 1.5 million people died here from the immediate consequences of starvation, exhaustion and illness. In the course of forced collectivisation, "debaisation" and sedentarisation, Kazakhstan lost between 36.2 percent (immediately perished) and 64 percent (emigration and demographic losses) of its total population within just a few months.

Given the horrendous extent of the deprivation, want, impoverishment and death it unleashed, starvation proved too much for the internal cohesion of Kazakh society to bear. Crime rates reached unprecedented levels, while reports of rampant cannibalism horrified the public. Completely overburdened local authorities reacted to the devastating conditions by cramming starving people into trucks, transporting them to remote regions and leaving them there to fend for themselves. Refugees who had been caught before making it to safety across the border were placed in barracks and left to starve. Minors were taken by the authorities to overcrowded children's homes, which were also stalked by hunger, illness and death.

As in the crisis areas of Ukraine, the meagre aid granted by the Politburo after a long period of hesitation in the summer of 1933 was insufficient to reach all those in need. The main aim of the support measures was to prop up Kazakhstan's collapsing economy. Saving people from starvation was at best the second priority.

Not only had 1.5 million people lost their lives at the end of the catastrophic famine, but nomadism as the dominant form of life of the Kazakhs had also ceased to exist. To make matters worse, from the late 1920s large areas of Kazakhstan had been confiscated and converted into camps for the construction of the country's largest Gulag zone—the KarLag. More and more people were driven out of their ancestral homelands. Many of the farmers who were dependent on nomadic grazing defended the areas vital for their herds by force of arms.

The period leading up to the complete resettlement of the Kazakh nomads from the KarLag zone to the barren steppe areas of the country was marked by repeated uprisings and conflicts: in the founding phase of the KarLag between February and May 1930 alone, 372 peasant riots were quelled. Between 1929 and 1933, the Soviet secret police, the OGPU, the forerunner of the NKVD, sentenced more than 13,000 people to detention in camps for terms ranging from three to ten years. Another 3,386 people were sentenced to death. The Kazakh intelligentsia also fell victim to the systematic persecution and arrest campaigns of the Soviet secret police. In two major waves of persecution in 1928/29 and in the wake of the mass terror of 1937/38, most of the country's intellectuals were banished, sentenced to forced labour or executed. The Stalinist policy of terror, the forced collectivisation and the associated exodus of the Kazakh population slashed the population from 5.8 to 2.4 million between 1930 and 1934.

Kazakhstan's Sovietisation was also accompanied by Russification, which envisaged the settlement in Kazakhstan of ethnic Russians alongside immigrants from other Soviet republics. These mainly comprised ethnic groups expelled and deported from the western Soviet territories, such as the Volga Germans and Crimean Tatars.

The consequences of the catastrophic famine, compulsory collectivisation and forced Sovietisation were concealed and downplayed for decades. Only during perestroika—the socio-political liberalisation that took place under Soviet head of state and party leader Mikhail Gorbachev—was the silence broken. 1986 marked the first protests and local uprisings in Kazakhstan against Soviet power and for the independence of the country. This was proclaimed in October 1990, following the election of the former Prime Minister of the Council of Ministers of the Kazakh Soviet Republic and former First Secretary of the Communist Party as President of the Republic of Kazakhstan.

Nursultan Nazarbayev repeatedly emerged victorious from the subsequent elections; he and his followers were, however, accused of obstructing the elections and of "irregularities". These also concern the constitutional referendum held in 1995, in which an unlikely 90 percent of voters ostensibly voted for the curtailment of the powers of the parliament in favour of the president.

In Kazakhstan, the process of coming to terms with the past is aimed at generating national awareness and is focused on the repression associated with the famine and the Gulag, in particular the establishment of the KarLag. For this purpose, various memorials have been set up and funded by the state. In many cases, the Office of the President or the President himself is involved in the construction and inauguration of the memorials. The victims of repression are commemorated each year on 31 May, but the perpetrators have never been brought to justice. Civil society organisations are still being suppressed to this day.

Monument to the Victims of Political Repression

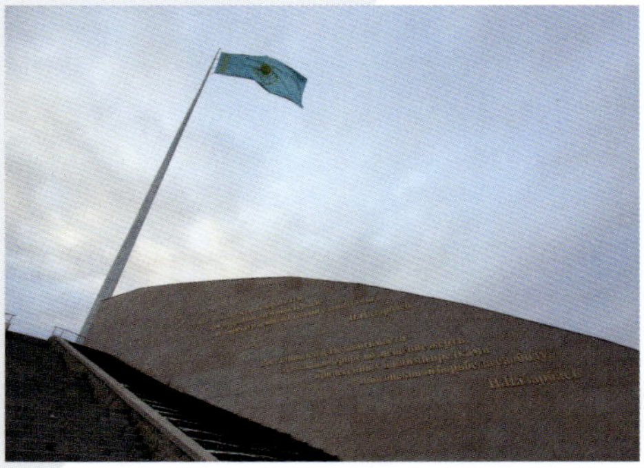

Monument to the Victims of Political Repression

Astana. The Memorial to the Victims of Political Repression is located on the site of the "Atameken" national memorial in the capital Astana. Built on 6 June 1997 on the initiative of Kazakh President Nursultan Nazarbayev, the 27-metre-high hill (Kurgan) commemorates the victims of political repression, in particular the detainees in the numerous Gulag labour and detention camps throughout Kazakhstan. Among other prominent national architects and artists, Timur Suleimenov, President of the Designers' Union of Kazakhstan, was commissioned to design the complex. The memorial was paid for by the Kazakh Presidential Foundation.

The architectural basis of the complex is a traditional Kazakh tomb construction, the "kurgan": a 27-metre-high mound that can be climbed via a staircase. At its highest point, a stele towers into the sky. The path to the top of the memorial is lined by a bas-relief with allegorical scenes of suffering to express the repression of the Kazakh people during Soviet rule.

Inscription

Kazakh: Біб—алтын кун бедеперген / кы байрағынə пей иіктерінде / жепбіреткен бейбітшіл епдің азаматымыз / Н. Назарбаев

Russian: Восстановление независимости— / это законномерное возмещение жертв, / принесенных нашими предками / в многовековой борьбе за свободу. / Н. Назарбаев

English: *Restoration of independence — this is the lawful compensation of the sacrifices made by our ancestors in the age-old struggle for freedom. / N. Nazarbayev*

Location: Astana, Qabanbay Batyr Avenue 6

Memorial to the Victims of the Famine of 1932 – 1933

Astana. The Memorial to the Victims of the Famine of 1932 – 1933 in Kazakhstan was inaugurated by President Nursultan Nazarbayev on 31 May 2012, the national Day of Remembrance of the Victims of Political Repressions. The memorial consists of a group of sculptures and a 23-metre-long memorial wall, the "Wall of Grief". The opening date marks the 80th anniversary of the artificially caused famine. Within a few months, the famine in the Central Asian republic claimed about 1.5 million victims and destroyed the country's centuries-old nomadic culture.

The dominant part of the memorial is a sculpture of a woman stretching her arms desperately towards the sky. Next to her stands the figure of an emaciated boy. Surrounding them are several mourning figures, such as were traditionally placed at the burial sites of indigenous Kazakhs. The middle of the black marble memorial wall behind it is designed in the form of a scissor grille. The designers used this symbolism to evoke traditional elements of nomadic living in Kazakhstan: the domed roofs of their yurts are held up by wooden scissor grilles. At the same time, it also represents the destructive power of forced sedentarisation.

Inscription
Kazakh: *1932 – 1933* Жылдардағы /
Ашаршылық Құрбандарының Рухына /
Мәңгілік Тағзым!

English: *Eternal remembrance of the famine victims of 1932 – 1933!*

Location: Astana, at the intersection of Respublica Ave and Abay Ave

►
Memorial to the Victims of the Famine of 1932 – 1933

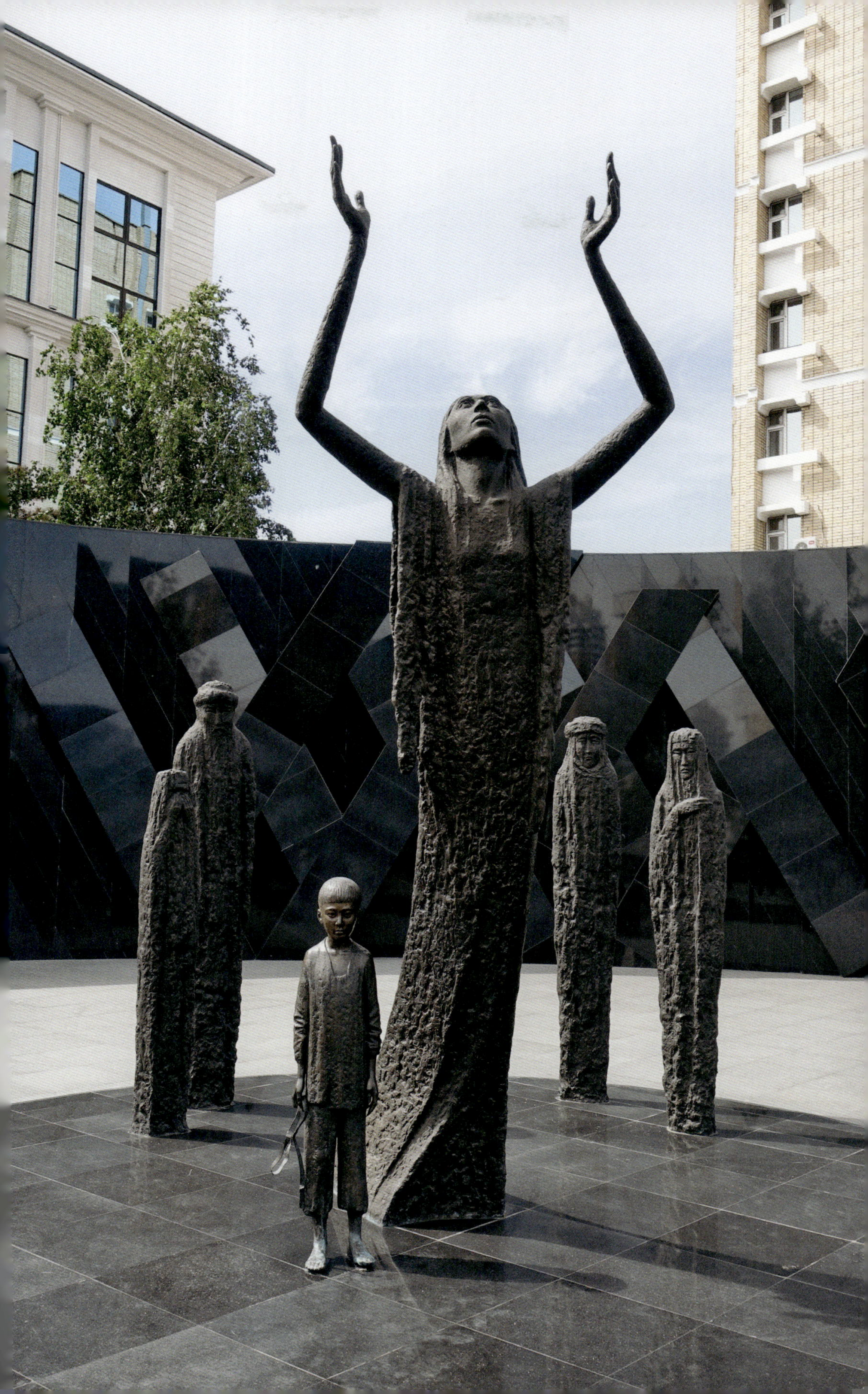

Memorial to the Prisoners of the ALZHIR Women's Camp

Akmol. The memorial inaugurated by Kazakh President Nursultan Nazarbayev on 31 May 2007, the national Day of Remembrance of the Victims of Political Repressions, is located at the historical site of the former "Akmol Labour Camp for Wives of Traitors to the Motherland". From December 1937 until its dissolution in June 1953, the ALZHIR camp was the central place of detention for the wives and children of victims of political persecution stigmatised as "enemies of the people". Today, the site houses a museum for the victims of political repression and totalitarianism, a memorial park, several groups of sculptures, the monumental buildings making up the "Arch of Sorrow" and a granite wall with the names of the 7,259 women who were held here.

Based on Order No. 00486 of 15 August 1937 "On the repression of wives and children of enemies of the people", the family members of prisoners were also arrested according to the principle of collective guilt. Troikas—consisting of the regional NKVD leader, the local party secretary and a representative of the public prosecutor's office for the region—were deployed all over the country by the NKVD headquarters and assumed the fundamental collective guilt of the persons identified as "traitors to the people" and their relatives. There were three special camps for family members in the Soviet Union: one in Mordovia, which mostly held the wives of disgraced high military officials, one in Western Siberia near the city of Tomsk, and one in Akmol. These camps were integrated into the existing structures of the "corrective labour camps" on the respective sites.

The ALZHIR was subordinated to the complex of Karagandinsk camps, the KarLag. It was located in an area isolated from the other detention sites on the shores of Lake Selonas near Akmol, which means "white grave" in Kazakh. The first consolidated transport with almost 8,000 "family members of traitors" arrived in ALZHIR in December 1937. Among the prisoners were not only female Soviet citizens but also numerous foreigners from European countries such as Bulgaria, the Baltic countries, Czechoslovakia, Poland, Romania and Sweden, but also from Korea and Japan.

ALZHIR was subject to a stricter camp regime than the other KarLag sites. This went hand in hand with the isolation of political prisoners but also with the ban on all correspondence, heavy physical labour and higher labour demands. Nearly 1,500 women worked twelve-hour shifts to produce embroidery in one of the most important production plants in the special camp. In addition to clothing and household textiles of all kinds, the start of the war required the women also to produce uniforms and winter clothing. Other inmates were assigned work in the fields or on road construction.

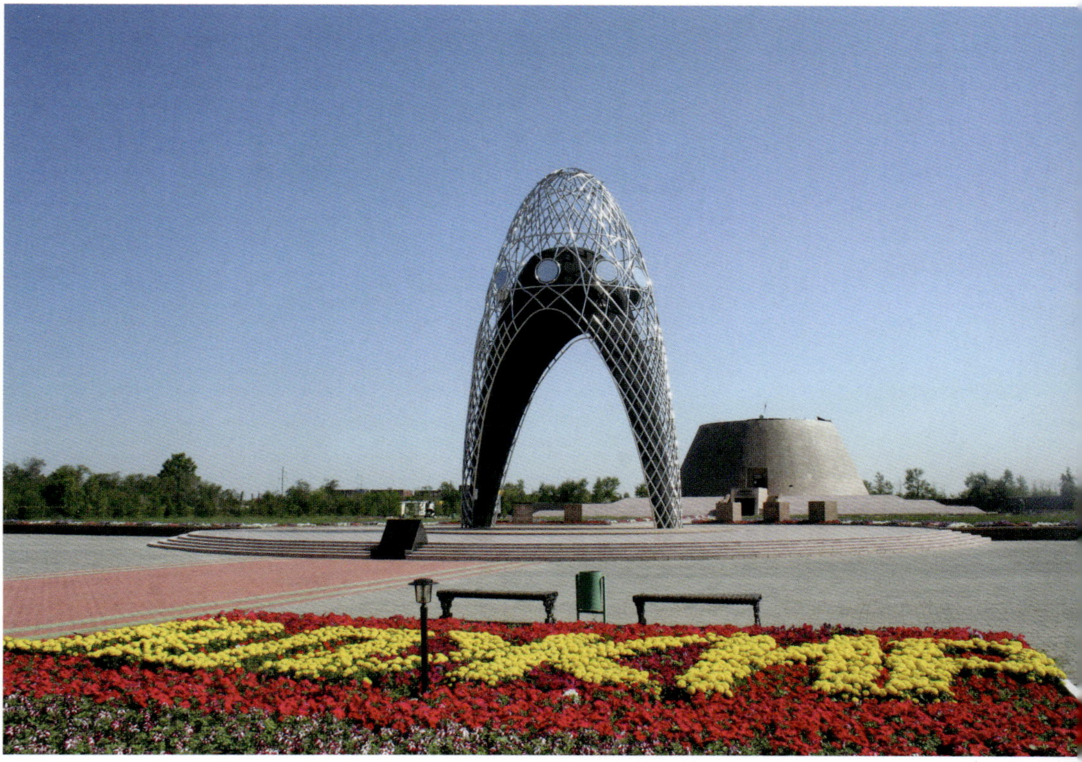

Outer grounds of the memorial to the prisoners of the ALZHIR women's camp

As early as September 1938, by which time 64 transports from 24 municipal remand prisons and 13 "correctional labour camps" in different parts of the Soviet Union had reached Akmol, ALZHIR was completely overcrowded. In October 1938, a "special branch" of the women's camp was opened in Spassk, near the town of Karaganda. Until its conversion into a POW camp in the 1940s, around 3,000 women were imprisoned there. In total, more than 18,000 women went through the special camp near Akmol, 7,259 of them serving their entire term of imprisonment here. In most cases, this was five to ten years.

The exhibition of the Museum for the Victims of Political Repression and Totalitarianism deals on the one hand with the history of the origin of the "corrective labour camps" and their political, administrative and economic significance in the state structure of the Soviet Union from the 1930s to the 1950s. On the other, considerable space is also given to the depiction of the individual fates of victims of the Soviet repression policy. Their only "offence" was to be the mothers, wives, daughters or sisters of men stigmatised as "traitors to the Motherland".

The exhibition contains original archive documents, letters and contemporary witness reports, photographs, clothing, preserved objects of daily use and other historical artefacts. The first part of the museum's two-part permanent exhibition presents the "political history of Kazakhstan in the 19th and 20th centuries". The country's Sovietisation, the forced collectivisation of agriculture, the famines of the 1930s and the Jeltoqsan riots in December 1986 which initiated the struggle for Kazakhstan's independence from the Soviet Union, are addressed. The second part of the exhibition, "The prisoners of ALZHIR", documents everyday life in the prison and the internment regime of the Akmol women's camp based on original certificates and mock-ups of the camp factory, the prisoners' barracks and command rooms. The museum organises a wide range of events such as readings and lecture series on the subject of repression and persecution as well as discussions with former inmates and the screening of thematically related documentaries.

Before the construction of the present memorial complex, a small museum had been built on the former camp cemetery site in 1989 on the initiative of the Director-General of Akmola-Fenix, Ivan Ivanovich Sharf. Its holdings were transferred to the memorial created in 2007. A massive archway of black granite under a dome woven from steel nets forms the entrance to the modern-day memorial. Also on display on the grounds are the faithful reproduction of a prisoner's barracks and the sculpture compositions entitled "Despair and Powerlessness" and "Fight and Hope". The first bronze sculpture shows a crouching man with his head bowed in mourning. Opposite him is the sculpture of a woman who, although emaciated, has a look of hope on her face. The memorial wall engraved with the names of the women imprisoned in ALZHIR bears **inscriptions** in Kazakh, Russian and English. They read:

Kazakh: ХХ ғасрдың *1930 – 1940* жәнe / *1950*—жылдарының басындағы / саяси қуғын—сүргін және / тоталиризм құрбандарын / еске алу—қабырғасы // Ада болып үміті, арманы да, / торғайлардай қамалды торға мына. / Ойларына не келсе, соны істеді. / Жазықсыздың жазыксыз жарларына

Russian: Стена памяти / жертв политических / репрессий / и тоталитаризма *1930 – 1940*х / и начала *1950*х годов ХХ века // А здесь в глухом чаду пожара / остатки юности губя, / мы не единого удара / не отстранили от себя

English: *Memorial / for the victims of political / repression during / the 1930–1940s / and early 1950s // And wasting our youth / we were facing / every blow / of a fierce life //* А. Ахматова

Location: Akmolinsk region, Akmol
Internet: www.museum-alzhir.kz

Museum of Political Repression Victims' Memory

Dolinka. The museum commemorating the victims of political repression, built on the initiative of Kazakh President Nursultan Nazarbayev, opened on 31 May 2010, the national Day of Remembrance of the Victims of Political Repressions, after extensive restoration work. It is located in the former headquarters of the Karaganda Corrective Labour Camp (KarLag), which was built between 1933 and 1935 by forced prisoner labour. Until the dissolution of the KarLag in 1959, the entire camp system on the territory of the Kazakh SSR was managed from here.

The KarLag was one of the largest and most enduring complexes of the Gulag and included 450 camps with thousands of main camps and subcamps that were established at different times and used for varying lengths of time. Its foundation dated back to the establishment of new detention camps in the Asian part of the USSR, Siberia and the Far East, as set out by the Council of People's Commissioners on 7 December 1929. This decision was preceded a few months earlier, on 13 May 1929, by a decree from Stalin, according to which the manpower of the prisoners sentenced to more than three years in prison was to be used in the fulfilment of the first five-year plan. The restructuring of existing Gulag sites and the establishment of new camp units in remote but economically promising regions of the Soviet Union were intended to help meet the planned increase in industrial production.

In the almost 30 years of its existence, the KarLag, with its various types of camp, reflected the development of the Soviet forced labour system. The original agricultural camp included the "Akmol Labour Camp for Wives of Traitors to the Motherland" (ALZHIR), special camps with a strict prison regime, and camps for repatriated individuals and prisoners of war. Prisoners were used not only in agriculture but also in various fields of construction work, coal and iron ore mining, the manufacture of equipment and the manufacture of armoured and infantry mines during the "Great Patriotic War". Particularly qualified inmates worked in the KarLag's agricultural and veterinary research laboratories, which cooperated with the Academy of Sciences in Moscow. Just a few months after the camp had been put into operation in May 1930, its detainees already numbered some 10,000; when it was dissolved in July 1959, the figure was around 17,000. During the time of the "Great Terror" and in the war years, the number of inmates fluctuated considerably, as was also the case in other Gulag sites. From 1936 to 1938, between 20,000 and 40,000 prisoners were taken in; during the "Great Patriotic War" the number rose to 50,000. However, the

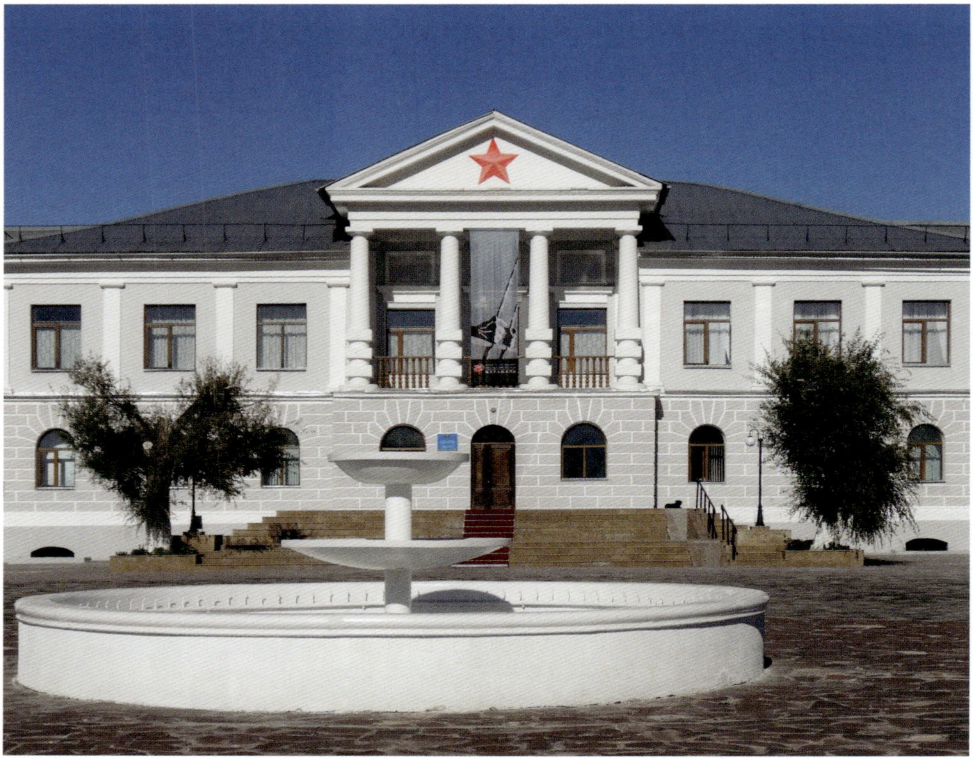

Façade of the Museum of Political Repression Victims' Memory

highest occupancy rate was in 1948, when 65,000 people were being held in the KarLag.

The camp's territory gradually expanded. The complex, divided into eight sections, covered an area of up to 17,129 square kilometres. The prisoners were spread over 72 camp sites. In the course of this expansion, ever larger sections of the Kazakh population were driven out of their traditional habitat.

The KarLag also included the third camp at Kengir, which became widely known through one of the largest prisoner uprisings in the history of the Gulag system, in May/June 1954. After the death of Stalin in March 1953 and the shooting of former NKVD leader Lavrentiy Beria, there were uprisings in the northern camps in Norilsk and Vorkuta. The amnesties issued only three weeks after Stalin's death pardoned over 1.2 million Gulag inmates but ruled out the release of "political" prisoners and all prisoners detained in the special camps.

The approximately 4,000 insurgents in the Kengir camp—including partisans and resistance fighters from Western Ukraine and the Baltic States as well as veterans of the Red Army—were calling above all for the reduction of all prison sentences, the abolition of exile after imprisonment, a relaxation of the prison regime through better living conditions, the abolition of prison cells and more contact with family members. On the morning of 26 June, 40 days after the strike began, 1,700 armed soldiers, 98 attack dogs and five tanks crushed the prisoner uprising. The "40 Days of Kengir" gained notoriety through the book "The Gulag Archipelago" by Russian dissident and Nobel Prize winner Alexander Solzhenitsyn.

The KarLag was wound up between 1956 and 1959, and the official date of closure was 27 July 1959. The agricultural camp sites were transformed into more than 50 state-owned estates for animal and plant production, which employed local and recruited workers alongside ex-prisoners and former warehouse personnel.

The Museum in Memory of the Victims of Political Repression in Dolinka has a permanent exhibition in 17 rooms, which examines the local history of the unjust regime in Kazakhstan, with particular reference to the KarLag. Visitors are also familiarised with the historical context of the Soviet Gulag system. The exhibition on the first floor uses historical documents, objets d'art, objects of daily use, various memorabilia and mock-ups to illustrate the history of the great famine in Kazakhstan in the early 1930s, the political repression of Kazakh intellectuals and the history of the development and economic activity of the KarLag.

The presentation also sheds light on the system of persecution and deportation operated by the Soviet secret police, which led to the exile of thousands of displaced persons and special resettlements from various parts of the USSR to Kazakhstan. Other rooms are dedicated to the acts of repression in the years after the death of Stalin and the development of Kazakhstan since its proclamation as an independent state on 16 December 1991. In the reconstructed cellars of the building, installations give an impression of the espionage, interrogation and torture practices of the Soviet secret police. These rooms are designed in clear contrast to the exhibition halls on the first floor: effigies of prisoners, guards, bureaucrats and officers of the secret police in recreated barracks, along with hospitals and carcases and interrogation, torture and execution rooms serve to shed light on the prison regime, the process by which victims were arrested and the course of the criminal investigations.

A virtual tour through all rooms of the museum is available on the institution's website. The texts of the exhibition are available in Kazakh, Russian and English. The museum offers guided tours of the exhibition and excursions to the nearby Mamochkino cemetery. The graves of mothers and children who died in the camp between 1930 and 1940 are located here.

Location: Karaganda region, Dolinka, Shkolnaya uliza 39
Internet: www.karlagmuseum.kz

Memorial to the Victims of Famine

Pavlodar. The Memorial to the Victims of Famine was ceremonially inaugurated on 31 May 2012, the Day of Remembrance of the Victims of Political Repressions in Kazakhstan. It is located at the entrance to the Muslim cemetery where the remains of famine victims were buried in the 1930s. In Kazakhstan, about 1.5 million people died during the great famine catastrophe of 1932/33. In the Pavlodar region alone, the "Great Famine" claimed around 300,000 lives.

The centrepiece of the Memorial to the Victims of Famine in Pavlodar is an approximately three-metre-high sculpture on a circular pedestal, which depicts the emaciated figure of a boy crying in a desperate gesture to his mother

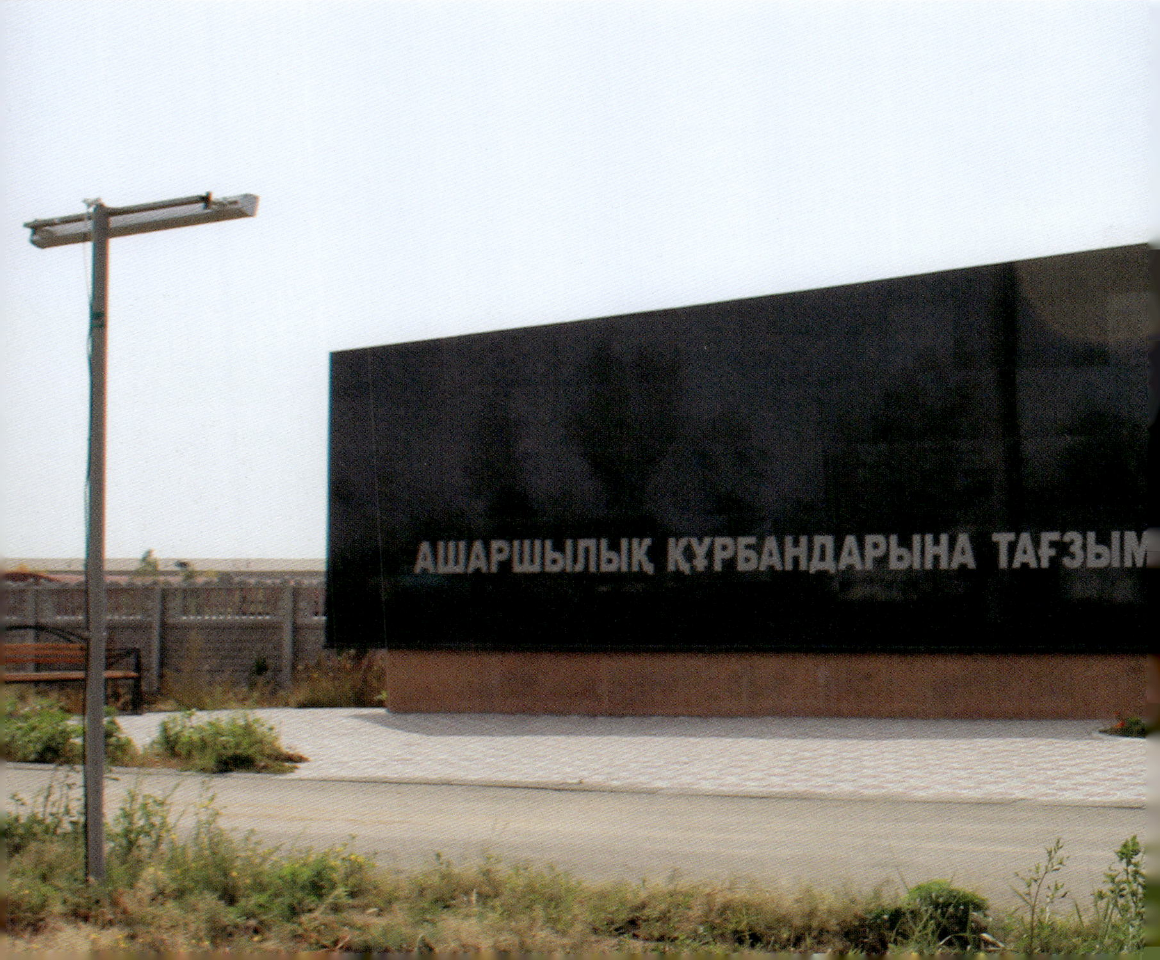

who has died of hunger and exhaustion. In the middle of the black granite memorial wall behind it are the broken contours of a shanyrak, the circular opening at the top of a Kazakh yurt. The artist Marat Abylkasimov considers the nomads to be the main victims of the famine in the Central Asian Republic.

Inscription
Kazakh: Ашаршылық құрбандарына тағзым // *1929 – 1933*

English: *We bow before the victims of the 1929 – 1933 famine*

Location: Pavlodar, opposite the Lenina district administration

Further reading:

Hedeler, Wladislaw: Sippenhaft im „Großen Terror“ 1937/38: Das „Akmolinsker Lager für Ehefrauen von Vaterlandsverrätern“ (ALŽIR) und seine deutschen Häftlinge. In: Weber, Hermann et al. (eds.): Jahrbuch für Historische Kommunismusforschung. Berlin 2005, pp. 81 – 101. / Hedeler, Wladislaw (ed.): Das Grab in der Steppe: KARLag. Das Karagandinsker „Besserungsarbeitslager“ 1930 – 1959: Dokumente zur Geschichte des Lagers, seiner Häftlinge und Bewacher. Paderborn, Munich 2008. / Kindler, Robert: Stalins Nomaden. Herrschaft und Hunger in Kasachstan. Hamburg 2014. / Mark, Rudolf: Die Hungersnot in Kazachstan. Historiographische Aufarbeitung im Wandel. In: Osteuropa, 2004, Vol. 54, No. 12, pp. 112 – 130.

Memorial to the Victims of Famine

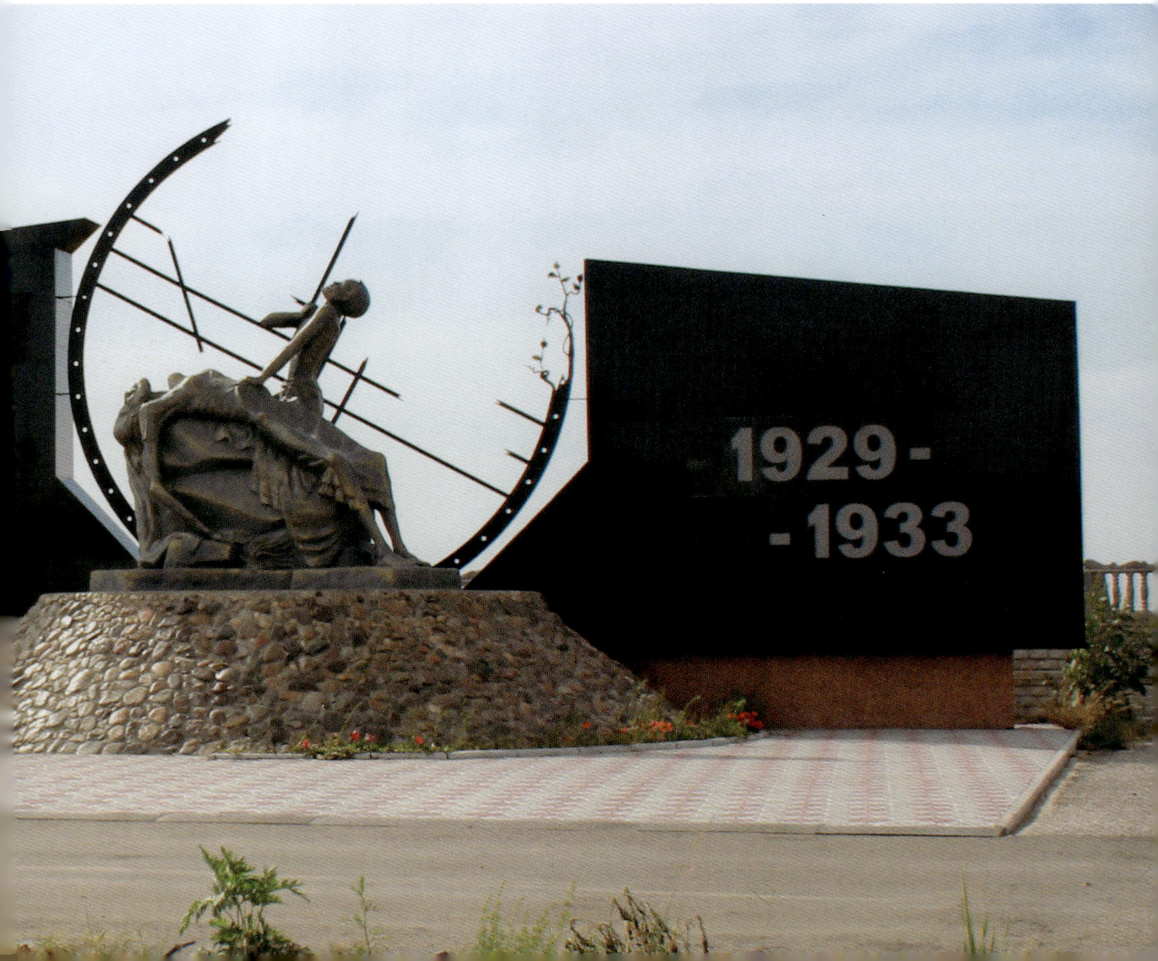

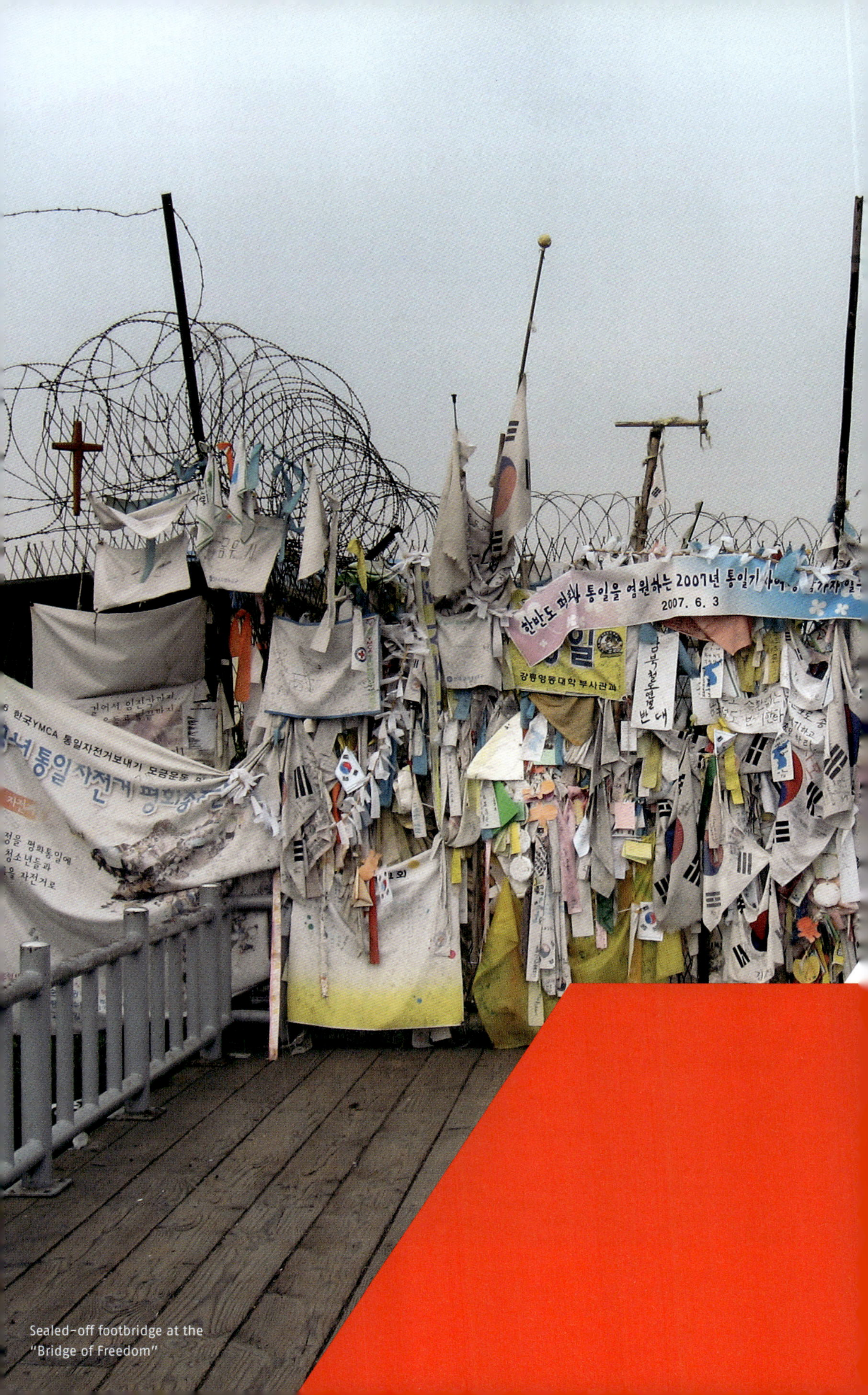

Sealed-off footbridge at the
"Bridge of Freedom"

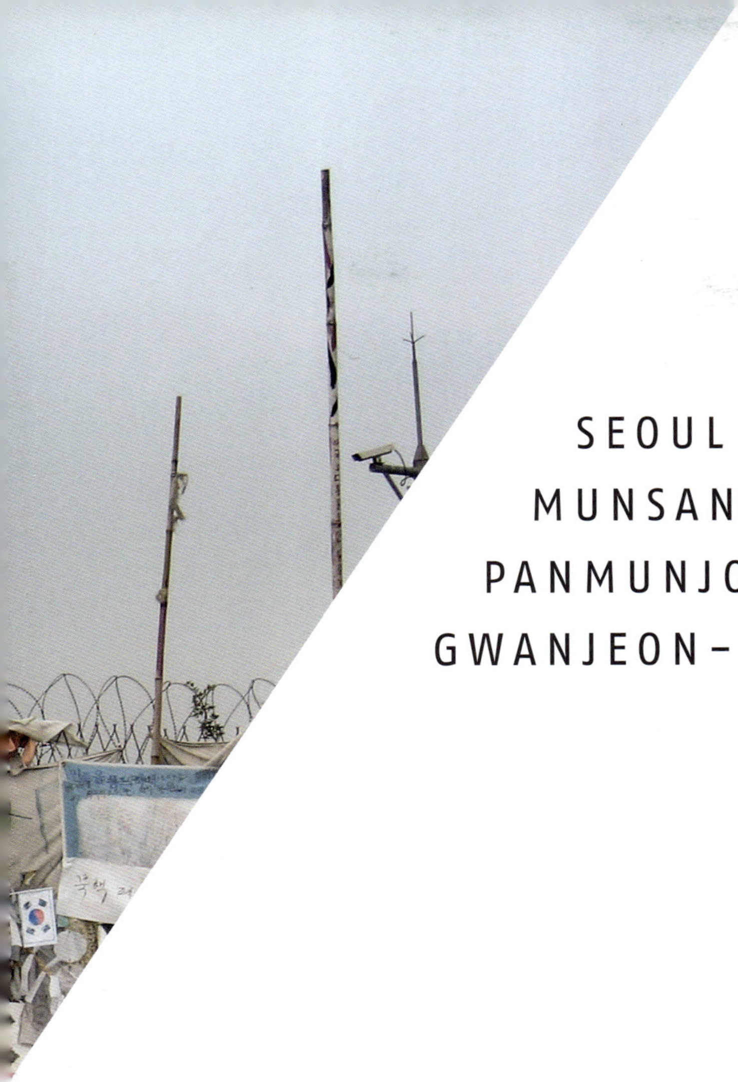

SEOUL
MUNSAN-EUP
PANMUNJOM
GWANJEON-RI

Korea

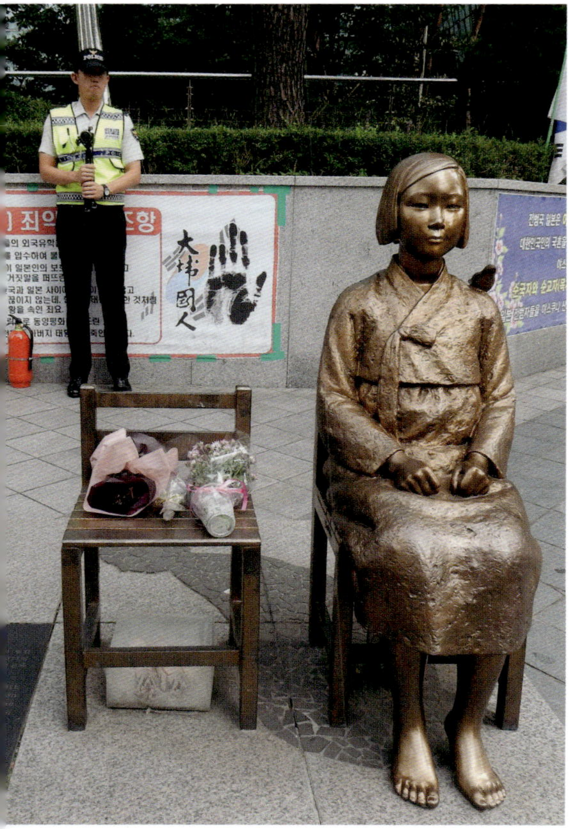

◄

In 2011, the Statue of Peace commemorating the so-called "comfort women" was set up in front of the Japanese Embassy in Seoul.

►

Border fortifications between North and South Korea

North Korea is one of history's most brutal communist dictatorships and, along with China, Cuba and Vietnam, one of the few communist regimes still in existence. Although there are numerous camps, prisons and execution sites in the country, where tens of thousands of people are held prisoner, there are, of course, no memorials there. The memory of the victims is maintained by institutions and memorials in the south of the divided country.

Korea came under Japanese rule after the Russo-Japanese War of 1905, after which the country was modernised and the Korean language and culture were suppressed. Especially during the Second World War in which Japan participated as an ally of Germany and Italy, Korean civilians were conscripted as forced labourers and Korean women recruited as slave prostitutes for Japanese soldiers.

After the surrender of the Japanese Empire in August 1945, the Japanese troops in Korea were handed over to the Red Army and the US troops along the 38th parallel north. Until 1947, the two Allies of the Second World War engaged in fruitless negotiations on the future of a united and free Korea. After the negotiations failed, the United States called on the United Nations to secure the withdrawal of all foreign troops from North and South Korea. This troop withdrawal was complete by the end of 1948.

After elections supported by the USA in the south and the formation of a Korean government, the Korean People's Republic was founded in the north as a communist dictatorship with Soviet support on 9 September 1948. In 1950, troops from the communist north invaded the south with

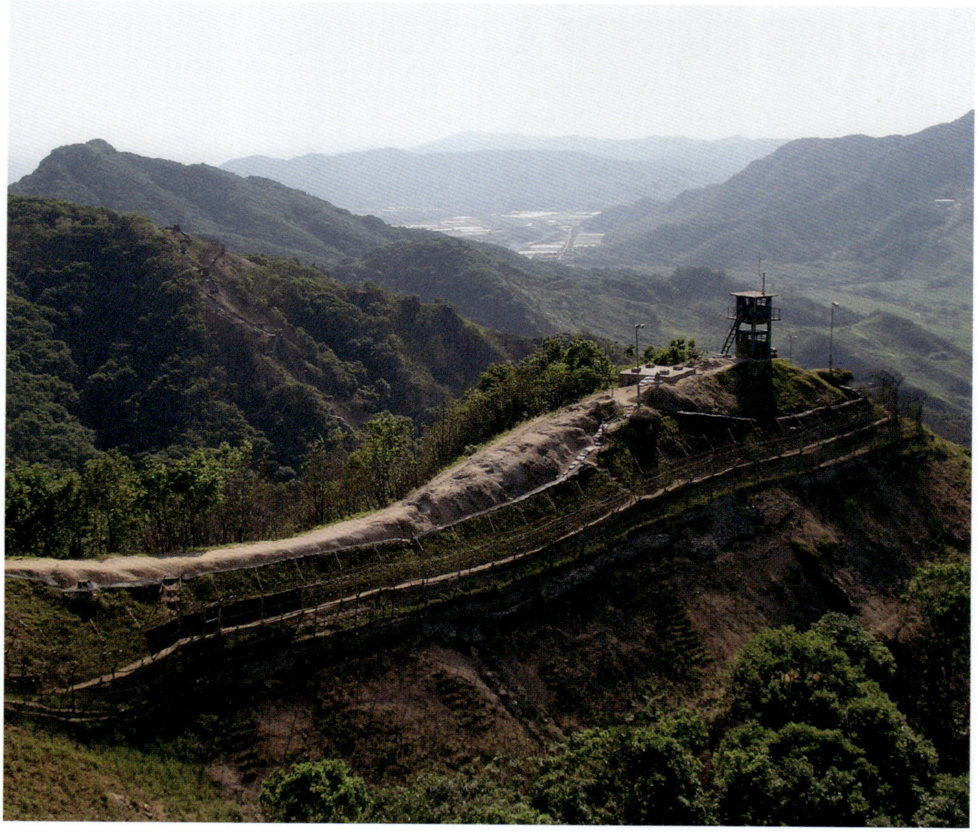

the aim of reuniting the country by force of arms and managed to take almost the entire peninsula. After initial support from the people of the South, any sympathy quickly turned into rejection and resistance when the North Korean communists tried to impose their rule in the South with forced collectivisation and by waging terror on the civilian population.

In this bloody conflict, which was the first proxy war in the Cold War between the Soviet Union and the USA, South Korean UN troops led by the USA beat back the North Korean troops. In 1953, in the Panmunjom Armistice Agreement, a demarcation line was finally agreed along the 38th parallel, separating the communist north from the democratically governed south. This demarcation line is one of the most heavily guarded and mined regions in the world.

While South Korea has developed into a stable parliamentary democracy since the end of the military dictatorship in 1988, North Korea has become the most isolated country in the world, where massive human rights abuses are a daily occurrence. Mismanagement and natural disasters led to continued famine that claimed thousands of lives. Coupled with an absolute cult of leadership centred around the dynasty of the country's founding president Kim Il Sung, his family and descendants, all forms of deviant behaviour are severely punished. Time and again, reports of executions in even the closest circle surrounding the current leader Kim Jong Un filter out into the public domain. So far, about 30,000 people have managed to escape from the isolated country to South Korea.

The official goal of both states remains the reunification of Korea.

War Memorial of Korea

Seoul. The War Memorial of Korea in Seoul was inaugurated on 10 June 1994 on the grounds of the former army headquarters. The extensive complex houses a comprehensive exhibition on Korean military and war history from its beginnings to modern times, with a prominent role afforded to the Korean War and the subsequent division of the country. In addition to the permanent exhibition, which is housed in the Joint Chiefs of Staff building, various military vehicles and armaments can be seen in the outer grounds. A memorial hall with the names of fallen soldiers completes the ensemble. In addition, various memorials commemorate the victims of war and division.

The grounds of the memorial also feature various commemorative markers and sculpture complexes. One of them is the memorial in memory of the Korean War. The eight-metre obelisk, consisting of two parts to symbolise the two parts of the country, North and South Korea, is the central memorial to the victims of the war. It is surrounded by two semi-circular groups of bronze sculptures depicting soldiers, civilians and refugees. In front of the memorial is a basin-shaped depression that can be reached via steps. This leads into the foundation of the obelisk, in which a memorial hall has been set up.

Also not far from the war memorial is the 18-metre-wide and eleven-metre-high memorial entitled "The Two Brothers". The elaborately designed sculpture composition shows the moment when two soldiers from the South and North Korean armies fall into each other's arms. This gesture of brotherhood expresses the will of the Korean people to unity and forgiveness. The soldiers stand on a freely accessible semi-circular pedestal of granite pieces gathered from different parts of the country. A crack runs through the middle of the platform, symbolising the division of the country. Inside the pedestal, wall reliefs show various scenes from the Korean War.

Location: Seoul, No. 8 1-ga Yongsan-dong
Internet: www.warmemo.or.kr

► Statue of Brothers

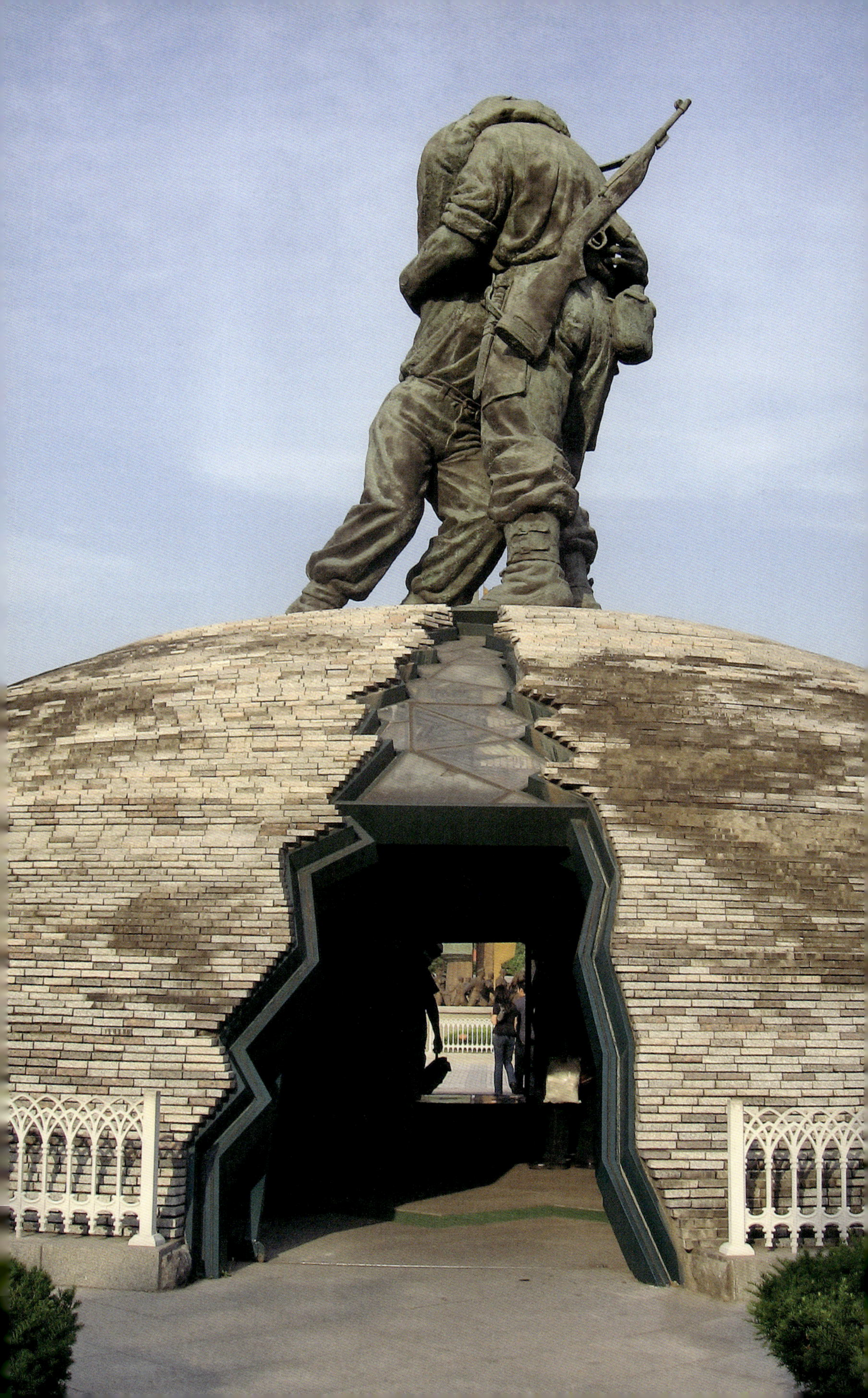

"Bridge of Freedom"

Munsan-eup. The "Bridge of Freedom" is the only link between North and South Korea. The modern bridge was built in 1998 to replace the old railway bridge that originally bore this name and is closed to visitors. A wooden connecting bridge leads to the edge of the fenced-off structure. Visitors have placed countless flags and notes here. Next to the bridge stands a memorial to the history of the building, which was inaugurated in 2000 on the 50th anniversary of the beginning of the Korean War.

The "Bridge of Freedom" was built at the beginning of the 20th century as a railway connection across the Imjin River. It consisted of two adjacent bridges over which trains could travel north or south. With the division of Korea into an American and Soviet Occupation Zone, the bridge became an important traffic hub between the two parts of the country. It was under Allied control until the North Korean troops overran it on June 25, 1950. In the course of the military conflict, a section of the bridge was destroyed, leaving only one functioning track. Allied troops recaptured the bridge, which played an important strategic role as a reinforcement and supply line until the end of the Korean War.

With the start of the armistice negotiations at the nearby Truce Village of Panmunjom in 1953 and the imminent withdrawal of troops behind the demarcation line, the bridge was reinforced and extended in makeshift fashion by American troops. It became particularly important when the exchange of prisoners of war commenced in May 1953. A neutral zone was created around the bridge where Allied prisoners were collected on the North Korean side and sent to South Korean territory for release. There was a temporary camp where the released prisoners could receive medical care. Under the impression of these events, during which more than 12,500 people were released, the bridge was given the name "Bridge of Freedom". In 1998, a new four-lane "Bridge of Freedom" was built on the same site and officially inaugurated on 15 June.

Imjingak Park for the reunification of Korea is also located in the immediate vicinity of the memorial. In 1972, a North Korea Centre was inaugurated here, which also houses an exhibition on the history of the neighbouring communist state. Named after the border river Imjin, the park features numerous memorials commemorating the Korean War and the division of the country.

Location: Munsan-eup, Paju-si, Gyeonggi-do

► Memorial next to the bridge

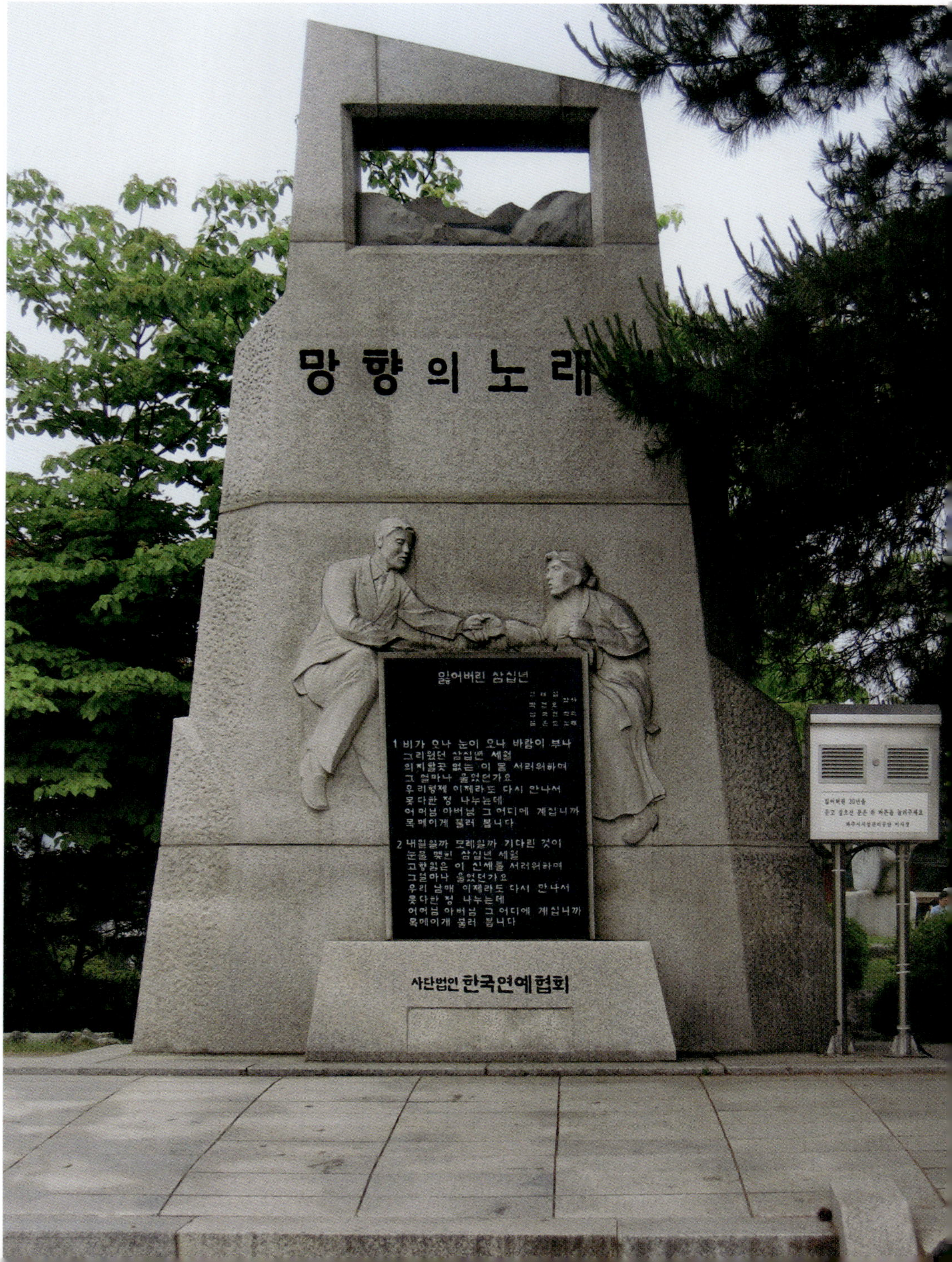
망향의 노래
잃어버린 삼십년
1 비가 오나 눈이 오나 바람이 부나
그리웠던 삼십년 세월
의지할곳 없는 이 몸 서러워하며
그 얼마나 울었던가요
우리형제 이제라도 다시 만나서
못다한 정 나누는데
어머님 아버님 그 어디에 계십니까
목메이게 불러 봅니다
2 내일일까 모레일까 기다린 것이
눈물 맺힌 삼십년 세월
고향잃은 이 신세를 서러워하며
그얼마나 울었던가요
우리 남매 이제라도 다시 만나서
못다한 정 나누는데
어머님 아버님 그 어디에 계십니까
목메이게 불러 봅니다
사단법인 한국연예협회

Panmunjom

Panmunjom is the name of a military complex located directly on the inner-Korean border under the administration of the International Ceasefire Commission. It is part of the common security zone between North and South Korea and still serves as a negotiating ground for delegations from both sides. Panmunjom is also the only official border crossing point between the two countries.

From 1951, delegations of the opposing parties in the Korean War met in Panmunjom to discuss an end to the military conflict. The negotiation site got its name from a nearby village of the same name, and the ceasefire agreement was concluded here in July 1953. The agreement to establish a demilitarised zone (DMZ) on both sides of the border required the resettlement of all inhabitants of the area. Only Panmunjom remained as a military outpost and was expanded in the coming years. Three blue barracks, half of which stand on North and half on South Korean soil, straddle the line marking the border. Official meetings took place there before North and South Korea erected their own buildings a few metres apart, in each case on their own territory.

There are also many commemorative markers in Panmunjom, including a memorial stone for the Allies who died defending the border. This stone, erected on the initiative of the Government of the Republic of Korea, is encircled by the flags of all Allied states involved in the conflict on the side of South Korea. It was installed to mark the 10th anniversary of the signing of the ceasefire agreement on 27 July 1963. Nearby, there is also a memorial stone explicitly commemorating the signing of the ceasefire agreement. The stone was inaugurated on 27 July 2003—the 50th anniversary of the signing—on the initiative of the United Nations High Command troops. Canadian officer David Dumont designed the pyramid-shaped obelisk, which features not only a text but also the flags of all Allied states.

Location: Panmunjom, Gyeonggi-do

► at the top: View of North Korea from the South at the "Joint Security Area"

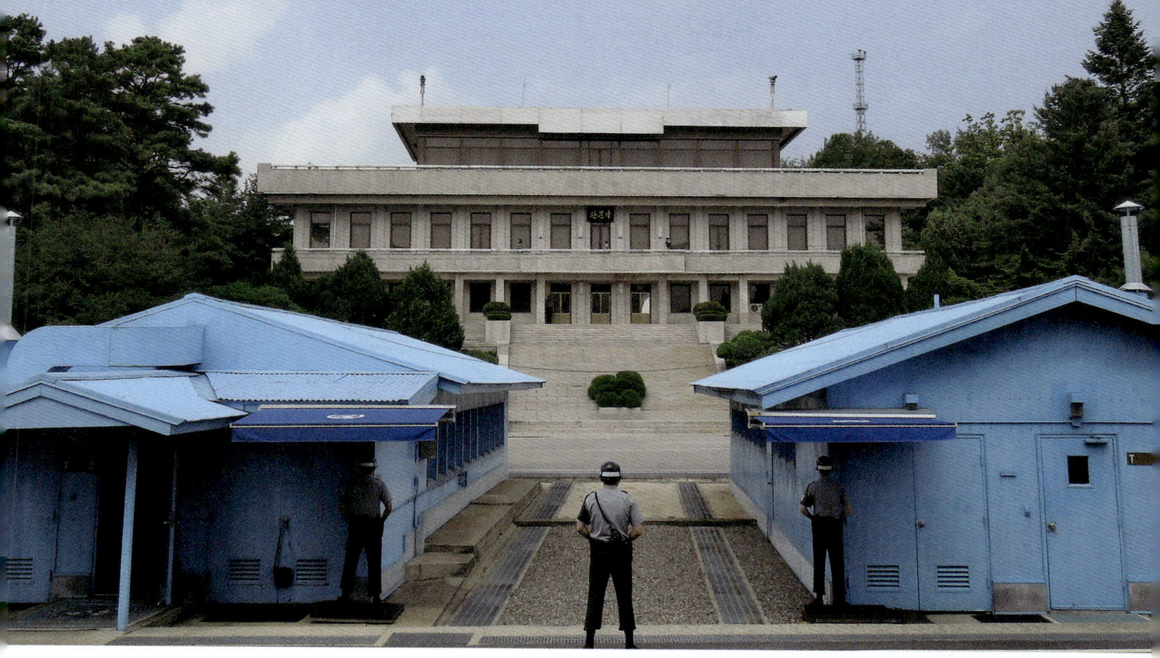

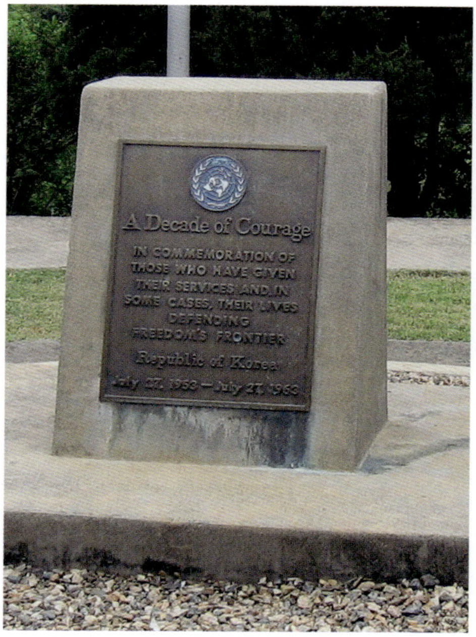

Memorial stone for the allies who died defending the border

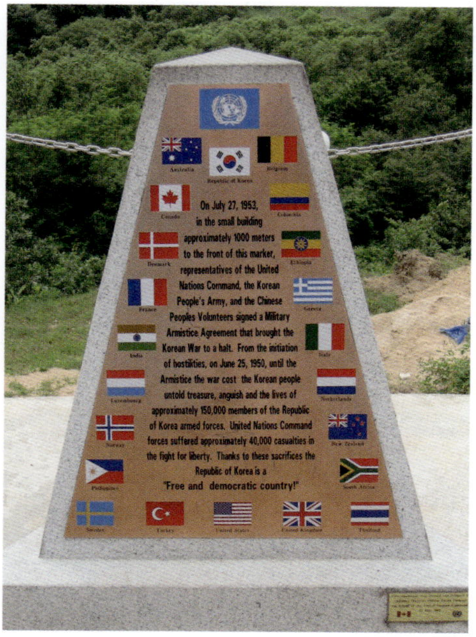

Memorial stone commemorating the signing of the Korean Armistice

Ruin of the Workers' Party Headquarters

Gwanjeon-ri. The ruin of the Workers' Party headquarters stands in the north-western part of South Korea. Until the outbreak of the Korean War in 1950, the building, erected in 1946, housed the Cheorwon regional headquarters of the Communist Party of Korea. The building was destroyed during the war. Later, mass graves with the remains of people executed by the communist security apparatus between 1945 and 1950 were discovered there. Plaques commemorate the history of the house, which was added to the list of South Korean national monuments in February 2001.

Cheorwon County was annexed to the Soviet Occupation Zone in 1945 after the liberation of Korea from Japanese occupation. In the same year, the Korean Communist Party began construction of an administrative building for the regional party committee. Hundreds of people from the surrounding area were press-ganged as construction workers and special taxes levied to finance the building, which was completed just one year later. After 1947, Cheorwon's Party Committee and Communist security forces coordinated propaganda campaigns aimed at influencing the people of the southern territories under US administration. In addition, the basement of the building served as a prison and execution site for opponents of the Soviet occupying power and the local communists. Countless people were executed here and buried in mass graves at the back of the house. With the outbreak of the Korean War in 1950, the party building found itself in the heart of the war zone and was badly damaged in combat. Since the 1953 ceasefire and the establishment of a new demarcation line, it has been part of South Korean territory.

Location: Gwanjeon-ri, Cheorwon-gun, Gangwon-do

Further reading:
An overview of memorial sites for the victims of communist dictatorships in the Republic of Korea is available in the online publication of the Federal Foundation: www.bundesstiftung-aufarbeitung.de/uploads/pdf-2009/eo_korea.pdf / Eun-Jeung, Lee/ Mosler, Hannes (eds.): Länderbericht Korea. Bonn 2015.

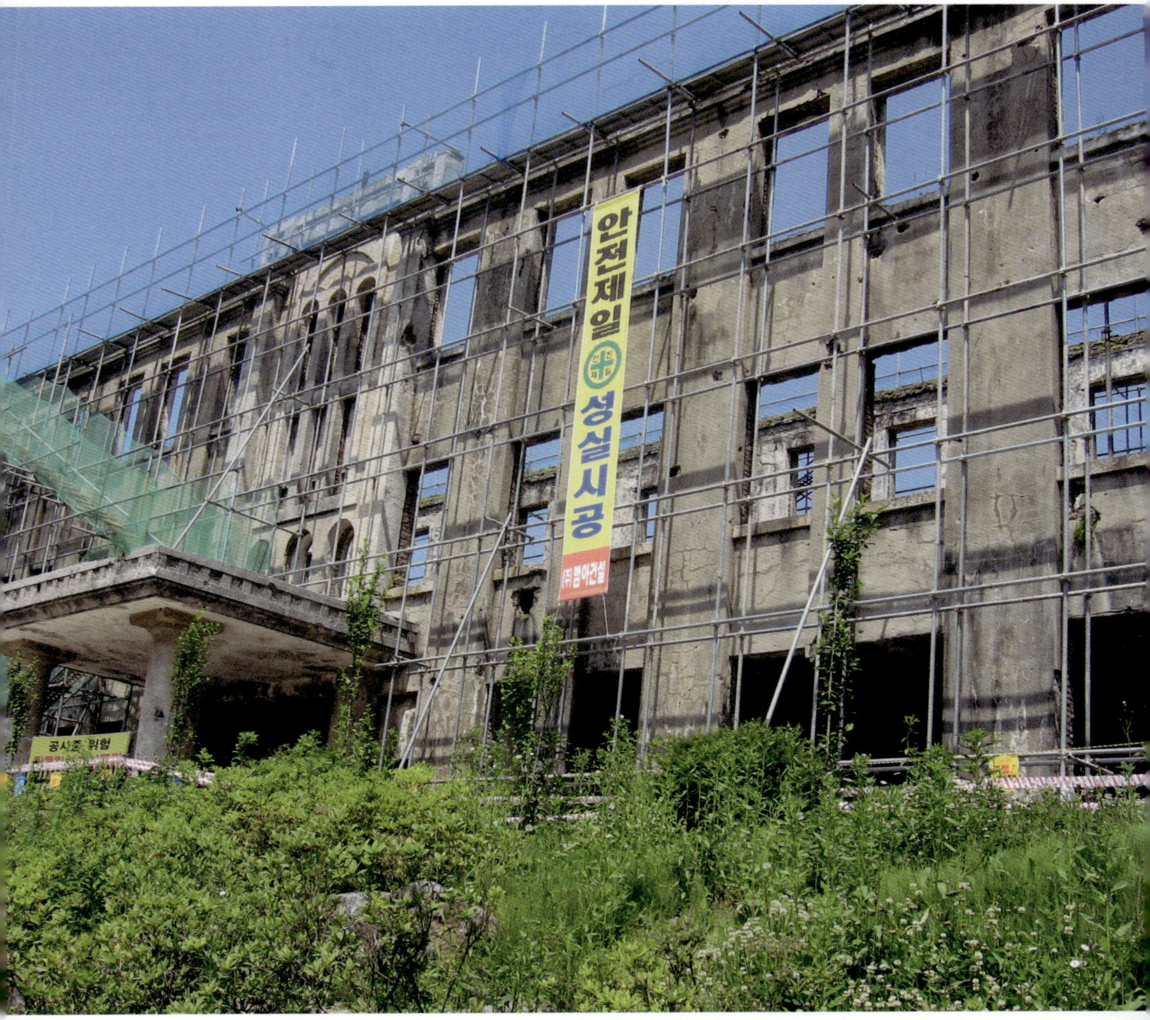

Façade of the ruin of the Workers' Party Headquarters

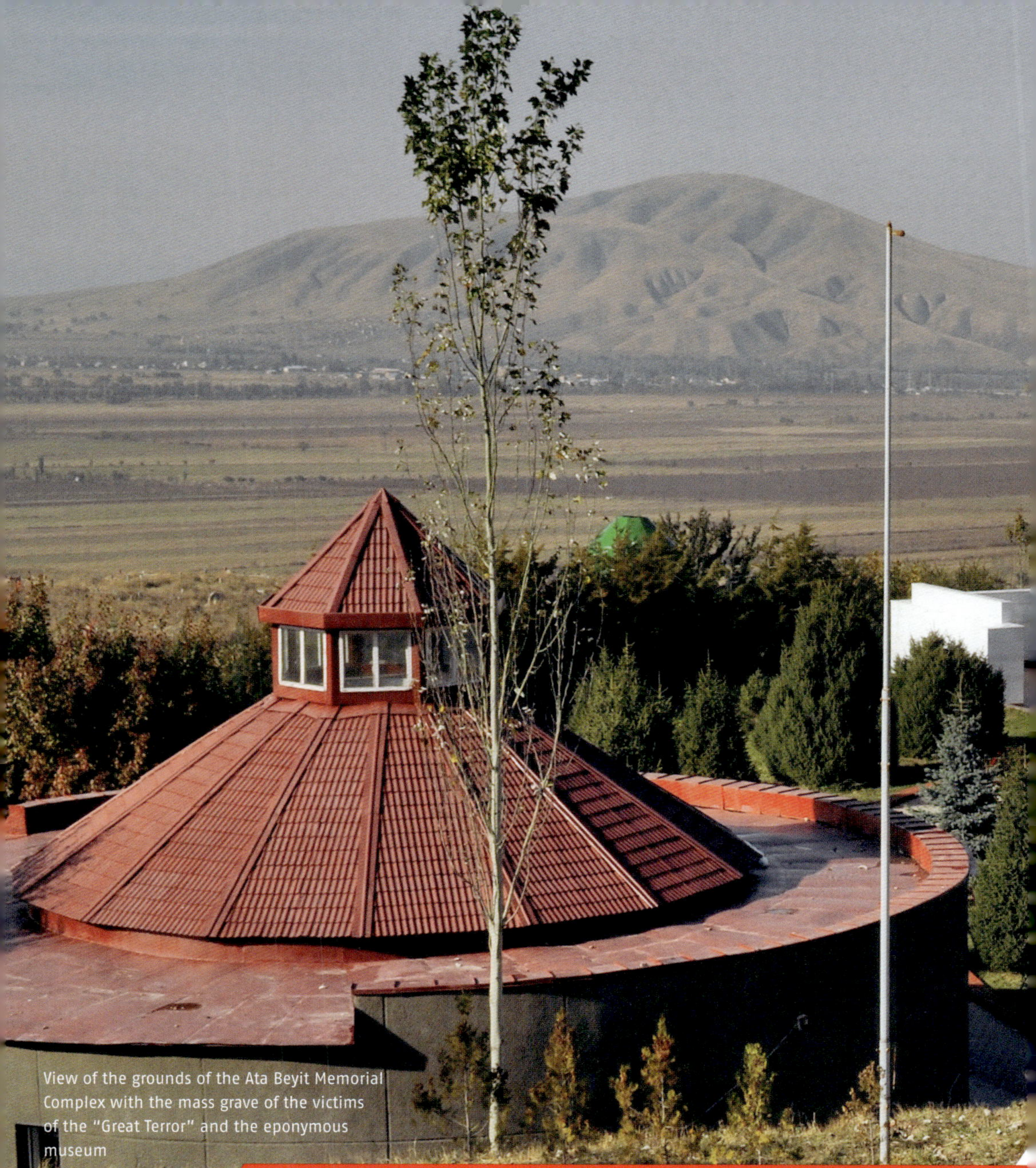

View of the grounds of the Ata Beyit Memorial Complex with the mass grave of the victims of the "Great Terror" and the eponymous museum

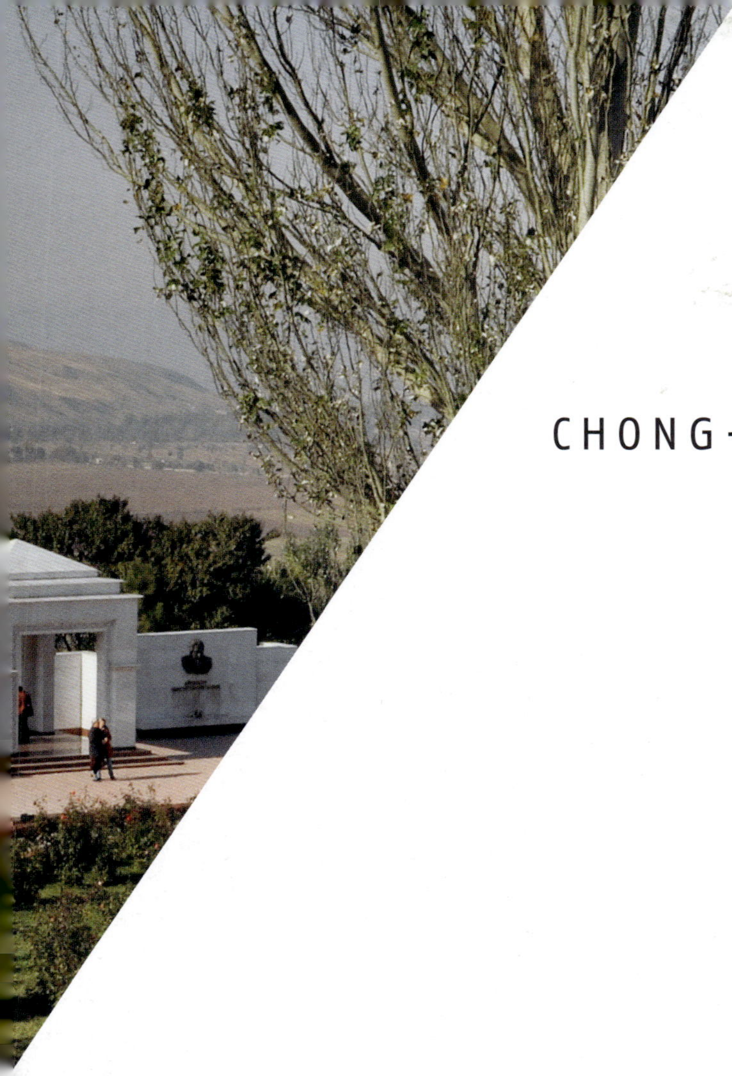

CHONG-TASH

Kyrgyzstan

Since the middle of the 19th century, Kyrgyzstan had belonged to the Russian Tsarist Empire. With the overthrow of tsarist rule in 1917, Kyrgyzstan gained its independence, but this was short-lived: in February 1918, Red Army troops occupied the country and deposed the government established in 1917. In 1918, Kyrgyzstan became part of the Turkestan Soviet Federative Republic, and, four years later, this region was merged with Turkmenistan, Uzbekistan and Tajikistan to form the Turkestan Autonomous Soviet Socialist Republic. The violent integration of the area into the Soviet Union was met with armed struggle and resistance. It was not until the mid-1920s that the area was brought under Soviet control. In 1926, the Kyrgyz ASSR was founded as an autonomous republic, which was renamed the Kyrgyz Soviet Socialist Republic in 1936.

With the introduction of Soviet power, the violent transformation of society also began in Kyrgyzstan, with a declaration of war on "backward" traditional ways of life. Nomadism, which was the predominant way of life for a large part of the population, was wiped out by forced sedentarisation. Private livestock, the livelihood of nomadic economies, was forcibly collectivised. Cattle and land owners regarded as wealthy were defamed as "kulaks", deported and murdered. Shamanism, once part of the traditional way of life and culture, was suppressed, as was the application of traditional healing methods. The fight was also taken to the Muslim religion rooted here, and almost all mosques were closed. The repression of traditional lifestyles and social structures was accompanied by forced modernisation. In accordance with Lenin's assertion that communism meant literacy plus electrification of the whole country, compulsory education was introduced and a comprehensive health system established, the implementation of which would require the enforced settlement of the population.

The Kyrgyz people did not simply acquiesce without resistance to the brutal transformation of their way of life and society. Many families fled to China and Afghanistan. To avoid the confiscation of their cattle, many people slaughtered their livestock. Famines and the collapse of the rural economy resulted. All the decisions were made in Moscow where knowledge of the situation on the ground was scant, with the result that it took a long time for the courses set by bad decisions to be reversed. It was not until the 1940s that the centralisation of livestock was reversed and grazing permitted in decentralised herds.

Just as in the other regions of the Soviet Union, the Great Terror raged in Kyrgyzstan in 1937/38 and was directed against both party cadres and "dangerous elements". It is still unclear how many people fell victim to the terror and the purges. It is estimated that hundreds of thousands died.

Populations considered unreliable—such as Volga Germans, Crimean Tatars and inhabitants of the Caucasus region—were deported from the west of the Soviet Union to Kazakhstan and Kyrgyzstan and forced to settle there. This led to demographic distortions, and the Kyrgyz people eventually became a minority. Since the war had forced the evacuation of many branches of industry from the western parts of the Soviet Union threatened by the German Wehrmacht to the Central Asian and Ural regions, industrialisation also took hold in Kyrgyzstan, where it had a lasting influence on the society. The collective memory of the years leading up to Stalin's death is marked by violent changes in lifestyle and society, forced collectivisation, famine, terror and death.

Only under Khrushchev and, especially, Brezhnev did people see a gradual improvement in their living situation. The food supply stabilised and the restrictive cultural policy was also relaxed. Gorbachev's reform policies of glasnost and perestroika led to a noticeable strengthening of the Kyrgyz opposition. It became possible to speak more openly about grievances and crimes of the past. The press was liberalised, and settlement bans that had shaped the lives of many people in the Soviet Union were lifted, allowing critical individuals to come together and form groups. At the same time, the easing of pressure and the loss of state authority resulted in an increase in violence. Previously suppressed ethnic conflicts, which had their origin in the forced resettlement of other population groups in Kyrgyzstan during the Soviet era, now erupted unhindered.

The final years of the Soviet Union saw repeated massacres of various ethnic groups in the border regions with Uzbekistan. In addition, people fought for access to the scarce water and pasture resources. Demands for the democratisation of political structures and the implementation of economic reforms increased. On 15 December 1990, Kyrgyzstan declared itself a sovereign state —albeit within the Soviet Union—and, on 31 August 1991, the Kyrgyz parliament proclaimed the country's national independence. When the Soviet Union was disbanded barely a year later, Kyrgyzstan remained part of the Commonwealth of Independent States (CIS) which had emerged from the Soviet Union.

The years of independence were marked on the one hand by political and economic reforms that initiated the democratisation of the country and demanded great sacrifices of the population. Poverty increased dramatically, causing even the modest standard of living under Brezhnev to be remembered fondly as a phase of relative general prosperity. On the other hand, the presidents, with their greatly increased powers, strengthened their authoritarian stranglehold on the country. Electoral fraud was a constant cause of concern. Hundreds of people died in unrest and mass demonstrations against the government in 2005 and 2011, but also in interethnic outbreaks such as the massacre of Uzbeks in Osh in 2010. Oppositionists were arrested, and their rights curtailed. Notwithstanding all the restrictions, Kyrgyzstan is now regarded as the only democracy in Central Asia.

The process of coming to terms with the past was slow: on the one hand, former communist cadres remained in power even after independence and continued to determine Kyrgyzstan's political development. On the other hand, many people struggled with the consequences of change.

Ata Beyit Memorial Complex

Chong-Tash. Initiated by former Kyrgyz President Askar Akayev and the well-known national writer Chingiz Aitmatov, the Ata Beyit Memorial (English: Grave of Our Fathers) was inaugurated on 8 July 2000 and is dedicated to the victims of political persecution in the Kyrgyz Republic of the Soviet Union. It is located on the site of the mass grave where 137 victims of the 1937/38 terror were buried by the NKVD. A museum of the same name is attached to the memorial. It contains 400 square metres' worth of personal belongings and archival documents about the people murdered at the site, as well as a history of political persecution in Kyrgyzstan. The memorial was funded by the presidential administration.

Above the central staircase is a group of stone sculptures. The emaciated figures of three men are depicted in a crouching position. Another memorial plaque is placed in the centre of the approximately two-hectare complex: above a smooth surface made of black stone, which slopes towards the sides and is framed by red granite slabs, is a tunduk made of red tubes. The tunduk is the highest point in the traditional yurts of the Kyrgyz nomads, where the two main structural supports cross. The stylised representation of a tunduk plays an important role in the symbolism of Kyrgyz statehood and is very present in public awareness—not least as the national coat of arms on the national flag.

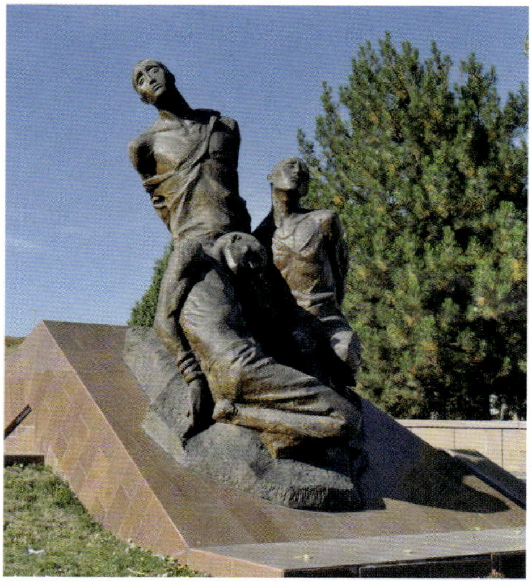

Group of sculptures commemorating the victims of the "Great Terror"

Below this construction, the mortal remains of the victims of mass terror lay buried. Accused of "counterrevolutionary activity" and defamed as "enemies of the people", 137 representatives of Kyrgyz intelligence, officials of the party and state apparatus, writers, teachers and students were executed in just four days between 5–8 November 1938. Their names are engraved on the red granite slabs surrounding the memorial plaque. For decades, the execution site had been kept secret and was eventually completely forgotten. Only after perestroika were excavation and exhumation works carried out at the beginning of 1992 on the initiative of Bübüra Kydyralieva. Kydyralieva's father—a witness to the events of November 1938—had revealed to his daughter the secret of the executions and the place where the remains of the dead were buried. Instrumental in the reburial and solemn funeral of the victims and in the design of the memorial complex was well-known Kyrgyz writer Chinghiz Aitmatov, whose father Torekul Aitmatov had been executed here in 1938. Since June 2008, Chinghiz Aitmatov's grave of honour has also been located just a few metres to the right of the central memorial square.

On 16 November 2011, a memorial to the victims of the coup d'état in April 2010 also opened on the site. This includes a 19-metre-long and 1.9-metre-high memorial wall of black and red granite on which the names of the victims are engraved. In addition, 27 black granite gravestones engraved with portraits of the deceased were erected. The ensemble is completed by an 8.5-metre-high mausoleum-like structure made of red granite and white marble.

On the basis of a presidential decree, a memorial ensemble commemorating the victims of the Central Asian Revolt of 1916 was also ceremoniously unveiled to the public at the memorial site in September 2016. In the centre of the composition is a 21-metre-high sculpture. On three massive stelae covered with red granite rests a tunduk, symbolising the convex roof of a yurt. Empty stirrups hang from it on metal cords of varying lengths, representing the enormous loss of life resulting from the revolt. Scenes on the 3.5-metre-high bas-reliefs on both sides of the sculpture illustrate the history of the Kyrgyz people during the 1916 National Uprising and the subsequent Soviet period.

8 November is the official Day of Remembrance for the Victims of Political Repressions in Kyrgyzstan, specifically commemorating the victims of the 1937/38 Great Purge.

Location: Chong-Tash, about 20 kilometres south of Bishkek

Further reading:

Kyrgyssstan. Memorialnyj kompleks schertwam repressij „Ata Beyjt". Pamjatniki schertwam polititscheskich repressij na territorii bywschego SSSR. [Kyrgyzstan. Memorial complex to the victims of repression "Ata Beyit". Memorials for the victims of political repression in the territory of the former USSR]. Sakharov Centre. Available online at: www.sakharov-center.ru/asfcd/pam/?t=pam&id=357&pic=5 (last accessed on: 16/11/2017). / Owen, Catherine: Memorial Ata Beyjt: Kyrgyssstan sakrywaet wosmoschnost dialoga s sowetskim proschlym. [Ata Beyit Memorial: Kyrgyzstan closes off the possibility of dialogue with the Soviet past.] 2011. Available online at: www.cogita.ru/pamyat/istoricheskaya-politika/memorial-ata-beiit-kyrgyzstan-zakryvaet-vozmozhnost-dialoga-s-sovetskim-proshlym (last accessed on: 16/11/2017). / Schmitz, Andrea/ Trevisani, Tommaso: Neuanfang im Schatten der Krise. Kirgistan nach dem Regimewechsel. In: SWP-Studie Stiftung Wissenschaft und Politik; Deutsches Institut für Internationale Politik und Sicherheit. Berlin 2011.

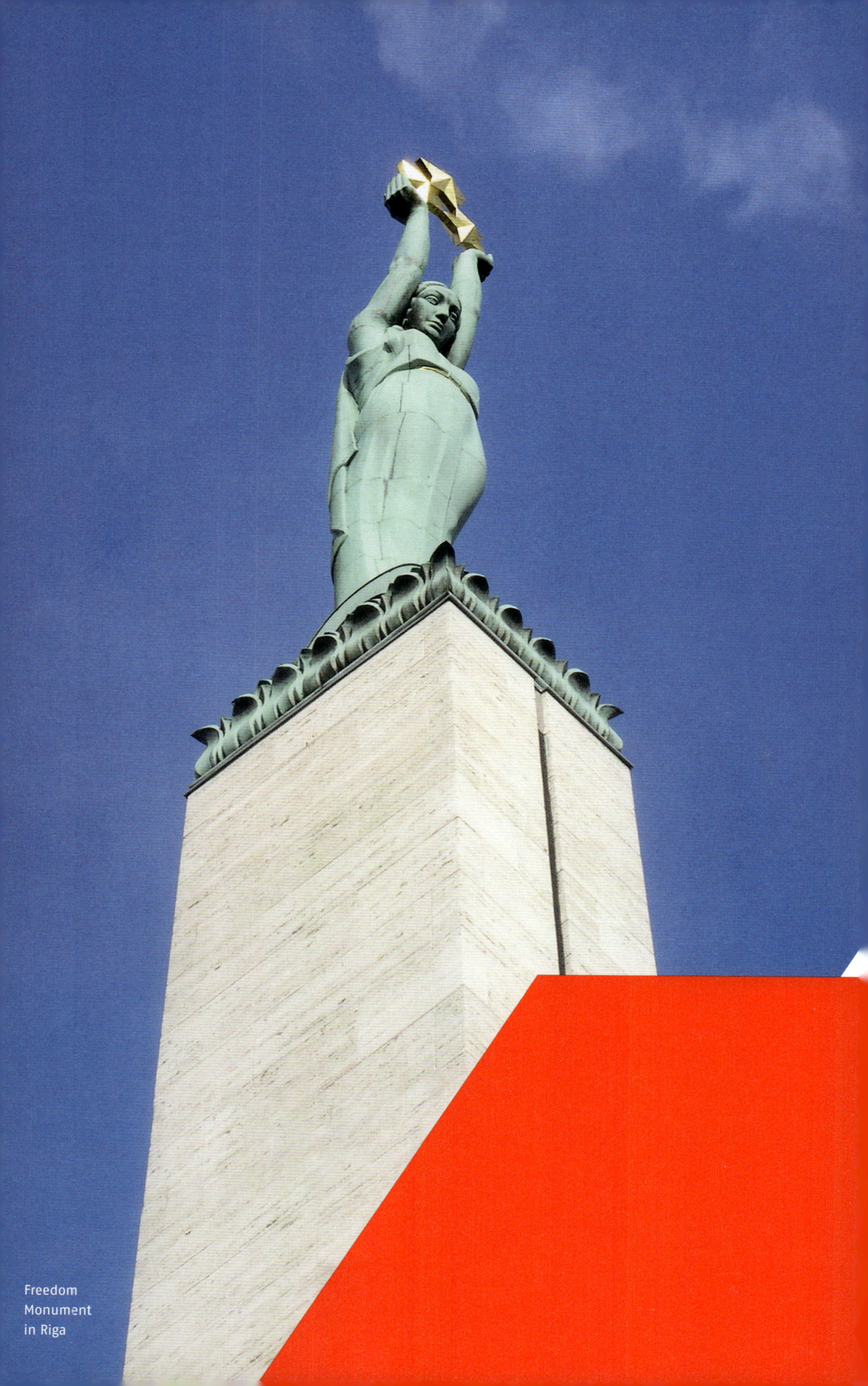

Freedom
Monument
in Riga

RIGA

Latvia

With the signing of the Molotov-Ribbentrop Pact on 23 August 1939, with its secret additional protocol dividing the states of Eastern Europe into spheres of influence between Hitler and Stalin, Latvia was placed under Soviet control. In October 1939, the Latvian government was forced to agree to the stationing of Red Army units in the country. In June 1940, the Kremlin issued an ultimatum, calling for the establishment of a pro-Soviet regime in Latvia and an increase in Soviet military presence. Only a short time later, the Red Army occupied the country. A so-called "people's government" under Moscow's influence took over the affairs of state. One month later—in July 1940—the People's Seimas announced the establishment of a Soviet government and applied for Latvia's accession to the Union of Soviet Socialist Republics, to which the USSR's Supreme Soviet agreed on 5 August 1940.

Soviet power having been established in the country, Soviet tools of repression, such as the NKVD, were also introduced. Sovietisation was accompanied by brutal force and the arrest and murder of politicians, clergy, intellectuals and artists; industry and banks were nationalised. In the early days of the forced collectivisation of agriculture, landowners were expropriated and kolkhozes established. The state controlled religious policy was to confiscate church estates and close houses of prayer. Members of the clergy were detained and murdered. In several places, remand prisons with interrogation, detention and execution rooms were established and mass arrests, deportations and executions prepared.

In the "Year of Horror" ("Baigais gads") in 1940/41, around 23,000 Latvians were arrested, deported or executed for political reasons. The first Soviet occupation was followed by the Nazi German occupation from July 1941 to September 1944. With the memory of Soviet reprisals still fresh, the Germans were initially welcomed as liberators by large sections of the Latvian population who were hoping for a return to independence. It soon became apparent, however, that the old occupying power had simply been replaced by a new one. Latvia was integrated into the "Reichkommissariat Ostland". Latvian collaborators and, later, press-ganged recruits were also involved in the extermination actions of the National Socialist occupying forces.

Almost all the approximately 70,000 Jews living in Latvia at the end of June 1941 were murdered; only 3,000 survived the Holocaust. Of the 20,000 Jews deported from Austria, Czechoslovakia and Germany to Latvia, only about 1,000 survived the massacres. Among the victims of the National Socialist regime of terror were approximately 20,000 Latvian communists and resistance fighters as well as several tens of thousands of Latvian citizens imprisoned and deported to Germany. Numerous Latvians joined resistance movements against the German occupying forces and participated in underground groups.

After Latvia was reconquered by the Red Army, the second phase of Stalinist repression began, lasting until the dictator's death in 1953. On the pretext of persecuting collaborators with the Nazi occupation regime, mass arrests and executions were again carried out. Actual and alleged collaborators became the victims of these measures, as did members of the national Latvian resistance movement—from 1944 onwards, about 15,000 "Forest Brothers" banded together as partisan units against the renewed Soviet occupation of the country—and the political, spiritual and cultural elites, who were declared "subversive elements". In 1949 alone, lists with names of about 42,000 persons were drawn up and their bearers deported to Siberia between 25 and 27 March 1949. By 1953, about 150,000 Latvians had been killed, imprisoned or exiled. After the death of Stalin, the first deportees were granted amnesty, but upon their return from the camps they were neither reunited with their confiscated property nor were they allowed to choose Riga as their place of residence.

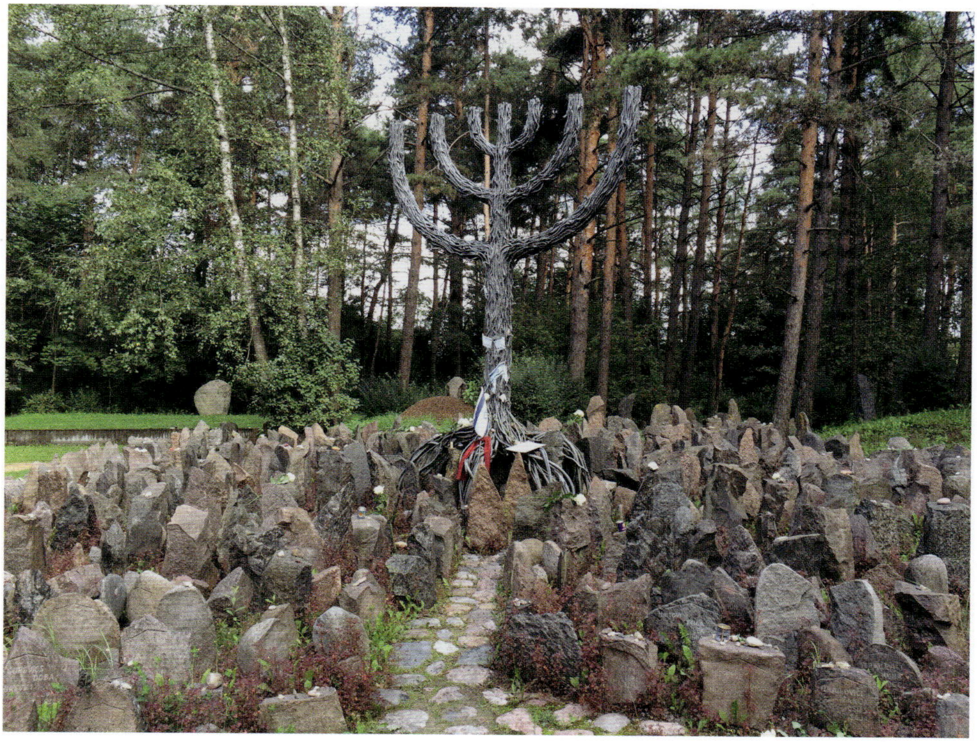

Memorial to the victims of the Holocaust
in Rumbula Forest

Activists and dissidents in Latvia campaigned after 1953 for human rights to be respected. However, these efforts only really picked up steam with Mikhail Gorbachev's policy of reform of glasnost and perestroika. In 1986, a Helsinki Group was set up in Latvia to promote respect for human rights and historical truth. Their activities were resisted by the state, as were earlier attempts to organise resistance and opposition. The members were perceived primarily as nationalist freedom fighters, arrested and finally forced into exile.

On 14 June1987, the anniversary of the beginning of the mass deportations from Latvia in 1941 to the Gulag camps, thousands of people laid down flowers at the Freedom Monument in Riga. This was repeated on 23 August 1987, the anniversary of signing of the Molotov-Ribbentrop Pact. In the face of mass protests, the Soviet leadership changed its nationality policy in the three Baltic Soviet republics. For example, the Latvian language was incorporated into the Constitution as a national language at the end of 1988. In October the same year—in parallel with the independence movements in Lithuania (Sąjūdis) and Estonia (Rahvarinne)—the Popular Front of Latvia (Tautas Fronte) was founded as a rallying point for the country's political reform forces.

On 23 August 1989, the fiftieth anniversary of the Molotov-Ribbentrop Pact, more than two million people formed a human chain through all three Baltic republics—Estonia, Latvia and Lithuania—to demonstrate their desire for national independence. The "Baltic Way" spanned over 600 kilometres and took in Tallinn, Riga and Vilnius, the capitals of the three Baltic countries. The national popular fronts in Latvia, Lithuania and Estonia thus demonstrated to the central authorities in Moscow that they could mobilise large crowds of people to enforce their desire for independence. The Tautas Fronte redoubled its demands for a sovereign Latvia. After winning the parliamentary elections on 18 March 1990 by a large majority and assuming key positions in the new government, the new parliament announced the "restoration of independence" of the country on 4 May 1990. This statement was accompanied by a condemnation of the Stalinist crimes and the occupation by the Soviet Union in 1940.

Following the intervention by Soviet special forces in the Lithuanian capital Vilnius on the night of 12–13 January, the democratic forces of the government, supported by the population, also prepared for military intervention in Riga. Despite the deployment of special forces of the Soviet Ministry of Internal Affairs in the city centre of Riga in January 1991, the Soviet regime could no longer hold on to power. During the subsequent conflicts in which Riga was defended against the advancing Soviet troops, eight people were killed. The unsuccessful coup against state and party leader Mikhail Gorbachev in August 1991 was used by the popular front to finally achieve national sovereignty on 21 August 1991.

The Soviet occupation regime and the injustices committed were designated as criminal by the Latvian parliament as early as 1990. Members of the Communist Party who were active after 1991 were stripped of their right to stand for election. Nor were they entitled to adopt Latvian citizenship. In 1997, the use of Soviet and Nazi symbols was banned and has been a punishable offence ever since.

A law passed in 1998 expunged the criminal records of victims of political repression. This gave them legal standing to claim for restitution of, or compensation for confiscated property or

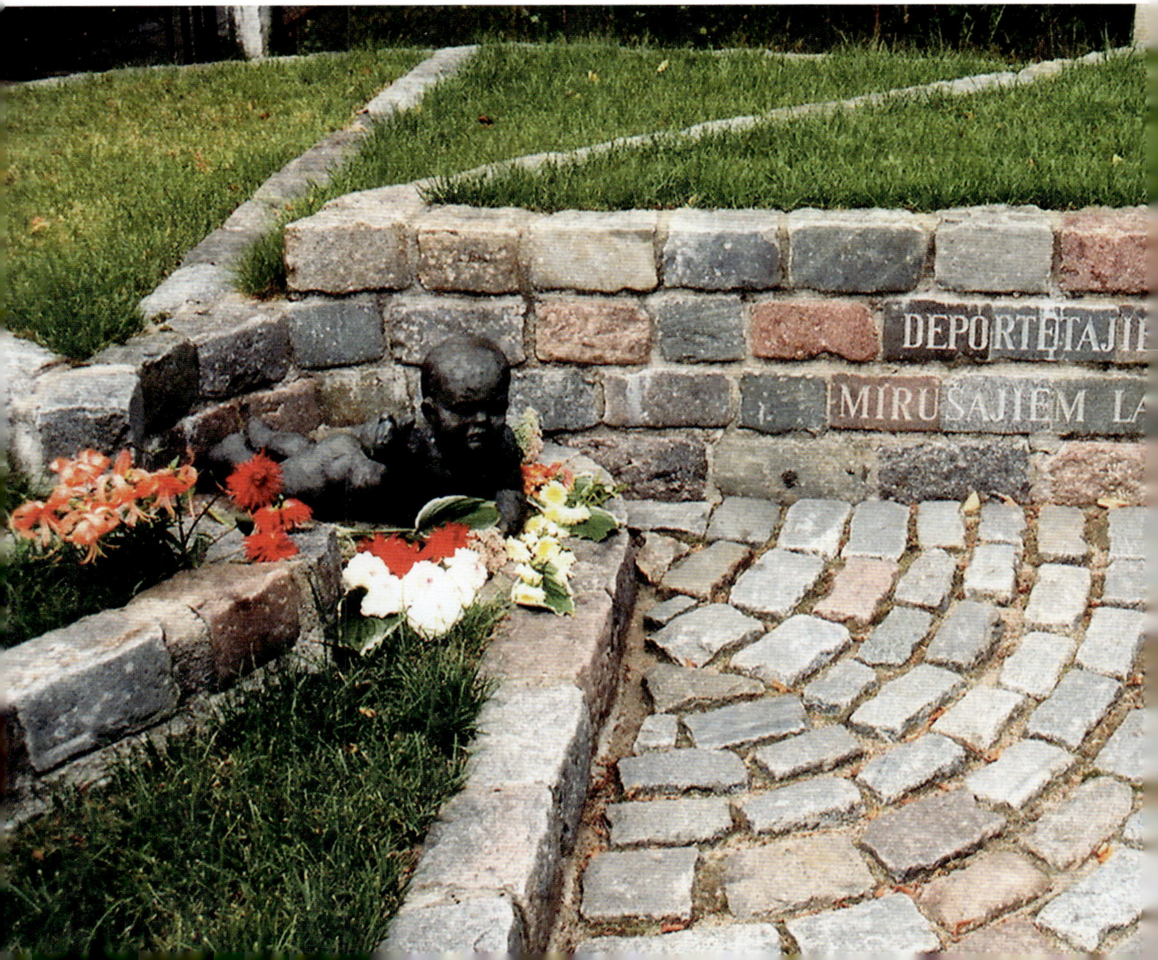

to apply for compensation payments for deportation, imprisonment and repression pursuant to provisions put in place in 1995. Overall, however, the social situation of formerly repressed people remains poor, as the periods of persecution have had an impact especially on pensions, with the consequence that many people are forced to live at subsistence level.

The KGB files were handed over to the Centre for the Documentation of the Consequences of Totalitarianism, which is part of the Latvian Constitutional Protection Bureau. In 2018, the decision was made to open and transfer the files into a separate archive. For certain positions in the state and administrative apparatus, there is an obligation to check whether the candidates are former employees of the KGB. Only in a few exceptional cases have criminal charges been brought against high-ranking communist leaders for the mass deportations and the communist regime in Latvia.

The central act of commemoration in Latvia is dedicated to the two major waves of deportations in 1941 and 1949. Throughout the country there are small monuments commemorating these deportations and their victims. A central monument to the victims of communist persecution does not yet exist. However, in the centre of the Latvian capital, the privately initiated Museum of the Occupation commemorates the victims of both the Soviet and Nazi occupation of the country.

Commemoration events are held in Latvia on 25 March (commemorating the victims of the deportations of 1949) and 14 June (in memory of the recurrence of the same events of 1941). Since 2009, the victims of the National Socialist and Communist regimes have been commemorated each year on 23 August.

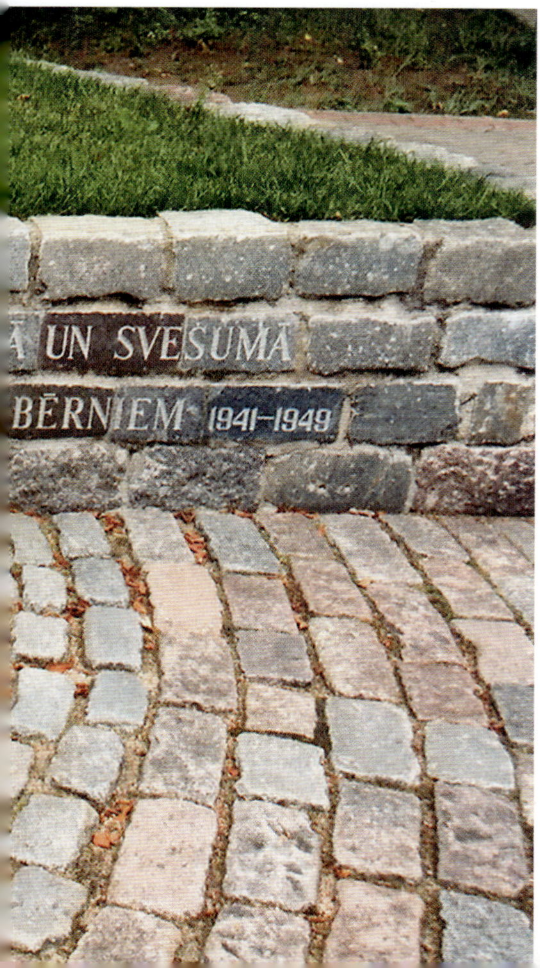

◄ Memorial to the Latvian children who died in Riga during deportation

Freedom Monument

Riga. The Freedom Monument (Brīvības piemineklis) in the centre of Riga is a symbol of Latvia's national sovereignty and was first conceived in the early 1920s after Latvia gained its independence for the first time on 18 November 1918. It was built between 1931 and 1935 during the moderate dictatorship of Karlis Ulmanis, with the help of donations from the population, on the same spot where a statue of the Russian Tsar Peter the Great had stood from 1910 to 1915. The official inauguration took place on 18 November 1935, which is National Independence Day.

The works of sculptor Kārlis Zāle were decisive for the implementation of the design by architect Ernests Štālbergs. Above a large monolithic base bearing the inscription "Tevzemei un Brivibai" ("For Fatherland and Freedom") are scenes and figures from Latvian mythology as well as reliefs symbolising work, family and the unity of the nation. Atop a 19-metre obelisk stands a nine-metre freedom figure in the shape of a young woman, popularly known as "Milda". This figure holds three golden stars up towards the sky. The stars were originally meant to represent the three Latvian provinces of Kurzeme (Courland), Vidzeme and Latgale but were interpreted during the Soviet occupation as a symbol of the unity of the three Baltic Soviet republics. All attempts by both the German and Soviet occupying forces to politically exploit or remove the monument ultimately failed because of the resistance of the Latvian population.

The monument, which over the course of time became increasingly symbolic as a sign of national self-determination and the fight against oppression, was one of the central sites of the "Atmoda", the Latvian liberation movement of the late 1980s. In the spring of 1987, the human rights group "Helsinki 86", which had been founded a year earlier, called for an unauthorised demonstration at the Freedom Monument. On 14 June, the anniversary of the Soviet deportations of 1941, almost 5,000 people gathered in front of the Brīvības piemineklis to express their will for independence. In the course of the Singing Revolution from 1987 to 1991, the monument was the starting and end point for numerous demonstrations.

Location: Riga, Brivibas bulvaris

► Freedom Monument as a symbol of Latvian national sovereignty

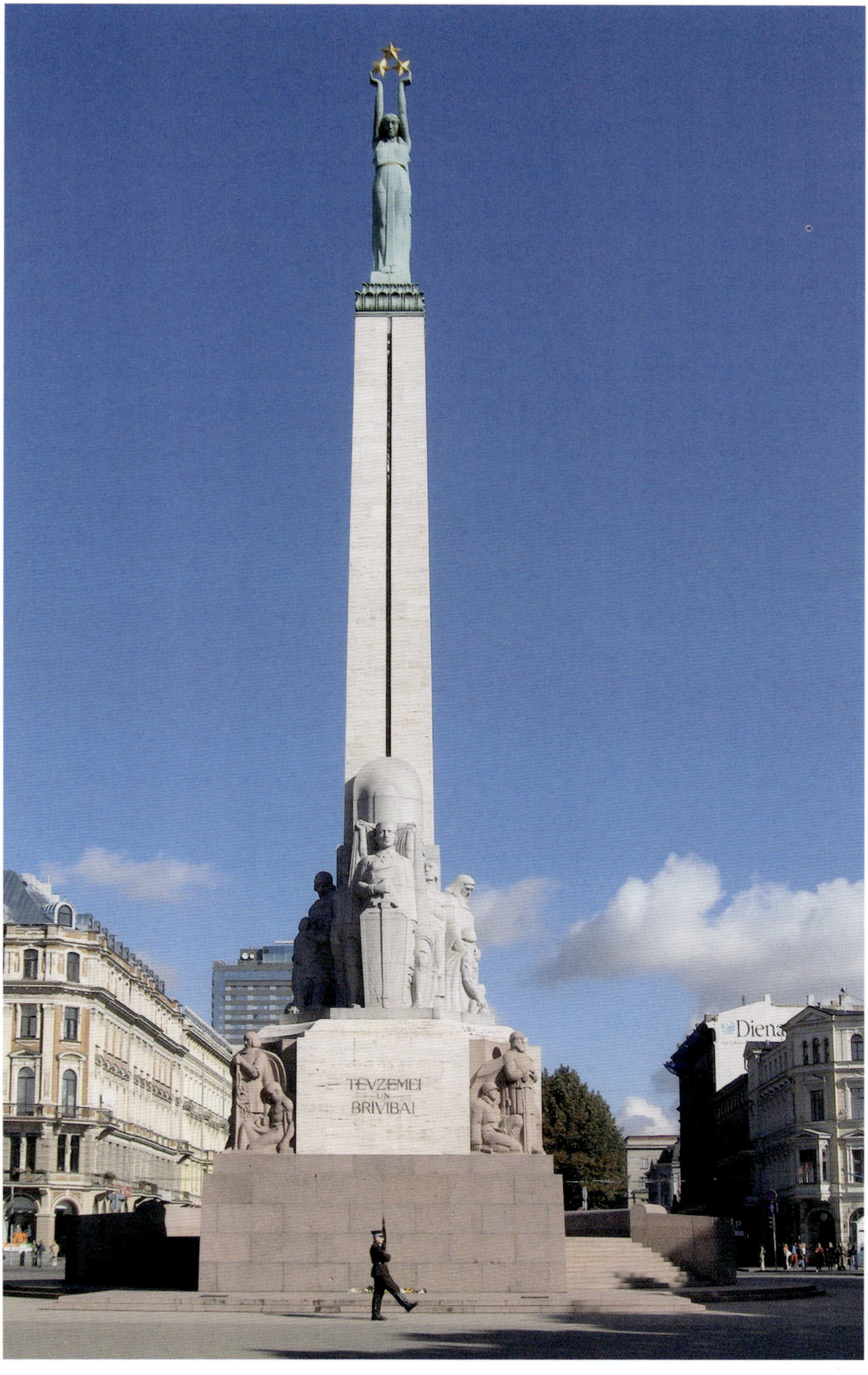
TEVZEMEI
UN
BRIVIBAI
Diena

Museum of the Occupation of Latvia 1940–1991

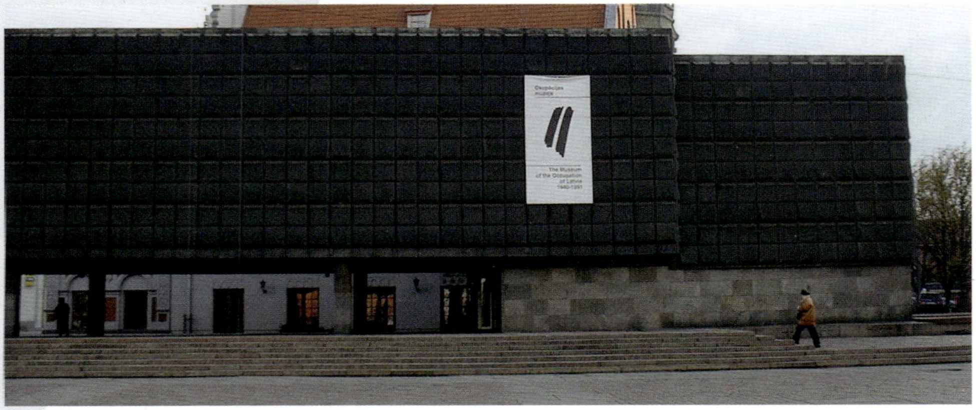

Exterior view of the museum

Riga. The Museum of the Occupation of Latvia opened on 1 July 1993 in the building of the former Latvian Riflemen's Battalion Museum. These were armed military units that allied themselves with the Bolsheviks at the end of the First World War and fought alongside the Red Army to enforce communist rule. The museum opened in 1970 but closed again in 1990—still in Soviet times. After minor structural changes, the Occupation Museum moved into the building in 1993. It owes its existence mainly to the commitment of Latvian emigrants from Western Europe and overseas who, after independence, supported the establishment of an institution to commemorate the occupation of Latvia by Nazi Germany and the Soviet Union. The Occupation Museum Foundation was established for the same purpose. In 1997, the Latvian state took over the patronage of the museum.

The permanent exhibition shows the history of the occupation regimes in Latvia after 1940. It begins with the effects and consequences of the Molotov-Ribbentrop Pact of 23 August 1939, whose secret additional secret protocol divided Eastern and Central Europe between the two dictatorships, placing Latvia under Soviet control. Following the first Soviet occupation in 1940/41, the presentation proceeds chronologically with the Nazi German occupation from 1941 to 1944 and the Holocaust. A third focus is on the portrayal of the second Soviet occupation from 1944, which came to an end with the independence movement in the 1980s. The aim is to show the impact of the respective political systems on the Latvian population. The numerous testimonies from

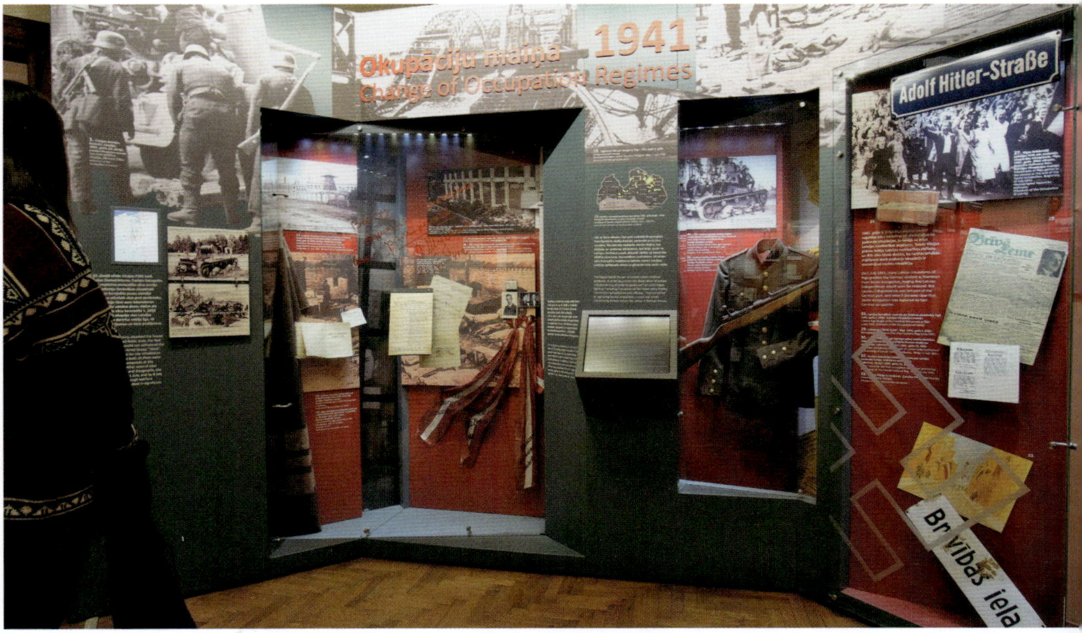

View of the exhibition in the Museum of the Occupation

everyday civilian life but also from the community of exiles and the camps are supplemented by official documents and audiovisual media.

On 20 September 2016, the Latvian parliament recognised the museum as an "object of national importance". An extension designed by Latvian-American architect Gunnar Birkerts is planned to enlarge the exhibition area. The permanent exhibition has been revised. While maintaining the conceptual chronological structure, a new focus has now been placed, among other things, on multimedia.

Location: Riga, Raiņa bulvāris 7 and Strēlnieku laukums 1
Internet: www.okupacijasmuzejs.lv

Barricades Museum

Riga. In August 2001, on the occasion of the 10th anniversary of the restoration of Latvian independence, a museum was opened in the Old Town of Riga to commemorate the conflicts between the Latvian national movement and the Soviet security forces. The museum is sponsored by the Association of Participants of Barricades of 1991.

As early as the 1980s, a citizens' movement, the so-called "Atmoda" (Awakening), which actively campaigned for independence from the Soviet Union, was organised in Latvia. As its success grew, so did the resistance of the Soviet government to national independence aspirations. When the Communist Party was defeated in the early 1990 elections to the national parliaments in all three Baltic republics, Moscow imposed economic sanctions and threatened military intervention. After 14 people were killed in the storming of the television tower by Soviet forces in Vilnius, Lithuania, on 13 January 1991, over 500,000 people gathered on the banks of the Daugava River in Riga at noon the same day. They expressed their

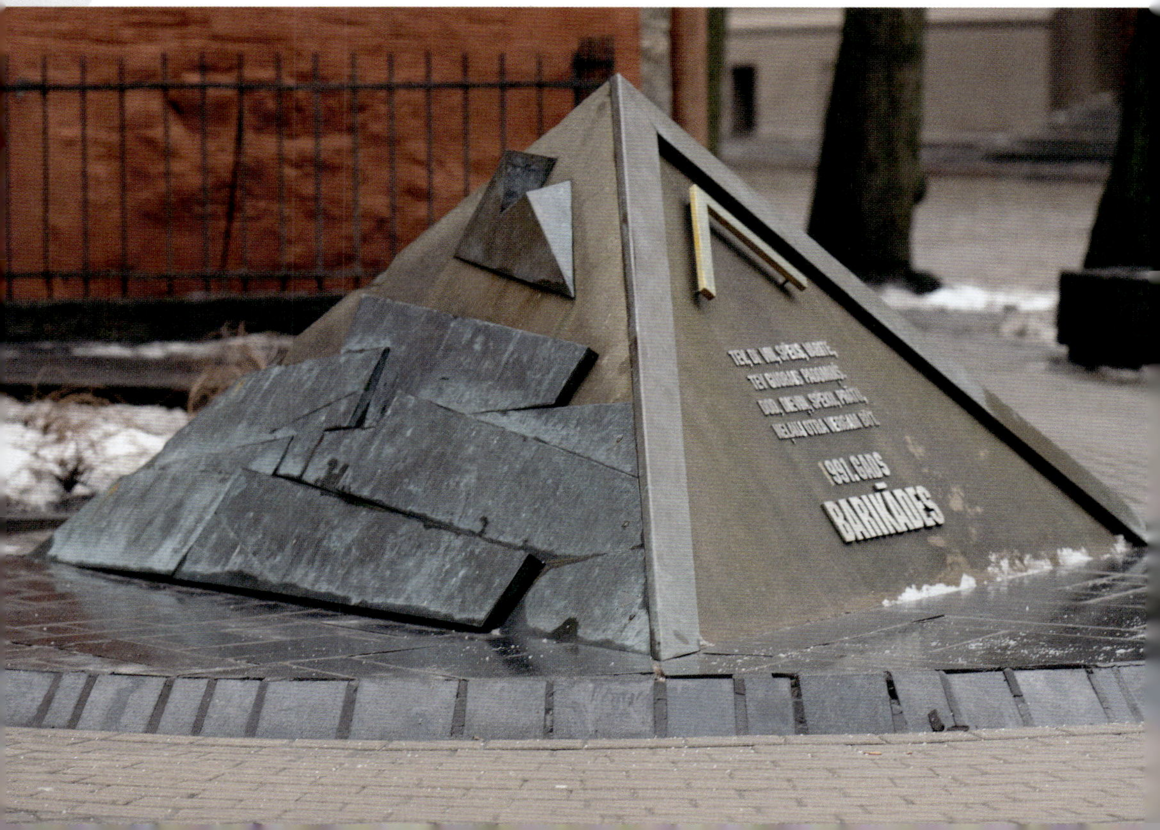

solidarity with their Lithuanian neighbours and demonstrated for the full restoration of Latvia's national independence. On the same day, the opposition movement led by the Popular Front of Latvia called on the population to erect street barricades to oppose the advancing Soviet troops. As most of the buildings and facilities of national importance were located in Riga's Old Town, this area became the central scene of the conflict. This culminated on the evening of 20 January in the storming of the parliament building by Soviet special purpose units of the OMON militia, during which six people lost their lives.

To commemorate these events, three exhibition halls in the museum trace the conflicts between the Latvian independence movement and the Soviet security forces in January 1991. The central part of the exhibition is a model of the barricades on Cathedral Square in January 1991, supplemented by contemporary photographs and films. In addition to guided tours of the exhibition rooms in Latvian and English, the museum offers educational programmes for students.

Location: Riga, Krāmu iela 3
Internet: www.barikades.lv

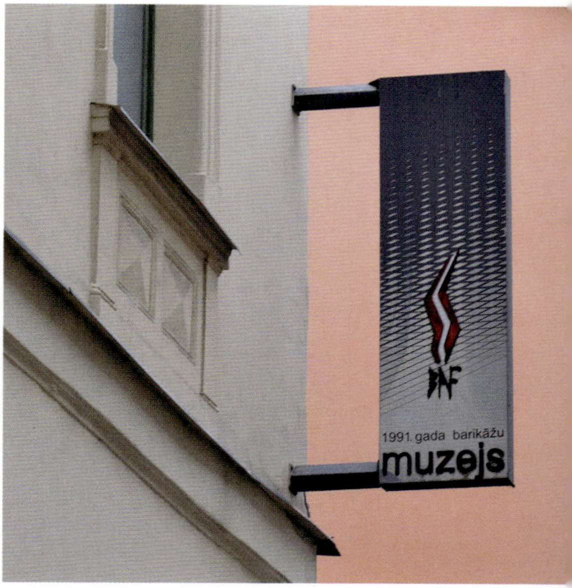

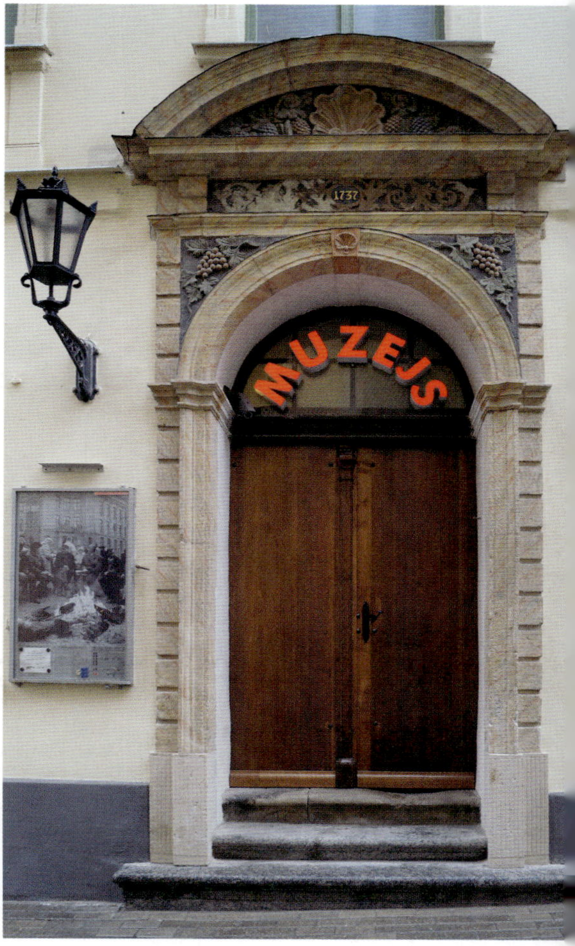

◄ Memorial commemorating the barricades of 1991

► Entrance to the museum

Former KGB Building "The Corner House"

Riga. At the junction of Stabu and Brīvības Street, Riga's most prominent boulevard, with its famous Freedom Monument, stands the former headquarters of the Soviet secret police, popularly known as the "Corner House" (Stūra māja). Built in 1912 as an apartment and office building, as the headquarters of the Soviet secret police.it became a symbol of the repression and terror practised by the totalitarian Soviet regime during the Soviet occupation.

During the first Soviet occupation between June 1940 and July 1941, the Soviet secret police seized the building, which had previously been used by the Latvian Ministry of the Interior, in August 1940. A remand prison with interrogation, detention and execution rooms was set up on the ground floor and in the basement of the building. Between 15 January and 22 June 1941, 186 death sentences were carried out here. The mass deportations of 14 June 1941, during

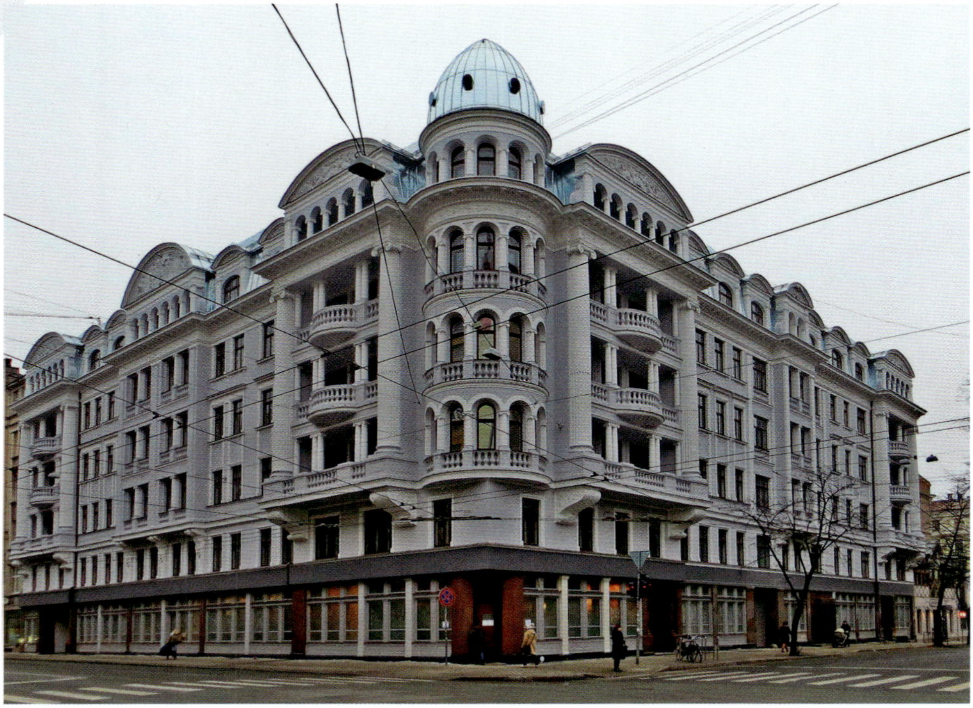

which some 15,000 Latvian citizens were deported to Soviet penal camps in Siberia, also started here. The lists were drawn up in the "Corner House" and the corresponding arrest warrants documented. In a grim joke, the "Corner House" became known as the highest building in the city—it was said that you could see all the way to Siberia from the uppermost floors.

During the Nazi German occupation from July 1941 to September 1944, various offices of local government used the building. On 13 October 1944, the Red Army occupied Riga again, and, shortly afterwards, the Soviet secret police moved back into the "Corner House". It was from here that the persecution of alleged and actual collaborators with the National Socialist occupation regime was conducted, the suppression of the national Latvian resistance movement organised and the removal of potentially "subversive elements" enforced. During the entire period of the second Soviet occupation of the country, the "Corner House" served the communist regime as a place for the imprisonment, torture and psychological humiliation of thousands of people.

It was not until the Singing Revolution and the attainment of national independence on 21 August 1991 that the KGB abandoned the building on Brīvības Street and authorities of the Latvian Republic moved in. Until July 2008, it was the headquarters of the Latvian state police and was subsequently handed over to the state-owned real estate agency "Valsts nekustāmie īpašum". One year later, the building complex was awarded the status of a nationally protected cultural object. On 14 June 2003, the Museum of Occupation inaugurated the "Black Threshold" memorial here, commemorating the deportations organised in this house.

◄
Façade of the "Corner House"

When Riga became the European Capital of Culture in 2014, the former KGB building was opened to the public as "File No. 1914/2014: The Corner House". After being closed temporarily, it re-opened in February 2015. An exhibition conceived and overseen by the Museum of Occupation in Riga provides information in Latvian, English and Russian on the activities of the Soviet secret police in Latvia and describes the various forms of resistance against the repressive regime. In addition, a virtual tour of the entire former KGB building is offered on the Internet.

Installed in 14 July 2003 and complemented by a symbolic step made of black granite, a commemorative plaque by sculptor Gļebs Panteļejevs and architect Andris Veidemanishas on the façade of the building commemorates the victims of Soviet repression.

The **inscription** in Latvian and English reads: *Padomju/okupācijas laikā/valsts drosibas/iestāde čeka/savus upurus/seit ieslodzīja./mocīja./nogalināja un/morāli pazemoja// Stūra māja/1940–1941/1944–1991/Corner House//During the Soviet/Occupation the/State Security/Agency KGB/Imprisoned./Tortured. Killed/and Morally/Humiliated Its/Victims in This/Building*

Location: Riga, Brīvības iela 61
Internet: www.kgbbuilding.lv

Museum of the Popular Front of Latvia

Riga. The Museum of the Popular Front of Latvia documents the process of Latvian independence and sheds light on the role of the Popular Front movement in the regaining of national sovereignty after 1990.

Much like the independence movements in Lithuania (Sąjūdis) and Estonia (Rahvarinne), the Latvian Popular Front (Tautas Fronte) became the most influential political force in the country shortly after it was founded on 9 October 1988. As an umbrella organisation of various smaller groups and reform movements, it quickly grew to over 230,000 members. In contrast to the radical wing of the opposition, the Latvian National Independence Movement, the Popular Front initially pursued a moderate course. It advocated the democratisation of the country modelled on perestroika but initially held back with demands for the restoration of state independence. With the growing urge for more independence in the population, the positions of the popular front also shifted.

On 23 August 1989, the 50th anniversary of the Molotov-Ribbentrop Pact, the mass protests in the Baltic Republics reached their apogee: from Tallinn via Riga to Vilnius, almost two million people formed a 600-km-long chain— the "Baltic Way". The national popular fronts in Latvia, Lithuania and Estonia thus demonstrated to the central authorities in Moscow that they could mobilise large crowds of people to enforce their desire for independence. Once the Tautas Fronte had won the parliamentary elections on 18 March 1990 by a large majority and members of the popular front had taken key positions in the new government, the new parliament announced the country's independence from the Soviet Union in May 1990. Despite attempts to crush the national independence movement in January 1991, the Soviet regime could no longer hold onto power. The unsuccessful coup against state and party leader Mikhail Gorbachev was used by the popular front to finally bring about national sovereignty on 21 August 1991.

The Tautas Fronte Museum, located in the original premises of the former headquarters of the Popular Front Movement, commemorates the fundamental political and social upheavals occasioned by historical events. On four floors, the origins of the Popular Front and its development as a movement and party are presented up to its dissolution following the achievement of the political goals in 1993. Numerous multimedia areas, installations, original workspaces of the leadership of the popular front and a replica of a party congress meeting convey a realistic representation of the struggle for independence. Guided tours of the exhibition rooms are offered in Latvian, English and German.

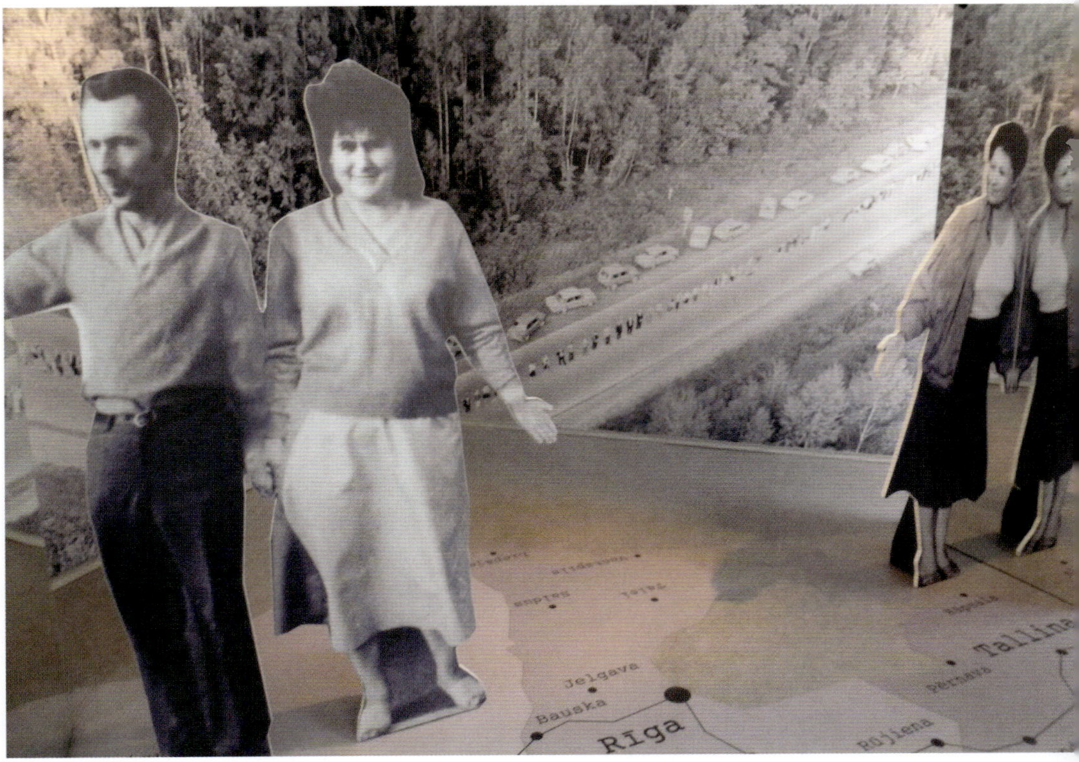

Exhibition segment on the "Baltic Way"

Location: Riga, Vecpilsētas iela 13/15
Internet: www.lnvm.lv

Further reading:
Čakstiņa, Kristīne / Pētersons, Rihards: 1918 – 1991. A Guide to Memorial Sites in Riga and Vicinity. Published by: Museum of the Occupation of Latvia. Riga 2017. / Nollendorfs, Valters: Lettland unter der Herrschaft der Sowjetunion und des Nationalsozialistischen Deutschland 1940 – 1991. Lettisches Okkupationsmuseum. Riga 2017. / Pārpuce, Rasa: Länderstudie Lettland. In: Honoring Civil Courage. Developing Suggestions to Improve the Situation of Victims of Communist State Crimes. Project Coordinator: Gedenkstätte Berlin-Hohenschönhausen 2015, Ref. No.: JUST/2011/JPEN/AG/2998Available online at: www.stiftung-hsh.de/assets/Dokumente-pdf-Dateien/EU-Projekt-Laenderstudien.pdf (last accessed on: 15/11/2017). / Welscher, Alexander / Beckmann-Dierkes, Norbert: Im dunklen Keller der Erinnerung. Published by: Konrad Adenauer Stiftung. Riga 2016.

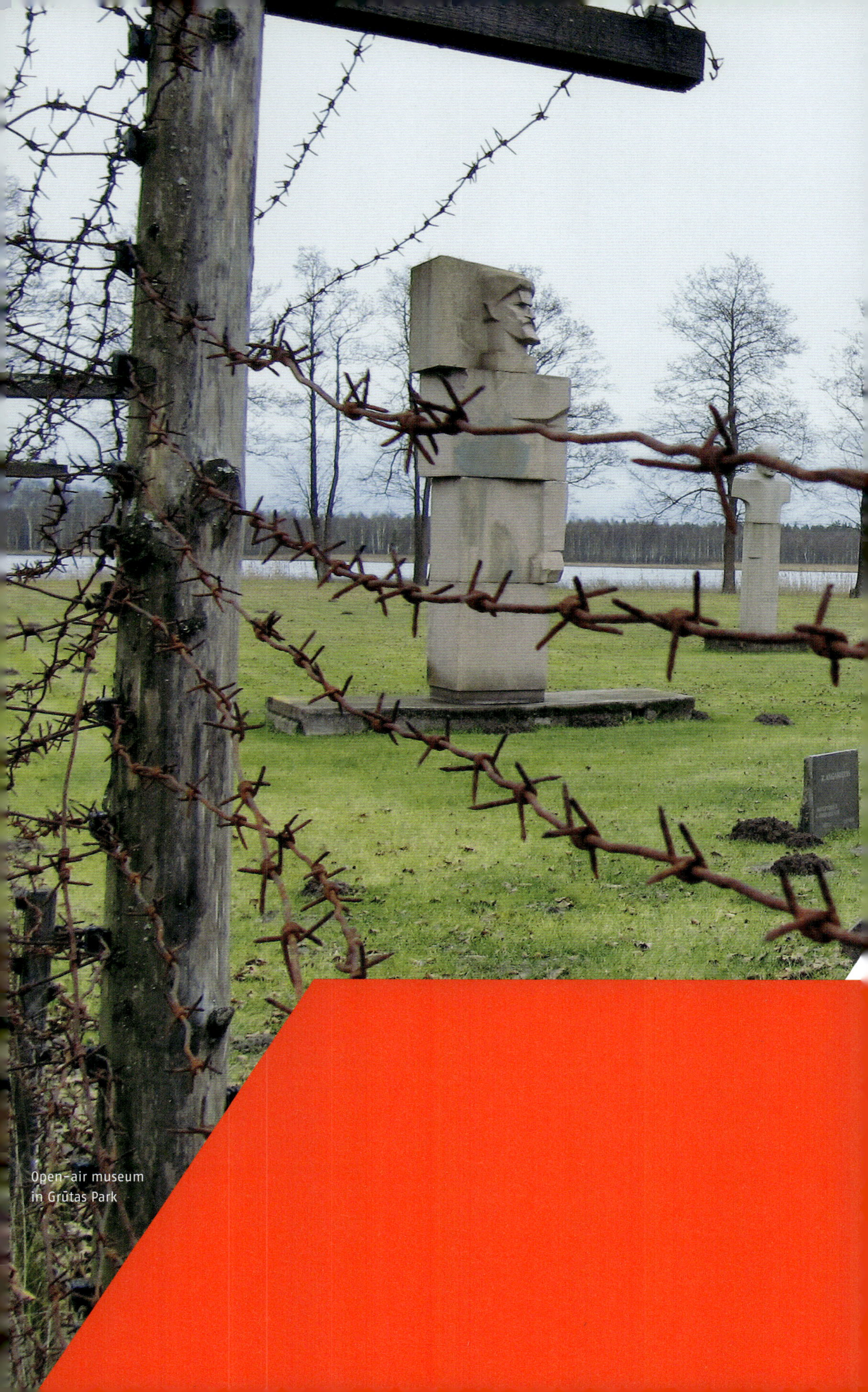

Open-air museum in Grūtas Park

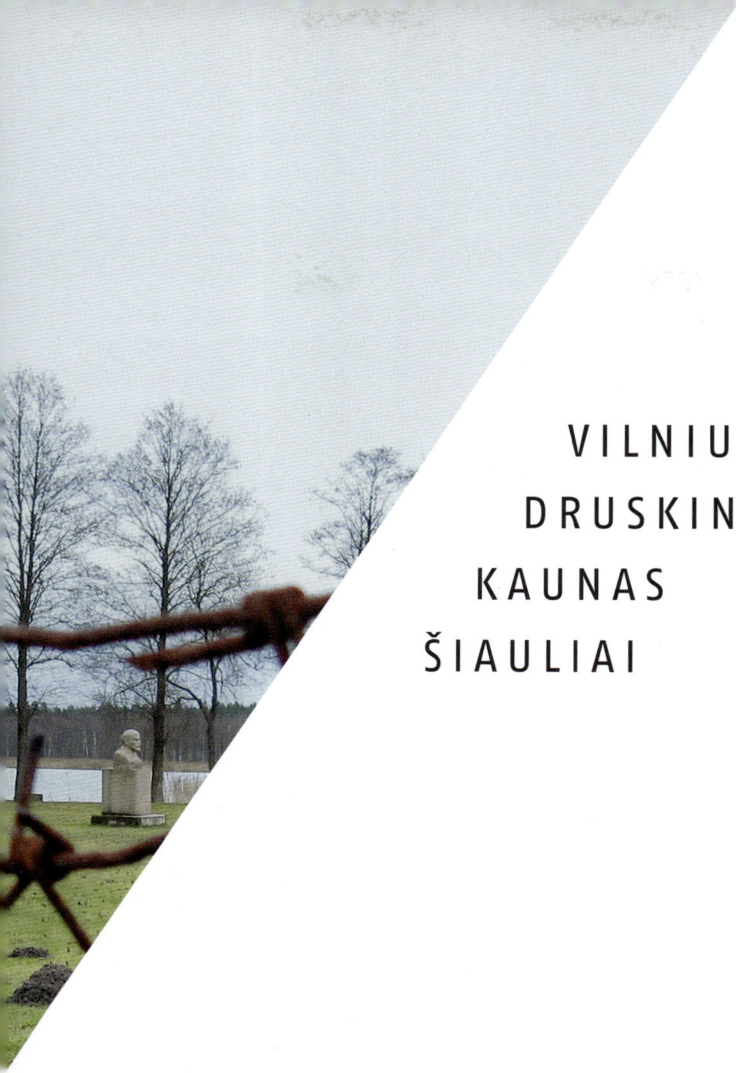

VILNIUS
DRUSKININKAI
KAUNAS
ŠIAULIAI

Lithuania

Like Estonia and Latvia, Lithuania was added to the Soviet sphere of influence by the secret additional protocol of the Molotov-Ribbentrop Pact and the German-Soviet Boundary and Friendship Treaty of 28 September 1939. After the occupation of eastern Poland and Vilnius, the Soviet Union forced the Lithuanian government—as it did in Latvia and Estonia—to conclude mutual assistance pacts and agree to the deployment of 35,000 Red Army soldiers. On 14 and 15 June 1940, the Kremlin issued an ultimatum to all three Baltic states demanding not only the stationing of an undetermined contingent of Soviet troops but also a change of government and new elections on the basis of uniform Communist lists. After the staged and rigged parliamentary elections, the so-called "People's Parliament" unanimously declared Lithuania a Soviet Socialist Republic on 21 July.

The puppet government under Justas Paleckis, who was loyal to Moscow, requested accession to the Soviet Union, which was granted on 3 August 1940. Sovietisation was accompanied by brutal force and the arrest and murder of politicians, clergy, intellectuals and artists; industry and banks were nationalised. During the forced collectivisation of agriculture, landowners were expropriated, and the establishment of kolkhozes was enforced. The state controlled religious policy was to confiscate church estates and close houses of prayer. Members of the clergy were detained and murdered. Between 14 and 21 June 1941, more than 30,000 Lithuanian citizens were detained without trial and either transported to the labour and prison camps of the Gulag system for forced labour or exiled to remote areas in Siberia.

Organised resistance coalesced shortly after the Soviet occupation. The nationalist Lithuanian Activist Front (LAF), which, at the height of the resistance struggle in the summer of 1941, had almost 36,000 members, was one of the underground organisations. On 22 June 1941, the day of the invasion of the Soviet Union by Nazi Germany, the activist front initiated an armed uprising against the Soviet occupation regime. However, an interim government set up by the LAF could only be maintained for a few days.

The advance of the Wehrmacht, which overran the country within a very short time, was initially perceived as a liberation from the "Red Terror". However, the Germans left the country in no doubt that Soviet oppression had been replaced by Nazi terror. Between June 1941 and the reconquest of Lithuania by the Red Army in July 1944, the country was once again subjected to dictatorship, repression and force. As in other occupied states, the National Socialist ideology appealed to the existing anti-Semitic resentments of nationalist population groups—especially among the members of the LAF. National police battalions also assisted the German troops in carrying out the Holocaust on Lithuanian territory. The Shoah, the National Socialist genocide of the Jewish population, killed 200,000 people in Lithuania—95 percent of the country's entire Jewish community. By the summer of 1944, another 75,000 Lithuanian citizens had been deported to the German Reich for forced labour, almost 20,000 men had been placed under the control of German troops, and more than 10,000 people had fled abroad.

Unlike the anti-Soviet resistance, the anti-Nazi opposition mainly used passive forms of resistance. Their activities were primarily directed at the sabotage of the Nazi occupation regime. The publication and distribution of underground newspapers and the establishment of a network of contacts with the Allies played an important role. Several politically motivated organisations, such as the Lithuanian Front, the successor association to the LAF and the Supreme Committee for the Liberation of Lithuania, an association of parties banned by the National Socialists, were active in the underground.

After the Battle of Stalingrad in early 1943, the Red Army stopped the advance of the Wehrmacht and began its own offensive. On its westward advance, it once again crossed the Lithuanian border into the north-east of the country on 4 July 1944. The Soviet re-occupation continued the repressive practices of 1940: forced collectivisation of the agricultural economy, systematic persecution and suppression of the clergy, elimination of the intelligentsia and renewed mass deportations. Between April 1945 and August 1952, almost 112,000 Lithuanian citizens were deported to Siberia for forced labour or exiled in several waves. During the March deportations in 1949 alone, by decision of the Soviet Council of Ministers, 33,500 Lithuanian citizens were transported into the interior of the Soviet Union in cattle cars.

The return of Soviet rule forced thousands of people in Lithuania and the other Baltic republics to go underground. In late 1945, about 30,000 men—organised in partisan groups—hid in the forests of Lithuania. The first resistance groups, popularly known as Forest Brothers, were recruited from the ranks of the LAF, the military organisation "Kęstutis" and men of various anti-Communist convictions. All agreed on the goal of preventing the permanent installation of Soviet power in Lithuania by all conceivable means. Among the subversive activities of the "Forest Brothers" were the sabotage of Soviet state assets, the removal of communist propaganda and the distribution of a nationally-oriented underground press. They also undermined local initiatives to support the establishment of Soviet administrative structures.

In the face of the Lithuanian partisans' resistance, the Soviet leadership ordered several reconnaissance and extermination campaigns against the armed units. In one of the large-scale operations between 28 June and 16 July 1946, the NKVD deployed 7,000 men, including special units of the secret police—"istrebiteli" ("destroyers")—to fight the Lithuanian partisans. After 1948, Soviet security forces increasingly infiltrated the underground. Whole units of the "Forest Brothers" were betrayed and liquidated. The resistance fighters realised that the Allies would not support the Baltic freedom struggle and the West would not intervene. Local conditions also deteriorated: due to economic recession, it became impossible for sympathisers to support anyone outside their own family.

The long years of hiding in the forest and the conspiratorial living conditions had worn down and demoralised many of the fighters. Attempts to revive and centralise the underground struggle under the "Union of Lithuanian Freedom Fighters", which was established in 1949, failed. The terror did not subside until the forced collectivisation of agriculture had been completed, the armed underground struggle of the "Forest Brothers" suppressed and the Lithuanian population decimated by repressive measures. By 1953, Lithuania had lost one-sixth of its population to deportation, war and punishment for resistance.

At the start of the "thaw period" under Nikita Khrushchev (1956 – 1964), the Lithuanian intelligentsia was fragmented and demoralised. Following the invasion of Czechoslovakia in 1968 by the Warsaw Pact troops, dissident movements called for greater freedom of expression and the preservation of national culture and tradition and were supported by the Catholic Church. On 15 May 1972, student Romas Kalanta set himself on fire in protest against the Soviet occupation regime, triggering mass demonstrations with the call of "Freedom for Lithuania!". At the same time, the Lithuanian underground press expanded its circulation. As in other Eastern Bloc countries, the CSCE Conference led to the establishment of local Helsinki Groups, which, citing the Helsinki Final Act, called for the granting of human and civil rights.

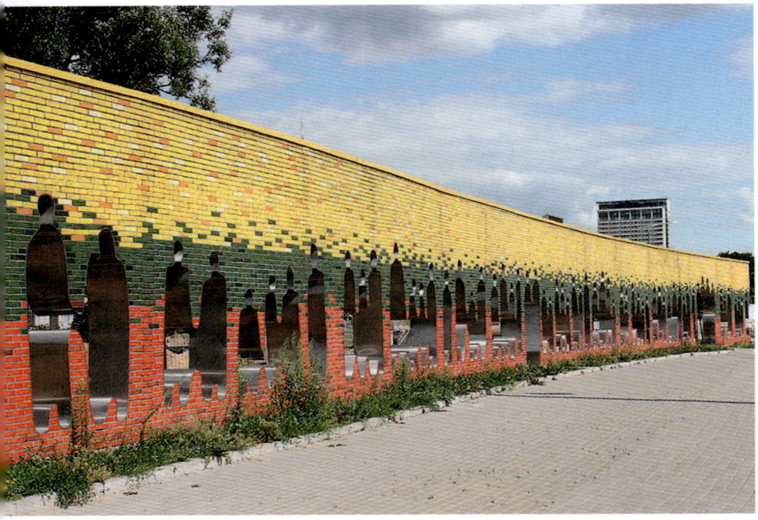

◄

Baltic Way Memorial Wall in Vilnius

►

Memorial stone for the first public demonstrations in 1987 in Vilnius

In Estonia and Latvia, too, resistance to the Soviet occupation had re-emerged as early as the 1960s. The demands of the dissident movements were marked by their desire for national independence. The first Helsinki Group was founded in Lithuania in 1976. As in the other Baltic republics, the Soviet occupying power reacted with a massive campaign of repression directed against the groups. Dissatisfaction with the nationality policy was increasingly expressed publicly. On the occasion of the 40th anniversary of the Molotov-Ribbentrop Pact on 23 August 1979, 45 Latvians, Estonians and Lithuanians wrote a "Baltic Appeal" to the UN, which led the European Parliament to adopt a resolution in 1983 decrying the unacceptable situation of the Baltic population.

The Helsinki groups were infiltrated, the activists arrested or driven into exile. In 1983, the Lithuanian group was finally dissolved. However, the reform policy pursued by Gorbachev in 1985 lent renewed momentum to the dissident movement in Lithuania. As in other countries, resistance was organised in the form of environmental and peace groups. In Lithuania, too, a mass rally to commemorate the occupation of the country in the wake of the Molotov-Ribbentrop Pact and the associated mass reprisals took place on 14 June 1987. In the face of mass protests, the Soviet leadership changed its nationality policy in the three Baltic Soviet republics. The Lithuanian language was incorporated into the Constitution as a national language at the end of 1988. The popular fronts founded in all three countries carried out joint actions against the Soviet central power and in support of national independence. The culmination of these actions was the 600-kilometre-long human chain between Lithuania and Estonia on 23 August 1989, the 50th anniversary of the signing of the Molotov-Ribbentrop Pact, which was joined by over two million people.

In the light of Lithuania's democratisation efforts—the country was the first to declare independence under Soviet occupation on 11 March 1990—Mikhail Gorbachev, the head of state and party of the Soviet Union, imposed an economic blockade that lasted several months. On the night of 12–13 January 1991, OMON troops attacked tens of thousands of protesters in Vilnius

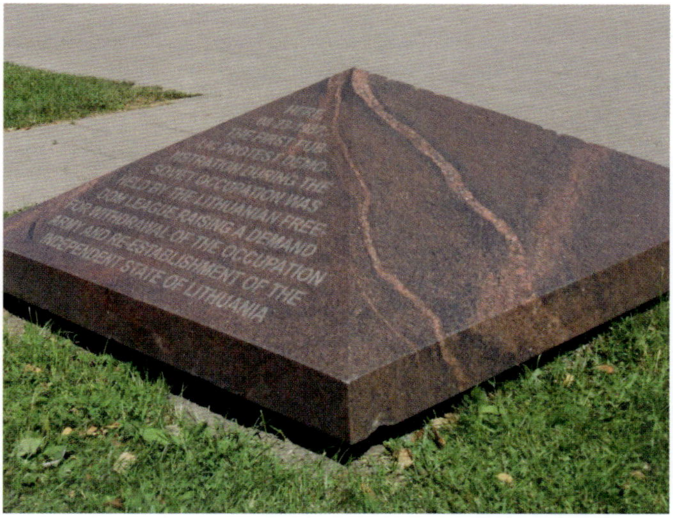

defending the television tower, parliament and other public buildings. 14 people were killed and hundreds injured over the course of these events. Despite the military intervention of Soviet troops, the first free parliamentary elections were held in February 1991.

Although the communist regime and its crimes were condemned, the rehabilitation of the victims took a long time. Since the convicted victims of repression were still considered criminals in accordance with laws that had not yet been repealed, proof had to be provided in the rehabilitation trials that they had been convicted innocently and wrongly. Rehabilitated persons received compensation and their property was reinstated. Ex-informers and spies were protected from unmasking if they pled guilty and expressed regret regarding their actions.

In 1992, the decision was made to establish the State Genocide Museum in memory of the victims of the two occupation regimes in Vilnius. Numerous memorials and monuments commemorate the victims of totalitarian rule in Lithuania.

The website of the Lithuanian Museum of the Victims of the Genocide and Resistance contains a list of all Lithuanian memorials.

Museum of Occupations and Freedom Fights

Vilnius. The Museum of Occupations and Freedom Fights was founded in 1992 on the initiative of Lithuanian prisoners' and deportees' associations. Since 1997, the institution has been part of the state-funded Genocide and Resistance Research Centre of Lithuania, an institution dedicated to research into the National Socialist and Soviet occupation of Lithuania.

Since its construction in 1899, the building in today's Aukų gatve 2 A, the "Street of the Victims", had served as a court, administration centre and school building. In June 1940, the NKVD moved into the building complex and set up more than 50 cells for prisoners on remand in the basement. During the German occupation of Lithuania between June 1941 and July 1944, the building was converted into the Gestapo headquarters. The cells continued to be used during the Nazi's regime of terror: numerous opponents to the Nazis were detained, tortured and liquidated here. With the second Soviet occupation of the country in July 1944, the NKVD returned to the building, and the prison was expanded with the addition of new cell wings, which were often overcrowded.

The exhibition, which is spread over three floors, deals with the persecution of the Lithuanian population by Soviet and German occupying forces. A large part of the exhibition area is set in the basement in more than 20 reconstructed cells. Documented here, in addition to the procedure for registering the detainees, are the conditions of imprisonment during the various periods of persecution and execution carried out by the KGB. The installation in the former execution cell serves as a central memorial room and keeps alive the memory of the approximately 1,000 people who were shot in prison or died in their cells and of all victims of totalitarian systems. Since 2011, part of the permanent exhibition has been dedicated to the memory of over 200,000 Lithuanian Holocaust victims. Along with the extermination regime of the Nazi German occupying forces, the exhibition traces the use of the Gestapo prison and the fates of its victims. The history of the Vilna Ghetto and the mass executions in the largest Lithuanian SS execution site in Ponary are also examined in detail.

Other exhibition rooms are dedicated to various aspects of the Soviet occupations of 1940/41 and again from 1944 to 1991. Overviews and individual biographies shed light on the repression of the country's political, cultural and intellectual elite and the ensuing mass deportations. Considerable space is devoted to the underground movement in the post-war years. The exhibition covers both the armed anti-Soviet resistance between 1944 and 1953, one of 20th-century Europe's most enduring partisan struggles, and the dissident movement of the 1960s and 1970s. It presents numerous original objects such as photographs,

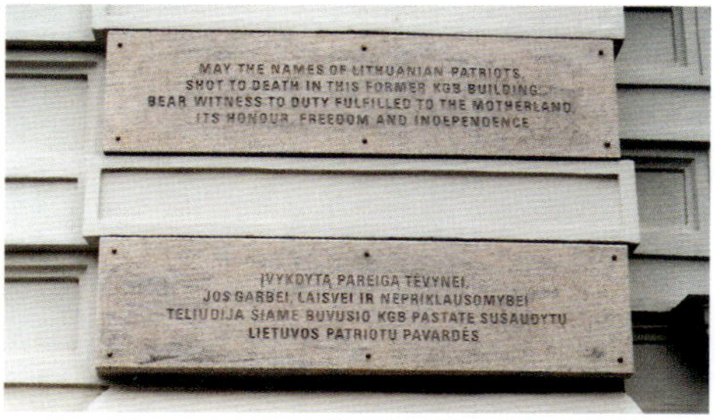

Names of the victims of execution in the former KGB prison engraved on the façade of the building

documents, letters and items of clothing, and various other historical memorabilia.

Since December 2008, the museum has also overseen the administration of the Memorial Complex of the Tuskulenai Peace Park. Between 28 September 1944 and 16 April 1947, the Soviet secret police carried out 767 death sentences in the basement cells of the former KGB prison. The remains of the victims were buried in mass graves on the grounds of the park. It was only during archaeological excavation work in 1994 that they were discovered and buried in a columbarium. The "Secrets of Tuskulenai Manor" exhibition in the former manor house of the complex, designed by the institution, provides information on the extermination apparatus of the totalitarian Soviet regime.

In addition to guided tours in Lithuanian and English, the museum also offers specially designed educational programmes, which include excursions and seminars.

The names of 199 Lithuanian citizens murdered between 1945 and 1946 which are engraved on the façade of the building commemorate the victims of the Soviet regime of repression.

Location: Vilnius, Aukų gatve 2 A
Internet: www.genocid.lt and www.tuskulenumemorialas.lt

The subject of the exhibition is the persecution of the Lithuanian population by Soviet and German occupiers.

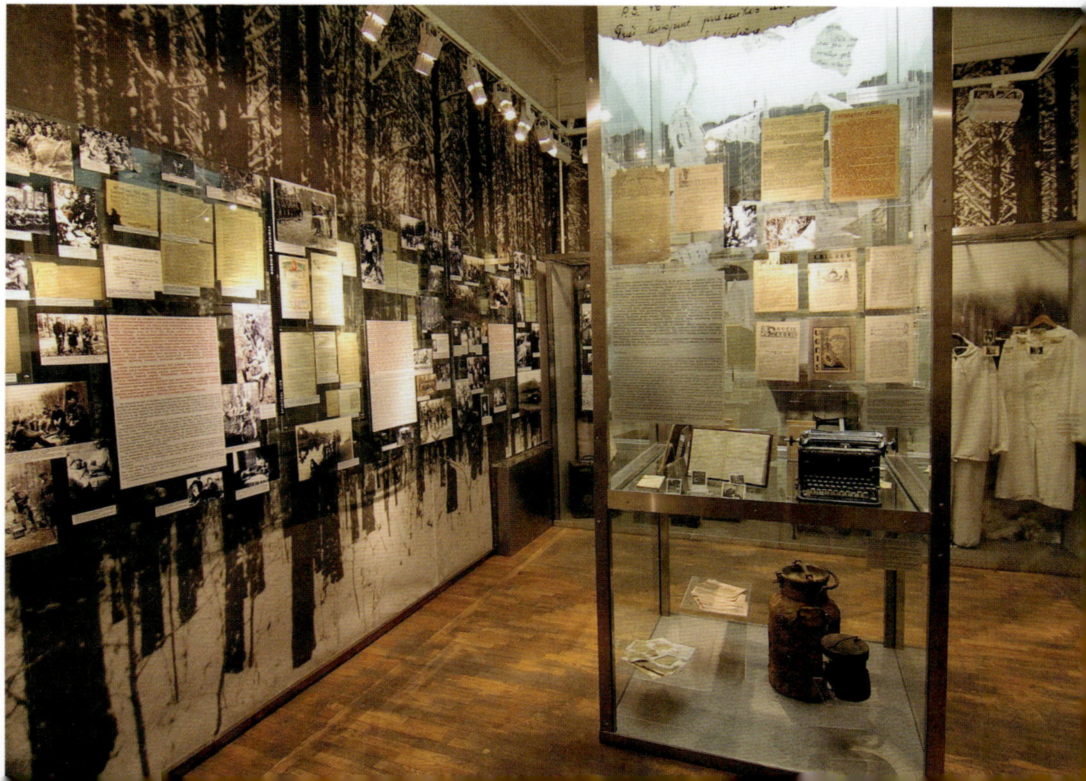

Museum and Memorial at the TV Tower

Vilnius. The television tower in Vilnius is the tallest building in Lithuania and stands near the centre of the capital. On the ground floor of the station is a memorial to the victims of "Vilnius Bloody Sunday", the violent suppression of the freedom demonstrations by Soviet special forces in January 1991.

Lithuania's Supreme Council (formerly the Supreme Soviet) proclaimed the country's independence from the Soviet Union on 11 March 1990. When provisional President Vytautas Landsbergis did not revoke the declaration of independence, armed troops of the Ministry of the Interior occupied strategically important buildings throughout Lithuania on 11 January 1991. Tens of thousands of people took to the streets of Vilnius. On the night of 13 January, local commanders instructed the OMON units to "clarify" the situation. 14 unarmed civilians died in an attempt to prevent the capture of the tower by forming a human chain. 700 others were injured. The day after the riots, over 100,000 people gathered in front of the parliament building, erected barricades and forced the Soviet troops to retreat.

Today, a small exhibition on the ground floor of the tower commemorates the events of January 1991.

The grounds of the broadcasting company have developed into a central memorial to the national independence movement. Relatives of the victims of Bloody Sunday have placed a commemorative plaque and several wooden crosses at the entrance to the memorial. The site also features a half-erected iron cross dedicated to the unarmed protesters run over by Soviet tanks.

On 15 June 2005, the eight-metre bronze sculpture entitled "Sacrifice" was unveiled in front of the television tower. Designed by Lithuanian sculptor Darius Bražiūnas and architect Artūras Asauska, the memorial shows the stylised figure of a young woman standing on a crown of bells, stretching her arms towards the sky. As a kind of statue of liberty, the sculpture is a symbol of national independence. The lyrics of the Lithuanian national anthem are engraved on the base of the bell. In memory of the victims, granite obelisks were installed and trees planted on the site of the broadcasting station. The streets around the tower bear the names of the victims of 13 January.

Location: Vilnius, Sausio 13-osios gatve 10

► Bronze sculpture "Sacrifice" by the TV tower in Vilnius

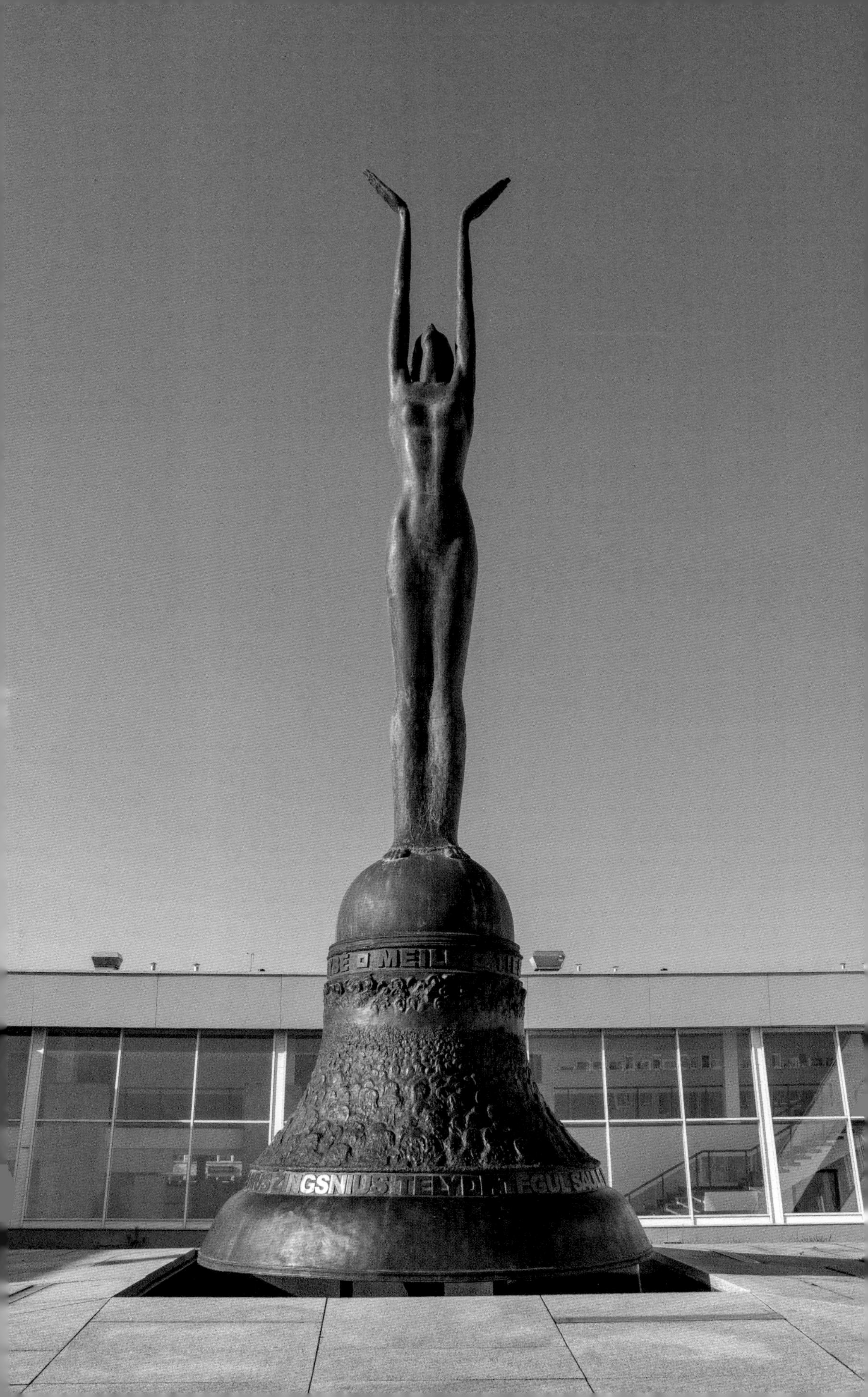

Grūtas Park — Soviet Sculpture Garden

Druskininkai. Since 1 April 2001, the Druskininkai National Park, 120 kilometres from Vilnius in the southwest of Lithuania, has been home to the Grūtas Sculpture Park. The 20-hectare forest site is dedicated to the display of relics of socialist art—sculptures, portrait busts, monuments and statues—which "adorned" countless streets and squares of the Lithuanian SSR until the collapse of the Soviet Union and Lithuania's independence, whereupon they were removed from public view. Stripped of their original symbolism, they are now intended to stimulate reflection on the country's past under Soviet foreign rule.

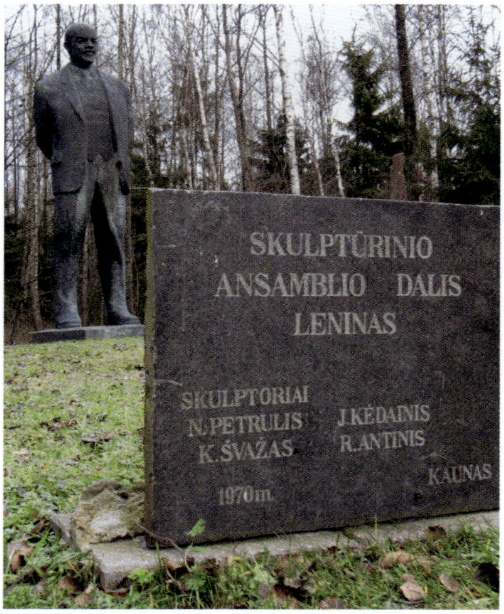

In 1998, the Lithuanian Parliament launched an initiative to preserve defunct Soviet monuments. The Lithuanian businessman Viliumas Malinkas prevailed with his idea of a sculpture park. The project, funded from his private assets, was highly controversial during the several years of the implementation phase. The main topic of discussion was the appropriate presentation and historical contextualisation of the exhibited objects, the significance of which is still controversial both within the Lithuanian population and among international visitor groups.

With its sculpture collection, Grūtas Park is presented as a place of remembrance. Statues, busts and reliefs on the extensive park grounds serve as part of an interactive educational experience. The 68 larger-than-life sculptures are arranged in thematically structured groups along a two-kilometre path. In addition to monuments to Lenin, Stalin and Marx, statues of high-ranking Lithuanian Soviet officials can also be seen here. These include Vincas Mickevičius-Kapsukas, the first chairman of the Lithuanian Communist Party, and Antanas Sniečkus, its first secretary. At the urging of the victims' associations, all the exhibits were

◄ Information boards were attached to all exhibits at the urging of the victims' associations.

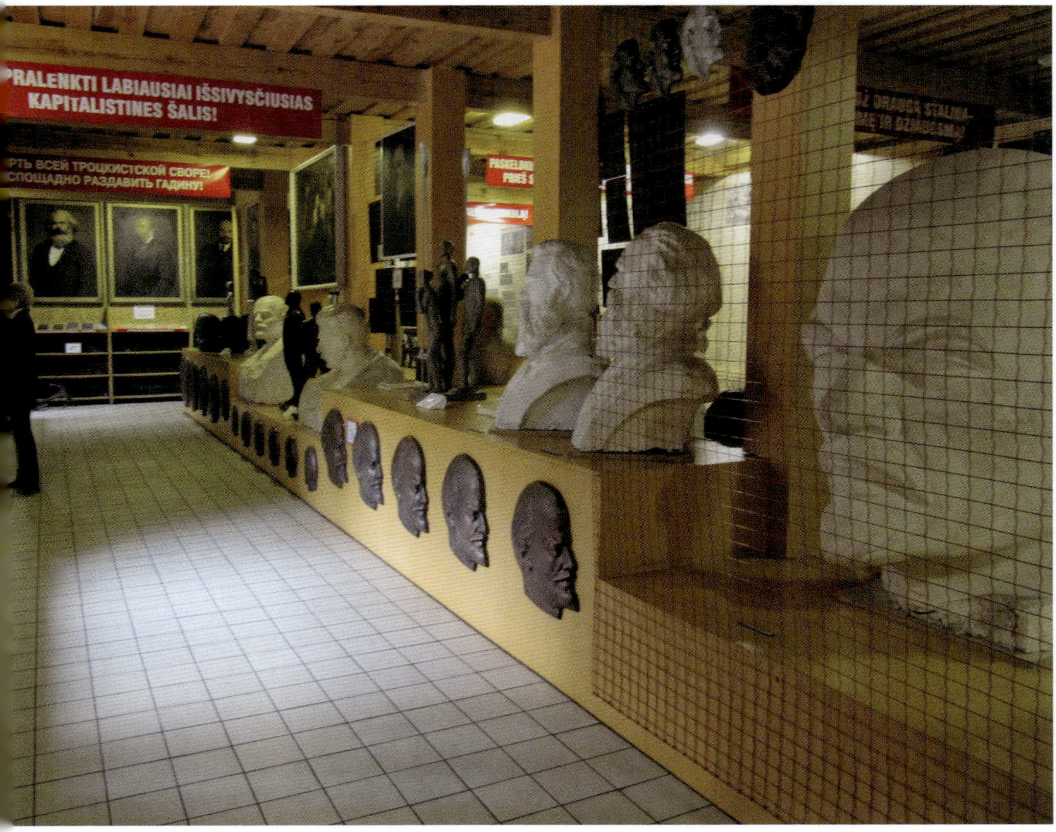

Collection of sculptures inside the museum

furnished with plaques. The texts provide information in Lithuanian and English about the sculptures, their former locations and the artists involved. A barbed wire fence surrounding the entire park area and several replica watchtowers erected on the perimeter of the complex refer to the mass repressions under Stalin, to which some 35,000 people fell victim during the first Soviet occupation between June 1940 and July 1941 alone.

The museum, which was designed in the style of the wooden cultural buildings of the 1940s and 1950s, provides information on the history of the Soviet occupation of Lithuania. Numerous films and audio recordings and photographs provide an insight into the ideologised culture and science of the Soviet era and reveal the effects of Soviet propaganda on the social value system. The objects on display reflect the cult of personality surrounding Soviet leadership idols such as Lenin and Stalin. Other works show common motifs of socialist work and everyday life and document the idealised representation of communist society.

Location: Grūtas, 66441 Druskininkai
Internet: www.grutoparkas.lt

Museum of Deportation and Resistance

Kaunas. The Museum of Deportation and Resistance was an initiative of the Union of Political Prisoners and Deportees of Lithuania and opened in June 1993. It stands on the site of Ramybės Park, which housed the municipal cemetery between 1847 and 1959. After demonstrations of solidarity with the Hungarian Revolution in 1956 and repeated meetings critical of the regime in subsequent years, the Soviet authorities levelled the memorial in 1959 and transformed the site into a recreational park. Since 1995, various memorial marks—sculptures, plaques and Christian crosses—have been installed to commemorate the victims of the uprising against the Soviet occupation in Kaunas in June 1941.

The Museum of Deportation and Resistance is one of five similar institutions set up by the victims' association in Lithuania's major cities. It documents the Lithuanian resistance struggle against Soviet and German rule between 1940 and 1990.

The museum collection contains about 6,500 objects, of which only about 800 can be presented in the two exhibition halls of the museum. In addition, the institution has an archive with numerous documents and photographs as well as personal testimonies of former resistance fighters.

The permanent exhibition focuses on the underground struggle of the "Forest Brothers", partisans, resistance fighters and guerrillas who resisted the Soviet occupation of the country after 1944. Also examined are various aspects of the Soviet policy of repression directed against the Lithuanian population—especially the deportations between 1940 and 1953. Uniforms, partisan badges, weapons, suitcases and numerous photographs are on display.

The museum works closely with schools and offers various excursions to local memorial sites, such as reconstructed "Forest Brothers" bunkers and the place where Romas Kalanta set himself on fire.

Location: Kaunas, Vytauto prospektas 46
Internet: www.lpkts.lt

Hill of Crosses

Šiauliai. The Hill of Crosses is a pilgrimage site not far from Šiauliai, an industrial town in northern Lithuania. On a saddle-shaped burial mound, enclosed by the valleys of the Kulpe River, are about 100,000 crosses and countless other Christian devotional objects. The historical memorial, which is visited by thousands of pilgrims every year, is a symbol of the Lithuanians' desire for freedom and national pride.

The origins of this pilgrimage site, first mentioned in 1850, are presumed to lie in the Polish-Lithuanian uprisings against tsarist rule by the Russian Empire. It is during the November Uprising of 1830/31, in which the occupied Poles and Lithuanians rebelled against the tsarist authorities, that the Lithuanian resistance fighters near Šiauliai are said to have suffered their greatest losses. Since the Russian occupation regime refused to bury the fallen, families, most of whom knew nothing of the whereabouts of the mortal remains of their relatives, erected symbolic memorial crosses on a hill near the River Kulpe. Around the turn of the century there are said to have been almost 150 crosses on the mountain. During the Lithuanian wars of independence between 1918 and 1920, further commemorative markers were added. The site became renowned as a symbol of living faith and a national spirit of resistance, a place of remembrance of the suffering endured and a beacon of hope for a better future. Until the first Soviet occupation

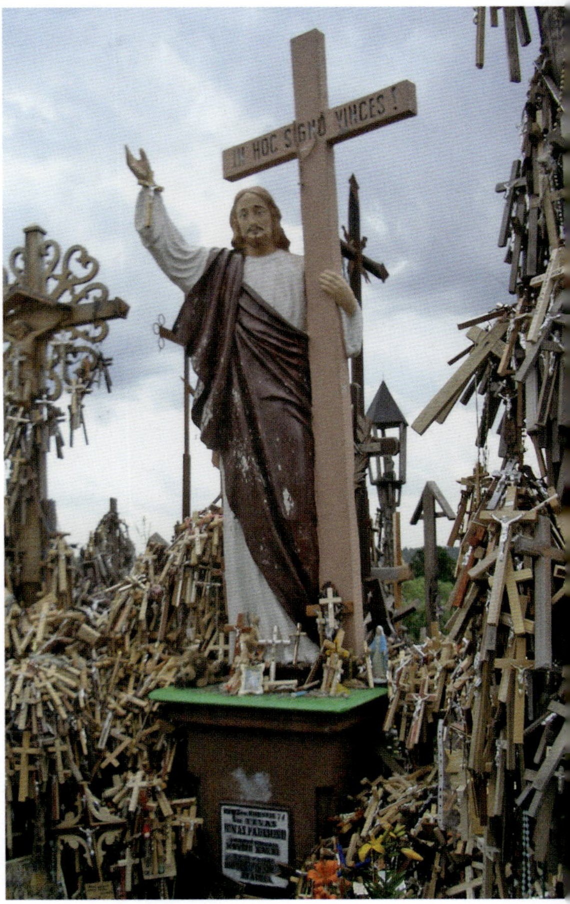

Figures of saints, prayer crosses and icons on the Hill of Crosses

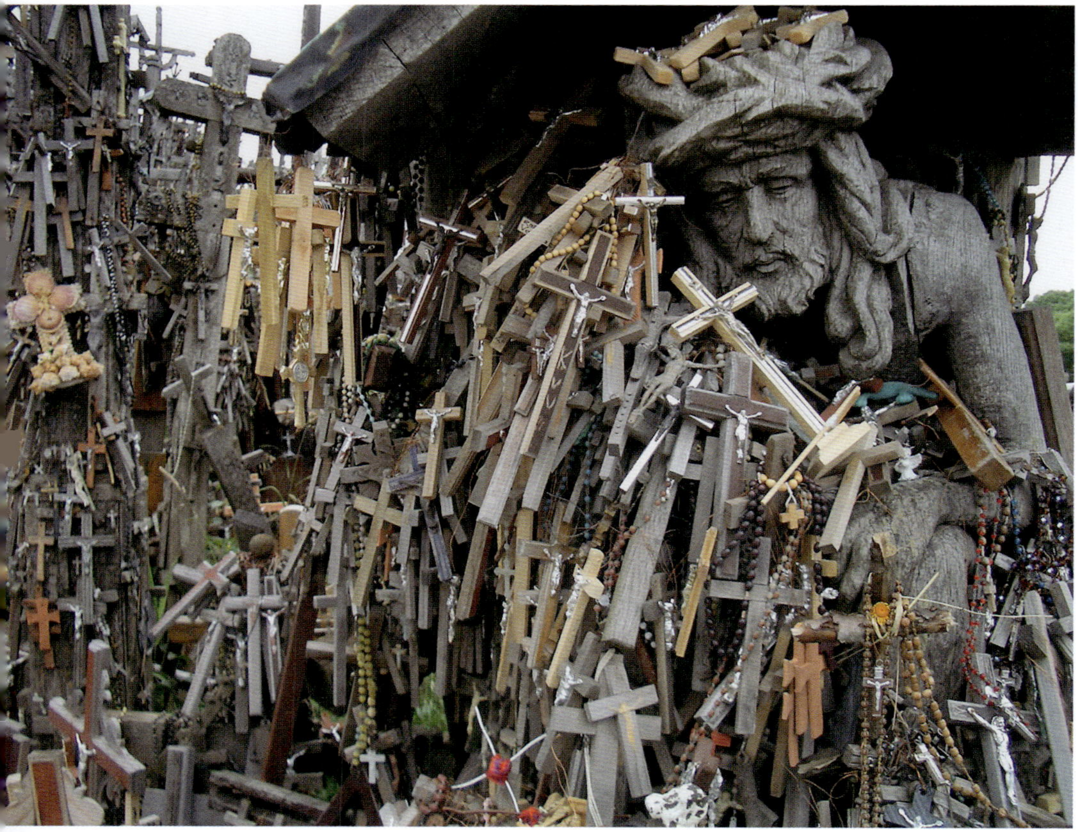

There are around 100,000 crosses and Christian devotionals at the memorial site.

of the country in June 1940, more than 400 crosses were erected in line with this tradition.

With the occupation of Lithuania by the Soviet Union and the subsequent Nazi occupation, the population was once again subjected to repression and violence. Despite state-imposed religious policies and the threat of persecution and punishment, the custom of erecting symbolic crosses continued even after the country was reconquered by the Red Army. Between April 1945 and August 1952, almost 12,000 Lithuanian citizens fell victim to Stalinist repression. The number of commemorative markers on the hill near Šiauliai increased rapidly. Under the cover of darkness, thousands of crosses were erected in memory of deported, interned and executed relatives, and others were put up to bear witness to the suffering of the individuals who had installed them. The site once again became an expression of civil disobedience to the Soviet regime and a symbol of religiously motivated resistance.

In June 1959, the Central Committee of the Communist Party of Lithuania reacted to the place of pilgrimage for the first time. In April 1961, the order was given to tear down more than 2,000 crosses. Iron crosses were processed into scrap metal; stone and concrete crucifixes were smashed, buried or sunk in the river; and the wooden crosses were burned. The hill was finally levelled by bulldozers. Within a very short time, however, the local population erected new crosses and commemorative markers on the same spot. Despite repeated attempts to destroy the site, the tradition could not be broken.

In the course of Gorbachev's reform policy, official toleration of this custom was enacted in 1985 with the inclusion of the site on the list of Lithuanian national cultural monuments. By the time the country gained independence from the Soviet Union in August 1991, over 55,000 crosses and crucifixes had already been placed on the mountain. Countless other Christian devotional objects, such as figures of saints, icons and devotional pictures, prayer wreaths and depictions of Lithuanian resistance fighters have been placed around the larger commemorative signs.

On 7 September 1993, on his first visit to predominantly Catholic Lithuania, Pope John Paul II celebrated a solemn Mass on the Hill of Crosses in front of a congregation of almost 100,000 people. An altar pavilion built especially for this purpose and a seven-metre wooden cross at the foot of the mountain were left to commemorate the religious ceremony. Since 2000, a monastery run by Franciscan monks, which serves as a novitiate for future monks and a place of contemplation, has stood on the grounds of this pilgrimage site.

Location: Twelve kilometres north of Šiauliai
Internet: www.hillofcrosses.com

Further reading:

Kuusi, Hanna: Prison Experience and Socialist Sculptures—Tourism and the Soviet Past in the Baltic States. In: Kostiainen, Auvo / Syrjämaa, Taina (eds.): Touring the Past. Uses of History in Tourism. Savonlinna 2008, pp. 105 – 122. / Motuzas, Alfonsas: The Origin of the Hill of Crosses, Devotional Practices and Music of the Pilgrimages. In: Scholarly Papers University of Latvia, Vol. 793. Oriental Studies Between East and West: Cultural and Religious Dialogue before, during and after the Totalitarian Rule. Riga 2013, pp. 79 – 84. / Peikštenis, Eugenijus: Das Museum für die Opfer des Genozids, Vilnius. In: Knigge, Volkhard / Mählert, Ulrich (ed.): Der Kommunismus im Museum. Formen der Auseinandersetzung in Deutschland und Ostmitteleuropa. Cologne, Weimar 2005, pp. 131 – 138. / Williams, Paul: The Afterlife of Communist Statuary: Hungary's Szoborpark and Lithuania's Grutas Park. In: Forum for Modern Language Studies, 2008, Vol. 44, No. 2, pp. 185 – 198. / Wirtualnyj musej gulaga. Kaunasskij musej ssylki i soprotiwlenija [Virtual Gulag Museum. Kaunas Museum of Deportation & Resistance]. Available online at: www.gulagmuseum.org/showObject.do?-object=1719266&language=1 (last accessed on: 22/01/2018).

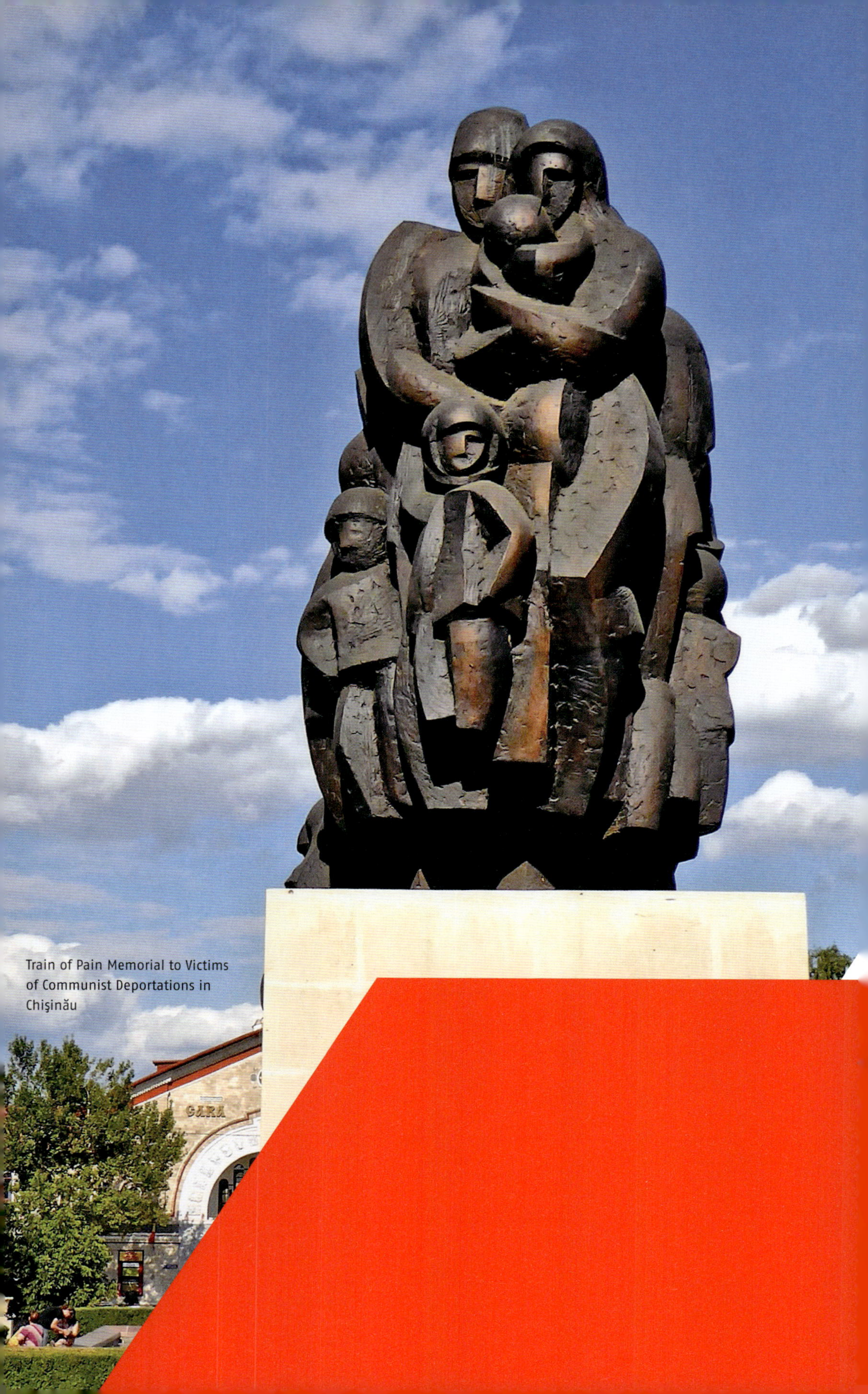

Train of Pain Memorial to Victims of Communist Deportations in Chişinău

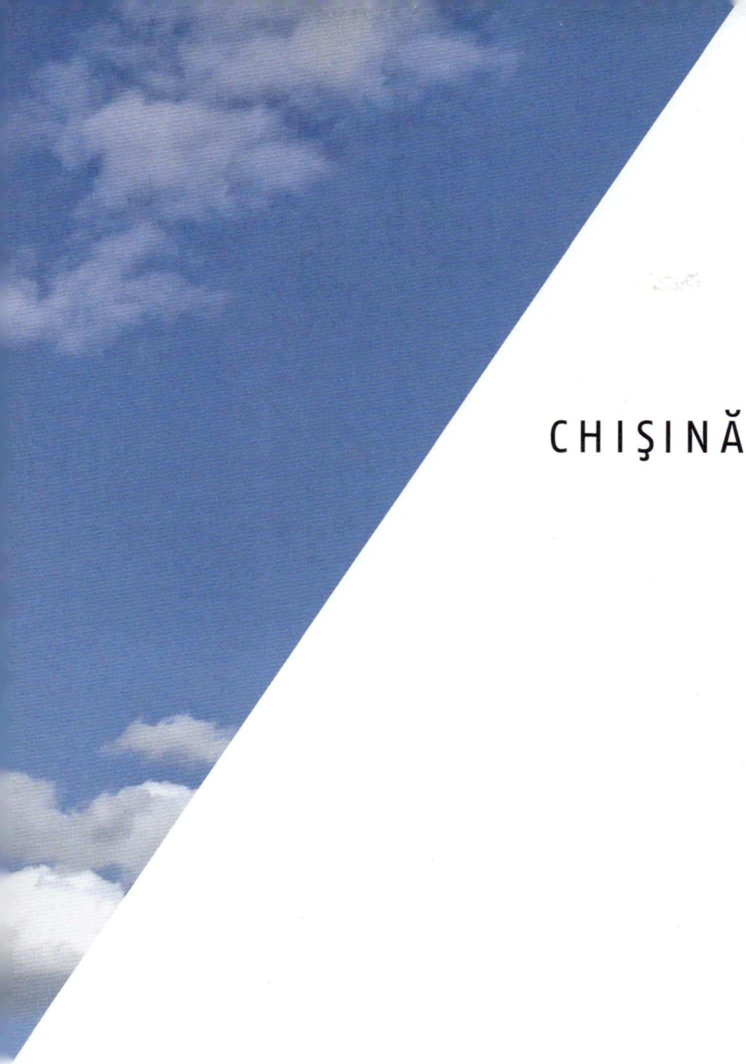

CHIŞINĂU

Moldova

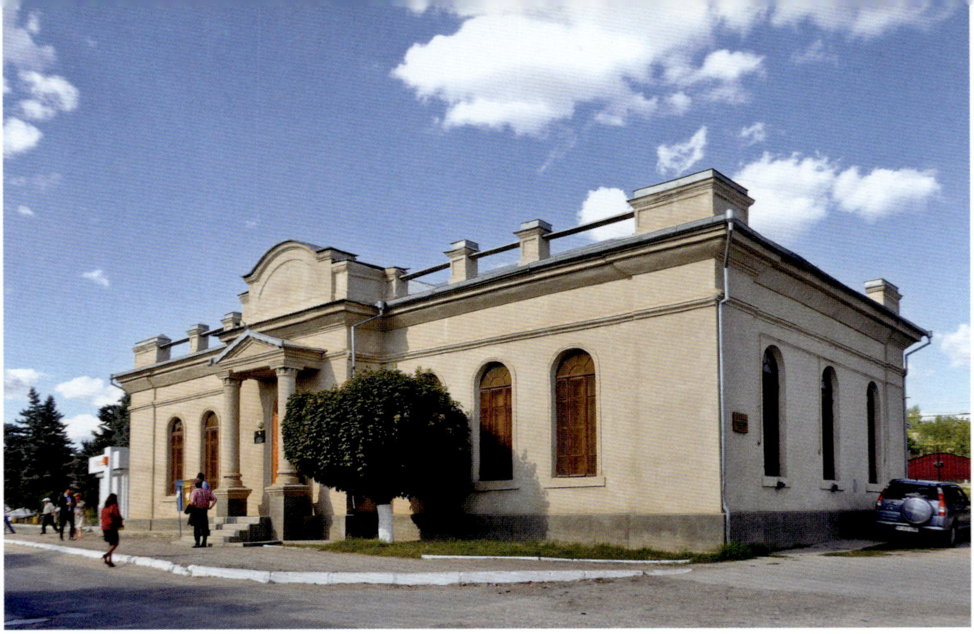

The Moldovan Democratic Republic was founded on 2 December 1917 as part of the Russian Democratic Federative Republic. At the same time, secret protocols between the victorious powers in the First World War and Romania determined that Bessarabia should be ceded to the Kingdom of Romania. However, Soviet Russia and, later, the Soviet Union continued to regard the region as their territory. The area east of the Dniester—Transnistria—was first annexed to the Ukrainian Soviet Socialist Republic and later to the Moldavian Autonomous Soviet Socialist Republic. A rigorous transformation of all political and public life in the territory belonging to the Soviet Union ensued in tandem with the parallel development in the other territories ruled by the Bolsheviks. Agriculture was collectivised, and wealthy farmers were defamed as "kulaks" and either murdered or deported along with their families and taken to camps and "special settlements". The pre-war political and intellectual elite was imprisoned and murdered; churches and monasteries were closed, and religious worshippers and priests arrested. The terror of the early days continued in the mass murders of the "Great Terror" in 1937/38.

On 28 June 1940, Soviet troops occupied Bessarabia, which belonged to Romania, and northern Bucovina in accordance with the terms of the Molotov-Ribbentrop Pact. This occupation was accompanied by the relocation, coordinated between Germany and the Soviet Union, of the approximately 3,600,000 inhabitants of German origin from these regions to the German Reich. These resettlement measures and the territorial redistribution had been agreed in the secret additional protocol to the Molotov-Ribbentrop Pact. Together with Transnistria, the territories of Bessarabia and Bukovina now formed the Moldavian Soviet Socialist Republic. After their accession to the Soviet Union, the population in these regions was subjected to forced expropriations, and the economy reshaped in the Soviet mould. About 250,000 people of Romanian descent were deported, and Russians, Belarusians and Ukrainians were resettled in the Moldovan territories.

In June 1941, Romania joined the German invasion of the Soviet Union, and these territories came under its control once again. Romanian associations, supported by the local population, carried out massacres of the Jewish population. Thousands were murdered or later deported to the German extermination camps.

◄

Open-Air Museum in Memory of the Victims of Political Repressions in Mereni

►

Memorial to the Victims of Political Repression in Tiraspol

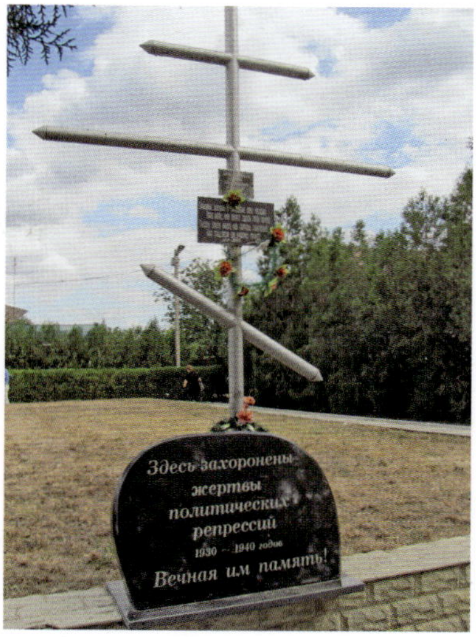

After the reconquest by the Red Army, Soviet power was restored. The terror against the Romanian population continued in the post-war period. Alleged and actual collaborators with the Romanian troops allied with Nazi Germany were arrested and murdered. In the post-war deportations between 1947 and 1950, an estimated seven percent of the Moldovan population—about 35,000 people—were deported to Siberia.

Thousands were killed or murdered. While the country was part of the Soviet Union, Moldovan citizens were not allowed to travel to Romania and vice versa. Family ties were severed and letters censored. Romanian, the mother tongue of a large part of the Moldovan population, was officially renamed "Moldovan" in a strategy to cut cultural ties with Romania. Relations between the peoples of the two countries only returned to normal after the fall of the Soviet Union.

In 1991, Moldova declared itself independent; Moldovan was introduced as a national language. Shortly after independence, fighting ensued between Transnistria, which was supported by the Russian government, and the government in Chişinău.

This ended with thousands dead and the secession of Transnistria from the Republic of Moldova. The regime in Tiraspol, the capital of Transnistria, rejected offers of regional autonomy, similar to that granted to Gagauzia, within the Republic of Moldova.

Coming to terms with the communist past has thus far only been of concern to a small minority. The main focus has been on the deportation of civilians: the opening by a private initiative of a museum in Chişinău dedicated to this subject is one example. A monument was also erected in front of the station from which the deportation trains departed, and a section on communist repression was opened in the National Museum of History.

In Transnistria, an autonomous region that strives for independence and still considers itself a communist country, there is a memorial built and maintained by a group of survivors and descendants of the victims of repression.

Exhibition on the Victims of Repression and Political Persecutions

Chişinău. Since June 2012, the basement of the Historical National Museum of the Republic of Moldova has housed the permanent exhibition "Soviet Moldova: Between Myths and Gulag". The exhibition was designed by the Museum of the Victims of Deportations and Political Repressions, a branch of the National Museum. The ceremonial opening took place in the presence of contemporary witnesses and survivors of Stalinist repression. Also present were numerous well-known personalities from the political and cultural life of Moldova.

More than 700 exhibits are presented in a darkened room on about 120 square metres of exhibition space. In an array of display cases, the exhibition features photographs, documents, geographical maps, personal effects of victims of political repression and Gulag detainees, eyewitness accounts by survivors of the Stalinist deportations of the 1940s and 1950s, and documents and materials from the former KGB archives.

Structured chronologically, the exhibition follows the establishment of the communist regime on the territory of the Moldavian Autonomous Soviet Socialist Republic, which was established in 1924: it examines the excesses of the "Great Terror" in 1937/38 and the occupation of Bessarabia and northern Bucovina following the signing of the German-Russian Nonaggression Pact in 1940, whose secret additional protocol partitioned Eastern Europe into the spheres of influence of Hitler and Stalin. The deportation waves of the 1940s and 1950s and the devastating famine of 1946/47 are also covered in detail. Forms of political repression and of resistance and opposition are outlined. Also presented and elucidated are the efforts made after the collapse of the communist system to commemorate the victims of the repressive regime.

Location: Chişinău, Strada 31 August 1989
Internet: www.nationalmuseum.md

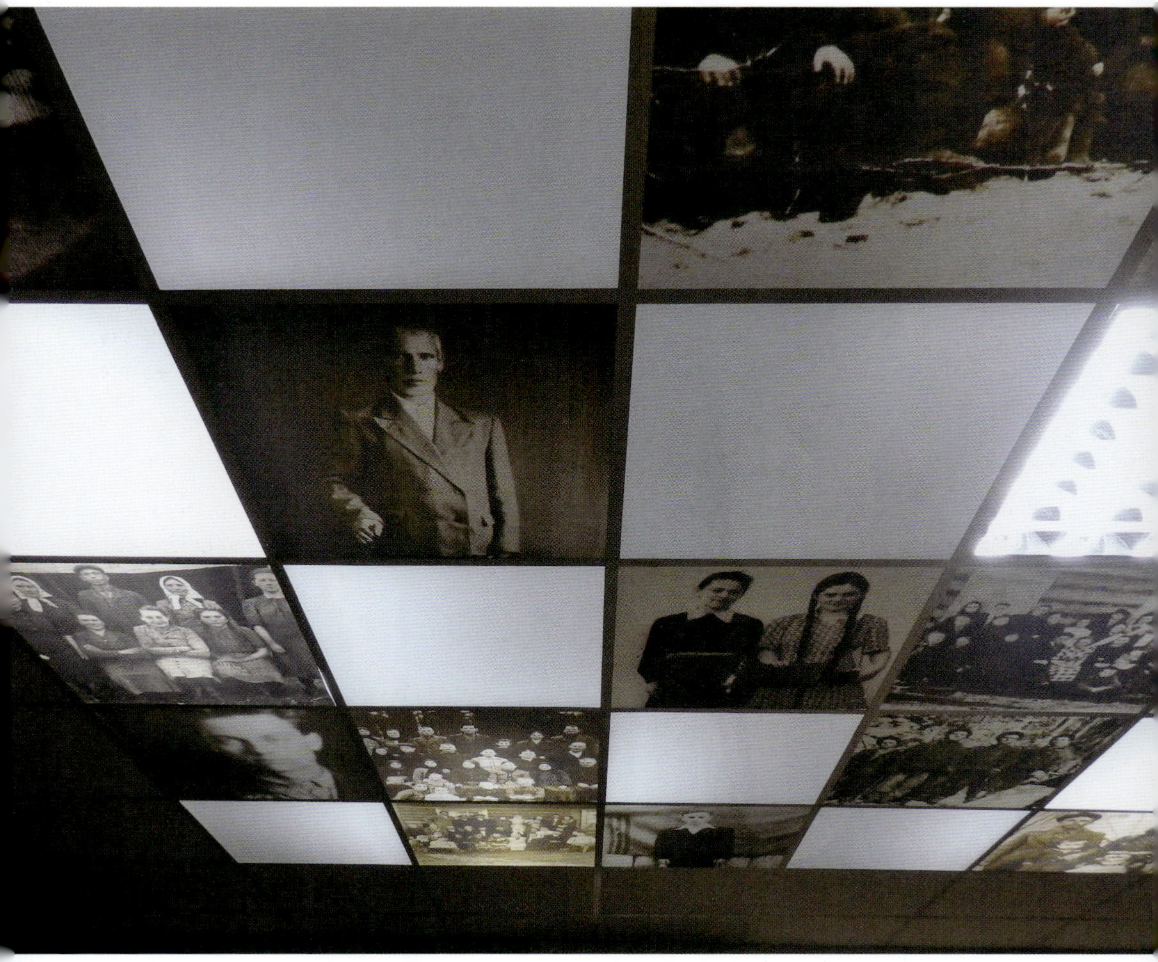

Ceiling of the exhibition hall with historic photographs

Train of Pain — Memorial to Victims of Communist Deportations

Chişinău. In 23 August 2013, the Memorial to Victims of Communist Deportations was inaugurated on the square in front of the train station in the Moldovan capital. The foundation stone for the construction of the monument was laid in 1990 on the initiative of the Association of Former Deportees and Political Detainees. However, it took another 23 years for the project, which was financed by the city government, to be completed.

The monument was finally unveiled to the public on the symbolic date of the 74th anniversary of the signing of the German-Russian Aggression Pact of 1939, whose secret additional protocol partitioned Eastern Europe into the spheres of influence of Hitler and Stalin. The inauguration ceremony was attended by the mayor of Chişinău, representatives of the city administration and journalists, and survivors of the deportations and their families. The bronze sculpture, also popularly known as the "Train of Pain", was created by the sculptor Iurie Platon. It stands in front of the station where the deportations from the annexed areas of Bessarabia and northern Bucovina to remote steppe areas of Kazakhstan and Siberia commenced in the 1940s and 1950s.

The sculpture, three metres high and twelve metres long, consists of an inclined stone base bearing representations of a densely packed throng of people cast in bronze. While the figures on the front of the monument are still recognisably human, the figures towards the rear merge to form an abstract "human train". At the back of the sculpture, only a suggestion of the axles and wheels of a deportation transport remains. Only a few metres away on the same square stands a monument to the victims of Stalinist repression.

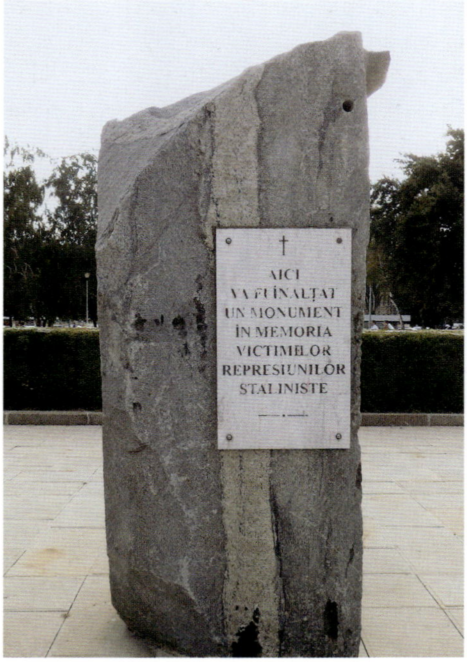

The Monument to Victims of Stalinist Repressions is located nearby

Inscription
Romanian: *IN MEMORIA / VICTIMELOR / DEPORTĂRILOR / REGIMULUI / COMUNIST*
English: *In memory of the deportation victims of the communist regime*

Location: Chişinău, Strada Piaţa Gării 1

Further reading:
Bochmann, Klaus / Dumbrava, Marina (eds.): Vademecum. Contemporary History Moldova. A Guide to archives, research institutions, libraries, associations and sites of memory. Commissioned by the Federal Foundation for the Study of the Communist Dictatorship in Eastern Germany. 2nd amended and expanded edition. Berlin 2015. / Hausleitner, Marianna: Deportationen als Mittel der Durchsetzung politischer Interessen in Südosteuropa bis 1944. In: Jahrbuch des Instituts für Geschichte „G. Baritiu" bei Cluj-Napoca (Klausenburg), 2006, Vol. XLV, pp. 169 – 178. / Postică, Elena: Expoziţia muzeală. „Moldova sovietică: între mituri şi gulag": In: Tyragedia, 2013, Vol. 7, No. 2, pp. 345 – 356. / Primăria Municipiului Chişinău: Monumentul în memoria victimelor deportărilor comuniste, inaugurat la Chişinău [Chişinău Town Hall: Monument to the Victims of Communist Deportations, inaugurated in Chişinău]. 2013. Available online at: www.bit.ly/2jylti5 (last accessed on: 30/11/2017).

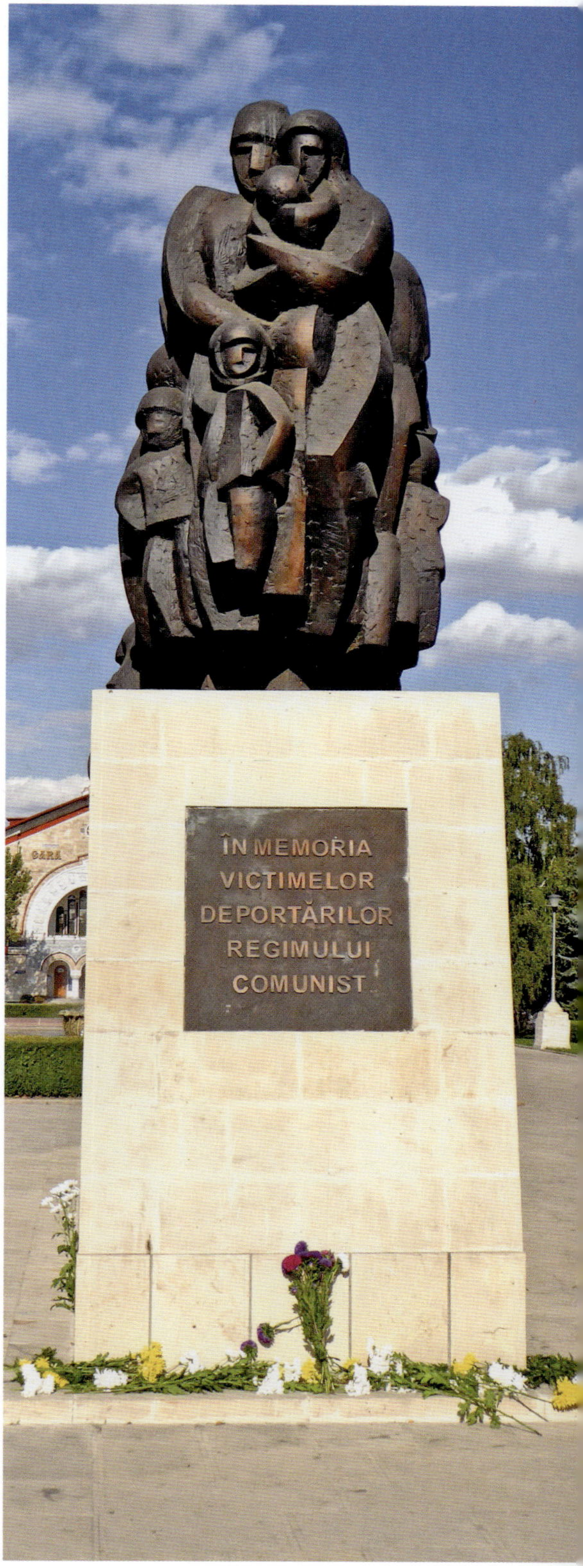

►
Front view of the Train of Pain Memorial to Victims of Communist Deportations

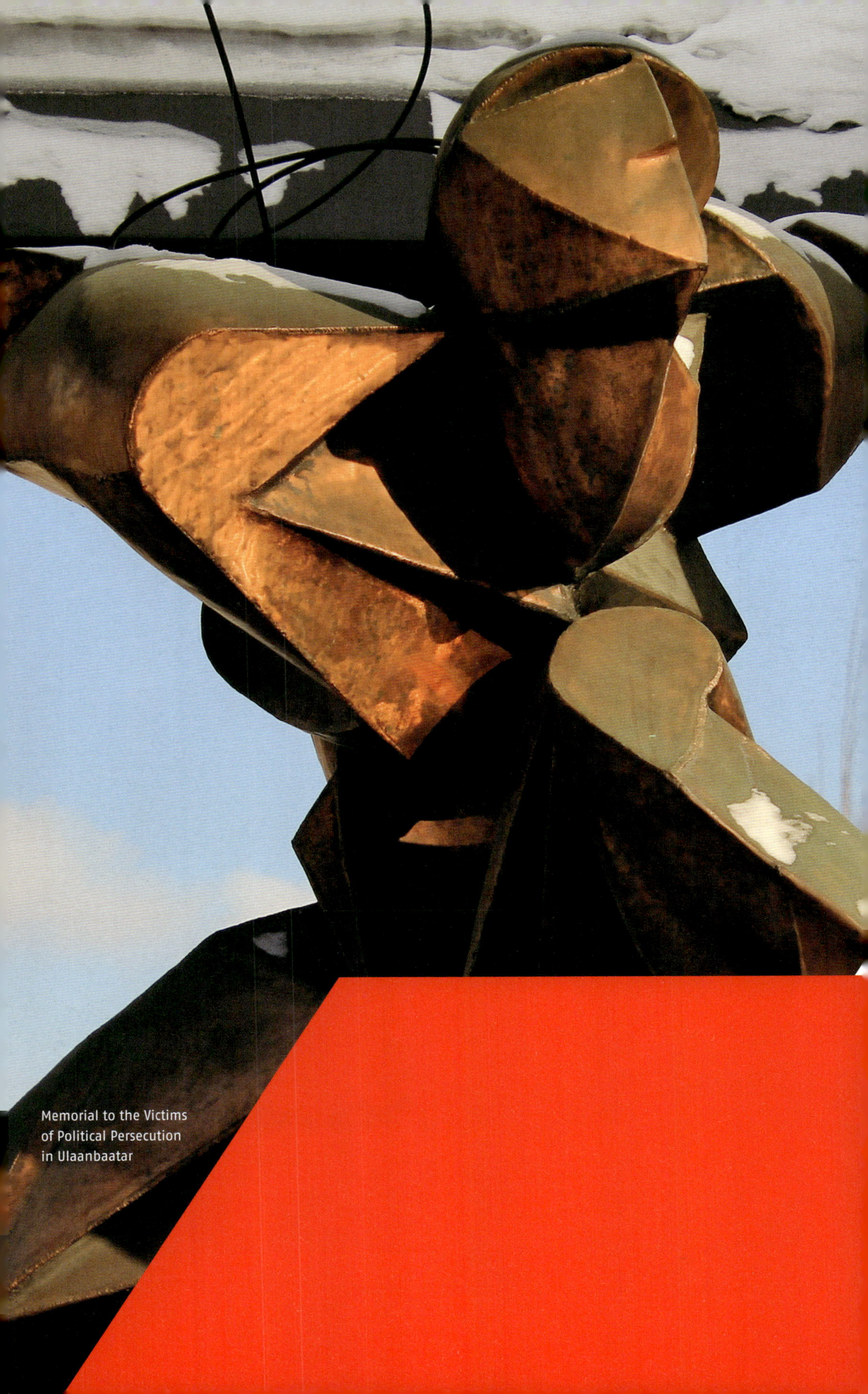

Memorial to the Victims of Political Persecution in Ulaanbaatar

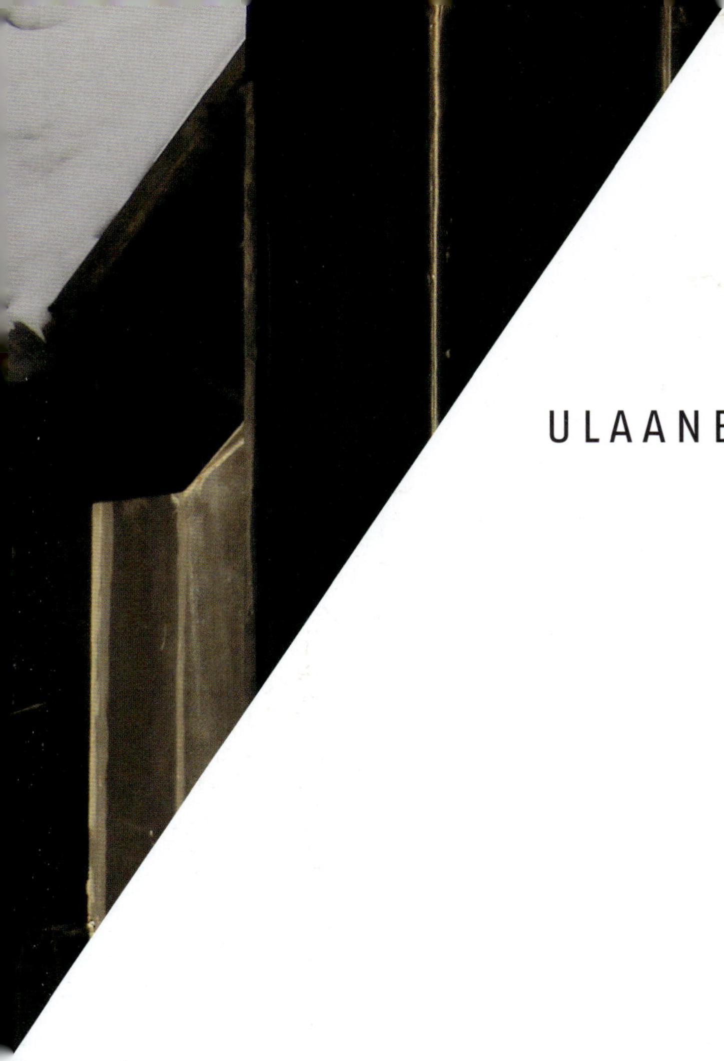

ULAANBAATAR

Mongolia

Until the end of the First World War, the territory of Mongolia was the subject of a dispute between the Russian Empire, China and Japan, each of which had its own territorial interests. These related primarily to the raw material deposits discovered in Mongolia. From the end of the First World War until 1919, Mongolia was ruled by China before it was once again occupied by Russians in the form of White Army troops. In 1921, fighters of the Mongolian Revolutionary People's Army, supported by 10,000 Red Army soldiers, seized the country's capital, Ulaanbaatar. While Inner Mongolia declared independence in 1921 and signed a treaty of friendship with Soviet Russia, Outer Mongolia remained under Chinese rule.

The Mongolian People's Republic was founded in 1924. The ruling Mongolian People's Revolutionary Party modelled its social transformation policy on that of the Soviet Union: the political "cleansing" of potential adversaries, the fight against the Buddhist religion, monks and worshippers, and a policy to eliminate nomadism shaped the lives of the approximately 500,000 inhabitants of the People's Republic. Moreover, Mongolia was not only politically but also economically and militarily dependent on the Soviet Union; Soviet soldiers were first stationed in the country in the 1920s.

The violent transformation of Mongolian society and the destruction of traditional lifestyles were seen as a fight against backwardness and feudalism. At the beginning of the 1930s, collectivisation was enforced, and livestock, pastures, water resources and mineral resources were expropriated and nationalised. Buddhist monasteries were also expropriated and several hundred monks murdered. At the same time, forced collectivisation was accompanied by the sedentarisation of the mostly nomadic population, thereby depriving them of their livelihoods. Some of the forcibly expropriated herds were brought to the Soviet Union, while some nomads chose to slaughter their animals rather than surrender them.

As in other Soviet republics, such as Ukraine and Kazakhstan, forced sedentarisation and collectivisation created the conditions for devastating famine. Thousands of families attempted to flee to neighbouring China, Japanese-occupied Manchuria and Tibet, and a third of all livestock died. This catastrophe prompted the peasants and nomads to rise up against the Soviet occupation. To calm the heightened tension in the region, repressive policies were relaxed in the mid-1930s. Some monasteries regained their property, the state relented in its fight against the Buddhist religion, and private ownership of livestock and pastures was once again permitted.

However, this phase was a brief one, as Mongolia fell prey to Stalinist repression between 1936 and 1938. Among the victims were cadres and functionaries of the ruling Communist Party who were regarded as "apostates", Buddhist worshippers and monks, and also individuals who had communicated with foreigners or been educated abroad. The Mongolian intellectual elite was destroyed, as was much of the cultural heritage, which was dismissed as backward. More than 35,000 people were abducted, executed and buried in mass graves that were not discovered until after 1990.

In response to this violence, insurgencies broke out again throughout the country but were bloodily suppressed. Soviet cadres, usually of non-Mongolian origin, were installed in the posts freed up by the assassination of local officials to guarantee Stalinist rule without national affiliation. During the Second World War, Mongolia became an important supplier of raw materials and supplies for the Soviet Union, while itself becoming the scene of battles between the Soviet Union and Japan.

Repressions continued after the end of the Second World War, albeit in a less overt form, especially after the death of Stalin. They now targeted so-called "anti-Soviet elements", who were deported to the Soviet Union. After the war, the Soviet leadership launched a large-scale campaign of industrialisation and for the introduction of nationwide health care and education based on the Soviet model. The goal was to completely suppress and eradicate the memory of the monastic schools that had existed in traditional Mongolian society and of traditional medicine.

Given these circumstances, there was no organised opposition until the 1980s, when the Mongolian government also officially began a process of rapprochement with China and the USA, leading to the establishment of diplomatic relations in 1987. Inspired by Gorbachev's policy of glasnost and perestroika, a nascent civil society began to develop, which also took steps to critically re-evaluate Stalinist crimes and repression in Mongolia. The first mass graves were located, and the extent of the crimes was publicly denounced. This was accompanied by increased hostility towards Russians, causing thousands of ethnic Russians who had settled in Mongolia under Stalin to flee to the Soviet Union.

As the Soviet Empire collapsed, Mongolians also took to the streets against communist rule in 1990, leading to the resignation of the government. In 1992, the Mongolian parliament adopted a new constitution that formally sealed the fate of the Mongolian People's Republic. While the reappraisal of the crimes had already begun in the late 1980s, the Mongolian government officially apologised to the victims of the persecutions and their relatives in 1996. 10 September was designated the National Day of Remembrance of the Victims of Political Repressions. Monuments commemorating the victims and the crimes were erected all over the country.

Memorial Museum of the Victims of Political Repression

Ulaanbaatar. The museum, which opened in 1996 in the centre of Ulaanbaatar, shows the various stages of political persecution in socialist-ruled Mongolia. The driving force behind it was Tserendulam Genden, daughter of the former President and Prime Minister of the Mongolian People's Republic Peljidin Genden, who was executed in Moscow in 1937 during the "Great Terror". The museum, which is privately funded, is located in Genden's former residence and is currently undergoing extensive renovation work.

The exhibition focuses on the development of the Mongolian socialist state in the 1920s and, above all, on the horrors of the mass terror from 1936 to 1938. Extensive space is also devoted to the reprisals against the Buddhist community in Mongolia. In addition to drawings, photographs, documents and contemporary objects of daily use, the exhibition features a showcase containing the mortal remains of victims of political repression.

Exterior view of the museum building

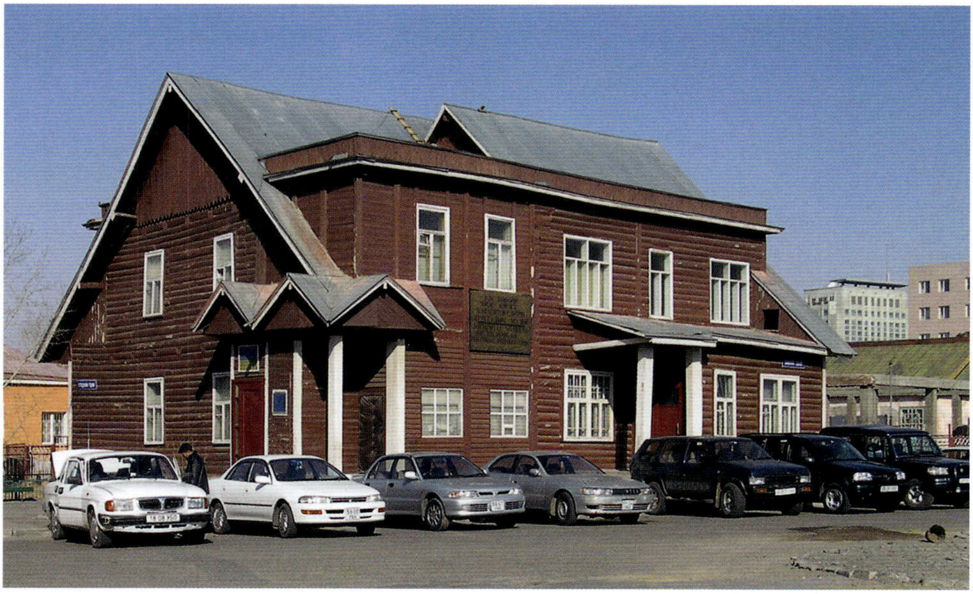

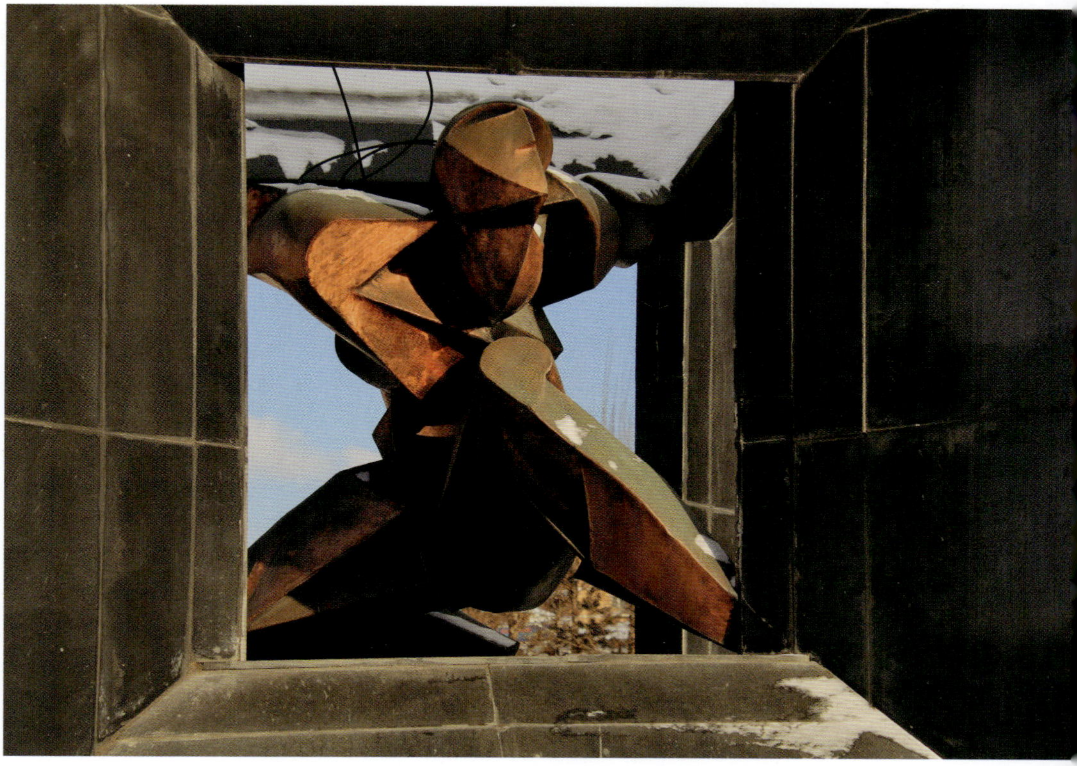

Memorial to the Victims of Political Persecution

Next to the museum is a memorial to the victims of political persecution in the 1920s and 1930s that was inaugurated in December 1997. The black stone walls of the cube-shaped memorial open out like a funnel. Wedged in the interior of the cube is the stylised effigy of a person crouching in a defensive position, who is pushing back against the narrowness of the walls closing in on it. A commemorative event is held here every year on 10 September, the National Day of Remembrance of the Victims of Political Repressions.

Another central memorial site dedicated to the victims of repression is the cemetery of honour at the foot of the Songino Khairkhan Uul Mountains outside Ulaanbaatar, which was opened in the early 1990s. This is located inside a cemetery that was created during the mass executions in 1937.

Location: Ulaanbaatar, Olimpijn Gudamsh 15

Further reading:

Kaplonski, Christopher: Blame, Guilt and Avoidance: The Struggle to Control the Past in Post-Socialist Mongolia. In: History and Memory, 1999, Vol. 11, No. 2, pp. 94 – 114. / Koller, Christian: Kollektivierte Nomaden: Die Gründung der Volksrepublik Mongolei vor 85 Jahren. In: Rote Revue — Zeitschrift für Politik, Wirtschaft und Kultur, 2009, 86/3, pp. 28 – 36. / Schmücking, Daniel / Helf, Rafaela: Die Aufarbeitung hat begonnen. Politische Verfolgung in der sozialistischen Mongolei. In: KAS Länderbericht 2017. Available online at: www.kas.de/mongolei/de/publications/47718/ (last accessed on: 16/11/2017).

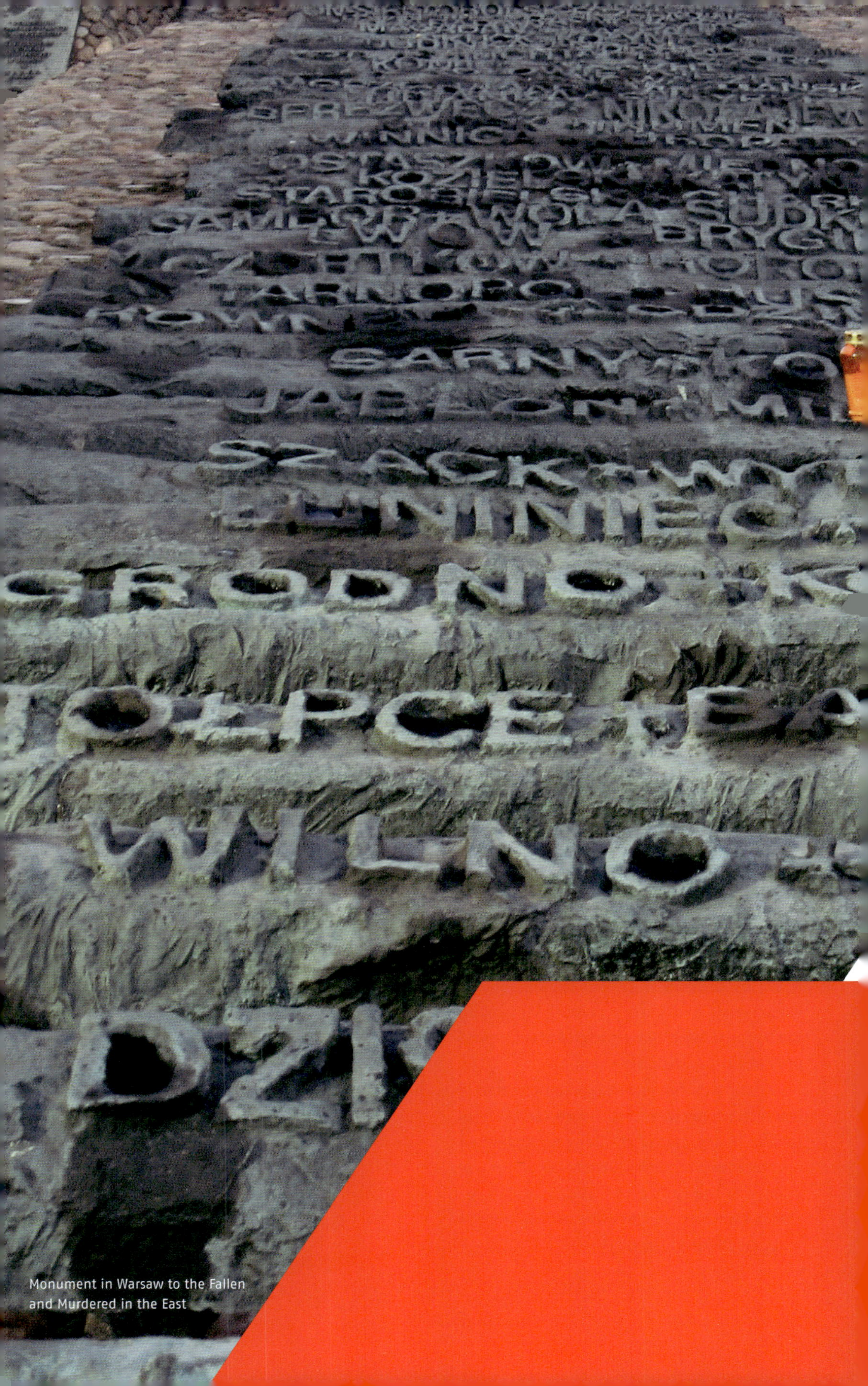

Monument in Warsaw to the Fallen and Murdered in the East

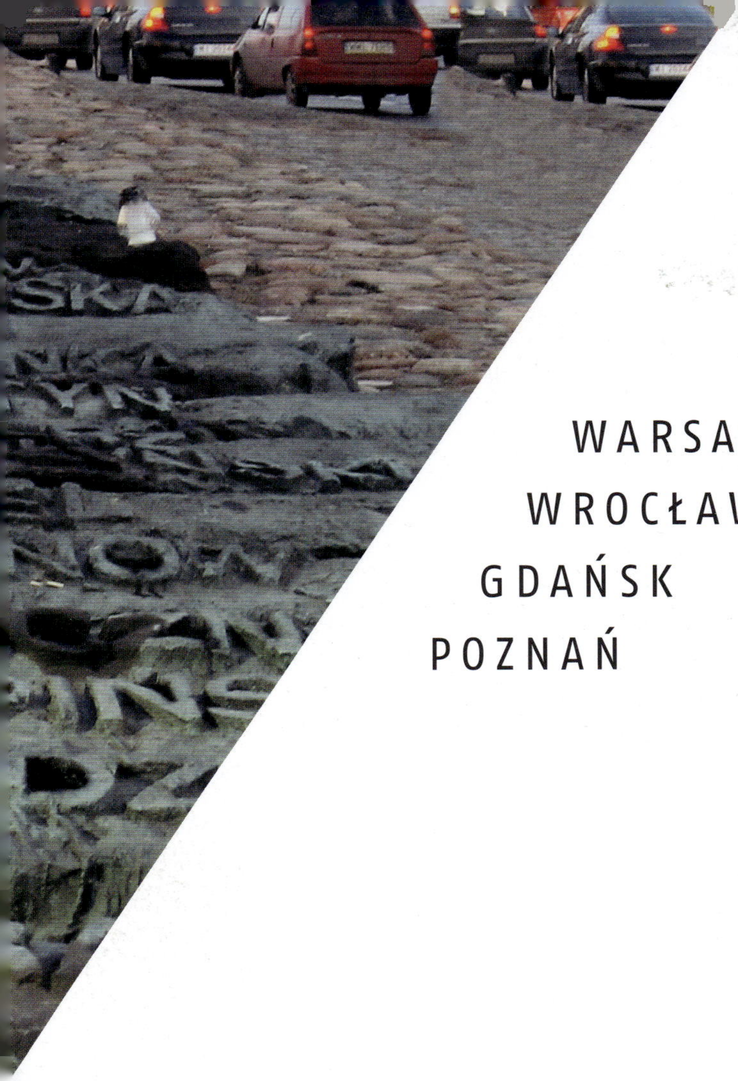

WARSAW

WROCŁAW

GDAŃSK

POZNAŃ

Poland

When Poland regained its independence after the First World War for the first time in over 120 years, the country was far from politically stable. On the one hand, there were territorial disputes with Germany and Czechoslovakia. On the other, tensions were mounting at the eastern border with the Russian Empire, finally culminating in the Polish-Russian War of 1920/21 in which Poland reconquered areas previously dominated by Russia.

In 1926, Józef Piłsudski established a regime that, notwithstanding its increasing authoritarianism, was welcomed by large sections of the population as it appeared to offer the prospect of stability after years of insecurity. However, the controversial demarcation of the borders following the Versailles Treaty continued to strain relations with neighbouring countries. Despite the conclusion of nonaggression treaties with the Soviet Union and Germany in 1932 and 1934, the latter two powers agreed in the so-called Molotov-Ribbentrop Pact of 23 August 1939 to carve up Eastern and Central Europe, including Poland. On 1 September 1939, the German Wehrmacht invaded Poland, thereby triggering the Second World War, which was waged as a war of aggression, extermination and conquest. On 17 September, the Red Army occupied eastern Polish territories as laid out in the pact and annexed them to the Soviet Union. Members of the Polish government fled to Paris (and then, after the German invasion of France, to London), where they formed a government in exile to organise resistance to the occupation of the country.

Nazi Germany and the Soviet Union proceeded to establish their respective occupation regimes in the occupied territories, blighting their populations with mass executions, mass deportations, the deprivation of rights and the annihilation of the political, military and cultural elites. The Soviet-occupied part of Eastern Poland was annexed to the Belarusian and Ukrainian Soviet republics, and the so-called Vilnius Region became part of Lithuania. Over 100,000 Polish citizens were arrested and deported to camps within the USSR. In addition, over 300,000 people (including entire families) were exiled to Siberia or Kazakhstan. The policy of the Soviet occupiers was directed against all potential opponents of the new power. Members of the intellectual, military and political elite were singled out in particular for liquidation. This policy reached its brutal apogee in the mass executions that became known as the "Katyń massacre". In the spring of 1940, on Stalin's orders, the Soviet secret police murdered over 22,000 Polish officers and arrested civilians who had fallen into the hands of the Soviet Union after the invasion of Eastern Poland.

In the part of the country occupied by Germany, the National Socialists pursued a policy of extermination against the population, above all against the approximately 3.5 million Polish Jews. Hundreds of thousands of civilians were deported to Germany for forced labour. In the German concentration and extermination camps built on Polish soil, millions of people were conscripted into forced labour, perished from hostile conditions or were murdered. About six million Jews from all the countries occupied by Germany were brought to the many extermination camps including Auschwitz-Birkenau, Treblinka, Sobibor, Belzec and killed. Hundreds of thousands of Sinti and Roma, as well as people regarded as "racially inferior", especially from Poland and the Soviet Union, also fell victim to the Nazis' racial fanaticism. After the German invasion of the Soviet Union on 22 June 1941, the Eastern Polish territory formerly annexed by the Soviet Union also came under German rule. During the Nazi occupation, Poland lost almost a fifth of its population.

Throughout the Second World War, Polish civilians and soldiers first fought in the regular Polish army and, after the surrender at the end of September 1939, as members of the "Home Army" ("Armia Krajowa") operating underground against the German and Soviet occupying forces. The Jewish uprising in the Warsaw Ghetto in the spring of 1943 in particular sent out a desperate signal that the Jews would not allow themselves to be slaughtered without resistance. During the Warsaw Uprising in August and September 1944, more than 150,000 Varsovians lost their lives in mass executions and bombardments.

When the Germans were forced to retreat on all fronts, the Red Army liberated Poland from National Socialist occupation. However, the country then came under Soviet rule. The Soviet Union finally annexed the Eastern Polish parts of the country and, in consultation with the Western Allies, agreed to compensate Poland for this loss with German territories after the end of the war. Poland's western border was moved 200 kilometres to the west, resulting in millions of expulsions and resettlements and the deaths of thousands of people.

After the end of the Second World War, a Communist regime was installed with the assistance of the Soviet Union: massive electoral fraud in a referendum in 1946 and "preparations" for the first Sejm elections in 1947 were intended to give the communist state power a veneer of "legitimacy". The enforcement of communist power was accompanied by the suppression of all forms of opposition and resistance against the communists and the new occupiers of the country.

In order to maintain communist rule, the security apparatus was constantly expanded. Founded in 1944, the Ministry of Public Security (Urząd Bezpieczeństwa, UB) asserted the claim to power of the communist Polish United Workers' Party (PVAP) through terror and violence. Between 1944 and 1947, the Ministry of Public Security conducted a brutal campaign against the underground groups, the most important being the Home Army and the "Freedom and Independence" organisation (Zrzeszenie Wolność i Niezawisłóść, WiN) that took on its mantle. Thousands of underground fighters became the targets of brutal attacks, persecution and deportation to the interior of the Soviet Union.

At the same time, the repressive measures were extended to the whole of society. Everyone was a potential target of the secret police: high officials of the pre-war period, but also members of the politburo, generals, partisans, peasants, young people and workers—anyone who might allegedly, actually or potentially have become active in the resistance to the communist regime.

By 1952, the security apparatus employed around 34,000 people and maintained a network of informers permeating all areas of social life. The aim of this network, which numbered 74,000 as early as 1949, was to keep the population in check through fear and to contribute to the atomisation of Polish society. According to official figures, the country's prison population included as many as 49,500 political prisoners by 1952. In January 1953, some 5.2 million people—one third of Poland's entire adult population—were also listed in the state security service's directories of "suspicious elements". The introduction of the planned economy was accompanied by mass expropriations and over-hasty industrialisation measures, which led to massive economic problems. By 1954, the number of prisoners interned in forced labour camps amounted to 84,200. It is estimated that some 50,000 people lost their lives between 1944 and 1956.

After the attempt to eliminate any opposition in the country, the Catholic Church remained as the only institution that could still function alongside the communist state apparatus. However, a compromise agreement negotiated in 1950 did not spare the church from repression: seminaries for priests and religious training were dissolved, and religious writings banned from public space, ecclesiastical jurisdiction was placed under state supervision and "acceptable" priests were placed in key clerical positions by the PVAP. The removal from office and imprisonment of the Polish primate Cardinal Stefan Wyszyński in 1953 was the culmination of the repressive measures against the Catholic Church.

The trajectory of all states occupied by the Soviet Union was similar, and Poland was no exception: The political opposition was eliminated, existing socialist movements were transformed into a communist one-party system, forced industrialisation was implemented and the church and religion were massively suppressed. Only after the death of Stalin in March 1953 did state terror subside to some extent. Some of the political prisoners were released "for health reasons", and the number of trials and arrests decreased. Nevertheless, these changes were only cosmetic at first: around 30,000 political prisoners remained incarcerated.

As it did in other Communist-ruled states, the 20th Congress of the CPSU in February 1956 finally gave the decisive impetus for de-Stalinisation. The secret speech by Soviet leader Nikita Khrushchev ("On the Cult of Personality and Its Consequences") not only condemned the Stalinist reign of terror but also discredited many Eastern European leaders who had previously worn their unconditional allegiance to Stalin as a badge of honour. The "thaw" that was set in motion also shook the position of state and party leader Bolesław Bierut and called his political course of an "iron socialism" into question. Under the surface, brewing ideological conflicts, differences of opinion and contradictions within the PVAP increasingly came to the surface.

The political power vacuum that suddenly arose in this heated atmosphere—Bierut died unexpectedly in March 1956—was initially filled by more moderate and reform-oriented successors in the offices of both Party Leader and First Secretary. They not only pleaded for a relaxation of strict press censorship but even went as far as making the content of Khrushchev's speech available to members of the party organisations—the only country in the Warsaw Pact to do so. The decision of the commissioned print shops, taken on their own authority, to increase the production run meant that the text of the speech became available to practically all interested parties within a very short time.

The growing number of party members and "ordinary citizens" who knew the content of the speech also amplified the voices of those questioning the PVAP's claim to government and power and criticising Poland's dependence on Moscow and also prompted increased speculation about the causes of Stalinist crimes. However, the demands increasingly articulated in Polish society for a fundamental change in state policy vis-à-vis the Catholic Church soon exceeded any degree of permissible criticism as intended by Khrushchev.

The systemic crisis of Stalinist-influenced socialism, the drop in living standards as a direct consequence of the planned economy, the huge expenditure on armaments, the (socio-)political shock of Khrushchev's revelations at the 20th Party Congress, the rapid increase in hostility towards the Soviet Union, the reports of thousands of released political prisoners after the amnesty of 27 April 1956 and the palpable loosening of state terror and the increase in opposition and resistance to communist rule led to a general strike by the workers of Poznań on 28 June 1956. This was the first major public uprising of the Polish population against the communist regime and was joined by large sections of the population. The uprising was bloodily suppressed: 74 people lost their lives, and tens of thousands were sentenced to long prison terms.

The events in Poznań were the prelude to numerous similar protests that convulsed the whole country until October 1956 and sparked unrest in other communist-ruled countries, such as Hungary. Immediately after the suppression of the Poznań uprising, however, the communist leadership attempted to discredit and stigmatise the events as a provocation by "foreign agents". In Poland, however, in contrast to many other countries, opposition and resistance to the communist regime remained clearly palpable and visible in the period that followed.

Time and again, the workers rose up against the ruling power in strikes and unrest. The protests reached new heights in March 1968, when thousands of students throughout the country marched in protest against communist power and in support of free elections, an end to Soviet occupation and democratic freedoms. In December 1970, strikes and uprisings against communist rule spread again in the shipyards of the Polish Baltic coast, only to be bloodily suppressed once again with significant loss of life.

Despite the brutal suppression of the protests and strikes, the resistance persisted. In June 1976, for example, there was further major unrest in Radom and Ursus. In 1976, the Workers' Defence Committee (Komitet Obrony Robotników, KOR) was founded to support the strikers, marking the first instance of cooperation between intellectuals and workers. In 1980, the repeated protests finally gave rise to the independent trade union movement Solidarity (Solidarność), which attracted nationwide support and became the most powerful organisation in Poland, with over 9.5 million members, including one million members of the PVAP. It was chaired by Gdańsk electrician and later Polish President Lech Wałęsa.

In December 1981, the state struck back and imposed nationwide martial law, which was only lifted in 1983. The leaders of Solidarity were arrested, and the union itself was banned in 1982. Once again, tens of thousands of people were imprisoned and persecuted. The children of imprisoned Solidarity supporters were taken to state foster homes, and security forces shot 25 people during strikes, such as the one in the Wujek Coal Mine in Katowice.

Defying its prohibition, Solidarność continued its underground resistance against communist power and its campaign for a free and democratic Poland. The systemic shift towards "market socialism" initiated at the end of 1988 and the participation of opposition representatives in the national Round Table Talks in February 1989 marked the beginning of the process of democratisation in Poland. Unlike in other communist countries, this did not unfold as a revolution but rather as a reform process (sometimes referred to as a "refolution"). The election of 1989 was the first semi-free election to be held in a country of the former Eastern Bloc, and representatives of Solidarity won in a landslide. Although the ruling Communist party had reserved 65 percent of the seats in the Sejm for itself and its satellite parties, this election ultimately marked the end of communist rule. Tadeusz Mazowiecki was appointed the first non-Communist head of state in the Eastern bloc.

Although the communist government had massively suppressed all forms of resistance for decades and had upheld the taboo on public discussion of violent excesses such as the Katyń massacre, the annihilation of members of the armed resistance and the bloody suppression of protests, strikes and unrest, the unofficial memory of the crimes perpetrated against the population had seared itself into the public consciousness. Operating underground, students, artists and Solidarity representatives organised events to commemorate the victims of these crimes. Citizens' initiatives such as KARTA in Warsaw addressed previously taboo issues and raised public awareness of hushed-up crimes and their victims.

After the change of regime, a process of historical reappraisal of and engagement with the "concealed" aspects of Polish history under communist rule began, but it was not until 1997, under Jerzy Buzek's centre-right government, that a genuine, state-supported reckoning with the communist past took place. On 18 June 1998, parliament passed a law condemning the communist regime and promising compensation for the injustices committed. The Institute of National Remembrance (IPN) with branch offices in all major Polish cities was henceforth responsible for investigating crimes against the Polish people, facilitating prosecution, conducting historical research and communicating this information to the public.

Although thousands of political prisoners had already been released in the process of de-Stalinisation under the amnesty granted after Stalin's death, it took until 1988 for their criminal records to be expunged. This act of exculpation was enshrined in law on 23 February 1991, annulling sentences handed down for acts of resistance against the occupation of Poland. At first, this only affected sentences imposed before the end of 1956. Later judgments were overturned in new hearings. In 2007, the law was amended to cover the entire period of communist rule from 1944 to 1989. Criminal expungement allows people who were wrongfully convicted to claim compensation and have periods of persecution added to their pension entitlement.

While these measures have benefited the victims of persecution, attempts to hold the perpetrators criminally accountable have proved largely unsatisfactory. Only very few have ever been tried in a court of law and hardly any convictions have been secured. A 2012 report by the president of the IPN was sobering: only 152 perpetrators had by then been convicted. Individuals responsible for depriving victims of their rights during communist rule were now enjoying all the rights and freedoms of the rule of law. While the foundation of the IPN in 1999 had allowed victims of persecution to view the records kept on them by the state security, former agents and collaborators could also avail themselves of this right. There is no provision for a regular review of the records of public servants.

Recent years have seen the establishment of various memorials and monuments to commemorate the injustices and crimes committed, and several commemorative events have been added to the public calendar, such as 1 March, the National Day of Remembrance of the "Cursed Soldiers", which commemorates those who took part in the armed resistance against the Soviet occupiers and communist rule. 13 April is Katyń Memorial Day, and 28 June is the National Day of Remembrance of the 1956 Poznań Protests. 23 August is the European Day of Remembrance for Victims of Stalinism and Nazism; 17 September is Sbirak's Day, when the country pays tribute to those deported to Siberia; and 13 December is Martial Law Victims Remembrance Day.

History Meeting House

Warsaw. The History Meeting House opened in 2005. The initiative for the construction of the house came from the non-governmental organisation KARTA Center Foundation, which has been dedicated to documenting and communicating the most recent contemporary history of Poland and Eastern and Central Europe since 1982. The aim of the house is to communicate the history of Poland and Eastern and Central Europe in the 20th century to the public through various historical exhibitions, educational projects, publications, discussions, readings, seminars, conferences and film screenings. One of the focal points of these educational programmes is the consequences of National Socialism and Communism.

The institution also includes a publishing house and an audio-visual library with a unique collection of digitised photographs, sound recordings and historical documents. The house's primary approach to engaging with history is its work with biographies. In cooperation with the KARTA Center, the institution maintains the largest oral history archive in the country. Over 5,500 biographical interviews provide a very personal experience of the history of the 20th century in Poland through the eyes of contemporary witnesses.

In cooperation with national and international partners, the History Meeting House offers a wide range of educational programmes targeted at schools and other groups with an interest in history. These include thematic events, interviews with contemporary witnesses, guided tours, workshops and educational games.

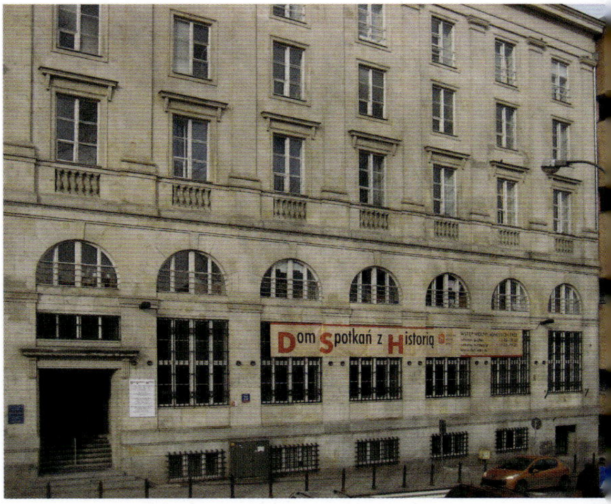

Entrance to the History Meeting House

Location: Warsaw, Ulica Karowa 20
Internet: www.dsh.waw.pl

Katyń Museum

Warsaw. The Katyń Museum in Warsaw was opened on 29 June 1993 in a section of the 19th century Russian fort known as Sadyba in the Mokotów district. Its collection comprises a vast array of memorabilia, most of which were found during the exhumations of the mass graves in Katyń, Mednoye and Kharkiv in the early 1990s. It also collects memorabilia from the relatives of the victims.

The museum was founded on the initiative of the Katyń Families Association, which wanted to create a worthy place for the recovered items. In cooperation with the Polish Army Museum, the association organised two exhibitions, in 1991 and 1992, featuring photographs and objects from the excavations. In December 1991, the decision was made to establish a Katyń Museum. After the necessary renovation of part of the historical Sadyba fortress, the museum was inaugurated in June 1993 by the then Vice-Minister of National Defence, Bronisław Komorowski, and the chairperson of the Katyń Families Association, Bożena Łojek. The building was blessed by military Ordinariate Leszek Sławoj Głódź and Prelate Zdzisław Peszkowski, a survivor of the Kozelsk camp.

The museum's holdings continued to grow through the addition of finds from the mass graves. Over the years, the initial exhibition area of 200 square metres was expanded to 500 square metres, but, even so, only a small proportion of the holdings could ever be presented in the exhibition halls and the "hall of remembrance". After the museum vacated Fort Sadyba in September 2011, it temporarily moved in with its parent institution, the Polish Army Museum, before finally relocating to the Warsaw Citadel, a 19th century fortress complex, in 2015. The new exhibition was expanded and updated to feature multimedia presentations. The 2.5-hectare area outside the museum has deeply symbolic elements, with a parade

Main museum entrance

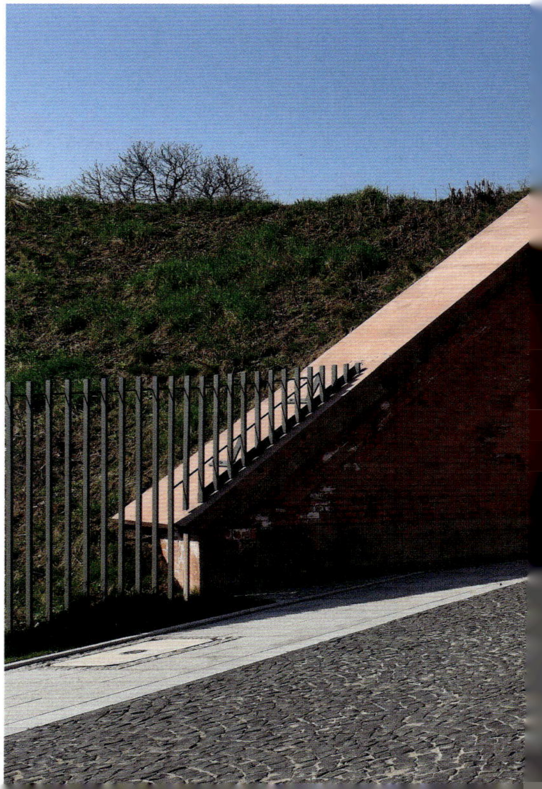

ground, a wooden cross and a small patch of forest intersected by the "Avenue of the Absent". The avenue is made up of over 20,000 cobblestones—one for every victim of the massacre. The names of the dead are engraved in an epitaph consisting of 15 plates. A bell with a bullet hole symbolises the execution of the prisoners.

The entrance to the museum leads through a darkened tunnel, on the right-hand wall of which the "shadows of the victims" are projected. The exhibition is divided into "discovery" and "testimony" levels. The first of these depicts the history and execution of the massacre, its instrumentalisation by the German discoverers and the Soviet perpetrators, the concealment of the acts of violence and defamation of those who protested against them, and finally their official revelation. Documents, photographs, posters and multimedia elements are presented in wooden military boxes.

On the second level of the museum, the more than 6,000 personal items from the victims found during the exhumations of the mass graves are on display in tall display cases, many of which are subdivided into sections. Each item—spectacles and combs, items of uniform and canteens, rosaries and chess pieces, wallets and bags—is positioned in a small chamber bathed in warm light. The last room before the exit to the outdoors confronts the visitor with the perpetrators of the Katyń massacre.

The publication "Erinnerungsorte für die Opfer von Katyń" (Memorial Sites for the Victims of Katyń), published by Leipzig University in 2013 and researched by the Federal Foundation for the Study of the Communist Dictatorship in Eastern Germany, provides an overview of 178 memorial sites in 18 countries.

Location: Warsaw, ul. Jana Jeziorańskiego 4 (Warsaw Citadel)
Internet: www.muzeumkatynskie.pl

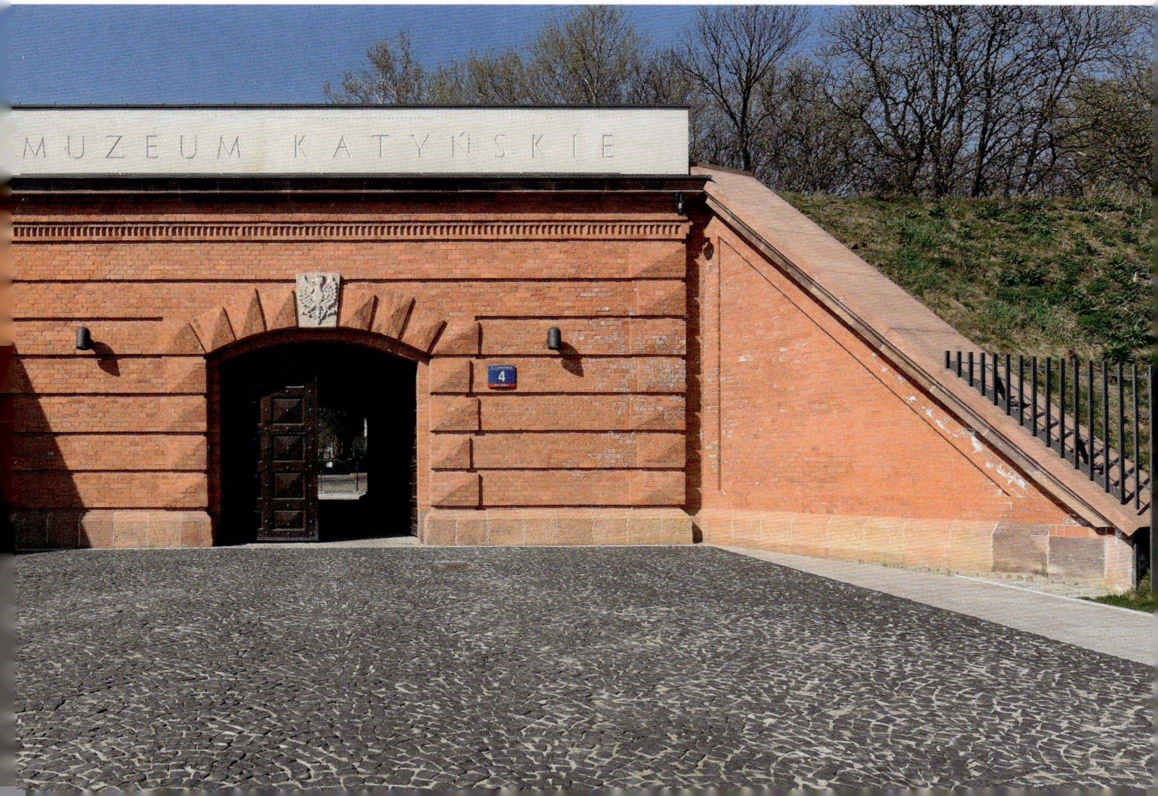

Monument to the Fallen and Murdered in the East

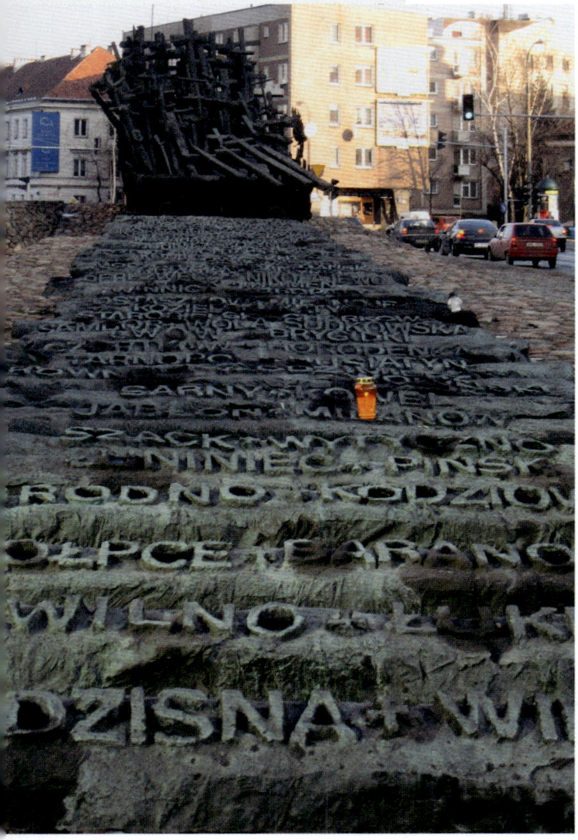

Monument to the Fallen and Murdered in the East

Warsaw. The Monument to the Fallen and Murdered in the East was inaugurated on 17 September 1995 on the central reservation of Muranowska Street. It consists of a recreation of a railway platform and an eight-metre-long open freight wagon. The monumental bronze sculpture by Maksymilian Biskupski features countless crosses connected by barbed wire which lean in different directions. In front of it, on another incline paved with fieldstones, are 40 railway sleepers, also cast in bronze and bearing the names of those camps and execution sites on the territory of the Soviet Union that played a part in the suffering and murder of Polish citizens. The bronze coat of arms of the Polish Armed Forces, a crowned eagle perched on a shield, is attached to one side of the wagon. The eagle is trussed with rope, and the shield at its feet bears the date "17 IX 39"; on this day, the Red Army attacked Poland under the terms of the Molotov-Ribbentrop Pact and occupied the eastern areas of the country. Christian and Orthodox crosses and tombstones with Jewish and Muslim symbols are placed on the wagon to raise awareness of the denominational diversity of the victims. One of the crosses is dedicated to the priest Stefan Niedzielak, provost at the Borromeo Church in Warsaw, who is presumed to have been murdered on 20 January 1989 because of his commitment to the commemoration of Katyń.

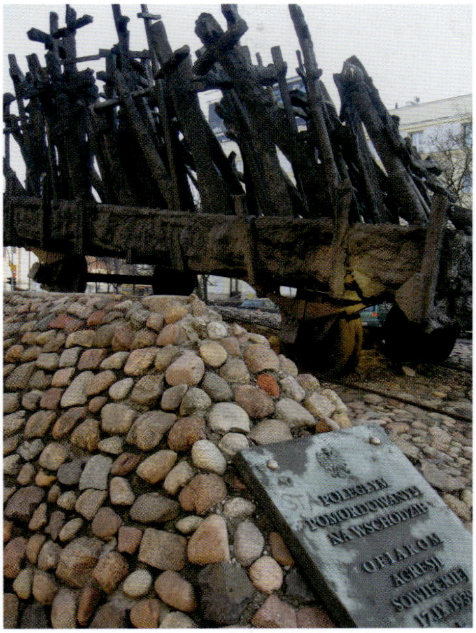

Central commemorative plaque on the Monument to the Fallen and Murdered in the East

The monument was erected by a foundation established in September 1989 under the direction of Wojciech Ziembiński. Its aim was to create an expressive central monument to the 500,000 victims of the mass deportations and persecution suffered by Poland during the Soviet occupation in World War II. A jury selected Maksymilian Biskupski's design in February 1991. It took four-and-a-half years to implement the design, to secure financing, mainly from government funds, and to find an appropriate location in Warsaw. The inauguration ceremony was attended by Polish President Lech Wałęsa, the Primate of Poland Cardinal Józef Glemp, the Chief of the General Staff of the Polish Armed Forces, the Mayor of Warsaw Marcin Święcicki and relatives of the victims.

During his seventh pilgrimage to his home country, Pope John Paul II prayed in front of the monument on 11 June 1999. Another memorial stone at the back of the monument commemorates this event.

Inscriptions

On the central commemorative plaque, Polish: *Poległym / Pomordowanym / na Wschodzie / Ofiarom / agresji / sowieckiej / 17 IX 1939 / Naród / 17 IX 1995*

English: *For the fallen [and] murdered in the East, the victims of the Soviet aggression of 17/09/1939. The Nation, 17/09/1995*

On the memorial stone for the Pope's visit, Polish: *Tu 11 czerwca AD 1999 / za ofiary agresji / sowieckiej / modlił się Ojciec / Święty / Jan Paweł II*

English: *On 11 June 1999 AD, the Holy Father John Paul II prayed here for the victims of Soviet aggression*

Location: Warsaw, Ulica Muranowska

The Anonymous Pedestrians—Monument to the Victims of Martial Law

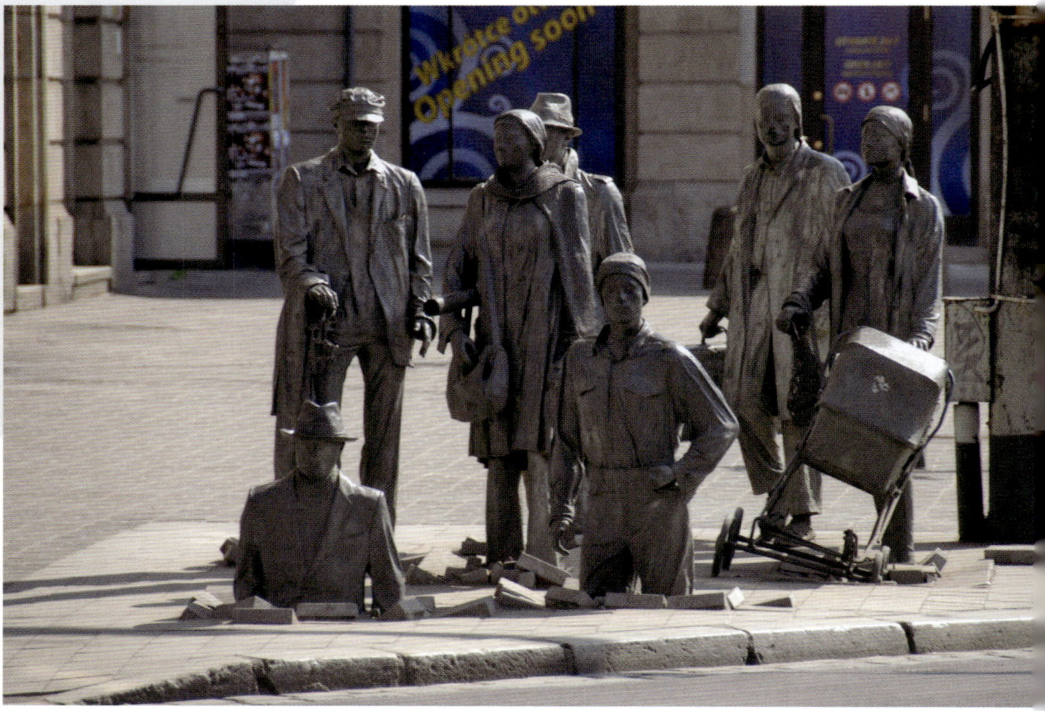

Wrocław. This monument was inaugurated in a solemn ceremony on the evening of 12–13 December 2006—the 25th anniversary of the declaration of martial law on 13 December 1981. It commemorates the victims of martial law who lost their lives in clashes with the state security forces, were detained in internment camps without court sentences or suffered countless reprisals. It also reminds us of all those who were forced underground after 13 December 1981 to resist the repressive regime and commemorates the hundreds of thousands of Poles driven into exile by communist tyranny. The bronze monument designed by famous Polish sculptor Jerzy Kalina consists of 14 statues: seven figures sinking into the ground on Piłsudskiego Street and another seven rising up from the "underground" on the other side of the road on Świdnicka Street.

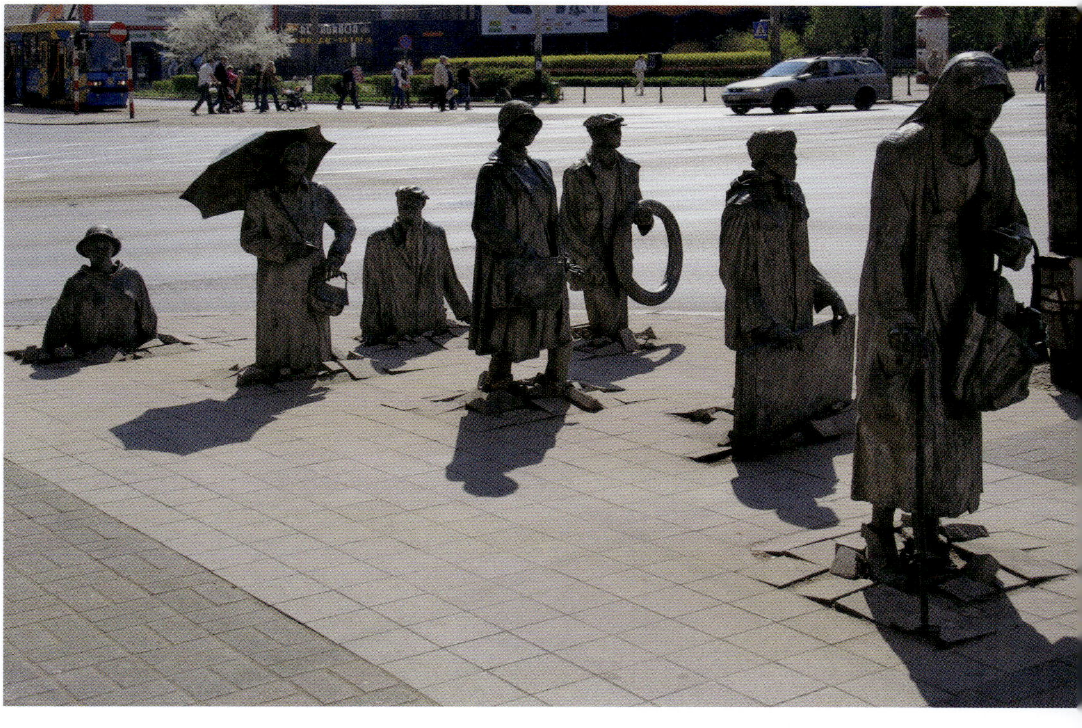

View of the monument on Piłsudskiego Street

◀

The Anonymous Pedestrians—Monument to the Victims of Martial Law

Location: Wrocław, at the junction of Piłsudskiego and Świdnicka Street

Monument to the Fallen Shipyard Workers of 1970

Gdańsk. The monument to the fallen shipyard workers, unveiled at a ceremony on 16 December 1980, commemorates the victims of the dramatic events of December 1970. The workers' strikes in numerous cities on the Polish Baltic coast, triggered by price increases, were crushed by the state security forces in Gdańsk. Dozens of workers at the Lenin Shipyard lost their lives. The memorial, which was built during the communist regime, was initiated by the free trade union Solidarity.

Shortly after the strikes in the winter of 1970, wreaths were laid by the wall of the shipyard in Gdańsk, only to regularly disappear overnight. In the following years, more and more people gathered in this place every December to commemorate the victims—by 1979, the crowd had grown to around 6,000 people. Lech Wałęsa, one of the Gdańsk strike leaders and later President of the Republic of Poland, spoke at the shipyard that year and demanded the erection of a monument. As the Solidarity trade union movement, which itself originated in the Gdańsk shipyard, gathered pace in the summer of 1980, the events of December 1970 and 1976 once again became a heated topic of debate. In a compromise between the party, the trade union and the church, the construction of the memorial to the casualties of the 1970 uprising in front of the Gdańsk shipyard Gate No. 2 was approved as part of the Gdańsk Agreement in August 1980.

The 42-metre-high monument, which was funded by donations, consists of three Latin crosses, each bearing an anchor in a symbolic representation of the crucified Christ. The composition is intended to symbolise the faith and the martyrdom of the Polish people on the one hand, and to express their unshakable hope on the other. On the lower part of the crosses are reliefs with scenes from the everyday life of the shipyard workers and the tragedy of December 1970, as well as panels on the history of Solidarity.

Behind the memorial, popularly referred to as the "Three Crosses Monument", is a memorial wall. At its heart is an engraved quotation from the speech given by Pope John Paul II during his first visit to Poland in 1979. The wall also lists the names and ages of the shipyard workers who died in December 1970. Right in front of the memorial wall stands the sculpture of a shipyard worker desperately reaching up with his arms. To its left, engraved in the memorial wall, are excerpts from Psalm 29 and fragments of the poem "Capo di Fiori" by Czesław Miłosz beginning with the words "You who wronged a simple man / bursting into laughter at the crime". The monument stands in front of the entrance to the European Solidarity Centre.

Location: Gdańsk, Solidarity Square

Memorial wall with the sculpture of a shipyard worker next to the Three Crosses Monument

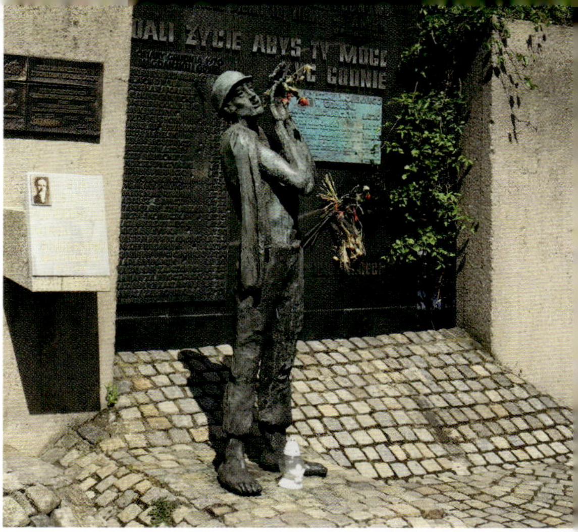

Monument to the Fallen Shipyard Workers of 1970 in Gdańsk

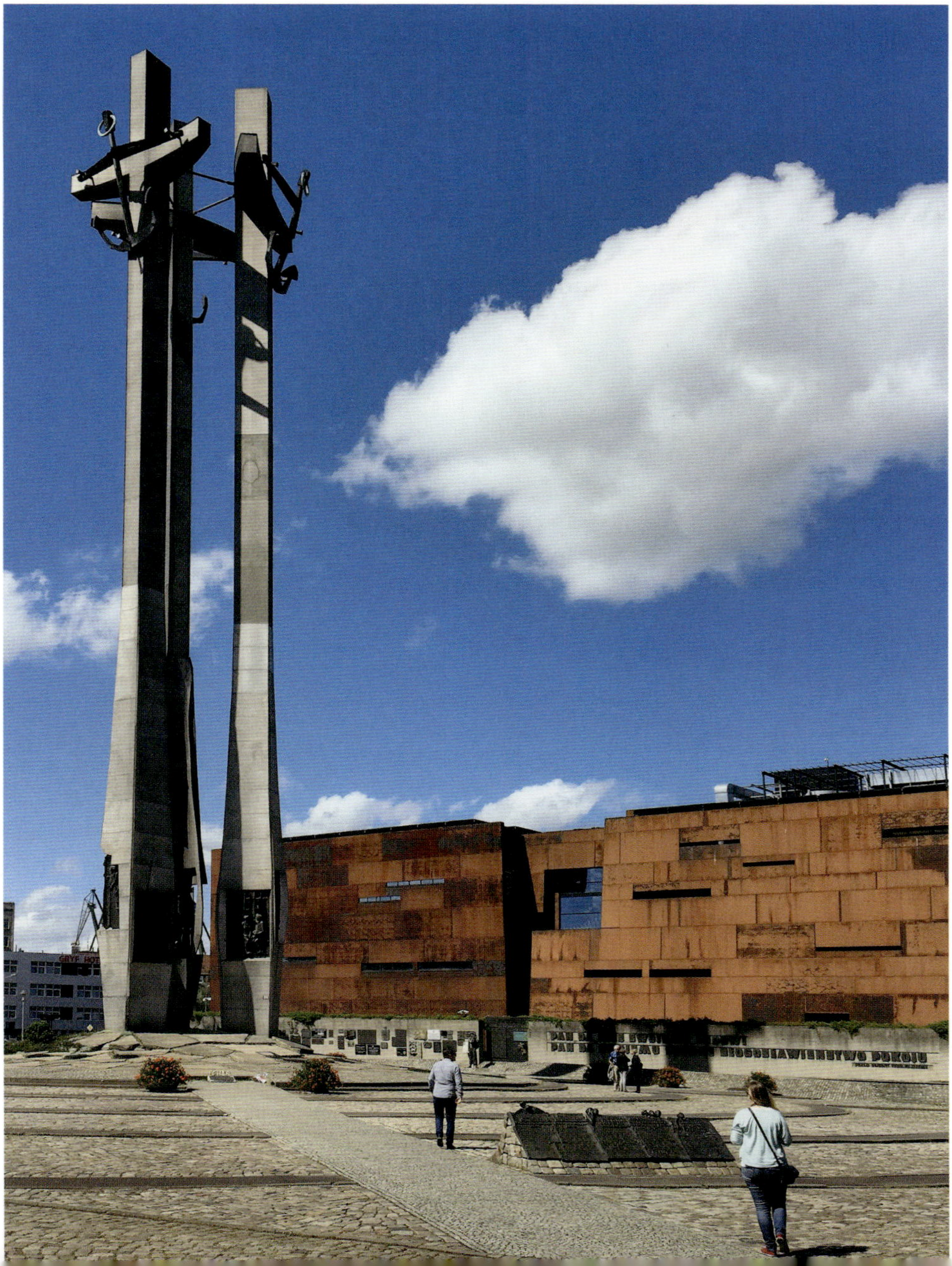

European Solidarity Centre

Gdańsk. The European Solidarity Centre, which opened on 30 August 2014, stands on the site of the former Lenin Shipyard. The exhibition there tells the story of the Solidarity free trade union in Poland and the civil movements in other Central and Eastern European countries. The establishment of the institution dates back to an initiative launched in the autumn of 2007 by the Polish Ministry of Culture and the trade union federation, NSZZ Solidarity. The 20,000-square-metre building complex comprises a museum, a central archive, a multimedia library, a research and education centre and offices for civil society organisations. New architectural elements as well as historical sites of remembrance are integrated into the vast grounds.

The overall concept includes the historic Solidarity Square, where the Monument to the Fallen Shipyard Workers is also located, the famous Gate No. 2 of the Lenin Shipyard and the former Health and Safety organisation building, which the trade union activists used as a conference hall during the legal phase of their work and which now serves as a memorial. The ensemble is completed by the modern building complex that houses the permanent exhibition.

On two floors and a total area of 3,000 square metres, it provides detailed information on the history of the origins and activities of the trade union movement. In six chronologically designed thematic units, it details the decline of communism in Poland and the other states of the former Eastern Bloc. The first room, "The Solidarność", charts the history of the movement from the initial opposition activity against the backdrop of the summer of strikes of 1980 to the founding of the first free trade unions in the People's Republic of Poland. Other rooms use interactive installations, multimedia presentations and numerous original documents and exhibits to shed light on aspects of everyday life in socialist Poland, the influence of the anti-Communist opposition before 1980, the actions of the repressive regime, the "Road to Democracy" and the "Triumph of Freedom". The last room, named after Pope John Paul II, is a place of silence that invites visitors to reflect on what they have seen.

The elaborately designed permanent exhibition is characterised not least by the successful combination of numerous original historical exhibits and multimedia elements. For example, over 2,000 yellow helmets fixed to the ceiling serve as a projection surface for original film documents, while a massive canteen table has been converted into a multimedia screen. At the same time, unique original exhibits offer a special view of history as actually experienced. These include the control cabin of the crane operator Anna Walentynowicz, whose politically motivated firing was the immediate cause for the 1980 summer strike

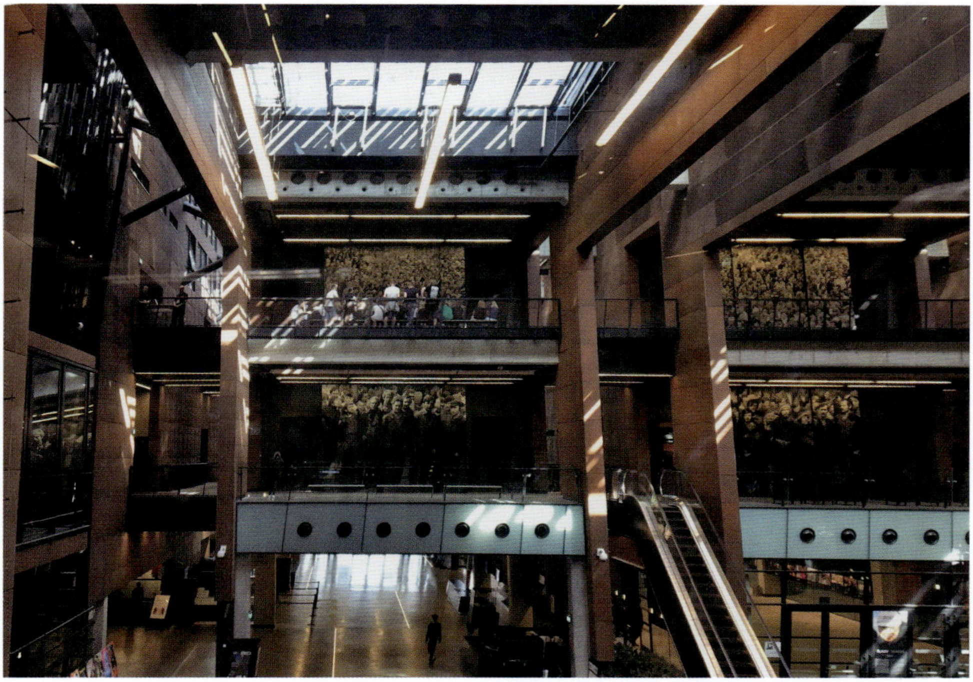

Interior view of the European Solidarity Centre

wave, the well-known banner "Proletarians of all factories unite" and, in particular, the two panels with the 21 demands of the strikers, which have been added to the UNESCO's World Heritage List. Contemporary witnesses regularly come to speak at the centre.

The entire exhibition is presented in Polish and English and is accessible to people with disabilities; audio recordings and braille texts are included for people with impaired vision. The educational work of the centre, which has existed as a cultural institution since 2008, is supplemented by conferences, seminars, concerts and film screenings. Its research work has yielded more than 122,000 historical documents, posters and leaflets and an archive of around 42,000 original photographs. In addition, the accounts of 800 contemporary witnesses have been recorded on film. A special "games department" allows children and young people to engage with the museum's subjects in an age-appropriate way. The series of publications issued by the centre disseminates information about Polish and European resistance to communism, including the history of the Solidarity movement and the opposition in the countries of Eastern and Central Europe.

Location: Gdańsk, Solidarity Square 1
Internet: www.ecs.gda.pl

1956 Uprising Monument

Poznań. With the rise of the Solidarity movement in Poland in the late 1970s, the memory of the striking workers of 1956 was rekindled. In 1980, a committee led by writer Roman Brandstaetter publicly supported the construction of a memorial to the victims. On the 25th anniversary of the uprising, on 28 June 1981, the monument was inaugurated to great public sympathy. Two tall interlocking concrete crosses designed by sculptor Adam Graczyk and architect Włodzimierz Wojciechowski commemorate the victims of the uprising. To the right is a stylised bust of the Polish heraldic eagle, which bears the motto of the insurgents: "O Boga, za wolność, prawo i chleb" (English: "Oh God, for freedom, justice and bread").

Location: Poznań, Adam Mickiewicz Square

Further reading:

Friszke, Andrzej: Geschichte der polnischen Opposition. In: Biografisches Lexikon Widerstand und Opposition im Kommunismus 1945 – 91 Federal Foundation for the Study of the Communist Dictatorship in Eastern Germany 2016. Available online at: www.dissidenten.eu/laender/polen/oppositionsgeschichte/1/ (last accessed on: 06/12/2017). / Gańczak, Filip: Länderstudie Polen. In: Honoring Civil Courage. Developing Suggestions to Improve the Situation of Victims of Communist State Crimes. Project Coordinator: Gedenkstätte Berlin-Hohenschönhausen 2015, Ref.-No.: JUST/2011/JPEN/AG/2998. Available online at: www.stiftung-hsh.de/assets/Dokumente-pdf-Dateien/EU-Projekt-Laenderstudien.pdf (last accessed on: 06/12/2017). / Paczkowski, Andrzej: Polen, der „Erbfeind". In: Courtois, Stéphane et al. (eds.): Das Schwarzbuch des Kommunismus. Unterdrückung, Verbrechen und Terror. Sonderausgabe. München, Zürich 2004, pp. 397 – 429. / Peters, Florian about Golak, Pawel/ Kerski, Basil/ Knoch, Konrad (eds.): Wystawa stała Europejskiego Centrum Solidarności. Katalog [The Permanent Exhibition oft he European Solidarity Centre. Catalogue]. Gdańsk 30/08/2014. In: H-Soz-Kult 2015. Available online at: www.hsozkult.geschichte.hu-berlin.de/index.asp?id=205&view=pdf&pn=rezensionen&type=rezausstellungen (last access on: 16/11/2017). / Weber, Claudia: Krieg der Täter: Die Massenerschießungen von Katyń. Hamburg 2015.

►

Monument to the 1956 Uprising in Poznań

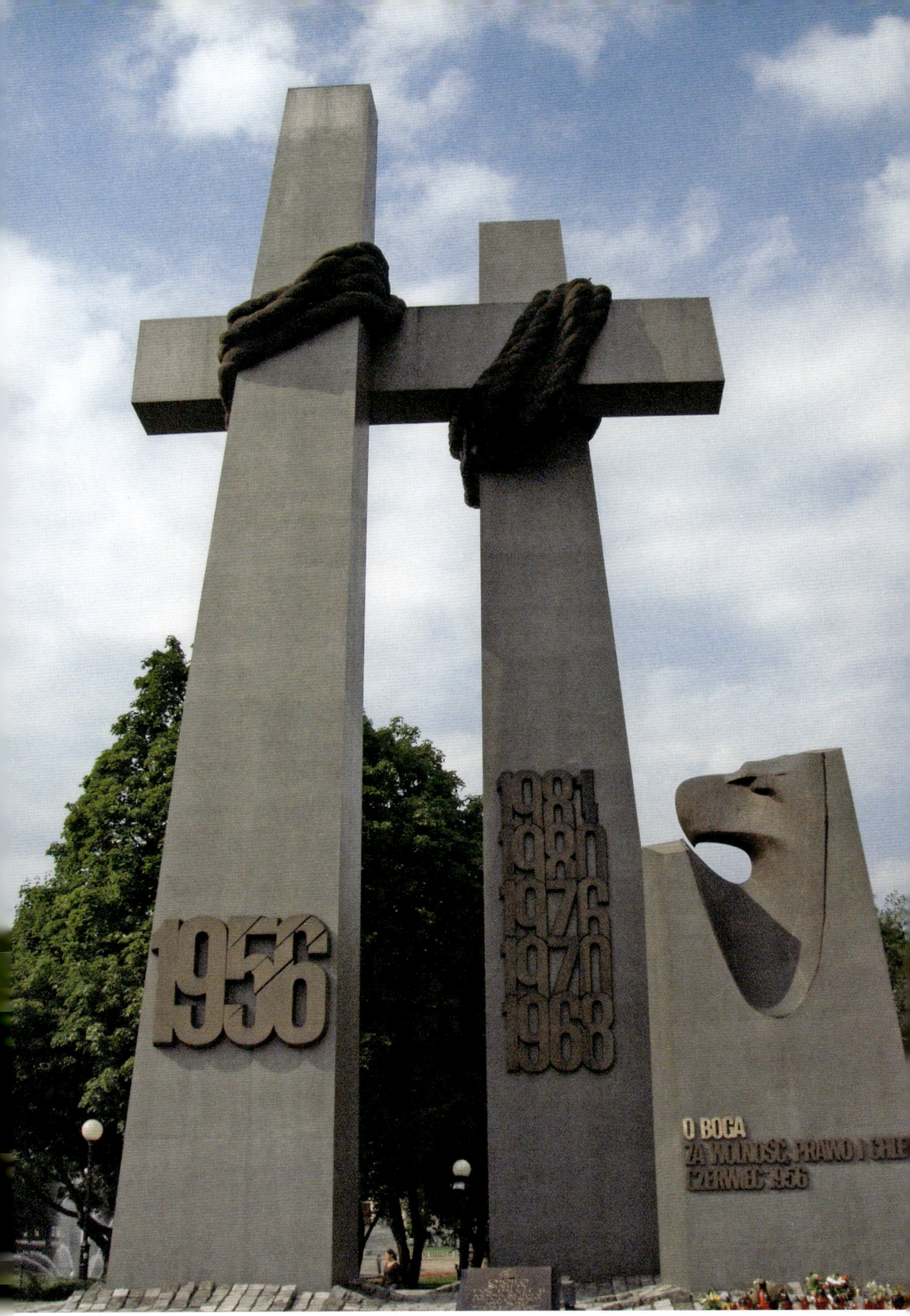
1956
1981
1980
1976
1970
1968
O BOGA
CZERWIEC 1956

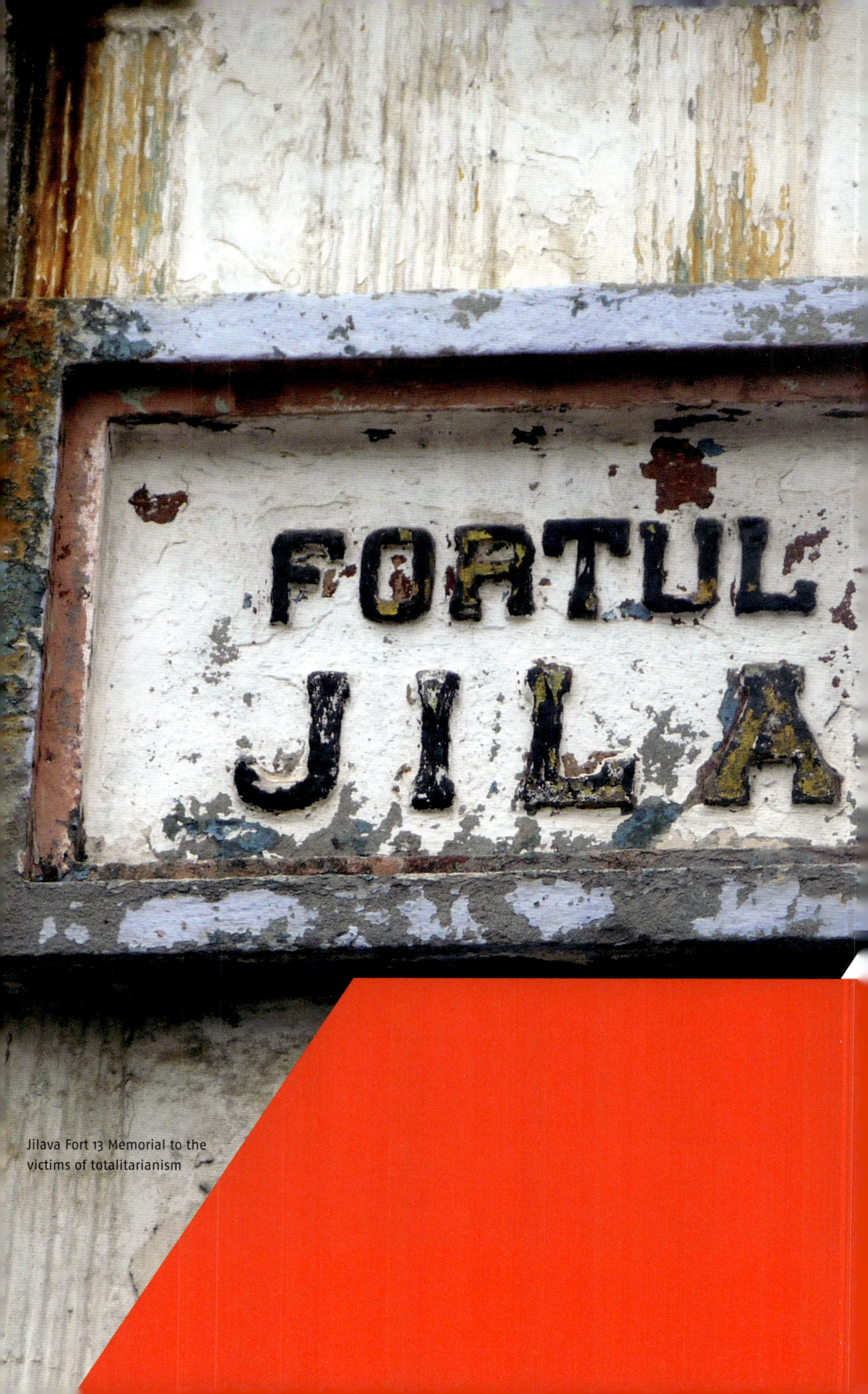

Jilava Fort 13 Memorial to the victims of totalitarianism

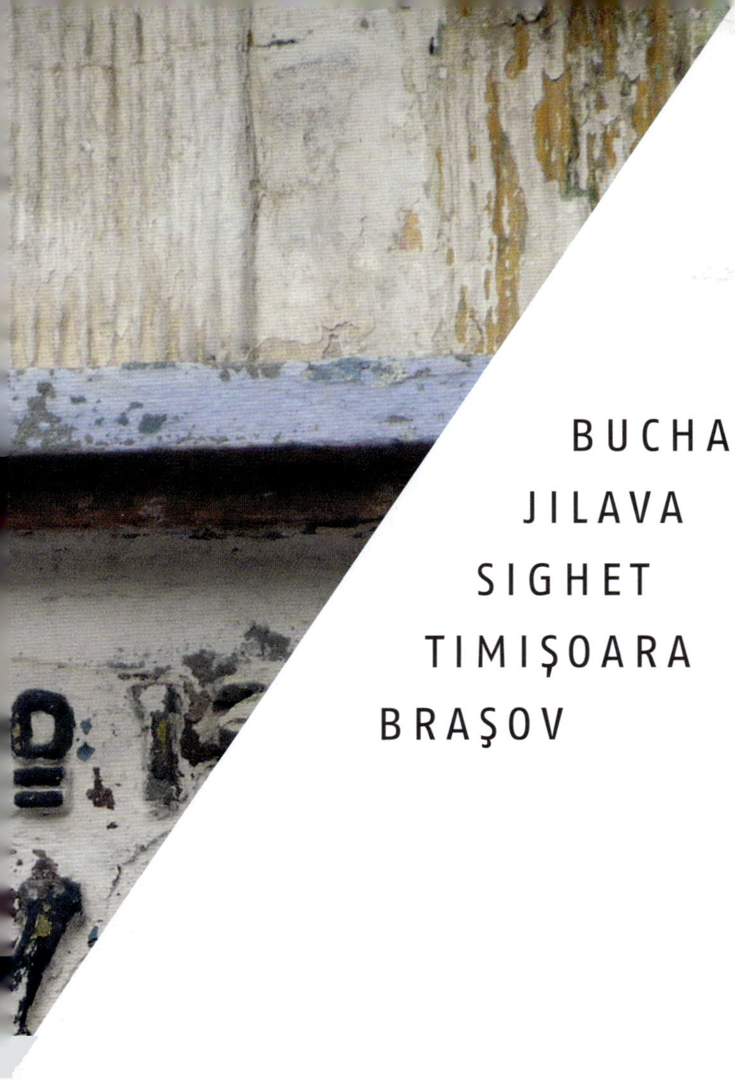

BUCHAREST
JILAVA
SIGHET
TIMIŞOARA
BRAŞOV

Romania

Under the terms of an agreement reached with Nazi Germany, Soviet troops occupied Romanian Bessarabia and northern Bukovina on 28 June 1940. This annexation and the resettlement of some 1,800,000 inhabitants of German origin from these areas to the German Reich was enshrined in the secret additional protocol to the Molotov-Ribbentrop Pact. After the Wehrmacht invaded the Soviet Union, the Romanian army fought alongside the German troops stationed in the country.

The fascist military dictatorship of Marshal Ion Antonescu, which was allied with the Axis powers, was overthrown by King Michael I in the summer of 1944. Romania now entered the war on the side of the Allies and fought against the German troops. For its part, the Soviet Union stationed Red Army units in Romania and considered the country to be under its rule, a stance which was later confirmed at the Yalta Conference. Armed resistance groups similar to the partisan movements in Poland, Ukraine and the three Baltic states formed against Soviet occupation. With the progressive Sovietisation of Romania after the rigged elections in November 1946 and the forced abdication of King Michael I, the country was officially declared a People's Republic on 30 December 1947.

As early as January 1945, large sections of the population who were of German descent were deported to the Soviet Union to make "human reparations". At the same time, tens of thousands of members and supporters of both fascist and bourgeois parties were arrested, and many executed. As in other Soviet occupied countries, the forced collectivisation of agriculture and the nationalisation of industry were enacted, accompanied by mass arrests and reprisals. Members of the churches and the intelligentsia, students and teachers were also persecuted. By 1949, the communist Romanian secret police Securitate had infiltrated and wiped out most of the partisan groups. Their members were either liquidated immediately or sentenced to long prison sentences or death as members of "gangs" and "terrorist groups".

Until the late 1950s, protests, strikes and acts of resistance measures were a regular thorn in the side of the Stalinist regime under Gheorghe Gheorghiu-Dej, which attempted to quash them with the open use of force. In the autumn of 1956, hundreds of students protested against the suppression of the Hungarian Revolution in the university towns of Cluj and Timişoara, likewise triggering harsh reprisals. In 1958, strikes and protests against land expropriation, compulsory collectivisation and forced industrialisation were staged in various parts of the country where the population was faced with deteriorating living conditions. Armed resistance continued sporadically until the early 1960s. After that, massive campaigns of repression against dissenters and critics of communist rule and the vast expansion of the Securitate thinned out the resistance's numbers, thus greatly diminishing the threat it posed.

More than 230 camps, prisons and psychiatric institutions were set up throughout Romania for the internment and detention of opponents of the regime, including 44 main prisons and 72 labour camps. By 1989, several hundred thousand people had been imprisoned and compelled into forced labour under inhumane conditions. In the early 1950s alone, around 180,000 people were detained for political reasons. Some 40,000 people were enslaved in forced labour camps between 1950 and 1954 and again between 1958 and 1963, for example during the construction of the Danube-Black Sea Canal. In a series of internal purges within the ruling communist party itself, alleged deviants were excluded from the party, some of whom were arrested or even executed. Overall, the Romanian Communist Party (PCR) excluded 192,000 of its own members.

Between 1962 and 1964, several amnesties were issued for political prisoners. In 1965, Nicolae Ceauşescu suceeded Gheorghe Gheorghiu-Dej as Secretary General of the Communist Party. The transfer of power was initially associated with a certain easing of reprisals. The cultural "thaw" initiated by Ceauşescu and, above all, his condemnation of the bloody suppression of the Prague Spring by Soviet troops in August 1968 also led the new "Conducător" initially to be regarded as a representative of "socialism with a human face", a view which earned him great plaudits, especially in Western countries, until the 1980s.

Initially, hopes for a de-Stalinisation of society spread among the Romanian population. However, timid attempts to critically engage with the terror of the 1940s and 1950s were soon blocked, and their initiators excluded from the Communist Party and the artists' and writers' associations. Many authors, artists and intellectuals were banned from publishing and performing. Critics and opponents of the socialist regime were monitored, harassed and placed under house arrest; many received death threats or were forcibly imprisoned or committed to psychiatric wards.

The Securitate took heavy-handed steps to suppress the popular outpouring of solidarity with the human rights movement in the ČSSR and the free trade unions in Poland and the Soviet Union, which inspired the foundation of the Free Trade Union of the Working People of Romania (SLOMR) in February 1979. All known 2000 members of trade union movement were arrested and either sentenced to several years in prison for charges such as "parasitism" or "hooliganism" or else committed to psychiatric institutions.

The miners' strike in the Jiu Valley in August 1977, with about 35,000 participants, was the biggest protest until the revolution in December 1989. After initially giving in to the miners' demands, the authorities moved military units to the mining sites, declaring the entire region a restricted area and firing around 4,000 miners. After the infiltration of the mining administration by Securitate employees, the strike leaders either disappeared under mysterious circumstances or died in "accidents".

In the 1970s and early 1980s, protests were also organised by members of national minorities in Romania. The Hungarian diaspora, which accounted for about 7.9 percent of the total population, published samizdat writings critical of the regime and actively resisted Ceauşescu's "systematisation programme". This called for the destruction of entire villages for the purpose of national "homogenisation" and the forced resettlement of villagers in so-called agro-industrial towns.

The country's architectural and cultural heritage was also destroyed, as old districts in Bucharest and many other towns and cities were demolished to make way for grand socialist buildings. A cultural opposition emerged: some writers abandoned the strict guidelines of socialist realism, Ana Blandiana's poetry gained a powerful reputation for its criticism of the prevailing circumstances, and, in the 1980s, professor of French Doina Maria Cornea from Cluj-Napoca emerged as one of the most important opposition personalities. Despite years of persecution by the authorities, she was unwavering in her criticism of Romanian Communism and her solidarity with those persecuted by the Securitate.

At that time, the country, whose elite cultivated an opulent lifestyle, was in a politically and economically desolate state. Despite widespread poverty and destitution, severe food shortages and rationing of energy, the "Conducător" indulged in his cult of personality, threw his weight behind lavish construction projects and claimed the successful development of Romanian socialism. In 1983, Radu Filipescu was arrested for distributing critical flyers in Bucharest; in the same year, the authorities arrested Iuga Dumitru, an electrician at the state broadcasting company who tried to form an opposition movement. The following year, several of his comrades-in-arms were also arrested. Protests by workers, for example in 1987 at a car factory in Braşov, were brutally suppressed by the Securitate.

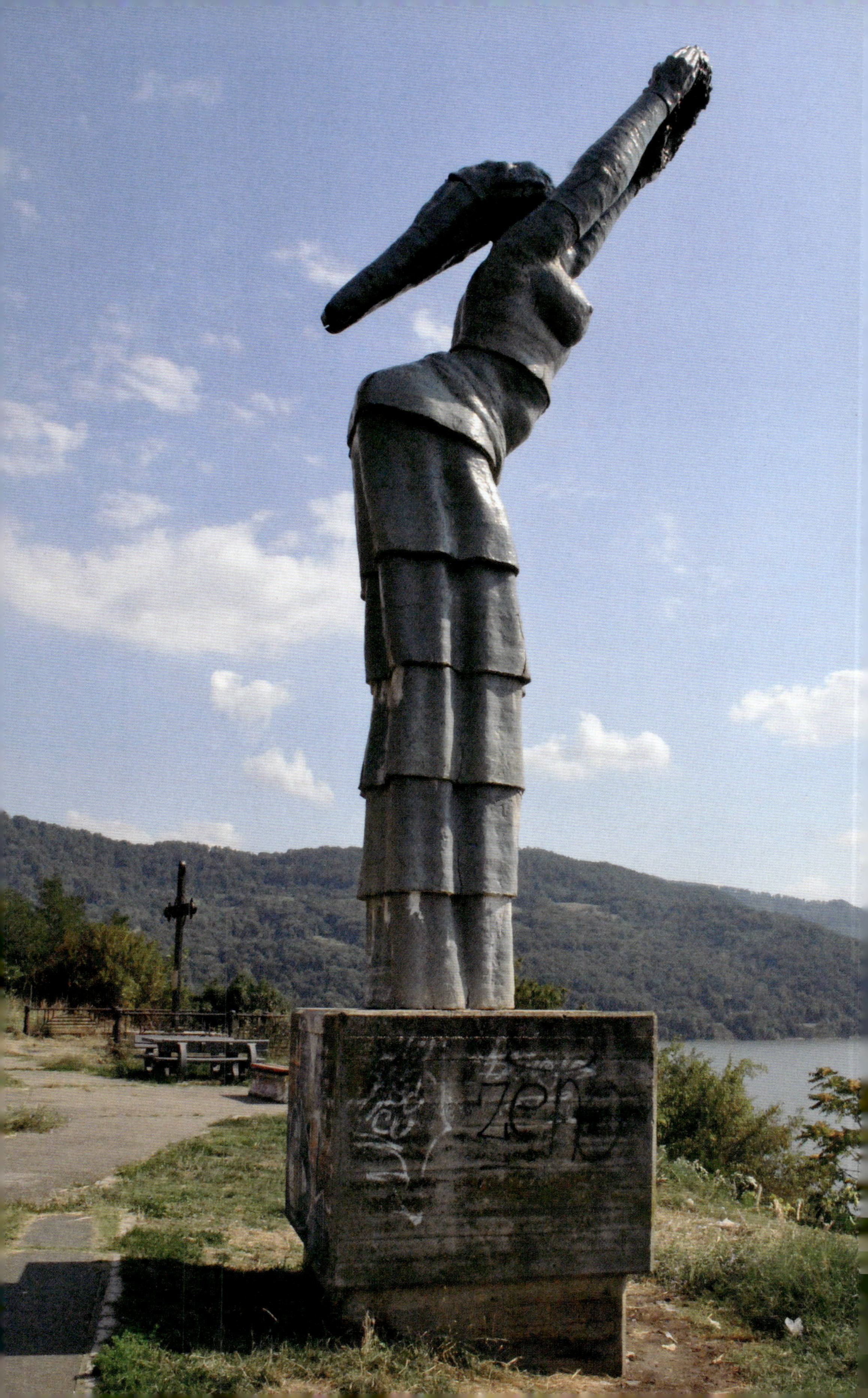

Swept along by the upheavals in other communist-ruled countries, protests also erupted in Romania in December 1989, triggered by the planned forced removal of pastor László Tőkés from Timişoara to a remote village. When the army and Securitate took action against the protesters with armoured vehicles, the protests spread to the entire country. Seven days later, on 22 December, the dictator Nicolae Ceauşescu was overthrown in Bucharest. More than 1,100 people lost their lives in the clashes between the state security forces and the protesters. After their capture, Nicolae Ceauşescu and his wife Elena were sentenced to death in a show trial held by an Exceptional Military Tribunal and executed on 25 December 1989.

After the change of regime, the process of reckoning with the crimes of the communist regime got off to a slow start. The Securitate was dissolved and transformed, the PCR fell apart and communist ideology was condemned as criminal. But many positions of power remained in the hands of former communist cadres, and there was a lack of neutral judicial bodies. Thus, after the execution of Elena and Nicolae Ceauşescu, only four charges were brought against former torturers, most of which did not result in convictions. Former political prisoners have been able to apply for their sentences to be expunged since 1990, but they were not entitled to compensation until 2009. 2005 saw the establishment of the Institute for the Investigation of Communist Crimes, which also has the power to initiate criminal investigations.

In part due to the tense social and economic situation in the country, attempts to come to terms with the experience of two dictatorships, publicly commemorate the victims and install memorials have all proved time-consuming and arduous. Nevertheless, in the decades since the collapse of the communist regime, a multifaceted "memorial landscape" of monuments, museums, memorials and commemorative markers has come into being. Often located at historical sites such as the Sighet Memorial or Jilava Fort 13, they commemorate repression, suffering and, above all, the victims of tyranny.

Various memorials and monuments have been set up in the country's border regions to keep the memory of refugee victims alive. In 1996, for instance, the "Danubia" monument, created by the sculptor Patriciu Mateescu, was unveiled near the town of Orşova and commemorates all those who lost their lives trying to escape from Romania to Yugoslavia.

The construction of further monuments, for example in the city of Sânnicolau-Mare where one of the last escape victims died—is planned. At the same time, in recent decades, commemorative markers and institutions dedicated to resistance, liberation, and democratic change have been created, such as the Museum of the 1989 Revolution in Timişoara or the Memorial of Rebirth in Bucharest.

◄
"Danubia" monument near Orşova

Memorial of Rebirth

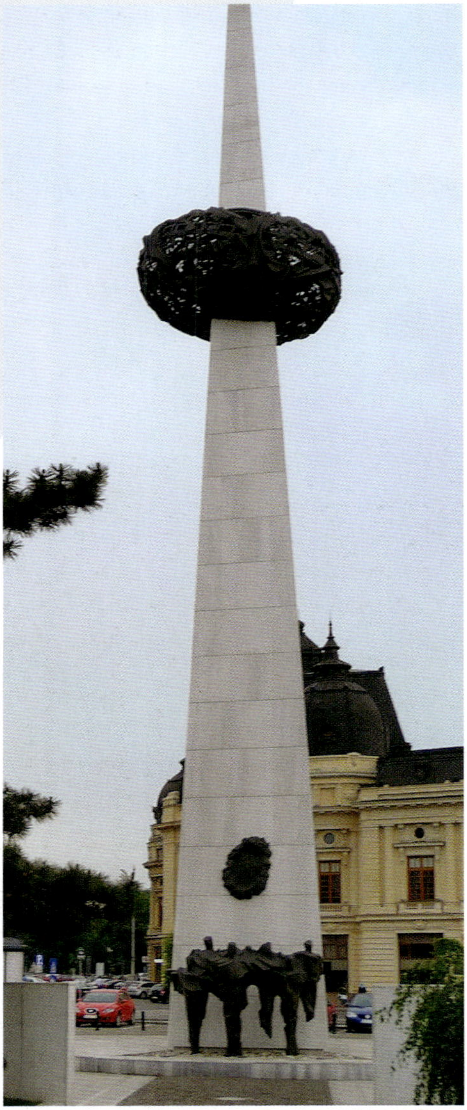

Bucharest. The Memorial of Rebirth is located on Revolution Square in Bucharest. This is the spot where the demonstrations against the communist regime of Nicolae Ceauşescu began on 21 December 1989. The monument ensemble designed by Romanian sculptor Alexandru Ghilduş in honour of the victims of the revolution was ceremonially unveiled to the public on 1 August 2005 following a period of heated public debate.

The monument consists of several elements whose names have a symbolic meaning. The centre of the monument is the Calea Biruinţei, the Path of Victory, a path lined on both sides with oak trees and marble benches. This symbolises Romania's path to the democratic transformation on the threshold of which the country stood poised at the dawn of the revolution. At the centre of the circular memorial site is a 25-metre-high obelisk of white marble with a stylised metal crown close to the top. This pays homage to the fallen revolutionaries for the sacrifice they made.

In the gravel bed at the front of the obelisk is an abstract bronze sculpture group. The fused figures are intended to express the unity, courage to embrace change and longing for freedom of the Romanian population as expressed

◄
Memorial of Rebirth on Revolution Square in Bucharest

in the demonstrations of December 1989. The memorial is framed by a semi-circular wall of remembrance. The names of the 1,058 victims of the revolution are engraved on the inside on brass plates.

Inscription on the Wall of Remembrance
Romanian: *EROI MARTIRI AI REVOLUTIEI DIN DECEMBRIE 1989*

English: *The martyr-heroes of the December 1989 Revolution*

Inscription on a plaque
Romanian: *MEMORIALUL RERENASTERII // GLORIE ETERNA EROILOR / SI REVOLUTIEI ROMANE / DIN DECEMBRIE 1989.*

English: *THE REVIVAL'S MEMORIAL // ETERNAL GLORY TO THE / ROMANIAN REVOLUTION / AND ITS HEROES / FROM DECEMBER 1989.*

Since 1990 there has been a cemetery for the Martyr-Heroes of the December 1989 (Cimitirul Eroii Martiri ai Revoluţiei din Decembrie 1989) near the Freedom Park in Calea Serban-Voda No. 237. This cemetery commemorates the 281 victims of the violent conflict who came from Bucharest. Dedications to, and the names of the victims are engraved on the uniform white marble tombs. A white wall framed by flower-beds bears the names of all the victims of the revolution engraved on metal plates. Next to this wall is a white memorial cross. On the initiative of the December 21 Association, the Church of the Martyr-Heroes of the Revolution was dedicated on the grounds of the cemetery in 2003.

Location: Bucharest, Piaţa Revoluţiei

Central memorial in the Cemetery of the Martyr-Heroes of December 1989 in Bucharest

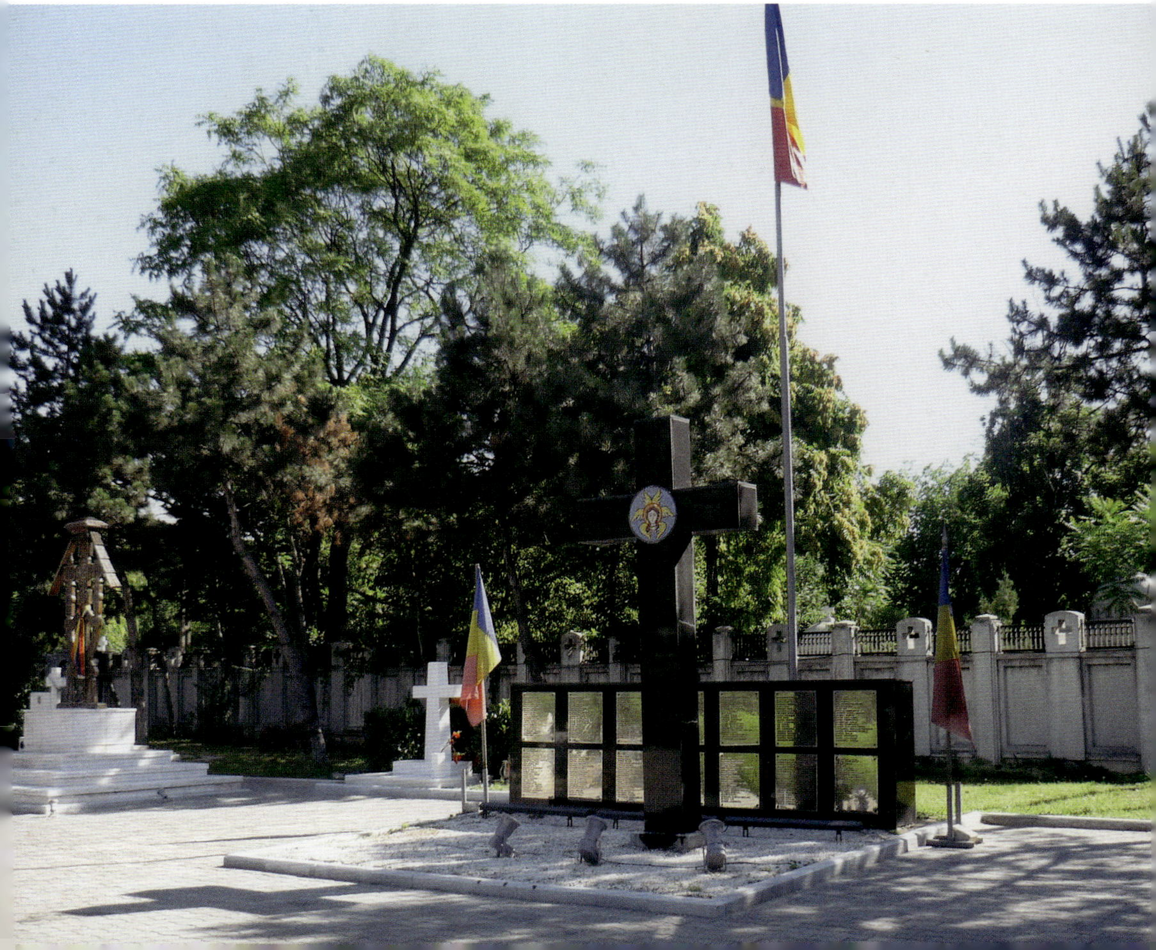

Aripi Monument in Memory of the Anti-Communist Resistance 1945 – 1989

Bucharest. The Aripi (Wings) monument to the anti-communist resistance between 1945 and 1989 was ceremonially unveiled to the public on 30 May 2016 on Free Press Square. It stands directly in front of one of the most important buildings of the Stalin era from the 1950s, the Casa Sânteii. The initiative for the 20-metre-high monument came from the Association of Former Political Prisoners in Romania, and it was largely funded by donations from local and national government agencies. The 100-tonne steel construction by sculptor Mihai Buculei, erected on the plinth of a demolished statue of Lenin, takes the form of three connected wings.

Inscription on the memorial plate in front of the memorial:
Romanian: *ARIPI // IN MEMORIA LUPTATORILOR / DIN REZISTENTA ANTICOMUNISTA // 1945 – 1989 // Autor Mihai Buculei*

English: *Wings — in memory of the anti-communist resistance 1945 – 1989. Author Mihai Buculei*

Location: Bucharest, Piata Presei Libere

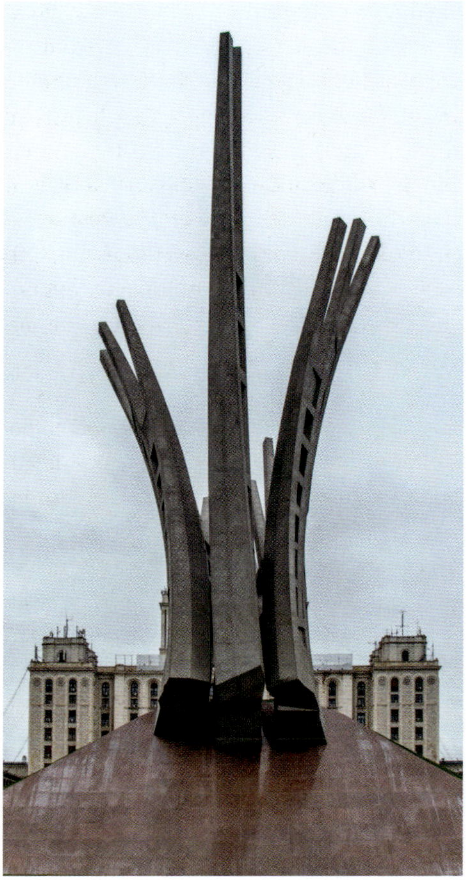

Aripi Monument in Memory of the Anti-Communist Resistance 1945 – 1989 on Free Press Square

Jilava Fort 13 Memorial

Jilava. The memorial to the victims of totalitarianism known as Jilava Fort 13 stands on the grounds of the prison of the same name. Located ten kilometres south of Bucharest, the fort was built in the second half of the 19th century as part of a fortification network. Until the early 1970s, Fort 13 served as a high-security and transit prison and execution site. Until 1989, Jilava was one of the most notorious prisons in Romania, ranking alongside the prisons in Piteşti and Sighet.

The history of the former prison reflects the political changes in Romania in the 20th century, having served all regimes as a place of detention for political opponents and as an execution site. In November 1940, more than 60 dignitaries of the Jewish community in Bucharest were murdered here. After the end of the war, the Red Army used the prison to incarcerate and execute former supporters of the fascist regime along with opponents of the communist transformation of the country. In June 1946, for example, Ion Antonescu and other leading politicians of the deposed pro-German Romanian government were executed here. Antonescu, whose government was responsible for the extermination of the Jewish population in Transnistria and the deportation of Sinti and Roma, had previously been sentenced to death as a war criminal in a public trial alongside former

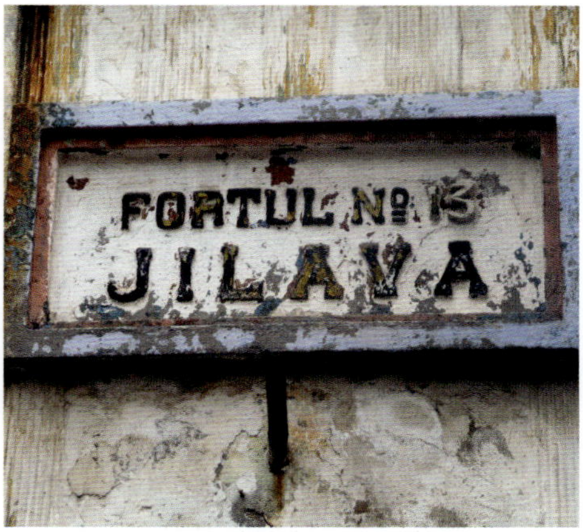

Jilava Fort 13 Memorial to the victims of totalitarianism

Governor of Transnistria, Gheorghe Alexianu, and the wartime Foreign Minister Mihail Antonescu. With the progressive Sovietisation of Romania after the rigged elections in November 1946 and the forced abdication of King Michael, the country was officially declared a People's Republic on 30 December 1947. The forced collectivisation of agriculture and the reprisals against the church and clergy provoked resistance in parts of the population, which the Stalinist regime under Gheorghe Gheorghiu-Dej met with open violence. Jilava was the place of incarceration not only of members of the political opposition and resistance fighters from all parts

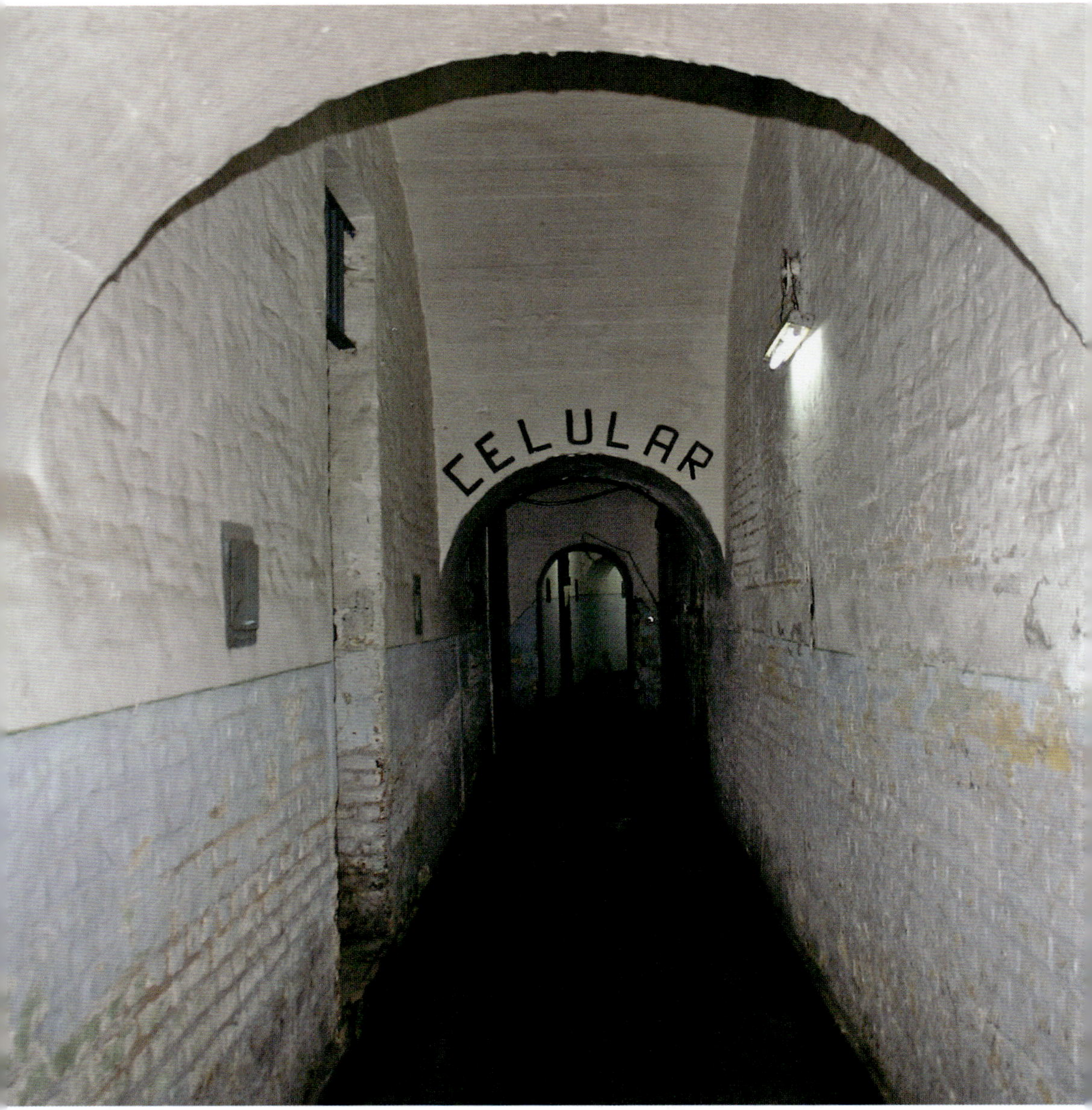

Entrance to one of the cell wings in the former high-security prison in Jilava Fort 13

of the country but also of disgraced Communist Party officials. Following the Soviet model, control of the prison was transferred from the military to the Ministry of Internal Affairs in 1948.

Under the dictator Gheorghiu-Dej, the conditions in Jilava were particularly harsh and brutal. Between 1948 and 1964, some 3,000 prisoners were interned in the 52 detention cells every year prior to trial or transportation to another detention centre or to one of the labour camps set up to build the Danube-Black Sea Canal. Their term of detention in the transit prison could last for anything from a few weeks to several years.

On arrival, the prisoners were subjected to violent humiliation rituals and mistreatment by the guards. Women and men were housed in separate sections, and the inmates included members of democratic parties such as the Christian Democratic National Peasant's Party (PNT) or the liberal-conservative National Liberal Party (PNL), communists who were victims of internal purges, former supporters of the fascist Iron Guard, war criminals and people accused of "treason" or of membership in "subversive organisations". In most cases, the prisoners in Jilava were charged with "crimes against state security". With the appointment of Nicolae Moromete as head of the guards and interim prison director—he held both posts from 1949 to 1952—the already strict prison regime was further tightened: fear, torture, hunger and terror dominated the daily life of the prisoners.

The 1964 general amnesty for political prisoners also led to changes in the Jilava prison. Following the completion of a new building in the city in 1970, detention operations at Jilava Fort 13 were discontinued. Along with other disused prisons, however, the fort was held in reserve for exceptional situations, such as that which occurred almost 20 years later during the revolutionary events of December 1989. When the protests and unrest in Timişoara spread to Bucharest within a very short time, more than 60 people were detained in a 15-square-metre cell in the fort.

After the collapse of the communist regime in Romania at the end of 1989, the entire prison complex was shut down. In the 1990s, the fort was used as a warehouse. Since 2012, the site, which also includes four above-ground inner courtyards, was opened to the public as part of the "Memorial to Totalitarianism, Repression and Resistance, Jilava Fort 13" project. The project, initiated by former Romanian President Emil Constantinescu in collaboration with the Association of Former Political Prisoners in Romania, serves as a memorial to oppression and a clarion call for resistance against totalitarianism. A virtual tour of the entire site of the former prison is available on the memorial's website.

Location: Jilava, Strada Sabarului 1
Internet: www.memorialuljilava.ro

Memorial of the Victims of Communism and of the Resistance

Sighet. The Memorial of the Victims of Communism and of the Resistance was established in 1994 by the Civic Academy Foundation (Fundatia Academia Civica) and opened to the public in 2000 after extensive renovation work. The initiative for the construction of a memorial and meeting place in the former prison for political prisoners goes back to the writer Ana Blandiana and her husband Romulus Rusan. In the more than 80 cells converted into exhibition rooms, which are spread over three floors of the building, various aspects of political persecution in Romania from 1944 to the revolution in 1989 are illustrated by historical overviews and individual prisoner biographies. Sighet also serves as a place of remembrance and commemoration. One of the institution's main goals is to educate the Romanian and international public about the forms taken by oppression and resistance to the communist dictatorship.

Sighet Prison was built in 1897 as a prison under public law. Between 1918 and 1945, it served as a regular prison for common criminals. After 1945, Sighet was initially used as a point of transit for prisoners and deportees from the Soviet Union. When the communist Romanian Workers' Party took power in 1947, the prison developed into one of the most notorious political prisons in the country. Until 1964, the regime of dictator Gheorghe Gheorghiu-Dej detained over 200 people in Sighet without a trial or court order, including almost the entire political, religious and intellectual elite of the country. More than 50 people died as a result of ill-treatment and miserable prison conditions. For the most part, the mortal remains were buried at night in a field outside the city. Only when the mass graves were uncovered in 1994 could the bones of the dead be reburied in separate graves.

From 1955 to 1977, the prison once again served as a regular prison. When General Secretary of the Romanian Communist Party Nicolae Ceauşescu, who came to power in 1965, launched a campaign to educate prisoners in the workplace in 1977, the prison was closed. In the following years, the building served as a salt depot, vegetable warehouse and broom factory. For several years after the collapse of the communist regime in December 1989, homeless people found refuge here. It was only in the mid-1990s, when the Civic Academy Foundation took charge of the decaying building, that the history of the institution was reconstructed and presented in a museum exhibition.

The cells, transformed into thematic presentation spaces, illustrate the widespread system of repression in communist Romania. The "Map Room" provides a topographical illustration of the more than 230 places of detention, forced labour, resettlement, deportation, repression and forced psychiatric treatment where some 600,000 people were held between 1945

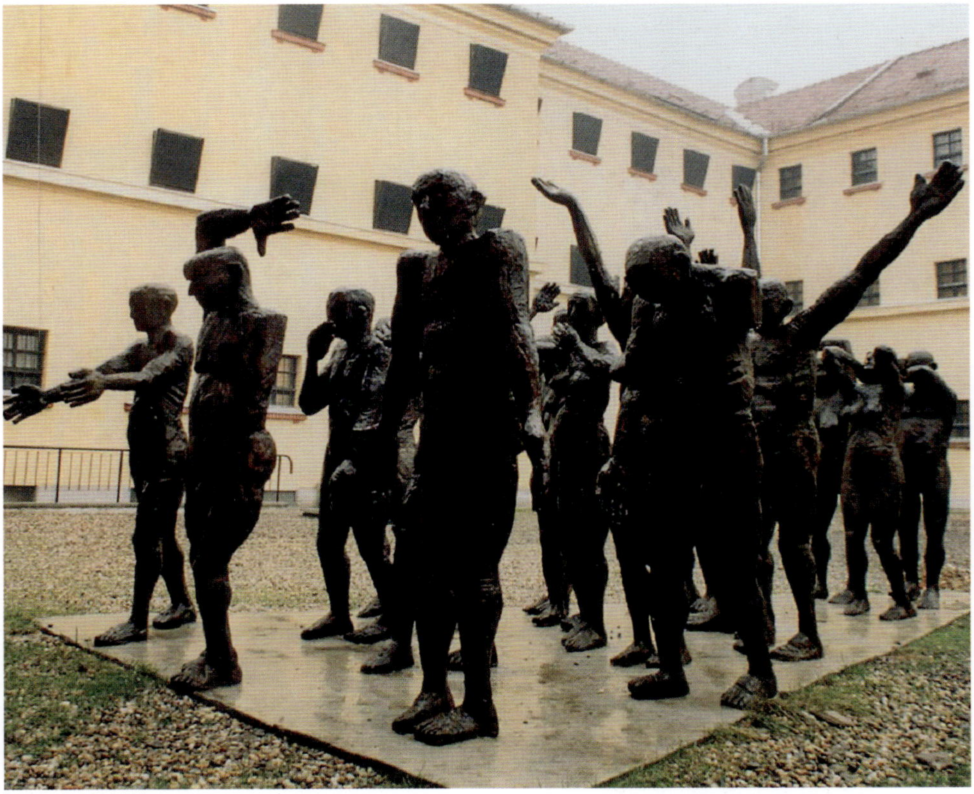

Sculpture composition "The Convoy of the Victims" in the inner courtyard of the memorial

and 1989. Hundreds of thousands were detained for up to ten years without ever being granted a trial under the rule of law.

Objects and facsimiles illustrate everyday life in prison, while graphics and information texts present the functions and special features of the communist penal system in Romania. Another important topic covered is the so-called "Piteşti Experiment" conducted in the years 1949 to 1952, when the newly founded secret police, the Sicuritate, sought to re-educate prisoners as "new people" through torture and humiliation.

Other parts of the exhibition document the elections of 1946 which were blatantly rigged to the benefit of the Workers' Party, the systematic elimination of established democratic associations and the final elimination of the multi-party system in favour of a one-party dictatorship in February 1948. The forced abdication of King Michael on 30 December 1947 is also examined in this context. Also presented are the persecution of the various denominational communities—from the material destruction of church property to the physical annihilation of clergymen—and the reprisals against the German, Jewish and Hungarian minorities in Romania. Finally, the exhibition turns a spotlight on the forced collectivisation and industrialisation campaigns and their devastating effects. A green furrow symbolises the rural resistance and the victims associated with it.

Other exhibition rooms are dedicated to forced labour in Romania, to the use by the communist regime of prisoners on construction sites, in mines and in factories. Between 1949 and 1954 and, again, from 1958 to 1963, some 40,000 forced labourers were employed

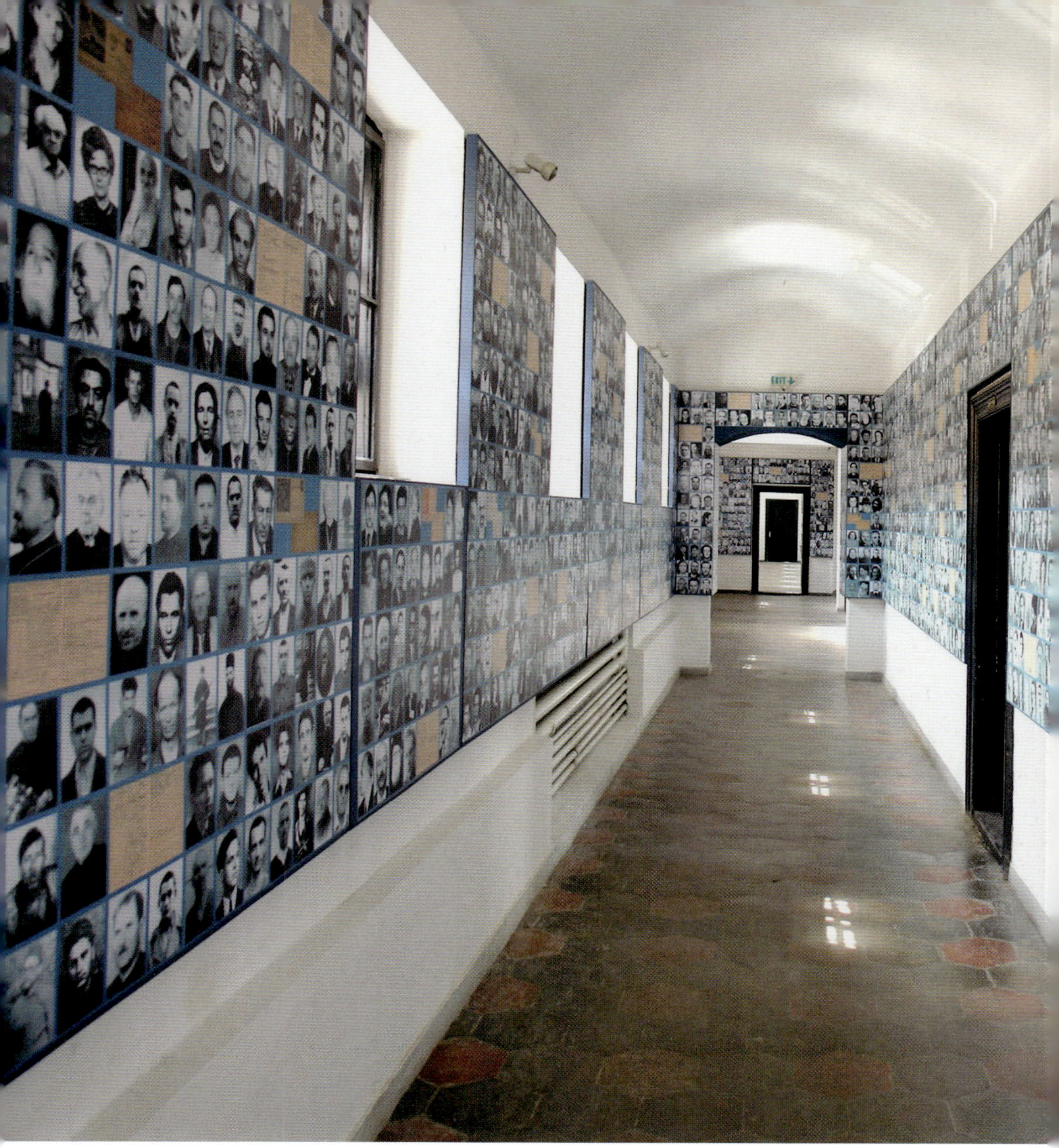

Photos of the victims of the communist regime on the walls of the exhibition

on the country's most prominent construction site, the artificial waterway of the Danube-Black Sea Canal. Sighet functioned as a "special labour unit"—as a "Danube colony" for the country's bourgeois elite. In April 1950, the Securitate was ordered to find reasons to prosecute "all the elements that have played a role in the political life of the country".

On the night of 5–6 June 1950, 80 people who had shaped Romania before the communist dictatorship were brought to Sighet. Further waves of arrests followed. In August 1951, the Ministry of the Interior legalised these measures with Decision No. 334 and sentenced the detainees to 24 months in forced labour camps. When the two years were up, on 6 August 1953, the ministry extended these sentences, which could not be appealed, by a further 60 months. The exhibition gives an impression of the

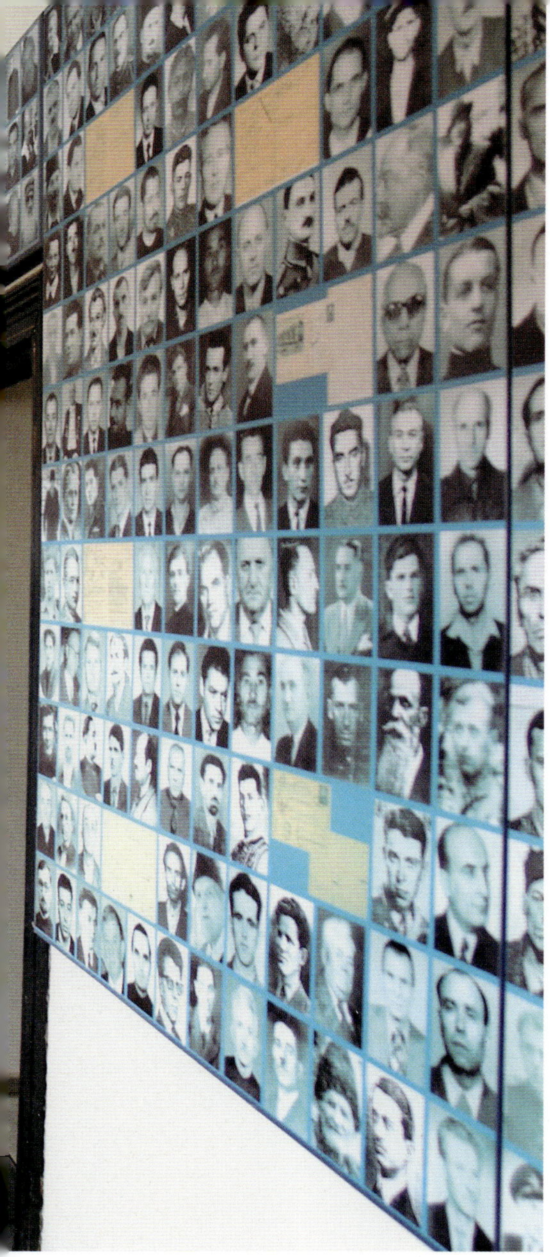

prison conditions in the small, mostly overcrowded cells and portrays the everyday life of the prisoners in Sighet and other prisons in the country.

Engraved on the walls of the ramp to the underground prayer room are the names of the 8,000 victims of the communist dictatorship identified so far. In the so-called cenotaph, a sacral rotunda, visitors are invited to a moment of meditation and reflection. In the middle of the room is a round stone slab covered with water, which reflects the cross-shaped opening in the dome-like ceiling. In the inner courtyard of the memorial are stone slabs bearing the names of other former Sighet inmates and the sculpture composition "The Convoy of the Victims" designed by Romanian artist Aurel Vlad. The 18 amorphous bronze figures moving towards the prison wall symbolise a society in agony.

The memorial also includes a paupers' cemetery not far from the complex. Some of the 53 people who died in prison between 1950 and 1955 were anonymously buried here. To commemorate them, trees were planted, and an altar was erected in 2005, dedicated as a memorial to the victims of all communist prisons, camps and deportation sites.

The Sighet Memorial organises numerous conferences, symposia and training courses in addition to its core education and information services. Since 1998, the institution has organised an annual international summer school whose participants are selected in an essay competition. The International Centre for Communist Studies, based in Bucharest, is affiliated to the Civic Academy Foundation, where scientific research is promoted by supporting archives and documentation. On 9 May 2013, an outpost of the memorial was opened in Bucharest.

Location: Sighetu Marmaţiei, Strada Corneliu Coposu 4 and Bucharest, Strada Jean Louis Calderon 66
Internet: www.memorialsighet.ro

The Museum of the 1989 Romanian Revolution in Timişoara

Timişoara. The "December 16 – 22, 1989 Revolution Memorial" Association, founded on 26 April 1990, set up a documentation and research centre under the direction of Traian Orban. With state support, a building in central Timişoara was restored and extended, and now houses the museum's exhibition rooms, a library and an archive. In the courtyard of the Documentation Centre is an ecumenical chapel as a place of remembrance and commemoration.

Timişoara, near the Hungarian border, is the largest city in Western Romania, with around 360,000 inhabitants. This is where the Romanian Revolution began on 16 December 1989, finally resulting in the execution of the dictator Nicolae Ceauşescu and his wife Elena on 25 December and the overthrow of the communist regime. The protests were triggered by the forced reassignment of the Hungarian Reformed Church pastor László Tőkés, who had been under observation for some time by the infamous Securitate secret police for remarks critical of the regime.

During 16 December, more than 1,000 people gathered in the city centre, making socio-political demands and calling for the removal of Ceauşescu. The Securitate tried to disperse the crowd with rubber truncheons, arresting dozens of protesters, but could no longer control the riots. The next day, many workers joined the protests: the crowd chanted anti-Communist slogans, and there were acts of brute violence and looting. The emergency forces took extremely violent action against the insurgents, and by the afternoon many people had been injured or killed. On 20 December, after more than 100 people had lost their lives in Timişoara, the armed forces stationed there finally took the side of the people. Timişoara became the first city in Romania to free itself from the Ceauşescu dictatorship.

After taking over a wing of the former army barracks No. 1079, the museum was able to expand its exhibition area in 2011. Comprehensive photo documentation, posters and information boards, video and audio presentations, reproductions and original exhibits present the history of the 1989 Revolution. Special attention is paid to the events in Timişoara, which, according to various historians and contemporary witnesses, still pose some unresolved questions. Visitors can take part in guided tours of the museum. These are offered in Romanian, English, German, French, Italian, Hungarian and Serbian.

On 20 December 2012, the anniversary of the Romanian Revolution, Klaus Christian Olasz, Consul of the Federal Republic of Germany, and

► Memorial to the Victims of the 1989 Revolution in the municipal cemetery in Timişoara

Dr Traian Orban unveiled an original segment of the Berlin Wall on the museum grounds as a memorial to the fall of the Iron Curtain in Europe. The donation by the Berlin Senate was made at the suggestion of Dr Anna Kaminsky, the managing director of the Federal Foundation for the Study of the Communist Dictatorship in Eastern Germany. Twelve sculptures and memorials were erected in central locations in memory of the events of 1989.

Between 1990 and 1999, on the initiative of the Timişoara "December 16 – 22, 1989 Revolution Memorial" Association, a memorial installation for the victims of the December Revolution was erected in the municipal cemetery. Designed by Romanian architects Pompiliu Alâmoreanu, Ionel Pop, and Liviu Brebe, it features symbolic graves for the more than 70 known dead, with their names engraved on the uniform black gravestones. Next to an open chapel made of black and white marble is the central memorial of the complex: a high wall, likewise made of black and white marble blocks, with a golden cross embedded in the middle. An eternal flame burns in a stone container directly in front of the memorial wall.

Location: Timişoara, Strada Popa Şapcă 3 – 5
Internet: www.memorialulrevolutiei.ro

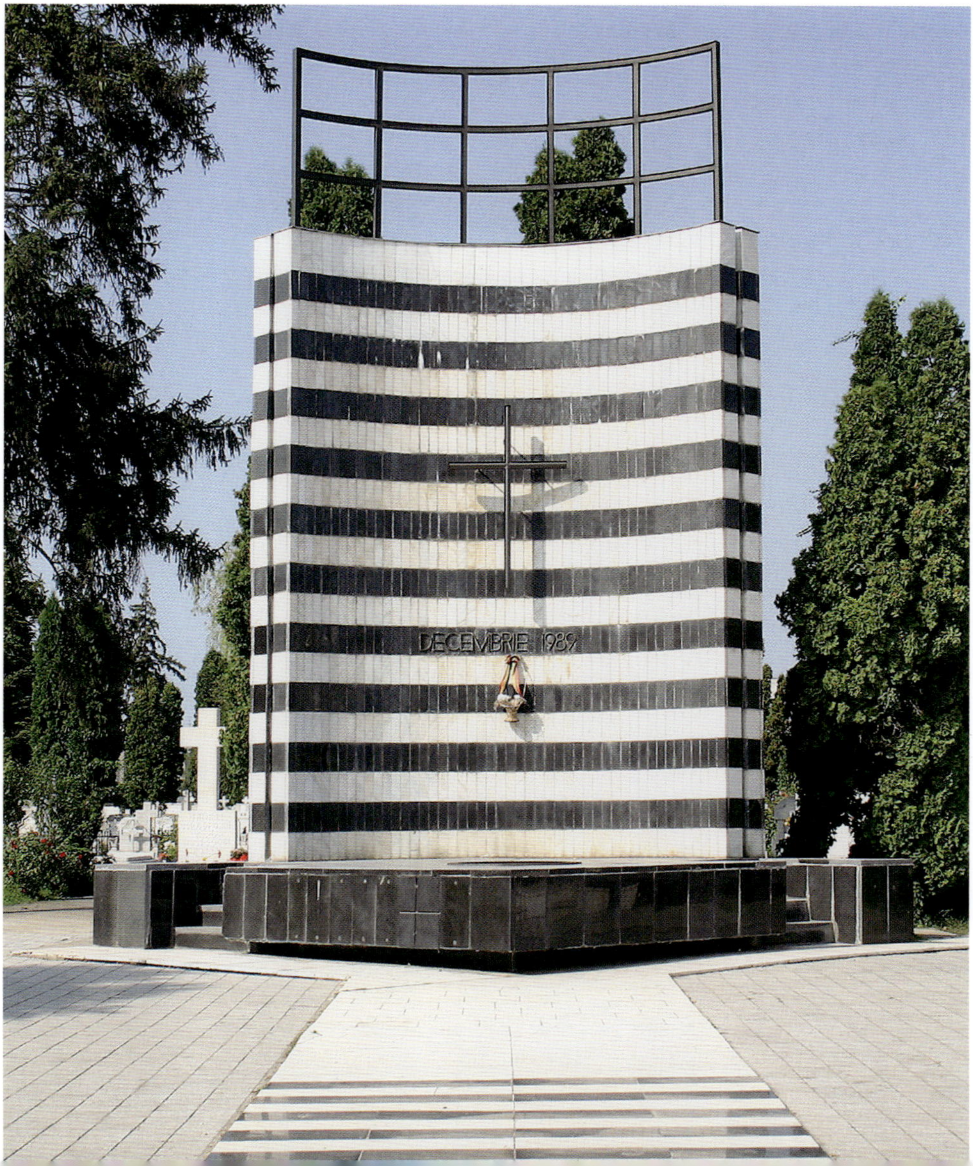

Memorial to the Rebellion of Braşov on 15 November 1987

Braşov. On the tenth anniversary of the workers' uprising on 15 November 1987 that became known as the Rebellion of Braşov, the monument was unveiled in 1997 on the initiative of the "15 November 1987 Association". The votive cross with its memorial plaque in honour of the freedom fighters is located on Calea Bucureşti, a section of the route covered by the protesters on their protest march to the city centre during the rebellion. The Rebellion of Braşov ranks alongside the miners' strike in the Jiu Valley in 1977 and the revolution that started in Timişoara in December 1989 as one of the most important protests in communist Romania.

Inscription on the pedestal of the monument Romanian: *A fost ridicat acest sfânt monument în cinstea braşovenilor care în acest loc, la 15 noiembrie 1987, învingându-şi teama şi dispreţuind moartea au cântat imnul »Deşteaptă-te, române!« şi au scandat »Jos comunismul!«*

English: *This sacred monument was erected in honour of the Braşovians who, on 15 November 1987, overcame their fear and scorned death to sing the hymn "Wake up, Romanians!" and to chant "Down with communism!"*

Location: Braşov, Calea Bucureşti (opposite Judeţean Braşov district hospital)

Monument to Anti-Communist Fighters 1944–1989

Braşov. The Monument to Anti-Communist Fighters was inaugurated and unveiled to the public on 14 September 2002. The initiative for the erection of the memorial goes back to the Braşovian chapter of the Association of Political Prisoners in Romania. The former political prisoner Octav Bjoza and Horia Salcă, the son of former prisoner Alexandru Salcă, played a major role in the realisation of the memorial. The red and black sandstone monument was funded with the support of local city and district authorities. It consists of an accessible circular platform, framed at the front by a low wall. On the opposite side is a curved wall with a stylised lattice window, barbed wire and cross. In front of the wall is a hemispherical stone container in which an eternal flame burns.

Inscriptions

Front side, Romanian: *ÎN FAŢA ACESTUI SIMBOL AL JERTFEI PENTRU LIBERTATE, CREDINŢĂ ŞI DEMNITATE NAŢIONALĂ DESCOPERIŢI-VĂ!*

English: *Bare your heads before this symbol of sacrifice for freedom, faith and national dignity!*

On the wall, Romanian: *ÎN MEMORIA LUPTĂTORILOR ANTICOMUNIŞTI 1944–1989*

English: *In memory of the anti-communist fighters 1944–1989*

On the circular platform, a star is formed by the intersection of four red lines, along which the names of places and regions associated with imprisonment, torture or politically-motivated murders between 1944 and 1989 are arranged according to their cardinal directions relative to Braşov.

Inscription (clockwise from the right of the eternal flame) with information about the place in square brackets:

TIMIŞOARA (prison, political psychiatry, mass graves, murders and executions)—LUGOJ (prison)

FĂGĂRAŞ (prison)—CODLEA (prison)

AIUD (prison)—GHERLA (prison, mass graves, murders and executions)

NISTRU (labour camp)—CAVNIC (labour camp)—BAIA SPRIE (labour camp)

SIGHET (prison and mass graves)—
SUCEAVA (re-education prison, mass graves, murders and executions)—

CERNĂUŢI (in present-day Ukraine)—
MIERCUREA CIUC (prison)—

SIBERIA—BĂLŢI (in modern-day Moldova)—
CHIŞINĂU (also in Moldova)—

GALATA IAŞI (prison)—ONEŞTI (labour camps and political psychiatric institute)—

DELTA DUNĂRII (labour camp)—GALAŢI (prison, mass graves, murders and executions)—

RÂMNICUL SĂRAT (prison)—

BALTA BRĂILEI (deportation centre and labour camp)—

CANALUL DUNĂRE—MAREA NEAGRĂ (labour camps, deportation centres, mass graves, murders and executions)—

PITEŞTI (re-education prison, mass graves, murders and executions)—JILAVA (transit prison, mass graves, murders and executions)—

VĂCĂREŞTI (prison hospital)—

TÂRGŞOR (prison for pupils)—
MISLEA (women's prison)—

CARANSEBEŞ (prison, mass murders and executions)—

OCNELE MARI (re-education prison, mass murders, and executions)—
CARACAL (camp)—CRAIOVA (prison, mass murders and executions)

Location: Braşov, Piaţa Teatrului

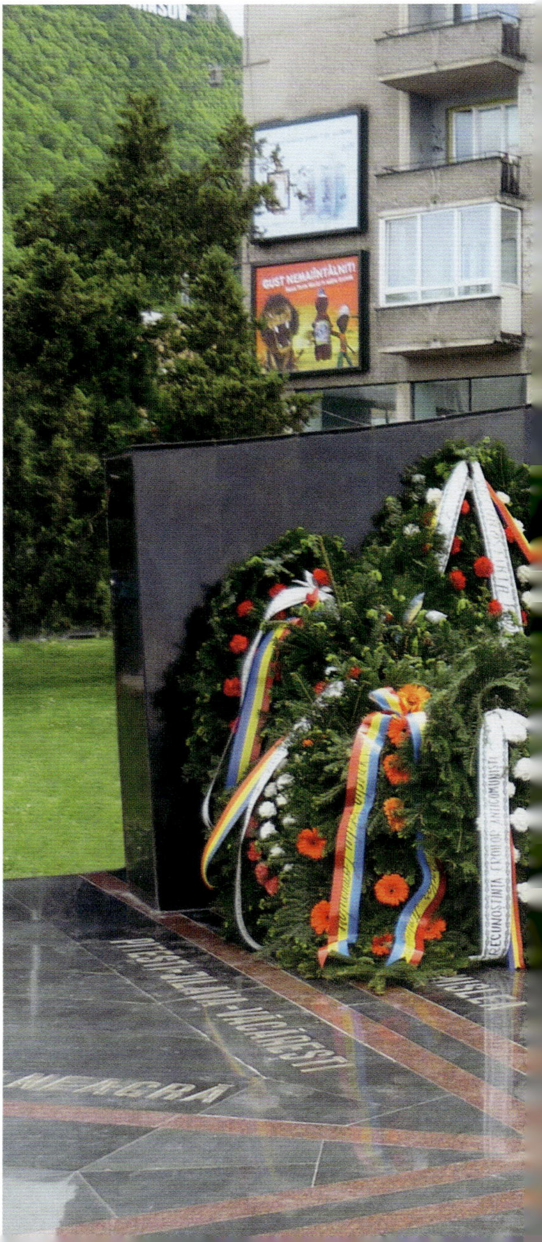

Memorial to the Victims of Communism 1944–1989 in Braşov

Further reading:

Grancea, Mihaela: Case Study on Romania. In: Honoring Civil Courage. Developing Suggestions to Improve the Situation of Victims of Communist State Crimes. Project Coordinator: Gedenkstätte Berlin-Hohenschönhausen 2015, Ref.-Nr.: JUST/2011/JPEN/AG/2998. Available online at: www.stiftung-hsh.de/assets/Dokumente-pdf-Dateien/EU-Projekt-Laenderstudien.pdf (last accessed on: 15/11/2017). / Hausleitner, Mariana: Politischer Widerstand in Rumänien vor 1989. In: Halbjahresschrift für südosteuropäische Geschichte, Literatur und Politik, 1996. Available online at: www.halbjahresschrift.homepage.t-online.de/radu1.htm (last accessed on: 15/11/2017). / Jung, Martin: In Freiheit. Die Auseinandersetzung mit Zeitgeschichte in Rumänien (1989 – 2009). Berlin 2016. / Oprea, Marius / Stejarel, Olaru: The day we won't forget: 15 November 1987, Braşov. Iaşi 2003. Rusan, Romulus (2008): Chronologie und Geografie der kommunistischen Unterdrückung in Rumänien; Zählung der zwangsinternierten Bevölkerung (1945 – 1989). Bucharest: Fundaţia Academia Civică.

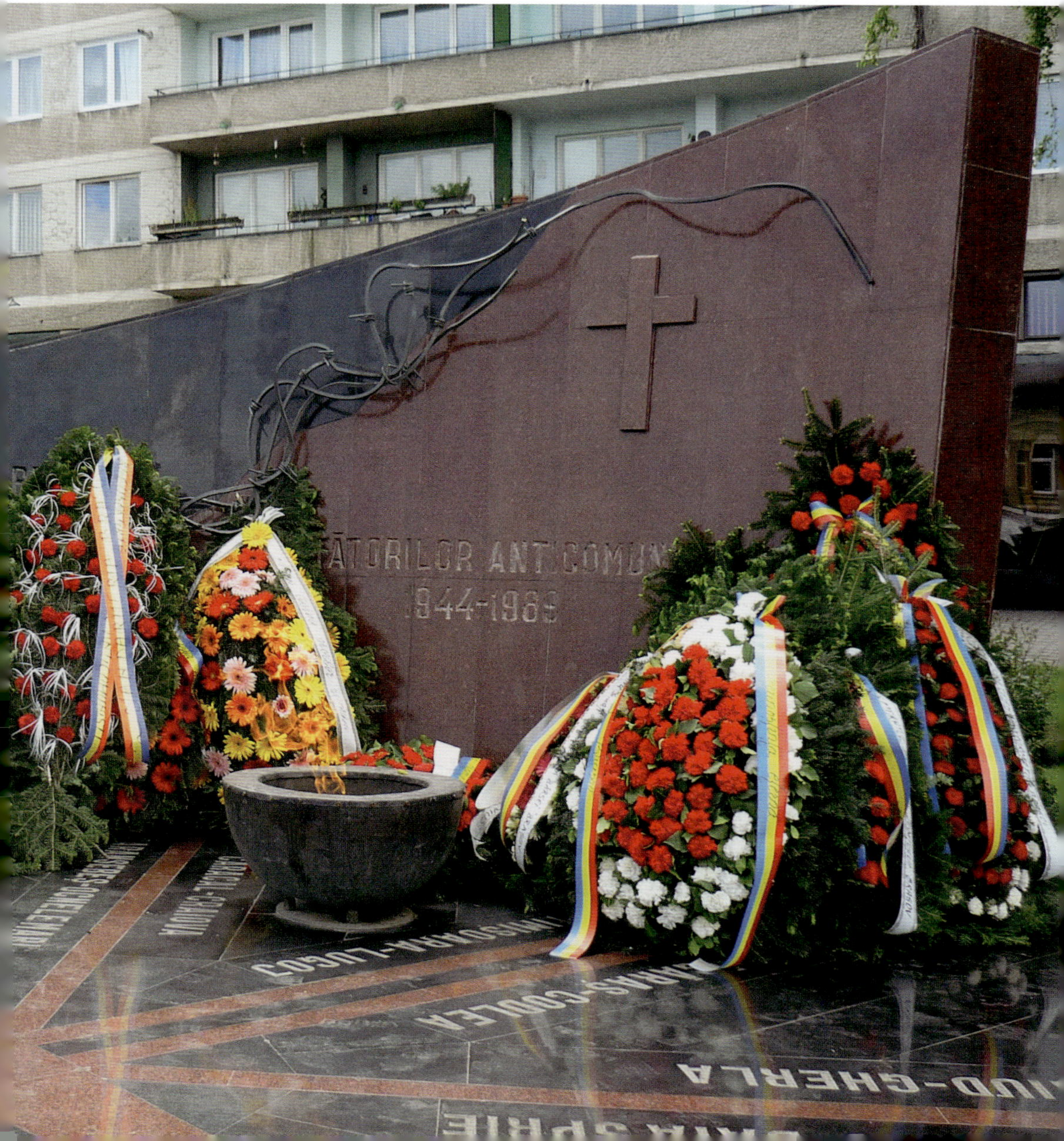

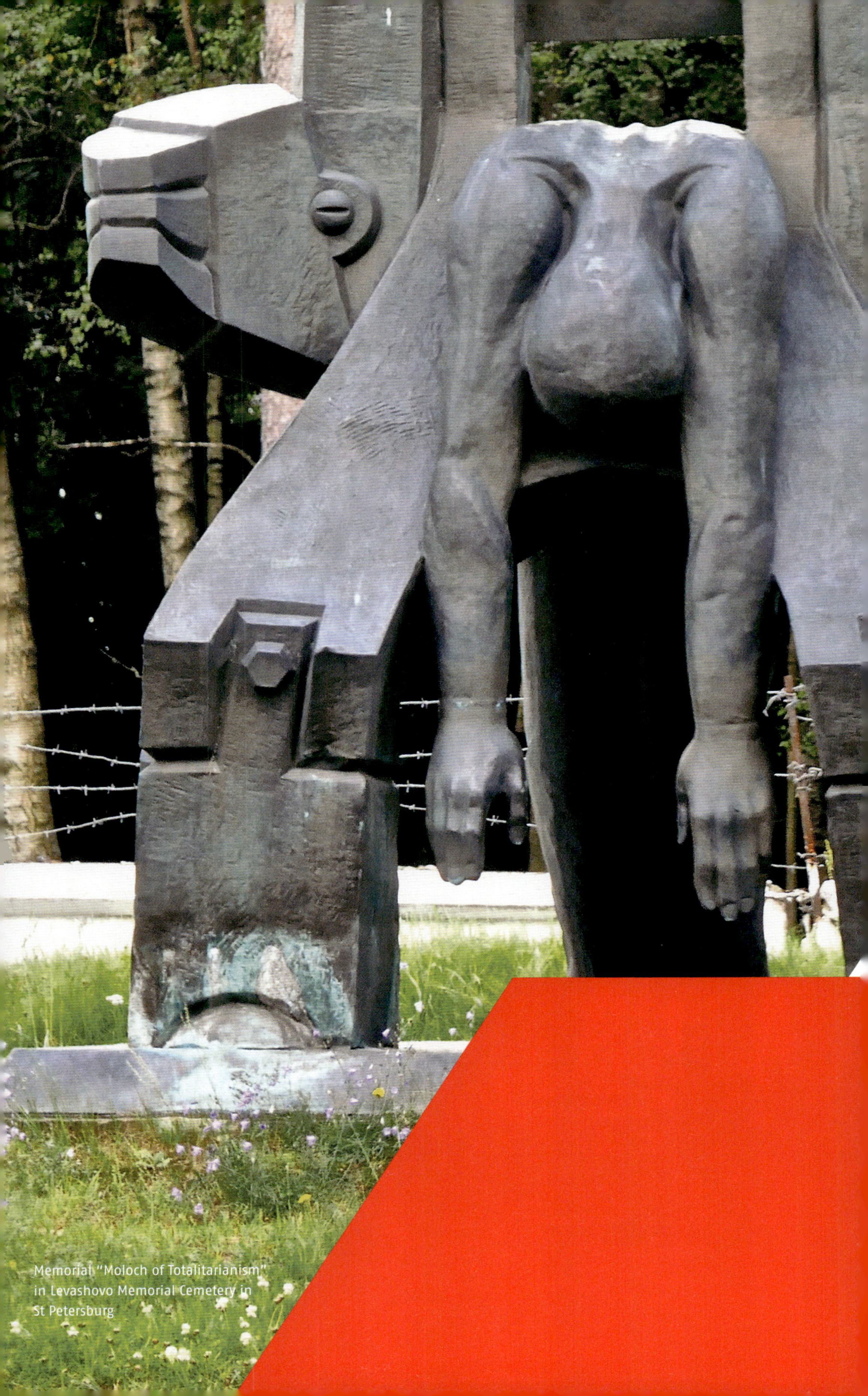

Memorial "Moloch of Totalitarianism" in Levashovo Memorial Cemetery in St Petersburg

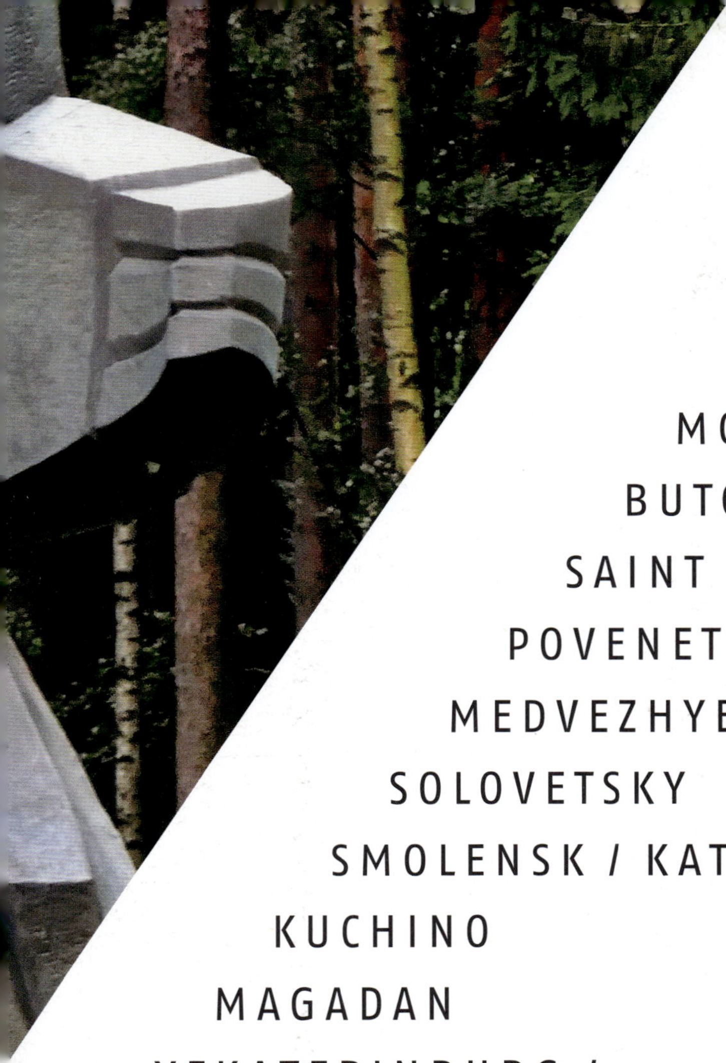

MOSCOW
BUTOVO
SAINT PETERSBURG
POVENETS
MEDVEZHYEGORSK
SOLOVETSKY
SMOLENSK / KATYŃ
KUCHINO
MAGADAN
YEKATERINBURG /
SHIROKAYA RECHKA

Russia

On 7 November (or 25 October according to the Old Style Russian calendar) 1917, the Russian Bolsheviks under the leadership of Vladimir Ilyich Lenin seized power in the so-called October Revolution and ended the government of social revolutionaries and Bolsheviks under Alexander Kerensky, which had been in place since February 1917. This marked the end of the almost eight-month attempt to make the shift from tsarist authoritarian rule to a bourgeois-democratic parliamentary system. In the following year, the Russian Social Democratic Labour Party was renamed the Russian Communist Party. After the founding of the Soviet Union, it first became the All-Union Communist Party and then, from 1952 onwards, the Communist Party of the Soviet Union (CPSU).

After the coup, the country was plunged into civil war: the Red Army led by Lenin and his Bolsheviks faced units of the so-called White Army, consisting of officers and troops affiliated with the tsarist or bourgeois order, alongside foreign intervention troops. The Russian Civil War claimed about eight million lives on all sides, including a great many civilians who were caught between the warring parties, before the Red Army finally emerged victorious. In 1922, the Soviet Union was founded, comprising the Russian Soviet Republic and the Ukrainian, Belarusian and Transcaucasian Soviet Republics, the latter consisting of Armenia, Georgia and Azerbaijan. Over the decades to follow, many other countries were forcibly annexed to the Soviet Union.

During the Civil War, the Bolsheviks had already introduced "war communism" in the territories they controlled. This provided for the expropriation of land and factories, the introduction of compulsory levies, and the forced recruitment of soldiers for the army as well as the use of "Red Terror" to secure Bolshevik rule. On 5 September 1918, the decree by the Council of People's

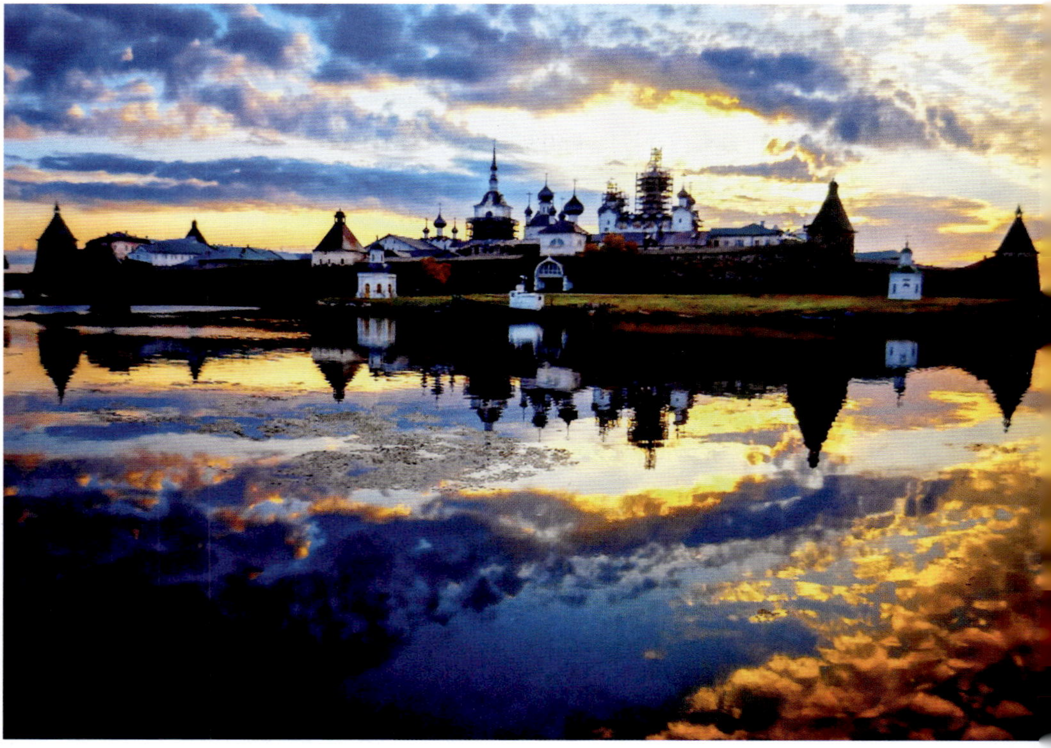

Deputies "On Red Terror" officially provided for the establishment of concentration and internment camps for the imprisonment of people who were considered enemies of the new order. One of the first camps was built on the Solovetsky Islands in the White Sea.

After the end of the Civil War, Lenin ordered the introduction of the New Economic Policy, which allowed farmers greater leeway in growing and selling their products, thus helping to rebuild the economy in the war-ravaged country. When Lenin died in 1924, Stalin took power and cemented his position with new waves of terror and mass reprisals. Step by step, domestic rivals and critics of his policies were deprived of power and driven into exile or, like the fate that later befell Trotsky, murdered. Their sympathisers were imprisoned in camps, compelled into forced labour or murdered. Stalin's rise to power effectively ended the phase of economic liberalisation in 1927, and the agricultural sector was forcibly collectivised. Under this pretext, tens of thousands of farmers lost their land and were stigmatised as "kulaks" and deported or murdered along with their families. The violent transformation of agriculture and the massive-scale persecution of farmers led to a famine which killed several million people, particularly in Kazakhstan, Ukraine and Crimea. The Soviet leadership also used famine as a means of disciplining sections of the population considered critical of the government.

As early as 1918, the foundation stone was laid for the construction of the camp system which later covered the entire Soviet Union. From the beginning of the 1930s, it was consolidated under the name Gulag (Glavnoye upravleniye ispravityelno-trudovykh lagerey: Main Administration of Corrective Labour Camps). The Gulag included a vast network of forced labour camps that covered the entire Soviet Union from the Solovetsky Islands in the White Sea to Magadan and Vladivostok in the Far East; from Murmansk and Vorkuta on the Arctic Circle to Alma-Ata and Ulaanbaatar in Central Asia; from the centre of Moscow to the centre of Leningrad. The term Gulag became synonymous with the repressive Soviet regime—inhumane living conditions, extreme physical labour, draconian punishments, malnutrition, exhaustion, illness and death.

As early as 1918, Lenin ordered the merciless suppression of all resistance and demanded that suspects be locked up in concentration camps outside the cities. In this widely ramified network of labour and penal camps, camps with criminal and political prisoners, women's and children's camps, and transit and special camps, alleged and actual opponents of the Soviet Union were isolated from the rest of society.

Starting in the late 1920s/early 1930s, the manpower of the prisoners was exploited during forced collectivisation and forced industrialisation for the accelerated infrastructural and economic development of the country. Artists, scientists and intellectuals were sent to the camps for "re-education" and had to perform forced labour tasks, for example in the construction of the Baltic Sea Canal and other major industrial projects.

Soviet rule also paved the way to an all-out assault on religious freedom: the practice of religious rites was banned entirely, numerous priests and worshippers were imprisoned or murdered, and church property was confiscated, deliberately destroyed or, in some cases, sold abroad to obtain funds for forced industrialisation. So-called museums of atheism were

◀
Centuries-old monastery converted into a camp complex on the Solovetsky Archipelago

established, exhibiting cult objects to warn the "New Man" of the dangers of religion and to make fun of the faithful. Churches were repurposed as stables and warehouses, swimming pools, crematoria and prisons.

The forced labour system, which enslaved prisoners under inhumane conditions in completely undeveloped and climatically extreme regions and forced them to perform the heaviest of physical labour tasks meant that the Gulag was at times the largest economic enterprise in the Soviet Union. Prisoners were used in all conceivable industrial sectors: from logging, mining, factory work, precious metal extraction, canal, railway, road and house building, agriculture, oil and radium extraction through to the development of guns, aircraft and machines in the secret research laboratories of the NKVD, the "sharashkas". After passing through the "meat grinder" of arrests, interrogations and confessions extracted under torture, they were transported in unheated cattle wagons to remote regions of the Soviet Union.

The number of camps increased drastically after the start of mass reprisals. Over the years, at least 476 large camp complexes were built with thousands of individual camps and subcamps, which held between a few hundred and several thousand people each. Added to this was the terror that shaped everyday life and society as a whole, culminating in the "Great Terror" of 1937/38. Within a few months, over two million people were arrested by the NKVD, 1.345 million of them sentenced under the notorious Article 58 of the Russian Criminal Code, and some 700,000 people shot. Over 27,000 wives and 36,000 children of so-called "enemies of the people" were deported to camps where they had to perform forced labour tasks.

The military leadership of the country was also swept up by the "Great Terror" and its purges. Almost the entire Red Army officer corps was murdered, for which the Soviet Union paid dearly with a massive loss of human life when Nazi Germany invaded on 22 June 1941. But even during the Soviet population's fight for survival against the war of aggression and annihilation waged by the Germans, repression continued unabated within the country.

The Second World War saw a huge increase in the number of people imprisoned in camps or exiled. Hundreds of thousands of people from all Soviet-occupied territories were brought to the Gulag, as were prisoners of war: for instance, up to 50,000 Germans were imprisoned in the Vorkuta camp complex alone. After the end of the war, renewed waves of repression brought hundreds of thousands more people to various camp sites. At the time of peak occupancy in 1950, the number of people detained in the Gulag camps exceeded 2,561,300.

Altogether, around 20 million people were imprisoned in the Gulag. Millions of people were murdered in its camps or fell victim to inhumane conditions. However, especially at the height of Stalinist mass terror in 1937/38, the difference between a life lived inside and outside the barbed wire fence was more a matter of degree than a fundamental change. It was often said that a prisoner released from the Gulag was only transferred from the "little zone" to the "big zone". All life was focused on unconditional submission to the ideology and aims of the Communist Party; any deviancy could result in deportation, imprisonment or death for the individual concerned and their family.

Soviet policy during Lenin's reign and that of Stalin in particular was aimed at depriving people of their personal histories and identities. Children and families were arbitrarily given new names and rigorous efforts made to sever any connections between the generations. Traditions, whether religious or cultural, were replaced by new Soviet rituals, and the old customs were banished from public life under the threat of punishment.

Even after the end of the Second World War, in which the Soviet Union paid the highest blood toll in terms of human lives and yet emerged as one of the victorious powers, the oppression of the population continued. More and more new groups were accused of conspiracies against Stalin or communist rule, and their members were subjected to show trials and, in many cases, executed. It was not until Stalin died in March 1953 that the killing ended. After his death, a process of de-Stalinisation under the new head of state and party Nikita Khrushchev began, which also brought about the gradual dissolution of the Gulag system and, relative to the conditions under Stalin, a degree of liberalisation of everyday life.

Political prisoners were released from the camps and rehabilitated but often discriminated against with regard to their choice of place of residence, education or occupation. Cities, streets and factories formerly named after Stalin were renamed. On 27 March 1953, almost 1.2 million prisoners were released in a mass amnesty. However, almost all prisoners detained for political reasons for "counter-revolutionary activity" under the notorious Article 58 of the RSFSR Penal Code were excluded from early release.

The slow and only selectively implemented efforts to reform the prison system caused anger and frustration within the camp complexes, which in turn resulted in work stoppages, strikes, assaults and mass uprisings against the guards and camp administration in 1953/54. Northern locations within the Arctic Circle, the GorLag, a special camp of the NorriLag system, the Vorkuta special camp RetchLag and the Kazakh special camp No. 4 in Kengir in particular saw the outbreak of violent conflicts in the summers of 1953 and 1954, which were bloodily suppressed by the state security authorities.

At the same time, the first mass redundancies presented the societies of the Soviet republics with enormous rehabilitation policy challenges. People who returned from captivity and exile, formerly reviled as "enemies of the people" and "nationalists"—especially in the Baltic regions, Ukraine, Belarus and Moldova—were denied access to identity documents, housing, work and pensions.

The cultural "thaw" and ensuing de-Stalinisation under head of state and party Nikita Khrushchev were a political balancing act for the highest echelons of the government of the USSR. After Stalin's death, the Gulag was successively dismantled as an all-encompassing system of oppression, and no further attempt was ever made to use the camp system as an integral part of the Soviet economy or to imprison millions of people. Nor were the secret police ever again granted such sweeping authority to encroach into the economic life of the country as they were under Stalin.

This is not to say, however, that repression and persecution ceased from this point. The camps as a means of state oppression never completely disappeared from the Soviet penal system but continued to be used to break political, national or cultural resistance. Soviet prisons were not fully integrated into the regular prison system, which only held criminals. Instead, the instruments of state oppression underwent a change. While the arrests during Stalin's rule were characterised by pure arbitrariness—without exception, anyone could be arrested "for nothing" at any time for any reason—arrests in the post-Stalinist period, especially during Leonid Brezhnev's reign, were made on the grounds of literary, religious or political opposition to the Soviet system. After the abolition of Article 58, arrests were now made under either the new Article 70 of the Penal Code on "Anti-Soviet agitation and propaganda" or Article 72 on "Organisational activity directed towards the committing of especially dangerous State crimes, and equally membership of an anti-Soviet organisation".

The first major politically motivated wave of arrests after the death of Stalin took place in the aftermath of the Hungarian Revolution in October 1956, which was violently suppressed by Soviet troops. Nearly 2,000 people who had sympathised with the popular uprising were incarcerated in the camps. Almost 10,000 political prisoners imprisoned between the early 1960s and late 1980s—dissidents, human rights activists, writers and dissenters such as Alexander Solzhenitsyn, Andrei Sakharov, Vasyl Stus, Arseny Roginsky and Sergei Kovalev—served their sentences in isolated camp complexes in the Mordovia and Perm regions.

It was only with the beginning of perestroika, the process of socio-political and economic modernisation of the USSR initiated by state and party leader Michael Gorbachev in early 1986, that the final decline of the Soviet penal camp system began. In 1987, in the spirit of glasnost and perestroika, Gorbachev called in his speech on the 70th anniversary of the October Revolution for light to be cast on the "dark spots" of Soviet history and for the taboo aspects of Soviet history and Stalinism to be addressed.

In the second half of the 1960s, an opposition human rights movement took root in the Russian heartland of the Soviet Union. Poetry readings, which had previously taken place in Moscow's Mayakovsky Square from 1958 to 1960, played an important role in their development. The so-called Glasnost demonstration in Moscow in 1965, protests against the arrest of the poets Andrei Sinyavsky and Yuli Daniel in 1965/66 and the conviction of Alexander Ginsburg in 1968, and the suppression of the Prague Spring in Czechoslovakia were important milestones for the opposition movement.

In the following years, increasing numbers of dissidents, such as Andrei Sakharov, Sergei Kovalev and Igor Shafarevich, became involved in the samizdat publication "A Chronicle of Current Events". During the 1970s, so-called Helsinki groups emerged in several Soviet republics calling for the human rights agreed at the 1975 CSCE Helsinki Final Conference. In the course of perestroika and the gradual easing of Soviet repressive policies, these activities expanded considerably. In many cities, human rights groups such as Memorial, the Sakharov Centre in Moscow and other civil society organisations were formed to address issues that had been hushed up for decades, especially the truth about the "Great Terror" and the Gulag and their millions of victims.

In many places, local initiatives succeeded in erecting monuments commemorating the victims of terror and repression, and exhibitions in the local museums were able to address previously glorified or taboo topics. These included not only the Gulag and Stalinist repression but also the wars in Afghanistan and Chechnya, as evidenced, for example, by the museum run in Yekaterinburg by veterans of the Afghan occupation. Official commemorative days were introduced in memory of the victims of repression, such as 5 August, the day on which the "Great Terror" was officially ordered in 1937, and 30 October, which became the Day of Remembrance of the Victims of Political Repressions.

Since the rise to power of Vladimir Putin, a former KGB officer, in 2000, the conditions for an independent historical reappraisal have become steadily less favourable. On the one hand, the official view of Russian history has shifted away from the "negative" sides of Soviet and Russian history in favour of a more positive interpretation. This has led to the downplaying of Stalinist repression and the associated reinterpretation of state-sponsored persecution, as has taken place, for example, in the only Gulag museum found in a historical camp, Perm-36. This has not been a consistent trend, however, since the state-run Gulag Museum in Moscow, which opened in 2015, does not follow the lead of Perm in its rewriting of the history of the camps and persecution at the hands of the state.

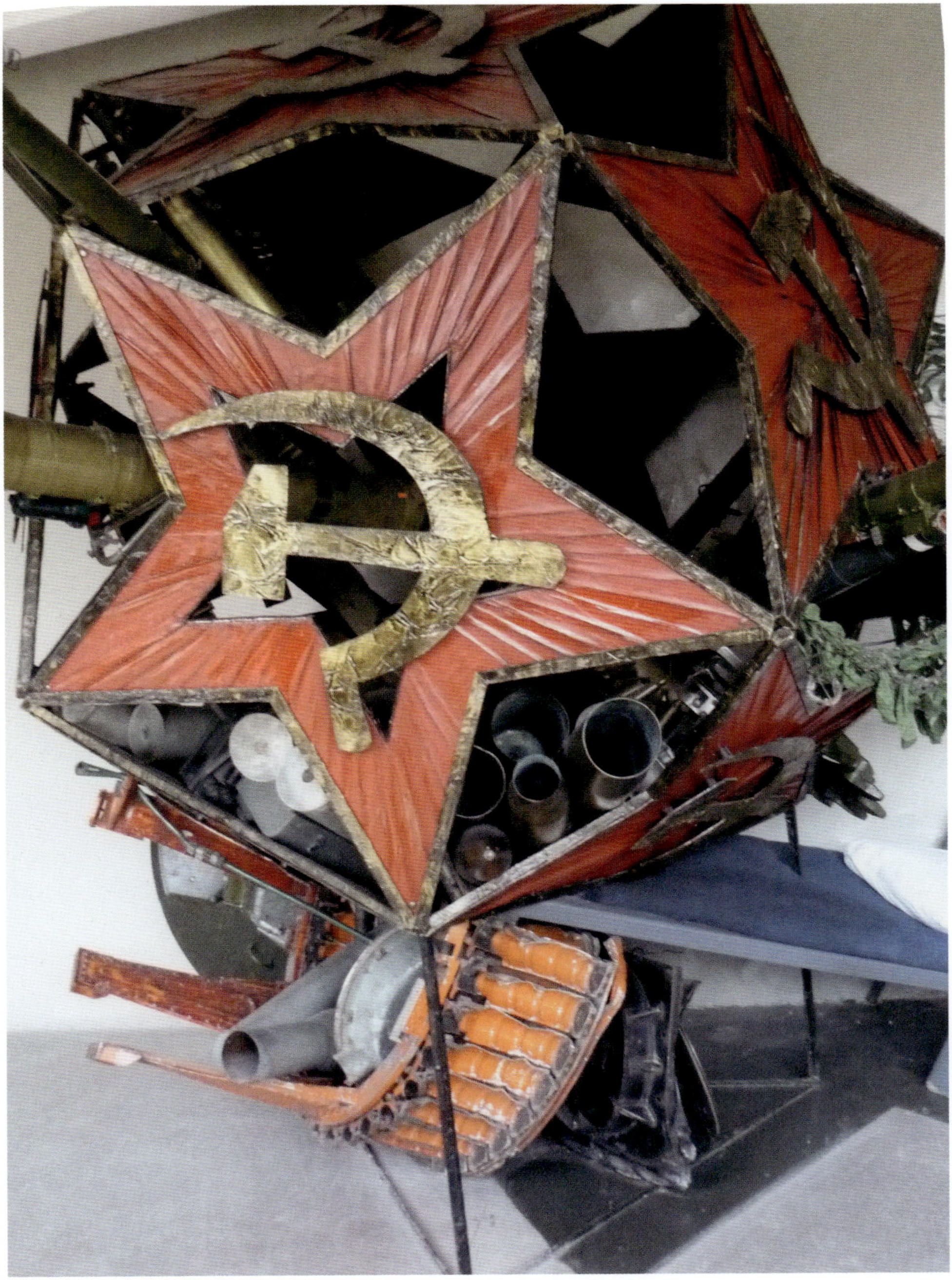

Memorial in the exhibition
"Weapons Behind Red Star"

Nevertheless, non-governmental organisations are increasingly being hindered in their work and put under pressure to register their activities pursuant to the "Law on Foreign Agents" passed in 2012. In late 2016, Memorial was declared a "foreign agent". In 2016, the well-known memorial activist Yuri Dimitriev, who was instrumental in locating Stalin-era mass graves in Karelia, was arrested. In a development that can hardly be written off as coincidence, a spurious study published by Petrozavodsk University at the time of his arrest declared that the mass graves found in Sandarmokh were not the result of NKVD killings but were instead the final resting place of prisoners of war killed by Finnish troops.

In parallel with the continued intimidation and obstruction of independent organisations such as Memorial, state institutions such as the History Memory Foundation were established in

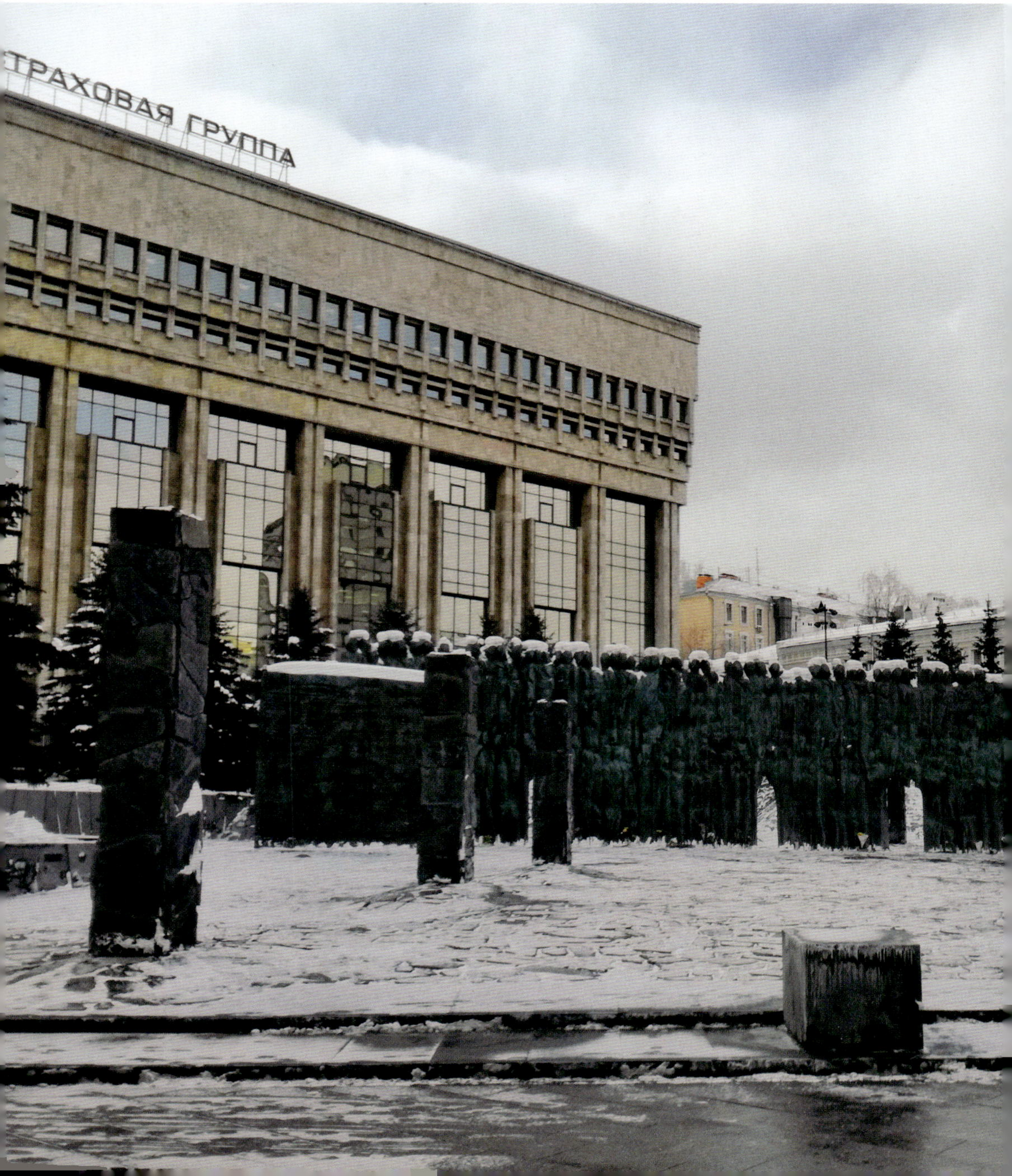

2008 to disseminate official government accounts of the country's history. Evidence of the self-contradictory nature of Russian policy regarding the culture of remembrance was provided by the inauguration of "The Wall of Grief", a state-funded monument to the victims of political impression, at the intersection of Garden Ring Road and Academician Sakharov Avenue in central Moscow on 31 October 2017.

An overview of the monuments in memory of the victims of Stalinist terror can be found in Anna Kaminsky's book "Erinnerungsorte an den Massenterror 1937/38" (Memorial Sites for the Mass Terror), Berlin 2007.

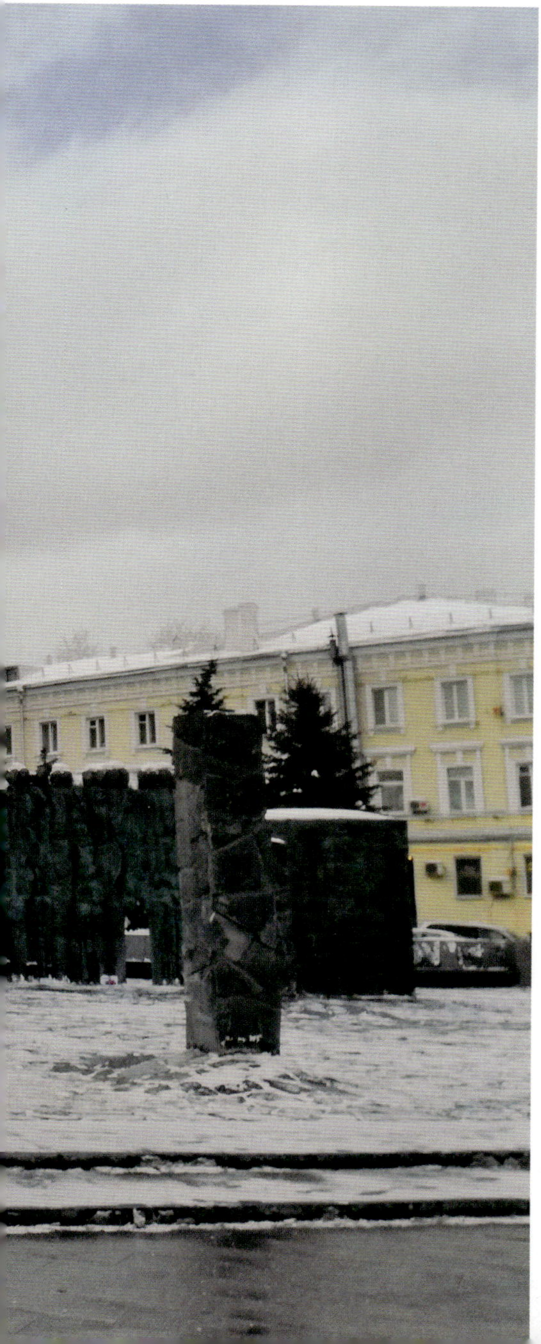

◄
"The Wall of Grief" in Moscow

Donskoy Cemetery

Moscow. Donskoy Cemetery, directly adjoining the monastery of the same name, is one of the largest and most important burial sites in Moscow.

At the beginning of the 20th century, the cemetery was considerably expanded. The construction of the church of St. Seraphim of Sarov and Anna of Kashin, which was completed and consecrated in 1914, began in 1904 on the area known as the New Donskoy Cemetery. After 1917, the church was closed and the first crematorium in the city was later installed in the building. The complex was commissioned in 1927, on the occasion of the 10th anniversary of the October Revolution, and remained in use until the early 1970s.

The Soviet forces of repression used both the cemetery and the crematorium to eliminate all traces of the victims of political persecution, whose remains were cremated here and buried in mass graves. The first documented cremations were carried out by the Soviet secret police, the NKVD, in early 1935. However, the possibility cannot be ruled out that the facility was already in use at an earlier date, probably directly after its commissioning in 1927. At that time, however, the individuals brought by the secret police to Yauzskaya Hospital and Vagankovo Cemetery were mostly those who had been sentenced to death.

A first major wave of cremations began in 1936 and lasted until the beginning of 1937. The main victims were people who had been wrongfully sentenced by the Military Collegium of the Supreme Court when the Great Terror began. More than 4,000 cremations have been documented for 1937 alone. The sheer number of executions was too much for the crematorium to handle, so several hundred non-cremated bodies were buried anonymously in mass graves.

Executions were mainly carried out in the Lubyanka Building and the Butryka and Lefortovo prisons, and the bodies brought to Donskoy for cremation immediately afterwards. Burtryka was probably the only one of these to continue to host executions after the war. There is also documentary evidence of executions in other court buildings and prisons.

A special unit of the secret police was in charge of the cremations, overseeing both the bureaucratic procedure and the disposal of the ashes. According to the director of the cemetery, who served in the post for many years before being arrested in 1941, he was personally entrusted with scattering the ashes in precisely defined places around the crematorium. The existence of the mass graves was known only to him and the members of the secret police involved.

► The church in Donskoy Cemetery housed the only crematorium in Moscow after 1927.

The total number of victims of political persecution at Donskoy Cemetery is impossible to determine with precision. Research by Memorial and historians shows at least 7,000 cremations, but the actual number is estimated at ten to eleven thousand. The ashes were removed to various parts of the cemetery over the decades, necessitating the creation of three mass graves. The ash fields for the years 1935 – 1941 are located at the back of the cemetery, immediately adjacent to the graves for the years 1942 – 1944. The casualties of the years 1945 to 1953 found their final resting place in the immediate vicinity of the crematorium.

The three mass graves at Donskoy Cemetery were discovered in the late 1980s. In the course of efforts to clear the names of politically persecuted individuals in Moscow, mainly backed by the Cheremushkinsk group led by Mikhail Borisovich Mindlin, the search also began for the graves of those executed between 1937 and 1953. Research in the archives of the former

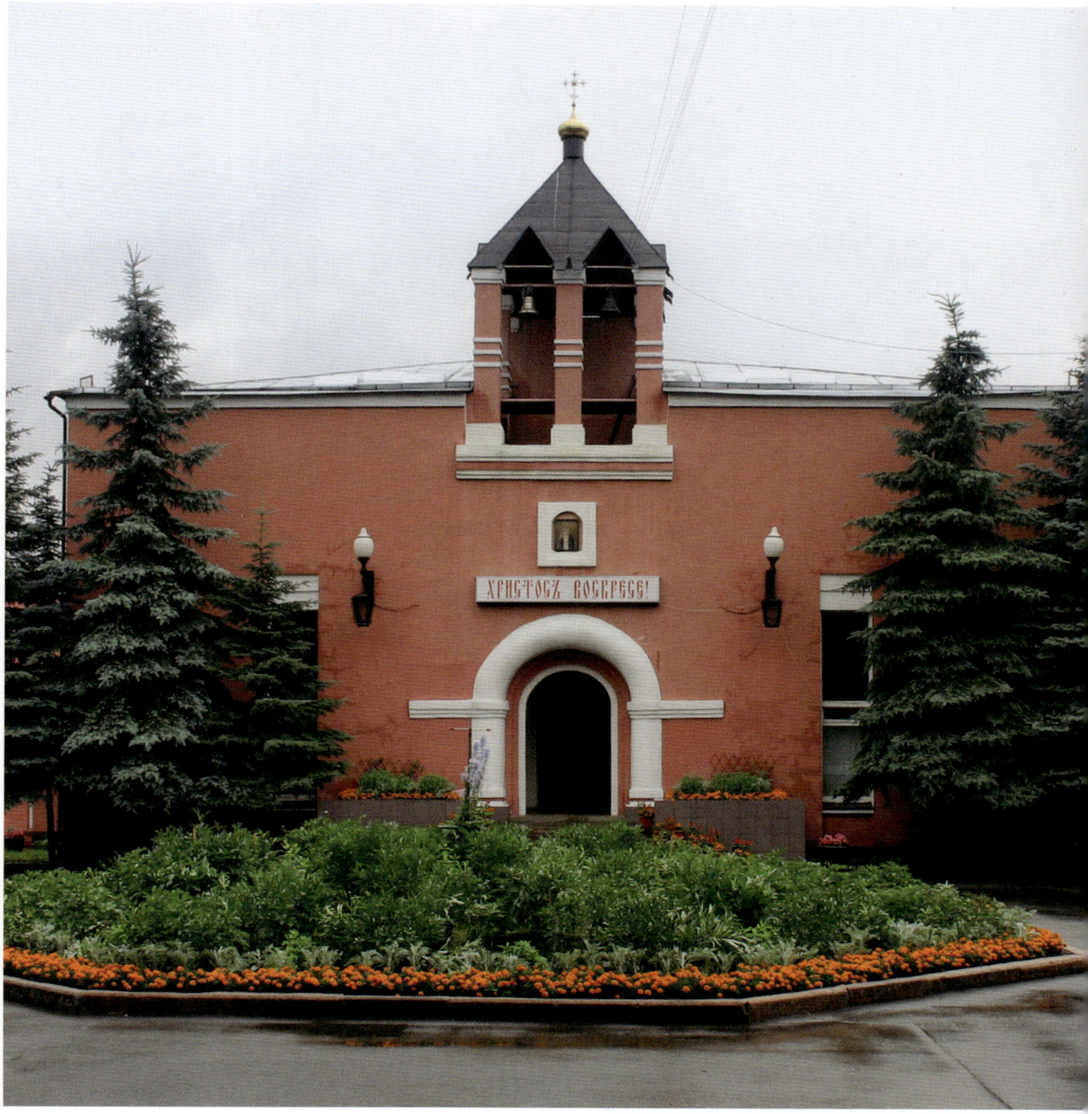

secret police confirmed the existence of three mass graves where the dead of various periods of persecution had been interred. The installation of the first memorial stone on the grave of the victims of the mass terror of 1937/38 in August 1991 marked the beginning of the gradual transformation of the plots into memorial sites that would pay due honour to the victims.

In the course of the inauguration of the memorial to the victims of the "Leningrad affair", one of the largest cleansing campaigns in the party and state apparatus of the Soviet Union after the mass terror of 1937/38, a commemorative site was created on Mass Grave No. 3. In the centre of the circular memorial is a sculpture of a kneeling woman. In front of her is a plaque commemorating the victims of persecution from 1945 to 1953.

Several national memorial stelae around the square commemorate Hungarian, Polish, Japanese, Austrian and German victim groups. 927 German citizens who were extradited from the GDR to the Soviet Union were sentenced to death by Soviet military tribunals between 1950 and 1953, shot dead in Moscow and buried in Donskoy Cemetery. In the presence of relatives of the victims, a memorial stone for the German victims of Stalinist persecution was officially inaugurated in July 2005.

Memorial Moscow, the Historical Research Institute Facts & Files and the Federal Foundation for the Study of the Communist Dictatorship in Eastern Germany have published comprehensive documentation with short biographies of the German victims entitled "Erschossen in Moscow..." (Shot Dead in Moscow...).

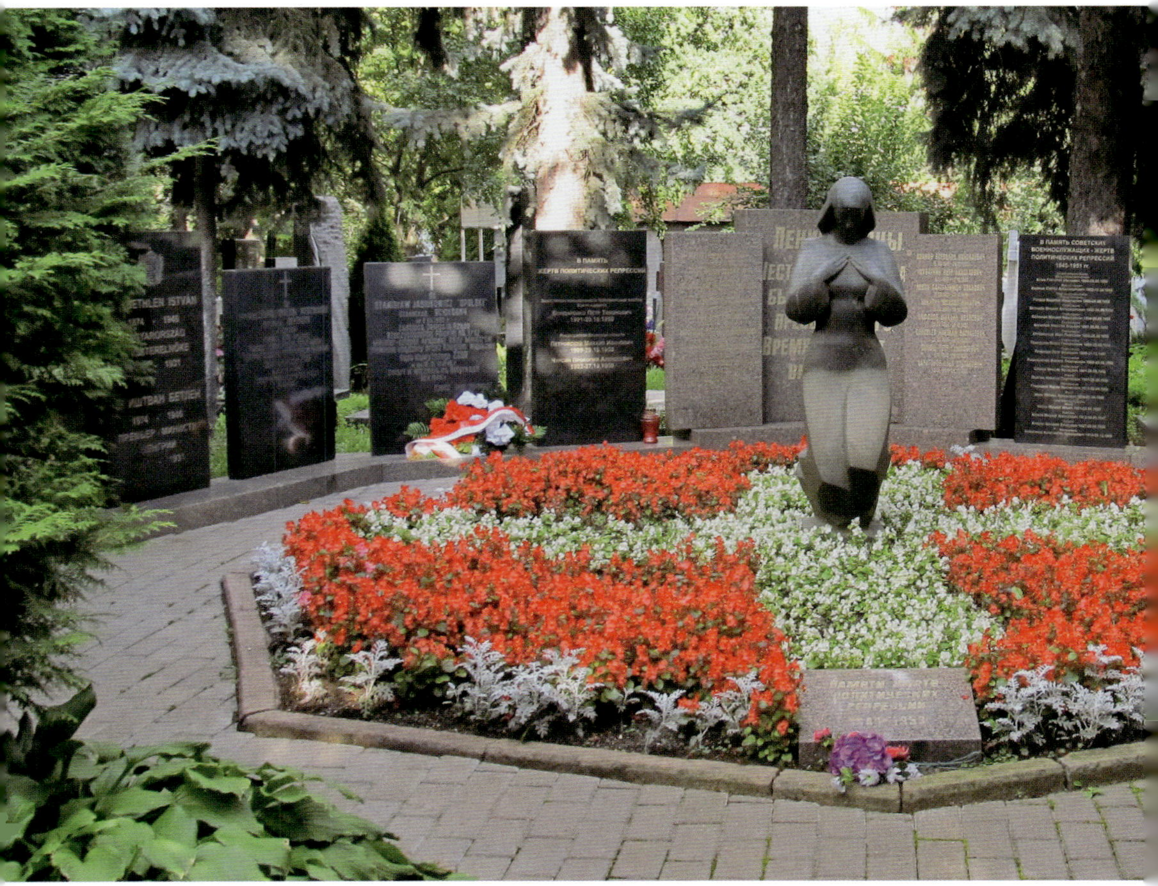

The memorial was made possible with funding from the Moscow City Government. Today, all three mass graves feature numerous individual and official commemorative markers. Every year on 30 October, the Russian Day of Remembrance of the Victims of Political Repressions, memorial ceremonies are held in the cemetery.

Inscription on the memorial stone at Mass Grave No. 3,
Russian: Памяти жертв политических репрессий 1945–1953

English: *In memory of the victims of political repression 1945–1953*

Mass Grave No. 3 in Donskoy Cemetery

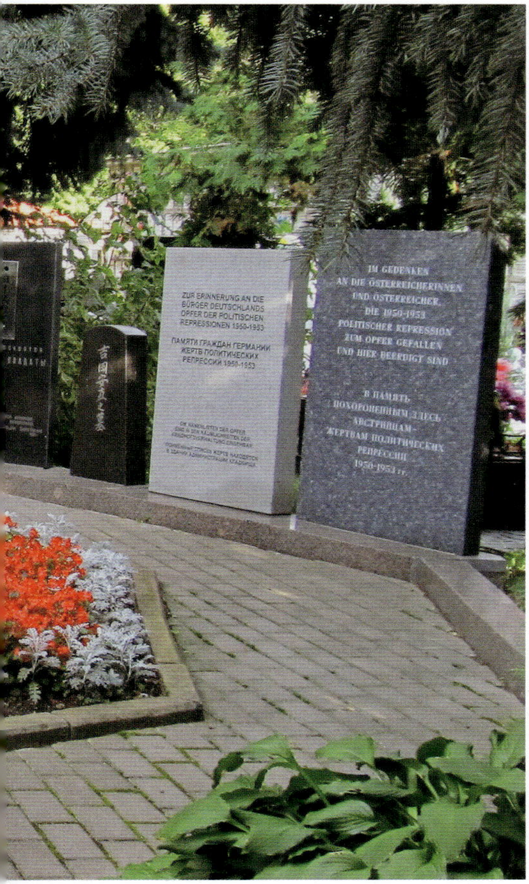

Inscription on the memorial stone for the victims of political repression at Mass Grave No.1,
Russian: Здесь захоронены останки невинно замученых и расстрелянных жертв политических репрессий 1930–1942. Вечная им память! // Общая могила № 1. Захоронение невостребованных прахов с 1930–1942 включ.

English: *Here lie the remains of innocent victims of political repression who were tortured and shot 1930–1942. Eternal memory! // Shared Grave No. 1. Grave of the unclaimed ashes. 1930–1942*

The **inscription** on the memorial stone for the German victims of political repression,
German / Russian: *Zur Erinnerung an die / Bürger Deutschlands Opfer der politischen / Repressionen 1950–1953*
Памяти граждан Германии / жертв политических / репрессий 1945–1953

English: *In memory of the citizens of Germany who fell victim to political repression 1950–1953*

Die Namenslisten der Opfer / sind in den Räumlichkeiten der / Friedhofsverwaltung einsehbar
Поимённые списки жертв находятся в здании администрации кладбища

English: *The lists of names of the victims are available to view in the cemetery administration building*

Location: Moscow, ulitsa Ordzhonikidse 4
Internet: www.topos.memo.ru/donskoe-kladbishche-novoe

Butovsky Poligon Memorial

Butovo. The Butovsky Poligon Memorial is located on the south-western outskirts of Moscow, near the village of DroshiNo. The Butovo Firing Range was located on what used to be a private estate that belonged to Muscovite merchant Soloviev until 1917. Between 1920 and 1995, it was a restricted area under the administration of the Soviet, and later Russian, secret police. In 1995, ownership was transferred to the Moscow Patriarchate of the Russian Orthodox Church.

Between 1937 and 1938, at the height of the mass terror, more than 21,000 people were shot and buried in mass graves by the NKVD. Among them were over a thousand clergymen. More than a third of all the people shot in Butovo were also prisoners of the Dmitlag, who were set to work on the construction of the Moskva-Volga Canal and executed once the canal was completed in 1938.

Numerous politicians, scientists and artists from pre-revolutionary Russia found their final resting place in Butovo. Among them were the President of the 2nd State Duma F.A. Golovin, the former Governor-General of Moscow V.F. Dzhunkovsky and his adjutant V.S. Gadon, and N.N. Danilevsky, one of the Russian aviation pioneers. Numerous members of the old Russian nobility and the tsarist army were also buried here. The lack of reliable sources means that the exact number of deaths is still unknown.

Since 1993, various restoration initiatives, including Memorial Moscow and the Russian Orthodox Church, have been working to transform the cemetery into a fitting memorial to the victims of the mass terror of 1937/38. When public debate about Stalinist crimes began under Gorbachev in the late 1980s, former prisoners, relatives, historians and journalists set about investigating the fates of the victims of mass terror. The first casualty lists were compiled after the archives were opened in the early 1990s.

The former killing ground of the NKVD in Butovo was first unearthed by the group "For the preservation of the memory of the victims of repression", founded in 1992 under the leadership of former Kolyma prisoner Mikhail Borisovich Mindlin. In June 1993, a first inspection of the cemetery took place after an expert commission of the Russian secret service, the FSB, had officially confirmed the existence of the "Butovo" execution site.

The first memorial stone was inaugurated on 10 October 1993 in the presence of numerous relatives and survivors of the mass terror. In the former secret service school at the edge of the cemetery, the parish set up a Sunday school, which also houses a small exhibition on the history of the cemetery. This is primarily dedicated to the fates of the religious dignitaries of the Russian Orthodox Church who

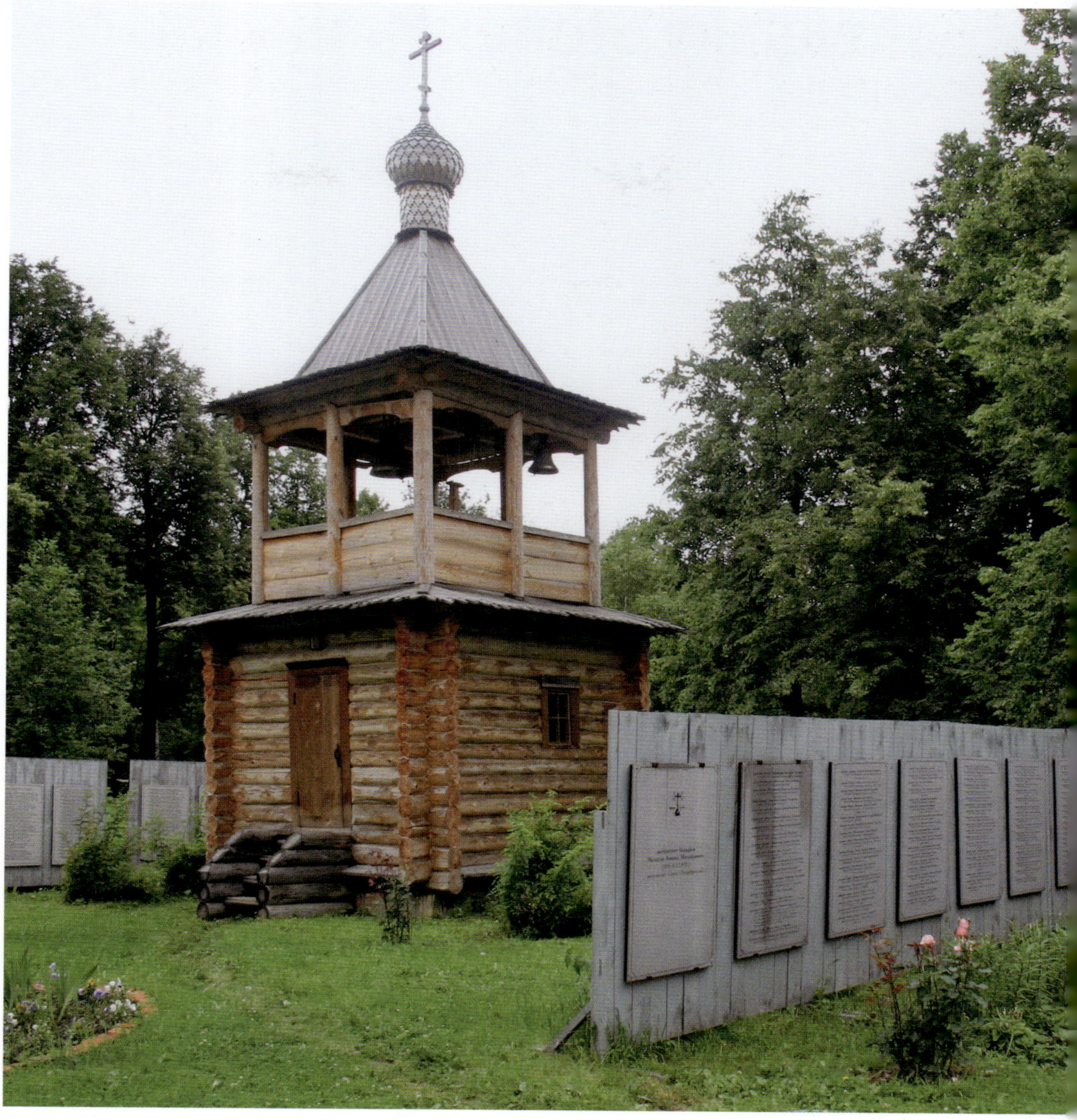

were shot in Butovo and who make up one of the largest groups of victims.

Today's memorial site includes the mass graves marked in the nineties, a wooden church—a "church on the blood"—consecrated in 1996, a wooden bell tower and a votive cross erected in May 1994. Numerous other commemorative markers have been placed in memory of the more than one thousand ecclesiastical dignitaries executed in Butovo.

Memorial chapel and plaques listing the names of the executed clergymen

Location: Butovo, ulitsa Yubileynaya
Internet: www.martyr.ru

Solovetsky Stone

Moscow. The Solovetsky Stone for the victims of political repression was inaugurated on 30 October 1990 in front of the headquarters of the former Soviet secret police at the edge of Lubyanka Square. The stone is one of the first great memorials to the victims of political persecution on the territory of the former Soviet Union. It was initiated by the Memorial Society, which brought the stone to Moscow and placed it on a marble plinth.

The Moscow City Government contributed financially to the enterprise, which was, however, largely funded from donations collected by Memorial. The design for the memorial, initially intended as a temporary solution, was provided by the artist S.I. Smirnov and realised by architect V. E. Korsi. An inscription explaining the meaning of the stone is engraved on the base. In the 1990s, a panel was erected at the edge of the square, providing further information in Russian and English.

When the Memorial Society was founded in 1988, the demand for a monument to the victims of political persecution in the Soviet Union became one of its most important concerns. The Soviet state and party leadership resisted the construction of such a memorial for a long time but eventually had to give in to public pressure, whereupon the project was initiated by Memorial. In the spring of 1990, when an expedition of the Soviet Memorial Initiative in Arkhangelsk set sail for the Solovetsky Islands to find a stone for a memorial to the victims of political repression in the city, Memorial joined this enterprise and ordered its own stone for the Moscow memorial.

The inauguration took place with the support of the Moscow City Government. The symbolic site in front of the headquarters of the Soviet secret police, known as Lubyanka, was deliberately chosen. Even before the monument was inaugurated, the name of the square had been changed back from Dzerzhynsky Square to its original name, Lubyanka Square, although the monument to the founder of the Soviet secret police Felix Dzerzhinsky was left standing until August 1991. The Solovetsky Stone brought to Moscow was placed a short distance away from Lubyanka Square in a garden in front of the Polytechnic Museum. Thousands of people filed through the streets of Moscow for the inauguration on 30 October 1990. Presiding over the inauguration were former Solovetsky prisoner Oleg Volkov and the exiled priest Gleb Yakunin. Anatoly Zhigulin and Sergei Kovalev spoke on behalf of Memorial. The intention was for the unhewn stone to be replaced in time by a new, "finished" memorial. Despite various initiatives in the following years, the temporary Solovetsky Stone remained in place, but its symbolic significance endured and increased.

Inscription on the stone
Russian: Этот камень с территории Соловецкого лагерия особого назначения доставлен обществом »Мемориал« и установлен в память о миллионах жертв тоталитарного режима. 30. октябрь 1990 года День политзаключенного в СССР

English: *This stone from the territory of the Solovetsky camp was brought here for special use and erected in memory of the millions of victims of the totalitarian regime. 30 October 1990 / Day of Political Prisoners in the USSR*

Inscription on the information board
Russian: За годы террора в Москве по ложным политическим обвинениям были расстреляны более 40 тысяч человек. В 1921–1926 годах расстреляных хоронили на территории кладбища Язской больницы (ныне больница № 223), в 1926–1935 г. г.— на Ваганьковском кладбище, а начиная с 1934 года и по крайней мере до 1950-х г. г. Расстрелянных кремовали в Московском (Донском) крематории. Начиная с 1937 года в качестве мест захоронений использовались также два полигона НКВД в ближнем Подмосковье—в Бутово и близ совхоза »Коммунарка«

English: *During the years of terror, more than 40,000 people were shot dead in Moscow on trumped-up political charges. In 1921–1926, those who were shot were buried in the cemetery of Yauzskaya Hospital (now Hospital No. 223), in 1926–1935 in Vagankovo Cemetery. From 1934 until at least the 1950s, those who were shot were cremated in the Moscow (Donskoy) crematorium and buried in mass graves. From 1937 onwards, two firing ranges of the NKVD in the suburbs of Moscow—Butovo and a site near the Sovkhoz Kommunarka—were also used as burial grounds.*

Location: Moscow, Novaya Ploshchad 3/4

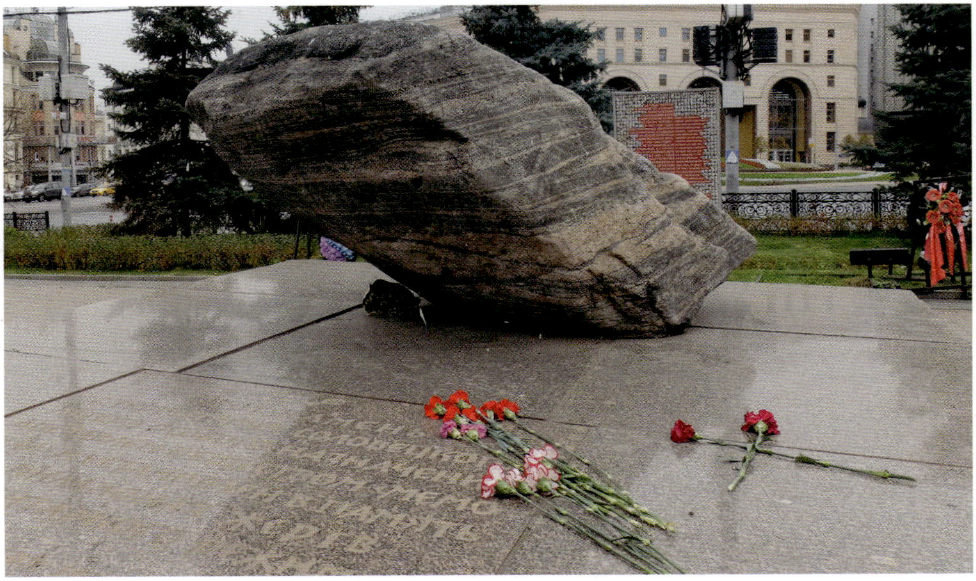

Solovetsky Stone for the victims of political repression

Memorial: The International Historical, Educational, Charitable and Human Rights Society

Moscow. Memorial, the oldest and best-known human rights organisation in Russia, arose from the "Group for the Preservation of the Memory of Soviet Repression Victims", which was founded in 1987. At the point of its official constitution at the founding conference in January 1989, Memorial became the first organisation in the Soviet Union not to have been established by party decree; it was instead established independently of the government through the socio-political self-organisation of interested citizens and former political prisoners.

Today, Memorial, whose first chairman was the nuclear physicist, Nobel Peace Prize winner and pioneer of the Soviet dissident movement Andrei Sakharov, maintains a network of over 70 regional and national branches and subsidiary associations in Russia, Ukraine, Belarus, Kazakhstan, Latvia, the Czech Republic, Poland, Germany, Italy and France. The organisation's primary tasks include the historical reappraisal of communist crimes and the preservation of the memory of the victims of political repression.

Since its foundation, another statutory objective of the organisation has been "the complete and public rehabilitation of the victims of repression". To this end, Memorial actively participated in the drafting of the law "On the Rehabilitation of Victims of Political Repression", which came into force in 1991. To this day, the organisation's central fields of activity include social and legal support for the politically persecuted and their relatives as well as assistance in the assertion of claims for compensation and medical care. Every year, Memorial takes part in the memorial events on 30 October, the Day of Remembrance of the Victims of Political Repression in Russia, with the aim of bringing the memory of the victims of the unjust Soviet regime into the focus of public awareness. This day has been celebrated by Soviet political prisoners as a day of solidarity and resistance since 1974, informally at first, and then, following the collapse of the communist regime, officially.

On 30 October 1990, on the initiative of Memorial, the Solovetsky stone was erected on Lubyanka Square, in front of the infamous headquarters and torture prison of the Soviet secret police. Since 2007, the "Return of the Names" event initiated by Memorial has been held here every year on 30 October. Throughout the day, the names of persons executed in Moscow during the years of the "Great Terror" in 1937/38 are read out. Since 1999, the society has sponsored the nationwide secondary school competition entitled "People and History, 20th Century Russia", for which more than 35,000 essays have already been submitted. In addition, Memorial organises and hosts a diverse programme of historical and political education, both independently and in cooperation with partners.

Another special project is the "Virtual Gulag Museum" of the Memorial Research and Education Centre in Saint Petersburg. The online database is a comprehensive compendium of testimonies to the era of Soviet terror. It presents detailed information in English, Russian and German on monuments and memorials as well as the remains of former camp sites.

Since 1990, the premises of Memorial Moscow have housed a museum collection containing more than 4,000 original exhibits of camp art and items of everyday prison life.

In 2004, the organisation was awarded the Alternative Nobel Prize for its work in defending human rights. In 2009, Memorial was awarded the European Parliament's Sakharov Prize for Freedom of Thought. In recent years, however, Memorial has repeatedly faced state restrictions: in October 2016, the organisation was obliged to register as a "foreign agent" on the instructions of the Russian Ministry of Justice in order to continue its activities. The derogatory designation "foreign agent" was introduced by a law passed in 2012 and concerns all institutions that try to "influence public opinion" and receive funds from abroad. This law is controversial because of the associated restrictions on freedom of expression and the activities of independent institutions and not least because the choice of words is reminiscent of the Stalinist era and the "Great Terror".

Location: Moscow, Karetny Riyadh 5/10
Internet: www.memo.ru

The Memorial Society has created a unique archive on the victims of political repression

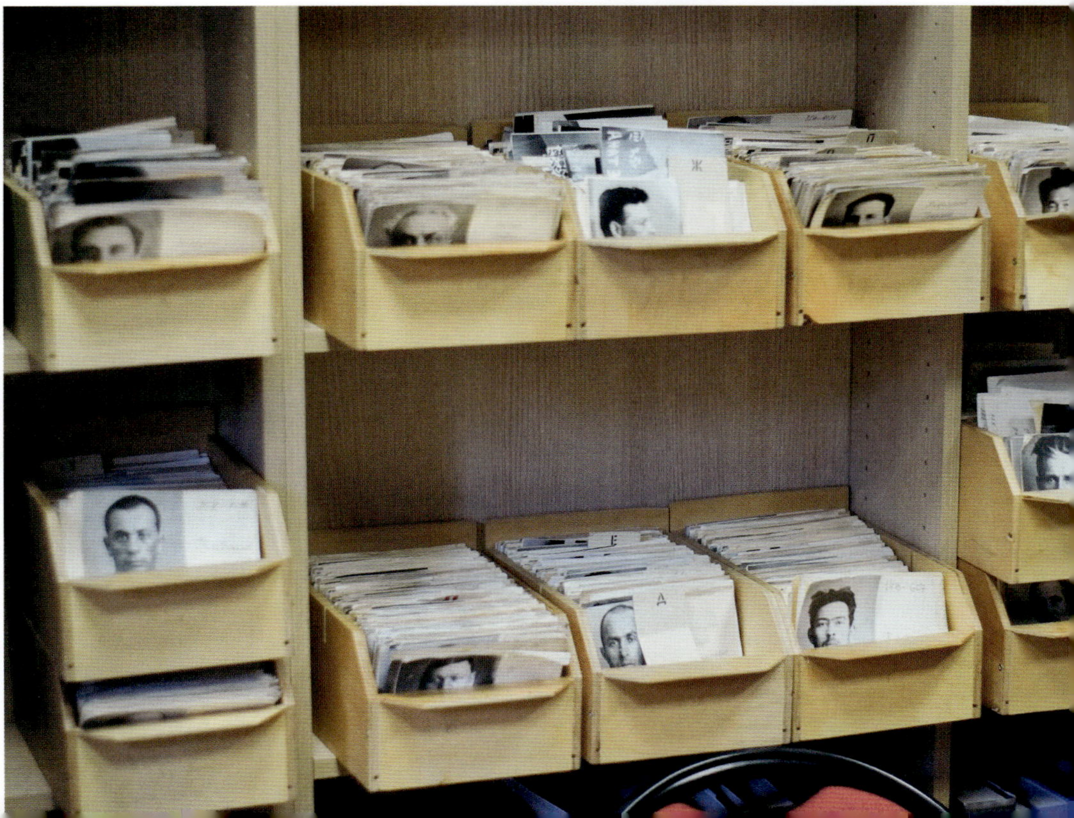

Andrei Sakharov "Peace, Progress, Human Rights" Museum and Public Centre

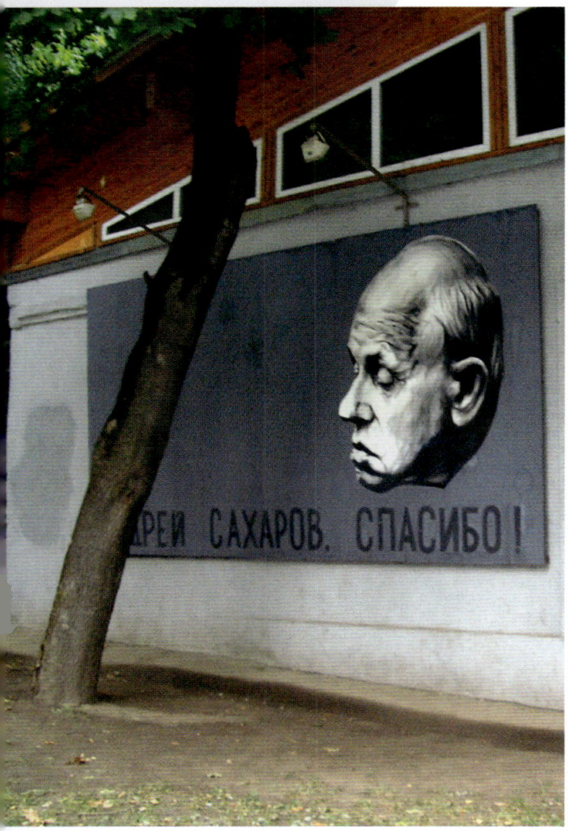

View of the museum façade

Moscow. Founded in 1994, the Andrei Sakharov "Peace, Progress, Human Rights" Museum and Public Centre offers a broad forum for discussions and events relating to current civic, political and cultural challenges. The museum's permanent exhibition sheds light on the history of (un)freedom in the USSR and is dedicated to the life and work of Nobel Peace Prize winner and dissident Andrei Sakharov.

The Sakharov Centre Museum views the history of the Soviet Union from the perspective of political repression. The first part of the exhibition, "Totalitarian Past", divided into four sections, deals with Soviet "mythology and ideology". The mechanisms of the totalitarian system and its effects on society and the individual are examined in detail. The following section, "The Way Through Gulag", uses biographies to cast light on the complex of camps and prisons during the waves of Stalinist persecution. Forms of resistance and defiance are then presented, starting with uprisings in the camps and the anti-Stalinist circles of the post-war period up to the dissident movement of the 1960s and 1970s. The third section regularly hosts temporary exhibitions dealing with the current problems of society in Russia. The final part is dedicated to the biography of Andrei Sakharov and his work.

In addition to the permanent and temporary exhibitions, the centre hosts an extensive library with video and audio collections. The holdings of the centre's museum include around 600 pieces of art—paintings, graphics, drawings and sculptures—an extensive collection of photographs, newspapers and samizdat and the personal effects of well-known Russian dissidents. The Sakharov Foundation organises conferences and seminars and, together with its international partners, the centre offers annual training courses on the protection and enforcement of human rights.

Location: Moscow, Zemlyanoy whale 57
Internet: www.sakharov-center.ru

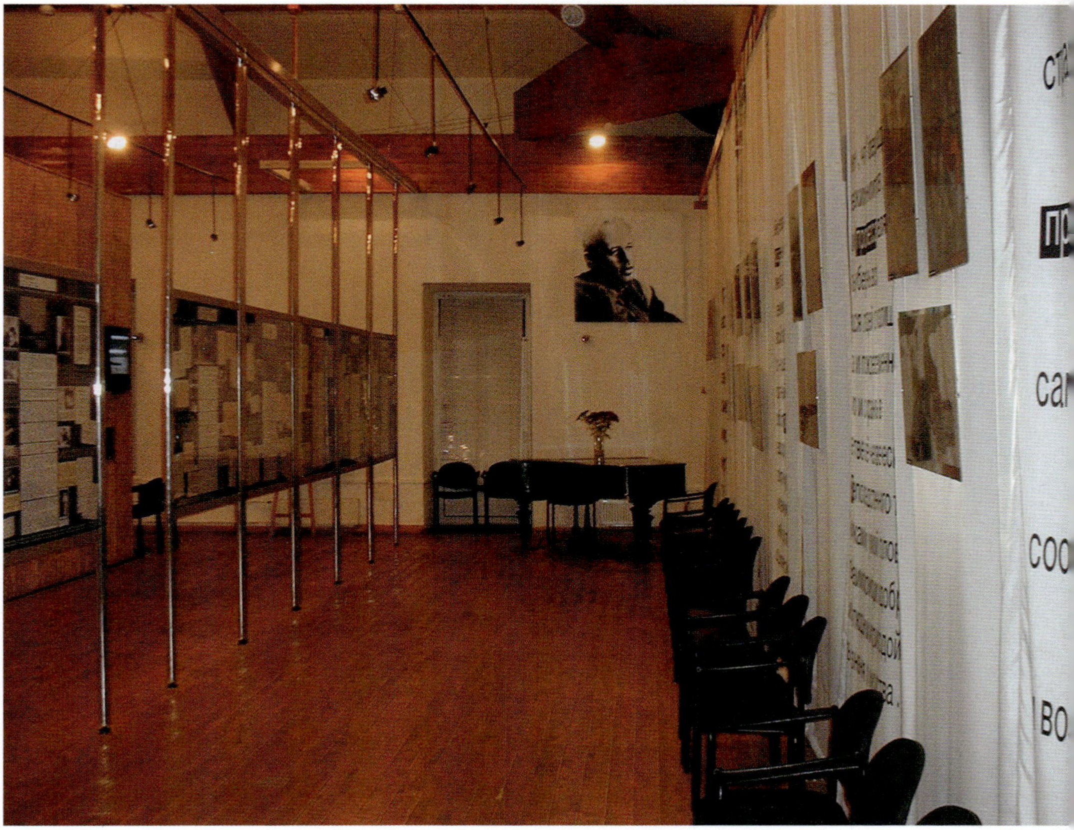

View of the exhibition

Gulag History State Museum

Moscow. The Gulag History State Museum was opened on 30 October 2015, the Day of Remembrance of the Victims of Political Repressions. The idea for the establishment of a museum dealing with the history of the Soviet forced labour camps dates back to an initiative of victims, relatives and historians and the prominent publicist and former camp prisoner Anton Vladimirovich Antonov-Ovseyenko. The museum's mission is to present the history, development and dissolution of the vast system of "correctional labour camps" on the territory of the former Soviet Union.

On more than 860 square metres of exhibition space, central aspects of the system of forced labour camps that shaped Soviet society, politics and the economy for many years are portrayed. The permanent exhibition, "National Memory of the Gulag", illustrates the history of political repression in the Soviet Union and focuses on more than 100 exhibits—everyday objects, documents, photographs, video interviews—collected from 25 museums throughout the country, which give an impression of camp life through the eyes of the Gulag prisoners.

In addition to the permanent and temporary exhibitions, the museum also hosts a research centre and a library. The new building also houses a volunteer centre, a screening room for films and a publication office. The museum owns a document archive with letters and oral histories of former Gulag prisoners and an extensive collection of pieces of art created by camp inmates and contemporary authors by way interpretation of the Soviet history of repression. The educational programme is supplemented by various events on the topic of repression: readings, film screenings, concerts, seminars and presentations. Guided tours through the exhibition are offered in Russian and English.

Location: Moscow, 1. Samotechny pereulok 9, Boulevard 1
Internet: www.gmig.ru

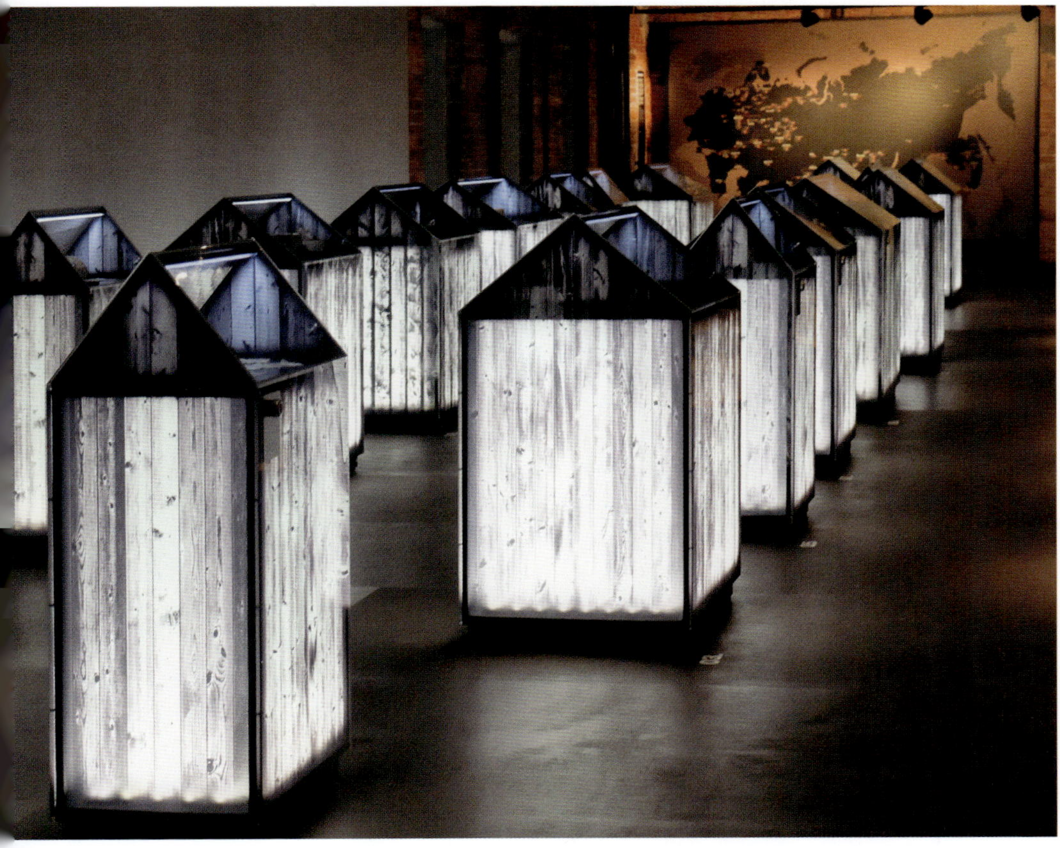

Display cases with exhibits

"Muzeon" Park of Arts

Moscow. Inaugurated in 1992, the Park of Arts is in the immediate vicinity of the Tretyakov Gallery of Modern Art and hosts the country's largest open-air exhibition of sculptures by Soviet and contemporary Russian artists. More than 700 exhibits with historical-political, avant-garde and modern subjects are presented here on more than 23 hectares of exhibition space.

At the end of 1990, the Moscow City Government decided to set up a sculpture garden on the current site of the Park of Arts. Originally planned as an artistic project, this project quickly gained new significance. After the suppression of the August Coup in 1991, the removal began in Moscow of a number of Soviet memorials which had until then been on display at many important sites in the capital.

In October 1991, the Moscow City Duma made the decision to collect the dismantled statues and sculptures and transfer them to the newly established park so that they would not be destroyed. Under the direction of Mikhail Pukemo, the "Muzeon" association was founded in early 1992 to work on the design and administration of the park. The development of the open-air exhibition began in the following years and has not yet been completed.

The historical section of the sculpture park contains numerous well-known monuments and statues that shaped Moscow's cityscape until 1991. One of the best-known exhibits is the sculpture of Felix Edmundovich Dzerzhinsky, the founder of the Soviet secret service. The statue created by renowned Soviet sculptor Yevgeny Vuchetich was unveiled in 1958 in front of the headquarters of what used to be the NKVD headquarters, the Lubyanka Building. It stood there until 24 October 1991, when, to great public dismay, the city government ordered its removal.

A granite statue of Stalin created by Sergei Merkurov in 1938 for the 1939 New York World's Fair served as a reduced-scale model for a sculpture more than 30 metres high to be erected in front of the Bolshoi Theatre in Moscow. Also in the park are statues of Lenin, Kalinin, Sverdlov, Brezhnev and other state and party officials as well as numerous monuments to the so-called Heroes of Socialist Labour.

In addition to "programmatic" works of socialist realism, the "Muzeon" also features works by Soviet avant-garde sculptors who, due to the restrictive Soviet state ideology, were unable to make their works accessible to the general public. These include sculptures by Evgeny Chubarov and numerous metal and stone expressionist pieces by Alexei Grigoryev and Leonid Rabens. On the initiative of the park management, Chubarov designed a memorial in memory of the victims of political repression. Behind a statue of Stalin, the artist erected a wall covered with a metal grid, the interior of which is filled with 283 heads made of stone. Above it is a wooden barrack roof with a barbed wire crown to evoke the camps of the Gulag.

Between 2012 and 2016, the park area was expanded and transformed into a spacious recreational area as part of an urban development initiative. In addition to various guided tours in Russian and English, the park operators also offer training courses, seminars, workshops and discussion events on various cultural and urban policy issues.

Location: Moscow, Krymsky Val 10
Internet: www.muzeon.ru

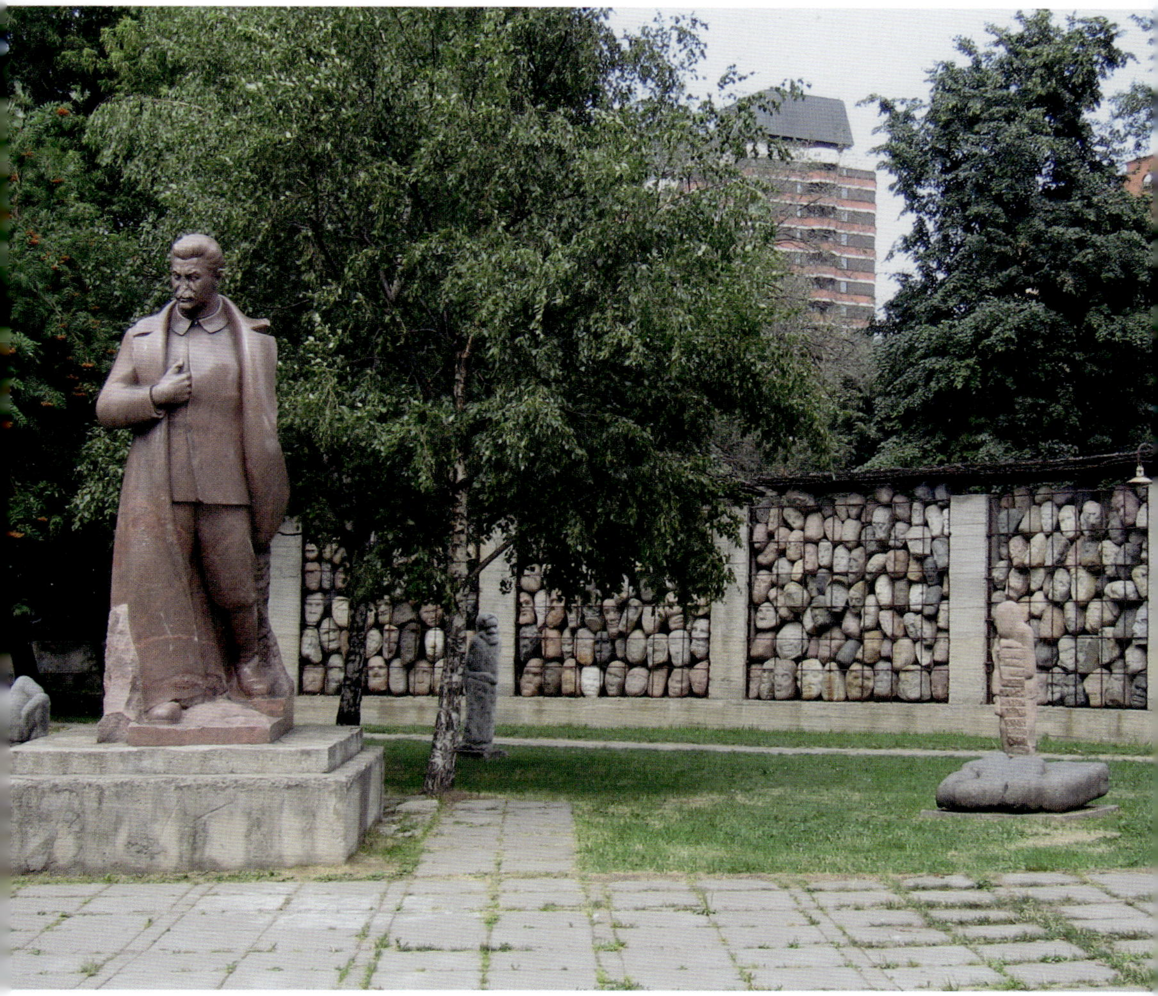

Statue of Stalin in front of the memorial to the victims of repression

Levashovo Memorial Cemetery

Saint Petersburg. Levashovo Memorial Cemetery is located on the outskirts of Saint Petersburg (known as Leningrad until September 1991). Between 1937 and 1954, the area was used by the Soviet secret police as a mass grave for over 24,000 people.

The history of the Levashovo cemetery is closely linked to the beginnings of mass terror in the Soviet Union. At the end of July 1937, the head of the local secret police administration, the NKVD, was ordered to execute more than 4,000 "spies, traitors, and enemies of the people" over the next few months. So that the mortal remains of the victims could be removed as inconspicuously as possible, a site was selected in the Pargolovsk forest near the Levashovo railway station. The area was fenced in during the summer months and closely guarded. The removals of mortal remains, which were then buried here in mass graves, probably began in early September 1937. According to eyewitnesses, although some of the executions were carried out on the spot, most took place in the cellars of the headquarters of the Leningrad NKVD, the "Bolshoy Dom" (Big House).

The exact number of people buried in Levashovo is unknown, as no evidence as to the whereabouts of the dead has been uncovered in the documents of the secret police. According to official figures, a total of 40,000 people were shot in Leningrad and the surrounding area between 1937 and 1938 alone, and about 24,000 were allegedly buried in Levaschovo. Memorial and historians estimate the total number of people buried here until 1954 at up to 45,000. Among them were some well-known scholars, Japanese specialists N. A. Nevsky and D. P. Shukov, Byzantine scholar V. N. Beneshevich, physical theorist M. P. Bronstein, poets Nikolay Oleynikov and Boris Kornilov and philosopher Pavel Florensky. The last victims of Levashovo included the members of the state and party apparatus who fell victim to the so-called "Leningrad affair" and were executed in 1949.

The last burials were probably in 1954. But it was not until 1965 that the head of the secret police, the KGB, of Leningrad ordered the cemetery to be permanently closed. After that date, the area remained restricted and was disguised as a military site. Secret police guarded the area. In the mid-1970s, the fencing was restored, and the mass graves, which had subsided in the meantime, were filled in with sand.

The cemetery was discovered in the spring of 1989 by members of the "Poisk" group ("The Search") under the direction of V. T. Muravsky, which had been searching for mass graves from the 1930s in the area covered by the Saint

"Moloch of Totalitarianism" memorial by the field of graves

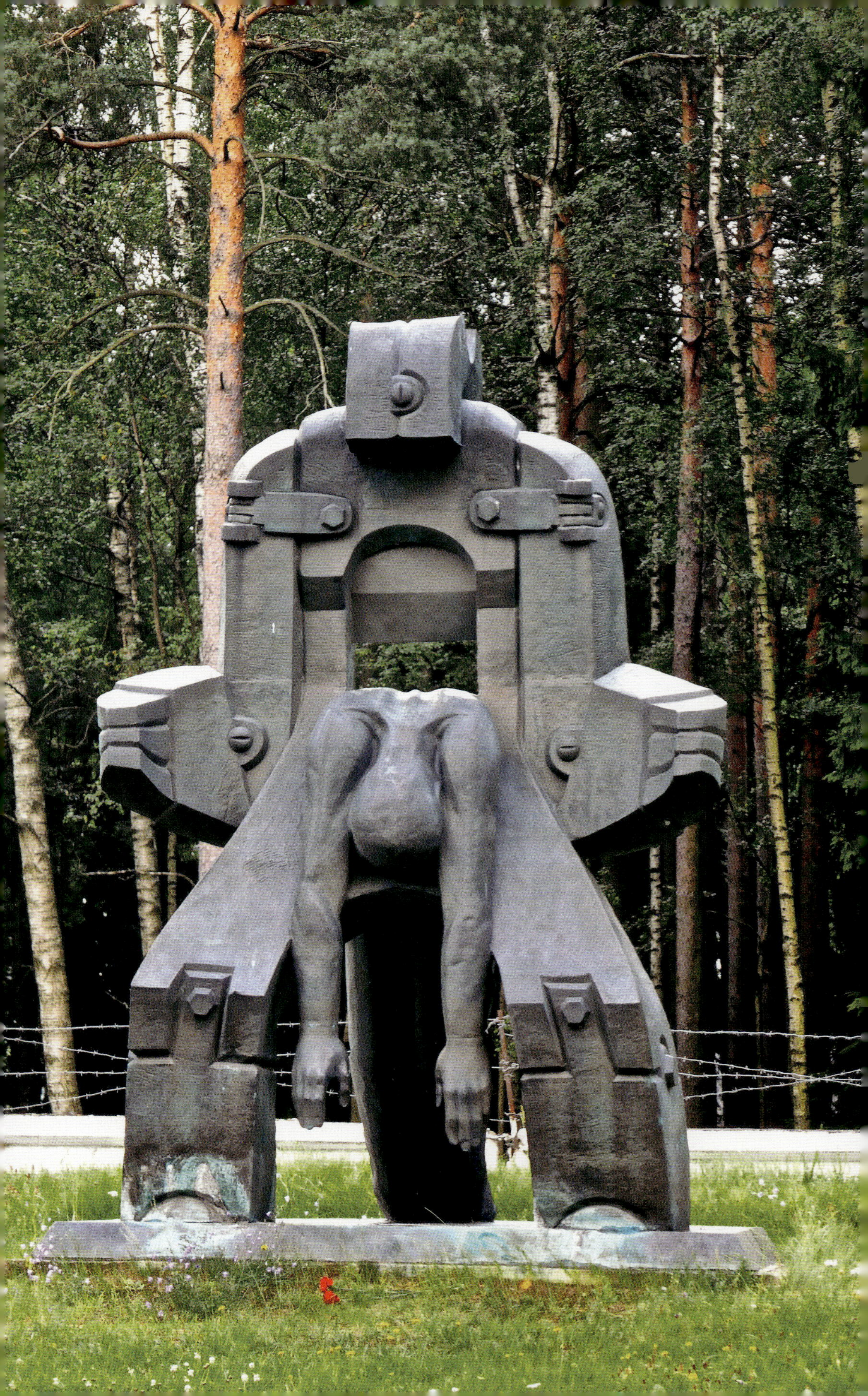

Petersburg section of Memorial since 1988. The Levashovo meadows, to which access was still restricted, were identified from testimonies given by contemporary witnesses. After these results became known, a fact-finding commission was set up by the Leningrad city administration in June 1989 that was officially tasked with the discovery of mass graves.

This commission submitted an official request to the KGB for clarification of the history of the Levashovo cemetery, which was rejected on the grounds of a lack of documents. However, the simultaneous handover of the first death lists from the secret police archives in Leningrad and Moscow confirmed the suspicions. On 18 July 1989, the city administration officially recognized the site as a memorial cemetery for the victims of political repression. In the autumn of that year, the restricted area was opened to a limited public and a first memorial service was held on 21 October 1989. On the initiative of victims' associations and the churches, a memorial stone, which no longer exists, was erected during the service. In the following months, geologists from Leningrad and Moscow carried out investigations and discovered numerous mass graves in the middle and at the northern end of the site. On 1 June 1990, the KGB officially transferred ownership of the site to the city of Leningrad. A group of nine architects and artists led by A. G. Lelyakov was commissioned to develop concepts for the transformation of Levashovo into a fitting memorial.

Since then, various victims' associations, the city administration, and victims and their relatives have been working on the construction of a memorial. To commemorate the victims of repression, a first exhibition on the history of the cemetery and the mass terror in Leningrad was opened on 30 October 1993 in the former guard house, organised by members of the "Association of Victims of Unlawful Repression" under L. A. Bartashesky.

In the following years, the development of the area began. Since the opening of the cemetery, countless individual and commemorative markers have been created. With the inauguration of the memorial "Moloch of Totalitarianism" on 15 May 1996 by the mayor of Saint Petersburg, Anatoly Sobchak, the cemetery was given a central memorial. The development work has not yet been completed, but the Levashovo Memorial is open to the public. Its offices and a small exhibition are located in the former guard's building.

Location: Saint Petersburg,
Gorskoye shosse 135
Internet: www.gulagmuseum.org

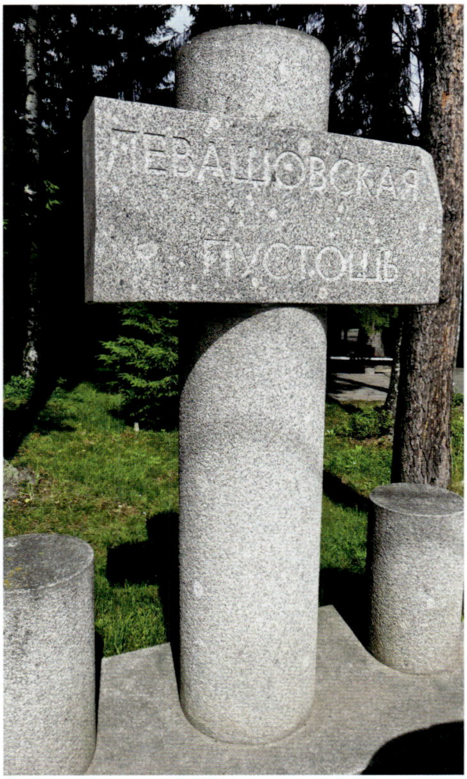

◄
Entrance to Levashovo Memorial Cemetery

State Museum of the Political History of Russia

Saint Petersburg. The State Museum of the Political History of Russia was opened to the public in 1920 as the State Revolution Museum. The museum is dedicated to the political, economic and cultural transformation processes of the 19th to 21st centuries in Russia and highlights the most important stages of change in the country's history. The museum's holdings include numerous original objects relating to the political parties and social movements, the central state bodies of the country (State Duma, Federal Council and Government) and the institutions of the individual members of the Federation.

The permanent main exhibition is divided into two major thematic units: "Man and Power in Russia in the 19th—21st Centuries" and "Soviet Epoch: Between Utopia and Reality". When passing through the first part of the exhibition, which consists of 25 interactively designed modules, visitors are informed about the development of central political trends and key events in Russian history. The decisive events and consequences of the February Revolution of 1905 and the "Great Socialist October Revolution" of 1917, as it was called by the Bolsheviks, are examined in detail. Also portrayed are the horrors of the "Red" and "White Terror" during the civil war years as well as the caesuras that these historical upheavals caused in the individual lives of people. Among other things, the causes and effects of forced industrialisation and the significance of the Gulag camp industrial complex for politics, economy and society in the country are illustrated. Also discussed are the course and significance of the "Great Patriotic War" in the Soviet Union as well as aspects of war communism and the New Economic Policy, forced collectivisation in agriculture and the phenomenon of the Soviet nomenklatura.

Other topics include the "thaw" initiated by head of state and party Nikita Khrushchev—a policy of cultural and social de-Stalinisation—and the modernisation course initiated by Mikhail Gorbachev under the slogans "glasnost" and "perestroika". The last block is devoted to developments since the failed coup in August 1991. It concludes with a presentation of the political and social conditions in the Russian Federation in the 1990s, which culminated in Vladimir Putin's accession to power at the end of 1999.

The second major part of the main exhibition, "Soviet Epoch: Between Utopia and Reality", sheds light on the everyday life and work of several generations under the changing policies of the political leadership, tracing the ideological pathos that accompanied life in all areas and outlining the forms of resistance chosen by human rights activists and dissidents in response to the authoritarian values and norms of the state.

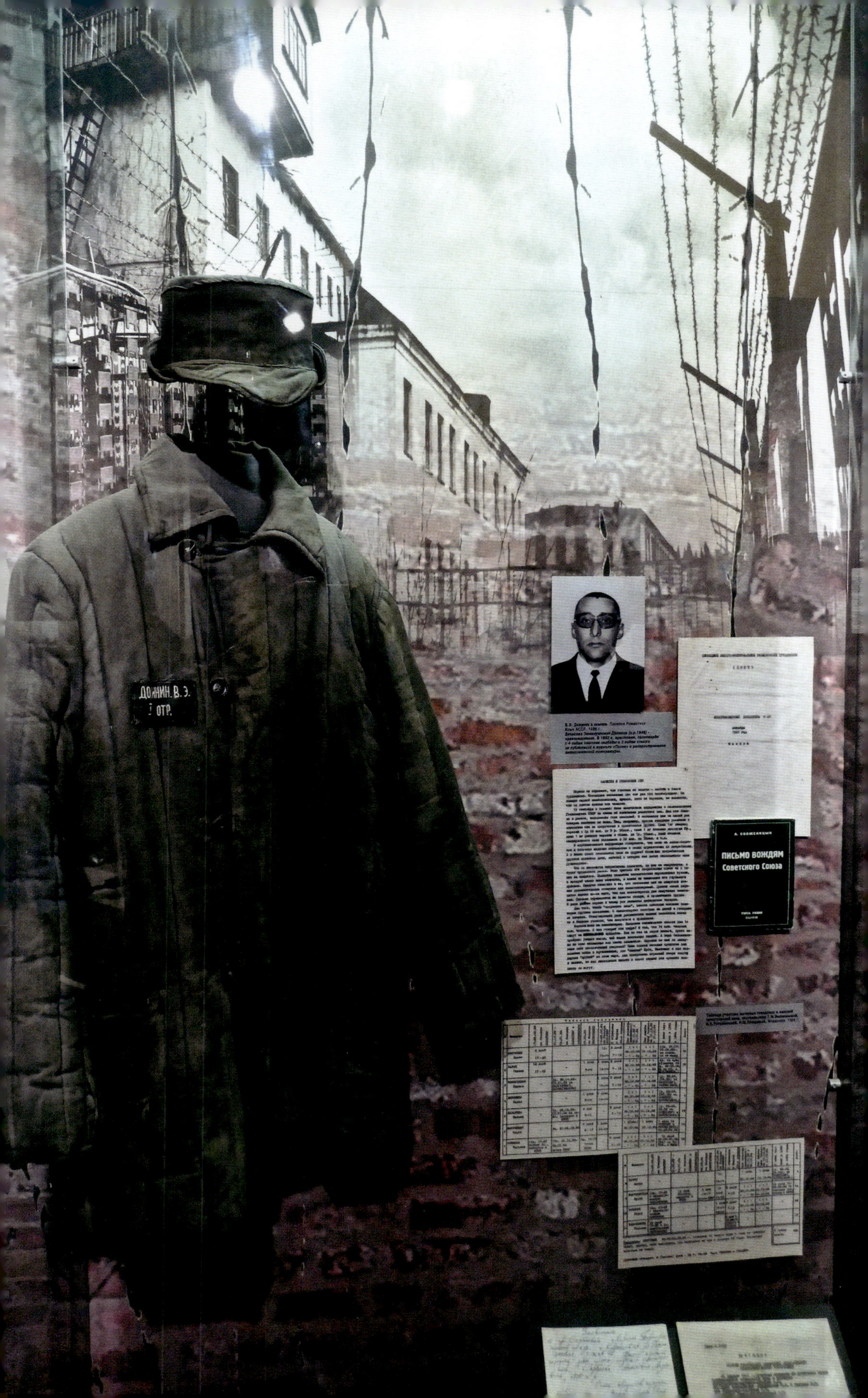
ПИСЬМО ВОЖДЯМ
Советского Союза

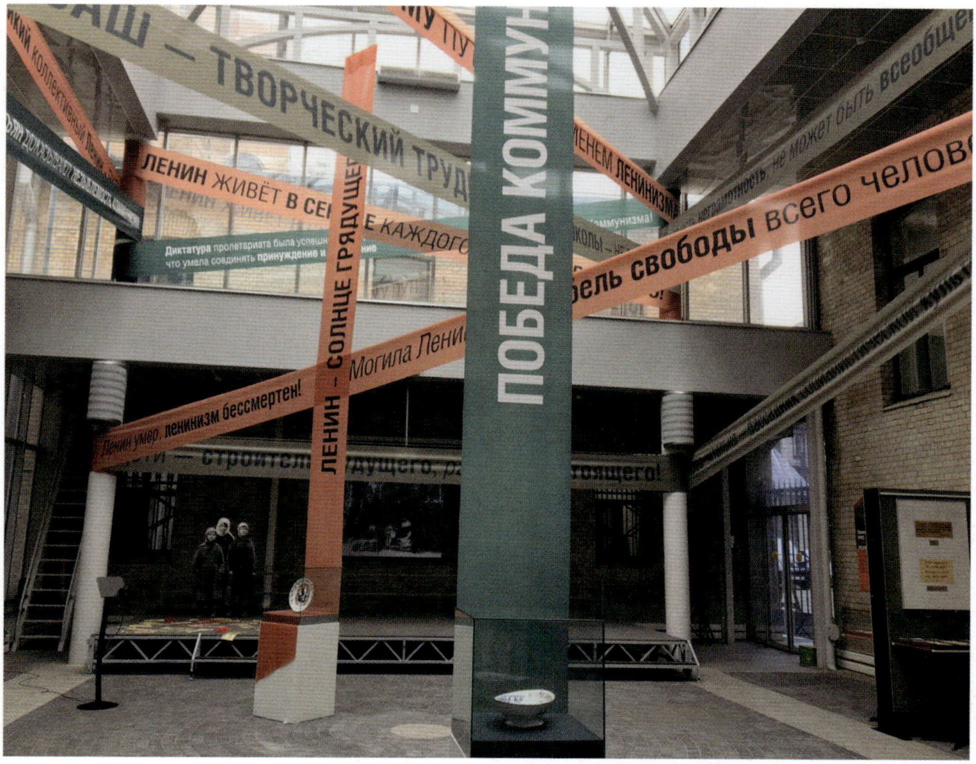

View of the museum's entrance hall

Many of the exhibits on display today have been loaned to the museum or donated by contemporary witnesses. In addition to the two main exhibitions, the museum also hosts solo and temporary exhibitions on a wide range of topics. Web users can take a virtual tour of the building on the institution's website. The museum has two other branches dealing with specific aspects of Russian political history. At the location in Gorokhovaya Street 2, the focus is on the history of the Soviet secret police and the Russian state security authorities. The branch at 13 Bolotnaya Street houses a children's museum, which conveys the history of Russia and the Soviet Union in a child-friendly manner.

Location: Saint Petersburg, Kuibyshev 2 – 4 roughy, Gorochovaya 2 roughy, Bolotnaya roughy 13
Internet: www.polithistory.ru

◄
View of the exhibition at the State Museum of the Political History of Russia

Exhibition in the Lutheran Church of Saint Peter and Saint Paul

Saint Petersburg. The Lutheran Church of Saint Peter and Saint Paul was built between 1833 and 1838 according to the designs of architect Alexander Pavlovich Brullov and is the largest Protestant church in Russia. Until its compulsory closure at the time of the "Great Terror" in 1937, it housed the congregation of the St. Peter's community founded in 1710.

It was then used as a warehouse; the magnificent fixtures and fittings of the building were confiscated, and the pastors Paul and Bruno Reichert were arrested and executed in 1938. In the 1950s, it was converted into a swimming pool which opened in 1962 and was used until 1993. After the swimming pool was closed, the building was handed over to the Evangelical Lutheran Church in Russia in the same year with the aim of restoring it to its original state. Due to the technical complexity and enormous financial expenditure involved, the renovation has not yet been completed.

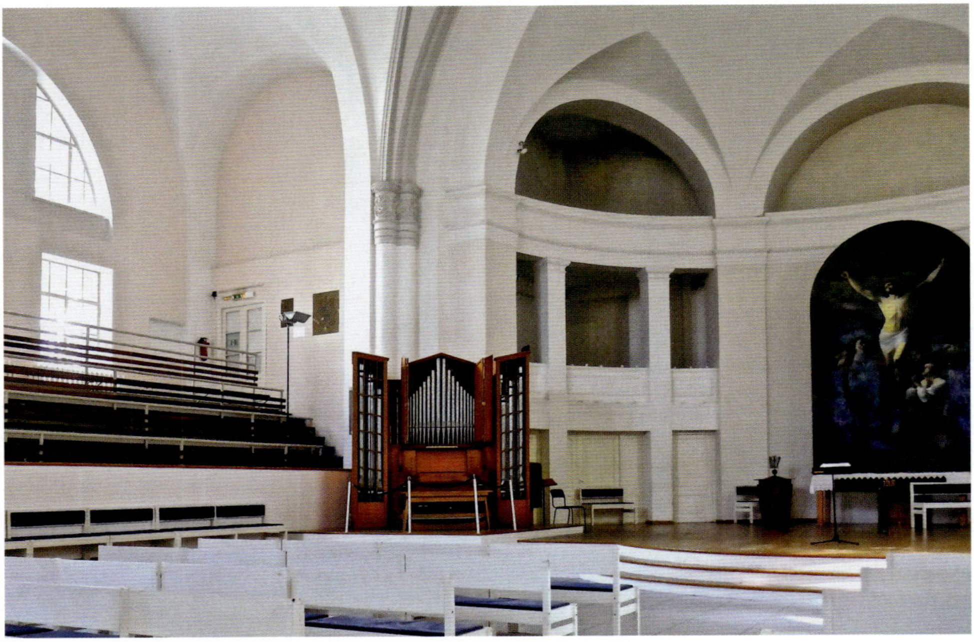

Reconstructed hall of the Church of Saint Peter and Saint Paul

The swimming pool was covered to restore the church hall, which is now located one floor lower. The basement and parts of the ground floor now form the "catacombs". Below the altar area is a representation of the history of the Russian Germans from 1937 to 1956, designed by artist Adam Schmitt in the form of a six-part mural. The former swimming pool can be entered through two openings in the wall. The room is occasionally used for temporary exhibitions and theatre performances. The outer layer of the basin was painted in 2007 by American artist Matt Lamb with subjects in an abstract-naïve style. A permanent exhibition also provides information about the eventful history of the building and casts light on the suppression of religion in the Soviet Union.

Location: Saint Petersburg,
Nevsky prospectus 22 – 24
Internet: www.petrikirche.ru

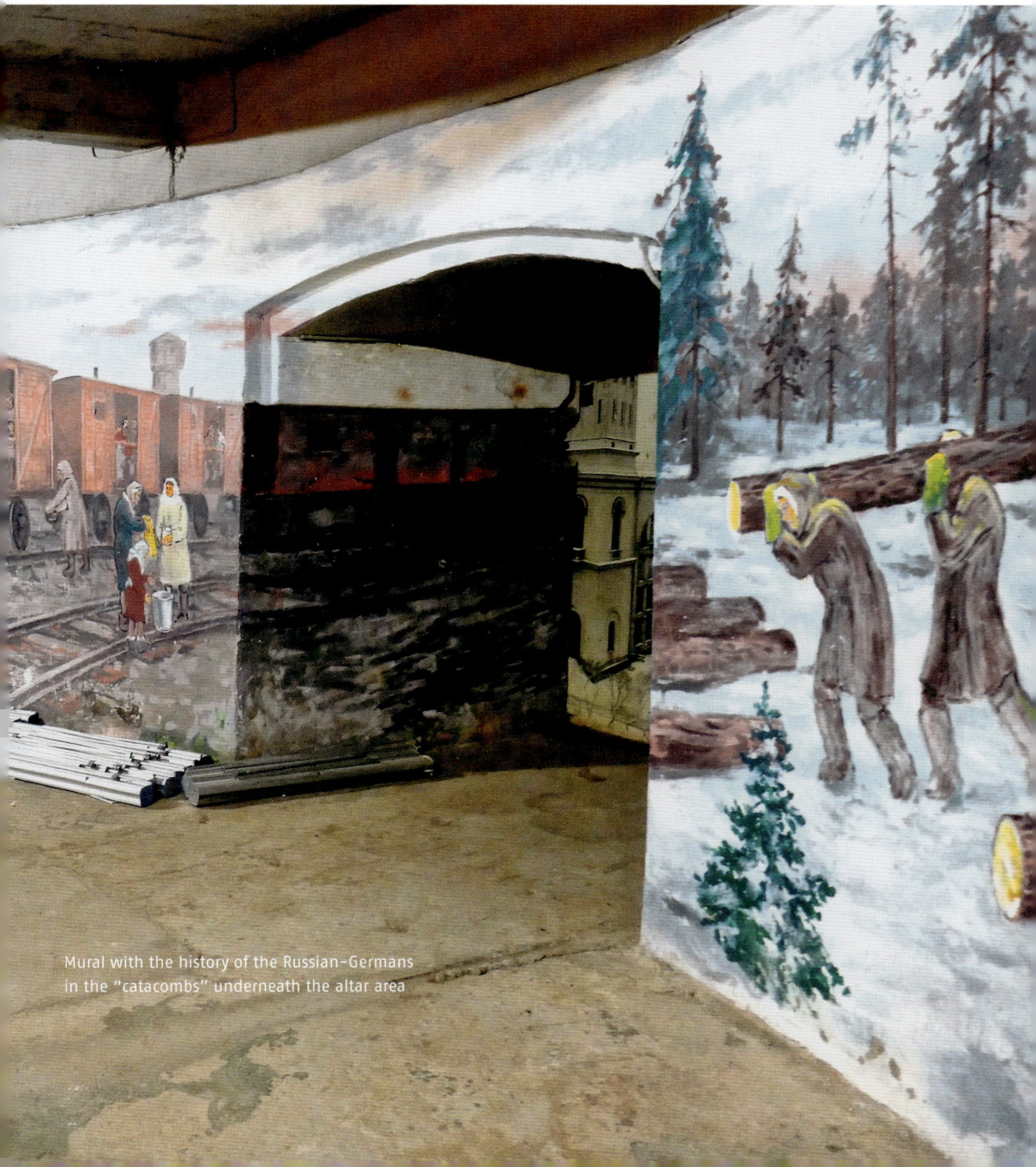

Mural with the history of the Russian-Germans in the "catacombs" underneath the altar area

Memorial Stone for the Victims of the Construction of the White Sea–Baltic Sea Canal (Belomor Canal)

Povenets. The Belomor Canal, an artificially constructed shipping route between the Baltic Sea and the Arctic White Sea, was a major construction project initiated by Stalin and built between 1931 and 1933. Like other labour-intensive construction projects of the 1930s, such as the steelworks near Magnitogorsk and the numerous "socialist cities" that sprouted from the steppes and swamps in the course of state-sponsored industrialisation, the Belomor Canal was also a prestige project of the Soviet leadership. Unlike many other construction projects, however, the extreme speed of the construction work, its particular importance for Stalin and, above all, the attention it attracted made its construction a unique undertaking. The White Sea–Baltic Sea Canal was the only project of the Gulag system that focused on Soviet propaganda both at home and abroad. The memorial stone in memory of the prisoners who died during the construction of the Baltic Sea Canal is located near lock No. 2 in Povenets. It was inaugurated in 1996 on the initiative of Memorial Saint Petersburg.

For administrative and practical reasons, the first prison camps of the Belomor Canal were created from the structures of the "Solovki special camp" (SLON). The prisoners used for the construction work and their guards were accordingly drawn from the Solovetsky Islands. The immediate canal work throughout the entire production period was supervised by Naftaly Frenkel. Himself a former prisoner of the Solovezk prisons, he quickly became one of the main players in the camp hierarchy responsible for the further development of the camp structures in the archipelago.

With the transfer of the SLON complex to the White Sea–Baltic Corrective Labour Camp Directorate (BelBaltLag) structures established in November 1931, the operational supervision of the project now came into the hands of the newly created canal bureaucracy. The political responsibility for the success of the construction project rested with Genrikh Yagoda, head of the Soviet secret police, the OGPU. Despite all efforts to make the work efficient, the working and living conditions were characterised by chaos, primitiveness and an economy of scarcity. A lack of technical equipment meant that construction work on the canal bed, which began in September 1931 after only seven months of surveying and development work, had to be carried out with the simplest of tools.

The approximately 170,000 prisoners and forcibly resettled individuals who were press-ganged into completing the project in the record time of 21 months had to make do with makeshift wooden spades, hand saws, pick-axes and wheelbarrows. As the construction work along the emerging canal progressed, the prisoners had to build new camp sites in completely undeveloped places in Karelia. In view of the inadequacy of the detention conditions, compliance with the deadlines set by Stalin required "creative" means of accelerating the work. A "socialist competition" between work brigades to meet performance targets was announced. In addition, there were "storms" in which work was carried out "voluntarily" for 24 to 48 hours without interruption. The cult of the "shock worker", the "udarnik", who exceeded the set targets, was fuelled by the prospect of privileges such as special meals and reduced prison terms.

For each period of three consecutive days of peak performance, workers were "compensated" with a reduction in their sentence of one day. This led to the release of 12,484 prisoners on 2 August 1933 once the project had finished on schedule. Numerous others were awarded medals and badges of honour. However, 25,000 people lost their lives during the construction of the Belomor Canal due to the rushed nature of the construction work and the difficult working and living conditions. These figures do not include all those people who were retired from the construction work due to illness or accidents or who died as a result of secondary symptoms.

The official opening of the canal on 5 August 1933 was accompanied by a wide-ranging publicity campaign. After Stalin's inspection trip on 17 August 1933, 120 well-known artists and writers, such as Aleksey Tolstoy and Mikhail Zoshchenko, took a steamboat trip on the canal under the direction of Maxim Gorki. Only one year later, 36 of them published an anthology that justified the unjustifiable in the style of socialist realism. The 600-page publication "Belomor—Kanal imeni Stalina" (The Canal Named After Stalin) lauds "the spiritual transformation of prisoners into shining examples of Homo Sovieticus". Only a short time later, the economic benefit of the canal proved to be insignificant. Due to its shallowness, it was unsuitable for industrial shipping.

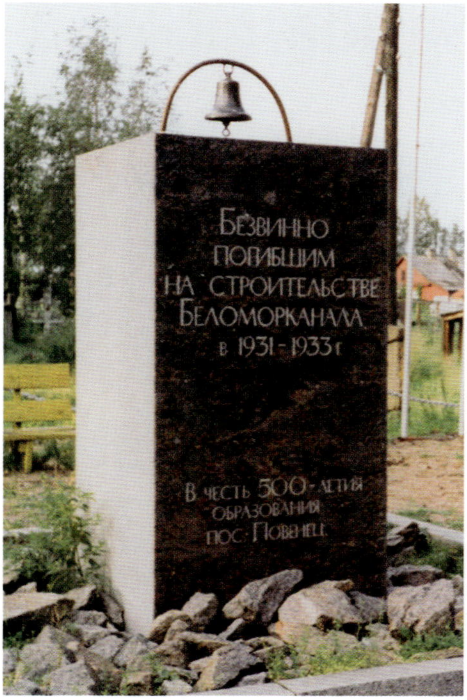

Memorial Stone for the Victims
of the White Sea–Baltic Sea Canal

The reddish-brown granite memorial stone in Povenets has a bell at the upper end and is surrounded by a fence of grey stone slabs.

Inscription
Russian: Безвинно / погибшим / на строительстве / Беломорканала / в 1931 – 1933 // В честь 500—летия / образования / пос. Повенец.

English: *The innocent who died during the construction of the Belomor Canal 1931 – 1933. In honour of the 500th anniversary of the Povenets settlement.*

Location: Povenets, on the main road near the second canal lock
Internet: www.gulag.memorial.de

Sandarmokh Memorial Cemetery

Medvezhyegorsk. Sandarmokh Memorial Cemetery is located 16 kilometres north of the town of Medvezhyegorsk in the direction of Povenets, near the village of the same name. After the graves were discovered in the summer of 1997, a cemetery was built here in memory of the thousands of victims of political persecution shot here between 1937 and 1938. Numerous monuments and memorials have since then been installed. In 2002, the Chapel of Saint George was consecrated in honour of the victims of repression. In accordance with an Orthodox burial tradition which dictates that each cemetery must have a church, the construction of the chapel was initiated by the Russian Orthodox Church with the support of victims' associations and Memorial.

The discovery of the cemetery at Sandarmokh owes a debt to the research done by SLON. Since 1988, members of the leading Russian human rights organisation Memorial, supported by relatives and the museum on the Solovetsky Islands, have been trying to shed light on the fate of prisoners murdered during the mass terror of 1937/38. In the course of this research in 1995, A. Soshina, a staff member of the Solovetsky Museum, discovered a list in the archive of the Russian secret service, the FSB, bearing the names of 1,111 camp inmates who were executed on the orders of the Leningrad administration of the Soviet secret police between October 27 and November 4, 1937. However, the documents did not provide any information about the exact place of execution.

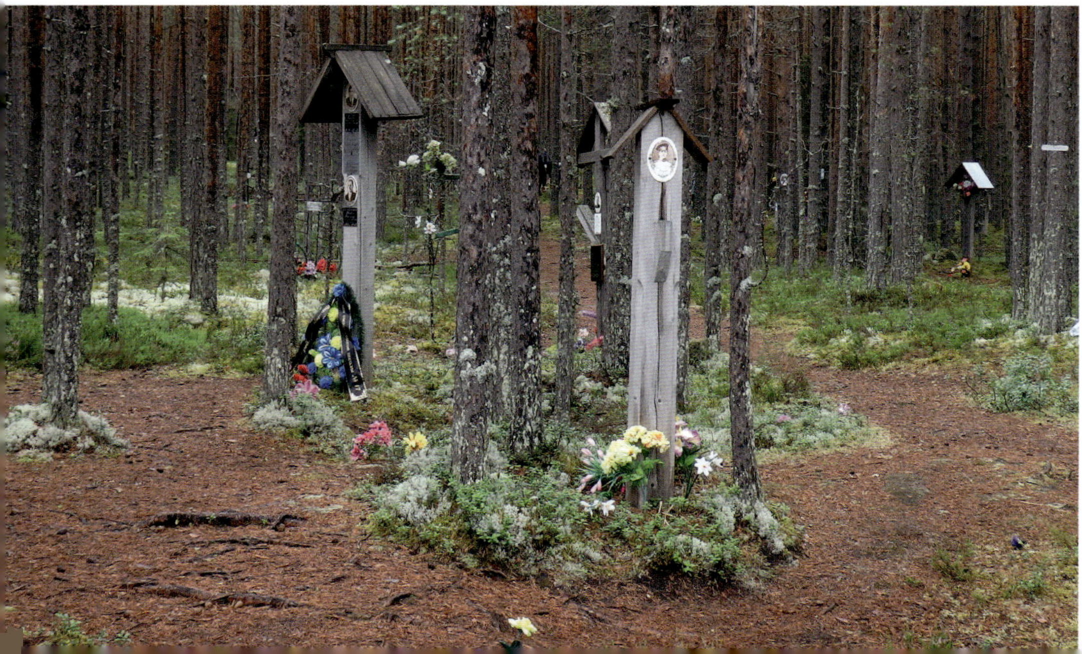

It was not until the interrogation protocol of Matveyev, the NKVD official responsible for the executions, was discovered in the autumn of 1996 that the location could be determined. In February 1997, Memorial set itself the goal of finding the mass grave by the 60th anniversary of the massacre in October the same year. Search groups were organised, which, together with the local administrations and the public prosecutor's office, interviewed contemporary witnesses in the area. On 30 June and 1 July 1997, with the help of army units, the search groups of Memorial Saint Petersburg and Memorial Karelia began their first search expeditions in a forest near Sandarmokh. They unearthed bones on the very first day. A total of five mass graves were opened, and about 150 dead exhumed. The medical forensic examinations revealed that this was undoubtedly the last resting place of the SLON prisoners.

The news of the discovery of the mass grave met with a huge public response in the following weeks. On 14 August 1997, the Commission for the Rehabilitation of the Victims of Political Repression of the Republic of Karelia made the decision to transform the site into a memorial cemetery and, at the suggestion of Memorial, declared 27 October a Day of Remembrance for the victims of Sandarmokh. The local authorities supported this request and provided funds to build a road to the cemetery, which was in place by the 60th anniversary of the massacre.

On 27 October 1997, a first memorial service was held in Sandarmokh. In the presence of about 900 people, two memorial crosses were blessed, and the foundation stone for a memorial was laid. At the urging of victims' associations, historical reappraisal initiatives, political parties and relatives, memorial signs were

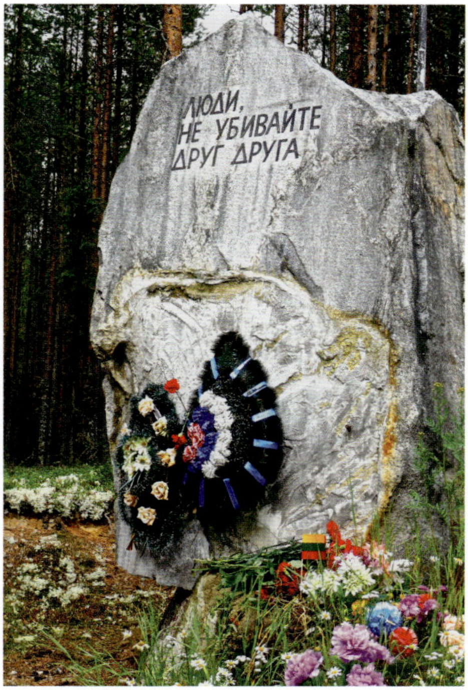

Memorial stone for the victims of Sandarmokh with the inscription "People, remember us! Don't kill each other!"

set up in memory of the individual groups of victims who found their final resting place in Sandarmokh. The 362 mass graves located to this day have been uniformly marked with denominationally neutral wooden poles, taking into account the different religious traditions. The Russian Orthodox Church supported the construction of a memorial church, which was consecrated in 1998. In 1999, the Day of Remembrance for the victims of Sandarmokh was moved to 5 August, the anniversary of the beginning of the mass terror. Since then, the central commemoration events have been held on this day.

◄

Numerous memorials and commemorative markers for the victims of repression

Location: Medvezhyegorsk, at kilometre 16 of the Medvezhyegorsk–Povenets road
Internet: www.sand.mapofmemory.org

Memorial to the Prisoners of the Solovetsky Camps

Solovetsky. The memorial to the prisoners of the Solovetsky camps (SLON) stands outside Solovetsky Monastery in the place where the STON special prison (Solovki Prison for special use) and an execution site were located between 1937 and 1939. Today, a memorial stone installed in 1989, a memorial cross erected in 1997 and a museum commemorate the camps and their victims. On the initiative of Memorial Saint Petersburg, the local history museum and the district administration, the memorial stone was inaugurated on 7 June 1989 as one of the first commemorative markers for the victims of the Gulag and political repression in the former Soviet Union. The occasion marked one of the first excursions to the Solovetsky Archipelago to commemorate the victims of the camp and to locate sites of mass executions.

At the same time, the first exhibition on the history of the Gulag opened at the Solovetsky Museum of Local History. The grey granite boulder, about two metres high, had no inscription at that time. The granite slab that can be viewed today was installed during a commemoration ceremony on 14 August 1999 on the initiative of Memorial Saint Petersburg. It bears the Russian inscription "Соловецким Заключенным" ("For the Solovetsk prisoners"). Since 1989, the stone has been the central meeting place and memorial site for the annual memorial events on the Solovetsky Islands. Meanwhile, further memorial stones have been installed on the grounds, for example for the deported and murdered Poles, Ukrainians, Russians and Armenians, and for the socialists and anarchists. The camp museum commemorates the history of the camp and the people captured and murdered on the islands.

The Solovetsky Archipelago, an isolated group of islands in the White Sea only 160 kilometres south of the Arctic Circle, was the "original cell" and the experimental site for the later Stalinist camp complexes. This is where the new methods of "perekovka", the "re-forging" of delinquents into true specimens of "Homo Sovieticus", were first put to the test with the systematic use of "corrective labour". The knowledge acquired in the archipelago was later used by the Soviet secret police in the realisation of major Stalinist construction projects such as the Belomor Canal and, from 1934 in particular, in the expansion of the Gulag system.

The first SLON camps were set up at the beginning of the 1920s as mainland camps in the northern Russian regions of Arkhangelsk and Karelia and were intended to be isolation prisons for political prisoners. After major restructuring, the existing mainland camps were disbanded and the inmates transferred to the Solovetsky Islands in the summer of 1923. The centuries-old monasteries of the archipelago

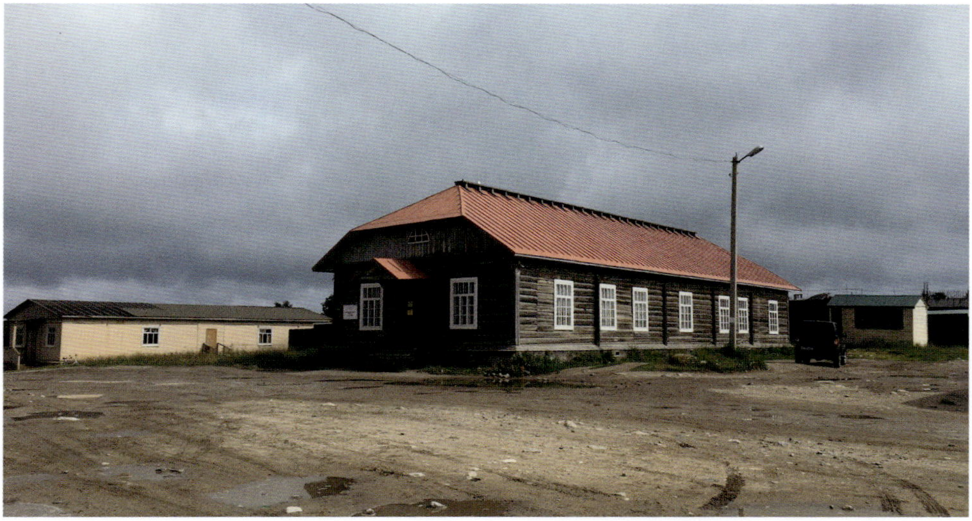

Camp museum in Solovetsky

with their monastic cells and workshops offered ideal infrastructural possibilities for the camp complex. On the personal insistence of Felix Dzerzhinsky, head of the Cheka and later of the OGPU, the entire monastery site and the camp management were placed under the administration of the secret police on 13 October 1923.

Compared to individuals sentenced during the Stalin era, the prisoners of the SLON prisons had to serve relatively short prison sentences of three to five, or in very rare cases, up to ten years. The Solovetsky Islands became a camp for the pre-revolutionary elite—rarely had so many artists, clergymen and politicians been imprisoned in such a small area. The prisoners were divided into three categories—"political prisoners", "counterrevolutionaries" and "criminals". The "political prisoners"—social revolutionaries, Mensheviks, and anarchists—enjoyed extensive special rights within the SLON hierarchy because of their connections to Western countries until they were transferred to political isolation camps in the interior of Russia in the mid-1920s. Together with the "counterrevolutionaries", who included tsarist officers, clergy of all denominations, nobility, Brasov sailors, businessmen, "Russians from abroad" and other social subgroups, they initially made up the majority of Solovetzk prisoners.

The "criminals", initially a low-status contingent on the islands, rose to the top of the prisoner hierarchy in 1928/29 after the transfer of the "political prisoners" and, from that point onward, dominated everyday life in the camp. With the implementation of a system of privileges and close cooperation between the internal prisoner government and the OGPU, an internal camp system was established which later became the predominant model for the Stalinist Gulag complex.

In the course of preparations for the Winter War with Finland in 1939/40, the decision was made to liquidate the entire camp complex. All prisoners and detainees were transferred to other sites of the BelBaltLag, the Belomor-Baltiysky work camp. Between 1939 and 1947, the monastery served as a military base for the Soviet Northern Fleet. From 1942 to 1945, a naval school was located here, where cadets were rushed through accelerated training for front-line naval operations during the "Great Patriotic War". During this time, the archipelago was declared a restricted area. In the 1960s, the

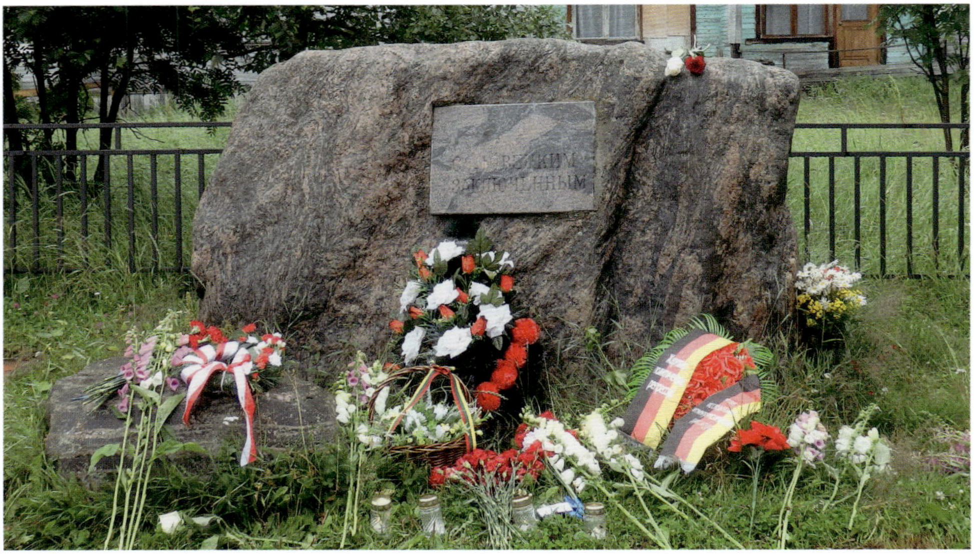

Memorial stone for the inmates of the Solovetsky camp

policy of de-Stalinisation under head of state and party Nikita Khrushchev finally paved the way to some renovation work on the buildings. The Solovki State Historical, Architectural and Natural Museum was established in 1967. An exhibition designed by Yuri Brodsky in 1989 sheds light on the history of the camp complex on the archipelago.

A memorial cross was placed at the memorial on 27 June 1999 on the initiative of V. Zhukov and A. Smirnov from Arkhangelsk. The commemorative marker, which had previously been blessed by the head of the Solovetsky Monastery, commemorates the closure of the special prison in November 1939. On the outer wall of the monastery is another memorial cross in memory of the prisoners of the Solovetsky camps. The inauguration took place on 7 June 1989. Memorial Saint Petersburg and the Solovetsky Museum and National Park Administration played a major role in the construction. The seven-metre-high Russian Orthodox wooden cross was erected opposite the memorial stone for the prisoners of Solovetsky. It is embedded in a natural stone base and bears no inscription.

Location: Solovetsky, ulitsa Pavla-Florenskogo Street
Internet: www.gulag.memorial.de

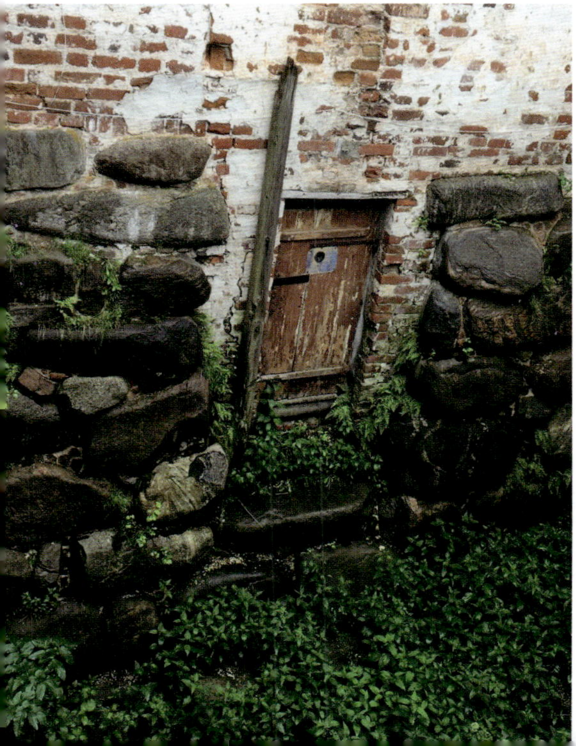

◄
Even today, there are visible traces of the monastery's history as a camp.

Katyń State Memorial with Polish military cemetery

Smolensk / Katyń. Since the discovery of some 4,400 bodies of Polish officers in the spring of 1943, the forest of Katyń, just under 20 kilometres west of Smolensk, has become a symbol of the Soviet mass murder of Polish prisoners of war. In July 2000, a memorial was opened here with three separate sections dedicated to the various groups of victims murdered at this site: the Soviet victims of Stalinist terror executed in 1937/38, the Polish officers shot by the NKVD in 1940 and the Soviet prisoners of war executed by German task forces in 1943. Prior to then, Katyń had for half a century been one of the most controversial places in European history: the Soviet Union continued vehemently to deny responsibility for the mass murder of Polish soldiers until 1990 and accused the German Wehrmacht of being the perpetrator. The story of Katyń thus become one of secrecy and repeated cover-ups.

There is no doubt today that, of the almost 15,000 Polish prisoners of war and roughly 7,000 other Polish prisoners from the eastern Polish territories annexed by the Soviet Union in 1939 who were murdered in accordance with a decision by the Politburo of the CPSU in the spring of 1940, about 4,400 of them, all officers, died in *Katyń*. They had previously been interned in a special camp of the NKVD on the grounds of the former Optina Pustyn Orthodox monastery in Koslsk and were probably transported to the Gniosdovo station in railway wagons, taken from there to the nearby forest and shot so that their bodies would fall into pre-dug graves.

Despite the strict secrecy of the executions, their bodies were discovered in the following years by the local population and Polish forced labourers. After this came to the attention of the German occupying forces, they used the unearthing of the mass graves in April 1943 for a large-scale anti-Soviet propaganda campaign. At the same time, the dead were exhumed under the supervision of an international group of experts who confirmed Soviet responsibility for the crime. After completion of the work, employees of the Technical Committee of the Polish Red Cross provisionally reburied the remains; the two generals identified, Bronisław Bohatyrewicz and Mieczysław Smorawiński, were given individual graves.

After the Red Army reconquered the Smolensk area in September 1943, a Soviet commission led by Nikolay Burdenko attempted to prove that the Poles had been shot by the advancing German troops in the autumn of 1941. The provisional cemetery was destroyed. Thereafter, the site remained hermetically sealed and could not be visited for decades. Nevertheless, after the 1960s, several monuments were erected in Katyń that backed the Soviet version of mass murder by fascists. A two-metre-high obelisk made of black granite was replaced in 1974 by a larger complex consisting of two, later four, graves set in concrete and a 1.7-metre-high stone wall with an ornamental grille in the centre.

Meanwhile, notwithstanding the Soviet insistence on German guilt, criticism of the theory of German responsibility for the mass murder grew from the early 1980s in Polish exile circles in the West and also among the opposition in the People's Republic of Poland. The proclamation of perestroika by the Soviet head of state and party Mikhail Gorbachev allowed Polish citizens once again to enter the cemetery in 1988. During a visit on 2 August that year, a Polish delegation was able to erect an oak cross donated by the Primate of the Catholic Church in Poland, Cardinal Józef Glemp, to express hope for the construction of a new memorial. When, less than two years later, on 14 April 1990, Wojciech Jaruzelski, the first Polish President, visited Katyń, the inscriptions on the memorial there had been hastily removed—the day before, the Soviet Union had officially conceded that responsibility lay with the NKVD.

The political transformation allowed Polish experts to re-examine the mass graves in 1994 and 1995 and to confirm the findings that the NKVD had perpetrated the massacre. After lengthy negotiations, a Polish-Russian agreement on the construction of a memorial was signed on 25 March 1995 in Katyń and in Mednoje, the final resting place of thousands of Polish police officers. This provided for separate Polish military cemeteries within the framework of common memorials dedicated to all victims of totalitarian violence. On this basis, the foundation stone for the Polish cemetery in Katyń, previously consecrated by Pope John Paul II, was laid by Polish President Lech Wałęsa on 4 June 1995.

The Polish sections of the memorials in Katyń and Medny and the joint cemetery in Kharkiv were designed by a group led by Zdzisław Pidek from Gdańsk and Andrzej Sołyga from Warsaw which won an international competition in October 1996. The group of artists proposed a vertical memorial wall, an underground bell and an altar table with a cross as central elements of all three cemeteries. This concept varied slightly during implementation to suit the local conditions.

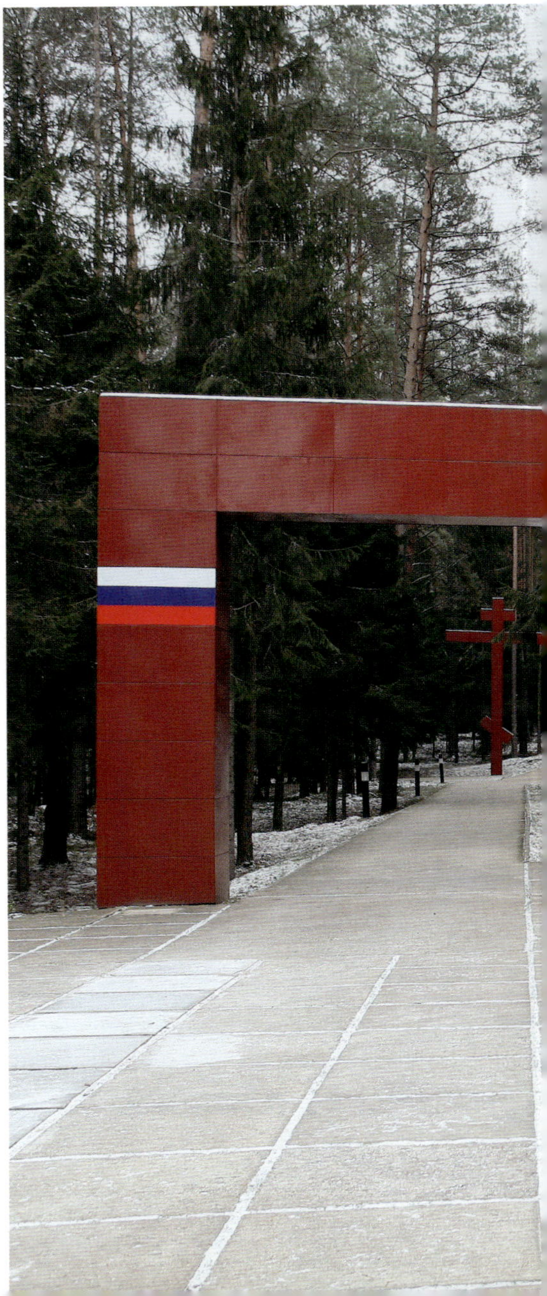

►
Entrance to the Katyń State Memorial

In March 1998, M. D. Khazanov was chosen to design the Russian part of the memorial. After the two concepts had been agreed, construction of the memorial, which was mainly financed by funds from the Polish and Russian states, began in May 1999 and was finally officially inaugurated on 28 July 2000—60 years after the historic event. The solemn inauguration ceremony was attended by relatives of the victims, Polish Prime Minister Jerzy Buzek, Russian First Deputy Prime Minister Victor Khristenko, the Primate of the Catholic Church in Poland, Cardinal Józef Glemp and honorary companies of the Polish and Russian armed forces.

Visitors enter the memorial through an open earth wall, whose sides are connected by a glass wall. Inside the wall are the offices of the memorial and a permanent exhibition on the history of the town. On the way through the forest to the graves is a square with two stylised metal gates crossing each other. From here, separate paths lead to the Polish and Russian

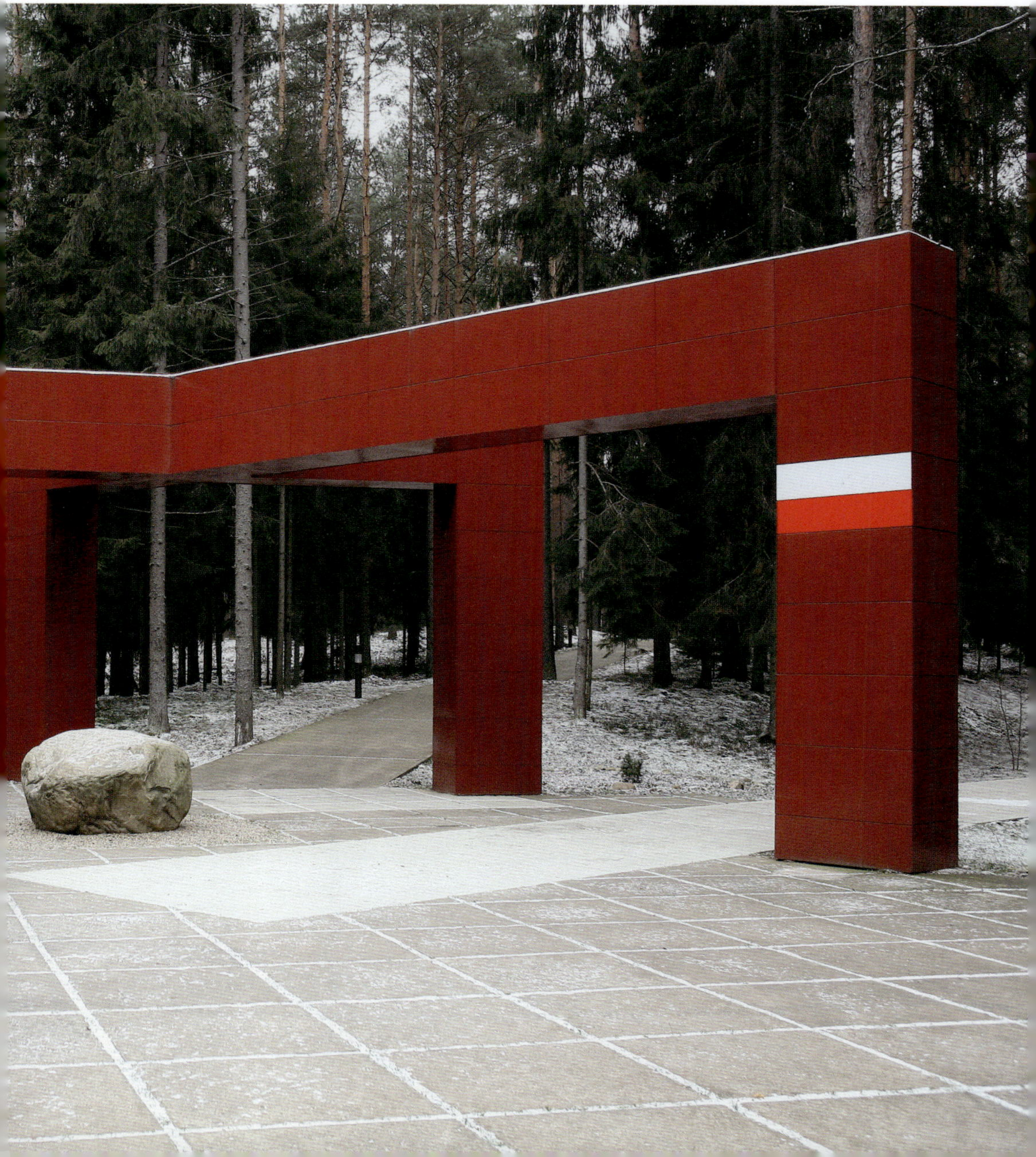

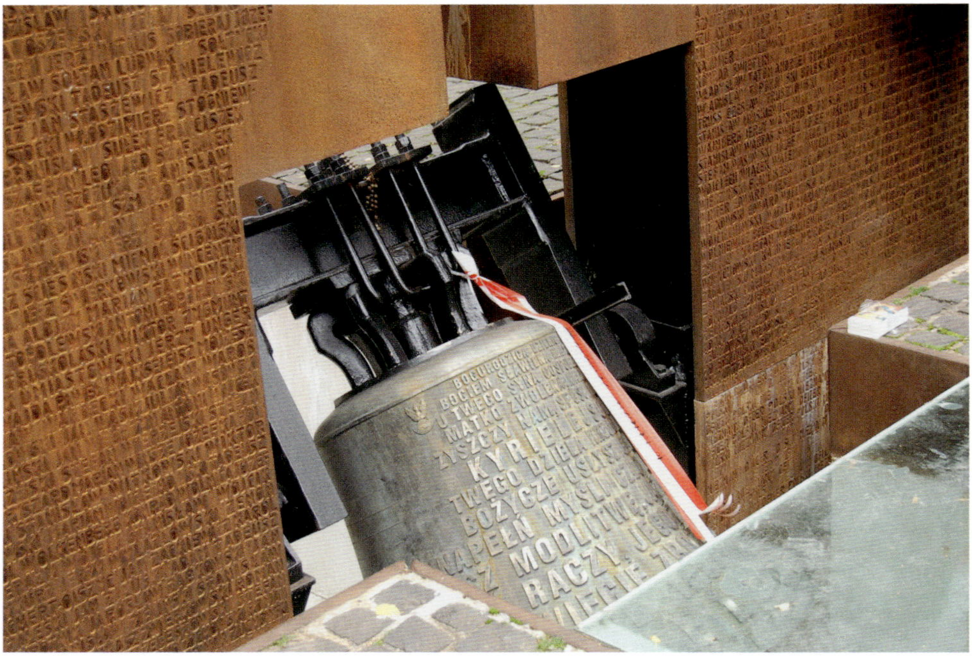

Memorial bell with inscription at the Polish military cemetery / Katyń State Memorial

sections of the memorial and to the "Avenue of Memory and Polish-Russian Reconciliation". The national flags of Russia and Poland attached to the upper cross-beams of the gate indicate the separate areas. There is also an Orthodox cross and a commemorative plaque for the 500 Soviet prisoners of war who were murdered at Katyń in 1943 by German task forces.

The entrance to the cemetery of Polish officers shot in 1940 is flanked by two iron columns bearing the coat of arms of the Polish army. The official name of the "Polish Military Cemetery Katyń" is embedded in the paved ground. Shortly behind the entrance on the left side is the wooden cross donated by the Polish Primate in 1988. The cemetery is divided into two areas: the former death pits where the officers were shot and buried, and the actual graves to which they were moved after their exhumation in 1943. The sites of the death pits are covered with iron plates, while the six mass graves laid out in 1943 in the centre of the cemetery are marked by iron borders with an iron cross in the centre. In addition to the mass graves, there are two individual graves for two identified generals, installed in 1943, which are marked by inscribed iron tombstones. The entire area of the graves is elevated one to two metres above the level of the surrounding forest and is surrounded by a wall with iron epitaphs with the names, dates of birth and death and military ranks of the 4,400 murdered officers.

The central axis of the Polish cemetery runs between the graves and is bordered at one end by four low iron stelae with symbols of the Catholic, Jewish, Orthodox and Muslim faiths whose adherents found their last resting place in the cemetery. At the opposite end of the axis is the centre of the complex: the iron altar with a six-metre-high iron memorial wall, with the names of the victims engraved on the surface. In the middle, the wall is interrupted by a narrow gap, behind which a slender iron cross rises above the wall. Between the two parts of the memorial wall, a bell hangs below ground level, bearíng the verses of the medieval hymn "Bogurodzica" (Mother of God) and the inscription "KATYŃ". The muffled sound of the underground bell is intended to evoke the failure of decades of attempts to conceal the truth about the casualties of Katyń. In front of the altar, the central commemorative plaque is embedded in the floor. Finally, the Polish part of the complex contains oversized iron recastings of the Polish medals "Virtuti Militari" and the "Cross of September Campaign", which were awarded posthumously to the officers murdered in Katyń.

The cemetery of the Soviet victims of the 1937/38 "Great Terror" is located on the opposite side of the gated square. At its entrance stands a ten-metre-high orthodox memorial cross made of metal. Since the terrain of the Soviet mass graves has not been thoroughly explored, it is in places only accessible via footbridges so as not to disturb the peace of the dead. Nine localised graves are marked by small hills surrounded by a low fence. The Polish and Russian parts of the memorial are connected by an "Avenue of Memory and Polish-Russian Reconciliation". A memorial stone was placed in 2009 in the "Valley of Death" outside the memorial site, where another 200 Soviet victims lie buried.

On the occasion of the 70th anniversary of the Katyń massacre, on 7 April 2010, the memorial was visited jointly by Russian Prime Minister Vladimir Putin and his Polish counterpart Donald Tusk. Together, they laid the foundation stone for an Orthodox church with an adjoining educational centre next to the main entrance to the memorial complex. On the way to another memorial service a few days later, the presidential plane containing Polish President Lech Kaczyński and the Polish delegation accompanying him crashed during its approach to the Smolensk airfield, killing all on board. On the first anniversary of the death of Kaczyński and his companions, 11 April 2011, his successor Bronisław Komorowski and Russian President Dmitry Medvedev came together to commemorate the victims of Katyń. This marked the first time a Russian head of state had visited the scene of the massacre. On 15 July 2012, next to the memorial, the Orthodox "Church of the Resurrection of the Lord", dedicated to the memory of the Russian victims killed there but also to reconciliation with Poland, was consecrated by Moscow's Patriarch Cyril I.

The publication "Erinnerungsorte für die Opfer von Katyń" (Memorial Sites for the Victims of Katyń), published by Leipzig University in 2013 and researched by the Federal Foundation for the Study of the Communist Dictatorship in Eastern Germany, provides an overview of 178 memorial sites in 18 countries.

Location: Katyń, Oblast Smolensk

Memorial Historical Centre of Political Repression "Perm-36"

Kuchino. The memorial on the site of the former prison camp Perm-36 was unique in the Russian Federation. The institution owes its existence to the long years of persistent reconstruction work by committed activists. After 1993, the regional department of the Russian human rights organisation, Memorial, in Perm and former prisoners of the camp made particular efforts to make the site accessible to the public. In the 20 years of its existence, Perm-36 developed under civil society leadership from a regional memorial in the Urals into an internationally renowned museum, memorial and educational centre. In addition to practical seminars, summer schools, youth meetings and international education programmes, the well-known "Pilorama" forum for civil society was also held here. Human rights activists, researchers, artists, politicians, journalists, Soviet dissidents and former camp inmates from Germany and abroad came together every year at this event to discuss the historical reappraisal of the Soviet regime and to conduct a critical dialogue on democracy, human rights and political and social issues.

Following Vladimir Putin's return to the presidency in May 2012, the memorial—headed by Tatyana Kursina and Viktor Lubirov—was subjected to legal repression and nationalised in 2014 under pressure from the local government. Since then, the entire area, together with the redesigned exhibition and the historical remains, has been under the ownership of the Perm Regional Administration. The new concept of the exhibition as a national-patriotic reinterpretation of history minimises and relativises the history of repression and the suffering of the victims of the communist dictatorship, while at the same time promoting the systematic dissemination of a falsified view of history by the state.

With the expansion of the camp industrial complex under Stalin, some 170 Gulag sites were established in the Perm region. The prisoners had to perform forced labour tasks in the construction of roads, railway lines and power stations and in the agricultural and timber industries. In 1946, Corrective Labour Camp No. 6 (ITK-6) was established in the village of Kuchino. The first inmates to be detained here were alleged criminals and persons accused of stealing socialist property. The prisoners were mainly used for logging work in the surrounding forest areas. After the death of Stalin in 1953, new party leader Nikita Khrushchev initiated the transformation of the Soviet penal camp system, under which the gradual dissolution of the Gulag was proposed.

►

Reconstructed watchtower on the site of the former "Perm 36" penal camp in Kuchino

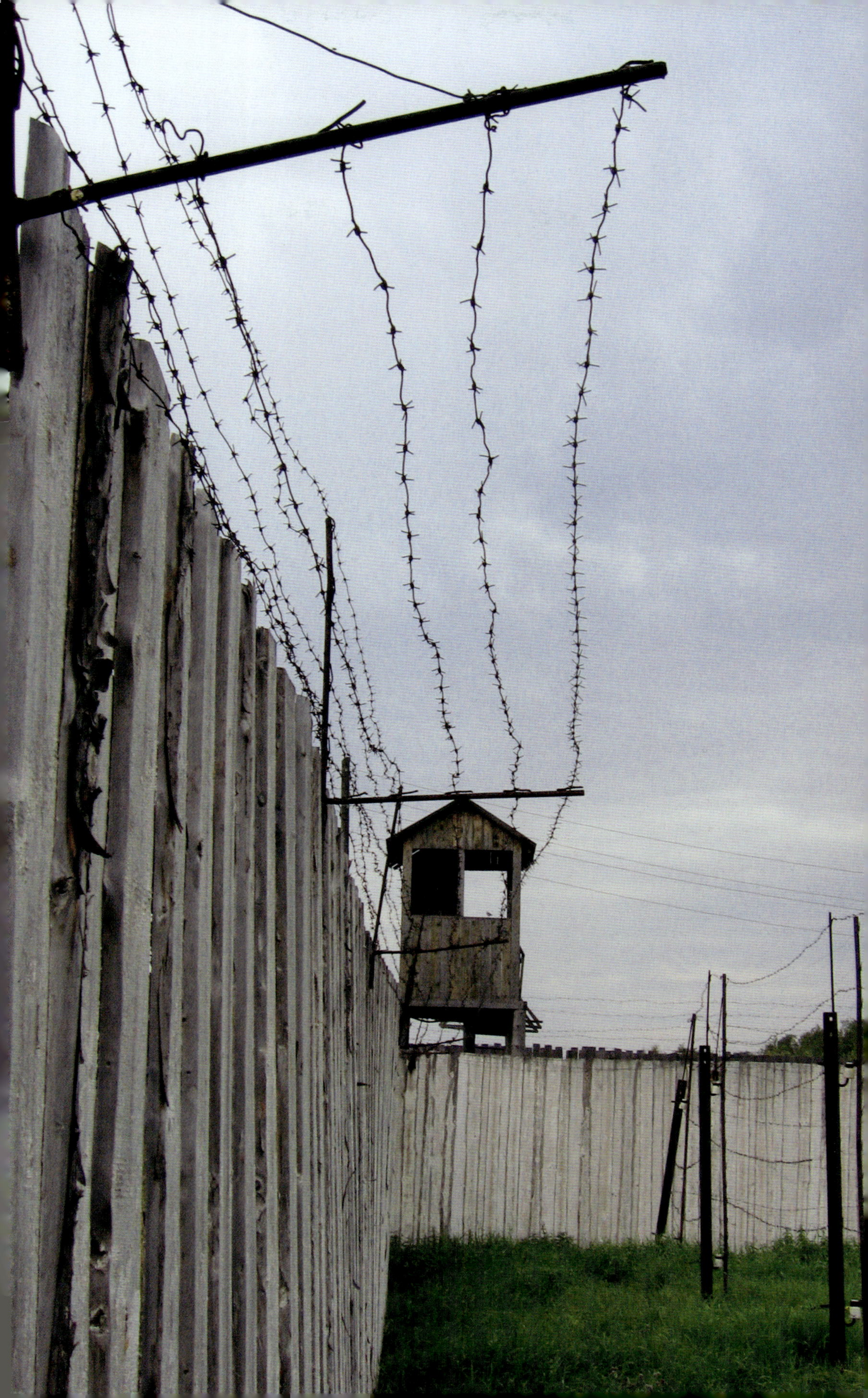

As a result of the mass amnesty issued on 27 March 1953, almost 1.2 million prisoners were released. However, the vast majority of political prisoners convicted under the notorious Article 58 of the Criminal Code of the RSFSR were excluded. Despite Khrushchev's "thaw" —the gradual de-Stalinisation of social and cultural life—numerous camps were maintained in and around Perm until the perestroika era. After the execution of former NKVD leader Lavrentiy Beria in December 1953, former officials of the Stalinist security apparatus served their symbolic prison sentences in ITK-6 in Kuchino between 1954 and 1972. Since the former NKVD employees, generals and officers, judges and police officers had themselves been involved in the persecution, conviction and internment of numerous people just a few years earlier, they were familiar with the infrastructure and the guard system of the camps, and the security precautions in Kuchino were considerably tightened as a result.

In the early 1970s, reprisals against human and civil rights movements in the Soviet Union intensified. The late 1950s and the 1960s had seen repeated confrontations between the liberally-minded majority of the intelligentsia and the officially decreed authoritarian views of the state apparatus. Soviet criminal law took action against this politically motivated dissent with sentences for "Anti-Soviet agitation and propaganda" or for "Organisational activity directed towards the state". Almost 10,000 political prisoners were given prison sentences in camps and regular prisons between the early 1960s and late 1980s. Quite a few found themselves in forced psychiatric care.

The "corrective labour camp" in Kuchino also changed into a detention site that mainly housed political prisoners. After the contingent of Stalinist officials had left the camp, the first political prisoners from camps in Mordovia were transferred to Kuchino on 13 July 1972 by top-secret order. At this time, the two camps known as VS-389/35 and VS-389/37 (Perm-35 and Perm-37) were also located in the immediate vicinity of Camp VS-389/36, the administrative designation of the Perm-36 political camp. The transfer of political prisoners to Perm was based in part on the fact that these sites had recently been examined by an international commission, meaning that no further checks were anticipated in the immediate future. On the other hand, Kuchino, some 1,200 kilometres away from Moscow, was considered sufficiently isolated to prevent any contact between the prisoners and the outside world. The respective camps differed only in the form of the prison regime—Perm-35 and -37 were camps with a "special regime" and Perm-36 was a camp with a "harsh regime". It was designed as a high-security prison, meaning that inmates were hardly ever allowed to leave their cells. Even the exercise yard was limited to a twelve-square-metre room with an open ceiling. The isolation of the prisoners was reinforced by the fact that the guards could be identified neither by their surname nor by their rank.

"Perm-36" was of particular importance in the persecution of dissidents. In 1980, a "special regime" zone was established here, in which activists of civil rights and national movements were isolated. The main prisoners were those whose involvement in such movements had already brought them into conflict with the Soviet system on several occasions. Among them were Sergei Kovalev, Levko Lukyanenko, Anatoly Marchenko, Lev Timofeev, Vasyl Stus and Balis Gayauskas.

It was with perestroika that the final decline of the Soviet penal camp system began. After an amnesty was issued in 1988, a small number of the inmates were released, and the remaining prisoners were transferred to Perm-35. Perm-36 was dissolved. It was not until February 1991 that the last inmates of the "Perm Triangle" were released, and the camp officially existed until 1992. After its closure, the secret service began the systematic destruction of the site. Almost all the buildings and security installations were levelled by bulldozers.

Originally supported by civil society organisations, the memorial housed the Gulag Museum, which was built in cooperation with the Andrei Sakharov Centre in Moscow and the Perm Regional Administration and opened in 1995. Two areas of the camp were reconstructed for museum purposes. In addition to the high-security area for "incorrigible" political prisoners and dissidents, parts of the "moderate camp zone" were rebuilt. In the high-security camp, the barriers, watchtowers, sleeping and working barracks were restored.

In addition to the reconstruction, the memorial has also carried out public relations work. In recent years, numerous publications have appeared and progress has been made in the establishment of a contemporary witness and video archive. The reconstruction of the camp site took place within the framework of international volunteer projects. Also involved in this work were pupils and students from the region. The museum has also developed travelling exhibitions on the history of political repression.

At the end of 2013, in the wake of severely criticised legislation cracking down on NGOs, the memorial management was forced to transfer the institution to state ownership to avoid stigmatisation as a "foreign agent"—a label earned by the receipt of foreign foundation funds. Beset by defamatory accusations, the co-founder and long-standing memorial site manager was replaced by a new administrator. Since the reopening of the museum, now under the exclusive auspices of the Perm Regional Administration, the focus has been on the contribution of the prisoners to the Soviet victory over Nazi fascism instead of commemorating the victims of repression. The repression is interpreted as a necessary evil to preserve the Soviet Union. The prisoners—according to the new account—contributed to the victory in the "Great Patriotic War" with their hard work. Guided tours of the exhibition emphasise that all prison inmates were "enemies of the Soviet Union" and "criminals" and were therefore justly imprisoned. New installations such as a medical examination room, a changing room and a camp library give the impression of reasonable detention conditions.

Location: Kutchino, 29 km outside Kemerovo
Internet: www.pmem.ru

Monument "Mask of Sorrow"

Magadan. The "Mask of Sorrow" memorial was inaugurated on 12 June 1996 on the summit of Krutaya Mountain in memory of the victims of the Dalstroy camp. Sculptor Ernst Neizvestny and architect Kamil Kasayev created the 18-metre-high concrete sculpture, which shows a human face with a cross worked into it. Today, the memorial is a central memorial to the suffering of the inmates of the Kolyma camps. The plant was built with funds from the Russian Federation and donations from the cities.

On the front of the memorial, the forehead, nose and eyebrow of the "mask" form a cross. From the left eye flows a tear with human heads embedded into it. The empty right eye socket of the sculpture houses a bell, under which the symbolic prisoner number 937 is carved. The central part of the rear of the monument houses a non-canonical crucifix and a bronze sculpture of a grieving young woman. The accessible interior of the monument houses a reconstruction of an isolation chamber and a symbolic replica of a grave site in the camp cemetery. Eleven stone blocks with the names of the most feared Gulag camps along the Kolyma River—Maldak, Butugychak, Chenikandzha, Dzhelgala, Elgen, Dnepropetrovsky, Serpantinka, Severnyj, Maglag, Kanyon and Kinzhal—stand on the first observation platform leading to the memorial. The steps leading to the second lookout point are lined with stone blocks engraved with religious symbols—the Christian cross, the Star of David and the Muslim crescent—and the communist emblem, the hammer and sickle.

Location: Magadan, on Mount Krutaja

►

The "Mask of Sorrow" is a central memorial to the suffering of the inmates of the Kolyma camps.

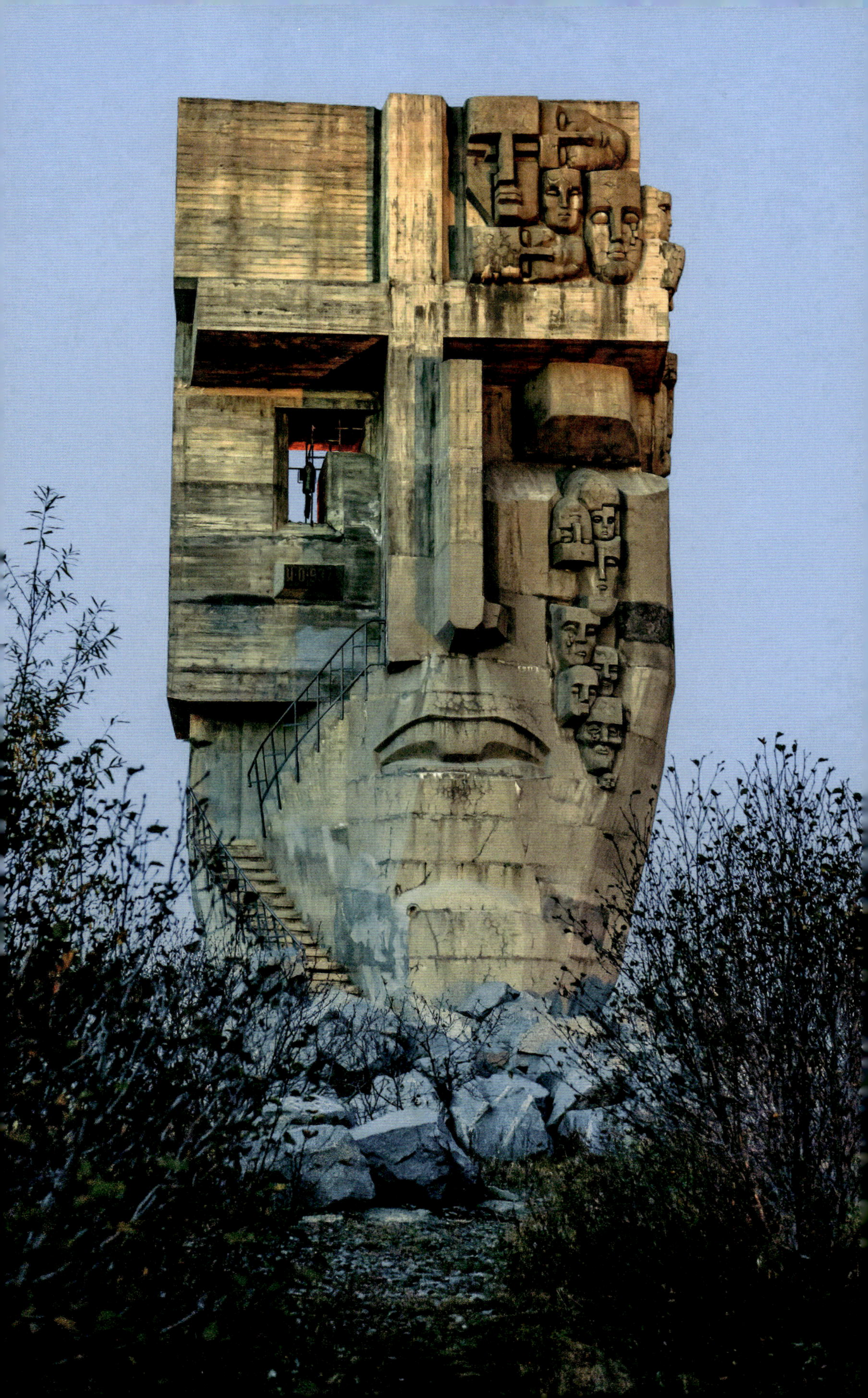

Memorial to the Victims of the Great Terror

Yekaterinburg / Shirokaya Rechka. The Memorial to the Victims of the Great Terror was inaugurated outside Yekaterinburg on 26 October 1996. The site is located at kilometre 12 on the road from Yekaterinburg to Moscow. The site was designed at the behest of the Association of Victims of Political Repression of the Sverdlovsk Oblast and the Yekaterinburg City Government.

The memorial is located at the site of mass executions of citizens of the Perm, Tomsk and Sverdlovsk regions. Between 1937 and 1938, death sentences were handed down by the regional troika—an extrajudicial tripartite body consisting of a local NKVD official, a party representative and the public prosecutor's office—and the victims executed at this site and anonymously buried. Since 1991, memorial services have been held on the grounds of the former restricted area of the Soviet secret police, the NKVD. In 1993, the Mayor of Yekaterinburg, A. M. Chernetsky, agreed to the erection of a memorial at this site. The funding was provided by the city administration. The designs were the work of architect A. L. Bulygin and the Chairman of the Prisoners' Association, A. A. Krivonogov. The central element is a several-metre-high votive cross made of black marble with a superimposed white cross to symbolise the innocence of the dead. Under the base of the cross is a mass grave. It lies in the middle of a radiant square, the entrances to which are bordered by brick walls. 46 metal plates list the names, birth and death dates of 18,475 people who were imprisoned in the camps of the Sverdlovsk and Perm Oblasts or otherwise became victims of political persecution. Facing the road is a wall made of white blocks.

Since 2004, a 1.5-metre-high grey granite obelisk with the symbols of the four great world religions has also stood on the site of the memorial. On the initiative of the Association of Victims of Political Repression in Sverdlovsk and with the support of the Yekaterinburg City Council, another memorial was erected to commemorate the nameless victims of the prisons and camps of the Gulag. Every year on 30 October, the Day of Remembrance of the Victims of Political Repressions, memorial events organised by the city administration in cooperation with the Victims Association are held here.

► Large devotional cross on the memorial grounds

Inscriptions

Russian: Мемориальный комплекс жертв политических репрессий 30–50 гг Здесь покоятся останки тысяч погибших безвинно расстрелянных наших соотечественников. Правда о местах массовых захоронений и причинах смерти скрывалась многие годы. Сегодня мы знаем их имена. Замедли шаг, обнажи голову перед братской могилой.

English: *Memorial to the Victims of Political Repression in the 1930s–1950s. Here rest the remains of thousands of our countrymen who perished, unlawfully shot. The truth about the location of the mass graves and the causes of death was concealed for many years. Today we know their names. Slow your pace, bow your head to the mass grave.*

Location: Yekaterinburg / Shirokaya Rechka at the 12th km of the Moscow motorway
Internet: www.ekmemorial.com

Further reading:

Applebaum, Anne: Der Gulag. Berlin 2003. / Baberowski, Jörg: Der Rote Terror. Die Geschichte des Stalinismus. München 2003. Hedeler, Wladislaw (ed.): Stalinistischer Terror 1934–1941. Eine Forschungsbilanz. Berlin 2002. / Kaminsky, Anna (ed.): Erinnerungsorte an den Massenterror 1937/38. Russische Föderation. Berlin 2007. / Kizny, Tomasz: Gulag: Solowezki, Belomorkanal, Waigatsch-Expedition, Theater im Gulag, Kolyma, Workuta, Todesstrecke. Hamburg 2004. / Roginskij, Arsenij / Drauschke, Frank / Kaminsky, Anna (eds.): „Erschossen in Moskau…". Die deutschen Opfer des Stalinismus auf dem Moskauer Friedhof Donskoje 1950–1953. 3. Fully revised edition, Berlin 2008.

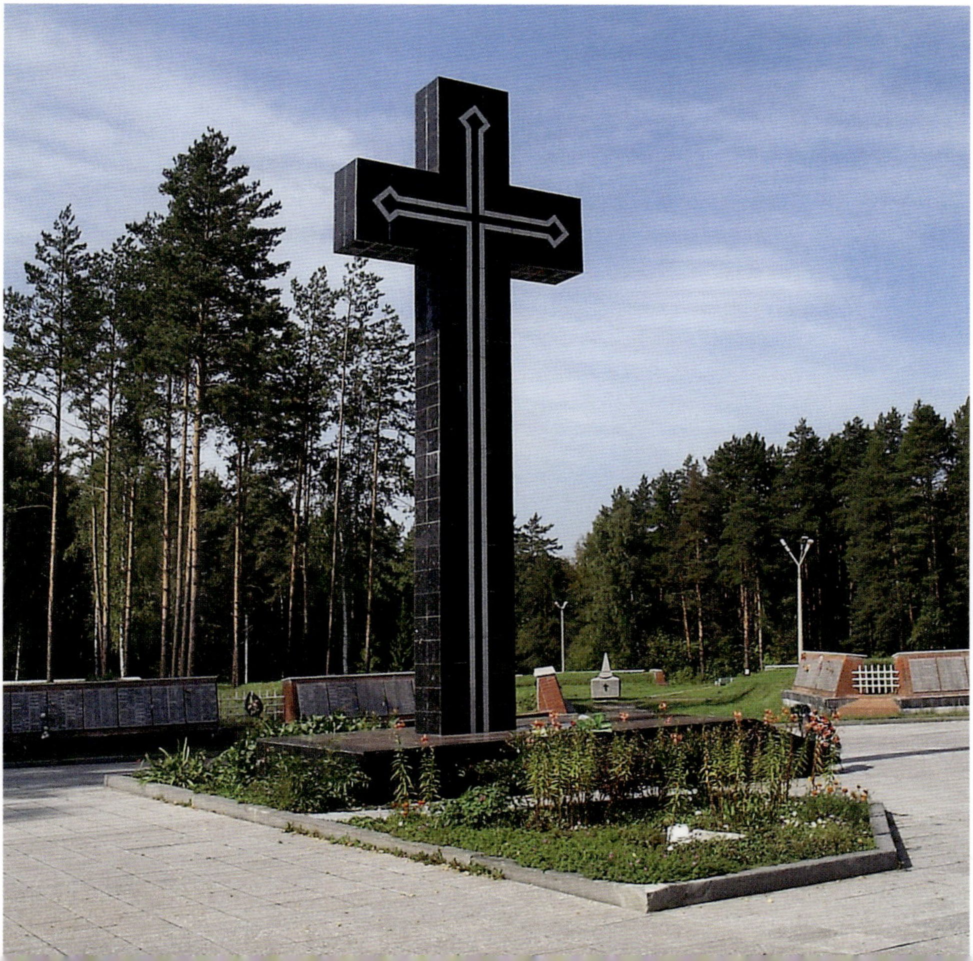

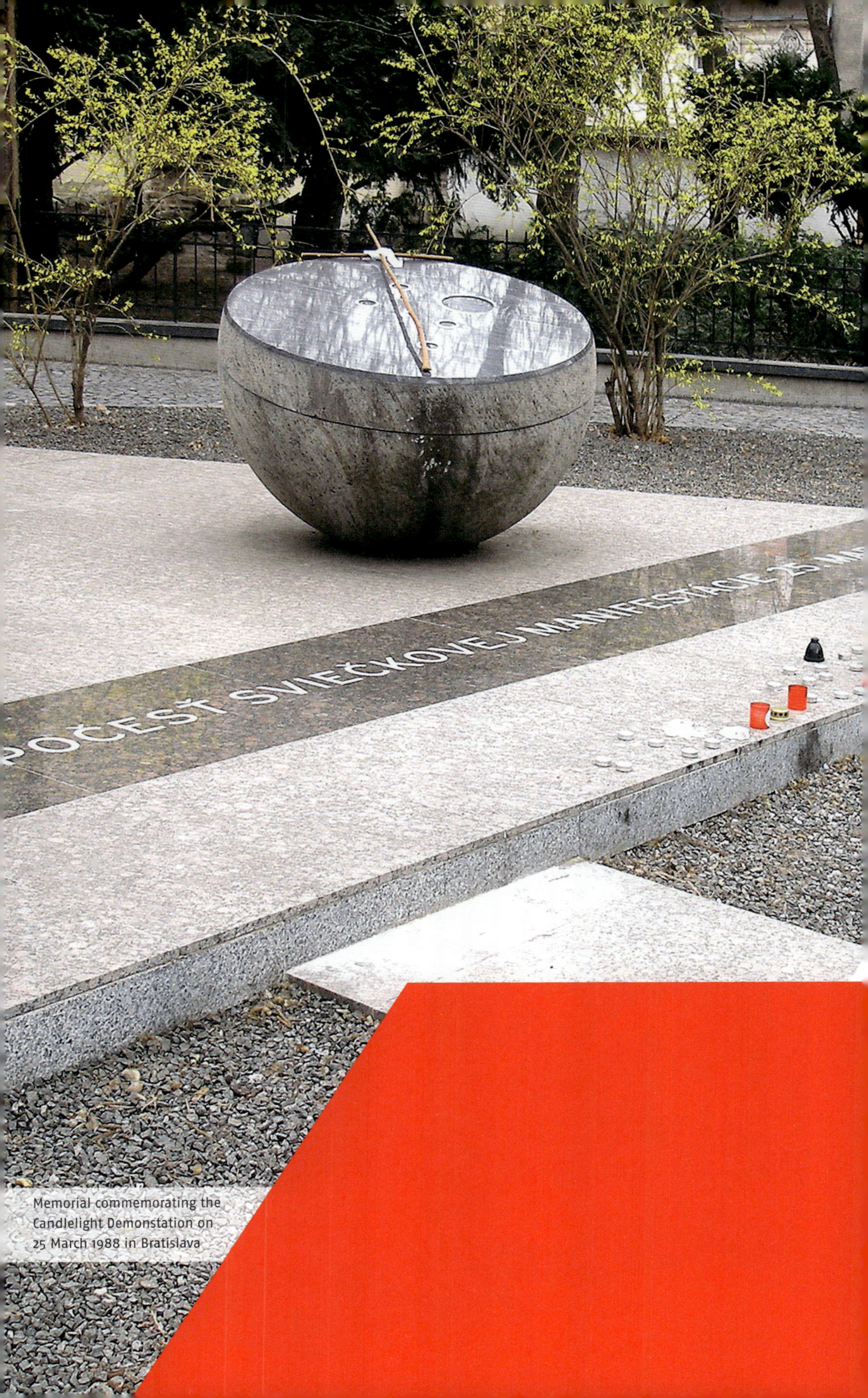

Memorial commemorating the Candlelight Demonstation on 25 March 1988 in Bratislava

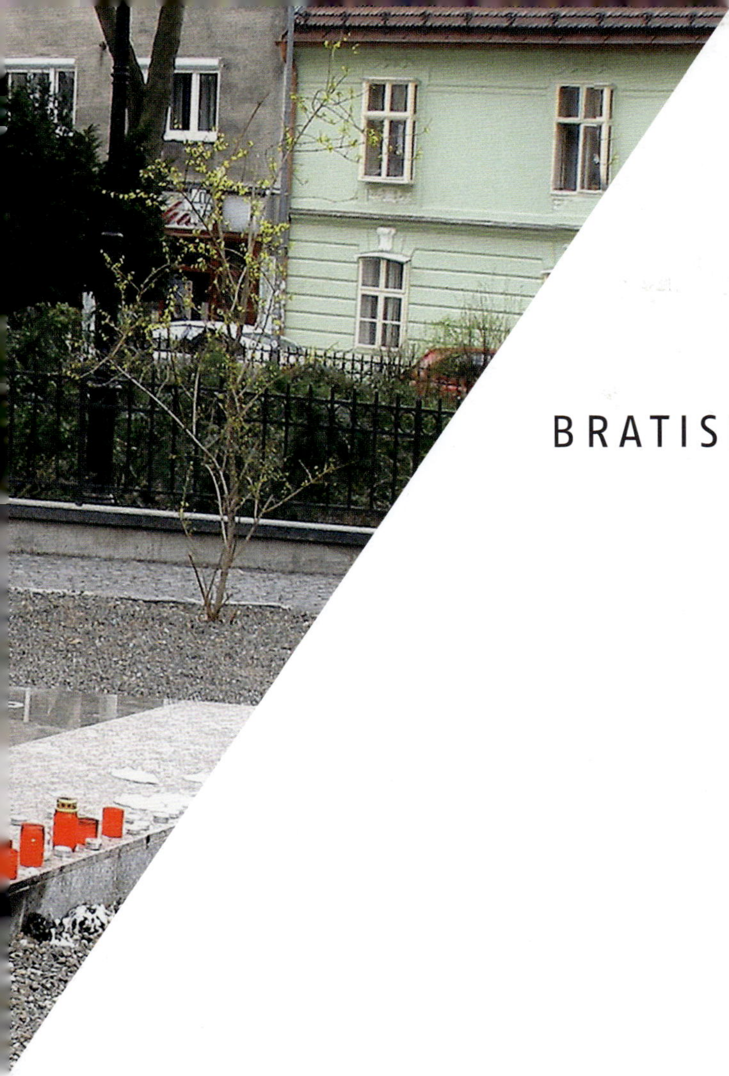

BRATISLAVA

Slovakia

Czechoslovakia was founded on 28 October 1918 just before the end of the First World War and was made up of Bohemia, which had previously been part of Austria-Hungary, and Slovakia, which belonged to the Hungarian part of the empire. The newly founded state of Czechoslovakia was home not only to Czechs and Slovaks but also to sizeable minorities of Hungarians and Germans. From the early 1930s onwards, dissatisfaction with the political and economic situation increased among the Slovak population. Nationalist aspirations and demands for greater autonomy became more pronounced.

After the Munich Agreement of 1938, in which the German Reich, Great Britain, France and Italy resolved to cede the Sudeten region, which, although part of Czechoslovakia, had a majority German population, to Nazi Germany, the Wehrmacht invaded the region on 1 October 1938 and incorporated it into the Reich. This marked the beginning of the destruction of Czechoslovakia, as other countries such as Poland and Hungary followed suit by occupying parts of its territory. On 15 March 1939, the Wehrmacht occupied the remaining territories of Czechoslovakia in breach of the Munich Agreement. Bohemia and Moravia were placed under German administration as protectorates. Under German pressure, the Slovak Republic declared independence on 14 March 1939. The new government under Jozef Tiso of the Slovak People's Party concluded a "protection treaty" with Germany, thereby, unlike the Czech part of the country, escaping occupation by German troops.

The Slovak Republic had little autonomy and was considered a vassal state by Hitler's grace. It became involved in hostilities early in the Second World War. As early as March 1939, Hungarian troops attacked Slovak territories, which were then annexed to Hungary after armistice negotiations at the beginning of April 1939. After the German invasion of Poland on 1 September 1939, Slovak associations became "Germany's first ally" in the war. From 1941 onwards, Slovak units also participated in the fighting against the Soviet Union. While Slovak Roma remained largely untouched by the Nazis' racial fanaticism, Slovak Jews were captured and deported to concentration camps in Germany. In 1942, the transfer of Slovak Jews to Germany was interrupted after protests by the Catholic and Protestant churches and the Vatican. After the occupation of the country by the Wehrmacht in August 1944 and the final suppression of the Slovak national uprising, the deportations resumed. Over 75,000 Slovak Jews were murdered.

As the inevitability of the defeat of Germany and its allies became increasingly apparent with the westward advance of the Red Army, more and more former allies turned against the German Reich. In late August 1944, an armed uprising broke out in Slovakia, in which large sections of the population participated. The aim of this uprising was to overthrow the clerical-nationalist puppet regime in Bratislava, which was loyal to the Third Reich. The German troops defeated the uprising and disarmed the Slovak associations.

In the spring of 1945, the Red Army finally occupied the country. The Slovak Republic once again became part of the re-established state of Czechoslovakia but was forced to cede the territory of Carpathian Ruthenia to the Soviet Union. After the communist coup in Prague in 1948, the Slovaks finally lost their political autonomy, which had in any case been severely curtailed since 1946. Slovakia was placed under the control of the central authority in Prague, which was now exercised by the Communist Party. Persecutions and political purges were directed against all those regarded as opponents of the new power. These included Slovak nationalists, bourgeois politicians and intellectuals, representatives of the clergy and members of the military resistance of 1944. By the mid-1950s, some 250 people had been executed for political reasons. About 70,000 Slovaks were arrested under the same pretext, and thousands were deported to the forced labour camps for uranium mining without even being sentenced in a court of law.

Until the 1950s, Czechoslovakia witnesses isolated, occasionally armed acts of resistance against communist rule. Political repression was accompanied by expropriations. Thousands fled to Austria to escape from persecution and oppression in their home country. About 450 people lost their lives in escape attempts between 1948 and 1989, and those who were caught fleeing were given long prison sentences.

In 1968, as a result of the reform process which included the demand for federalisation of the centralist state, Czechoslovakia and its capital Prague were occupied by troops of the Warsaw Pact. 180 people lost their lives in the fighting and hundreds suffered injuries. Once again, thousands tried to flee the country. Critical intellectuals were barred from their professions and rebellious youths placed in special homes. Family members and children of so-called class enemies were banned from working or not allowed to study. The population was monitored by the state security apparatus and thoroughly infiltrated by a dense network of informants.

It is estimated that at least 1,700,000 people left the country between 1948 and 1989; other estimates suggest that more than 250,000 fled Czechoslovakia between 1968 and 1989 alone. However, there are known cases from the 1950s in which the Czechoslovak secret police kidnapped refugees and returned them to the ČSSR, where, after their conviction, they disappeared in camps and prisons.

Throughout the period of communist rule there were repeated acts of resistance and civil disobedience. In the Slovak part of the country in the early 1970s, acts of opposition were carried out mainly by artists and writers, such as the groups known as "DG" (Degenerated Generation) or "Safran". In 1977, a few civil rights activists founded Charter 77 to protest against human rights violations throughout Czechoslovakia. The group was founded in the wake of the arrest of the members of the "Plastic People of the Universe" band after a concert in February 1976. The protests continued in the following years; members of the Charter were arrested and banished from the cities. However, these repressive measures were no longer able to contain the protest against the regime.

A special feature of the Slovak part of the country in comparison to the Czech Republic was the greater role played by Christian (Catholic) groups in the anti-communist opposition. These included, for example, an underground church recognised by the Vatican which, along with several other Catholic groups, was instrumental in organising social activity, publishing independent writings and supporting petitions demanding respect for human rights. Representatives of the Hungarian minority also participated in the Slovak opposition and maintained contact with the Hungarian resistance across the border.

The rise to power of Gorbachev in the Soviet Union in 1985 and his introduction of the policies of glasnost and perestroika bolstered the acts of opposition, which then spread to all parts of the country. In many cases, the protests had the support of the churches, and the demonstrations were organised by Catholic dissidents. On 25 March 1988, for example, thousands of people took part in the so-called Candlelight Demonstration in Bratislava, which called above all for religious freedom.

Barely a year later, between 15 and 20 January 1989, further unrest ensued on the occasion of the 20th anniversary of the death of Jan Palach, who had set himself on fire in January 1969 in protest against the suppression of the Prague Spring. The police brutally suppressed the protests. Leading opposition figures and dissidents such as Václav Havel were arrested. November 1989 saw open protests in many cities: hundreds of thousands of people demonstrated against communist rule and called for the democratisation of the country. The protest wave was set in motion by a small demonstration of about 300 students in Bratislava on 16 November 1989. After tens of thousands of people had demonstrated peacefully on Wenceslas Square in Prague on 17 November 1989, the protests in the Slovakian capital Bratislava also intensified; on 25 November, the protestors numbered 100,000.

When rumours arose that a student had died during the demonstration in Prague on 17 November, the situation escalated. Strikes and protests took place all over the country. Protesters occupied universities, theatres were taken over and demands made for the resignation of the government and the democratisation of the country. After the forced resignation of the communist government, the protest movement led by Václav Havel and representatives of the Communist Party began negotiations, which led to the formation in December 1989 of a government of communists and representatives of the protest movement. Václav Havel was elected president and the right to rule of the Communist Party removed from the constitution.

In the spring of 1990, the Czechoslovak Socialist Republic (ČSSR) was renamed the Czech and Slovak Federative Republic (ČSFR). The Communist Party of Slovakia (KPS), which had been founded in 1939 after the disintegration of ČSR and served as the regional branch of the KSČ between 1945 and 1989, changed its name to the Party of the Democratic Left in 1990. In 1991, the orthodox communists left the party and re-founded the Communist Party of Slovakia. In June 1990, the first free elections were held in Slovakia, from which the anti-Communist VPN, the Slovak counterpart of the Czech "Civic Forum", emerged victorious with almost 30 percent of the vote. Because of the peaceful nature of the protests, the revolution became known as the "Velvet Revolution". On 25 November 1992, the Federal Assembly passed Constitution Act 542, effectively dissolving the ČSFR to form two independent states. Slovakia gained sovereignty on 1 January 1993.

The reappraisal of communist rule began immediately after the Velvet Revolution. In 1990, the first rehabilitation law was passed, and compensation was granted to victims of political persecution. This included not only compensation for periods of detention but also reimbursement or compensation for expropriated assets. In May 1991, the parliament officially condemned communist rule as criminal, a move which was later reaffirmed by the newly independent Slovakia, with various laws passed in 1993 and 1996 declaring communist rule unlawful. At the same time, resistance to communist rule was classified as legitimate and honourable. Collective condemnation of the communist leadership was omitted; the focus was instead on the establishment of personal and individual culpability. In 2011, the justification or trivialisation of communist crimes became punishable by law.

As early as 1991, the first lustration law was passed in Czechoslovakia, providing for the review of certain positions in public institutions and ministries. After the dissolution of Czechoslovakia and the establishment of Slovakia as an independent state, the law expired in 1996 and was no longer renewed. Because of the suspension of background checks, many judges and prosecutors who had worked in the judiciary during the communist regime remained in office.

The prosecution of the perpetrators of abuses under communist rule has been unsatisfactory: to date there have been few convictions for communist crimes. Although the former chairman of the Communist Party and the head of the secret police were indicted, the trials came to nothing. One bone of contention was that, although defendants had the right to a defence lawyer at the expense of the state, those who had been persecuted politically at the time were forced to pay for their own legal representation. Trials against former leaders were protracted, and, in many cases, individuals who had been politically persecuted died before the trials could even begin. While attempts were made to sue former border guards for the killing of refugees at the border, these suits were dismissed on the grounds that the soldiers had acted in accordance with the law in force at the time.

The Memory Institute was founded in 2002. Its task is to document and investigate the crimes and, if necessary, to bring charges. This institute also holds the files of the secret police, which are generally available for anyone to inspect.

Memorial of Executed and Martyred Political Prisoners of Communism

Bratislava. The Memorial of Executed and Martyred Political Prisoners of Communism was inaugurated by Bishop Vladimír Filo on 28 October 1992 and was the first memorial site to be officially established on the territory of the Slovak Republic. Former political prisoners and other victims of the communist regime still meet here every year for commemoration ceremonies. The memorial, whose construction was initiated by the Association of Former Political Prisoners of Slovakia, stands near the main entrance to the Ružinov cemetery.

The memorial consists of three stone walls symbolising the prisons and detention centres of the communist regime. It bears plaques with inscriptions and, most importantly of all, a list, which is incomplete, bearing the names of the victims of political tyranny who lost their lives or were executed in prisons. In the centre of the space between the walls stands a 17-metre-high Latin cross.

The memorial, inspired by former political prisoner Pavol Cintavy, was created in 1990 to mark Pope John Paul II's first visit to Slovakia. Before it was relocated to the Ružinov cemetery, the cross stood at the altar at Vajnory Airport in Bratislava. Every year on 17 November, the Day of Struggle for Freedom and Democracy, memorial events and wreath-laying ceremonies are held here.

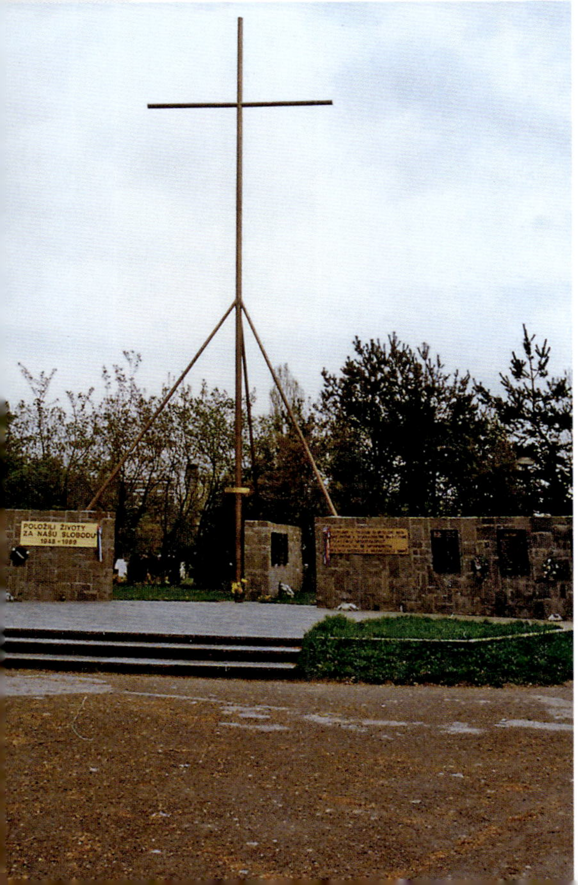

◄ Memorial to the Executed and Martyred Political Prisoners of Communism

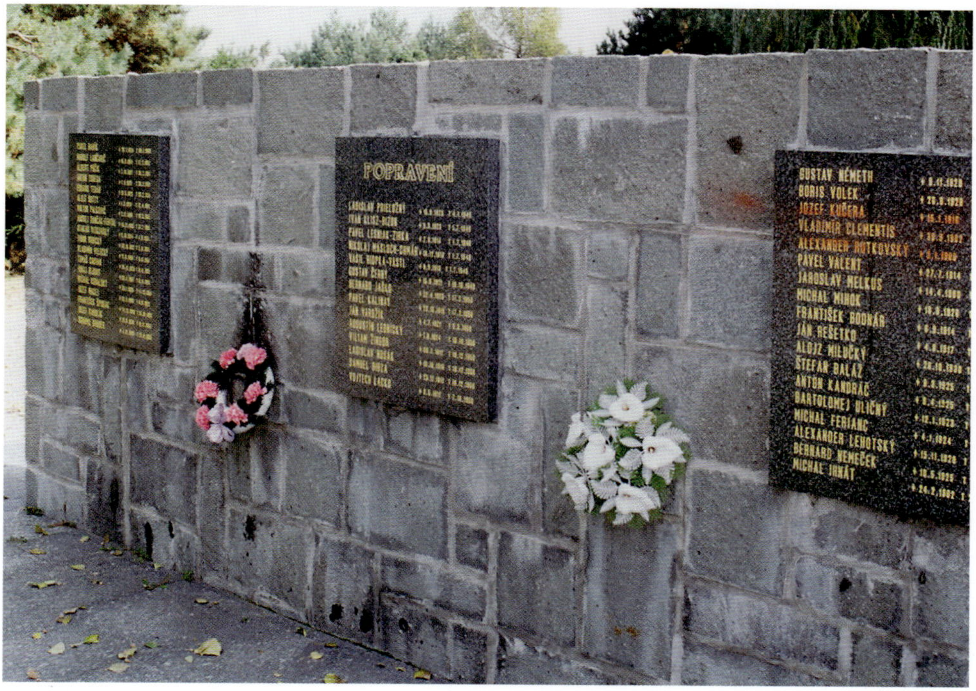

Memorial to the Executed and Martyred Political Prisoners of Communism

Inscription
Slovak: *POLOŽILI ŽIVOTY / ZA NAŠU SLOBODU / 1948 – 1989*
POSTOJME V TICHOM ZAMYSLENÍ NAD / UMUČENÝMI A POPRAVENÝMI MARTÝRMI / — OČAKÁVALI SPRAVODLIVOSŤ / DOSTÁVALO SA IM OPOVRHNUTIA / HLADALI SLOBODU A NACHÁDZALI SMRŤ

English: *They gave their lives for our freedom 1948 – 1989*
Let us remain in silent reflection on tortured and executed martyrs — they expected justice, they got only contempt, they sought freedom and found death

Location: Bratislava, on the grounds of Ružinov cemetery

Museum of Crimes and Victims of Communism

Bratislava. On 25 March 2013, the 25th anniversary of the Candlelight Demonstration in the Slovak capital in 1988, the Museum of Crimes and Victims of Communism was officially opened to the public. A few months earlier, on 17 November—the symbolic date of the Velvet Revolution in the former Czechoslovakia in 1989—the museum had staged a brief and provisional opening ceremony before closing again for completion.

The initiative to build the museum came from František Neupauer, chairman of the "Silent Heroes" civic organisation, and the Association of Former Political Prisoners in Slovakia. Until the change of government in March 2012, the project was actively supported by the then Prime Minister Iveta Radičová. At present, however, the institution does not receive any state support and is funded exclusively through donations. The exhibition rooms of the museum were provided by the Saint Elizabeth College of Health and Social Work.

On the college's spacious top floor, the exhibition uses display boards and authentic objects to document the period between the communist coup in February 1948 and the collapse of the regime in the autumn of 1989. The presentation focuses on the individual fates of the many "silent heroes" whose stories of resistance and opposition had not previously been made known to the public. Further expansion of the exhibition is planned with the long-term goal of documenting and providing information on totalitarian regimes outside Europe. In addition to guided tours of the exhibition, the museum staff also organises conferences, seminars and lectures and provides various educational programmes for schools.

Location: Bratislava, Námestie slobody 3
Internet: www.muzeumkomunizmu.sk

Further reading:

Gyarfášová, Soňa: Case Study on Slovakia. In: Honoring Civil Courage. Developing Suggestions to Improve the Situation of Victims of Communist State Crimes. Project Coordinator: Gedenkstätte Berlin-Hohenschönhausen 2015, Ref. Nr.: JUST/2011/JPEN/AG/2998Available online at: www.stiftung-hsh.de/assets/Dokumente-pdf-Dateien/EU-Projekt-Laenderstudien.pdf (last accessed on: 01/12/2017). / Katholisches Magazin für Kirche und Kultur: „Stille Helden" — Museum der Verbrechen und Opfer des Kommunismus in Preßburg eröffnet. 2012. Available online at: www.bit.ly/2kfMkof (last accessed on: 01/12/2017). / Marušiak, Jura / Kmeť, Norbert: Geschichte der slowakischen Opposition. In: Biografisches Lexikon Widerstand und Opposition im Kommunismus 1945 – 91. Federal Foundation for the Study of the Communist Dictatorship in Eastern Germany. Available online at: www.dissidenten.eu/fileadmin/user_upload/Slowakei/Oppositionsgeschichte/dissidenten_eu-Slowakische-Oppositionsgeschichte.pdf (last accessed on: 15/02/2018).

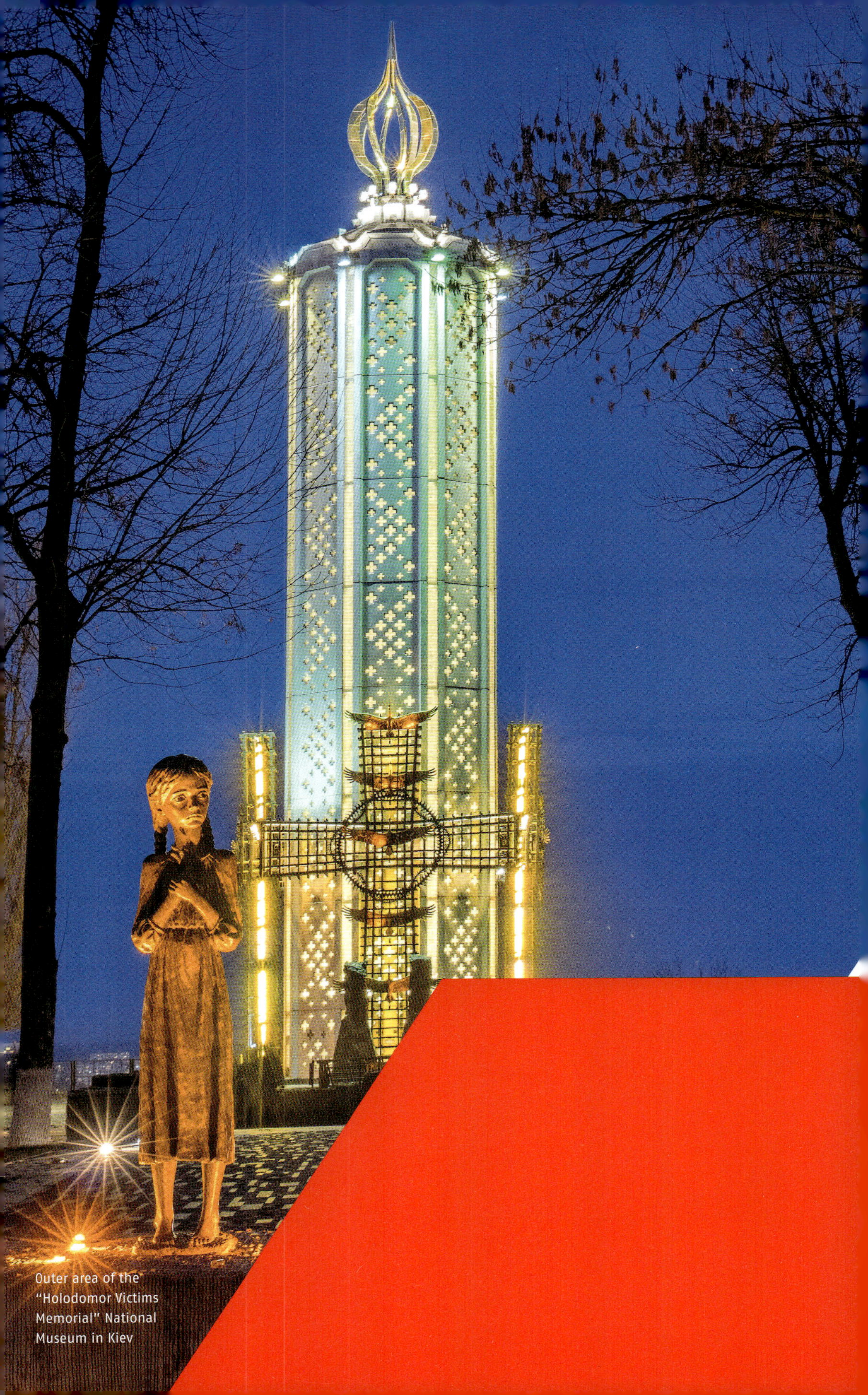

Outer area of the "Holodomor Victims Memorial" National Museum in Kiev

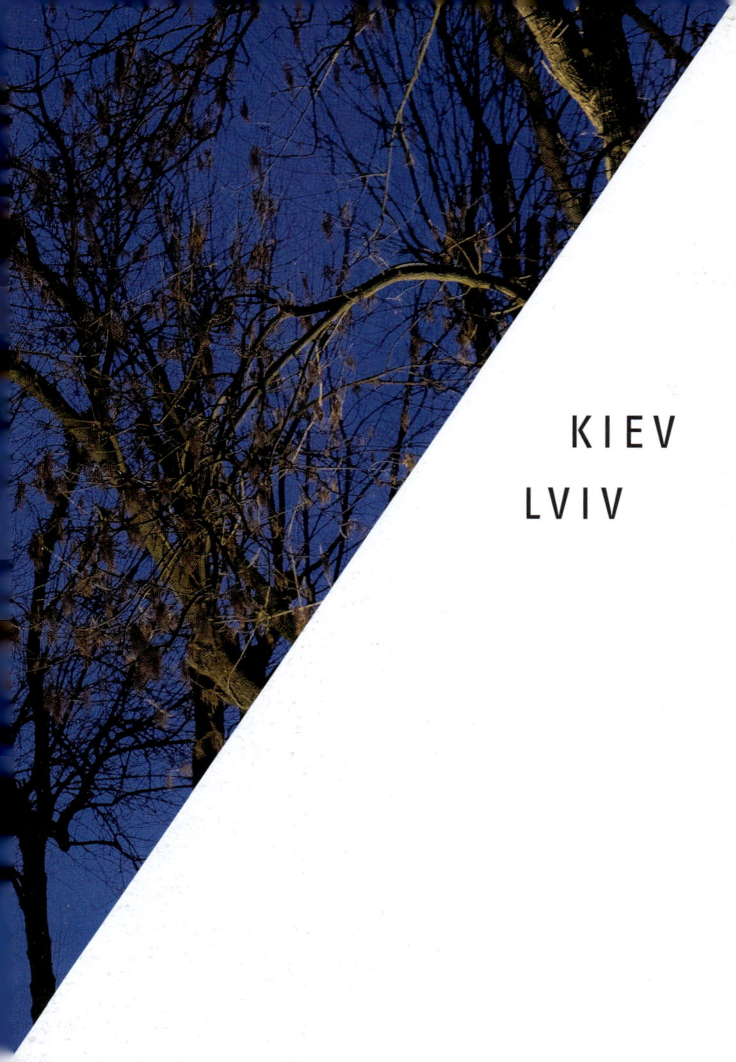

KIEV

LVIV

Ukraine

Between the partitioning of Poland in the 18th century and the end of the First World War, most of the territory of modern-day Ukraine belonged to the Russian Empire. Only Galicia, the Carpathians (Transcarpathia) and Northern Bucovina in the west and south-west were under the rule of the Habsburg Monarchy. As in other European countries, nationalist aspirations to the establishment of independent nation-states intensified at the end of the 19th century. After the overthrow of tsarist rule in Russia in February 1917, a Ukrainian Constituent Assembly was formed in Kiev, previously part of Russia, which sought Ukraine's autonomy within Russia.

In reaction to the Bolshevik Revolution in Petrograd, the Ukrainian People's Republic was declared in November 1917 as part of the Russian Republic, which had been dissolved by the Bolsheviks. Their stated goal was a federative structure for Russia. Right from the outset, this brought the new, initially socialist government in Kiev into conflict with the Russian Bolsheviks and their Ukrainian comrades who, although much weaker than their Russian counterparts, nonetheless asserted their right to rule the country. In late December 1917, the Russian Bolshevik Red Guards launched a military offensive in eastern Ukraine, with organised workers' revolts in Ukrainian cities taking place at the same time. Shortly before the first occupation of Kiev by Bolshevik troops, the People's Republic of Ukraine declared independence in January 1918.

After the Treaty of Brest-Litovsk, which was concluded between the Ukrainian People's Republic and the Central Powers in February 1918, the Bolsheviks were forced to leave Ukraine following a joint offensive by Ukrainian, German and Austrian troops. Ukraine remained formally independent but was occupied by German and Austrian troops. In the following years, the fighting spread to the whole of Central and Eastern Ukraine. After countless changes of government, foreign interventions, fierce battles between the "Reds" and the "Whites" and an all-out civil war, by the end of which everyone had fought against everyone else (during this time the government in Kiev changed hands no less than 15 times), the Bolsheviks finally won the upper hand. From 1920, the entire area of Central and Eastern Ukraine was under their control. The Ukrainian Soviet Socialist Republic became part of the Soviet Union in 1922.

The West Ukrainian People's Republic was founded in 1918 in Galicia in Western Ukraine, formerly part of Austria-Hungary. The unification with the Ukrainian People's Republic declared in January 1919 was largely a symbolic act. After the Polish-Ukrainian war of 1918 – 19 and until the Second World War, Galicia joined Poland, as did the Volhynia region in the northwest, which Soviet Russia was forced to cede to Poland in 1920 under the terms of the Treaty of Riga. At the same time, Carpathian Ruthenia was ceded to the newly founded Czechoslovakia, while northern Bucovina was integrated into Romania, which was greatly expanded after the First World War.

Soviet rule was enforced in the territories belonging to the Soviet Union: the clergy and religious worshippers were persecuted and members of previous governments and of the cultural and political elite arrested or murdered. Farmers were expropriated and forced into the newly established state kolkhozes; families defamed as kulaks were deported or murdered. The industrialisation of the coal-mining areas in eastern Ukraine began at the same time. In 1929, Stalin announced the final "liquidation" of all remaining free rural economies. The result was the mass expropriation, arrest, deportation and extermination of hundreds of thousands of people.

The "Holodomor", composed of the words "holod" (starvation) and "mor" (mass death), despite being one of the most horrific man-made famines of the 20th century, was long ignored by official Soviet history. Although the term was coined by the Ukrainian diaspora in the USA and Canada in reference to the deaths from starvation that afflicted in Ukraine at the end of the 1970s, it was only during perestroika that the Soviet Union took its first faltering steps toward ending the denial and cover-up of the "Great Famine". Today it is known that, in the whole territory of the USSR in the years 1932/33, about six to seven million people died of starvation and exhaustion. In Ukraine, where the Holodomor is now classified as a genocide (more than 20 countries in the world have adopted this definition), between 3 and 3.5 million people died of starvation. In its latest study from 2015, the Ukrainian Institute for Demography and Social Studies estimates that there were as many as 3.9 million direct victims.

The losses were also colossal in the territory of the former Kazakh Autonomous Republic (now Kazakhstan): More than 1.5 million people fell victim to starvation here. The famine was particularly catastrophic in the northern Caucasus, especially in the Kuban region, along the Don, in the vast regions of the Lower and Middle Volga, in the southern Urals, Western Siberia and the Kursk, Tambov and Vologda regions. Entire settlements were desolated within a few months, some areas appearing to be completely devoid of human life.

The "Great Famine" of the 1930s was not preceded by any natural disasters. Instead, it was the result of the Soviet state's extremely brutal policies. Without forced collectivisation—the forcible incorporation of small farms into larger state-controlled collective farms after 1929—and "dekulakisation"—the Stalinist campaign of repression against supposedly wealthy farmers—the catastrophe would not have occurred. On the one hand, the country's accelerated industrialisation was to be financed by ever-increasing grain exports. On the other, the measures served the final establishment of Soviet power in rural areas. The village, as the remaining bastion of tradition and faith which had so far been able to escape the "socialist system of values", was to be removed as the last obstacle to Stalin's totalitarian rule. Resistance to collectivisation and the brutal grain seizures associated with it had been manifest from the outset. However, Stalin viewed this not as a reaction to his brutal policy towards the peasantry but instead as "sabotage by grain-hoarding kulaks". The category of "kulak", which was as elastic as the whims of the Soviet leadership wanted it to be, was thus redefined to include supposedly wealthy farmers and anyone who refused to collectivise.

In Ukraine, famine spread in rural areas at the turn of 1931/32. By the spring of 1932, 144,000 people had already died of starvation. On 10 June 1932, in view of the critical situation, Ukrainian chairman of the Council of People's Commissars Vlas Chubar sent a request to the Premier of the USSR, Vyacheslav Molotov, for "urgent food relief". Rather than acceding to this request, Molotov proclaimed on several occasions that it was imperative to comply with the established requisition quotas. Without any prospect of help, Ukrainian farmers secretly tried to withhold part of the harvest to protect themselves against starvation. These desperate acts were punishable by execution or ten years' imprisonment in a camp.

Unrest and uprisings increased—of the 1,630 protests registered throughout the Soviet Union, 1,096 took place in the Ukrainian SSR and the ethnic-Ukrainian-dominated Kuban region. In Stalin's eyes, Ukraine had become the centre of political destabilisation. He had not forgotten the massive peasant revolts against collectivisation that had previously taken place there in 1930. Based on his view of nationalism, he conflated this resistance with the growing self-confidence of the Ukrainian functionary elites, whom he suspected of disloyalty to the overriding interests of the Soviet Union.

In the 1920s, as part of a relatively liberal nationality policy, the Bolsheviks had supported the non-Russian peoples integrated into the USSR. The Ukrainian language was introduced as an official language in 1923, and conscious attempts were made to promote national culture. However, nation-building was intended to serve as an instrument of Sovietisation—the republics were to be firmly anchored within the USSR: "national in form, Soviet in content". Strategically important Ukraine was increasingly perceived as an "island of autonomy" and the peasantry as a "class". In the eyes of the Soviet leadership, both were considered equally dangerous. The "sabotage" by the "kulaks and enemies of the kolkhoz system" was to be defeated by famine as an instrument of terror and the Ukrainian resistance smothered for good.

The number of victims in the Ukrainian villages was considerably higher than in other starving regions of the USSR. This was because of the draconian measures introduced throughout Ukraine, which were applied in other famine regions either only sporadically or in a less brutal form. On 18 November 1932, the Central Committee of the Communist Party of Ukraine imposed food sanctions: kolkhozes that did not meet their grain requirements—and the virtual impossibility of fulfilling these quotas meant that this applied to 90 per cent of them—had to forfeit 15 times their normal monthly ration of meat. If kolkhozes failed to fulfil the plan, they were placed on "black lists" from the beginning of December 1932. In effect, this meant the cessation of all trade, the confiscation of all food in the shops and the imposition of a total blockade on the villages. Deprived of all their winter supplies, the farmers were left to starve. By mid-December, 82 Ukrainian regions had been affected by the measures.

From mid-December 1932, the terror campaign was also extended to the Kuban region in the northern Caucasus, which was mainly inhabited by ethnic-Ukrainian Cossacks and peasants. In a secret meeting of the Council of People's Commissars of the USSR of 14 December 1932, it was decided that the OGPU secret police should intervene to stop the "sabotage of grain collection and sowing" in the North Caucasus and Ukraine. There followed the mass deportation of 60,000 to 100,000 Cossacks from their settlements to the far north, the Urals and Kazakhstan. 15,000 members of the regional Communist Party were arrested. These purges were the precursors to the later "national operations" that reached their peak during the Stalinist mass terror of 1937/38.

In the winter months of 1932/33, hundreds of thousands of farmers attempted to flee areas of Ukraine afflicted by famine to the neighbouring regions of Belarus and the Soviet Union to find food. On 22 January 1933, the party organs and the OGPU were ordered by Stalin and Molotov to seal off the borders with the North Caucasus and Ukraine. None of the famine regions in the Urals or the Volga was subjected to similar coercive measures. In those regions, hundreds of thousands of people were able to flee to northern Russia or the southern Caucasus to escape starvation.

The sealing off of the areas was intended to prevent the dissemination of information on the situation in rural areas and the stoking of social tensions in the regions by itinerant famine victims. By mid-March 1933, the OGPU had arrested 219,416 people in compliance with the directive of 22 January, of whom 186,588 were returned to their homes and 9,385 forced to stand trial. 10,657 people were placed in "filtration camps". The territorial isolation of the territories also made it possible to carry out the cleansing campaigns ordered by Stalin against so-called "national and anti-Soviet elements" of the Ukrainian elites in the education, party and agricultural sectors. For many people, this meant arrest, deportation and long-term detention in the Gulag camps.

Only in July 1933, when the terror inflicted by the famine had reached its greatest intensity and geographical extent, did the Soviet leadership approve aid for the areas affected by "supply difficulties". However, the allocations were insufficient. Although millions of people starved to death in rural areas, the Soviet Union continued its export of 1,830,000 tonnes of grain to raise funds. At the height of the famine disaster, state-controlled grain storehouses were holding over one million tonnes of grain reserves—enough to save millions of people from starvation.

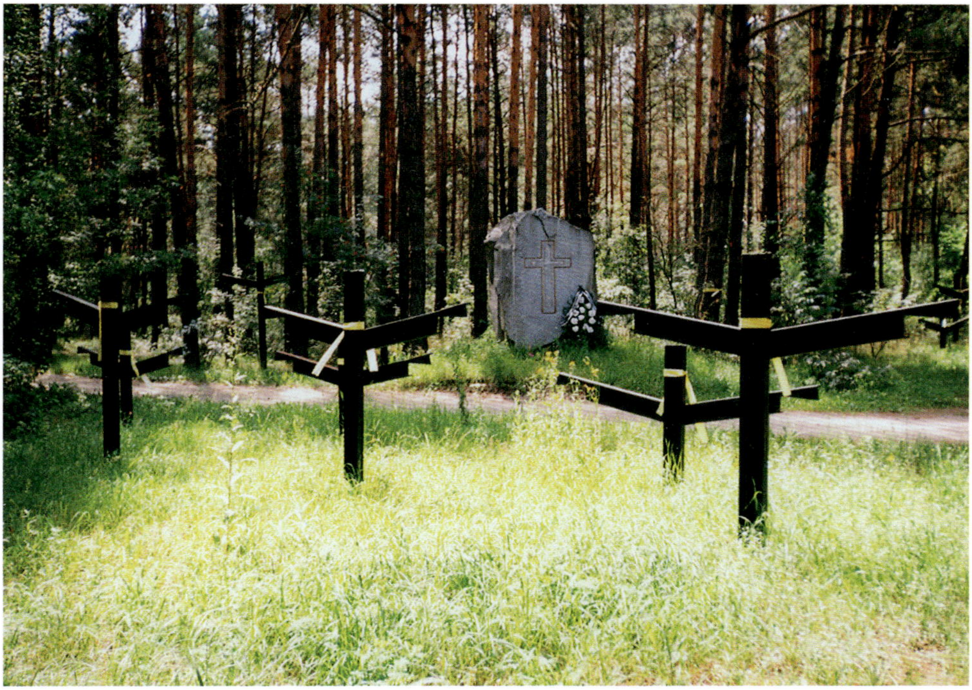

Memorial crosses for the victims of mass terror at the Bykivnya memorial near Kiev

Even once the disastrous famine had been overcome, however, the country still did not come to rest. Only a few years later, a new wave of mass arrests and executions began in the "Great Terror", to which hundreds of thousands of Ukrainians fell victim in the course of "national operations". Countless mass graves all over the country bear witness to murders by the Soviet secret police. To this day, neither the exact locations nor the number and identity of those murdered have been established; this is because the NKVD destroyed many documents after the German invasion to prevent them from falling into the hands of the Germans. Memorial chapels have been erected at many of the execution sites and mass graves located to date.

On 17 September 1939, shortly after the invasion of Poland by the German Wehrmacht, Soviet troops invaded Eastern Galicia and Volhynia. According to the agreements laid down in the Molotov-Ribbentrop Pact of 23 August 1939, Western Ukraine (Eastern Galicia and Volhynia), which had until then belonged to Poland, were to come under Soviet rule. In June 1940, the Soviet Union annexed what was then Romanian Northern Bukovina. In line with the practice that had been established in the Eastern Ukrainian regions in previous decades, Stalinist terror now also took hold here. Polish citizens (Poles, Ukrainians and Jews)—mainly politicians, clergy, intellectuals and people considered wealthy—but also Ukrainian nationalists were arrested, deported or murdered.

By the time the German Wehrmacht invaded the Soviet Union on 22 June 1941, hundreds of thousands of citizens had fallen victim to terror in the new areas of the Ukrainian SSR. In the light of these circumstances, the invasion by the German troops in June 1941 was welcomed by parts of the population as a liberation from Soviet rule. Ukrainian volunteers joined German troops in the fight against the Red Army, and massacres of the Jewish population also began immediately after the German invasion.

Hopes that the Third Reich would support Ukraine's independence efforts, however, were dashed very quickly. The OUN (Organisation of Ukrainian Nationalists) had proclaimed an independent Ukrainian state immediately after the German occupation of Lviv. This state was not, however, recognised by Nazi Germany, and its leaders, including Stepan Bandera, were arrested and transported to Berlin. From early 1942 to September 1944, they were imprisoned in the Sachsenhausen concentration camp. After the German invasion, it also became apparent in Ukraine that Nazi Germany was waging a criminal war of aggression, conquest and annihilation and regarded the people of Eastern Europe—such as Poles, Ukrainians, Belarusians and Russians—as subhuman, treating them accordingly.

With the invasion by the German troops, the systematic murder of the Jewish population began in Ukraine. Millions fell victim to the Nazis' racial fanaticism. In addition, the occupiers starved hundreds of thousands of Soviet prisoners in the camps on Ukrainian territory and deported hundreds of thousands of Ukrainians to Germany for forced labour. The entire infrastructure was destroyed. Timothy Snyder has described the areas in Ukraine, Belarus and Poland as "Bloodlands". Both nationalist and Soviet partisan associations formed against the German occupation. However, the Germans responded to their acts of sabotage with brutal retaliation against the civilian population.

With the advance of the Red Army on the territories held by the German Wehrmacht, the nationalist partisan associations broadened their campaign against the German occupiers to include the Soviet army. Some Ukrainian nationalists, who, in the light of the terror of the years 1939 to 1941, considered the Stalinist Soviet Union to be the greater of two evils, collaborated with the Germans and enrolled in combat units (the 1st Galician Division or the 14th Waffen Grenadier Division of the SS) to take part in the battles against the Red Army.

The UPA (Ukrainian Insurgent Army), founded in 1942, fought the German troops and the Polish home army (AK—Armija Krajowa) from 1943. The conflict with Poland that had been ongoing since the end of the First World War descended into a bloodbath in Volhynia as, according to various estimates, the UPA associations murdered between 35,000 and 60,000 Polish citizens (between 25,000 and 40,000 in Eastern Galicia) in 1943/44, and the AK killed thousands of Ukrainians in retaliation. At the end of the war, the UPA concentrated on fighting the advancing Soviet units. After the war, it continued its guerrilla war against the Soviet Union. It was not until the mid-1950s that Soviet troops were finally able to crush the UPA, although individual resistance cells persisted until the 1960s.

After the victory of the anti-Hitler coalition and the surrender of the German Wehrmacht on 8 May 1945, and in accordance with the Allied agreements, the entire territory of Ukraine, including the former West Ukrainian territories, came under Soviet control. In June 1945, Carpathian Ruthenia became part of the Ukrainian SSR under the treaty between the Soviet Union and Czechoslovakia.

Persecution continued in Ukraine after the end of the war. On the one hand, it was perpetrated against actual and alleged collaborators who had cooperated with the German occupying forces or been involved in crimes against the civilian population. At the same time, acts of terror were once again directed against anyone who was considered potentially dangerous. This included representatives of the Ukrainian independence movement, artists and intellectuals, or ordinary workers and peasants who were arrested on the flimsiest of pretexts and deported to Siberia.

After Stalin's death, the terror also died down in Ukraine, although diluted forms of repression continued. Although the Ukrainian language and culture were officially recognised and permitted, people who supported the promotion of free Ukrainian culture and liberalisation of the increasingly repressive Soviet system were persecuted and imprisoned as enemies of the state. This fate befell many dissidents, such as the Ukrainian poet Vasyl Stus, who died in mysterious circumstances in the Perm 36 camp in Siberia in 1985. In 1976, following the signing of the Helsinki Final Act on 1 August 1975, a Helsinki Group was set up in Ukraine to document human rights violations and promote democratisation.

National Museum "Holodomor Victims Memorial"

Kiev. The museum, which has been recognised by the state since 2010, opened to the public on 22 November 2008, which was Holodomor Remembrance Day that year. The museum with its extensive memorial complex is located on the hills of Petcherskyi (a district of Kiev) on the right bank of the Dnieper River. Inaugurated on the 75th anniversary of the famine disaster of 1932/33, the institution commemorates the several million Ukrainian victims who lost their lives in the course of the forced collectivisation of the agricultural economy, "dekulakisation" and the brutal grain procurement measures of the Soviet government.

The five-hectare memorial complex was designed by Ukrainian architect Yuriy Kovalyov and monumental artist Anatoly Haidamaka. In front of the entrance to the site are two cuboids of black granite which bear the inscriptions 1932 and 1933 respectively. A few metres further back, the sculptures of two kneeling angels mark the entrance to the memorial. The black paving of the path leading to the centre of the complex symbolises the regions of particularly fertile Ukrainian black soil, which were among the worst affected by the Holodomor.

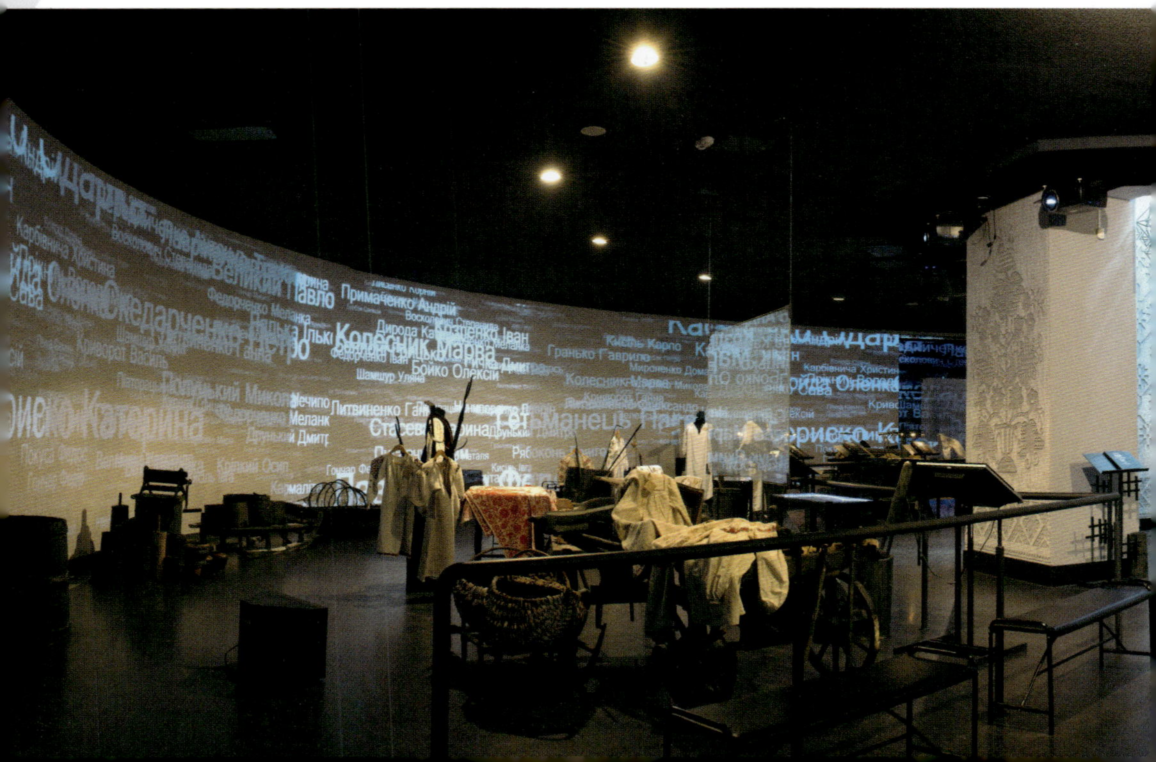

The path is lined on both sides with a total of twenty-four millstones and stone slabs engraved with the names of hundreds of villagers who lost their lives to famine. Halfway to the museum, on a circular concrete base, stands a life-size bronze sculpture of an emaciated girl. Looking into the distance, she holds three ears of grain in her hands crossed in front of her chest. The composition, known as "Bitter Memory of Childhood", is dedicated to all those children who died of hunger and exhaustion during the Holodomor.

The central square of the grounds is dominated by a thirty-metre-high monument in the form of a burning candle. The white façade of the memorial bears traditional Ukrainian embroidery patterns with cross-shaped glass inlays of different sizes. On the outside of the memorial are four Latin crosses made of black bars. At the point where the beams of the crosses meet is the bronze figure of a stork with outstretched wings. This symbolises the rebirth of the Ukrainian nation-state after the collapse of the Soviet Union.

Below the memorial is the museum with an exhibition on the Holodomor. The main items on display are everyday possessions of the Ukrainian rural population in the 1920s and 1930s. The exhibits come from the regions of the country particularly affected by the Holodomor. In the middle of the exhibition hall are books of the dead with the names of 900,000 victims of the famine catastrophe. Video installations with documents, photographs and film sequences provide information on the causes, course and consequences of the famine disaster.

Location: Kiev, ulitsa Lavrska 3
Internet: www.memorialholodomor.org.ua

Exhibition at the "Holodomor Victims Memorial" National Museum

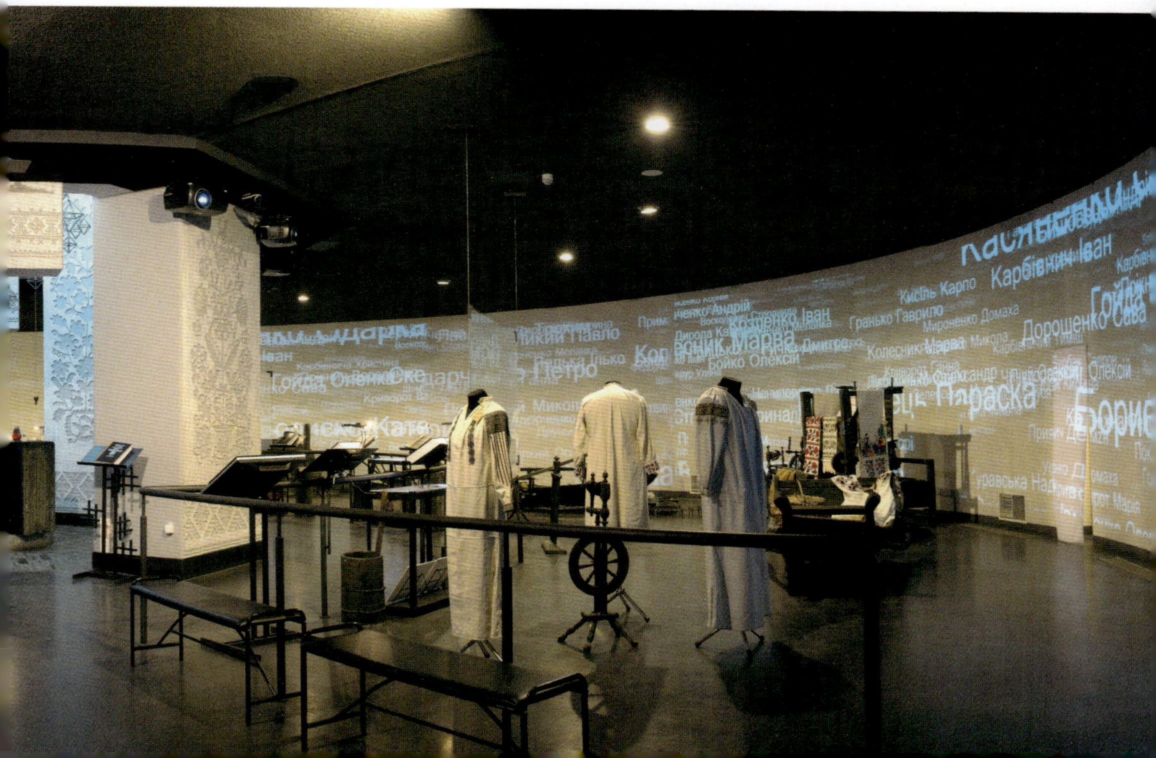

Monument to Victims of Famine in 1932/33

Kiev. The Monument to Victims of Famine in 1932/33 was inaugurated on Mykhailivska Square on 2 September 1993 on the occasion of the 60th anniversary of the famine catastrophe. The granite-and-bronze monument consists of a recessed cross with the silhouette of the "Mother-Protector", the national symbol of Ukraine, at its heart. The design for the simple memorial was presented by sculptor Vasyl Perevalsky and architect Mykola Kysly.

The monument was unveiled in the presence of President Leonid Kravchuk and is still one of the central memorials to the victims of the Holodomor in Ukraine. In recent years, Memorial Kiev has set up panels on the outer wall of St. Michael's Monastery to its rear to provide information about the famine catastrophe.

Inscription

Ukrainian: Мільйонам Українців— жертвам Голодомору Геноциду 1932–1933 років. / Встановлено 1993 р

English: *For the Millions of Ukrainians— Victims of the Famine-Genocide of 1932–1933 / Erected in 1993*

Location: Kiev, ploshchad Mikhailovskaya

► Monument in Kiev to the Victims of Famine in 1932/33

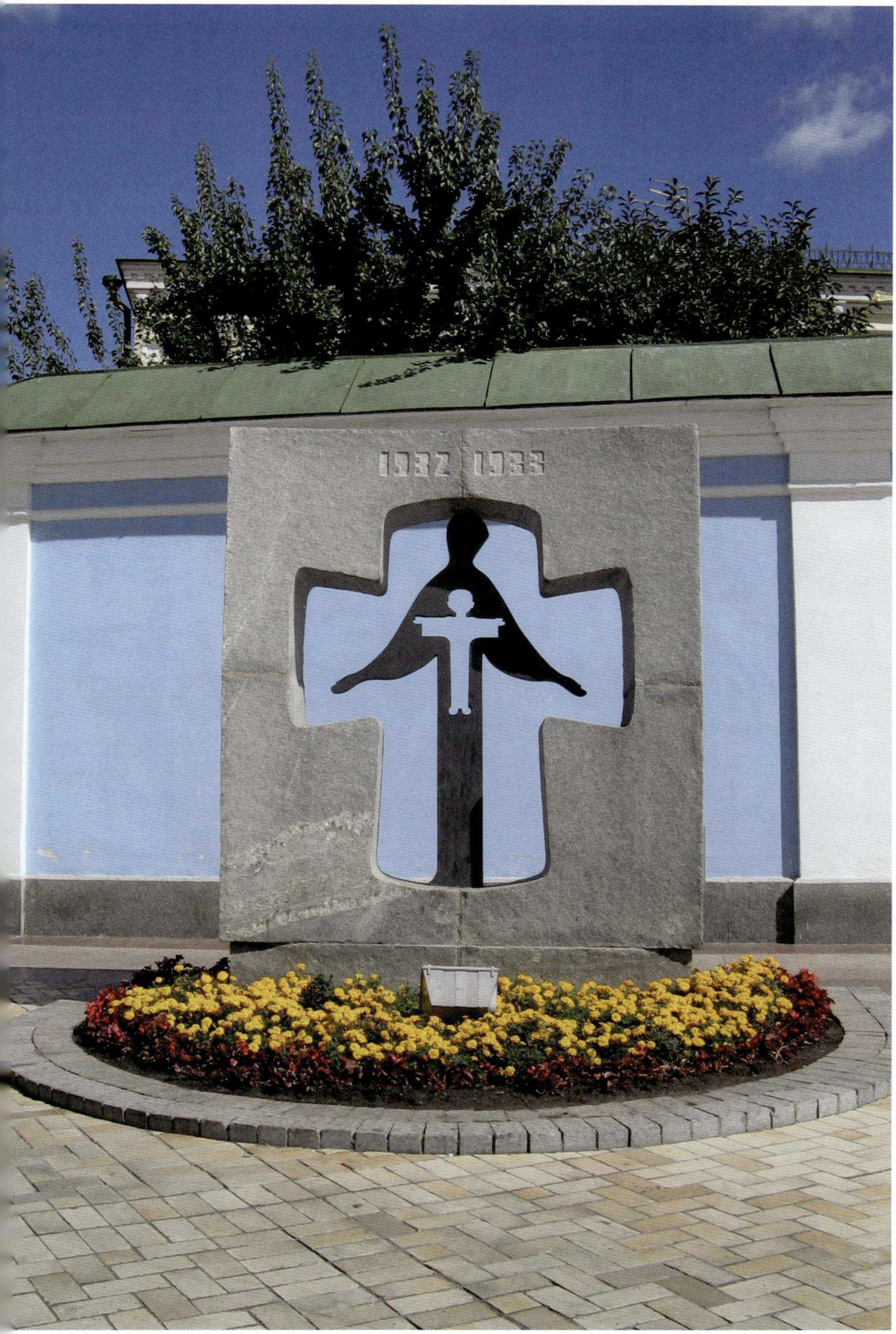
1932 1933

Museum of Soviet Occupation

Kiev. The Museum of Soviet Occupation began life on 30 November 2001 as a temporary exhibition in the headquarters of the Kiev-based organisation Memorial, entitled "Not to Be Forgotten: A Chronicle of the Communist Inquisition in Ukraine (1917–1991)". On the initiative of Memorial's board, the exhibition was renamed "Museum of Soviet Occupation" on 10 April 2007. It provides a chronological account of historical events between 1917 and 1991 and aims to inform visitors about the Soviet era of Ukrainian history. Other parts of the exhibition portray the fates of Ukrainian prisoners on the Solovetsky Islands and the history of Kiev during the Soviet period.

The main part of the "Chronicle of the Communist Inquisition" exhibition is divided into twelve thematic units. Using photographs, posters, archival materials and previously unpublished documents, it traces the outline of communist rule and its consequences on the territory of the Soviet Union and the Ukrainian Republic. Presented first is the "system of concentration camps in the USSR", in which not only members of other nationalities but also thousands of Ukrainians had to serve long prison sentences and perform forced labour tasks. With a huge network of at least 476 camp complexes and thousands of individual and subcamps, the reach of the Gulag extended throughout the entire Soviet Union.

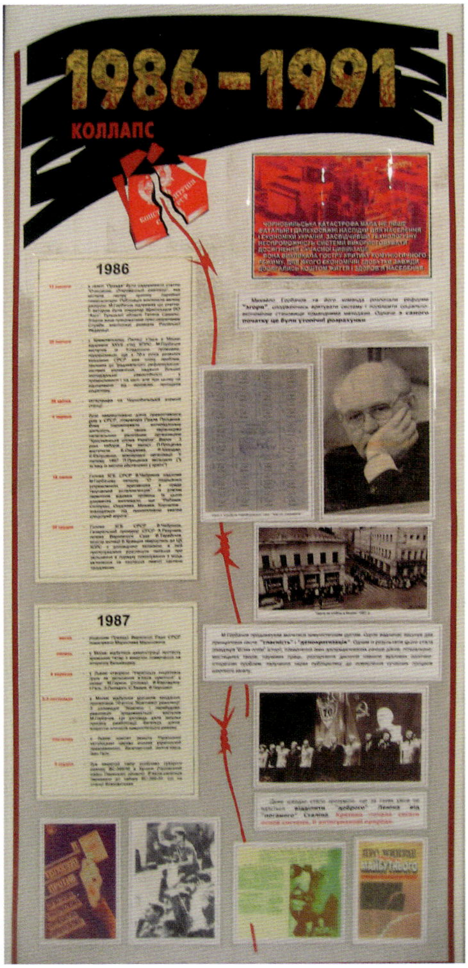

Information panel at the Museum of Soviet Occupation

Considerable space is devoted to a chronological presentation of communist rule on the territory of Ukraine. Beginning with the Bolshevik coup during the October Revolution of 1917, the exhibition traces the activities in Ukraine of the Soviet secret police under the direction of Felix Dzerzhinsky. It also sheds light on the horrors of the civil war years from 1918 to 1920 and the violence of the "Red" and "White Terror", at the end of which the Soviet's hold on power was fully established.

The next section portrays the consolidation of the Stalinist hold on power and the forced industrialisation that was to catapult the Soviet Union into modernity within a very short time. In this context, both forced collectivisation—the compulsory and brutal incorporation of small farms into state-controlled kolkhozes—and the "dekulakisation campaign" against supposedly wealthy farmers and all those who refused to follow the guidelines of the collectivisation diktat are covered comprehensively. The horrors of the Holodomor in 1932/33 are documented in particularly gruesome detail. In the Soviet Union, the famine, which was used as an instrument of Stalinist terror, claimed some six to seven million victims. Between 3 and 3.9 million people died within a few months from the direct consequences of deprivation, starvation, impoverishment and disease in Ukraine's grain surplus areas and the Kuban region of the Northern Caucasus populated by ethnic Ukrainians.

Further exhibition spaces offer insights into the Stalinist excesses of violence in the "Great Terror" in 1937/38, which, in their absoluteness and arbitrary brutality, had as their aim the "liquidation" of all remaining "enemies" within the party and state apparatus as well as in all social classes. Also discussed are the events and consequences of the "Great Patriotic War" and the last years of Stalinist rule before the death of the dictator on 5 March 1953. Other topics include the years of stability and stagnation during the Brezhnev era from 1965 to 1985 and the collapse of the Soviet system in August 1991. The process of Ukrainian nation-building after 1991 is also presented in chronological order.

The Kiev Memorial is complemented by an extensive collection of film material and scientific literature on communist crimes in Ukraine from the October Revolution in 1917 to the collapse of the Soviet Union in 1991. Guided tours of the exhibition are available in Ukrainian and Russian.

Location: Kiev, ulitsa Michaila Stelmacha 6A
Internet: www.memorial.kiev.ua/expo/eng/second.html

National Historical and Memorial Reserve "Graves of Bykivnya"

Kiev. A Polish military cemetery was built in 2012 on the eastern outskirts of the Ukrainian capital, Kiev, as the fourth cemetery, after those in Medny, Kharkiv, and Katyń itself, for the victims of the mass murders in Katyń. It is located on the grounds of the "National Historical and Memorial Reserve 'Graves of Bykivnya'", where the Soviet secret police, the NKVD, buried the mortal remains of the people they had shot since 1937. It is estimated that anywhere between tens of thousands and over 100,000 Ukrainian victims were shot by the NKVD in Kiev and transported here by lorry or on trams running through the forest.

The burial site of Bykivnya has been known since 1971 and, according to the official Soviet version, contained graves from the German occupation period between 1941 and 1943. It was not until the end of the Soviet Union that it became apparent that the people buried here had in fact been murdered by the Stalinist secret police. The suspicion soon began to circulate that it was Polish victims of the mass executions in the spring of 1940, known as the Katyń massacre, who lay buried in Bykivnya. This hypothesis was confirmed by exhumations by Polish archaeologists in 2001, 2006 to 2007, and 2011, who were able to identify 1,488 corpses as Poles on the basis of personal objects found in the graves. Although individual identification was only possible in a few cases, it can be assumed that these were the victims of the so-called "Ukrainian Katyń list". This contained the names of 3,435 Polish citizens held in the prisons of Western Ukraine, annexed to the Soviet Union in 1939, who were to be shot in the course of the Katyń operation.

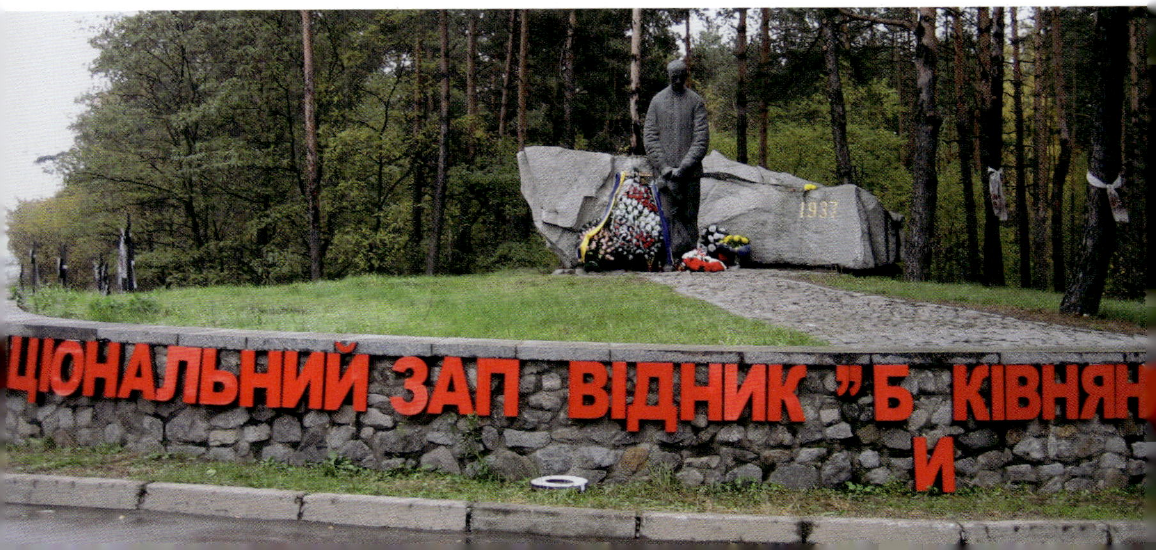

Entrance area to the "Graves of Bykivnya" memorial

After the exhumed bodies had been buried in provisional graves in October 2007 and September 2011, Polish President Bronisław Komorowski laid the foundation stone for the construction of a Polish military cemetery on 28 November 2011 in the presence of his Ukrainian counterpart, Victor Yanukovych. The design of the cemetery by the Air Projekt and Moderau Art groups is based on the existing grave sites in Katyń, Medny, and Kharkiv. Instead of the rusty iron used predominantly for those sites, however, light granite was chosen as the principal material for Bykivnya.

The central elements are a memorial wall bearing the names of all the victims of the "Ukrainian Katyń list" and a horizontal cross lying on a symbolic burial mound with the "Virtuti Militari" medal and the Polish Cross of September Campaign engraved on its sides. There is also a granite altar and a bell placed between four stelae in the centre of the memorial ensemble with the symbols of the confessions and religions of those murdered. This is surrounded by panels with individual epitaphs.

The Presidents of Poland and Ukraine officially inaugurated the cemetery on 21 September 2012. The Holy Mass during the inauguration ceremony was presided over by the Primate of Poland, Archbishop Józef Kowalczyk and Polish Military Ordinariate Józef Guzdek.

An ensemble of seven memorials to the Ukrainian victims of Stalinist terror had already been erected in Bykivnya in 1995. At the entrance to the site is a monument consisting of a larger-than-life sculpture of a man with his head bowed standing in front of two large granite blocks on which the year 1937 is engraved. Other memorial stones with short inscriptions and 87 stylised metal crosses are scattered along a funeral path in the forest. The memorial, designed by Volodymyr Chepelyk and Mykola Kyslyi, culminates in a granite cross at a mass grave discovered during the excavations. Small metal plaques with the names

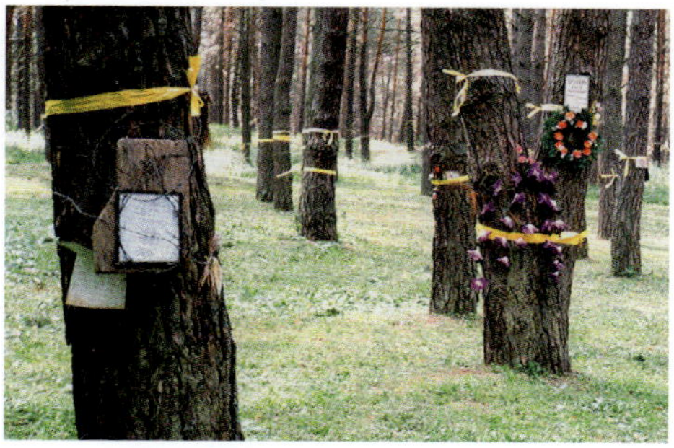

Trees with plaques and floral decorations on the grounds of the memorial

of individual victims and traditional shawls, which, according to Ukrainian custom, are given as a blessing on journeys, hang on many trees and crosses around the memorial.

The cemetery was declared a "National Historical and Memorial Reserve" in 2006. On 21 May the same year, Ukrainian head of state Victor Yushchenko attended the traditional memorial service in Bykivnya for the first time. In 2012, a new monumental memorial to the Ukrainian victims was erected next to the Polish military cemetery. This consists of a seven-metre hill of grey granite stones with ten large grey granite crosses arranged up its flank. The Ukrainian coat of arms is engraved on the uppermost cross. The memorial also includes two pairs of granite stelae, each of which feature an oversized bullet hole.

Location: Kiev, prospekt Brovarskyi, east of the Bykivnya District
Internet: ua.bykivnya.org/

Monument to the Victims of Communist Crimes

Lviv. The Monument to the Victims of Communist Crimes stands directly in front of the building of former Prison No. 1. The prison was built as an annex to the former Austro-Hungarian gendarmerie, with construction starting directly after the First World War in 1918 and ending in 1920. Before the Second World War, the Fourth Department of the Polish State Police detained political prisoners here. After the outbreak of the war in September 1939 and the invasion of Galicia by the Soviet army under the terms of the Molotov-Ribbentrop Pact, the Soviet political secret police, the NKVD, was headquartered in the building from 1939 to 1941.

During the German occupation, the building housed the Gestapo detention centre and

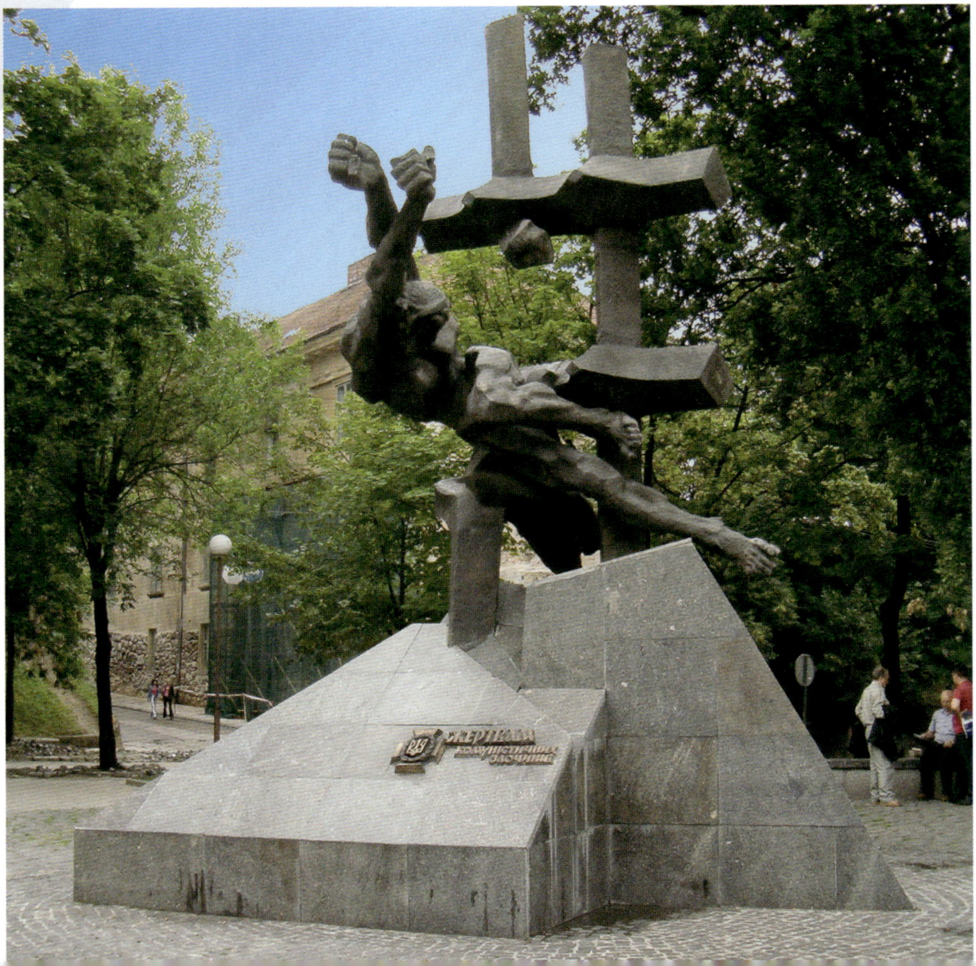

the SD Einsatzgruppen. The prison yard was paved with tombstones from the old Jewish cemetery. From 1944, the building was once again used by the NKVD and its successor organisations, the MGB and KGB. Even after the collapse of the Soviet Union, the building remained a prison for the first few years after the independence of Ukraine. It was used as a remand prison of the Ukrainian secret service SBU until its final closure in 1996.

The memorial was erected by the Association of Political Prisoners and various organisations of the Lviv region, with the participation of the population. On 23 June 1992, during a memorial ceremony to mark the 51st anniversary of the start of the NKVD massacres in Galicia, a memorial stone was placed here with the inscription "At this place a monument to victims of communist terror will be erected". The monument was inaugurated on 8 November 1997. The sculpture of a dying man on a pedestal in front of a stylised lattice window is dedicated to all the victims of communism. The composition was designed and created by sculptor Petro Shtayer and architect Roman Syvenkyi.

After the German invasion of the Soviet Union on 22 June 1941, the NKVD arrested huge numbers of alleged spies and saboteurs, particularly in the western regions annexed in 1939, where thousands were detained. They were taken to the prisons of the secret police, which were already overcrowded due to mass arrests and temporary detentions prior to deportation. The original plan was to evacuate all the detainees from the prisons and prisoner of war camps in the front-line areas to the interior of the country.

On 24 June 1941, Lavrentiy Beria, head of the NKVD, issued the order to release criminal prisoners but to evacuate political prisoners to the east. If this was no longer possible due to the proximity to the front, the prisoners were to be shot. In Galicia and Volhynia alone, more than 20,000 people (mostly Ukrainians but also numerous Poles and Jews) were murdered in the NKVD prisons in the first days of the war in June 1941.

Every year on the last Sunday in June, commemorations are held at the memorial, attended by representatives of all the denominational groups in the Lviv region.

◄
Monument to the Victims of Communist Crimes

Inscription on the base
Ukrainian: Жертвам / комуністичних / злочинів

English: *To the Victims of Communist crimes*

Location: Lviv, ploshchad Markiana Shashkevycha

Further reading:

Kaminsky, Anna (ed.): Erinnerungsorte an den Holodomor 1932/33 in der Ukraine. Leipzig 2008. / Kaminsky, Anna (ed.): Erinnerungsorte für die Opfer von Katyń. Leipzig 2013. / Krutsyk, Roman / Yeremenko, Artur: Educational Handbook to Accompany the Exposition „Not to be Forgotten. A Chronicle of the Communist Inquisition in Ukraine 1917 – 1991". The Kyiv City Organization of the All Ukrainian Memorial Society of V. Stus. 2003. Available online at: www.memorial.kiev.ua/expo/eng/second.html (last accessed on: 15/11/2017). / Simon, Gerhard: Holodomor als Waffe. Stalinismus, Hunger und der ukrainische Nationalismus. In: Osteuropa, 2004, Vol. 54, No. 12, pp. 37 – 56. / Werth, Nicolas: Die große ukrainische Hungersnot von 1932 / 33. In: Baberowski, Jörg / Kindler, Robert (ed.): Macht ohne Grenzen. Herrschaft und Terror im Stalinismus. Frankfurt, New York 2014, pp. 117 – 139.

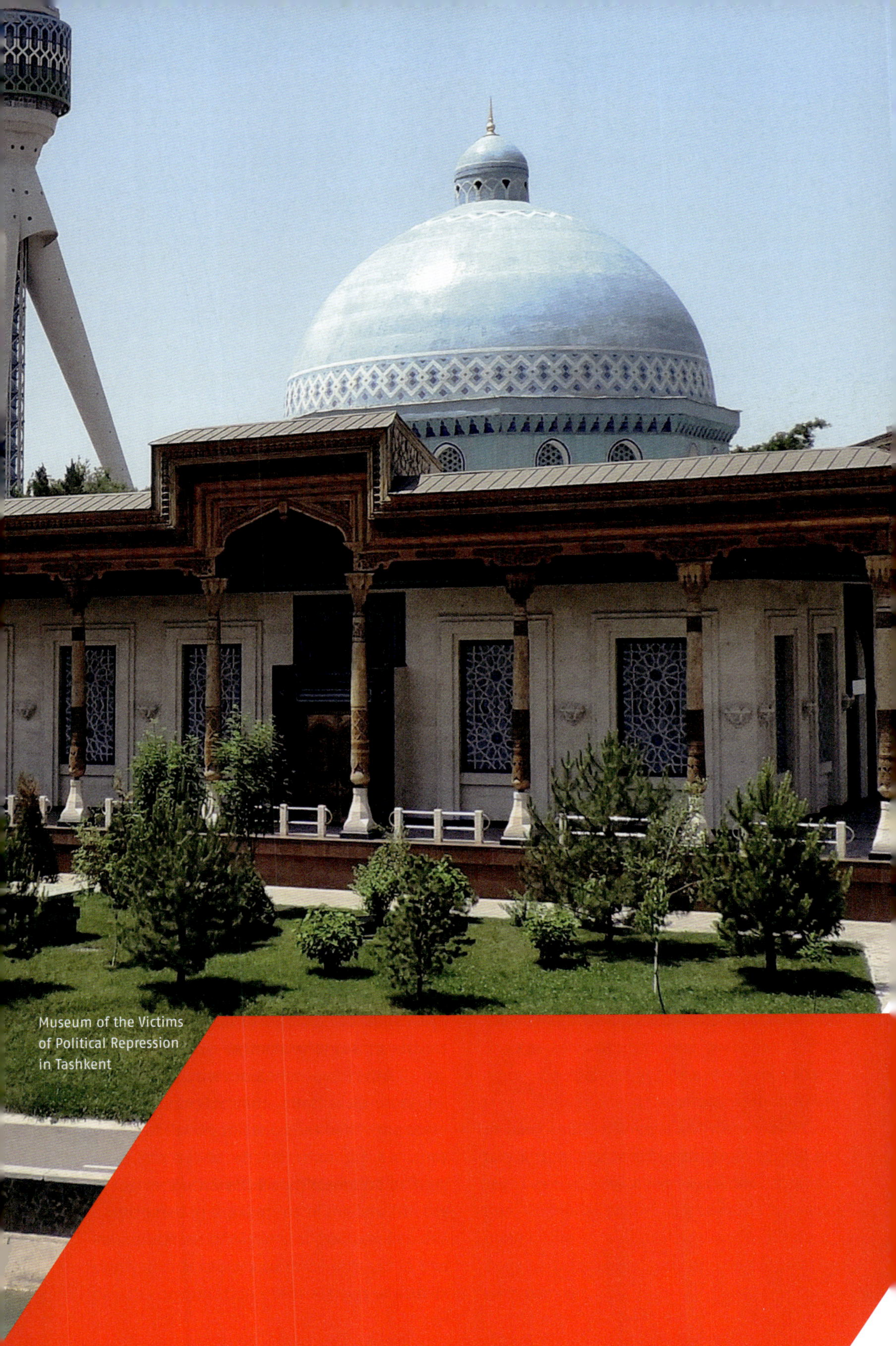

Museum of the Victims
of Political Repression
in Tashkent

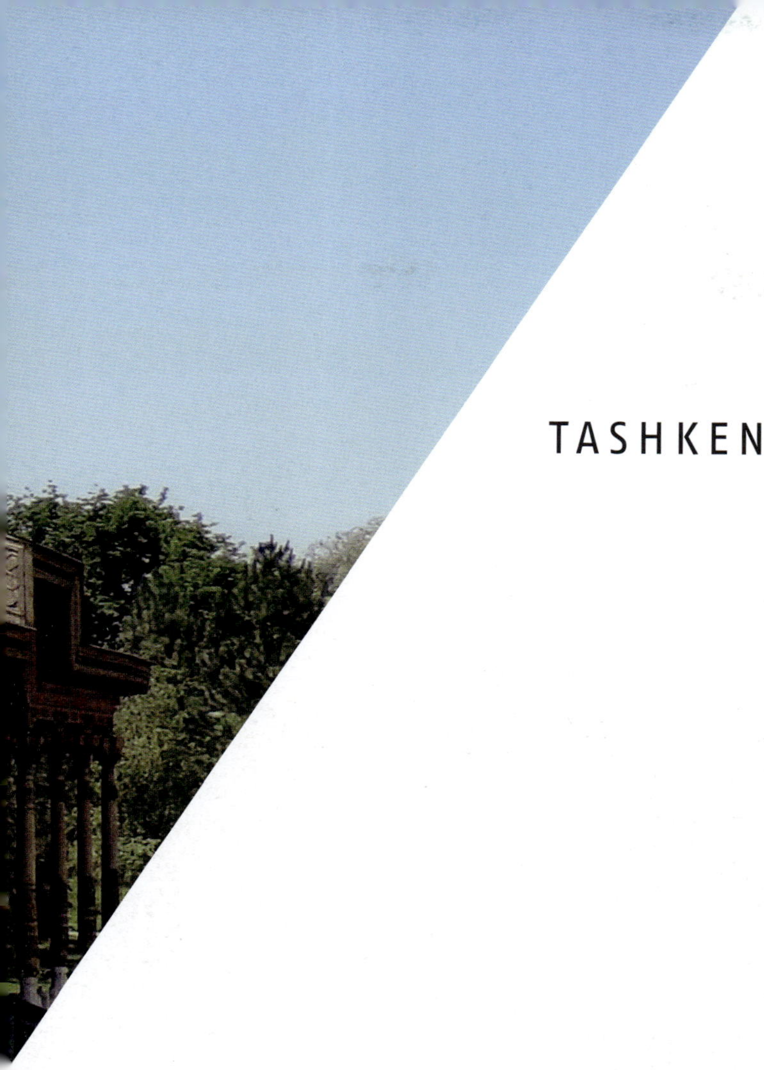

TASHKENT

Uzbekistan

Until 1918, Uzbek territory belonged to the Governor-Generalship of Turkestan and was part of the Russian Tsarist Empire. After the Bolsheviks took power in large parts of the Russian Empire and Tashkent in 1917, the Central Asian peoples were promised their national independence, a pledge repaid by strong local support for the Bolsheviks. During the ensuing civil war, however, the local elites were defamed as "nationalists" and declared enemies of the Soviet occupying power. In the civil war, local units fought against the Red Army; in 1922, the units were disbanded, although some units continued to offer armed resistance to the Bolsheviks until the mid-1930s. In 1922, the Turkestan Autonomous Soviet Socialist Republic was founded, which, with the inclusion of further territories, was renamed the Uzbek Soviet Socialist Republic in 1924 before acceding to the Soviet Union in 1925.

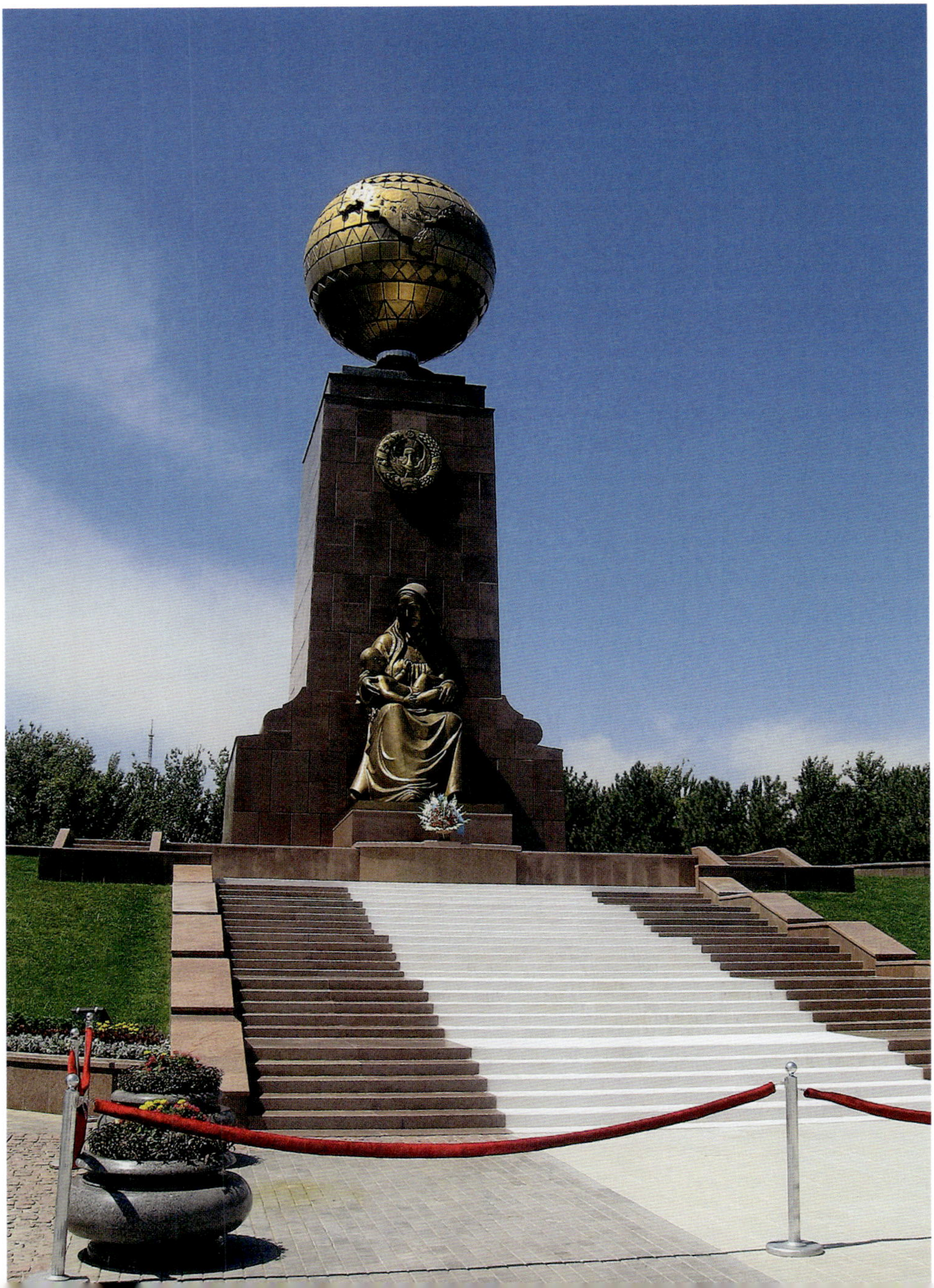

The establishment of communist power in Uzbekistan and the other Central Asian republics followed the same pattern as in the other Soviet republics: forced expropriations and collectivisation, destruction of the traditional way of life, forced industrialisation and the conversion of traditional agriculture to cotton monocultures, and the fight against the Islamic religion and its representatives. The violent transformation of society was accompanied by mass arrests, executions and deportations. During the "Great Terror", large swathes of the Uzbek party elite and intelligentsia were murdered.

After the German invasion of the Soviet Union, the country became a dumping ground and deportation destination for tens of thousands of people who were considered unreliable because of their ethnicity or origin and deported eastwards from the western parts of the Soviet Union. At the same time, the persecution of worshippers and Islamic religious leaders was suspended during the war as an attempt to bolster the morale of the troops and the population by allowing them to practise their religion.

Between the end of the war and the death of Stalin in 1953, little changed in the patterns of persecution and repression. As in the other parts of the country, new waves of repression were repeatedly perpetrated against different population groups. It was only after the death of Stalin and the 20th party conference of the CPSU in 1956 that the intensity of the reprisals lessened. A certain amount of cultural opening-up began, and the cultivation of some local traditions was permitted.

One constant bone of contention was the historical assessment of Central Asia's incorporation into the Russian Tsarist Empire: while the Bolsheviks regarded this as an act of modernisation that had enabled the peoples of Central Asia to leave behind medieval structures and traditions, the local population perceived their annexation by the Russian Empire as an act of colonisation. This view of history also applied to Soviet rule, the massive settlement of ethnic Russians, the suppression of the Uzbek language and the establishment of Russian as the official language.

With the invasion of Afghanistan by the Soviet Union in 1979, the Central Asian region took on a new strategic function because of its shared border with this newly invaded state. In the early 1980s, repression took hold once more, prompted in part by the so-called "cotton affair", in which the large-scale falsification of production figures in cotton cultivation was uncovered. This gave Moscow the opportunity to remove a large proportion of the local elite from their positions. Also criticised were ideological deviance and the lax treatment of Islam and its representatives. For the local population and elites, however, these conflicts—encouraged by Gorbachev's policy of glasnost and perestroika—offered an opportunity to point to the massive environmental problems caused by cotton monoculture and discrimination against Central Asian citizens, for example in the Soviet army and the administration.

In December 1991, following a referendum, Uzbekistan declared itself independent. Islam Karimov, the former chairman of the Uzbek Communist Party, was elected president and remained in office until his death in December 2016. Critical historico-political debates about the Soviet past are suppressed and required to follow the course set out by Karimov. The Communist Party renamed itself the People's Democratic Party; many cadres remained in their offices and positions. The former Soviet Uzbek secret police, the KGB, was renamed the SNB and has been the national security service ever since.

◄
Monument of Independence in Tashkent

Museum of Victims of Political Repression

Tashkent. Opened on 31 August 2002, on the site of the Memorial of the New Martyrs, the state-run museum addresses the issue of political persecution on the territory of present-day Uzbekistan. The museum stands on an area that served the Soviet secret police as an execution site between 1928 and 1941. The number of people murdered here is still unknown.

The exhibition focuses on the effects of the country's Sovietisation in the 1920s and 1930s, especially the "dekulakisation campaigns" and the development of collectivist agriculture. A second focus is on the reappraisal of Uzbekistan's history as a destination for deportations after the Second World War. Particular attention is paid to the fates of the Crimean Tatars and Koreans who were abducted and brought here. The historical contextualisation of the exhibition goes beyond the Stalinist phase: also presented are the conquest of the region by Russia in the 19th century and British attempts at annexation.

Since the completion of extensive expansion and renovation work in 2008, the Museum of Victims of Political Repression has been considered one of the most important symbols of Uzbek national independence. Visiting the institution is a mandatory for all pupils and students in Tashkent. Only a few metres from the museum is a 27-metre-high rotunda with a domed roof and a symbolic jade gravestone at its heart.

The exhibition, which is divided into ten thematic units, uses multimedia elements, photographs, documents and original objects to illustrate different periods of Uzbek history from the end of the 19th century to the attainment of national independence in September 1991. Structured chronologically, the showcases which first greet the visitor show the history of subjugation of the Central Asian states by the Russian Tsarist Empire. It is in this context that the anticolonial uprisings of the local population and their brutal oppression by the tsarist regime are illuminated and brought to the fore.

The parts of the exhibition dedicated to the Soviet period trace the seizure of power by the Bolsheviks in 1917 and the break-up of both the short-lived "Provisional Government of Autonomous Turkestan" in 1918 and the Basmachi "resistance movement". Considerable space is devoted to the repressive measures of dekulakisation and forced collectivisation, the Stalinist mass terror of 1937/38 and the history of the country as a destination for deportations, especially during and after the Second World War.

► View of the grounds of the Memorial of the New Martyrs

Uzbekistan's development during the Khrushchev and Brezhnev eras is omitted, and the narrative resumes with the "cotton affair" of the mid-1980s. As a result of the affair, Uzbek party and state officials were arrested and convicted en masse, and many committed suicide. The prosecution of this economic crime—years of embezzlement, corruption and falsification of data in the fulfilment of central planning targets for the cotton harvest—was just one of a long series of Soviet repressions. The exhibition concludes with a presentation of the memorial work carried out in Uzbekistan since the attainment of national independence in September 1991 for the victims of communist crimes.

Since 2001, by decree of long-standing President Islam Karimov, 31 August has been designated a Day of Remembrance for the Victims of Political Repressions. 9 May is also celebrated as a Day of Memory and Honour. Every year on this day, the museum hosts official commemorative events with the participation of key representatives from politics and society.

Location: Tashkent, Amir Temur ko'chasi, "Shahidlar xotirasi" maydoni
Internet: https://bit.ly/2tptZXo

Further reading:

Abashin, Sergei: Entsowjetisierung und Erinnerungspolitik in Zentralasien. In: Mählert, Ulrich et al. (eds.): Jahrbuch für Historische Kommunismusforschung. Berlin 2014, pp. 125 – 138. / Abashin, Sergei: Mustakillik and Remembrance of the Imperial Past. Passing Through the Halls of the Tashkent Museum in Memory of the Victims of Repression. In: Russian Politics and Law, 2010, Vol. 48, No. 5, pp. 78 – 91.

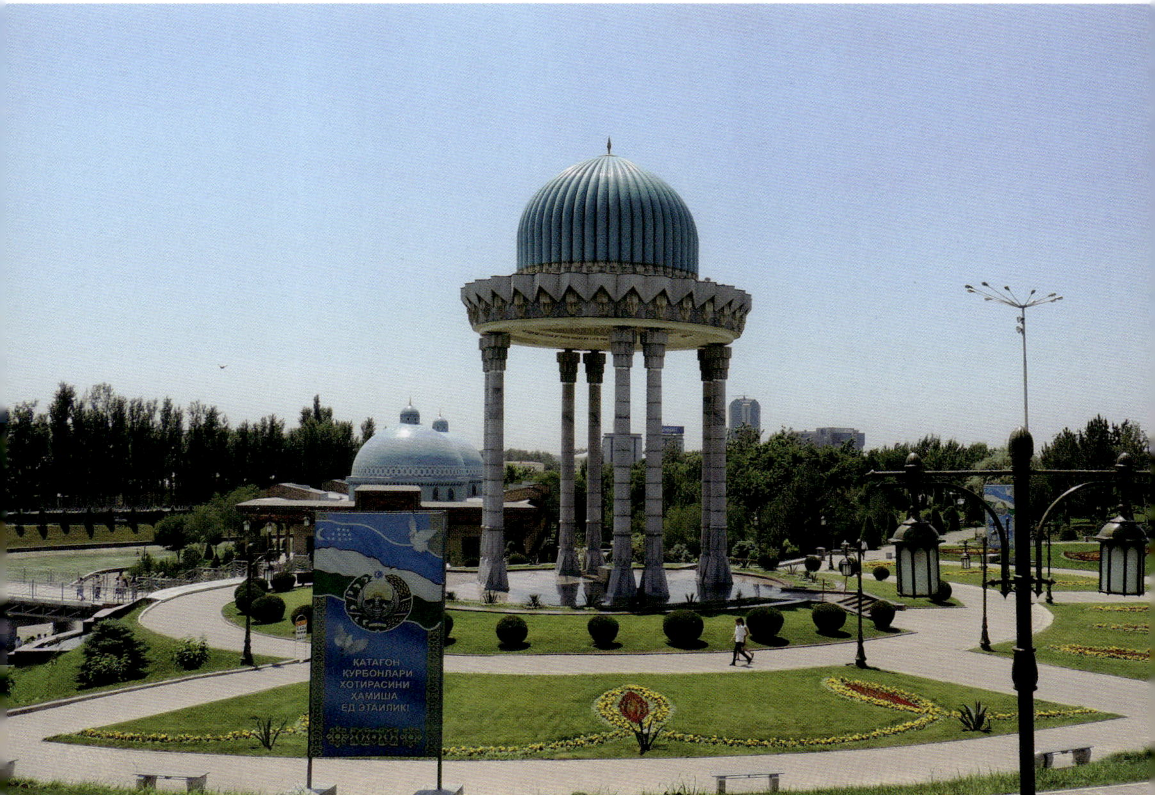

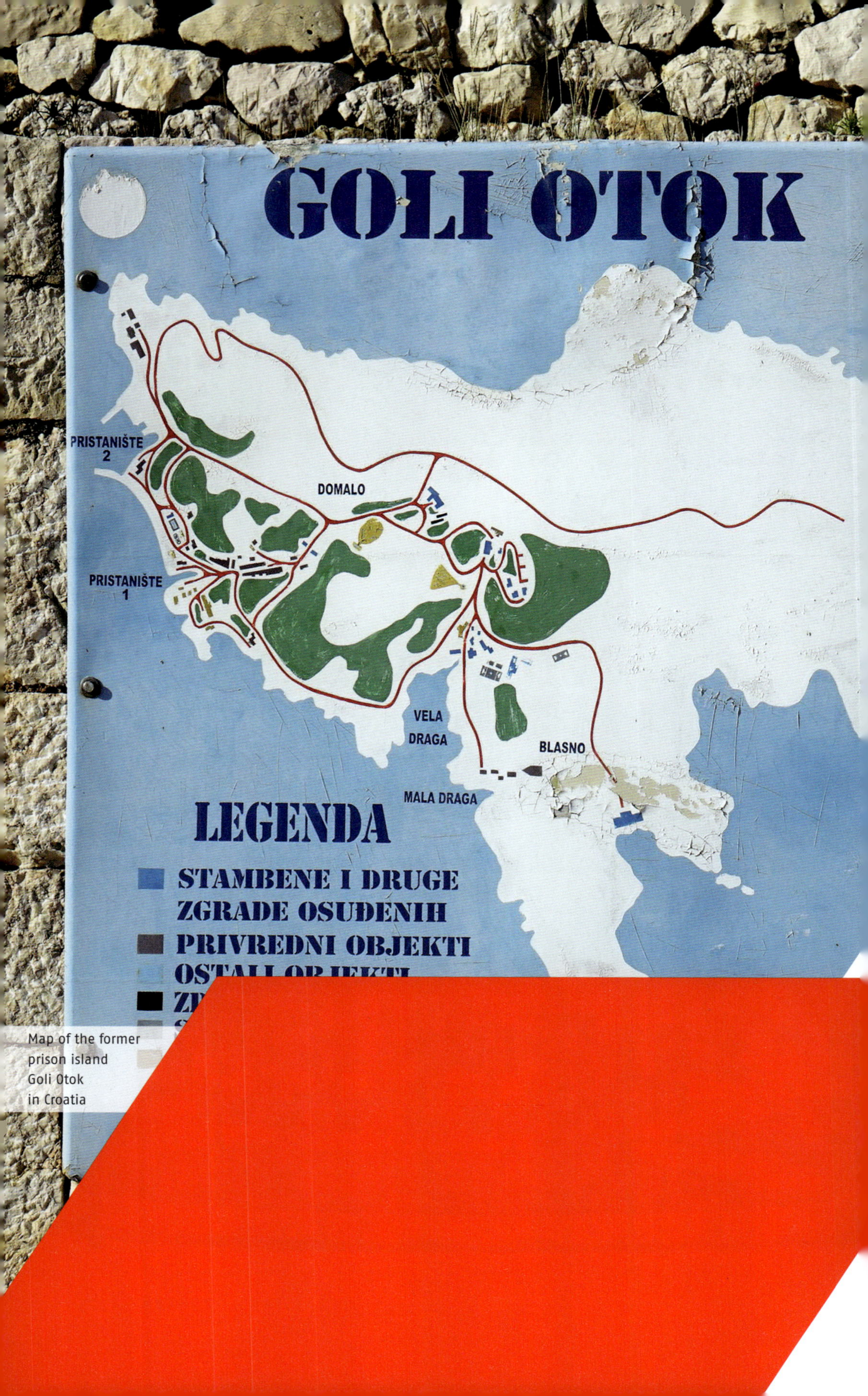

Map of the former prison island Goli Otok in Croatia

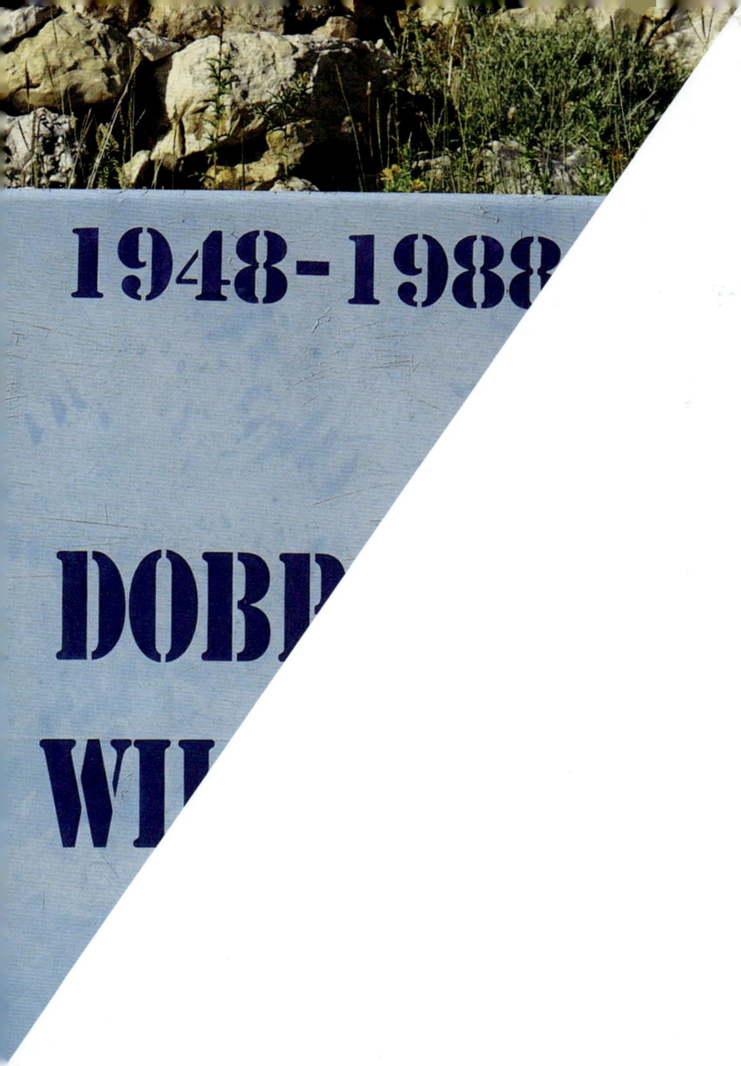

Former Yugoslavia

In April 1941, the German Wehrmacht attacked the Kingdom of Yugoslavia, occupying the country and annexing parts of it variously to the National Socialist German Reich, Mussolini's Italy and Italian-occupied Albania and Bulgaria. The Second World War was a complicated conflict in Yugoslavia, fought from 1941 to 1945 as a war of resistance to the occupying powers and their various local allies, as an ideological war between communists and anti-communists and fascists and anti-fascists and, last but by no means least, as an interethnic war. In Croatia, a fascist government came to power, adopting the German race laws and taking violent action against Serbs, Jews, Roma and Communists.

Various resistance movements formed in response to the occupation of the country, consisting primarily of communist-dominated partisan units and loyal Chetnik associations. The associations fought not just against the occupying forces and collaborators but also against one another, with the communist People's Liberation Army ultimately prevailing. Battles were also fought between different ethnic groups. The war was fought on all sides amidst bitter hardship and great losses for the civilian population. The partisans and their role were mythologised in post-war socialist Yugoslavia and formed an important part of the country's self-image.

At the end of the war, the communists led by Tito took power. The victory in the so-called People's Liberation War was a means to the legitimation of the seizure of power and the eagerly awaited revolution. The driving motivation behind this war, fought under the supreme command of the General Secretary of the Communist Party and Marshal of Yugoslavia Josip Broz, known as Tito, was the transformation of society according to Marxist-Leninist ideology in its Stalinist form. The declared goal of the revolutionary cadres of the Communist Party was a reckoning with capitalism, which they regarded as a spent force, along with all the forces that supported it, and the establishment of socialism by the dictatorship of the proletariat or, more precisely, of its avant-garde, endowed with the "proper consciousness". The idea was for revolution to emerge from victory in the war. Just how radical this approach was is evident from the numbers of people killed at the end of the war. Even according to the most conservative estimates, at least 70,000 people were murdered by Tito's partisans in the fury of the reckoning that took place in the spring of 1945. Source-based estimates today assume that communist retribution caused at least 80,000 deaths during World War II and its immediate aftermath.

The communist partisans and the secret police systematically eliminated actual and alleged collaborators, members of the political, cultural and religious elites and thousands of civilians who were regarded as sympathisers or relatives of "enemies". Despite the terror and the countless crimes perpetrated to install communist power in Yugoslavia, the Yugoslav version of communism was, and still is, considered comparatively moderate. This view stems from the special position of socialist Yugoslavia under Tito between the blocs during the Cold War and the effective liberalisation and decentralisation that took place in the 1960s and 1970s.

However, the number of victims in the years after 1945 and the extent of repression in Yugoslavia tell a different story. The expulsion, expropriation, detention and murder of Danube Swabians, Hungarian and Italian minorities and the crimes committed by the People's Liberation Army after the end of the war, such as the mass executions of "enemies of the people", were hardly discussed after 1945. It was only after the end of communism that the country began to come to terms with this era; prompted by the intensifying crisis that followed Tito's death, these crimes played an important role in various national and nationalist discourses. Most of the victims of 1945 were buried in mass graves, thrown into rock crevices, karst caves, or abandoned shafts, or bricked up alive; these sites have yet to be fully identified.

On 29 November 1943, a partisan parliament in the Bosnian town of Jajce voted to establish a "Democratic Federal Yugoslavia", consisting of the Republics of Slovenia, Croatia, Bosnia-Herzegovina, Serbia, Montenegro and Macedonia. The foundational myth of the new Yugoslavia, which was also intended to unite the various ethnic groups under the slogan of the "brotherhood and unity" of the Yugoslav peoples, was the role played by the anti-fascist resistance under communist leadership in the "people's struggle for liberation".

After Tito's break with Stalin in March 1948, persecution was extended to actual and alleged supporters of Stalin, thousands of whom were imprisoned under inhumane conditions on the almost completely barren prison island of Goli Otok in the northern Adriatic Sea. Opponents of the Yugoslav communists included the democratic opposition as well as representatives of the churches, worshippers, owners of land and industry, intellectuals and members of the pre-war political elite. Those who were considered nationalists and enemies of the "brotherhood and unity" of the Yugoslav peoples were also persecuted. Once any individual had been accused of being a supporter of Cominform or a fascist or nationalist, there was nothing to stop the secret police declaring them a suspect and arresting them.

In addition—and although freedom of religion was enshrined in the constitution—a brutal crackdown was conducted against the churches, especially in the first years after Tito's rise to power. Church estates were expropriated and religious schools converted into state institutions. Priests were arrested and harassed, some even murdered. Secret police informers infiltrated and monitored existing religious communities and the priesthood.

Although 118 Catholic priests had actively supported the "People's Liberation Army" under the leadership of the Communist Party during the war, and 43 Catholic priests lost their lives as members of the anti-fascist resistance, this did nothing to change the general attitude of the party towards faith and the church. In the best case, religion was declared a private matter for the individual, but under no circumstances could the authority of the party be permitted to be called into question.

In the 1950s, the open practice of terror abated. The repression of actual and alleged opponents of communist rule, however, continued. The Yugoslavian secret police blanketed the country with a dense network of spies. In the 1960s, the supply situation and, with it, the standard of living improved noticeably—not least because hundreds of thousands of Yugoslavian citizens went to the West for employment as so-called guest workers. Despite the repressive stance towards any national aspirations, ethnic conflicts repeatedly broke out, such as the "Croatian Spring" in 1971 and the protests in Kosovo after Tito's death in 1980 which were forcibly suppressed.

After the death of Tito, who ruled the country and held it together from 1945 to 1980, the economic situation deteriorated dramatically, and ethnic conflicts that had been suppressed in previous decades increasingly began to erupt. Nationalist forces gained traction in all sub-republics, first of all in Serbia in the mid-1980s, where Slobodan Milošević came to power in 1987. While anti-communist parties seeking national independence won the first free elections in Slovenia and Croatia in 1990, Slobodan Milošević prevailed in Serbia with his brand of nationalist Serbian socialism.

Under the influence of Serbia, a large part of the Serbian minority in Croatia did not recognise the democratically elected government in Croatia. Negotiations between the leaders of the various Yugoslav republics failed to bring about a solution. Following referenda, Slovenia and Croatia declared their independence on 25 June 1991 on the basis of statutory provisions enshrined in

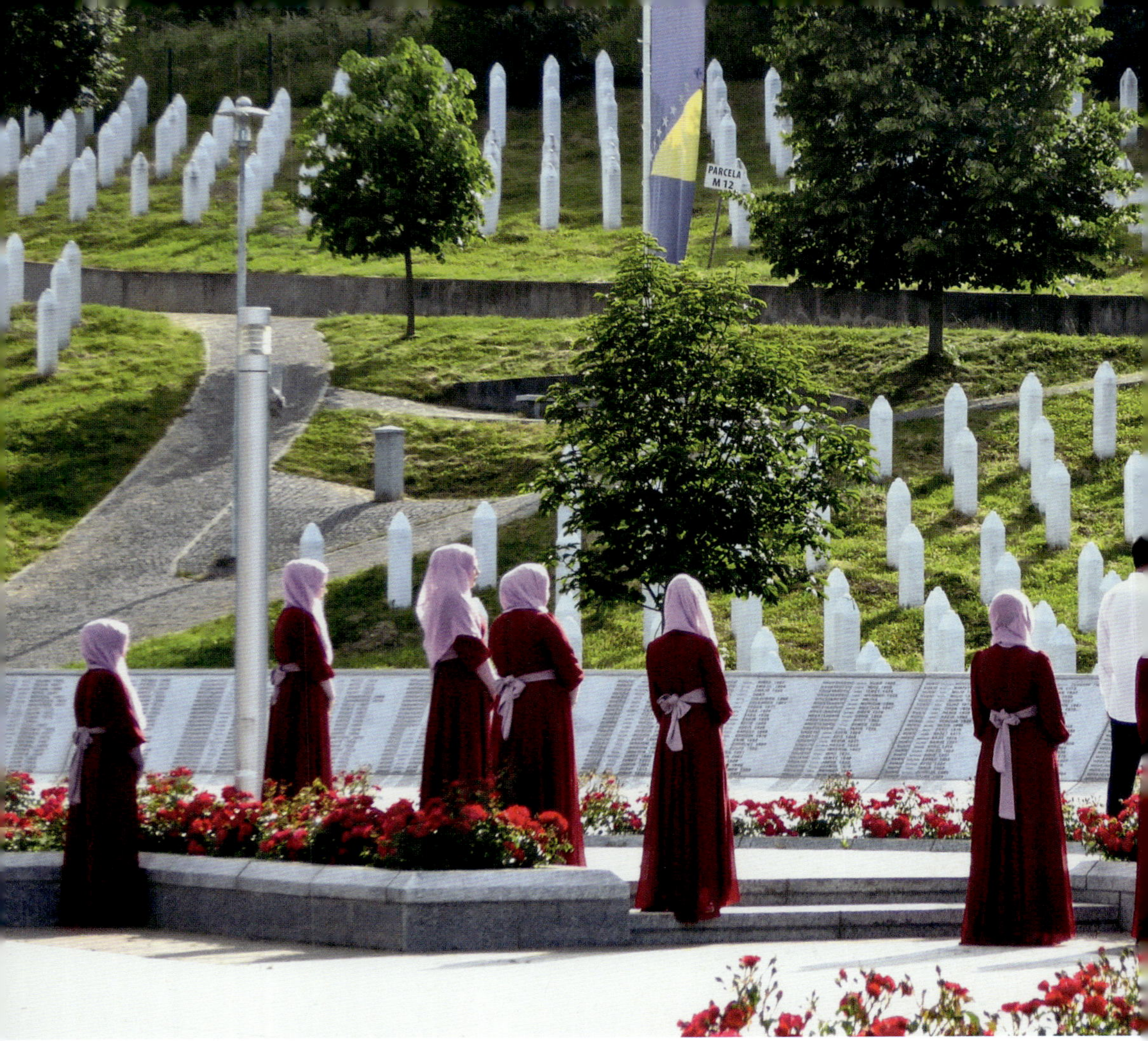

the 1974 Yugoslav Constitution. The Yugoslav People's Army and paramilitary associations controlled by Milošević tried to fashion a Greater Serbia by military force. Fighting flared only briefly in Slovenia. In Croatia, however, the result was open and bloody warfare, followed to an even greater extent in Bosnia-Herzegovina, which declared independence in March 1992.

The war in Bosnia-Herzegovina ended with the Dayton Agreement of 21 November 1995. A complicated regulation provides for Bosnia-Herzegovina to remain a sovereign and undivided state within internationally recognised borders, with Sarajevo as its capital. At the same time, Bosnia-Herzegovina consists of two entities: Republika Srpska, with 49 percent of the territory, and the Federation of Bosnia and Herzegovina, with 51 percent. In addition, the self-governing Brčko District straddles both sub-republics but is, however, subject to the Federal Government.

The massacre in Srebrenica in eastern Bosnia, which even the presence of Dutch blue helmet soldiers could not prevent, is considered the worst crime not only of this war but of post-war European history as a whole. Serbian militias, paramilitary units and Bosnian Serb army troops under the leadership of Ratko Mladić murdered thousands of Bosnian boys and men in the so-called UN Protected Area. This crime was classified as genocide by the International Court of Justice (ICJ).

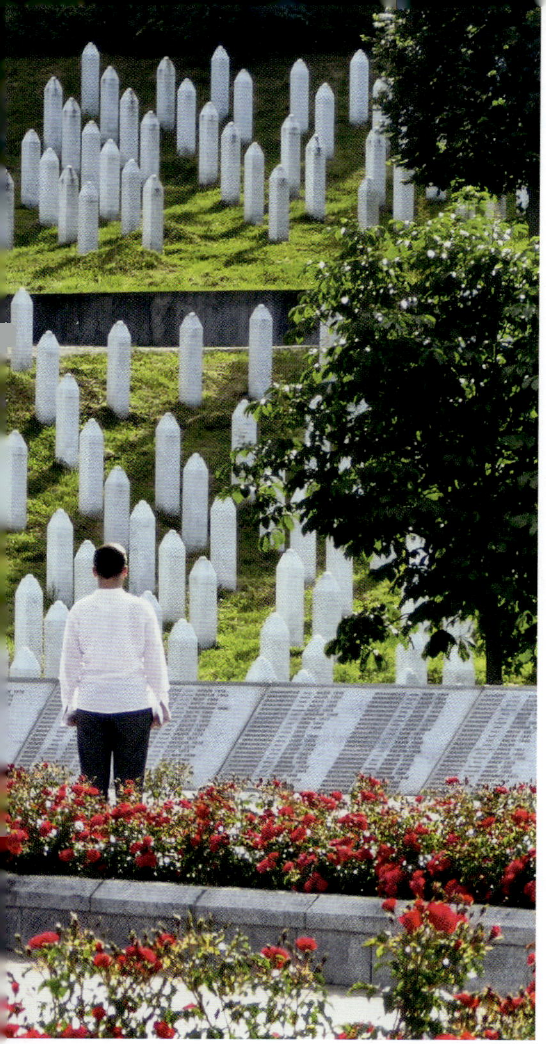

◄
Srebrenica-Potočari Memorial and Cemetery for the Victims of the 1995 Genocide

The wars of the 1990s in the former Yugoslavia claimed more than 100,000 lives and, in many ways, left behind a sea of wreckage. It is these conflicts that have also largely shaped the process of coming to terms with the past. The wounds run deep, and the memory of the victims of the war is too recent, especially in Bosnia-Herzegovina and Croatia, but also in Serbia and Kosovo.

In Slovenia and Croatia, the crimes of the immediate post-war period after 1945 have increasingly been commemorated since the end of socialism. Mass graves are being located and memorial initiatives launched at former camp sites. In some respects, the attention paid to post-war communist crimes is leading to the relativisation of the crimes committed against Jews, Serbs, communists and others during the Nazi occupation and under the rule of the fascist Ustaša regime in Croatia. This is reflected, for example, in the fact that there are no monuments or memorials to the victims of the communist regime in many of the former Yugoslav states.

Further reading:

Calic, Marie-Janine: Geschichte Jugoslawiens im 20. Jahrhundert. München 2014. / Sundhaussen, Holm: Jugoslawien und seine Nachfolgestaaten 1943 – 2011. Wien 2012.

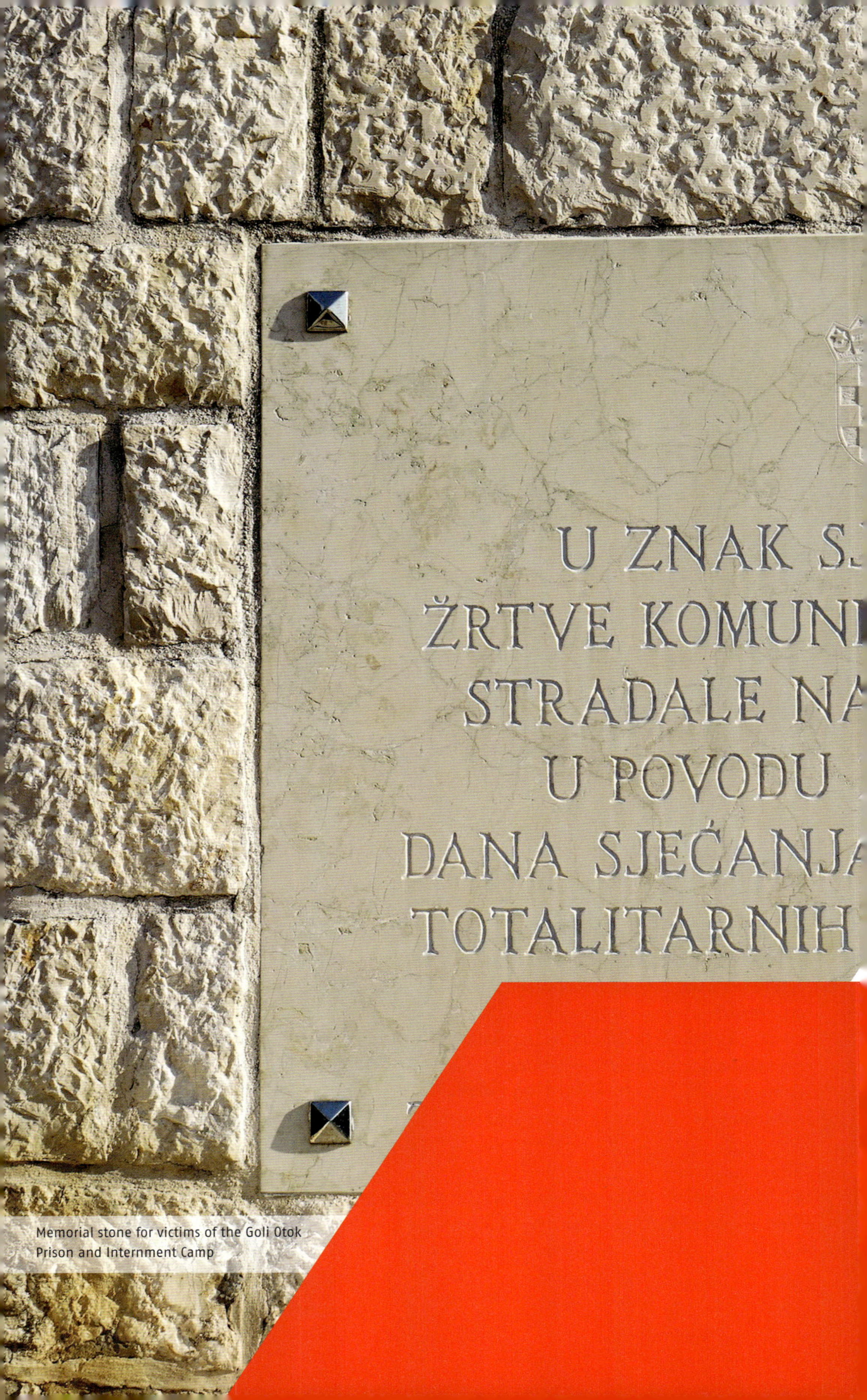

Memorial stone for victims of the Goli Otok Prison and Internment Camp

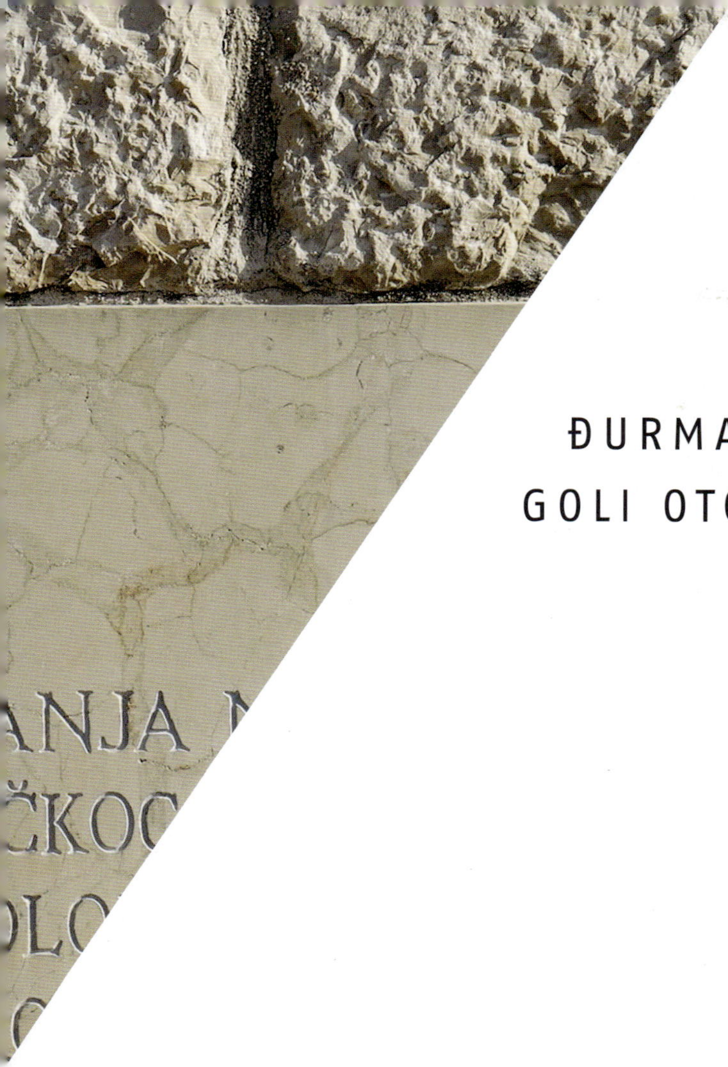

ĐURMANEC

GOLI OTOK

Croatia

On 1 December 1918, after the fall of Austria-Hungary in the southern Slavic territories, the union of the Kingdoms of Serbia and Montenegro and the State of Slovenes, Croats and Serbs, founded in October 1918, was proclaimed in Belgrade as the Kingdom of Serbs, Croats and Slovenes under Serbian monarch Alexander I Karađorđević. There were protests and resistance from the outset against the centralist structure of the state and Serbian dominance, especially in the non-Serb areas, as the Serbs, the ethnic group with the highest numbers, were accused of pursing a centralist Serbian-centred policy with flagrant disregard for the national autonomy of the other nationalities.

On 20 June 1928, while the parliament in Belgrade was in session, a member of the Serbian Radical Party shot the leader of the Croatian Peasant Party, Stjepan Radić, and four other Croatian members of parliament, two of whom died immediately. Radić died of his injuries seven weeks after the assassination attempt. This is now widely regarded as a symbol of the failure of the first Yugoslav state. After this assassination attempt on 6 January 1929, King Alexander assumed dictatorial powers and changed the name of the state to the Kingdom of Yugoslavia. Parliament was dissolved, and all political parties and the opposition press were banned.

Alexander wanted to instil Greater Serbian Yugoslavism as the ideology of rulership from the top down. All this ideology had in common with the notion of a federal Yugoslavia was its name. State-propagated Yugoslavism collapsed in the Second World War, together with the Yugoslav state, which had been weakened by conflicts of nationality.

The most radical resistance came from a Croatian nationalist movement called Ustaša, a right-wing extremist and terrorist underground association led by a former member of parliament of the Croatian Right Party, Ante Pavelić. He went into exile immediately after the dictatorship was proclaimed and vowed revenge for the murder of Croatian members of parliament. In its founding statute, the Ustaša committed itself to the armed liberation of Croatia and the Croats from the Serbs. In 1934, in an assassination orchestrated by the Ustaša, the King of Yugoslavia was murdered in Marseilles along with the French foreign minister during a state visit to France.

In 1939, shortly before the start of the Second World War, a compromise was finally reached between the Belgrade government and what was by far the strongest opposition party in the Croatian territories, the Croatian Peasant Party, to put Serb-Croatian relations on a new footing through the creation of a largely autonomous Croatian entity, the "Banovina of Croatia". This came too late, however; nor did it consider the interests of Bosnian Muslim sections of the population in Bosnia-Herzegovina. Under pressure from Nazi Germany, the Kingdom of Yugoslavia joined the Tripartite Pact between Germany, Italy and Japan on 25 March 1941.

Serbian officers mounted a coup after which Hitler, without formally declaring war, ordered the bombing of Belgrade and the breakup of Yugoslavia. On 6 April 1941, the invasion by the German Wehrmacht and its allies began. After the defeat of the Yugoslav army and Yugoslavia's rapid surrender after only ten days of blitzkrieg, the territory of the Yugoslav state was divided between the Axis powers, Germany and Italy, and their allies Hungary, Bulgaria, and Albania. The royal government fled to London.

After the leader of the Croatian Peasant Party, Vladko Maćek, refused to be installed in Croatia as the head of a puppet state controlled by Nazi Germany, Hitler turned to the leader of the radical Ustaša, at that time in exile in Italy. On 10 April 1941, the Independent State of Croatia was proclaimed, with Ante Pavelić as its "Poglavnik" ("leader"). He tried to emulate his fascist and National Socialist role models in both appearance and politics. The Ustaša state was characterised by mass violence against Serbs, Jews and Roma.

After the victory of the partisan army led by Tito, Croatia became part of Democratic Federal Yugoslavia which had been proclaimed during the war. From 1946, this composite state was known as the Federal People's Republic of Yugoslavia and, from 1963 until its disintegration in 1991, it bore the name of the Socialist Federal Republic of Yugoslavia (SFRY). In political purges, supporters and members of the Ustaša, actual and alleged supporters of, and collaborators with the Nazi occupation were systematically persecuted and murdered along with political opponents, civilians and arbitrarily selected victims. During communist rule, the liquidations of 1945 and the expulsions were a social taboo.

Agricultural land and businesses were nationalised and thousands of people driven into exile. The Yugoslav secret police persecuted emigrants who were considered dangerous even in exile abroad. At present, the names are known of about 100 opponents of the regime who were murdered while abroad. Since the church was the only major social institution in a position to resist communist power, its representatives and many worshippers were persecuted, priests and nuns murdered, and the church estates confiscated. Under the pretext of collaboration with the Nazi regime, the German minority in Croatia was also expropriated and almost completely displaced after 1945.

After Tito broke with Stalin in 1948, the Yugoslav communists developed their own model of socialism, which they referred to as "socialist workers' self-management". Repression relaxed once Yugoslavia had established itself internationally as a state under Tito and left behind the phase of "administrative socialism" in favour of "self-managing socialism". So-called "social ownership" dominated the economy, but private ownership of up to 20 hectares of land was permitted.

However, political activities outside the communist parties and organisations under their control were still not tolerated. In Croatia, this particularly affected those forces that promoted greater economic autonomy, cultural independence and the cultivation of the Croatian language. During the "Croatian Spring" reform movement between 1967 and 1971, the Zagreb party leadership also took up the demands for national autonomy and greater independence from the centre in Belgrade. In December 1971, Tito had the entire Croatian party leadership replaced by new cadres loyal to the party line and ordered the Yugoslav secret police to crush the reform movement. Numerous student leaders and cultural officials were arrested and demonstrations suppressed by police brutality.

After Tito's death in May 1980, the signs of crisis increased and protest movements in the individual Yugoslav republics gained momentum. In the wake of the upheavals throughout Eastern Europe at the end of the 1980s, Croatia and Slovenia in particular called for the transformation of Yugoslavia into a confederation and the introduction of parliamentary democracy. The Croatian Democratic Union (HDZ), which advocated an independent Croatia, emerged as the strongest force in the May 1990 elections. Even before Croatia's withdrawal from the SFRY, expulsions occurred and roadblocks were set up in areas populated by Serbs.

On 25 June 1991, Croatia and Slovenia declared themselves sovereign and independent states. In the aftermath of independence, Croatian cities such as Vukovar, Split, Karlovac and Dubrovnik were attacked and in some cases badly damaged by Serb paramilitary units and divisions of the Yugoslav People's Army. Thousands lost their lives in the attacks and the blockades imposed on these cities. After the international recognition of Croatia in late 1991/early 1992, the fighting in Croatia itself ceased and shifted to the territory of Bosnia-Herzegovina. After the reconquest in

August 1995 by the Croatian armed forces of occupied Croatian territory in Operation "Storm", many Serbs fled to Serbia from the regions that had rejected rule by Zagreb and proclaimed the Republic of Serbian Krajina with the ultimate goal of joining a future Greater Serbia.

After the collapse of Yugoslavian communism and Croatian independence, numerous associations, societies and family members of the persecuted and those who had died in 1945 undertook to mark the silent graves. However, the commemoration ceremonies were instrumentalised by all sides. While nationalist forces tried to portray the victims as fighters against communism and its innocent victims, others reviled them as fascists and Nazi collaborators.

The war from 1991 to 1995 eclipsed the memory of the period of communist rule and the reappraisal and prosecution of the crimes committed during that period. Although Croatia adopted a "declaration on the condemnation of crimes committed during the totalitarian communist regime" in 2006, this did not entail the prosecution of individuals. No one was held legally responsible for the crimes committed in 1945. It took until 2017 for Croatian Prime Minister Andrej Plenković (HDZ) to declare that the country would not only commit to a reappraisal of the fascist Ustaša regime but also take a more nuanced approach to its socialist past. To this end, a "Council for Dealing with Consequences of the Rule of Non-Democratic Regimes" was set up in March 2017 to draw up recommendations for a historical reappraisal and to remember and approach head-on the crimes and traumas of the 20th century.

After Croatian independence, confiscated property was returned, and expropriations of land and companies were reversed. The authorities tried to respect the rights, for example, of new owners or tenants of houses and apartments and to avoid inflicting unnecessary hardship on them. A law on the rehabilitation and compensation of political prisoners was adopted as early as 1992. Subject to the submission of the relevant documents, these former internees were to have their convictions overturned, and their terms of imprisonment were to be taken into account in the calculation of their pensions.

Memorial Cross and Stone for the Victims of the Goli Otok Prison and Internment Camp

Goli Otok. On this unpopulated island in the northern Adriatic Sea, measuring only 4.6 square kilometres, a devotional cross and a plaque commemorate the victims of the former penal and reform camp on Goli Otok in which political opponents of the Tito regime were detained. At present, on the initiative of the "Goli Otok Ante Zemljar" association and with the support of the Croatian government, a memorial to the former internees in the camp is being built. The association is a civil society organisation named after writer and former inmate Ante Zemljar who died in 2004. Ante Zemljar was imprisoned on Goli Otok between 1949 and 1953 and processed his experiences in literary form. Goli Otok was already in use as a prison island during the First World War. Under Tito's rule, an internment camp was opened here in 1949. The nearby islet of Sveti Grgur housed, among other things, an internment camp for women as part of the Goli Otok complex. After Goli Otok, Sveti Grgur is the second largest of the uninhabited islands between the Croatian islands Rab and Prvić.

After breaking with Stalin and driven by fear of internal party opposition, Tito ordered the expulsion of thousands of members of the Communist Party of Yugoslavia (CPY), which was renamed the League of Communists of Yugoslavia in 1952, and the arrest of alleged or actual Stalinists as "Informbirovci", or "Cominformists" (Cominform was the abbreviation by which alleged or real followers of the so-called Communist Information Offices controlled by Stalin and created in 1947 by the communist parties of France, Italy, Bulgaria, ČSSR, Romania, Poland, the USSR and Yugoslavia were known). The Communist Information Office existed between 1947 and 1956 as a supranational alliance of the communist parties in the former Eastern Bloc and was dominated by the CPSU (Communist Party of the Soviet Union); the CPSY was a member until June 1948.

Over the years, political opponents and dissenters were increasingly interned in Goli Otok for "re-education purposes" alongside party cadres. Aleksandar Ranković, head of the secret and military police, had been commissioned to set up the camp. Until its dissolution, Ranković ran the secret service known as OZNA (Odjeljenje za zaštitu naroda—Department for People's Protection) before going on to assume the leadership of the UDBA (Uprava državne bezbednosti—State Security Service) in 1946. In 1966, during the reform movement within the League of Communists of Yugoslavia (SKJ, successor of the CPY from 1952 onwards), Ranković was relieved of all offices.

When the first prisoners arrived in 1949, the island was still completely barren, and the prisoners had to build their shelters and houses for the guards and camp workers in sweltering heat.

The systematic "re-education" that followed mostly took the form of pointless and repetitive work. Without so much as a court sentence, most camp inmates were subjected to heavy physical labour, psychological oppression, malnutrition and, often, abuse. They were not released until they were considered ideologically acceptable from the regime's point of view.

Ruins of the former Goli Otok Prison and Internment Camp

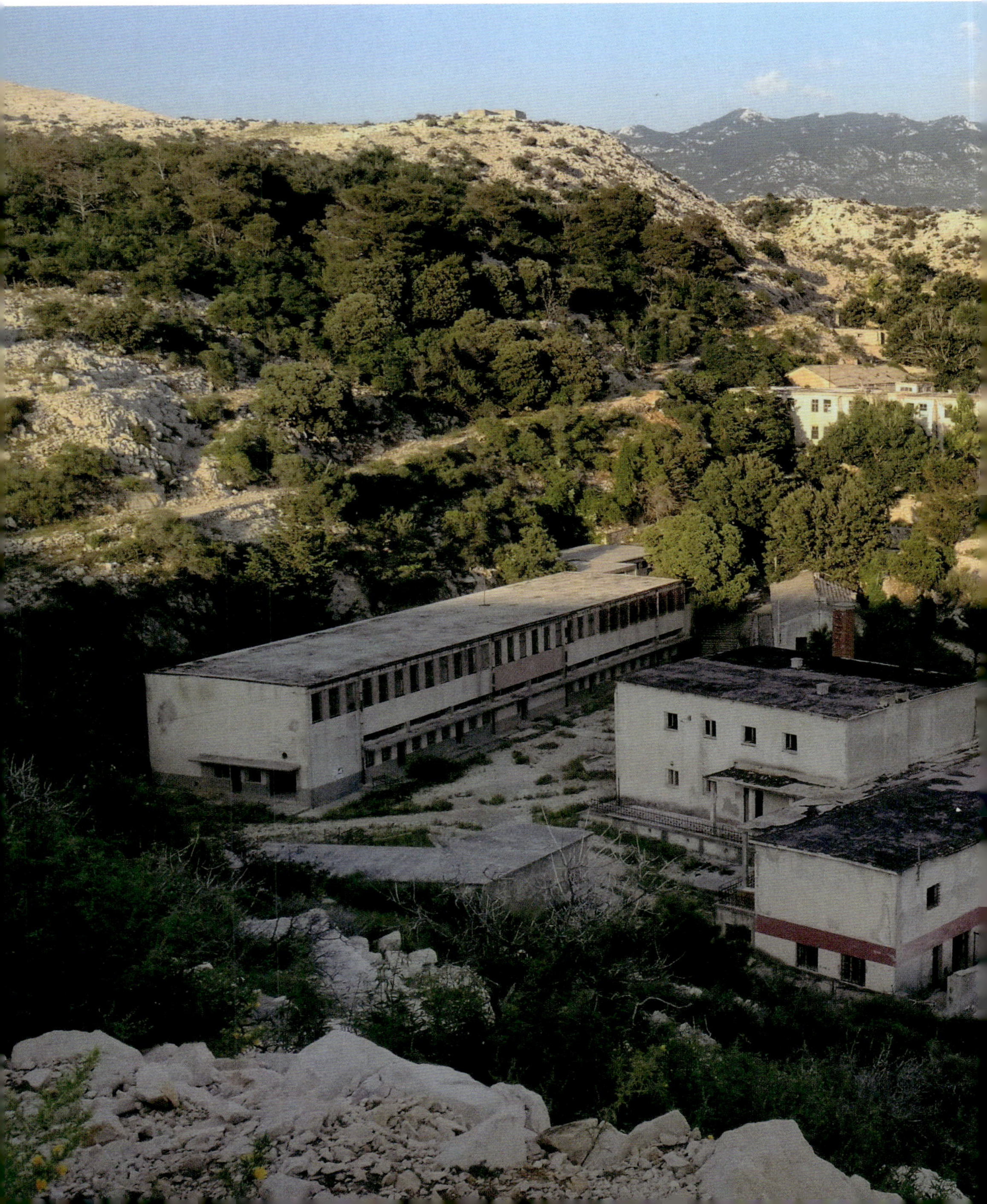

From 1956 onwards, the island served as a prison for felons. The exact number of camp inmates and deaths has not been determined to this day, since most of the files covering the camp period were destroyed in 1966. Even less is known about Sveti Grgur. According to some estimates, between 11,000 and 18,000 inmates were held in Goli Otok until 1956. At least 400 people did not survive the harsh prison conditions and the outbreaks of epidemics. Many committed suicide. Most attempts to reconstruct the history of Goli Otok rely on the memoirs of former prisoners, which mainly emphasise the psychological burden imposed by the "self-managing structure". Within the framework of the camp system, cooperation

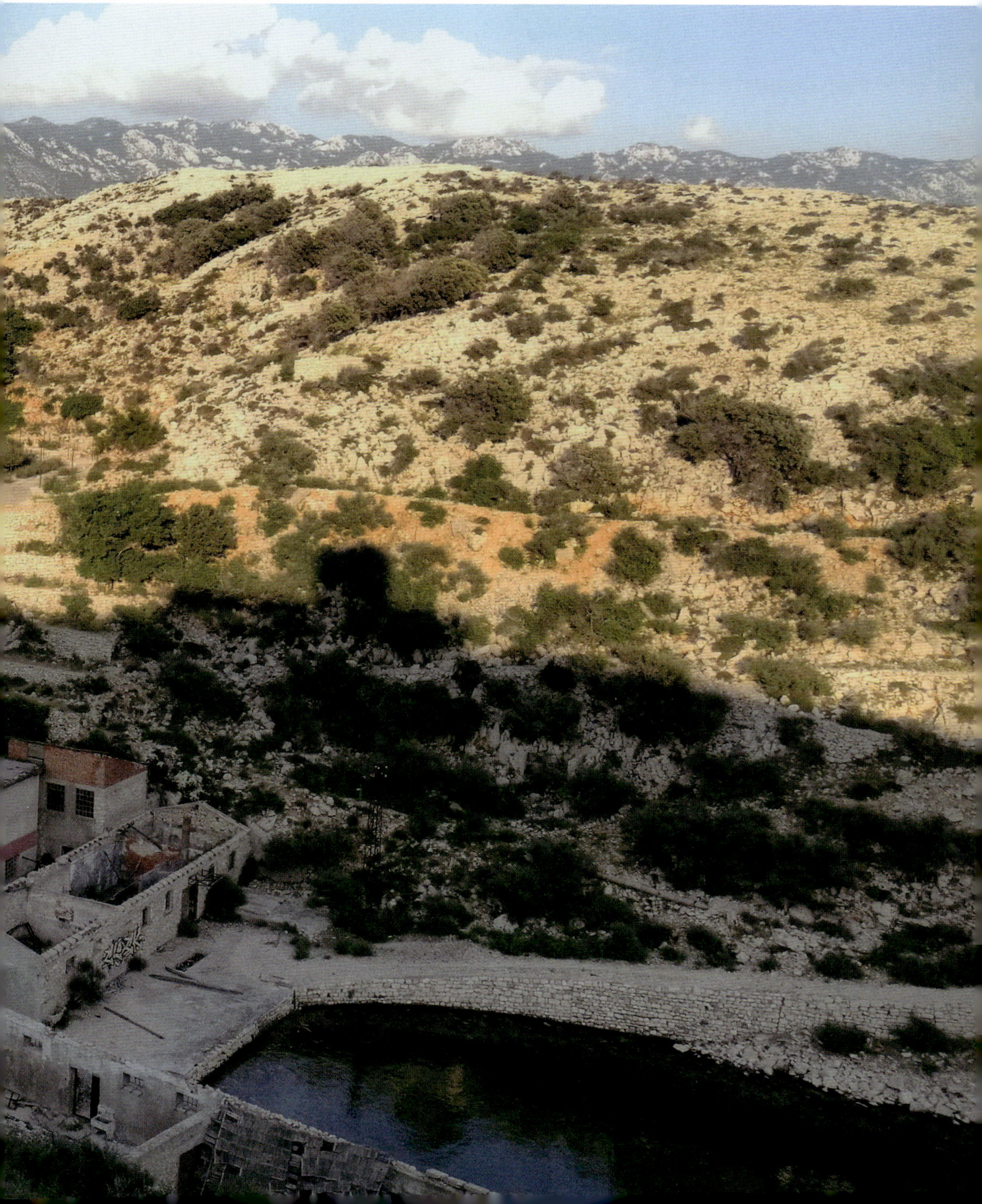

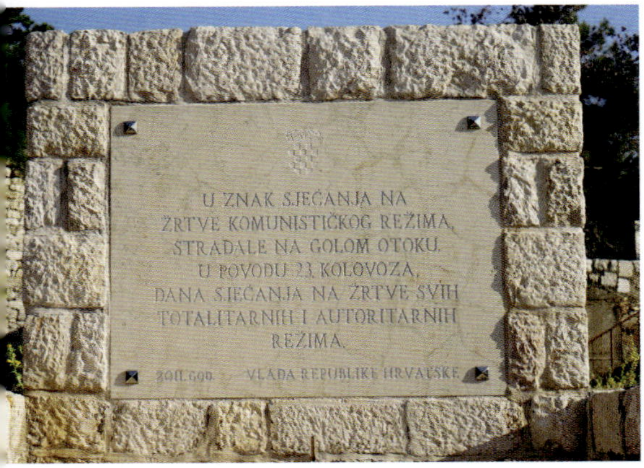

Memorial stone for victims of the Goli Otok Prison and Internment Camp

with the guards allowed inmates to climb up the hierarchy or enjoy privileges, which could, however, be revoked at any time on a whim. Visitors to Goli Otok can see some of the remains of the camp: about 15 barracks and a building used for the employees' leisure activities, as well as parts of the "hotel" which housed the camp administration. Other smaller buildings are preserved in fragmentary form. On Sveti Grgur, visitors can see the remains of the well-hidden 50 or so barracks.

On 23 August 2011, the then Croatian Prime Minister Jadranka Kosor unveiled two commemorative plaques, one on Goli Otok and one on Sveti Grgur, on the occasion of the European Day of Remembrance for the Victims of All Totalitarian and Authoritarian Regimes. The white plaques are engraved with blue inscriptions.

Inscription on the plaque in Goli Otok
Croatian: *U ZNAK SJEĆANJA NA ŽRTVE KOMUNISTIĆKOG REŽIMA STRADALIM NA SVETOM GRGURU, U POVODU 23. KOLOVOZA, DANA SJEĆANJA NA ŽRTVE SVIH TOTALITARNIH I AUTORITARNIH REŽIMA / 2011. GOD. VLADA REPUBLIKE HRVATSKE.*

English: *As a sign of remembrance of the victims of the communist regime who died on Goli Otok on the occasion of 23 August, the Day of Remembrance for the Victims of All Totalitarian and Authoritarian Regimes / 2011 / Government of the Republic of Croatia.*

Inscription on the plaque on Sveti Grgur
Croatian: *U ZNAK SJEĆANJA NA ŽRTVE KOMUNISTIĆKOG REŽIMA STRADALIM NA SVETOM GRGURU, U POVODU 23. KOLOVOZA, DANA SJEĆANJA NA ŽRTVE SVIH TOTALITARNIH I AUTORITARNIH REŽIMA / 2011. GOD. VLADA REPUBLIKE HRVATSKE.*

English: *As a sign of remembrance of the victims of the communist regime who died on Sveti Grgur on the occasion of 23 August, the Day of Remembrance for the Victims of All Totalitarian and Authoritarian Regimes / 2011 / Government of the Republic of Croatia.*

On Sveti Grgur, the Association of Croatian Camp Inmates (Udruga hrvatskih logoraša Svetog Grgura) has set up its own plaque. It reads: *UDRUGA HRVATSKIH LOGORAŠA KONCENTRACIJSKOG LOGORA OTOKA SVETI GRGUR 1959 – 1966. 23. 8. 2011 SVETI GRGUR.*

English: *Association of Croatian Inmates of the concentration camp on the island of Sveti Grgur 1959 – 1966. 23/08/2011 Sveti Grgur. The "Audio" agency has recently been commissioned by the Croatian government to present a concept for the construction of a memorial.*

Location: Goli Otok and Sveti Grgur

Memorial to Victims of the "Stations of the Cross" in the Regions of Macelj, Fruka and Đurmanec

Đurmanec. Đurmanec is located in the north of Croatia near the Slovenian-Croatian border. A memorial to the victims of the immediate post-war period was built here on the initiative of survivors of the "Stations of the Cross" (Križni put)—as the marches of Croatian prisoners are often called—and the pastor of the parish of St. George (sv. Juraj) with the support of the then Croatian government. The memorial consists of a tomb, the Memorial Church of the Passion of Jesus (Muke Isusove), stelae of the cross tracing the different "Stations of the Cross" and a memorial stone for the victims of communism.

Between 1941 and 1945, the Yugoslav People's Liberation Army (popularly known as the partisans) under Communist leader Josip Broz Tito fought against the Nazi occupying power and its allies, Italy and Hungary. The partisans included NDH (Nezavisna Država Hrvatska—Independent State of Croatia) troops, consisting of Ustaša militias and home-defence units (Domobrani). The NDH was founded after the Axis invasion of the Kingdom of Yugoslavia in 1941. Its reach extended over large parts of present-day Croatia, the whole of Bosnia-Herzegovina and parts of Serbia and Montenegro, and it remained in existence as an ally of the Third Reich until May 1945. The fascist Ustaša movement was installed to rule the country.

In May 1945, the NDH troops fled from the People's Liberation Army for Austria, in the company of Slovenian home guard units ("Domobranci"), Montenegrin Chetniks, Wehrmacht soldiers and SS troops, as well as numerous civilians. The Allies stopped the convoy of tens of thousands of people near the Austrian city of Bleiburg in Carinthia and turned it over to the Yugoslav People's Liberation Army, which brought the refugees back to Yugoslavian territory. After disarming the troops and crossing the Austrian-Slovenian border, the People's Liberation Army carried out mass executions. Military personnel who did not fall victim to the shootings or reprisals were driven with the civilians into the interior on hunger marches, which many did not survive.

Since the end of the communist rule, these ordeals have become known in Croatian parlance as "Stations of the Cross". The exact number of victims has yet to be determined; tens of thousands of deceased and missing individuals and victims of execution by shooting have been confirmed to date.

On 8 October 1991, the Croatian Parliament (Sabor) established a fact-finding commission to investigate the victims of the Second World War and the post-war period (Državna komisija za otkrivanje ratnih i poratnih žrtava). In June and August 1992, the Commission located

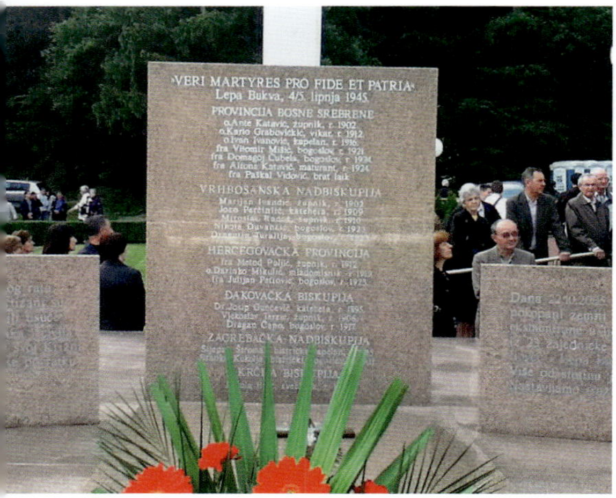

Memorial stone with the names
of executed priests

23 mass graves in Maceljsko Gorje (Macelj Mountains, Macelj) in the Lepa Bukva, Ilovec and Smiljanova Graba areas and exhumed the remains of 1,163 people, including 21 priests. The vast majority of the clergy were Franciscans from Bosnia and Herzegovina. The communist leadership had ordered their execution on the night of 4–5 June 1945.

The remains from the mass graves were transferred to Zagreb and stored in the Institute of Pathology at the University of Zagreb School of Medicine. In October 2003, the bodies were first transported to Mirogoj Cemetery in Zagreb to be buried there. In February 2004, however, the public tender for a memorial in Fruki near the city of Đurmanec in the area of Maceljsko Gorje was announced, and the construction of a crypt, designed to accommodate all the mortal remains, commenced.

On 22 November 2005, the ceremonial transfer of the victims of Zagreb to Đurmanec took place. The ceremony was presided over by the Archbishop of Zagreb, Josip Bozanić. Jadranka Kosor, the then Vice President of the Croatian government, attended the act of mourning. This was the largest communal funeral ever held in Croatia. The remains were placed in the crypt around an eight-metre high devotional cross on a marble pedestal. On another platform next to the memorial cross are two marble memorial stones. Engraved on the first are the names of the 21 priests who fell victim to the communist acts of violence. The second memorial stone bears the Croatian **inscription:**

22. 10. 2005 u ovoj su grobnici pokopani zemni ostaci 1163 žrtve eksumirane u ljetu 1992 godine iz 23 zajedničke jame na položaju Lepa Bukva, Ilovec und Smiljanova graba. Više od stotinu jama jos nije otvoreno. / Nastavljamo tražiti nase mučenike.

Provincija Bosne Serbrene
Dr Josip Gunčević, kateheta, r. 1895.,
o. Ante Katavić, župnik, r. 1902.,
o. Karlo Grabovičkić, vikar, r. 1912.,
o. Ivan Ivanović, kapelan, r. 1916.,
fra Vitomir Mišić, bogoslov, r. 1921.,
fra Domagoj Čubela, bogoslov, r. 1924.,
fra Alfons Katavić, maturant, r. 1924.,
fra Paškal Vidović, brat laik,

Vrhobosanska Nadbiskupija
Marijan Ivandić, župnik, r. 1902.,
Joza Perčinlić, kateheta, r. 1909.,
Miroslav Radoš, župnik, r. 1910.,
Nikola Duvančić, bogoslov, r. 1923.,
Dragutin Turalija, bogoslov, r. 1923.,
Herzegovacka Nadbiskupija
fra Metod Puljić, župnik, r. 1912.,
o. Darinko Mikulić, mladomisnik, r. 1919.,
fra Julijan Petrović, bogoslov, r. 1923.,
Vjekoslav Terzić, župnik, r. 1906.,
Dragan Čapo, bogoslov, r. 1917.,
Stjepan Štromar, bistrički kapelan, r. 1915.,
Branko Kukolja, bogoslov, r. 1921.,
Nikola Ilijić, svećenik, r. 1913.

English: *On 22/10/2005, the earthly remains of 1,163 victims were buried in this tomb, exhumed in the summer of 1992 from 23 different sites in the area of Lepa Bukva, Ilovec and Smiljanov. More than 100 sites remain sealed. We will continue the search for our martyrs.*

Bosnian Franciscan Province
Dr Josip Gunčević, catechist, born 1895.,
o. Ante Katavić, pastor, born 1902.,
o. Karlo Grabovičkić, vicar, born 1912.,
o. Ivan Ivanović, chaplain, born 1916.,
fra Vitomir Mišić, theologist, born 1921.,
fra Domagoj Čubela, theologist, born 1924.,
fra Alfons Katavić, graduate, born 1924.,
fra Paškal Vidović, lay brother,

Archdiocese of Vrhbosna
Marijan Ivandić, pastor, born 1902.,
Joza Perčinlić, catechist, born 1909.,
Miroslav Radoš, pastor, born 1910.,
Nikola Duvančić, theologist, born 1923.,
Dragutin Turalija, theologist, born 1923.,

Archdiocese of Herzegovina
fra Metod Puljić, pastor, born 1912.,
o. Darinko Mikulić, priest, born 1919.,
fra Julijan Petrović, theologist, born 1923.,
Vjekoslav Terzić, pastor, born 1906.,
Dragan Čapo, theologist, born 1917.,
Stjepan Štromar, chaplain, born 1915.,
Branko Kukolja, theologist, born 1921.,
Nikola Ilijić, priest, born 1913.

The opening ceremony was attended by representatives of the Croatian War Veterans Association (Udruga ratnih veterana—Hrvatski Domobran), the Association of Croatian Political Prisoners (HDPZ—Hrvatsko Društvo Politićkih Zatvorenika), and the Association of Officers Club 242 (Ćasnićki klub 242—Association of Croatian Troops 1942–1945), accompanied by Drago Brglez, parish priest of Đurmanec, all of whom had previously worked for the construction of the memorial. In 2007, the Memorial Church of the Passion of Christ (Muke Isusove) was built next to the crypt and consecrated by the Bishop of Varaždin, Josip Mrzljak. In 2011, sculptor Ante Jurkić finished the stelae of the cross on the route to the entrance of the church, symbolically recreating the "Stations of the Cross". The white wooden cross stelae stand on pedestals, each of which is engraved with Roman numerals starting with "I". Sculptures in memory of the victims were also placed on some of these platforms.

On 23 August 2011, the Europe-wide Day of Remembrance for the Victims of All Totalitarian and Authoritarian Regimes, a commemorative stone was placed in front of the memorial church on the initiative of the Croatian government to commemorate all victims of totalitarian regimes. It was inaugurated by former Croatian Prime Minister Jadranka Kosor.

Location: Đurmanec, at the Passion of Christ Memorial Church

Further reading:

Münnich, Nicole: Titos tabuisiertes „Hawaii". Zum Stand der Forschung über die jugoslawische Lagerinsel. Goli Otok und zur Frage nach Aufarbeitung. 2005. Online available at: www.de.scribd.com/document/75717790/Goli-otok (last retrieved: 16/01/2018). / "Politički zatvorenik" [The Political Prisoner], 2004, No. 148/149, 7–8, Zagreb. / "Politički zatvorenik" [The Political Prisoner], 2005, No. 163, 10, Zagreb.

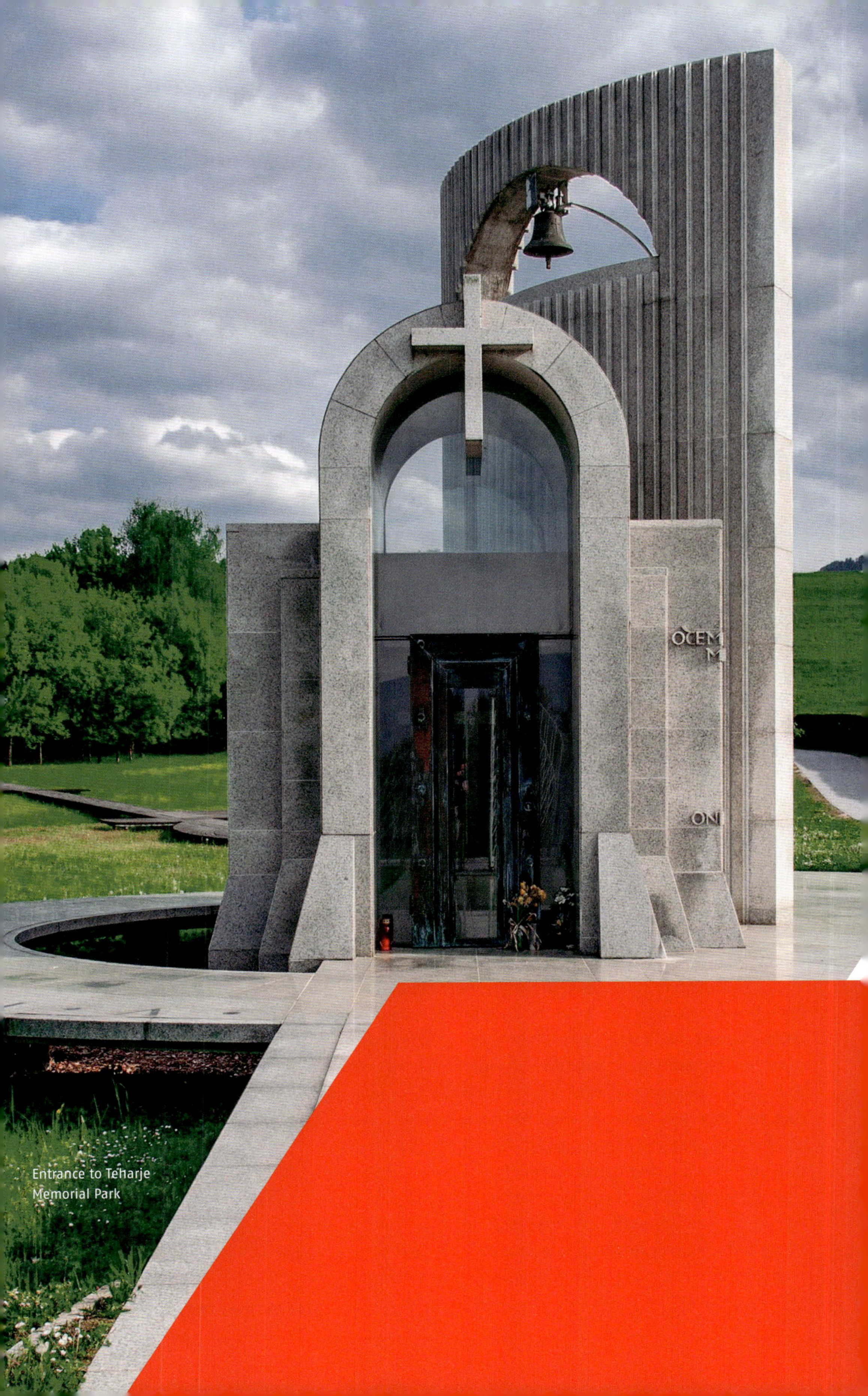

Entrance to Teharje
Memorial Park

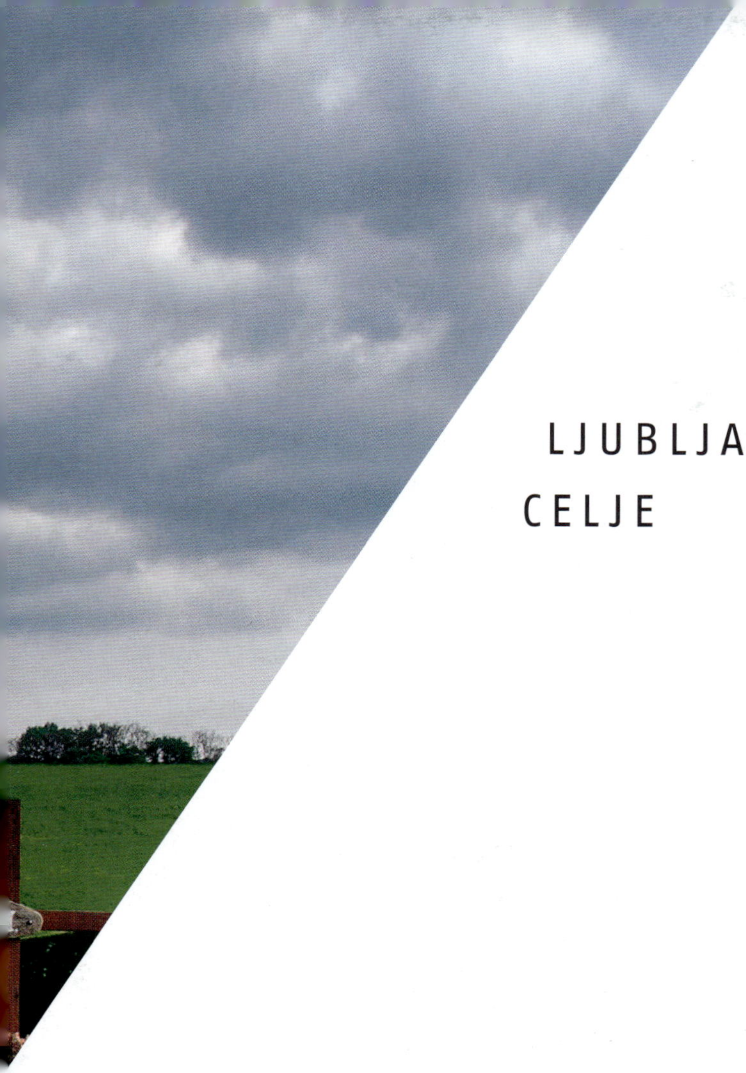

LJUBLJANA

CELJE

Slovenia

After the occupation of the Kingdom of Yugoslavia by the Axis powers in April 1941, the multi-ethnic state was divided up and the independent state of Croatia (Nezavisna Država Hrvatska—NDH) established on the territory of present-day Croatia and large parts of Bosnia-Herzegovina. The new state was an ally of the Axis powers between 1941 and 1945 and was ruled by the fascist Ustaša movement, which collaborated with the Nazi occupying power. The ethnic Slovenian regions of the former Kingdom of Yugoslavia were divided between Italy, Hungary and the German Reich during the fascist occupation. Nazi Germany annexed the northern part (Upper Carniola and Lower Styria) of the country. Mussolini's Italy occupied the province of Ljubljana and the southern part of Slovenia, while the Prekmurje region in the extreme northeast was annexed by Hungary. 80,000 Slovenes were deported to Germany, Bulgaria and Romania for forced labour.

After the occupation and division of the former Kingdom of Yugoslavia, armed resistance headed by the Yugoslav People's Liberation Army—known as partisans—under the command of the communist Josip Broz Tito, who went on to become head of state and the party in Yugoslavia, began first in Slovenia before spreading to all the occupied territories. In the interior of the country, the partisans engaged in armed conflicts with both the occupying powers and various local collaboration associations.

In Slovenia, these were predominantly units of "Domobranci" (home guard soldiers). This home defence force was founded after the Italian surrender in 1943 by order of the Nazi occupying power and fought with the Wehrmacht in the interior against the communist partisan groups. After the official end of the war in 1945, the People's Liberation Army engaged in reprisals against its wartime adversaries. Thousands of members of these units fled alongside units of the Wehrmacht and the Waffen SS but also with countless civilians to Carinthia in Austria and into British captivity, at which point they believed themselves safe from persecution by the Yugoslav partisans. The British occupying power, however, agreed to repatriate the prisoners and sent them back to Slovenia, where they were received by partisan units and executed without trial by the communist secret police OZNA (Odjeljenje za zaštitu naroda—Department for People's Protection) between the end of May and the end of June 1945.

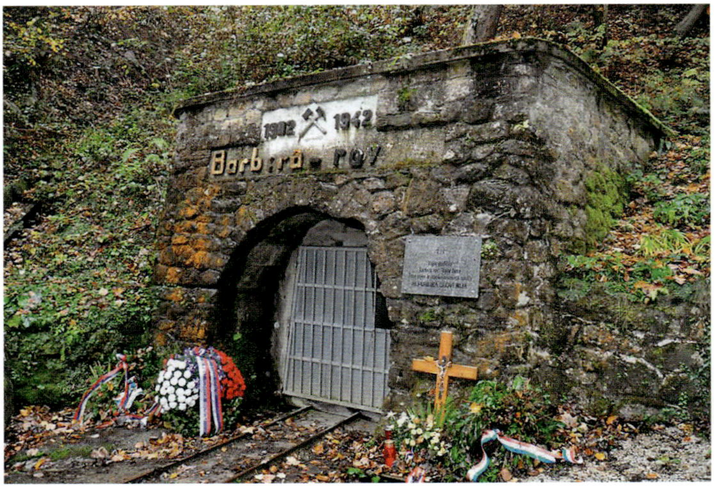

Mass graves in the Barbara Pit of thousands of prisoners of war and civilians liquidated by communist partisan units

Because the country shares a border with Austria, it was on Slovenian territory that most of these mass executions took place after the end of the war. Many of the mass graves and execution sites from this period have not yet been located. The search for them and the public discussion about post-war crimes only became possible after Tito's death in the 1980s and gathered pace in the 1990s. It is estimated that there are several hundred graves containing over 100,000 victims. Family members have placed simple wooden crosses or plaques on the supposed mass graves to commemorate their murdered relatives.

Although the mass executions ended in early August 1945, the acts of repression against the democratic opposition and all opponents of the communist regime continued. South of the capital Ljubljana, an area around the village of Kočevje was closed off, declared a military restricted area and turned into a huge camp complex with additional military installations. Thousands of people were imprisoned here, compelled into forced labour or murdered. All the detainees' property was confiscated, and members of their families were evicted from their homes.

The fight against the Church also continued. Priests and worshippers were attacked, including, in 1952, Bishop Anton Vovk, who was doused with gasoline and set on fire by youths. More than half of Slovenia's priests, who numbered more than 1,000, were arrested. Four out of the nine priests who were sentenced to death were executed. Show trials of Catholic clergy spread dismay and terror. The fight against the Church was so bitter mainly because the Communist authorities saw in it one of its strongest opponents.

Open terror did not cease until the 1950s, with surveillance by the secret police and the suppression of the democratic opposition remaining commonplace. In the 1970s and, especially after Tito's death, in the 1980s, national efforts to bring about independence intensified. After the first free elections in 1990, the forces supporting national independence on an anti-communist platform prevailed. Barely a year later, on 25 June 1991, Slovenia declared itself independent. In the war in the former Yugoslavia that followed the declarations of independence of various former Yugoslav states, Slovenia was spared the long-drawn-out fighting that raged elsewhere.

A critical examination of the past in respect of both the Nazi occupation and collaboration, post-war crimes and the communist regime did not take place until after the turn of the millennium; many former communist cadres remained in their posts, with no vetting of either civil servants or, in particular, holders of political office. The review of judges was an exception—in 1994, all judges had to reapply for their positions. The former communist secret police underwent structural transformation after 1990 in a process lasting several years. Its powers were changed to ensure that the new security service would no longer have any police powers. Security personnel also lost the right to carry weapons. Administrative reform was also implemented to prevent documents from being destroyed. In 2006, a law was passed regulating the opening of files, which, with the exception of documents containing sensitive personal data, have now been made public.

To this day, the topics of crimes committed during and after the war are still the subject of heated debate and are an object lesson in the potency of unresolved conflicts, even those which took place more than 70 years ago. The conflict fault lines run between the assessment of and approach to state collaboration with the Nazis and the crimes committed during German occupation on the one hand, and the assessment of the mass murders by the communist partisans and the secret police after the end of the war on the other. Whereas the first few weeks after the end of the war and the crimes and mass murders committed at that time by communist associations play a role in public discussions, the later period in communist Yugoslavia usually recedes into the background.

In recent years, monuments have been erected in various places for the Domobranci who fell during the Second World War or were murdered by communist partisans. Some of these were erected in the immediate vicinity of monuments to the victims of National Socialism, such as in Grahovo in southern Slovenia, provoking heated debate about not only how to approach the issue of collaboration with the Nazis but also the uncritical dedications that indiscriminately turn all the dead into victims.

In 2009, the Slovenian parliament voted to install memorial plaques with identical wording —"For the victims of war and post-war murders" or "The victims of war and revolutionary violence"—in places where members of the home guards fell during the Second World War and at sites of mass crimes committed during the post-war period. This indiscriminate marking of the memorials added fuel to the controversial discussion of the question of who should be regarded as a victim. The Študijski center za narodno spravo (Centre for National Reconciliation) was founded in 2008 on the initiative of the Slovenian government.

In 1996, the first law was passed to rehabilitate the victims of communism. This law also regulated the issues of reparation, pension payments and compensation for injuries or deaths suffered by political prisoners and their surviving relatives. In 2011, a separate compensation law was passed, covering both the victims of the war and post-war communist crimes. In addition, regulations have been adopted concerning the return of expropriated and nationalised property to its former owners.

There is as yet no special national day of remembrance of the victims of communist repression. However, wreath-laying ceremonies and commemorations are held at memorial sites.

National Museum of Contemporary History of Slovenia

Ljubljana. Located in Tivoli Park, the National Museum of Contemporary History sheds light on Slovenian history from the beginning of the First World War in 1914 to the present day. After Slovenia gained its national independence in August 1991, the exhibition—whose ideological focus had previously been on military history, the history of the Yugoslav communist regime and the socio-economic development of the country—was fundamentally revised and expanded. In addition to various works of art, decorations, textiles, coins and military equipment, the museum's collection also includes film, audio and visual documents. Since 1952, the institution has also maintained a department for documentary photography, which has grown to around two million photographs.

The permanent exhibition "Slovenia in the 20th Century", which opened in 1996 and has since been revised several times, uses multimedia elements, numerous original exhibits and installations to trace the most important events in Slovenian history. Political, economic and cultural developments in the country during the First World War and the 1920s and 1930s are examined. Also featured prominently is the fate of the Slovenes during the Second World War and the subsequent history of Slovenian society as part of the Socialist Federal Republic of Yugoslavia until Slovenia's separation from the Yugoslav federation and its declaration of independence on 25 August 1991.

The museum also highlights the events of the Ten-Day War—the fighting between the Yugoslav People's Army and the Slovenian Territorial Defence in July 1991—as well as Slovenia's admission to the United Nations in 1992 and the country's accession to the European Union in 2004 and to NATO a year later. Each of the thematic areas also features a section dedicated to the everyday work life and living conditions of the Slovenian population in the 20th century.

The permanent collections are supplemented and expanded by various temporary and travelling exhibitions. For example, the temporary exhibition "Huda Jama" (Evil Pit) that opened in December 2009 documented the liquidation and disposal of thousands of prisoners of war and civilians by communist partisan units in the Barbara Pit in Teharje in Slovenian Lower Styria between 1945 and 1946.

Location: Ljubljana, Celovška cesta 23
Internet: www.muzej-nz.si

Teharje Memorial Park Dedicated to the Memory of the Victims of Post-War Killings

Celje. Teharje Memorial Park is in the historical region of Lower Styria in Slovenia. In October 2004, the then President of the Slovenian Parliament, Feri Horvat, opened the memorial park for the victims of communism which had been designed by architect Marko Mušič. During the Second World War, between 1943 and May 1945, a military camp and, subsequently, a Wehrmacht prison stood on the grounds of today's park. After the official end of the war, the Yugoslav People's Liberation Army (NOV) continued to operate Teharje as a labour camp for prisoners of war until 1946. The detainees consisted mainly of soldiers from local collaborationist forces, many of whom were liquidated in mass executions without a court order.

At the centre of today's memorial park is a monumental sculpture of white marble. It consists of two large marble columns connected by a semicircle, modelled to resemble open handcuffs. Below the monument, a staircase leads to a catacomb-like small room that houses a white marble sarcophagus. In front of the entrance to the catacomb is a cross. A narrow concrete path leads through the complex to the monument and a small chapel.

The site of the concentration camp in Teharje is in the immediate vicinity of the former Huda Jama mine (Evil Pit). Several thousand prisoners of war and civilians, including prisoners from the Teharje labour camp, were liquidated and buried here between 1945 and 1946 by communist partisan units. In March 2008, the commission for hidden mass graves set up by the Slovenian government initiated the opening of the Barbara Pit near Huda Jama, which was used until 1942. Here, the researchers discovered 726 mummified corpses that have been undergoing forensic examination since 2016.

The first attempts having been made to identify the exhumed remains, it is now assumed that the victims were not confined to members of the Slovenian collaborationist associations, the Domobranci, but also included prisoners of war and civilians. In 1997, the Slovenian Society for the Identification of Concealed Gravesites erected the commemorative chapel of St. Barbara at the Barbara Pit to commemorate the mass grave. Since 2001, the Barbara Pit has been officially registered as a burial site. The Commission's investigations into hidden mass graves in Slovenia have so far uncovered more than 590 such mass graves, 30 of them in the Celje area alone.

Location: Celje, Bukovžlak 30

► Entrance to Teharje Memorial Park

Further reading:

Kladnik, Mateja Čoh (ed.): Slovenia in 20th Century: The Legacy of Totalitarian Regimes. Collection: Totalitarianism—Questions and Challenges, 6. Ljubljana 2016. / Lozic, Vanja: National Museums in Bosnia-Herzegovina and Slovenia: A Story of Making "Us". In: Building National Museums in Europe 1750–2010. Conference proceedings from EuNaMus; European National Museums: Identity Politics; the Uses of the Past and the European Citizen; Bologna 28–30 April 2011. EuNaMus Report No. 1, pp. 69–98.

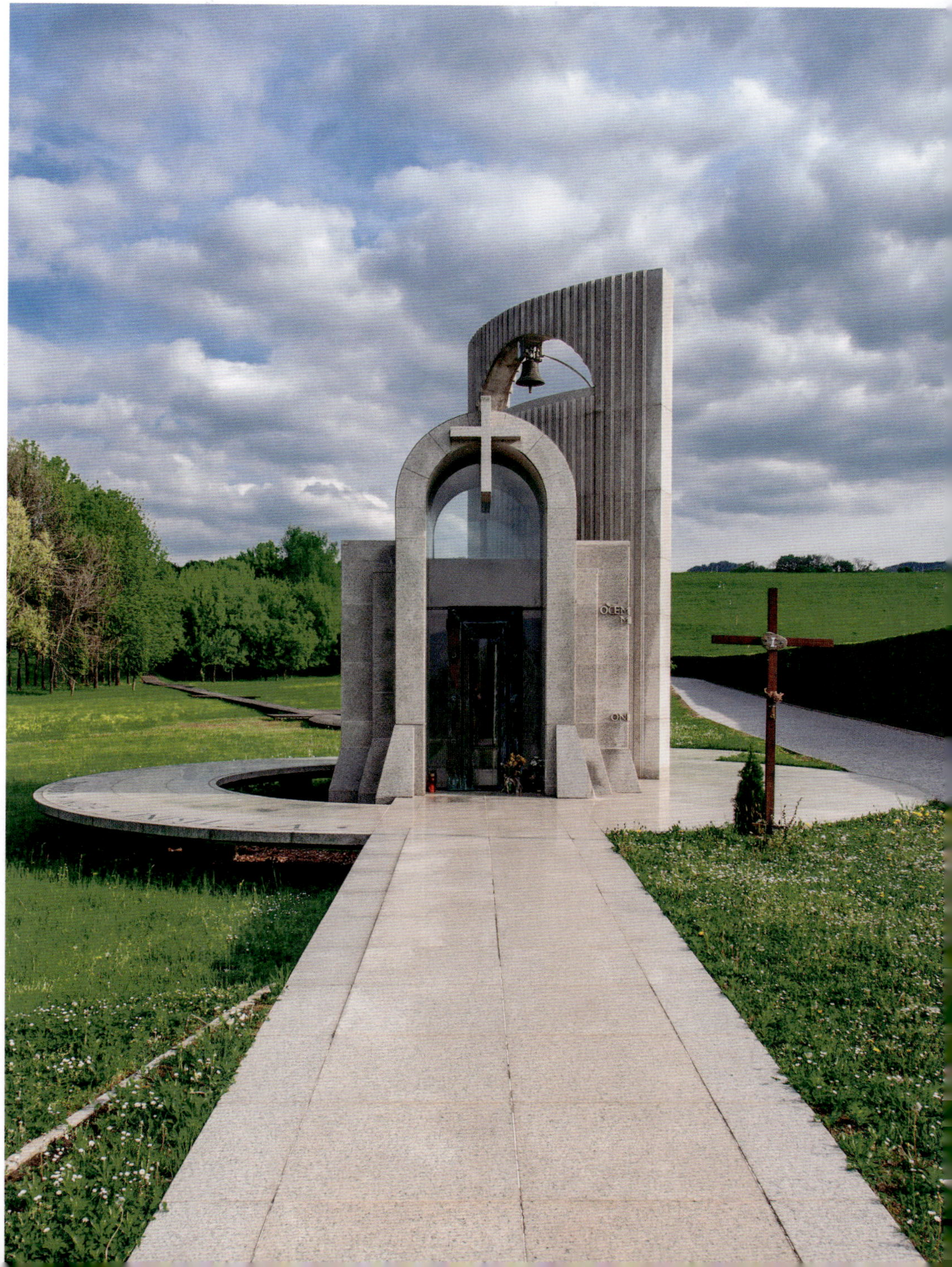

Museums and Memorials

Commemorating the Victims of Communist Dictatorships

Monuments commemorating the victims of communism are not only to be found in countries that were once subject to communist rule. Crimes and their victims are also commemorated in countries such as Austria, Australia, Belgium, Canada, France, Switzerland, the United Kingdom and the USA. Most of these monuments were erected on the initiative of exile communities and family members who managed to escape abroad. The majority of the monuments recall landmark events in the history of repression and resistance. For example, in Adelaide (Australia), London (Great Britain), Vienna (Austria) and Jersey City and Boston (USA), monuments commemorate the Katyń massacre and the 22,000 Polish civilians and military personnel murdered there by the Soviet secret police under Stalin's orders. Monuments commemorating the victims of the Holodomor in Ukraine are to be found in Washington D. C. (USA), and Edmonton and Regina (Canada). According to estimates, between six and twelve million people fell victim to this catastrophic famine which was artificially caused by the Soviet leadership. Last but not least, monuments have been erected to commemorate worldwide revolts against communist rule, such as those in Hungary in 1956 and Prague in 1968. For example, monuments to the Hungarian Revolution can be found in Andau, Austria, and in Paris; in Vevey in Switzerland, there is a memorial to the Prague Spring of 1968.

Since the fall of the Berlin Wall, over 300 monuments which draw on its symbolic significance to commemorate the inhumanity of the communist regimes and honour the memory of their victims have been installed throughout the world. These consist mostly of surviving segments of the Wall and have been built in over 50 countries. An overview of the Berlin Wall in the world has been compiled by the Federal Foundation for the Study of the Communist Dictatorship in Eastern Germany in its book "Where in the World is the Berlin Wall?".

Finally, there are two monuments that commemorate the victims of communism in general. These are in Washington D. C. (USA) and London (UK).

Countries with No History of Communist Dictatorship

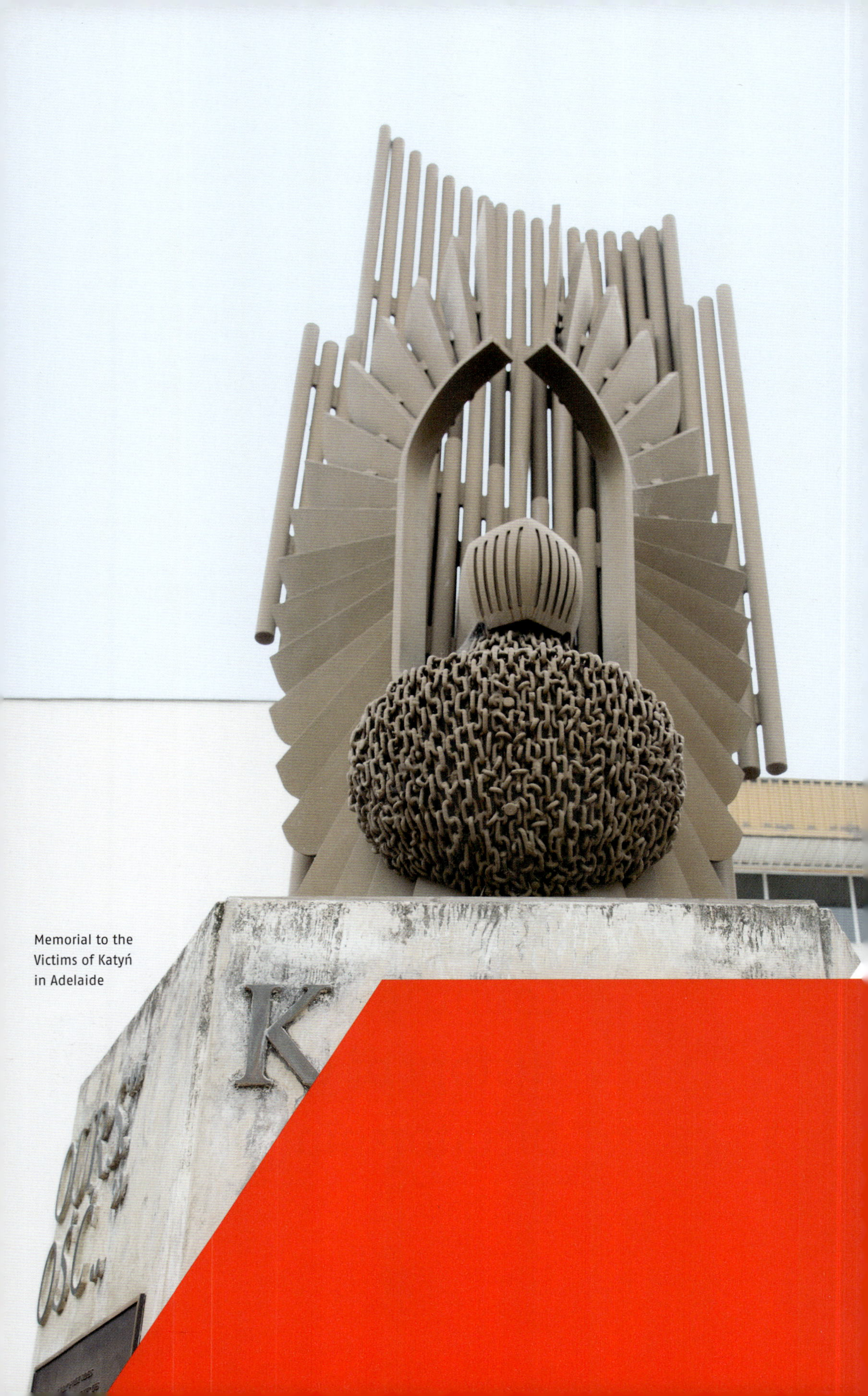

Memorial to the Victims of Katyń in Adelaide

ADELAIDE

Australia

Memorial to the Victims of Katyń

Adelaide. After the monument on Hindmarsh Island near Goolwa, the Katyń Memorial in Adelaide, capital of the state of South Australia, was the second monument erected in Australia to commemorate the victims of the mass murder of Polish officers by Soviet forces. It was initiated by the Polish Ex-Servicemen's Association in Australia under the patronage of the president of the Polish government-in-exile, which had been based in London since the Second World War and continued to claim to be the legitimate government of the Polish state in competition with the Communist People's Republic. The monument was inaugurated on 17 September 1977, the anniversary of the Soviet invasion of Eastern Poland in September 1939. It was celebrated with a mass in St Peter's Cathedral in Adelaide and a parade to the site of the monument in front of the "Dom Polski Centre".

The monument was designed by Stanisław Ostoja-Kostkowski and consists of a hexagonal base of white marble and a sculpture made of vertical metal struts of different heights, symbolising the forest of Katyń where the shootings took place. A helmet with hussars' wings sits in front of the metal forest. The artist thus evokes the tradition of Polish Winged Hussars which dates back to the 16th century and is the byword for soldierly bravery and chivalry.

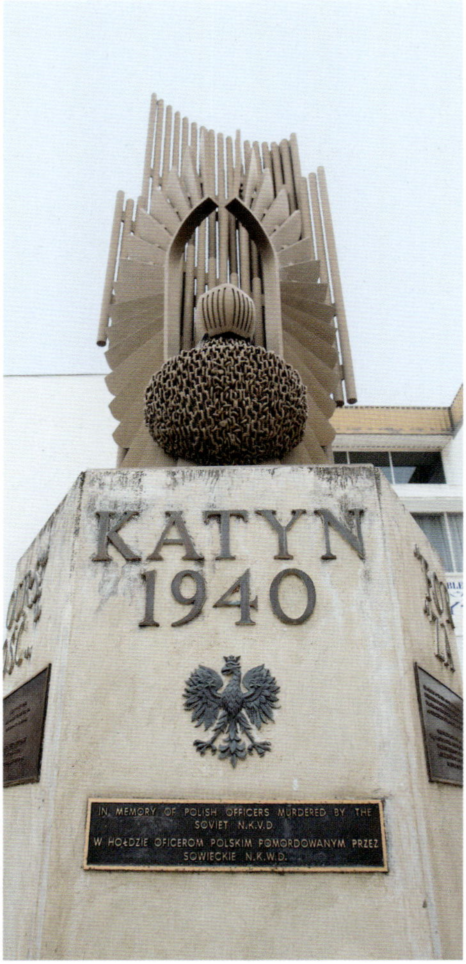

Memorial to the Victims of Katyń

The front of the marble base bears the **inscription** "Katyń 1940" and the crowned Polish eagle in large letters, while the traditional slogan of the Polish independence movement "*Za naszą wolność i waszą*" (*"For your freedom and ours"*) is written in two languages around the base. Below are metal panels with more detailed **inscriptions**.

Inscriptions

On the base, English / Polish:
Katyń 1940 For your freedom and ours /

Za naszą wolność i waszą

On the front, English / Polish:
In memory of Polish officers murdered by the / Soviet N. K. V. D.

W hołdzie oficerom polskim pomordowanym przez / sowieckie N. K. V. D.

On the front right, English / Polish:
The conscience of the world cries for truth to be witnessed / in remembrance of 14,500 Polish prisoners of war who disappeared / in 1940 from camps at Kozielsk, Starobielsk and Ostaszkow of whom / 4,500 were later identified in mass graves at Katyn near Smolensk.

Sumienie świata woła o świadectwo prawdzie / pamięci 14 500 polskich jeńców, którzy zniknęli w 1940 z obozów / w Kozielsku, Starobielsku i Ostaszkowie, a z których / 4 500 znaleziono później w zbiorowych mogiłach / w Katyniu koło Smoleńska.

On the front left, English / Polish:
This monument was erected by the Polish Ex-Servicemen's / Association in Australia with the support of the Polish / community and their Australian friends. / Unveiled by the President of the World Federation of / Polish Ex-Combatants' Association, major Stefan Soboniewski. / Blessed by His Lordship Bishop Szczepan Wesoły on the 17th september, 1977.

Pomnik ten zbudowany został przez Stowarzyszenie Polskich / Kombatantów w Australii wraz ze społeczeństwem polskim / i przyjaciółmi australiskimi. / Odsłonięcia pomnika dokonał Prezes Federacji / Światowej Stowarzyszenia Polskich Kombatantów / kol. Stefan Soboniewski. / Pomnik poświęcił J. E. ks. bp. Szczepan Wesoły dnia 17 września 1977 roku.

On the back, English / Polish:
In memory of Polish soldiers / sailors and airmen who gave their lives / during Second World War 1939 – 1945.

Żołnierzom Rzeczypospolitej Polskiej / którzy oddali swe życie / w Drugiej Wojnie Światowej 1939 – 1945.

Location: Adelaide, Polish House (Dom Polski Centre), 232 Angas Street

Further reading:
Kaminsky, Anna (ed.): Erinnerungsorte an die Opfer von Katyń. Leipzig 2013.

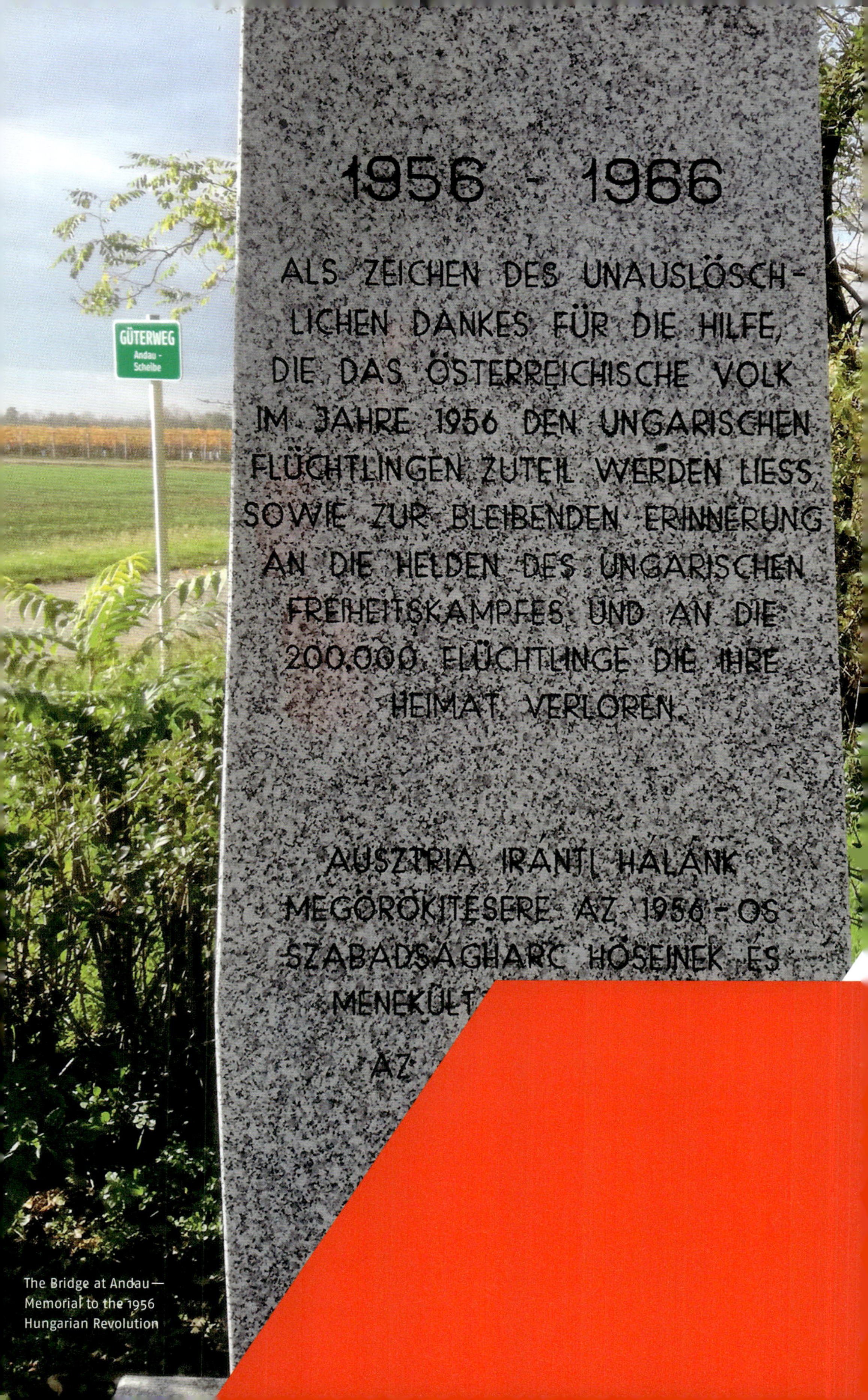

The Bridge at Andau—
Memorial to the 1956
Hungarian Revolution

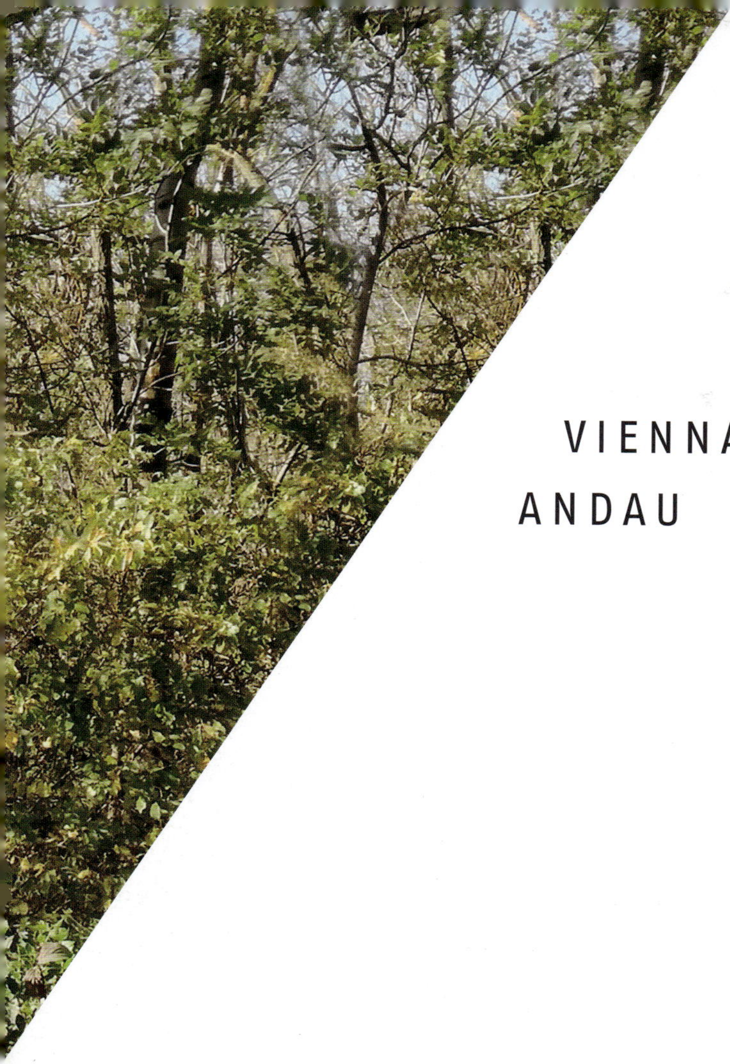

VIENNA

ANDAU

Austria

Memorial Stone for the Victims of Katyń and the Smolensk Air Disaster

Vienna. Since 2011, a simple memorial stone at the Polish church has honoured the victims of the mass murder of Katyń and the people who died in the air disaster near Smolensk in April 2010. Among them were Poland's President Lech Kaczyński and 95 other members of his delegation. On the white natural stone, the Polish national coat of arms with the crowned eagle and the red-and-white chessboard symbol of the Polish Air Force are engraved in red. The simple inscription "Katyń 1940 — Smoleńsk 10 IV 2010" is engraved between the two symbols.

The memorial stone was erected by the Polish Catholic Mission in Austria at the suggestion of the Polish community in Vienna. Its inauguration took place during a solemn mass on 10 May 2011. The ceremony was attended by a consul of the Polish Embassy in Vienna, Zuzanna Kurtyka, the widow of the President of the Institute of National Remembrance (IPN) who died in Smolensk, Janusz Kurtyka, and Andrzej Melak, brother of Stefan Melak, chairman of the Katyń committee, who also died in the plane crash.

A plaque on the cross commemorates the Smolensk plane crash in three languages.

Inscription

Polish: *Pamięci prezydenta RP Lecha Kaczynskiego / i 95 ofiar katastrofy lotniczej / pod Smoleńskiem w dniu 10 IV 2010 r., / którzy w 70 rocznicę katyńskiego ludobójstwa, / udawali się złożyć hołd polskim oficerom / zamordowanym przez sowieckie NKWD.*

German: *Zum Andenken an den Präsidenten der / Republik Polen Lech Kaczynski sowie / an die 95 weiteren Opfer des / Flugzeugabsturzes bei Smolensk, / die am 10. April 2010 auf dem / Weg zu einer Gedenkfeier für / die polnischen Offiziere — Opfer / des sowjetischen Massakers / von Katyń vor 70 Jahren — waren.*

English: *In memory of the President of the / Republic of Poland Lech Kaczynski and 95 other / victims who died in a plane crash near Smolensk / on April 10, 2010. On the 70th anniversary / of genocide in Katyń, they were on their way / to honor the Polish officers murdered there / by the Soviet National Commissariat / for Internal Affairs.*

Location: Vienna, Rennweg 5a at the Church of the Polish Catholic Mission

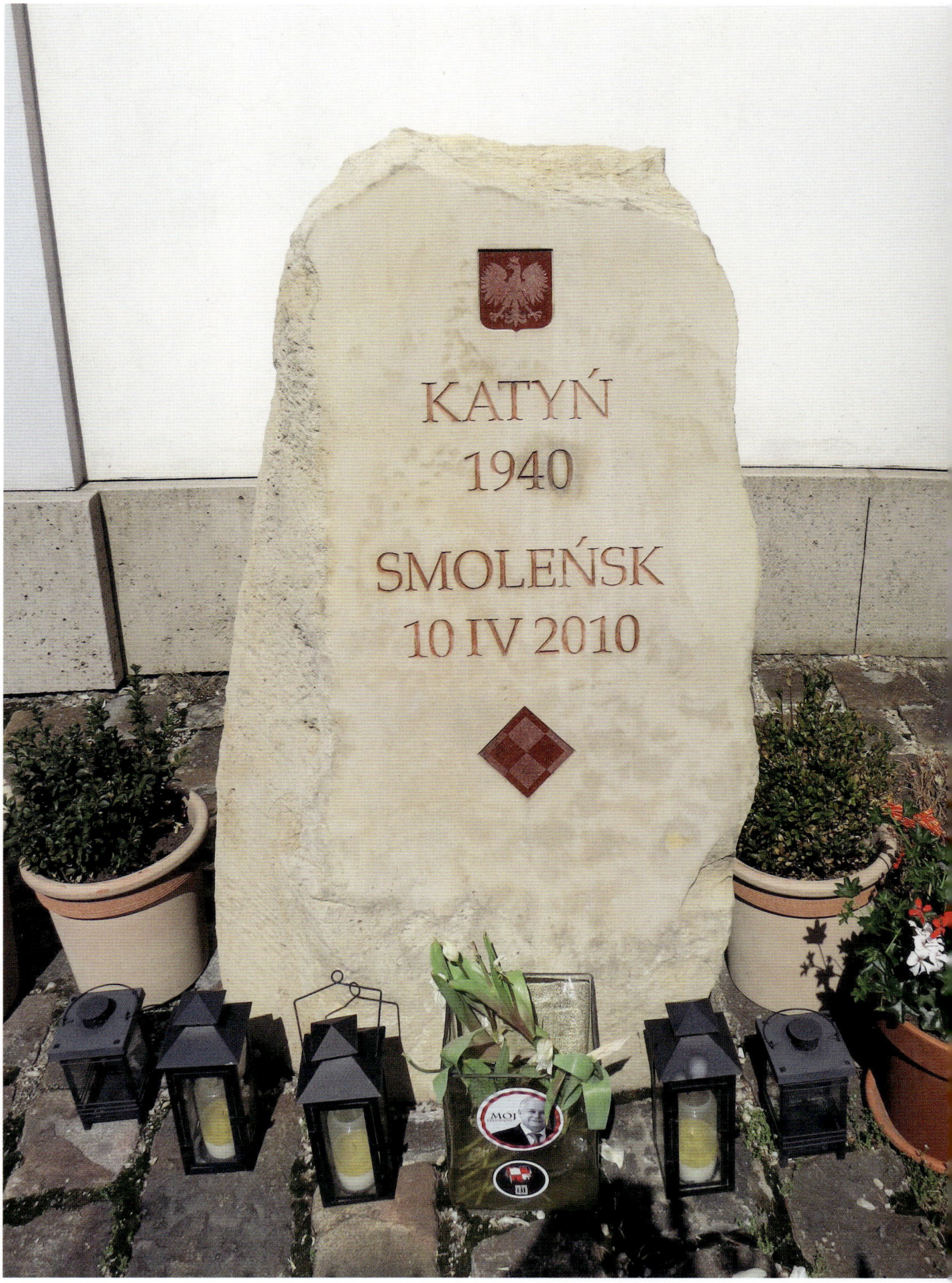

Memorial Stone for the Victims of Katyń
and the Smolensk Air Disaster

The Bridge at Andau—Memorial to the 1956 Hungarian Revolution

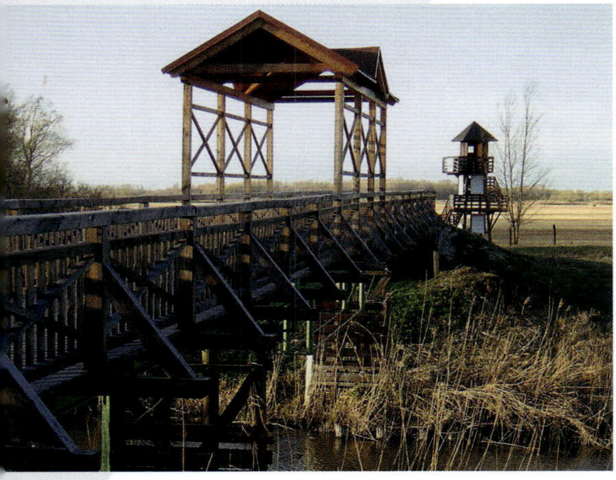

The reconstructed Bridge at Andau today

Andau. In the early hours of 4 November 1956, the Red Army began the violent suppression of the Hungarian Revolution. Around 200,000 Hungarians fled the country as a result. On the Austrian-Hungarian border, a small bridge over the Einser Canal served as an escape route to freedom for about 70,000 people. In the afternoon of 21 November 1956, however, the small wooden bridge was blown up by Hungarian border guards.

The bridge was reconstructed in 1996 on the initiative of the "Association for International Understanding—The Bridge at Andau" to commemorate the uprising and the solidarity between Hungarians and Austrians which enabled many people to flee. A first memorial was erected near the bridge on 12 November 1966 to mark the 10th anniversary of the uprising. The almost two-metre-high obelisk bears an inscription in German and Hungarian commemorating the event.

Over the years, artists from all over the world have built 90 further sculptures, monuments and installations along the "escape route", thus creating a unique open-air gallery. The commemorative markers were created during artists' symposia held by the "Association for International Understanding" in the town from 1992 to 1996. The sculptures and installations, most of which are made of wood, are visible signs of the "rejection of violence, intolerance, inhumanity, contempt of humankind and racism".

The Hungarian Revolution was one of the most important uprisings against the communist dictatorships behind the Iron Curtain. Like the popular uprising of 17 June 1953 in the GDR which preceded it and the Prague Spring that followed in Czechoslovakia in 1968, the revolution in Hungary was violently suppressed by the brutal intervention of the Soviet military.

► Historical photo of the inauguration of the memorial

Inscription

German: *1956 – 1966 / ALS ZEICHEN DES UNAUSLÖSCH-/ LICHEN DANKES FÜR DIE HILFE, / DIE DAS ÖSTERREICHISCHE VOLK IM JAHRE 1956 DEN UNGARISCHEN FLÜCHTLINGEN ZUTEIL WERDEN LIESS / SOWIE ZUR BLEIBENDEN ERINNERUNG / AN DIE HELDEN DES UNGARISCHEN / FREIHEITSKAMPFES UND AN DIE / 200 000 FLÜCHTLINGE, DIE IHRE / HEIMAT VERLOREN.*

Hungarian: *AUSZIRIA IRANTI HALANK/ MEGÖRÖKITESERE AZ 1956 – OS / SZABADSAGHARC HÖSEINEK ES / MENEKÜLTJEINEK EMLEKERE. / AZ AMERIKAI MAGYAROK*

English: *1956 – 1966 / As a sign of indelible gratitude for the help offered by the Austrian people to the Hungarian refugees in 1956 / and also as a permanent memorial / to the heroes of the Hungarian / freedom struggle and to the 200,000 refugees who lost their homeland.*

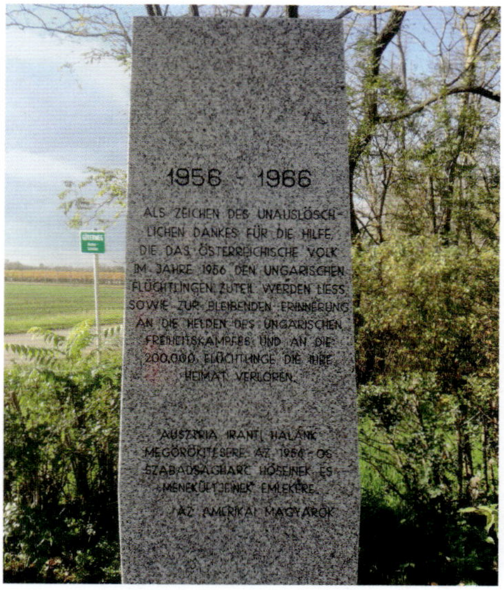

The Bridge at Andau — Memorial to the 1956 Hungarian Revolution

Location: Andau, Bridge at Andau

Further reading:

Kaminsky, Anna: Erinnerungsorte für die Opfer von *Katyń*. Leipzig 2013. / Tourismusverband Andau. Brücke von Andau. Ein Symbol der Menschlichkeit. Available online at: www.andau.info/bruecke-von-andau.26.0.html (last accessed on: 11/01/2018).

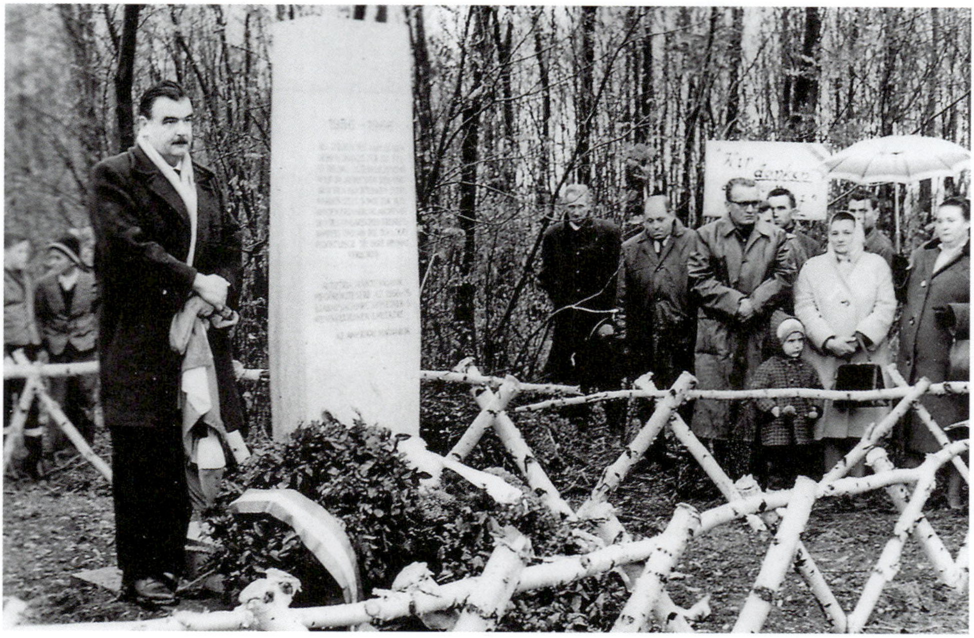

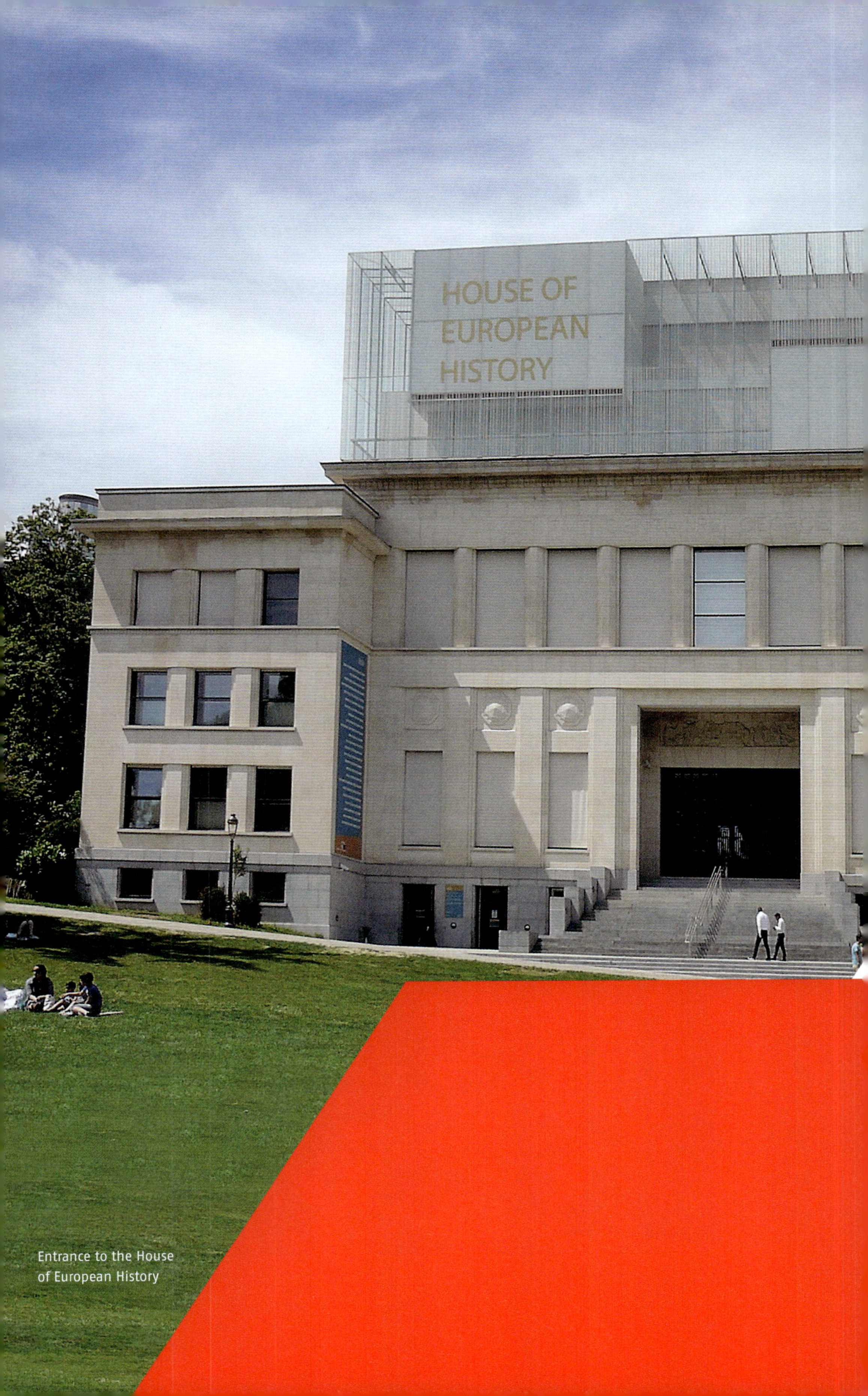

Entrance to the House of European History

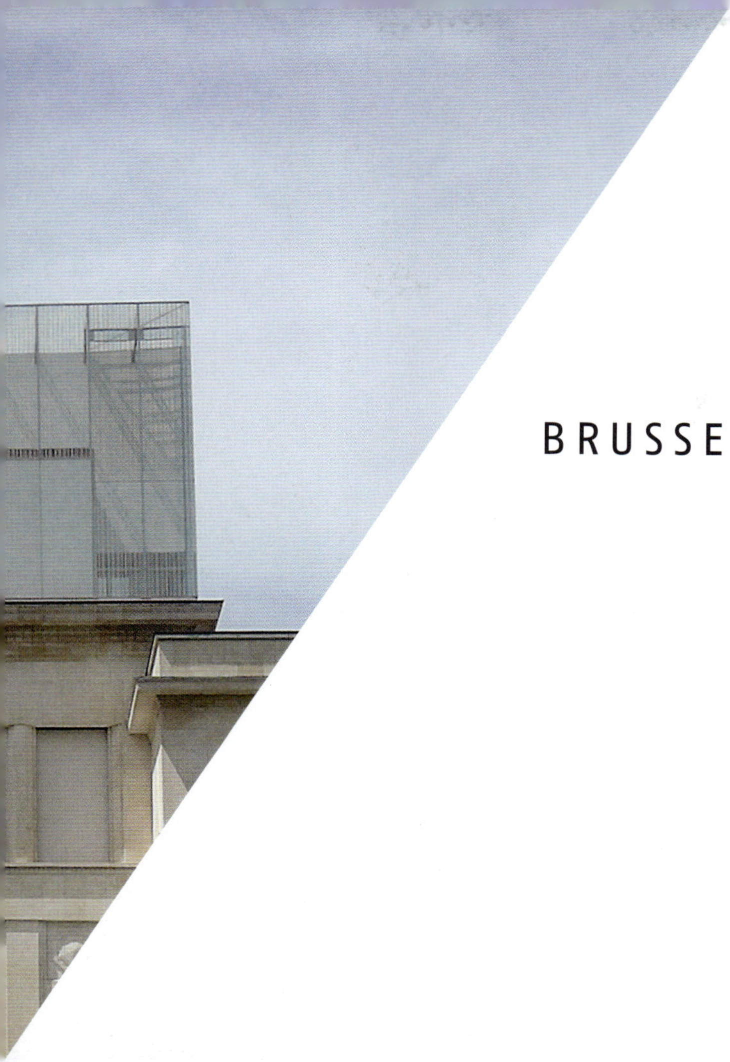

BRUSSELS

Belgium

House of European History

Brussels. The House of European History opened on 17 May 2017 in the Eastman Building in Park Leopold, in the heart of Brussels' European Quarter. Hans-Gert Pöttering, the then President of the European Parliament, proposed the initiative to establish this historic major EU project in 2007. The museum sees itself as a "reservoir of European memory". In keeping with the EU's slogan, "United in Diversity", its task is to elaborate a common understanding of European history. The cost of preparing the exhibition was borne by the European Parliament. Some of the current operating costs are covered by the European Commission.

The exhibition focuses on European history in the 19th and 20th centuries. Explanatory text is largely dispensed with; instead, explanations of the exhibits in all 24 official languages of the EU can be read on the tablets provided. More than 1,000 exhibits are presented on a total of 4,000 square metres of exhibition space. The first two floors of the building are reserved for temporary and travelling exhibitions.

The central artistic element of the building is the numerous metallic banners that wind along the ceilings above the exhibition concourse and finally become entangled, flowing down the open stairwell via the top floors. This "Vortex of European History" features various quotations in Latin, Greek and Cyrillic, including the words of the Swiss poet Adolf

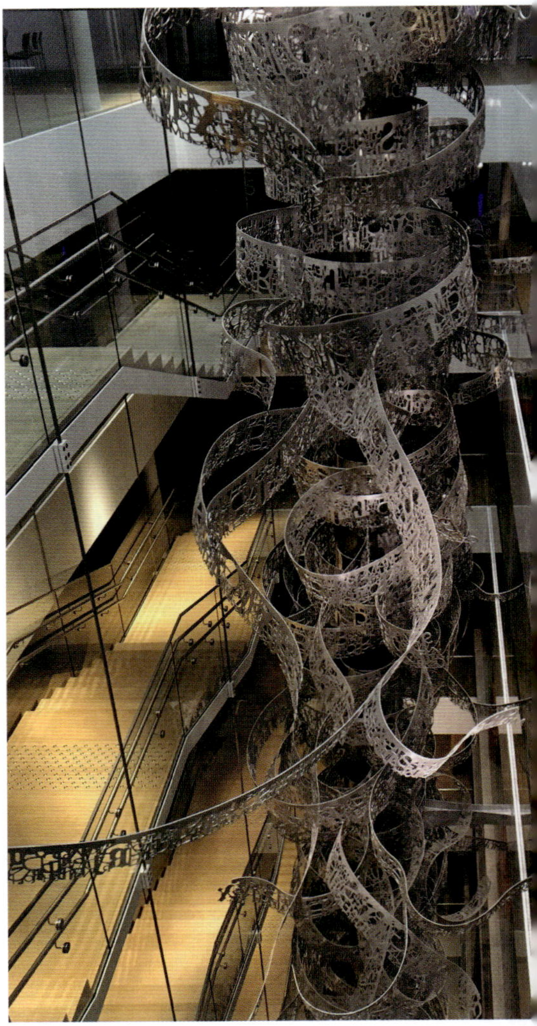

Metal banners winding their way down the open staircase via the top floors

Muschg: "What binds Europe and divides it is at its core one thing: the common memory."

At least since the two European enlargement rounds of 2004 and 2007, the most important EU institutions—Commission, Parliament and Council—have been striving to find an appropriate way to honour narratives of cultural memory throughout Europe. The places of remembrance of the victims of the Holocaust and National Socialism have now been joined by the official commemoration of the victims of the communist dictatorships. In a ruling in 2008, the European Parliament declared 23 August—the day the German-Soviet Non-aggression Pact was signed in 1939—to be a day of commemoration of the victims of Stalinism and Nazism. In 2009, the parliament also adopted a programmatic resolution on "European conscience and totalitarianism", which categorically rejects all forms of dictatorship, irrespective of their ideological orientation.

In addition to the contents of the exhibition, the institution also offers a wide range of educational opportunities for various target audiences. The auditorium regularly hosts discussions, conferences, workshops, short courses, concerts, films and residential events. A range of teaching materials designed for schools is available on-site or online. Annotated material is available on the Internet for teachers, and class and group activities are complemented by visual materials such as videos, photographs and reports. The museum's website, "My House of European History", presents the individual experiences of people from all over Europe and invites them to share their own history interactively on the website.

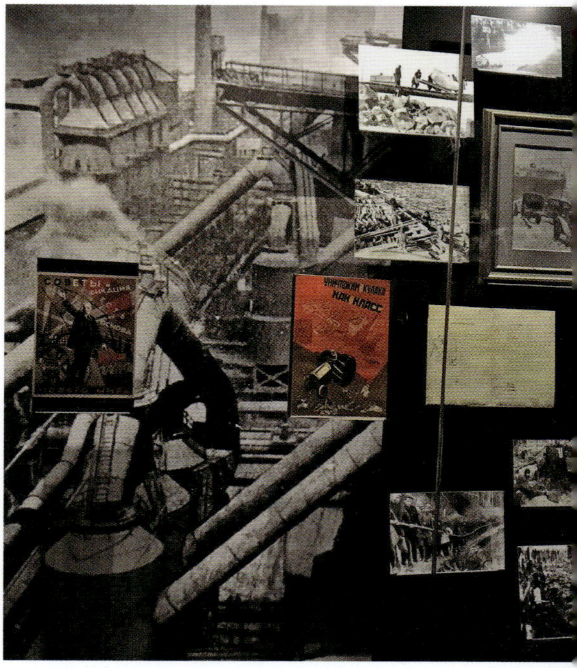

Exhibition detail in the House of European History

Location: Brussels, Rue Belliard / Belliardstraat 135

Internet: www.historia-europa.ep.eu and www.my-european-history.ep.eu/myhouse/myheh_project?locale=en

Further reading:

Troebst, Stefan: Eckstein einer EU-Geschichtspolitik? Das Museumsprojekt "Haus der Europäischen Geschichte" in Brüssel. Bundeszentrale für politische Bildung 2012. Available online at: www.bpb.de/geschichte/zeitgeschichte/deutschlandarchiv/144616/eckstein-einer-eu-geschichtspolitik?p=all (last accessed on: 11/01/2018). / Sachverständigenausschuss Haus der Europäischen Geschichte: Konzeptionelle Grundlagen für ein Haus der Europäischen Geschichte. Brussels 2008. Available online at: www.europarl.europa.eu/meetdocs/2004_2009/documents/dv/745/745721/745721_de.pdf (last accessed on: 11/01/2018).

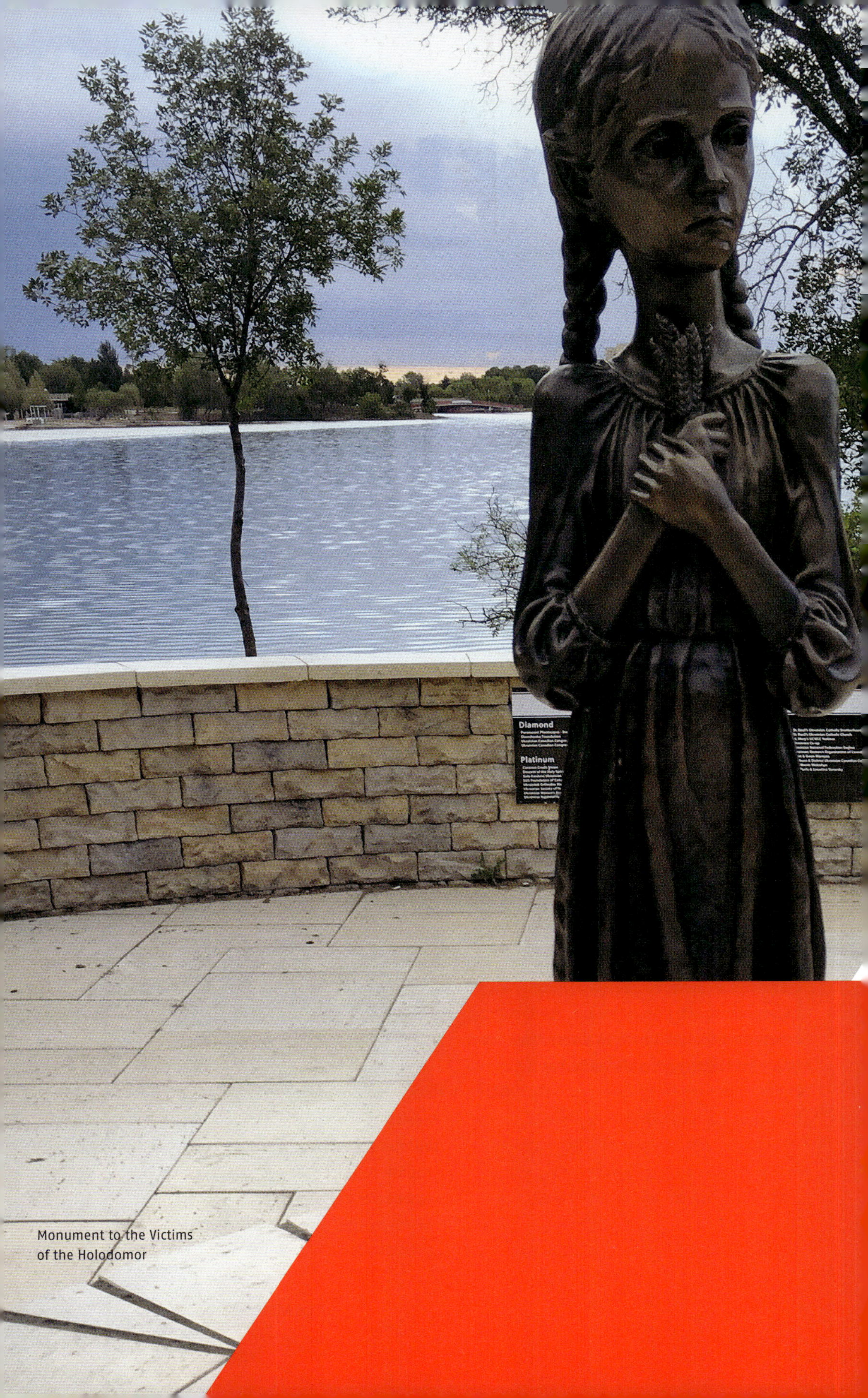

Monument to the Victims of the Holodomor

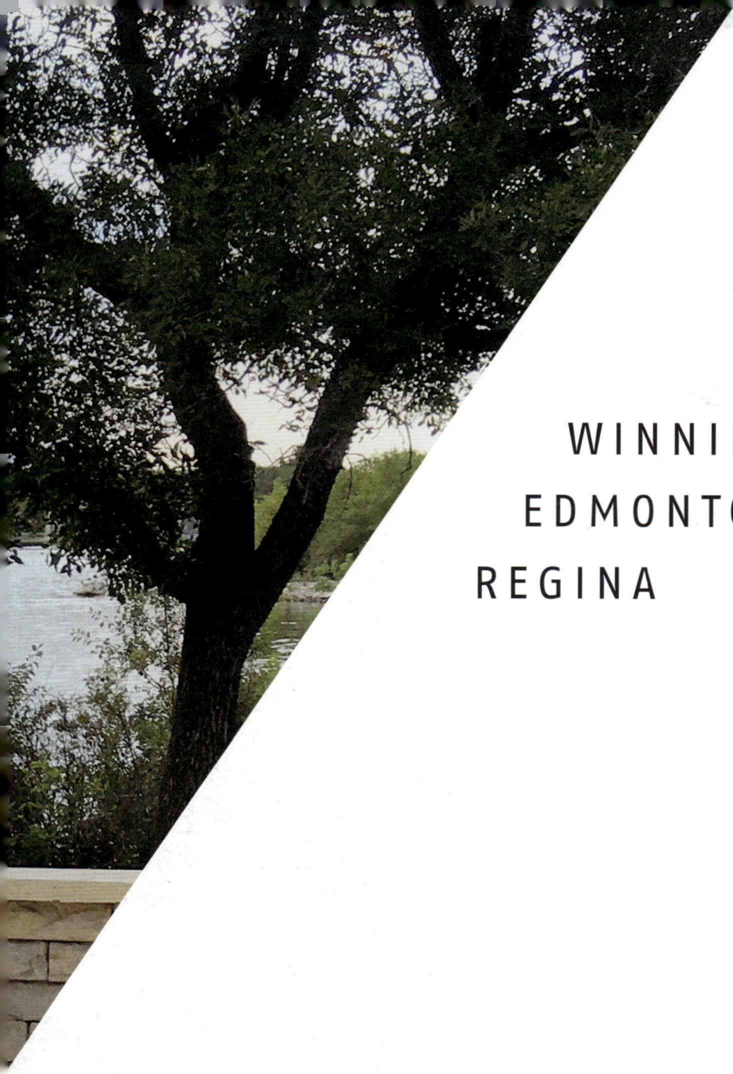

WINNIPEG

EDMONTON

REGINA

Canada

There are a number of monuments in Canada commemorating communist crimes and their victims, although Canada itself was not the scene of these crimes. The catastrophic famine of 1932/33 in Ukraine is commemorated, as is the 1940 Katyń massacre, during which more than 22,000 Polish military personnel and civilians were murdered by the Soviet secret police, the NKVD, on Stalin's orders. These monuments were initiated and created by the very sizable exile communities. Most of them are in central locations in Canadian cities.

While Canada is willing to commemorate crimes committed in other countries, a general memorialisation and commemoration in public spaces of the victims of Canadian state policy towards the "First Nations" is striking by its absence. For decades from the 1930s, indigenous peoples were subjected to severe persecution and repression in the form of forced assimilation measures. Children were taken from their parents and communities at four years of age and sent to "residential schools". There they were forbidden to use their indigenous names; their hair was cut off, and the use of their own language was forbidden. Mistreatment and sexual abuse were the order of the day in these schools, most of which were run by the church and, rather than educating the children, served instead to force them to assimilate and to alienate them from their families and communities of origin. The consequences of this policy have been devastating. Not only have traditional family and community structures in indigenous societies been permanently destroyed, but these societies are still afflicted by the highest suicide rates among Canadian young people and children, the highest rates of alcoholism, a lack of educational opportunity and inadequate health care. In very many reservations, the inhabitants still have insufficient access to both power and water.

The last of these schools was not closed until 1996. Two years later, the Canadian government set up a fact-finding commission to investigate the "cultural holocaust" of the indigenous population and make recommendations on compensation for the crimes committed and their consequences. Since 2007, the Canadian government has provided funds to mitigate the effects of forced assimilation.

Canadian Museum for Human Rights

Winnipeg. On 19 September 2014, the Canadian Museum for Human Rights opened at the confluence of the Red and Assiniboine Rivers in the capital of the Canadian province of Manitoba. It is the first national museum to have been built since 1967 and the only institution of its kind in Canada outside the capital, Ottawa. The idea for the project came from Izzy Asper, the founder of one of Canada's largest media companies, who played a major role in financing the museum. Constructed as a hemisphere consisting of five superimposed arches with glass panels and a 100-metre-high "Tower of Hope" in the centre, the facility houses 13 multimedia exhibition galleries dedicated to various modules covering the complex issue of human rights. A ramp made of Spanish alabaster and illuminated from the inside extends across the nine floors of the museum. The exhibition focuses mainly on Canadian society. Accordingly, various perspectives of indigenous peoples on human rights are discussed alongside testimonies bearing witness to violations of ethnic rights throughout the history of the country. Also subjected to critical examination are the position of human rights in Canadian society and the various measures taken to safeguard these fundamental values.

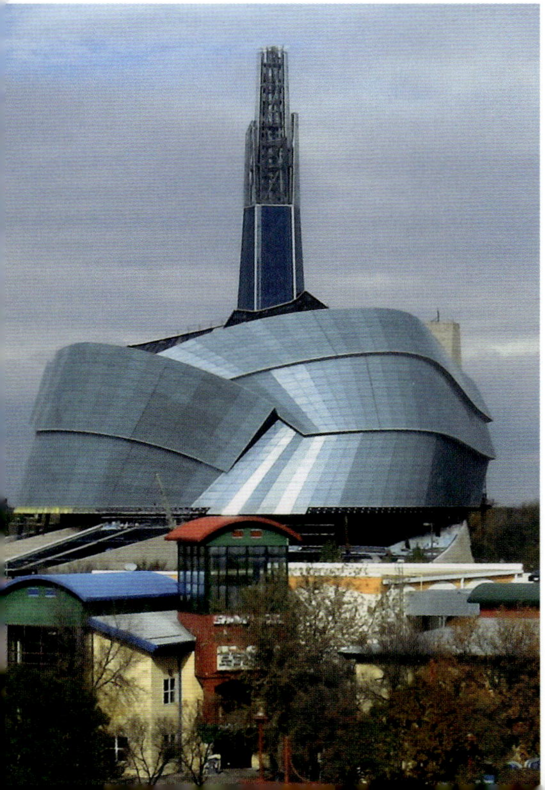

Canada's influential community of Ukrainians in exile also participated in the long-running public discussion of how the museum should be conceived and succeeded in ensuring that the Holodomor—the catastrophic famine of 1932/33 in Ukraine—was recognised as a genocide and featured in the museum alongside the genocide of the Armenians at the beginning of the 20th century, the genocide in Rwanda in 1994, the massacre in Srebrenica in 1995 and the Holocaust.

Location: Winnipeg, 85 Israel Asper Way

◄
Canadian Museum for Human Rights

Monument to the Victims of the Holodomor

Edmonton. The monument to the victims of the Holodomor was inaugurated in 1983. It was one of the first commemorative markers in Canada to be erected in memory of the victims of the famine disaster of 1932/33 and was initiated by the Ukrainian-Canadian Congress of Edmonton. The monument, designed by artist Ludmilla Temertey, consists of a broken metal circle displaying the silhouettes of emaciated hands. The square, black stone base features a depiction of the Ukrainian coat of arms and an inscription in English, Ukrainian and French that explains the significance of the monument.

Inscription
English: *In memory of the millions who perished / in the genocidal famine inflicted upon / Ukraine by the Soviet regime / in Moscow 1932–33 / Let us all stand guard against tyranny, violence and inhumanity.*

Ukrainian: Пам'яті мільйонів жертв / народовбивчого голоду в Україні, / спричиненого совєтським / режимом у Москві *1932–33* р

French: *À la mémoire des millions de victimes / de la famine génocide infligée à / l'Ukraine par le régime soviétique / de Moscou en 1932–33*

Location: Edmonton, at Winston Churchill Place

Monument to the Victims of the Holodomor

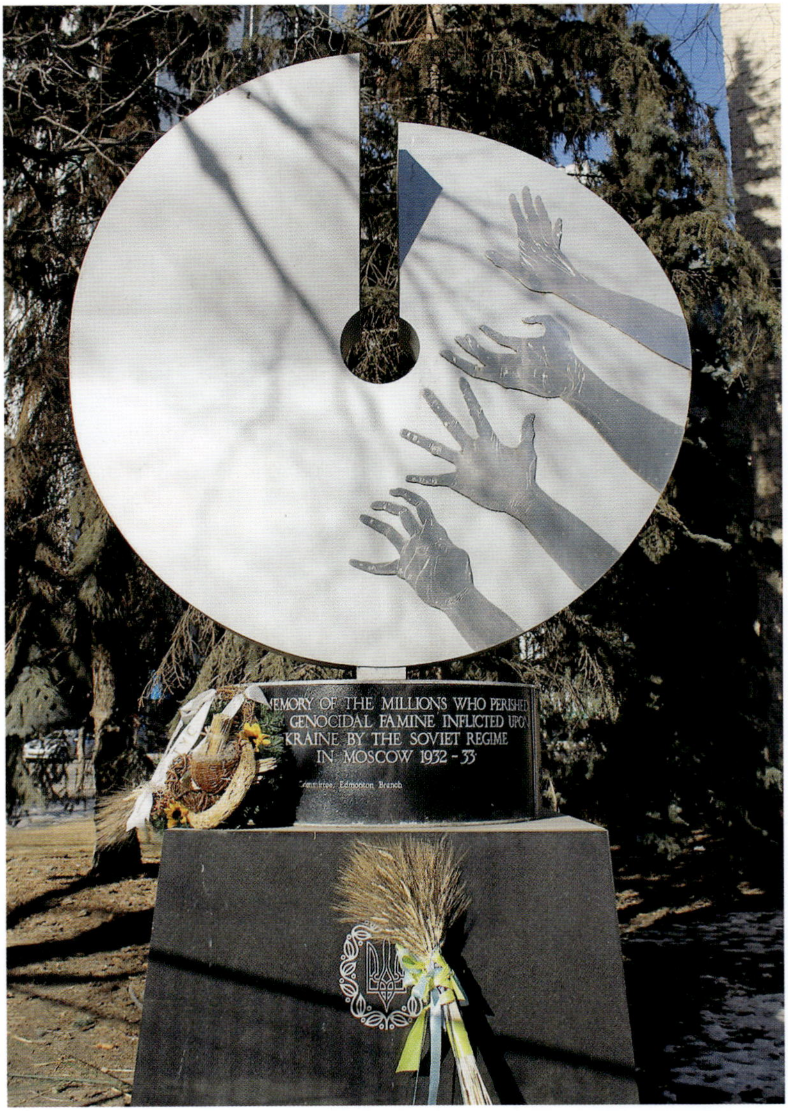
EMORY OF THE MILLIONS WHO PERISHED
GENOCIDAL FAMINE INFLICTED UPO
KRAINE BY THE SOVIET REGIME
IN MOSCOW 1932 - 33
Committee, Edmonton Branch

Holodomor Statue— "Bitter Memories of Childhood"

Regina. The monument to the victims of the Holodomor was unveiled to the public on 12 May 2015. The volunteer group of the Ukrainian Canadian Congress, an association of the Canadian-Ukrainian exile community in Canada, played a major role in the implementation of the project. The bronze sculpture created by sculptor Petro Drozdowsky is a life-size figure of an emaciated girl. Looking into the distance, she holds three ears of grain in her hands crossed in front of her chest.

The sculpture is an exact replica of the "Bitter Memories of Childhood" statue which stands at the entrance to the "Holodomor Victims Memorial" National Museum in the Ukrainian capital, Kiev. The monument commemorates the several million Ukrainian victims of the catastrophic famine of 1932/33 who lost their lives during the forced collectivisation of the agricultural economy, "dekulakisation" and the brutal grain procurement measures of the Soviet government.

Inscription

English: *Bitter Memories of Childhood // This monument commemorates the millions of victims of the / enforced starvation by Stalin's Communist regime during the / Holodomor famine Genocide in Ukraine 1932–1933. // On May 7, 2008 the Saskatchewan Legislature passed Bill 40, / the Ukrainian Famine-Genocide (Holodomor) Memorial Day Act / making Saskatchewan the first province in Canada / to recognize the Holodomor as genocide. // Ukrainian Canadian Congress Regina Branch 2015*

Location: Regina, in the Park Wascana Center southeast of the Parliament building on Lakeshore Drive

Further reading:

Archdiocese of Regina: Holodomor Memorial Statue Blessed. 2015 Available online at: www.archregina.sk.ca/news/2015/05/19/holodomor-memorial-statue-blessed (last accessed on: 11/01/2018). / Holodomor Research and Education Consortium. Monuments in Canada. Available online at: www.holodomor.ca/education/introduction/monuments/ (last accessed on: 11/01/2018). / Lerchenmüller, Franz: Marx und Mandela. Menschenrechtsmuseum in Winnipeg. taz.die tageszeitung article dated 11/10/2015. Available online at: www.taz.de/!5237252/ (last accessed on: 11/01/2018).

► Holodomor Statue— "Bitter Memories of Childhood"

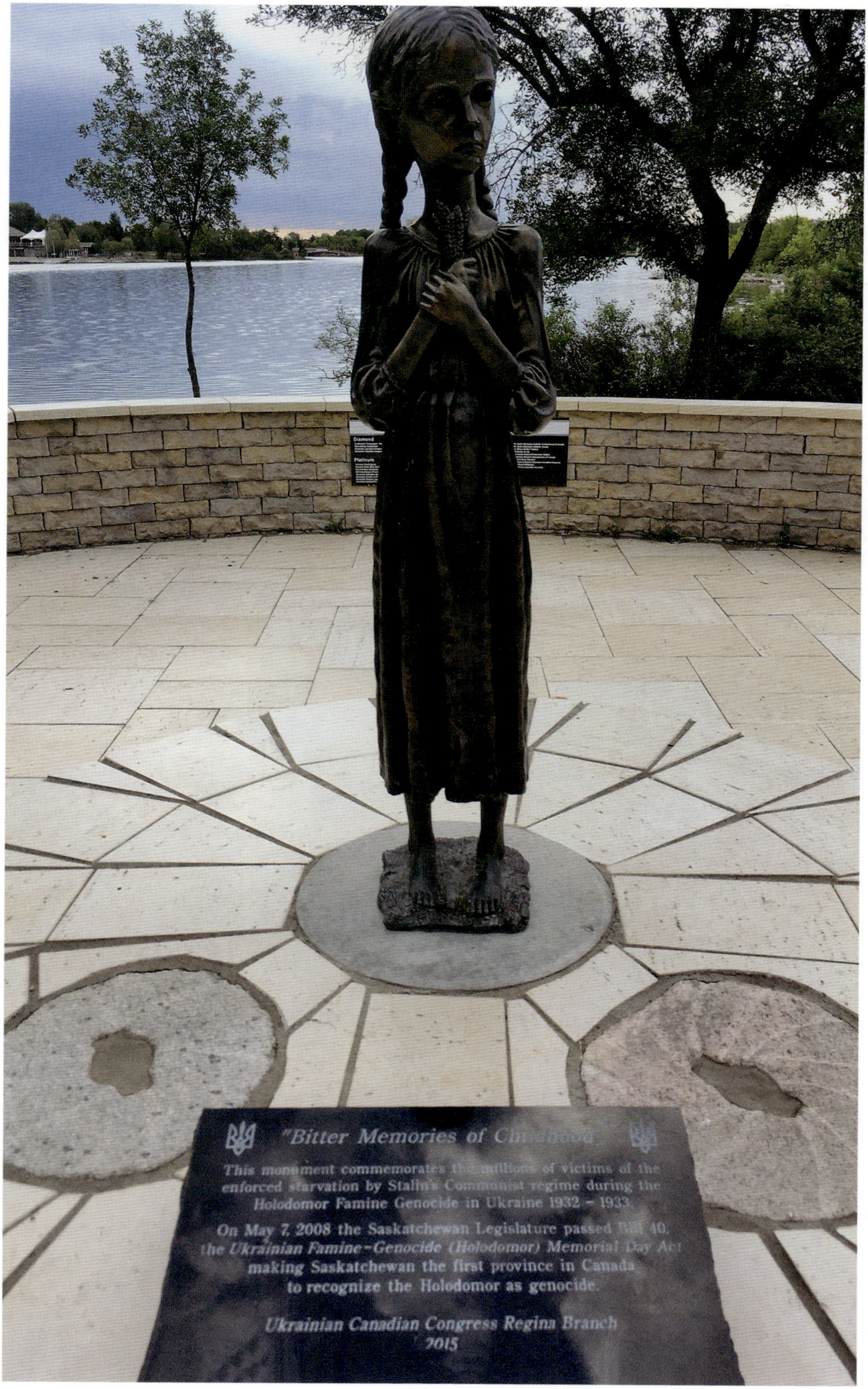
"Bitter Memories of
This monument commemorates the millions of victims of the
enforced starvation by Stalin's Communist regime during the
Holodomor Famine Genocide in Ukraine 1932 – 1933.
On May 7, 2008 the Saskatchewan Legislature passed
the Ukrainian Famine-Genocide (Holodomor) Memorial
making Saskatchewan the first province in Canada
to recognize the Holodomor as genocide.
Ukrainian Canadian Congress Regina Branch
2015

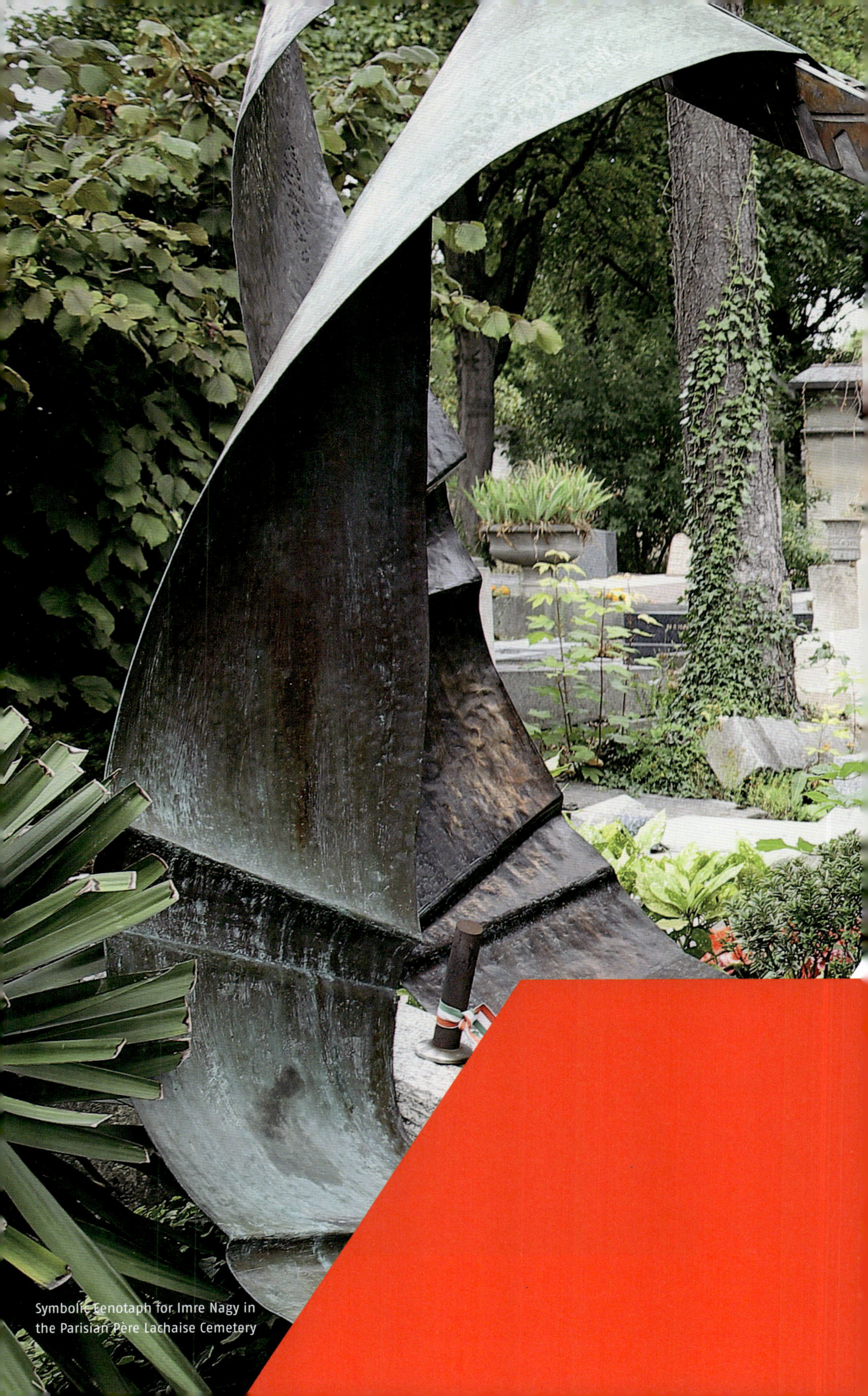

Symbolic Cenotaph for Imre Nagy in the Parisian Père Lachaise Cemetery

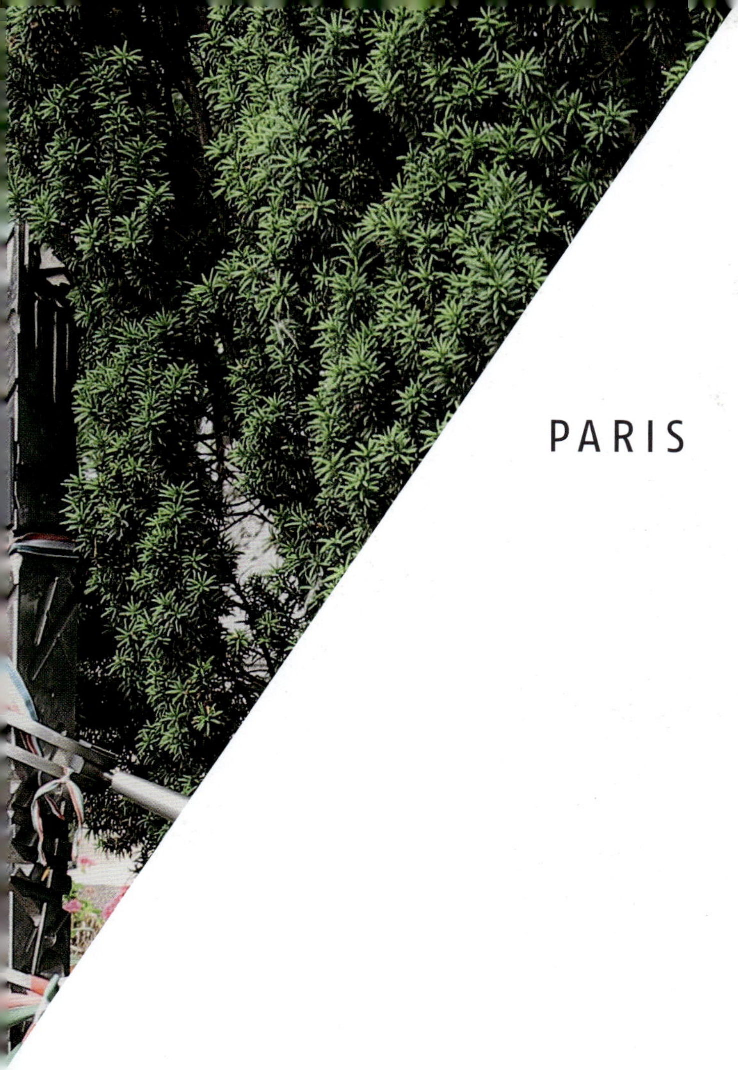

PARIS

France

Symbolic Cenotaph for Imre Nagy

Paris. The cenotaph for Imre Nagy was inaugurated at the Père Lachaise Cemetery on the 30th anniversary of Nagy's death in accordance with plans by Hungarian artist László Rajk. Rajk was one of the most important representatives of the democratic opposition in socialist Hungary in the 1970s and 1980s. His father of the same name held high office in the Hungarian Communist government and party but was arrested in 1949 on the charge of "leading a group of Titoist spies", sentenced to death and executed in a show trial. The symbolic tomb in Paris consists of two semi-circular metal elements bent upwards, with a grave marker in the Hungarian tradition placed in the middle. In front of the grave, a small granite slab embedded in the ground references Nagy's belated burial in Budapest.

Imre Nagy was born on 7 June 1896 in Kaposvár. After finishing high school, he completed an apprenticeship as a locksmith and signed up for military service at the outbreak of the First World War. In July 1916, he was taken prisoner in Galicia, where he first came into contact with the ideas of the Russian socialist movement, which had a lasting influence on him. In May 1920, he became a member of the Russian Communist Party.

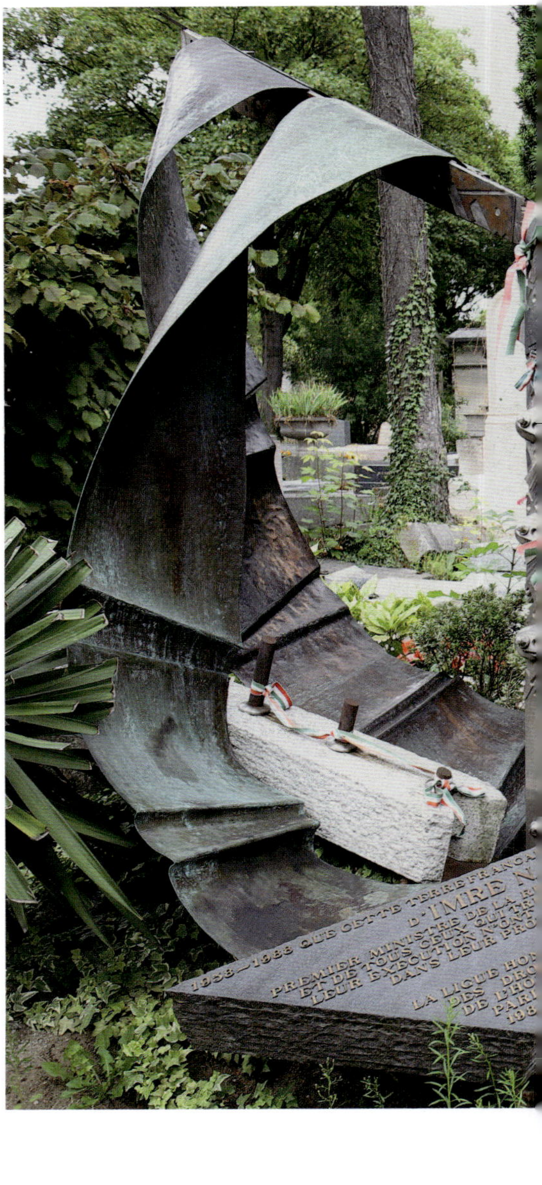

Symbolic Cenotaph for Imre Nagy
in the Parisian Père Lachaise Cemetery

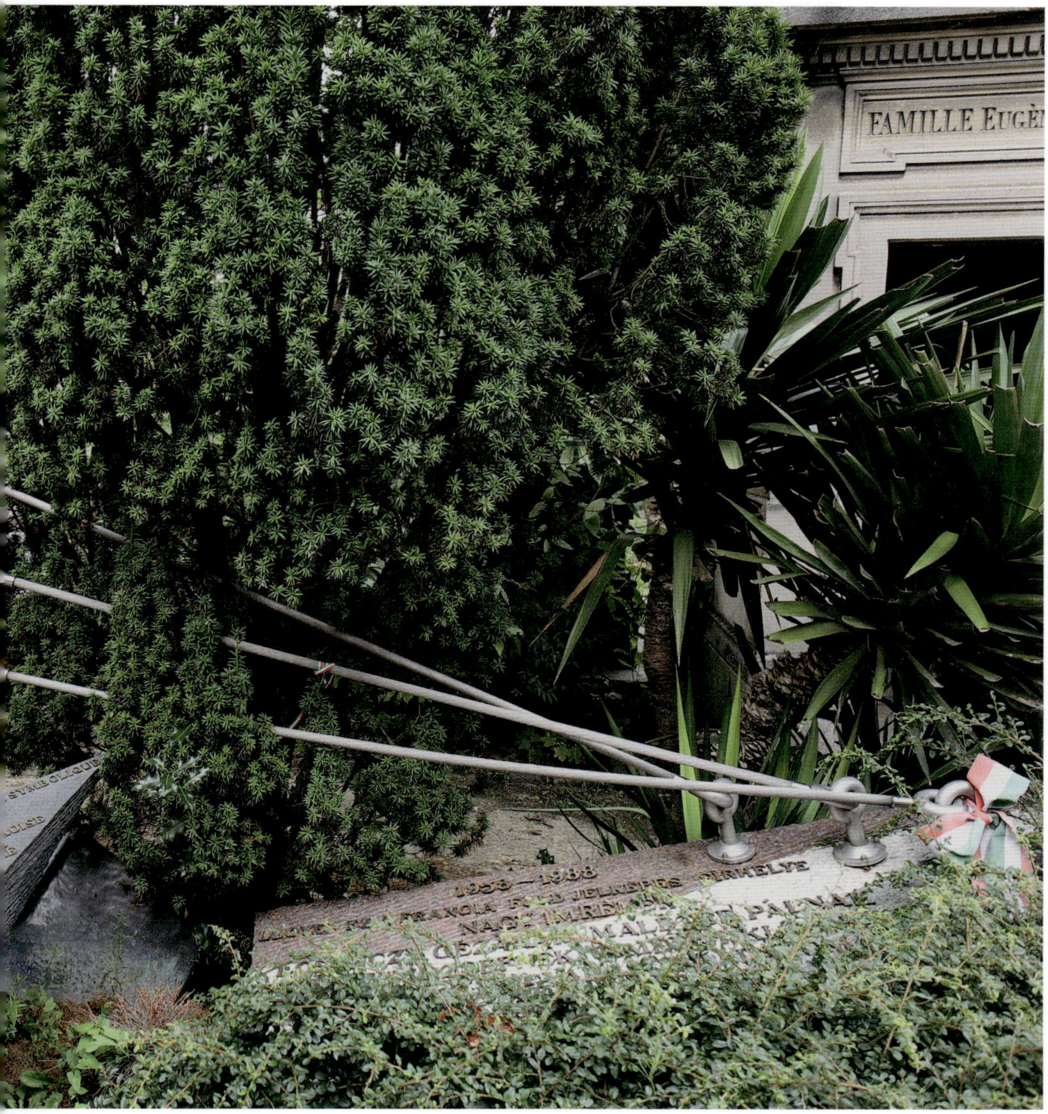
FAMILLE

After returning to Hungary in 1921, he became a member of the Social Democratic Party, from which he was expelled in 1925 because of his left-wing extremist positions. After two arrests in 1927, for which he was not convicted due to lack of evidence, Nagy went into hiding. In 1930, he emigrated to the Soviet Union, where he worked for the International Agricultural Institute until 1936. Nagy narrowly escaped the Great Purges after his denunciation by Béla Kun. During the Second World War, he worked for the Hungarian language service of Radio Moscow. In December 1944, he returned to Hungary. From 1947 to 1949, he was President of the Hungarian National Assembly. After his appointment as Prime Minister in 1953, he tried to carry out extensive economic and political reforms. In 1955, he was stripped of all his offices and expelled from the party. However, his ideas remained in circulation among elements of the Hungarian intellectual elite and were increasingly discussed in public from mid-1956 onwards.

Following the first demonstrations, Nagy returned to the highest leadership of the party on 23 October 1956 at the insurgents' request and was reappointed Prime Minister. In this function, he attempted to push through the most important goals of the revolution against the MDP, the Hungarian Working People's Party, and the Soviet leadership. He advocated the withdrawal of Soviet troops, a multi-party system and Hungarian neutrality.

On 30 October 1956, a new government was formed with Nagy at the helm. During the second Soviet invasion on 4 November 1956, he and his associates sought refuge in the Yugoslav embassy. On 22 November, Nagy and his family were arrested by Soviet officials and brought to Romania despite assurances by the new party leader János Kádár that this would not happen. On 12 April 1957, Nagy was officially arrested, and he was extradited to Hungary in June. On 15 June 1958, the Supreme Court People's Judicial Council sentenced Nagy to death for treason and conspiracy to overthrow the Hungarian government. Together with other alleged criminals, he was transferred to the prison in Kozma Utca where he was executed on 16 June 1958. His body was secretly buried in the courtyard of the institution. It remained interred there until 1961, when the mortal remains were exhumed and taken to plot 301 of the New Municipal Cemetery in Budapest. In June 1989, Nagy was ceremonially reburied on plot 301 to great public acclaim.

Location: Paris, Le Cimetière du Père Lachaise, plot 44

Memorial to the Victims of Communism in Romania

Paris. During a pilgrimage to the cemetery of Romanian heroes in the French town of Soultzmatt in June 1984, former political prisoner Cicerone Ioaniţoiu proposed to the exiled Romanians living in France that a marble monument be erected in Paris in honour of the Romanians executed in their homeland by the communist regime. At the time, his appeal did not elicit much in the way of response. Of the one million francs that would have been necessary for the construction of a monument, he only managed to raise 40,000. The creation of a memorial to the Romanians who had been murdered was given fresh impetus only when Remus Radina, a well-known former political prisoner and representative of the AFDPR, the Association of Former Political Prisoners in Romania, in France, came across a granite plaque in the Père Lachaise cemetery which General Charles de Gaulle had dedicated to the memory of the French resistance at the time. He then suggested to Cicerone Ioaniţoiu that they follow the example of the general. At this cemetery, a grave was bought near the entrance and a granite slab measuring one by two metres erected. The **inscription** reads:

French: *1944 – 1989 // Aux Roumains / tombes pour dieu / et la democratie // Les exiles / Roumains*

English: *1944 – 1989. The Romanians who died for God and democracy. The exiled Romanians.*

The symbolic tomb was inaugurated on 25 February 1990.

Location: Paris, Le Cimetière du Père-Lachaise

Further reading:

Rainer, János: Imre Nagy. Vom Stalinisten zum Märtyrer des ungarischen Volksaufstands. Eine politische Biographie 1896 – 1958, Paderborn 2006.

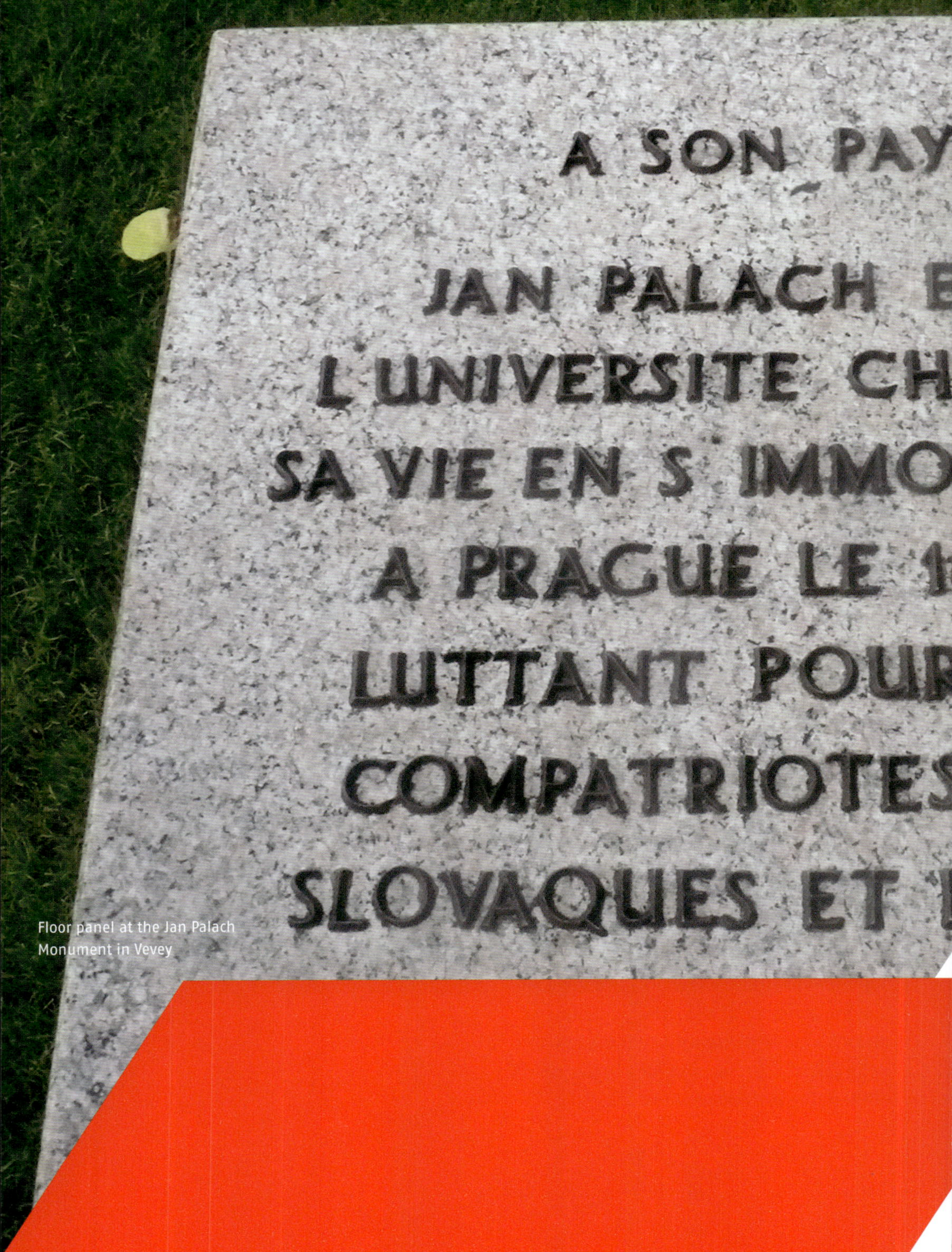

Floor panel at the Jan Palach
Monument in Vevey

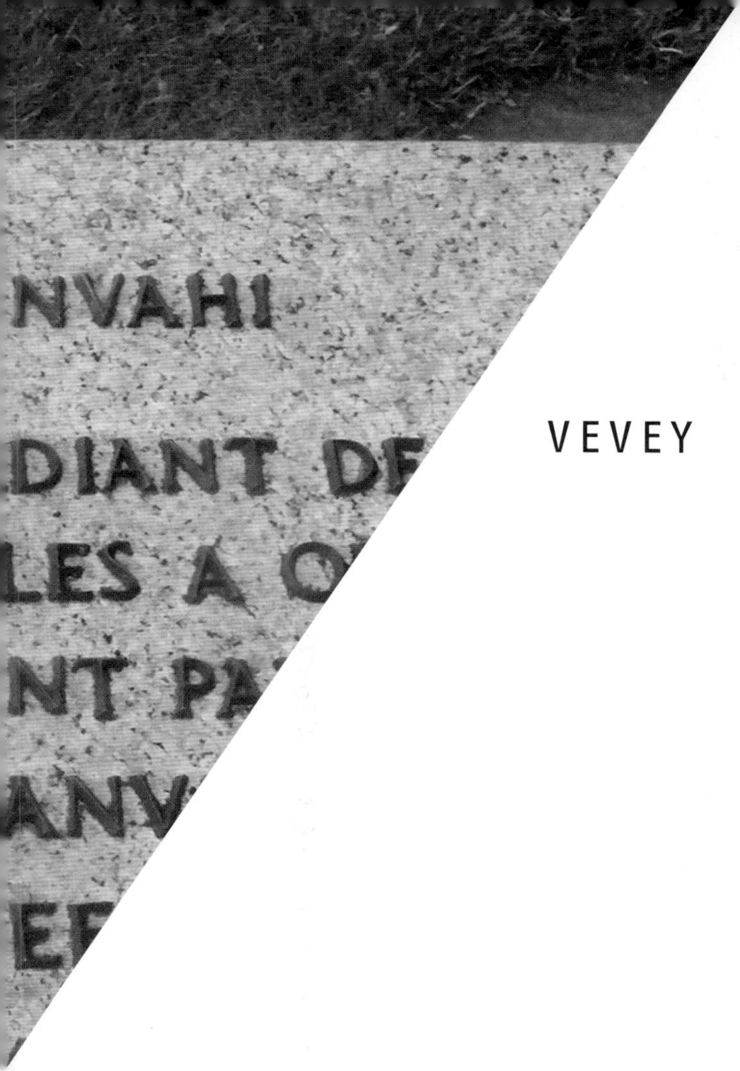

VEVEY

Switzerland

Jan Palach Monument

Vevey. On the shores of Lake Geneva, in the city of Vevey, a memorial to Jan Palach was unveiled to the public in 1997. The sculpture, created by Czech sculptor Josef Knobloch, shows a stylised flame on a reddish granite stele. On the front is a medallion with Palach's picture and an inscription dedicated to him. Embedded in the lawn is another panel commemorating Palach in French.

The impetus for the monument largely came from physician Madeleine Cuendet, who organised aid for Czechoslovak refugees in Switzerland after the suppression of the Prague Spring in 1968. When she learned of the self-immolations of Jan Palach and Jan Zajícs, she attempted to erect a monument to both of them. However, this idea met with resistance, with the result that implementation was delayed by almost 30 years. After the Velvet Revolution of 1989, Madeleine Cuendet organised medical supplies for Czechoslovakia and was awarded the medal "Pour le Mérite" by President Václav Havel for her dedication. In the early 1990s, the idea for a monument resurfaced, and implementation began with the support of the Czech Embassy and other associations.

Inscription
French: *À son pays envahi//Jan Palach, étudiant de/l'université Charles, a offert/ sa vie en s'immolant par le feu/a Prague le 16. janvier 1969,/luttant pour defendre ses/compatriotes tchèques et/slovaques et pour la liberté/si chère au cœur des Suisses*

English: *But they invaded his country. Jan Palach, a student at Charles University, gave his life in Prague on 16 January 1969, when he surrendered himself to the fire. He burned to defend his Czech and Slovak compatriots and to defend freedom that is so dear to the heart of the Swiss.*

Location: Vevey, on the shore of Lake Geneva, Quai Maria Belgia

Further reading:
Jan Palach. Multimediales Projekt der Karlsuniversität Prag. Orte der Erinnerung. Available online at: www.janpalach.cz/de/default/mista-pameti/vevey (last accessed on: 11/01/2018).

►
Jan Palach Monument

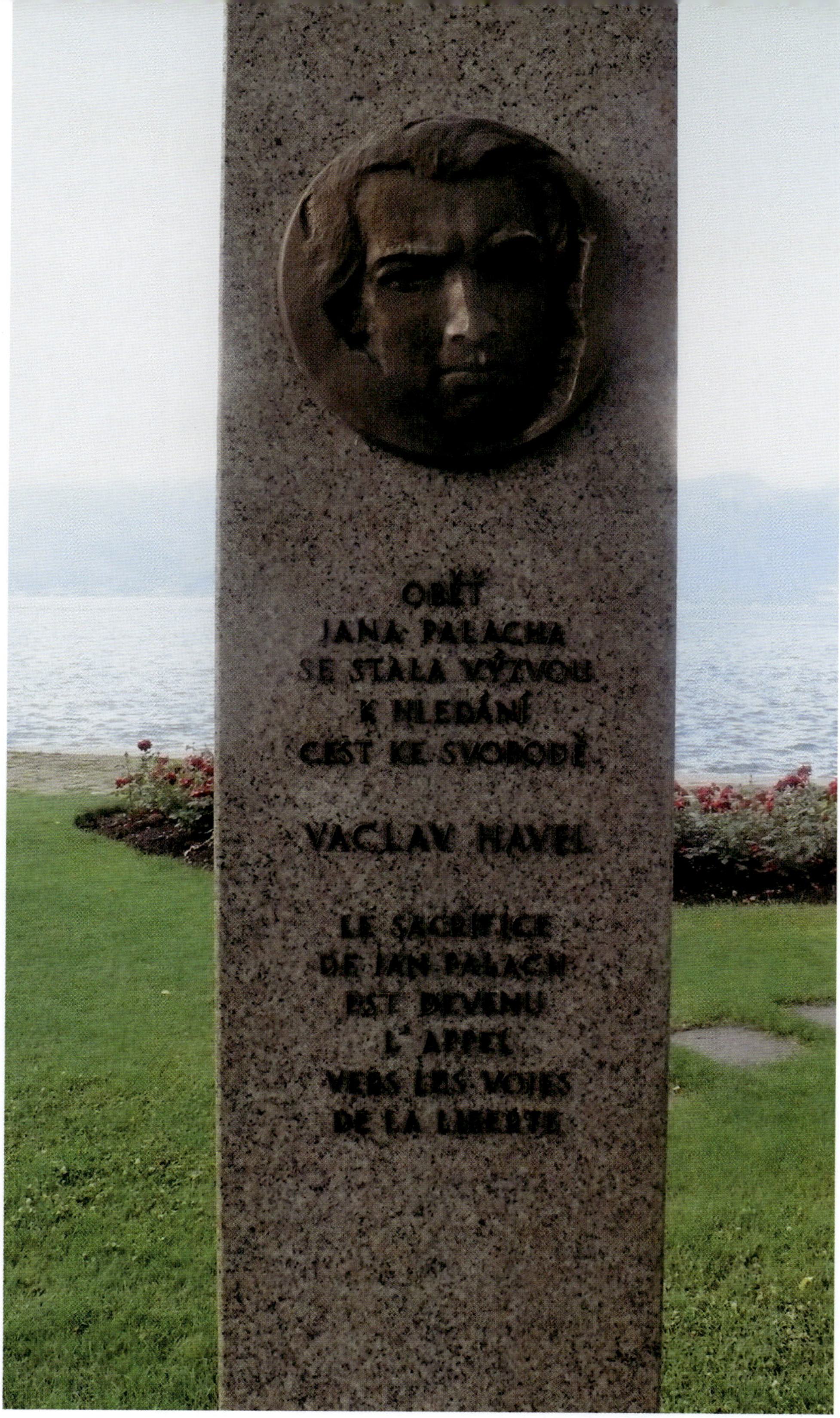
OBĚŤ
JANA PALACHA
SE STALA VÝZVOU
K HLEDÁNÍ
CEST KE SVOBODĚ
VACLAV HAVEL
LE SACRIFICE
DE JAN PALACH
EST DEVENU
L'APPEL
VERS LES VOIES
DE LA LIBERTE

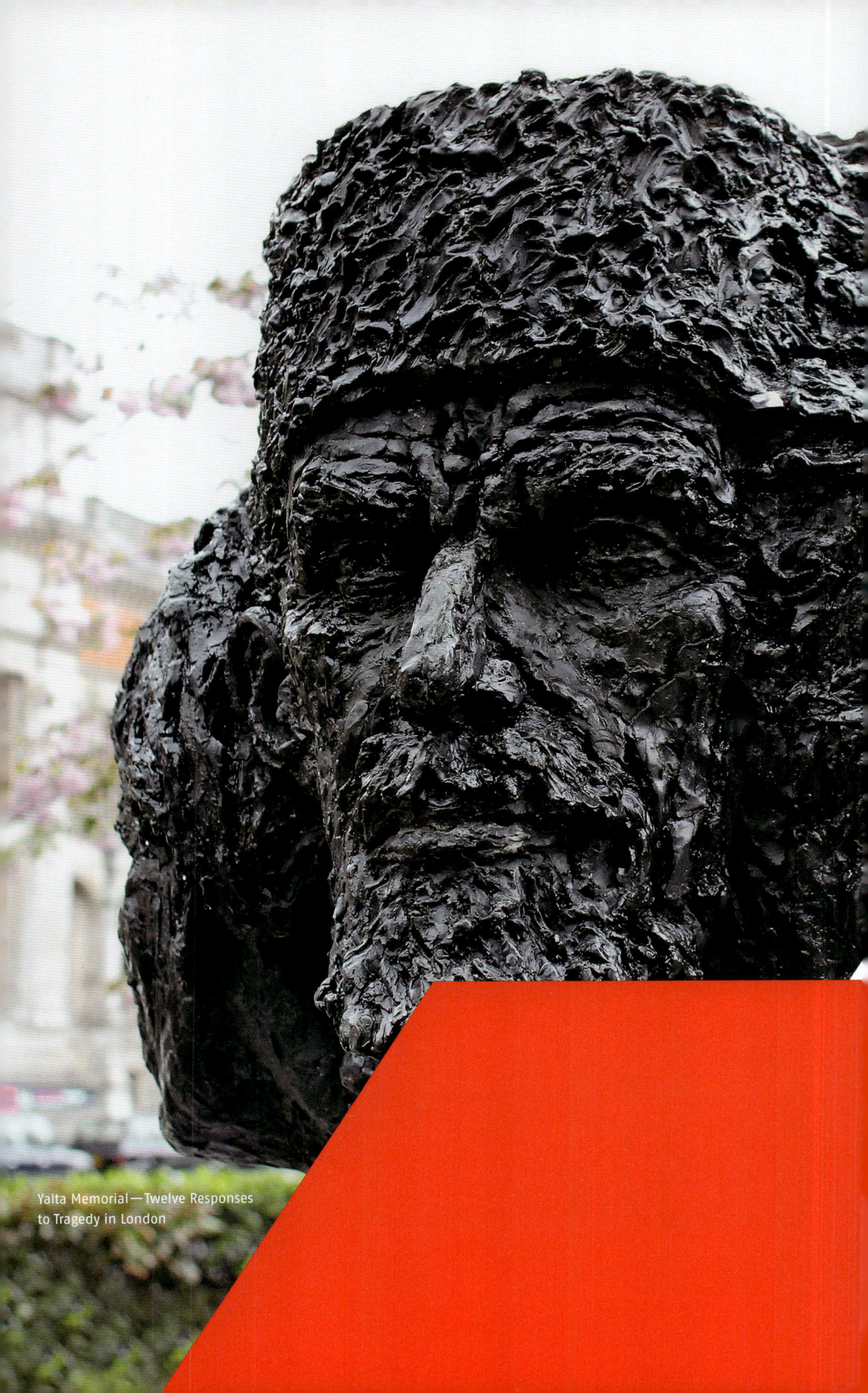
Yalta Memorial—Twelve Responses
to Tragedy in London

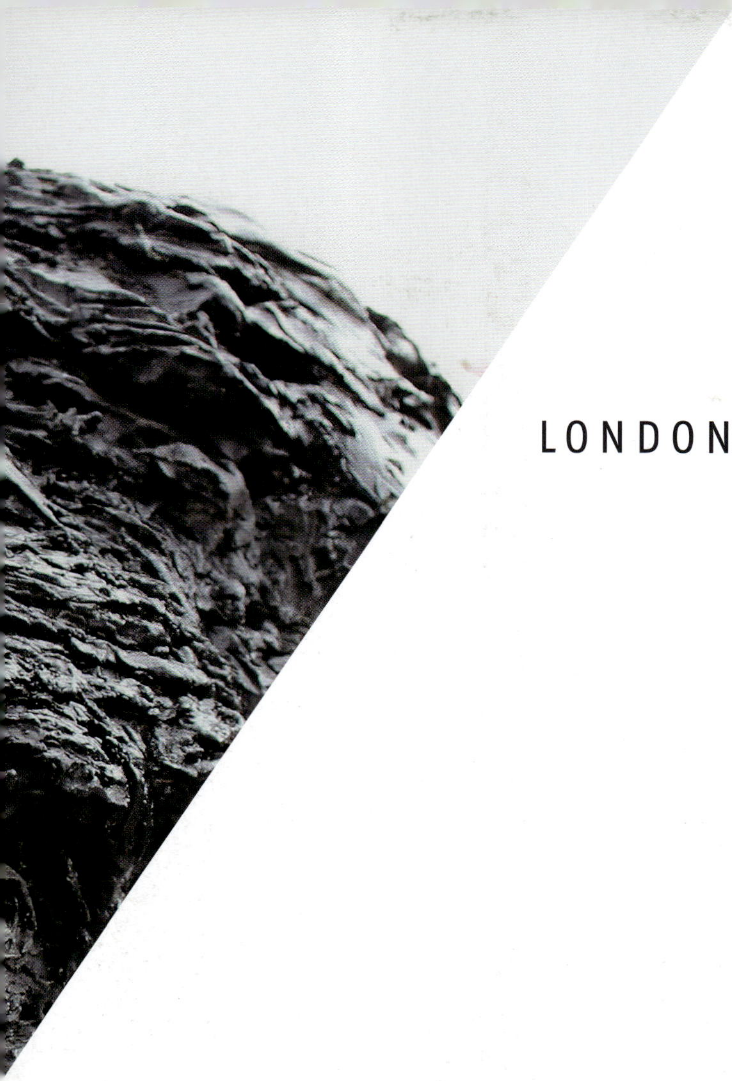

LONDON

United Kingdom

Yalta Memorial — Twelve Responses to Tragedy

London. The Yalta Memorial "Twelve Responses to Tragedy" was dedicated by Bishop John Klyberg of Fulham in South Kensington on 2 August 1986. The sculpture, designed by British sculptor Angela Conner, commemorates all those who were either expelled or forced to flee their homes as a result of the Yalta Conference in February 1945. The monument, which consists of twelve busts on a pedestal, replaced a monument that had previously been erected here in 1982 but had been vandalised.

The first plans for the construction of the original monument were drawn up as early as 1970. At the time, journalists Richard West, Patrick Marnham and Auberon Waugh wrote to the conservative British weekly "The Spectator" calling for the erection of a monument to keep alive the "the memory of the hundreds of thousands of innocent people who were forcibly repatriated by the Allies to the Soviet and Yugoslav authorities at the end of the second world war, a crime that was carefully hushed up at the time and even concealed from Parliament for fear of the outcry that would have resulted." The idea was taken up again a short time later in another letter to the "Times" by British politicians from various parties. In May 1980, in the face of resistance from the Foreign Office — the construction on British Crown territory of a memorial critical of the government was a major bone of contention — Prime Minister Margaret Thatcher finally decided to allow the monument to be built.

Inscriptions

On the east side:

This memorial was placed / here by members of all parties / in both Houses of Parliament / and by many other sympathisers / in memory / of the countless / innocent men, / women and / children from the Soviet Union / and other East European states / who were imprisoned and died / at the hand of communist / governments after being / repatriated at the conclusion / of the Second World War / May they rest in peace.

On the west side:

This sculpture was dedicated by / the bishop of Fulham / on 2nd August 1986 to / replace the previous / memorial dedicated by / the Bishop of London / on 6th March 1982 which / was later destroyed by vandals to whom / the truth was intolerable.

On the south side:

Twelve responses / to tragedy / by Angela Conner.

Location: London, opposite the Victoria & Albert Museum at the junction of Cromwell Road and Thurloe Place

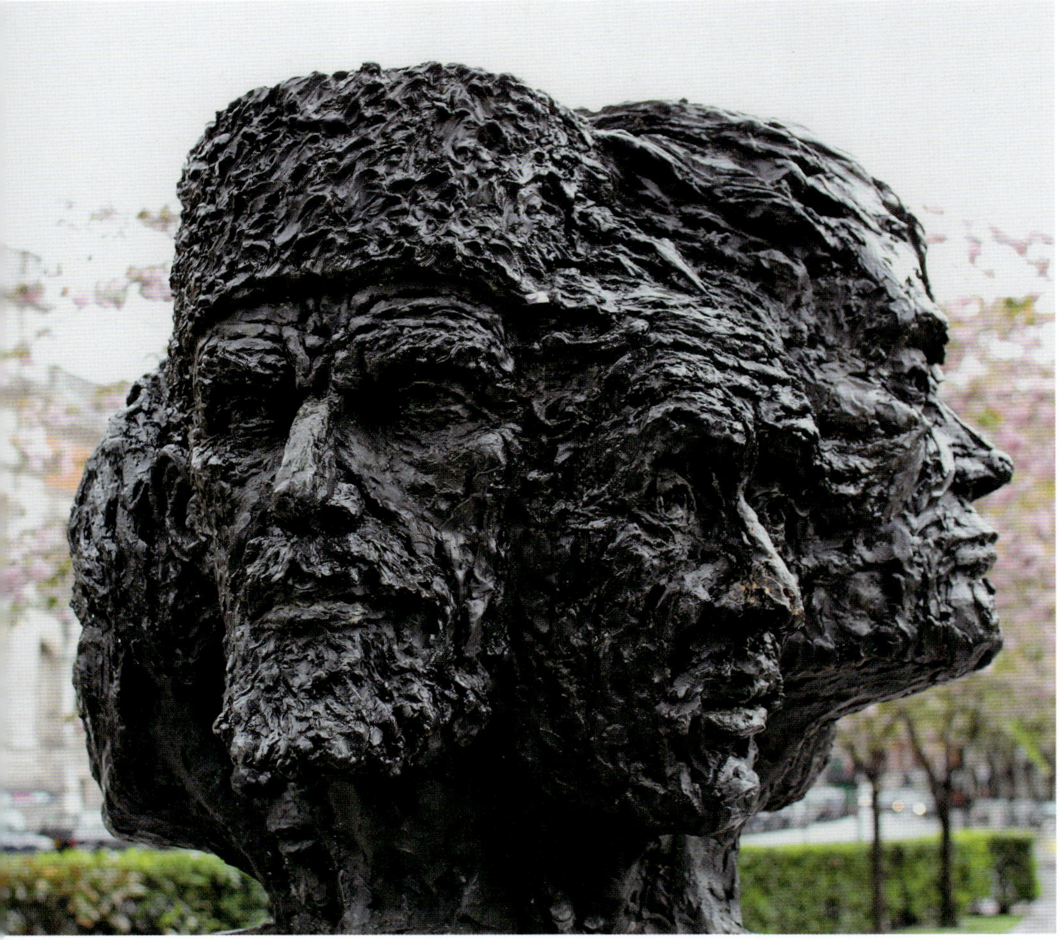

Yalta Memorial—Twelve Responses to Tragedy

Katyń Memorial

London. The first public monument to the victims of Katyń in Western Europe was erected in London's Gunnersbury cemetery in 1976. It was the most controversial of all the Katyń monuments worldwide: plans for it met with massive resistance from the Soviet Union and the Polish People's Republic, which tried to exert diplomatic pressure to prevent its erection to cover up Soviet responsibility for the crime.

The creation of the monument was first inspired by the efforts of exiled Poles in Great Britain in 1970 to build a central memorial to the victims of the mass murder of Polish civilians and military personnel by the Soviet secret police. The idea met with a considerable response in the British media, which led to the establishment of a Katyń Memorial Fund Committee in the British Parliament in 1971. An executive committee was also set up. In addition to British MPs, both committees included representatives of the Polish diaspora in Great Britain. The project was also supported by the umbrella organisation of Poles in the United States, the Polish American Congress in Chicago.

However, once the collection of the necessary funds had begun in December 1971, a conflict with the British government ensued that would drag on for many years. Out of diplomatic consideration for the Soviet Union, the government urged that the year 1940 be omitted from the monument. Explicit mention of this date would set Soviet culpability for the massacre in stone, and the Soviet Union wanted to prevent this at all costs.

Another difficulty was to find a suitable location for the monument. Four sites that had initially been considered in West London, where most of the exiled Poles lived, were not available for practical reasons. Another location had to be abandoned due to the continuing resistance of the Church of England. Finally, the multi-denominational cemetery in Gunnersbury, which is not under Anglican or state administration, was selected, clearing the last obstacle to the realisation of the monument.

The foundation stone was laid on 1 July 1976, and the monument was symbolically unveiled to the public on 18 September 1976 by Mary Chełmecka, the widow of one of the victims of Katyń. The Catholic Bishop of the Polish Diaspora, Władysław Rubin, dedicated it in the presence of representatives of the Polish Orthodox and Protestant Churches and the Association of Jewish Ex-Servicemen and Women. Afterwards, the president of the anti-communist Polish government-in-exile, Stanisław Ostrowski, laid the first of over 120 wreaths at the monument. The mayors of some

►
Katyń Memorial

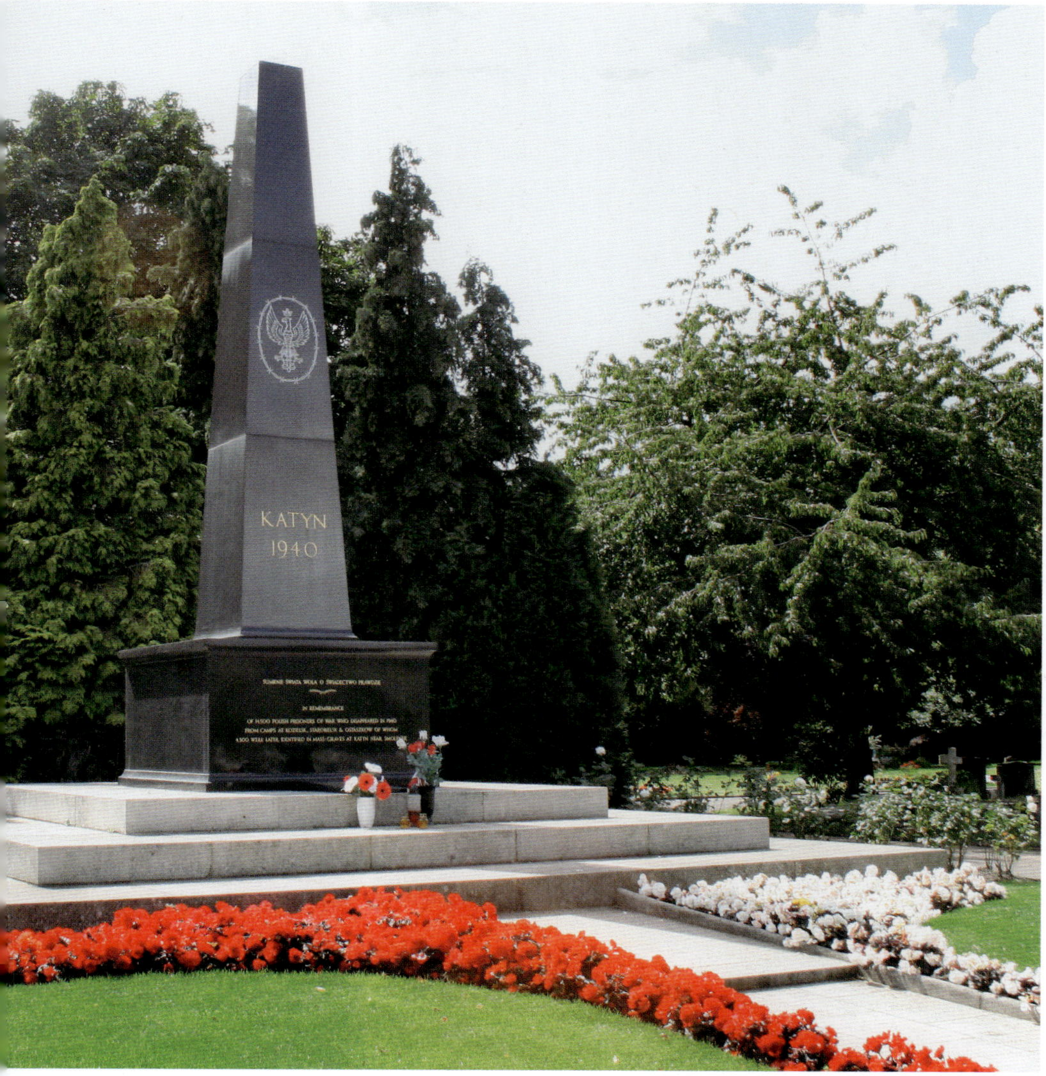
KATYN
1940
IN REMEMBRANCE

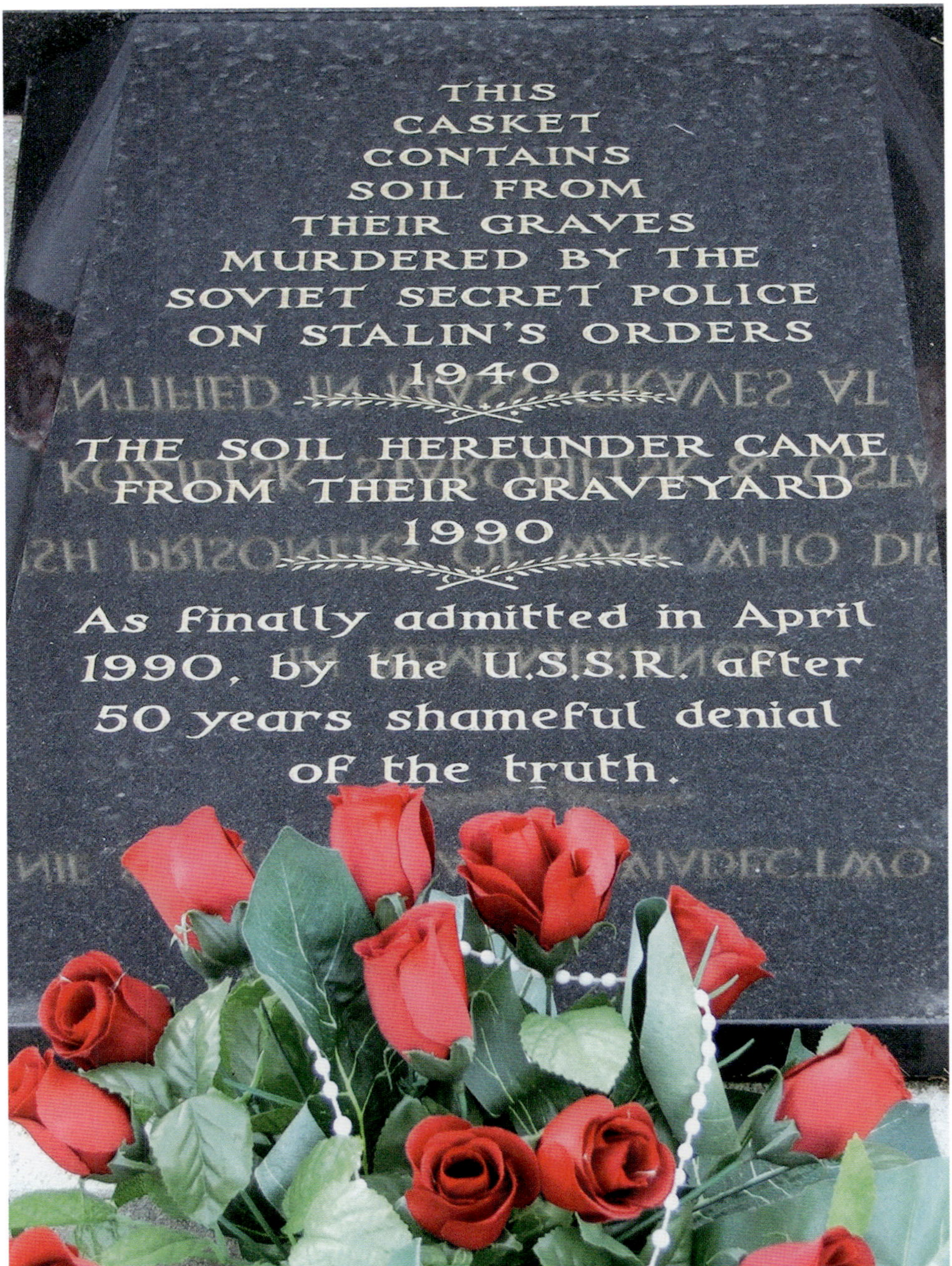

Base of the Katyń Memorial
with inscriptions

London boroughs and survivors of the POW camps at Kozelsk, Ostashkov and Starobilsk also attended the inauguration ceremony with a crowd estimated at 8,000.

The inauguration of the monument was accompanied by massive controversies. The Soviet Embassy lodged twelve official complaints with the British Foreign Office regarding the ceremony alone, with the aim of keeping the celebrations to a minimum. No representatives of the British government attended the ceremony. In response to a request from the Foreign Office, the British Minister of Defence, Fred Mulley, went so far as to forbid British officers who wanted to attend the inauguration ceremony in a private capacity from wearing uniform. This ban was demonstratively flouted by two reserve officers.

In the following years, the monument remained a hot-button issue. While the Labour government refused to officially participate in the annual commemoration ceremonies, Margaret Thatcher's Conservative government set diplomatic concerns aside in 1979 and thereafter, permitting a military ceremony to be held on the events.

The Katyń Memorial in Gunnersbury was designed by Ryszard Gabrielczyk and consists of a simple four-metre-high black marble obelisk with an attached relief of a crowned Polish eagle in a barbed wire wreath made of Nubian granite. The inscription "KATYN 1940" is engraved underneath. The obelisk stands on a black marble base with a dedication to the memorial, which in turn rests on a symmetrical, three-tiered pedestal made of light grey stone. Embedded in this pedestal is a capsule containing soil from Katyń.

Because Soviet culpability for the Katyń massacre is not explicitly mentioned in the monument's inscription but is only implied by the inclusion of the year 1940, representatives of radical anti-communist movements criticised the concept as too reserved. After the political upheaval in 1989, on 21 April 1990, an additional plaque was placed on the top step of the pedestal, naming the Soviet secret police as the perpetrators. The annual commemoration events organised by the Polish Ex-Combatants Association at the memorial, which until then had always taken place at the end of September to commemorate the Soviet invasion of eastern Poland on 17 September 1939, have since been moved to April, the month recognised in Poland for the commemoration of Katyń.

Inscriptions

On the base, Polish / English:

Sumienie świata woła o świadectwo prawdzie.

In remembrance / of 14 500 Polish prisoners of war who disappeared in 1940 / from camps at Kozielsk, Starobielsk & Ostaszkow of whom / 4 500 were later identified in mass-graves at Katyn near Smolensk.

On the podium, English:

This / casket / contains / soil from / their grave. Murdered by the / Soviet secret police / on Stalin's orders / 1940 / The soil hereunder came / from their graveyard / 1990 // As finally admitted, in April / 1990, by the U. S. S. R. after / 50 years shameful denial / of the truth.

Location: London, Gunnersbury Cemetery, Gunnersbury Avenue

Further reading:

Kaminsky, Anna (ed.): Erinnerungsorte für die Opfer von Katyń. Leipzig 2013.

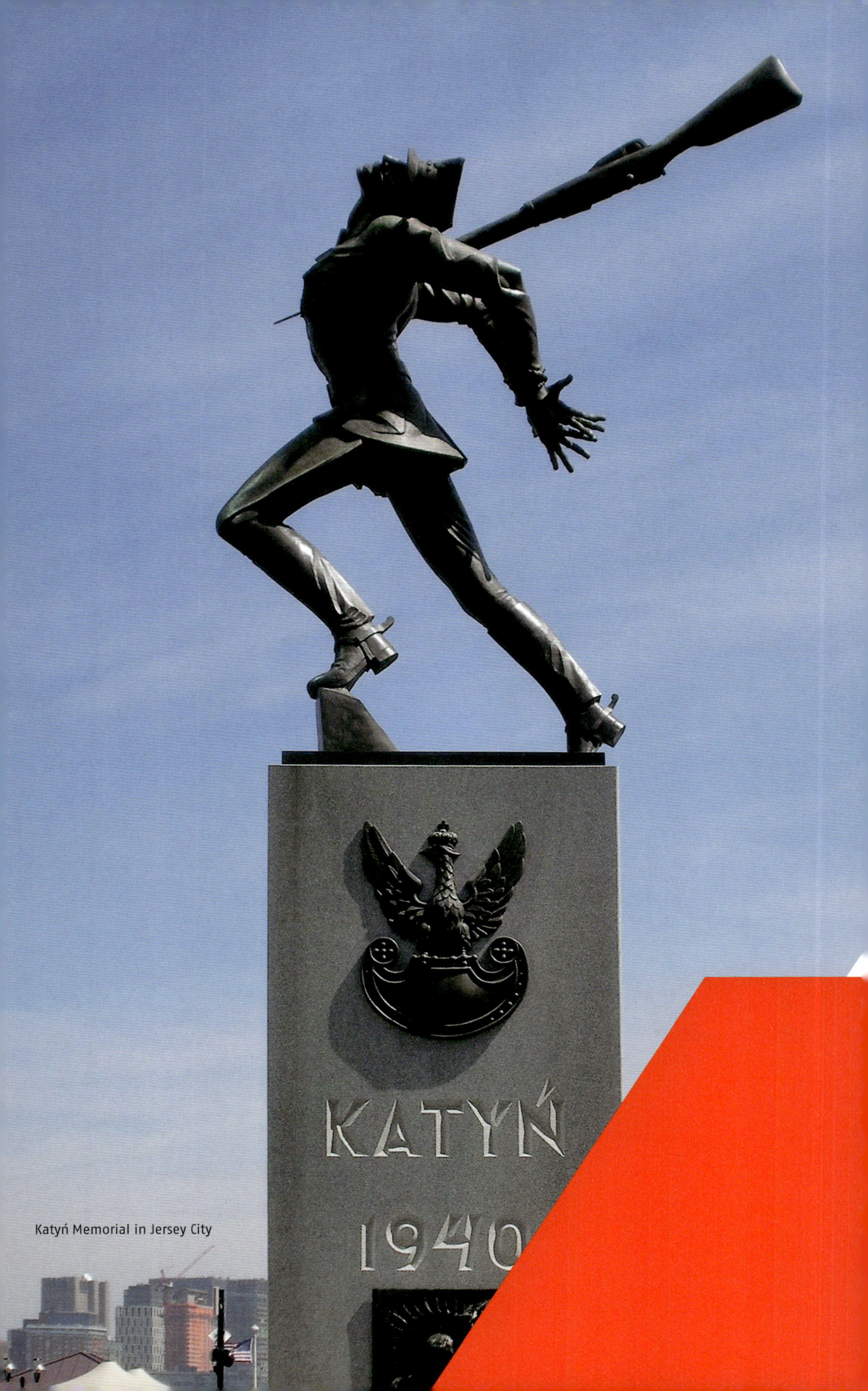

Katyń Memorial in Jersey City

WASHINGTON
JERSEY CITY
CULVER CITY
BOSTON

USA

Victims of Communism Memorial

Washington, D.C. The Victims of Communism Memorial was inaugurated on 12 June 2007 on the occasion of the 20th anniversary of the visit of the then US President Ronald Reagan to Berlin in 1987. The bronze statue erected near the Capitol Building is a replica of the ten-metre-high papier-mâché Goddess of Democracy, which Chinese students erected a few days before the bloody suppression of the rallies on Tiananmen Square in Beijing on 4 June 1989. At the same time, the three-metre-high sculpture of a young woman holding up a torch bears a clear resemblance to the New York Statue of Liberty. The inauguration ceremony was attended by US President George W. Bush and high-ranking representatives of the US government and international organisations.

The construction of the memorial has its origin in a decision by the US Congress to dedicate a monument in Washington to the global victims of communism. The first Act of Congress on this issue was passed in 1993 during the Clinton Presidency. In the following year, the Victims of Communism Memorial Foundation was founded, which agitated for the construction. In addition to US politicians, human rights activists and scientists such as Jeane Kirkpatrick, Bob Dole, Claiborne Pell and Jane Kirkland, it also included personalities such as Václav Havel, Lech Wałęsa, the wife of Andrei Sakharov, Elena Bonner, and Lithuanian President Vytaustas Landsbergis. The cost of the memorial was estimated at about 825,000 US dollars. After the amount had been raised through a worldwide fundraising campaign in the summer of 2006 and the site for the construction of the memorial negotiated with the city of Washington, the foundation stone was laid on 27 June 2006.

Inscription

At the base of the monument:

To the more than / one hundred million / victims of communism / and to those who love liberty.

Location: Washington, D.C., square between Massachusetts Avenue and New Jersey Avenue

► Victims of Communism Memorial

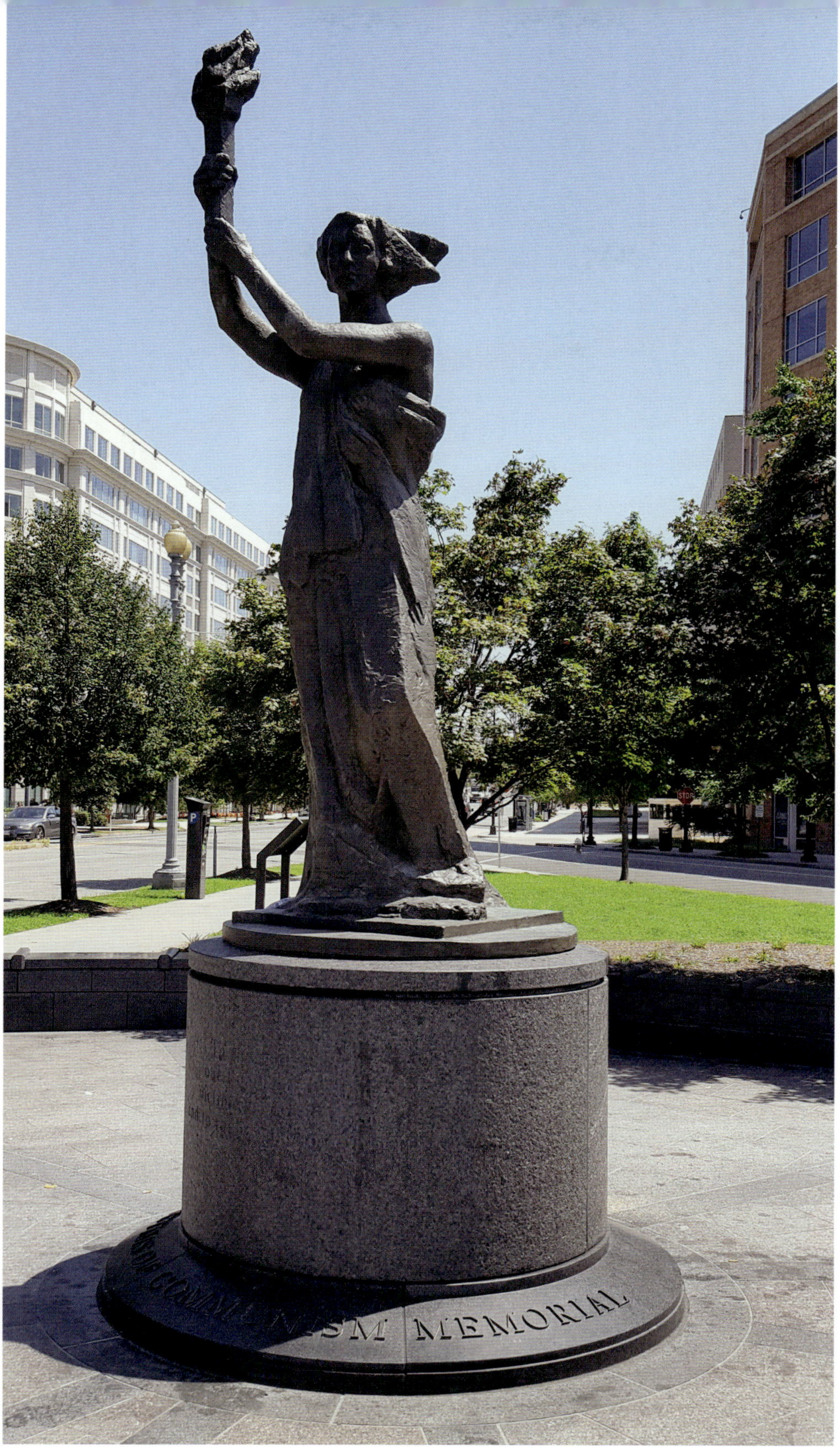
MEMORIAL

Holodomor Memorial to Victims of the Ukrainian Famine-Genocide of 1932–1933

Washington, D.C. The Holodomor Memorial was first presented to the public at a ceremonial inauguration ceremony on 7 November 2015. It commemorates the several million victims of the famine catastrophe in Ukraine in 1932/33. The monument was created on the initiative of the Ukrainian Congress Committee of America. The United States Senate approved the construction of the planned memorial in 2005. Funding was provided by the US National Park Service and the Ukrainian government. The front of the ten-metre-long bronze bas-relief depicts individually carved grain ears whose contours increasingly dissolve as they recede further towards the back of the composition. The grain field motif chosen by Ukrainian-American architect Larisa Kurilas symbolises the peasantry as the main victims of the famine catastrophe.

Inscription

English: *Famine-enocide / in Ukraine // In memory of the millions / of innocent victims / of a man-made famine / in Ukraine. Engineered and / implemented by Stalin's / totalitarian regime*

Ukrainian: У пам'ять про мільйони / невинних жертв штучного / голоду в Україні / спланованого та вчиненого / Сталінським тоталітарним / режимом.

Location: Washington, D.C., at the intersection of North Capitol Street, Massachusetts Avenue, and F Street N.W.

Holodomor Memorial to Victims of the Ukrainian Famine-Genocide of 1932–1933

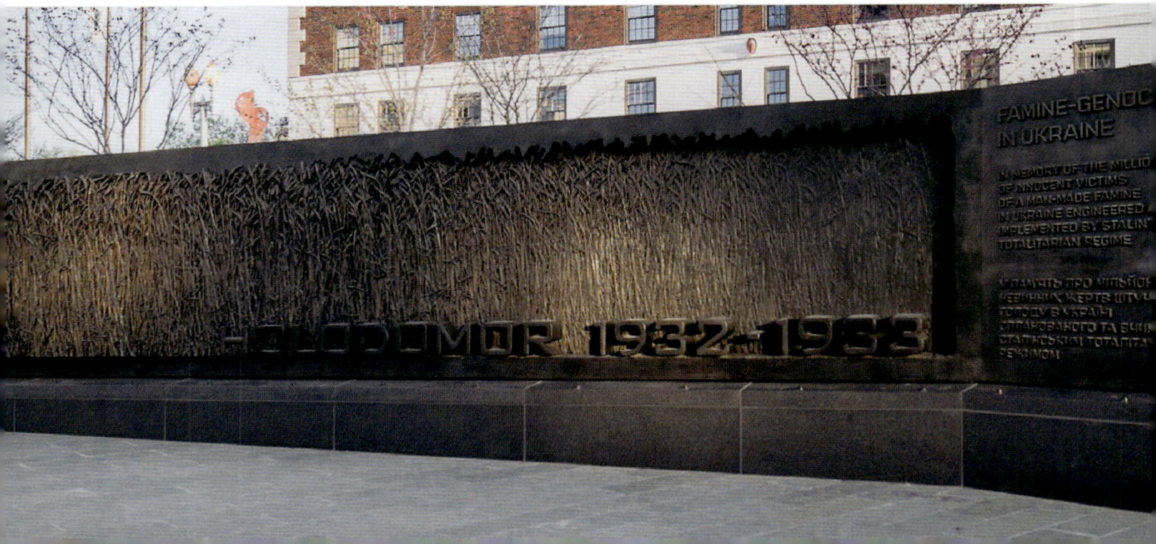

Katyń Memorial

Jersey City. The Katyń Memorial in Jersey City is the second monumental work by Polish-American sculptor Andrzej Pityński dedicated to the victims of Katyń after the Hussar monument "The Avenger" in Doylestown, which was created in 1988. In contrast to the monument in the Polish veteran cemetery near the small town of Doylestown, the Katyń monument in New Jersey was the first of its kind in a public space in the US at the time of its inauguration on 19 May 1991. It is located on Exchange Place in central Jersey City, right at the mouth of the Hudson River, across from the Manhattan skyline.

The monument was initiated by Stanisław Paszul and Joseph Płoński and the committee they founded to build a Katyń monument in Jersey City. It cost more than 250,000 dollars, which was put forward by Polish émigrés in North America and by the artist himself. The inauguration of the memorial was celebrated with a mass attended by 37 priests.

The memorial consists of a five-metre-high bronze sculpture standing atop a five-metre pedestal. The sculpture depicts a young, gagged, Polish officer whose hands are tied behind his back. Thrust in his back is the bayonet of a carbine. His head is pulled back so that he faces the sky. The composition symbolises the treacherous "stab in the back" dealt by the Red Army to the Polish troops while they were fighting against the German Wehrmacht in September 1939.

The words "KATYŃ 1940" are engraved in large letters on the front of the light grey granite base. Above it is a bronze cast of the coat of arms of the Polish army with the eagle and shield. While this side commemorates the Katyń massacre, on the opposite side of the pedestal is a bronze relief more than four metres high in the form of a cross displaying a mother with three children of different ages. The word "SIBERIA" and, above it, the year "1939" are written on the crossbeam of the cross. By the foot of the mother with the three children is an inscription. In it, a Polish poem and a text written in English recall the deportations from the Soviet-occupied Polish eastern territories to Siberia that began in 1939. Also mentioned there are the fighters of the anti-communist Polish underground murdered by the NKVD between 1944 and 1956.

On both sides of the pedestal are bronze plaques with an excerpt from a poem by the Russian poet Andrei Voznesensky about Katyń, a short dedication, and the key phrase from the 1952 final report of the fact-finding committee of the US House of Representatives. On the right side of the monument is a text in Polish, with a bronze cast of the crowned Polish eagle set underneath. On the left side, under the Great Seal of the United States with the bald eagle, is a panel with an English text. Another bronze plaque on the right lists the initiators and backers of the monument.

On 11 September 2004, another bronze relief dedicated to the victims of the 11 September 2001 terrorist attack on the World Trade Center was unveiled on the front below the main inscription "KATYŃ 1940". It shows the Mother of God embracing the burning twin towers in her arms. The silhouette of the Katyń monument is also superimposed over the skyline of Manhattan. The Mother of God's halo contains the words "United States of America".

Inscriptions

Polish: *Katyń 1940 / Katyń—to otwarty makabryczny skarbiec, / a w nim zamordowany kwiat narodu / polskiego, wojska, młodej inteligencji, / twórców, bohaterów którzy z szablami / rzucali się na czołgi. / Katyń—to skarbiec kłamstwa, stalinowskiego / i poststalinowskiego, globalnego załgania / rządów, komisji międzynarodowych, / pisarzy—to skarbiec hańby. / Katyń—to wygnanie z pamięci Boga. / Katyń—to skarbiec prawdy... / Boże daj ukojenie duszom niewinnie / zamordowanych w Katyniu / Fragment wiersza A. Wozniesienski, 1989 r / Poświęcono pamięci 15 400 polskich oficerów, intelektualistów, / liderów, więzniów wojennych, brutalnie zamordowanych / przez sowieckie N.K.W.D. na wiosnę 1940 roku i pochowanych w masowym grobie w lesie Katyńskim koło Smoleńska i w / innych nieznanych miejscach Rosji Sowieckiej. / ... Ten komitet jednomyślnie wykrył bez żadnej wątpliwości / że sowieckie N. K. W. D. popełniło masowy mord na polskich / oficerach, liderach, intelektualistach w lesie Katyńskim / koło Smoleńska w Rosji ... / Komitet Izby Administracyjnej / Kongres Stanów Zjednoczonych / Raport Nr. 2505 Washington, 1952. / Fundator tablicy—Wachmistrz Lucja Rutkowski.*

English: *Katyn 1940 / Katyn—a macabre treasury, and in it the murdered / flower of the Polish Nation, the army, the / young intelligentsia, the creators and the / heroes who armed with swords threw / themselves on tanks. / Katyn—a treasury of lies, stalinistic and post- / stalinistic, a subterfuge by governments, / international commissions, writers—a / treasury of infamy. /Katyn—a banishment of God from one's memory. / Katyn—a treasury of truth... / God, grant peace to the souls of the innocent / assassinated in Katyn. / Excerpt of poem by A. Wozniesienski, 1989 / Dedicated to the memory of the 15 400 Polish officers, / intellectual leaders, and prisoners of war brutally / massacred by the Soviet N. K. W. D. in the spring of 1940 and / buried in mass graves in the Katyn Forest near Smolensk, / and in other undisclosed sites in the Soviet Union. /... This committee unanimously finds, beyond any question or / reasonable doubt, that the Soviet N. K. W. D. (People's Commissariat / of Internal Affairs) committed the mass murders of the / Polish officers and intellectual leaders in Katyn Forest / near Smolensk, Russia ... / Committee on House Administration, United States House of / Representatives Report No. 2505 Washington, 1952 / In remembrance of my brothers—the ›Virtuti Militari‹ cross from / Monte Cassino, 1944—from 2nd Lt. Emil Kornacki, survivor of Ostaszkow camp.*

► Katyń Memorial

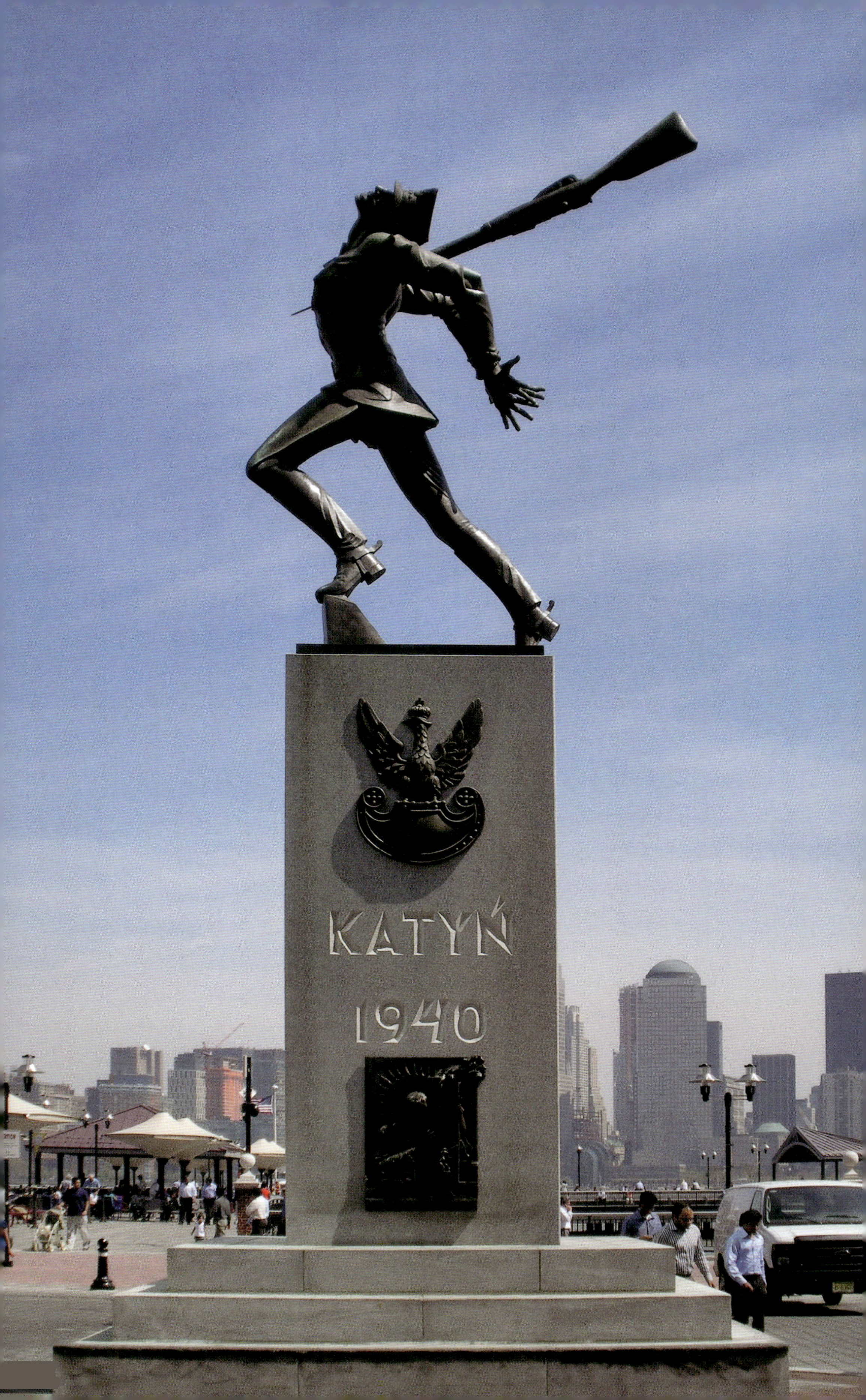
KATYŃ
1940

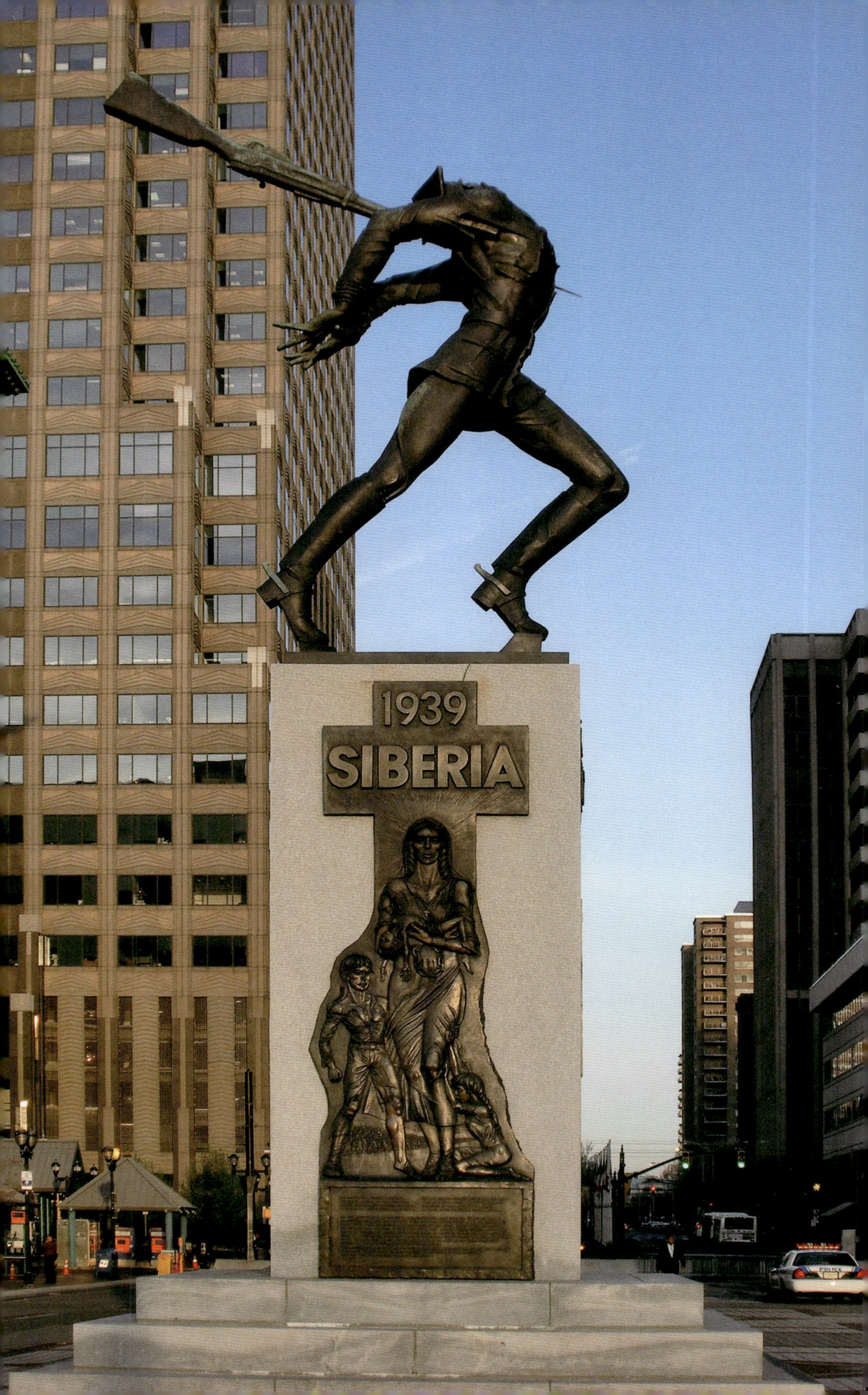
1939
SIBERIA

Relief "Siberia 1939"
Polish: *Skonały myśli i czyny i słowa / łzy tylko biegną nocami głuchymi / i pieśń niewoli złowieszcza grobowa / w akordach bólu ciągnie się po ziemi / I tylko czasem gdzieś w śniegach Tobolska / twarz smutna blada-białością opłatka / popatrzy w dal… Usta szepną: Matka / a potem ciszej smutniej szepną: Polska*

English: *On the seventeenth of September, 1939, the Polish Army, engaged in fierce combat / against the Germans, was attacked from the rear by the Soviet Army. In conspiracy / with Hitler (the Ribbentrop-Molotov Pact), Stalin seized forty-seven percent of / Polish land and annexed it to Soviet Russia. Two million Polish citizens, including / children, women, and senior citizens, perished en route to Siberia and at torturous / work in Soviet labor camps. From 1944 to 1956, thousands of Polish patriots—soldiers / of the underground armies of the A. K., N. O. W., N. S. Z., and W. I. N.—were heinously / murdered by the Soviet secret police (the N.K.V.D.). / This monument is dedicated to the millions of Polish citizens and heroes who offered / their lives in the fight against communism for our and your freedom. / Let them have honor and glory for all time.*

Relief for 11 September 2001
English: *Never forget! Pray for all the innocent / victims and heroes who died in the terrorist / attack on America, September 11 2001.*

Location: New Jersey, Exchange Place on Montgomery Street

◄
Katyń Memorial

Wende Museum

Culver City. The so-called Wende Museum opened in the summer of 2002. The initiator was the cultural historian and director of the institution Justinian Jampol. The house sees itself as a research archive as well as an art and educational institution. The museum's collection—the largest of its kind in the world—contains over 100,000 relics from the Cold War period, illustrating everyday culture and political developments in the GDR, Eastern Europe and the Soviet Union. One of the museum's primary objectives is to preserve the objects, to provide a greater understanding of the challenges and interrelationships of art, culture, and history at that time, and to explore their effects on the present. Since 2016, the facility has stood a former armoury of the US National Guard.

Only part of the collection can be curated and presented. However, after prior registration with the museum archive, all exhibits can be viewed on site or examined and used for educational and research purposes. Some of the objects can be accessed via an online gallery on the institution's website. In addition to a wide variety of consumer items, the holdings of the Wende Museum include numerous original works of art—drawings, photographs, graphics, sculptures and paintings—or reproductions thereof. The extensive archive, which comprises, among other things, Erich Honecker's personal estate from his time in Berlin's Moabit Prison in 1992, contains around 3,500 sound and film recordings. It also holds a comprehensive collection of contemporary furniture, socialist folk art, flags and banners as well as various design objects.

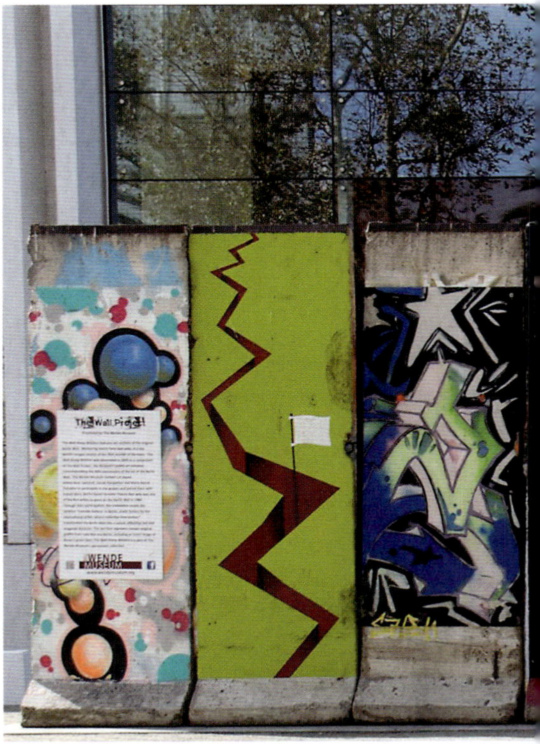

►
Original segments of the Berlin Wall in front of the former location of the Wende Museum

The museum's most complex and largest project to date is the exhibition "Facing the Wall: Living with the Berlin Wall". This traces the personal stories of four people connected to the museum: West Berlin wall artist Thierry Noir, former East German border guard Peter Bochmann, the West Berlin "Mauerspecht" (or "wall-pecker") Alwin Nachtweh and former Stasi officer Hagen Koch, who mapped the course of the Berlin Wall in 1961 and then oversaw its demolition in 1989. Through these contrasting biographical testimonies, the exhibition designers give visitors a personal point of entry into the history of the division of Germany and Europe and the realities of the Cold War. As part of the exhibition's festivities in November 2009, the museum installed another ten original segments of the Berlin Wall on Wilshire Boulevard in Los Angeles, featuring graffiti by well-known wall artists such as Thierry Noir and Kent Twitchell and by local artists.

Among the exhibition highlights of recent years are "Deconstructing Perestroika"—a compilation of hand-drawn poster designs created in reaction to the transformation processes of glasnost and perestroika initiated by head of state and party of the Soviet Union Mikhail Gorbachev—and the exhibitions "Competing Utopias", "Communism for Dinner" and "Face to Face". All these projects deal with a wide range of topics and were designed to inspire visitors to reflect on parallels between the antagonistic power blocs of the Cold War. The exhibitions point not least to the discrepancies between the ideologically charged promises of salvation offered by the communist regimes and everyday realities.

On its website, the museum provides digital access to all exhibition materials—works of art, artefacts, documents, films and contemporary witness reports. In addition, it organises readings, seminars, film screenings

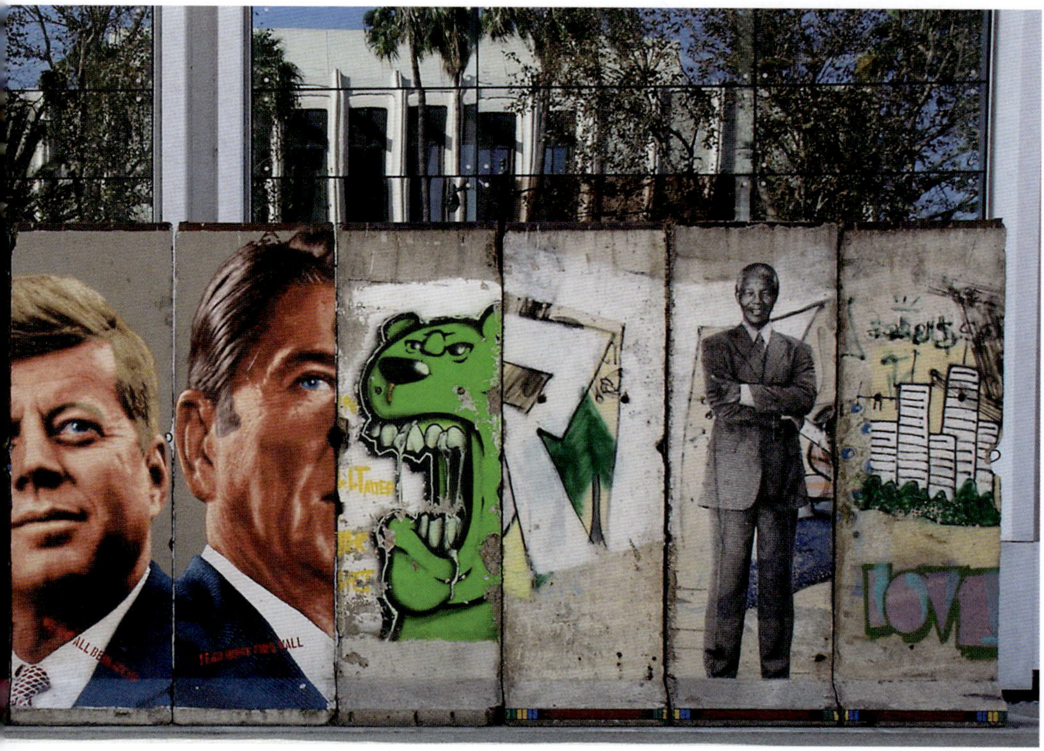

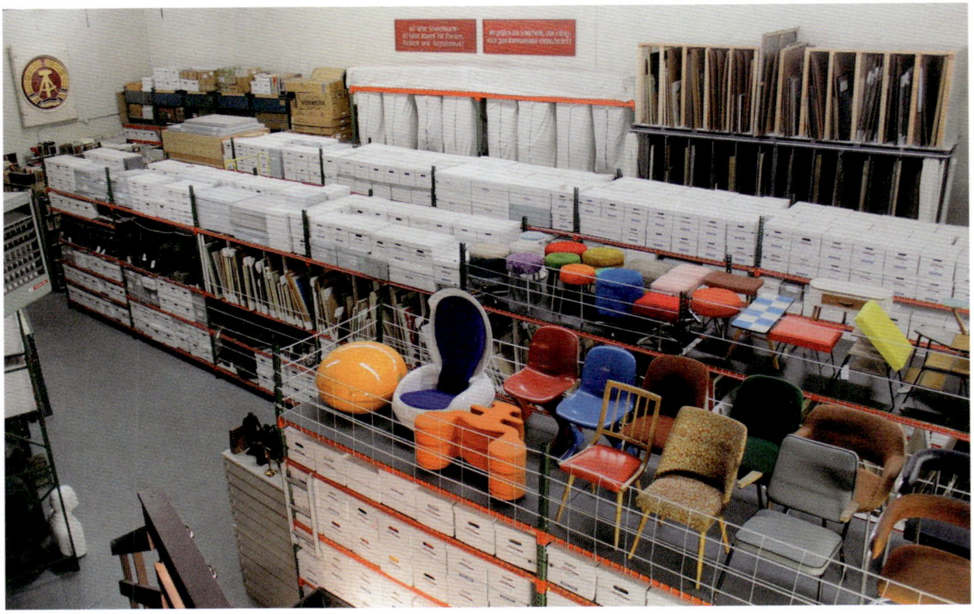

A view of the museum's archive holdings

and lectures and provides online materials on the topics of the construction of the Berlin Wall, post-war Europe and the Cold War for school classes. The museum's archive of contemporary witnesses also contains numerous audio-visual files and interviews with citizens from the states of Eastern Europe and the Soviet Union as well as former possessions of political prisoners and victims of state repression from Albania.

Location: Culver City, 10808 Culver Boulevard
Internet: www.wendemuseum.org

"The Partisans" Memorial

Boston. The memorial "The Partisans" by artist Andrzej Pitynski was inaugurated in front of the Boston World Trade Center on 7 September 2006. It commemorates those Polish civilians and military personnel who fought against the German and then against the Soviet occupation of Poland during the Second World War. The ten-metre-long, seven-metre-high and four-metre-wide aluminium sculpture composition shows the slumped figures of five mounted warriors.

The monument, which was erected in 1979, was opened to the public for the first time in 1983. In the following years, however, the installation had to change location several times and was last on display in Boston Common Park. It owes its current location to the advocacy of the Massachusetts Bay Transportation Authority after the Boston City Council had ordered the sculpture to be removed from the park in early 2006.

With this memorial, the artist wanted to commemorate the sacrifice of the Polish military in the fight against the two totalitarian powers. The monument also stands for all the so-called "cursed soldiers" (Polish: Żołnierze wyklęci)—those Polish resistance fighters who were active in the anti-communist resistance between 1944 and 1963 and who fought against the ruling regime in the Socialist People's Republic of Poland. Each of the riders in the monument is modelled on a commanding officer or soldier of the Polish resistance struggle. From front to back, using the respective pseudonyms of the fighters, these are: "Wolnyak" Jozef Zadierski, "Pulkownik" Michal Krupa, "Majka" Stanislaw Pelczar, "Garbaty" Adam Kusz and "Kula" Aleksander Pitinsky, the artist's father.

The term "cursed soldiers" was coined in the 1990s. They include members of various underground organisations such as Freedom and Independence (Zrzeszenie Wolność i Niezawisłóść; WiN), which emerged from the structures of the Home Army (Armia Krajowa; AK) and organised political and armed resistance in the early post-war years. Members of the National Military Union (Narodowe Zjednoczenie Wojskowe; NZW) and the National Armed Forces (Narodowe Siły Zbrojne; NSZ) were also among their ranks.

Although the Polish secret police, supported by special units of the NKVD, succeeded in taking down all the higher-ranking officers of the armed underground by 1951, around 1,300 different sections of the resistance were still active until 1955. In the hope of a radical change in the political situation in Poland, the partisans carried out operations against state security institutions, Soviet internment camps and prisons for political detainees. The last known "cursed soldier", Józef Franczak, was

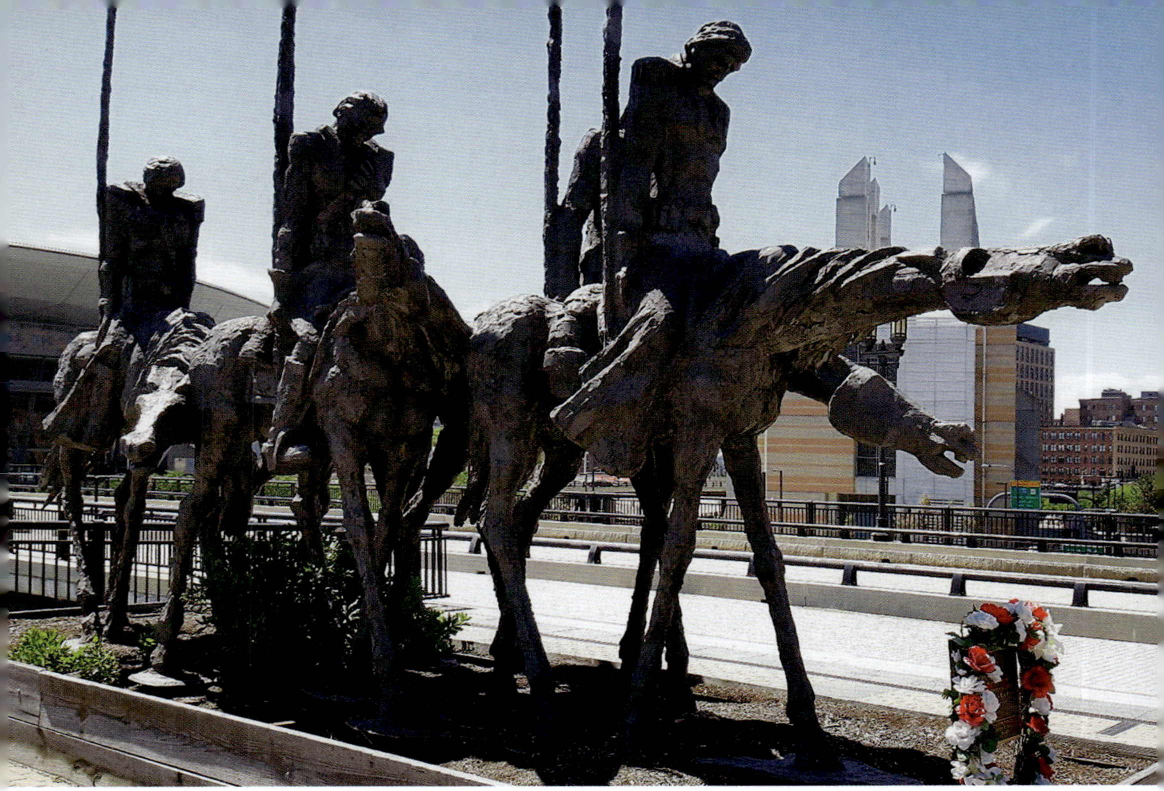

ambushed close to Lublin in October 1963, almost 20 years after the communists seized power in Poland.

It is estimated that about 22,000 soldiers, military officers and officials of the Polish socialist state and at least 1,000 employees of the Soviet secret police NKVD lost their lives due to the subversive operations of the armed resistance. On the side of the "cursed soldiers", some 8,000 were killed, around 5,000 were sentenced to death by the Polish judiciary, and another 21,000 underground fighters died in prisons and camps. Survivors, including those granted early release during the amnesty for political prisoners in 1947, were under constant observation and were socially and politically stigmatised until the collapse of the communist regime.

"The Partisans" Memorial

►

Inscriptions on the memorial

Since 2011, the National Day of Remembrance of the "Cursed Soldiers" has been celebrated in the Republic of Poland every year on 1 March—the anniversary of the execution of seven members of WiN—Freedom and Independence.

Inscription on the commemorative plaque in front of the sculpture composition:
The Partisans // by Andrzej Pitynski // 1979 // The sculpture depicts / Polish underground fighters / who battled the German and Soviet / forces during World War II / and later the Communist / regime of Poland.

Location: Boston, Summer Street in front of the Boston World Trade Center

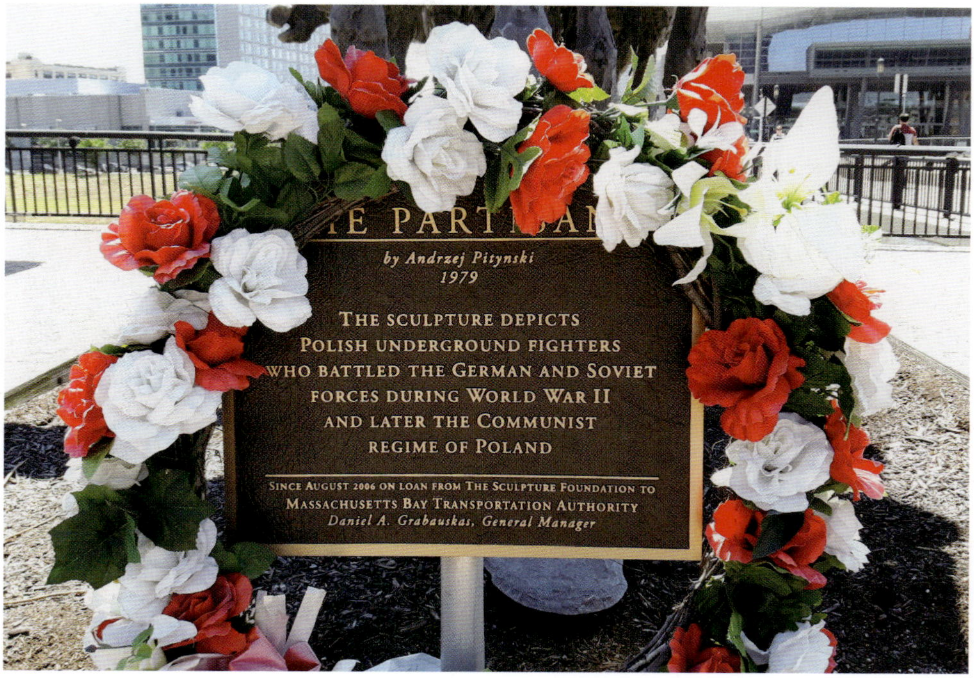

Further reading:

Blaylock, Sandra: Whither Alltag?: How the Wende Museum Revises East German History (and why it matters). In: Verges (2013): Germanic and Slavic Studies in Review 2.2. / European Network Remembrance and Solidarity. National day of Remembrance of the "Cursed Soldiers". 2016. Available online at: www.enrs.eu/pl/news/1167-1-march-the-national-day-of-remembrance-of-the-cursed-soldiers (last accessed on: 11/01/2018). / Kaminsky, Anna (ed.): Erinnerungsorte für die Opfer von Katyn´. Leipzig 2013. / Victims of Communism Memorial Foundation: The Victims of Communism Memorial. Available online at: http://victimsofcommunism.org/initiative/the-memorial/ (last accessed on: 11/01/2018). / Wesolowsky, Tony: Ukraine Famine Monument Erected in Washington. Radio Free Europe Radio Liberty article dated 06/08/2017. Available online at: www.rferl.org/a/ukraine-famine-monument-erected-in-washington/27174009.html (last accessed on: 11/01/2018).

Appendix

Selected Bibliography

Apelt, Andreas / Grünbaum, Robert / Togay, János Can (Hrsg.): Die ostmitteleuropäischen Freiheitsbewegungen 1953 – 1989: Opposition, Aufstände und Revolutionen im kommunistischen Machtbereich. Berlin 2014.

Applebaum, Anne: Der Gulag. Berlin 2003.

Applebaum, Anne: Der Eiserne Vorhang: Die Unterdrückung Osteuropas 1944 – 1956. München 2012.

Applebaum, Anne: Red Famine. Stalin's War on Ukraine. New York 2017.

Baberowski, Jörg: Der Große Terror: Die Geschichte des Stalinismus. München 2003.

Baberowski, Jörg: Der Feind ist überall. Stalinismus im Kaukasus. München 2003.

Behrends, Jan Claas / Katzer, Nikolaus / Lindenberger, Thomas (Hrsg.): 100 Jahre Roter Oktober. Zur Weltgeschichte der Russischen Revolution. Berlin 2017.

Bernhard, Michael / Kubik, Jan: Twenty Years After Communism. The Politics of Memory and Commemoration. New York 2014.

Bolton, Jonathan: Worlds of dissent: Charter 77, the Plastic People of the Universe, and Czech culture under communism. Cambridge 2012.

Brunnenbauer, Ulf / Troebst, Stefan (Hrsg.): Zwischen Amnestie und Nostalgie. Die Erinnerung an den Kommunismus in Südosteuropa. Köln 2007.

Chlewnjuk, Oleg: Stalin. Eine Biographie. München 2015.

Courtois, Stéphane et al.: Das Schwarzbuch des Kommunismus. Unterdrückung, Verbrechen und Terror. Sonderausgabe. München, Zürich 2004.

Diener, Alexander / Hagen, Joshua (Hrsg.): From Socialist to Post-Socialist Cities. Cultural Politics of Architecture, Urban Planning, and Identity in Eurasia. London, New York 2015.

Di Palma, Francesco / Müller, Wolfgang: Kommunismus und Europa: Europapolitik und -vorstellungen europäischer kommunistischer Parteien im Kalten Krieg. Paderborn 2016.

Dörr, Nikolaus: Die Rote Gefahr. Der italienische Eurokommunismus als sicherheitspolitische Herausforderung für die USA und Westdeutschland 1969 – 1979. Wien 2017.

Eichwerde, Wolfgang / Pauer, Jan (Hrsg.): Ringen um Autonomie. Dissidentendiskurse in Mittel- und Osteuropa. Berlin 2017.

Faulenbauch, Bernd: »Transformationen« der Erinnerungskulturen in Osteuropa nach 1989. Essen 2006.

Florin, Moritz: Kirgistan und die sowjetische Moderne: 1940 – 1991. Göttingen 2015.

Fröberg Idling, Peter: Pol Pots Lächeln. Eine schwedische Reise durch das Kambodscha der Roten Khmer. Frankfurt am Main 2013.

Gregory, Paul / Lazarev, Valery (Hrsg.): The Economics of Forced Labor: The Soviet GULag. Stanford 2003.

Hobsbawm, Eric: Das Zeitalter der Extreme: Weltgeschichte des 20. Jahrhunderts. 12. Aufl. München 2014.

Jung, Martin: In Freiheit. Die Auseinandersetzung mit Zeitgeschichte in Rumänien (1989 – 2009). Berlin 2016.

Kaminsky, Anna (Hrsg.): Erinnerungsorte an den Massenterror 1937 / 38. Russische Föderation. Berlin 2007.

Kaminsky, Anna (Hrsg.): Erinnerungsorte an den Holodomor 1932 / 33 in der Ukraine. Leipzig 2008.

Kaminsky, Anna (Hrsg.): Erinnerungsorte an die Opfer des Kommunismus in Belarus. Berlin 2010.

Kaminsky, Anna (Hrsg.): Erinnerungsorte für die Opfer von Katyń. Leipzig 2013.

Kaminsky, Anna (Hrsg.): Die Berliner Mauer in der Welt. Berlin 2014.

Kaminsky, Anna (Hrsg.): Orte des Erinnerns. Gedenkzeichen, Gedenkstätten und Museen zur Diktatur in SBZ und DDR. 3., überarbeitete und erweiterte Aufl. Berlin 2016.

Kashtalian, Irina: The Repressive Factors of the USSR's Internal Policy and Everyday Life of the Belarusian Society (1944 – 1953). Wiesbaden 2016.

Kilzer, Katharina / Müller-Engbers, Helmut (Hrsg.): Geist hinter Gittern. Die rumänische Gedenkstätte Memorial Sighet. Berlin 2013.

Kindler, Robert: Stalins Nomaden. Herrschaft und Hunger in Kasachstan. Hamburg 2014.

Knigge, Volkhard / Mählert, Ulrich (Hrsg.): Der Kommunismus im Museum. Formen der Auseinandersetzung in Deutschland und Ostmitteleuropa. Köln 2005.

Knigge, Volkhard (Hrsg.): Kommunismusforschung und Erinnerungskulturen in Ostmittel- und Westeuropa. Wien, Köln 2013.

Koenen, Gerd: Utopie der Säuberung: Was war der Kommunismus? Frankfurt am Main 2000.

Koenen, Gerd: Was war der Kommunismus? Göttingen 2010.

Koenen, Gerd: Die Farbe Rot. Ursprünge und Geschichte des Kommunismus. München 2017.

Kolář, Pavel: Der Poststalinismus. Ideologie und Utopie einer Epoche. Wien, Köln 2016.

Koposov, Nikolay: Memory Laws, Memory Wars: The Politics of the past in Europe and Russia. Cambridge, New York 2017.

Lehmann, Maike: Eine sowjetische Nation: Nationale Sozialismusinterpretationen in Armenien seit 1945. Frankfurt am Main, New York 2012.

Mark, Rudolf et al. (Hrsg.): Vernichtung durch Hunger. Der Holodomor in der Ukraine und der UdSSR. Berlin 2004.

Niegelhell, Anita / Ponisch, Gabriele: Wir sind immer im Feuer. Berichte ehemaliger politischer Gefangener im kommunistischen Albanien. Wien, Köln, Weimar 2001.

Raichevsky, Stoyan: Bulgarien unter dem kommunistischen Regime 1944 – 1989. Berlin 2016.

Schlögel, Karl: Das sowjetische Jahrhundert. Archäologie einer untergegangenen Welt. München 2018.

Smith, Stephen Anthony (Hrsg.): The Oxford handbook of the history of communism. Oxford 2014.

Snyder, Timothy: Bloodlands. Europa zwischen Hitler und Stalin. 2. Aufl. München 2010.

Teichmann, Christian: Macht der Unordnung. Stalins Herrschaft in Zentralasien, 1920 – 1950. Hamburg 2016.

Veen, Hans-Joachim / Knigge, Volkhard: Denkmäler demokratischer Umbrüche nach 1945. Wien, Köln 2014.

Weber, Hermann / Mählert, Ulrich (Hrsg.): Verbrechen im Namen der Idee. Terror im Kommunismus 1936 – 1938. Berlin 2007.

Weber, Claudia: Krieg der Täter: Die Massenerschießungen von Katyń. Hamburg 2015.

Wemheuer, Felix: Famine Politics in Maoist China and the Soviet Union. New Haven 2014.

Geographical Index

The following list contains in alphabetical order all places where memorials and museums are located.

List of Abbreviations

AFDPR
Asociaţia Foştilor Deţinuţi Politici din România (Association of Former Political Prisoners in Romania)

AK
Armia Krajowa (Home Army)

ALŽIR
Akmolinskij lager schjon ismennikow rodiny (Akmolinsk Camp for the Wives of Traitors to the Motherland)

ÀVH
Àllamvédelmi Hatóság (Hungarian Secret Police)

BelBaltLag
Belomorsko-Baltijskij isprawitelno-trudowoj lager (White Sea-Baltic Corrective Labour Camp Directorate, WSBC)

BKP
Balgarska Komunisticeska Partija (Bulgarian Communist Party)

BSSR
Belorusskaja Sowjetskaja Sozialistitscheskaja Respublika (Belarusian Soviet Socialist Republic)

CC
Central Committee

CIS
Commonwealth of Independent States

COMINFORM
(Information Bureau of the Communist and Workers' Parties)

COMINTERN
Communist International

CP
Communist Party

CPC
Communist Party of China

CPR
Partidul Comunist Român (Communist Party of Romania)

CPS
Communist Party of Slovakia

CPSU
Kommunisticeskaja partija Sovetskovo Sojuza (Communist Party of the Soviet Union)

CSCE
Conference on Security and Cooperation in Europe

ČSSR
Československá Socialistická Republika (Czechoslovakia)

ČSFR
Česká a Slovenská Federatívna Republika (Czech and Slovak Federative Republic)

CUHK
Chinese University of Hong Kong

Dalstroj
Glawnoje uprawlenije stroitelstwa Dalnego Sewera (Far North Construction Trust)

DERG
ደርግ (Provisional Military Government of Socialist Ethiopia)

Dmitlag
Dimitrowskij isprawitelno-trudowoj lager (Dmitrovskii Correctional Labour Camp)

DS
Derschawna Sigurnost (Bulgarian State Security)

DubrawLag
Dubrawnoje lagernoje uprawlenije
(Dubravny Camp Directorate)

EPRDF
Ethiopian Peoples' Revolutionary Democratic Front

GDR
German Democratic Republic

GMD
Guomindang
(a party of the Republic of China)

GorLag
Gorny Camp Directorate (mining camp)

GULag
Glawnoje Uprawjenije Lagerej
(Main Administration of Camps and Places of Detention)

IPN
Instytut Pamięci Narodowei
(Institute of National Remembrance)

JVA
Justizvollzugsanstalt
(term used for prison in Germany)

KarLag
Karagandinskij isprawitelno-trudowoj lager
(Karaganda Corrective Labour Camp)

KGB
Komitet Gosudarstwennoj Besopasnosti
(Committee for State Security)

KOR
Komitet Obrony Robotników
(Committee for the Defence of the Workers)

KPČ
Komunistická strana Československa
(Communist Party of Czechoslovakia)

KSSR
Kasachskaja Sovetskaya Sotsialisticheskaya Respublika (Kazakh Soviet Socialist Republic)

LAF
Lietuvos Aktyvistų Frontas
(Lithuanian Activist Front)

Laogai
System of Forced Labour Camps in the People's Republic of China

MEFESZ
Magyar Egyetemisták és Főiskolai Egyesületek Szövetsége (Hungarian Federation of University and College Students' Associations)

MfS
Ministerium für Staatssicherheit
(Ministry for State Security in East Germany)

MDP
Magyar Dolgozók Pártja
(Hungarian Working People's Party)

NDH
Nezavisna Država Hrvatska
(Independent State of Croatia)

NGO
Non-Governmental Organisation

NKGB
Narodnij Komissariat Gossudarstwennoi Besopasnosti (People's Commissariat for State Security)

NKVD
Narodnyi Komissariat Wnutrennich del
(People's Commissariat for Internal Affairs)

NOV
Narodnooslobodilačka vojska
(Yugoslav People's Liberation Army)

NPT
Nápravně Pracovní Tábor
(Czech Correctional Labour Camp)

NS
Nationalsozialismus
(National Socialism–Nazism)

NSDAP
Nationalsozialistische Deutsche Arbeiterpartei
(National Socialist German Workers' Party)

NSZ
Narodowe Siły Zbrojne (underground organisation "National Armed Forces")

NSZZ
Niezależny Samorządny Związek Zawodowy "Solidarność" (Independent Self-governing Labour Union "Solidarity")

NOP
Nacionalnaja objedinennaja partija Armenii
(National United Party of Armenia)

NVA
National People's Army in East Germany

NZW
Narodowe Zjednoczenie Wojskowe
(underground organisation "National Military Association")

OGPU
Objedinjonnoje Gossudarstwennoje Polititscheskoje Uprawlenije
(Joint State Political Directorate)

OMON
Otrjad Mobilny Ossobowo Nasnatschenija
(Special Purpose Police Unit)

OUN
Organisazija Ukrajinskich Nazionalistiw
(Organisation of Ukrainian Nationalists)

OZNA
Odjeljenje za zaštitu naroda
(Department for People's Protection of the Yugoslav Secret Police)

PDS
Partia Demokratike e Shqipërisë
(Democratic Party of Albania)

PSD
Partia Socialdemokrate e Shqipërisë
(Social Democratic Party of Albania)

PVAP
Polska Zjednoczona Partia Robotnicza
(Polish United Workers' Party)

RetschLag
Retschnoj lager (River Camp)

RSFSR
Rossijskaja sowetskaja federatiwnaja sozialistitscheskaja respublika (Russian Soviet Federative Socialist Republic)

SBZ
Sowjetische Besatzungszone
(Soviet Occupation Zone)

SDS
Sajus na Demokratitschnite Sili
(Union of Democratic Forces)

SED
Sozialistische Einheitspartei Deutschlands
(Socialist Unity Party of Germany)

SLON
Solowezkij Lager Osobogo nasnatschenija
(Solovki special camp)

SMT
Soviet Military Tribunal

SovLab
Soviet Past Research Laboratory

SS
Schutzstaffel (paramilitary organisation of the German Nazi Party)

StB
Státní bezpečnost
(Secret Police of Czechoslovakia)

STON
Solowezkaja tjurma Osobogo nasnatschenija
(Solowezker Gefängnis zur besonderen Verwendung)

TNP
Tábory Nucené Práce
(Czech forced labour camp for uranium mining)

TWO
Trudovo Vaspitatelno Obshezhitie
(Residential home for worker reeducation)

UB
Urząd Bezpieczeństwa
(Office for State Security of the People's Republic of Poland)

UDBA
Uprava državne bezbednosti
(State Security Service of Yugoslavia)

ÚDV
Úřad dokumentace a vyšetřování zločinů komunismu (Czech Office for the Investigation and Prosecution of Communist crimes)

UNESCO
United Nations Educational, Scientific and Cultural Organisation

UNO
United Nations Organisation

UPA
Ukrajinska Powstanska Armija
(Ukrainian Insurgent Army)

USSR
Union of Soviet Socialist Republics

ÚSTR
Ústav pro studium totalitních režimů
(Czech Institute for the Study of Totalitarian Regimes)

WiN
Zrzeszenie Wolność i Niezawisłóść
("Freedom and Independence" underground organisation)

ZISPO
Zakłady Metalowe Józefa Stalina w Jarzyna
(Joseph Stalin Metal Works in Poznań)

Image Credits

The photos were taken by the Federal Foundation for the Study of the Communist Dictatorship in Eastern Germany, mainly by Anna Kaminsky, Rainer Eppelmann, Ruth Gleinig, Anna von Arnim-Rosenthal, Markus Pieper, Ulrich Mählert and Sabine Kuder. Further photos were kindly provided by:

BunkArt · p. 24

Bundesstiftung Aufarbeitung, Harald Schmitt, Bild Schmitt336_neu · pp. 70, 74

Adam Lederer · p. 37

Georg Meusel · pp. 94, 98, 99

Elena Temper · pp. 38, 43, 44

Usewald Siniak · p. 46

Belene Island Foundation · pp. 59, 60, 61

Yasna Mindilikowa · p. 48

Felix Sternagel · p. 75

Gedenkstätte Berlin-Hohenschönhausen · p. 131

Gedenkstätte Sachsenhausen · p. 133

Jürgen Hochmut · p. 141

Florian Kindermann · pp. 107, 159, 274

Estonian Institute of Historical Memory · pp. 110, 111

KGB Cells Museum · pp. 100, 117

Modzzak, Spomenik ubijenim Franjevcima.jpg, online available at: https://commons.wikimedia.org/wiki/File:Spomenik_ubijenim_Franjevcima.jpg, Creative Commons Attribution-Share Alike 4.0 International https://creativecommons.org/licenses/by-sa/4.0/deed.de, no changes made · p. 392

Robert Lubej · pp. 394, 401

Chris Price · pp. 166, 171

Jens Schöne · pp. 173, 444, 451, 452

"ALZIR" Museum and Memorial Complex · p. 175

Cecilia Emmelhainz · p. 178

Dmitrij Filushin (Дмитрий Филюшин), Файл: Памятник жертвам голодомора в Казахстане (Павлодар).jpg, online available at: https://bit.ly/2HHfapw original source: http://www.panoramio.com/photo/81343227 Creative Commons Attribution-Share Alike 3.0 https://creativecommons.org/licenses/by-sa/3.0/deed.de, no changes made · pp. 180, 181

Wolfgang Hans Eminger · pp. 194, 198

Keane Lindblad · p. 184

Thijs Witters · p. 191 on top

Dietrich Wolf Fenner · pp. 229, 230

Aris Jansons · p. 212

DavidConFran—Own work, CC BY-SA 3.0, https://commons.wikimedia.org/w/index.php?curid=29676367 · p. 220

The Museum of Genocide Victims · p. 223

Martijn Munneke · pp. 216, 226, 227

Edda Ahrberg · pp. 211, 235

Torsten Baar · pp. 240, 245

Volker Assmann · p. 244

Adrian Grycuk—Praca własna, CC BY-SA 3.0 pl, https://commons.wikimedia.org/w/index.php?curid=61251259 · pp. 254, 255

Ronny Heidenreich · pp. 221, 253, 411

Oliver Igel · p. 265

Peter-Dietmar Leber · p. 270

Memorialul Victimelor Comunismului si al Rezistentei Sighet · pp. 279, 280, 281

Vera Dubina · pp. 296, 297

Memorial Moskau · p. 307

Wiktor Feduschtschak · pp. 323, 357, 367

Stanisław Kiełbowicz · pp. 330, 331

Instytut Pamięci Narodowej w Białymstoku Kiełbowicz · p. 332

Andrey Strelnikov · p. 339

Nadkachna—Own Work, CC BY 3.0, https://commons.wikimedia.org/w/index.php?curid=10670415 · p. 89

Vojna Memorial Lešetice · pp. 90, 91, 92

Kowalewskij Andrij, Jakimenko Julija, Burkazkaja Anastasija · p. 352

Joycelyn Pantaleon Hidalgo · pp. 360, 361

Kathleen Hiller · p. 363

Oleksandra Luchyk · p. 364

Leon Yaakov · pp. 370, 375

Benoist Guitton · pp. 426, 428, 429

Sarah-Rose Burke · pp. 436, 439

Simon P. White · p. 441

Malcom Edwards · p. 442

Ccyyrree—Own work, CC0, https://commons.wikimedia.org/w/index.php?curid=21959268 p. 421

Karen London · p. 423

James Daschuk · pp. 418, 425

Otto Gruber · pp. 408, 412, 413

Martin Gutzeit · pp. 432, 435

Hope Harrison · p. 447

Lindsay Fuller · p. 448

Wende Museum · pp. 454, 455, 456

Rob O'Leary · p. 225

Guy Delsaut—Own work, CC BY-SA 4.0, https://commons.wikimedia.org/w/index.php?curid=61503033 · p. 414

Юрочкин Роман—File: Монумент независимости Узбекистана.jpg, CC BY-SA 3.0, https://ru.wikipedia.org/w/index.php?curid=6215333 · p. 372

Ing. Mgr. Jozef Kotulič—Own work, CC BY-SA 3.0, https://commons.wikimedia.org/w/index.php?curid=14843389 · p. 342

US Embassy Slovenia Facebook—www.facebook.com/media/set/?set=a.10153712766513088.1073742173.53039228087&type=3, public domain, https://commons.wikimedia.org/w/index.php?curid=46724962 · p. 396

39751:FORTEPAN / Nagy Gyula · p. 158

40165:FORTEPAN / Nagy Gyula · p. 152

Kathleen Chapman · pp. 404, 406

Krystyna Samsonowska · p. 366

Legal Notice

Edited by Anna Kaminsky on behalf of the
Federal Foundation for the Study of Communist Dictatorship in East Germany
Kronenstrasse 5
D-10117 Berlin
www.bundesstiftung-aufarbeitung.de
buero@bundesstiftung-aufarbeitung.de

Specialist proofreading
Maria Matschuk

Proofreading
Sina Volk, Sandstein Verlag

Typesetting and reprographics
Jana Felbrich, Jana Neumann, Sandstein Verlag

Design
Bettina Neustadt, Jana Felbrich, Sandstein Verlag

Printing and finishing
FINIDR, s. r. o.
Český Těšín

Cover image
Memorial to the victims of the famine in Kazakhstan (©Jens Schöne)

The German National Library has listed this publication in the German National Bibliography; detailed bibliographic data are available on the Internet at http://dnb.dnb.de.

www.sandstein-verlag.de
978-3-95498-391-9